THE ULTIMATE BOOK OF RELATIONSHIPS

THE ASTROLOGICAL FORCES THAT INFLUENCE YOUR COMPATIBILITIES IN WORKING LIFE, FRIENDSHIP, FAMILY AND LOVE

THE ULTIMATE BOOK OF

RELATIONSHIPS

REVEALING THE SECRETS OF COMPATIBLE PARTNERSHIPS

CLARE GIBSON

Saraband

For Elaine and Jem Smallwood, a Sagittarius–Gemini couple who score 7/10 in theory, but far higher in practice.

Published by Saraband (Scotland) Limited
The Arthouse, 752–756 Argyle Street,
Glasgow G3 8UJ, Scotland
hermes@saraband.net

ISBN: 1-887354-35-2

Printed in China

10 9 8 7 6 5 4 3 2 1

EDITOR: Sara Hunt
ART DIRECTOR: Deborah Hayes
GRAPHIC DESIGN ASSISTANT: Phoebe Tak-Yin Wong

Photo Credits and Acknowledgments: The publisher would like to thank the following people: Dillon Bennett, Henriette Borner, Christina Cheong, Cathy Dolan, Nikki Fesak, Donna Freed, Chloe van Grieken, Lottie van Grieken, Keith Hunt, Maureen Hunt, Lex Lamb, Sallie Moffat, Peter Murray, Hannah Neufeld, Robert Outram, Kerry Ryan, Ken Schweitzer, Annika Warner, and Ross White.

The design of this book is based on Ziga Design's work for the companion title, *The Ultimate Birthday Book.*

The twelve illustrations each representing the signs of the zodiac are reproduced here courtesy of **Saraband Image Library**. All other photographs and illustrations in this book are **© 2002 Arttoday.com, Inc.** unless otherwise listed here. Grateful acknowledgment is made to the following individuals and institutions for permission to reproduce illustrations and photographs:

© 1999 PhotoDisc, Inc.: 69, 71, 74, 77; **Library of Congress, Prints and Photographs Division:** 41; **Saraband Image Library:** 25; **© Daisy N. Shiloh:** 42, 43, 48, 49, 54, 55, 60, 70, 74, 75, 76, 116, 137, 219, 389.

The photographs on the front and back cover, also shown on pages 1, 2, 7, 79, 159, 239, and 319 are reproduced courtesy of **AKG London**.

CONTENTS

Adapt yourself to the environment
in which your lot has been cast,
and show true love to the fellow
mortals with whom destiny has
surrounded you.

MARCUS AURELIUS, *Meditations* (SECOND CENTURY AD)

INTRODUCTION

None of us exists in a vacuum, and it is a rare day that passes without us having some form of contact with other people, whether we love, like, or even loathe them. And not only do our relationships with others have the power to send us soaring into the heady heights of happiness or sinking into the depths of deep depression, but they often give our lives meaning and purpose. Our relationships are therefore fundamental to our well-being, and when we truly gel with someone, feeling as though we have found a kindred spirit can be the most exhilarating of experiences. More often than not, however, we find ourselves arguing with our lovers, resenting the selfishness of our parents, children, or siblings, falling out with our friends, fuming at our bosses, or criticizing our workmates. Why are relationships so hard to get right? And is there a secret to getting along with each and every one of those who populate our personal worlds?

Harnessing the Help of Astrology

There is indeed a ready-made diagnostic and prognostic tool that will enable you to understand why you immediately click with some individuals, but instinctively feel hostile to, or threatened by, others, and that can give you an indication of how your relationships are likely to develop. That tool is astrology, a system that has been used to understand and predict human behavior for thousands of years in the West, in Mesoamerica, in India, in China, and elsewhere. Such is its accuracy that it has endured to this day, while once equally popular types of divination have long since fallen by the wayside (including, thank goodness, haruspicy, or the examination of the entrails of slaughtered animals and birds that ancient Romans priests were convinced enabled them to prophesy future events).

They may be unable to prevent themselves from glancing at their horoscopes in a newspaper or magazine, but many people dismiss the notion that the location of the planets and constellations in relation to us when we were born has a profound effect on our characters and consequently on the course of our lives. Yet no one can deny that the gravitational pull of the Moon influences the tides of the Earth's seas and oceans, and scientific research furthermore increasingly seems to corroborate astrological theories and conclusions. During the mid-twentieth century, for example, the French statistician Michel Gauguelin was startled to ascertain that the only link between many of those who had been outstandingly successful in high-performance athletic careers was sharing a ruling planet in Mars, which astrology associates with such go-getting traits as risk-taking, aggression, and determination. Scientists are forced to reassess their views time and time again, and astronomers most recently in 2003, with the discovery of a distant and significant object in our solar system by a N.A.S.A. team led by Dr. Mike Brown, of the California Institute of Technology. Named Sedna, for the Inuit

Above: *Ancient Romans consulted astrologers, or stargazers, to learn their future or fate.*

Right: *In* The Odyssey, *Homer tells us that the goddess, or nymph, Calypso instructed Odysseus (a Greek hero whom the Romans called Ulysses) to keep the constellation of the Great Bear on his left as he sailed for home. Odysseus is depicted here with an armillary sphere, an instrument that was once used to determine the position of the stars.*

sea goddess, there is a real possibility that this frozen mass may be classified as a planet. From personal experience, I can also attest to the way in which some skeptics waver when faced with an astrological analysis of their personalities, for following the publication of *The Ultimate Birthday Book*, my astrological interpretation of the nature of each day of the year, numerous bemused strangers told me that although they didn't believe in astrology, the page devoted to their birthday described them to a "T." So don't be too quick to reject astrology as a valid aid in assisting you to build better relationships: remain open-minded, consider the information and advice that the *The Ultimate Book of Relationships* gives you objectively, and don't be too surprised should many of the observations ring true.

It is important to remember, however, that even if they share the same zodiacal sign, no two people are ever the same, for if their places, dates, and times of birth differ, so, too, do the astrological influences that contribute to their personal makeup. (This caution even holds true for identical twins, for none emerge from the womb together, and however short the duration between their births, the slight shift in the position of the heavenly bodies overhead will inevitably result in subtle differences in their temperaments.) Your genes and upbringing also have a vital part to play in how you feel, behave, and react to others, regardless of any astrological considerations. Perhaps most importantly of all, we are blessed with free will, so that although astrological influences, nature, and nurture may predetermine or mold our mindsets to a certain extent, a split decision—be it conscious or unconscious—may cause you to behave out of character, and in so doing, set in motion dramatic life changes that may result in you dissolving old relationships and forming new attachments. In short, you have the power to overturn your astrological destiny and change your fate, whether for better or for worse.

This is not to say that if you are a Leo with a leonine lover, for instance, the page that analyzes your past, present, and future relationship is inaccurate. What it does mean, however, is that in order to benefit from a precise breakdown of

Above: *As well as looking like peas in a pod, identical twins can display similar characteristics. Yet while they may share the same arrangement of genes, they are nevertheless individuals with their own, unique personalities. And because none are born at the same instant, their astrological birth influences differ slightly from those of their sibling.*

***Right:** Those born during the year of the horse—one of the twelve creatures of the Chinese zodiac—are said to be independent, intelligent, and restless, much like people whose Sun sign is Gemini, the horse's Western equivalent.*

the myriad influences that affect your interaction with one another, you would both need to have your birth charts drawn up and interpreted by an experienced and reputable astrologer who also has a knowledge of psychology and will consequently be able to offer you informed advice on how to maximize the positives and minimize the negatives inherent in your relationship.

About This Book

The character assessments, plus points, potential pitfalls, guiding principles, and compatibility ratings contained in this book have all been based on the Western, Sun-sign astrological theories that have prevailed for millennia, largely because they have proved themselves so reliable, but also because we Westerners are generally more familiar with the solar calendar, twelve signs of the zodiac, and four elements than with the lunar calendar, twelve animals, and five elements of Chinese astrology, for instance. (And be advised that familiarizing yourself with that and other astrological traditions will give you a deeper and more detailed perspective on your own conduct and the way in which others relate to you, and you to them.)

If you aren't already acquainted with them, the following pages will introduce you to astrology's ten planets (the Sun, the Moon, Mercury, Venus, Mars, Jupiter, Saturn, Uranus, Neptune, and Pluto), the four elements (fire, earth, air, and water), the two polarities (masculine, or positive, and feminine, or negative), and the three quadruplicities (cardinal, fixed, and mutable) that in some combination make up our birth influences, whether we were born under the zodiacal sign of Aries, Taurus, Gemini, Cancer, Leo, Virgo, Libra, Scorpio, Sagittarius, Capricorn, Aquarius, or Pisces, whose astrological characters and qualities are also explained. Armed with this basic knowledge, you will then be in a better position to assess your relationships with others yourself, while always bearing in mind the words of the French philosopher Jacques Maritain: "We don't love qualities, we love persons; sometimes by reason of their defects as well as of their qualities" (*Reflections on America*, 1958).

Finally, it is crucial that you regard the observations and judgments that appear on those pages that have special significance to you as extreme examples of the best and worst that could befall you and your beloved, friend, parent, child, brother or sister, boss, or coworker. In addition, although you should certainly take any recommendations into account, don't feel compelled to follow them slavishly lest your relationship otherwise falls apart. Neither should you let yourself be too buoyed up or cast down by the number of hearts or smiley faces accompanying a particular entry, nor conclude that an encouragingly high overall rating or a dispiritingly low mark out of ten means that astrology has blessed or cursed your love affair or friendship. For the beauty of astrology is that it both warns against complacency should you blithely have thought that you needn't work on improving your rapport with someone, only to read that a number of serious stumbling blocks are likely to trip you up, and heartens you when you fear that you and your loved one have reached rock bottom, but then learn that you can overcome the obstacles that are blocking the path that leads to mutual contentment. Nothing is inevitable or unchangeable in life, least of all in the fluid realm of human interaction, so let astrology be an instructive and constructive guide in helping you to transform your relationships, and therefore also your life, for the better.

Left: *Forewarned is forearmed, which is why learning more about both your own and your lover's astrological character, and how you are likely to interact as time goes by, will help you to keep on track as you set off into the unknown together.*

The Planets

The theories and principles of astrology evolved thousands of years ago, before scientific advances had enabled the nature of the solar system to be understood properly (and even today, astronomers are still making new discoveries), at a time when it was believed that the heavenly bodies revolved around the Earth, not the Sun. This not only explains why astrology classifies the Sun (actually a star) and the Moon (Earth's satellite) as planets, but why the zodiacal signs of Scorpio, Aquarius, and Pisces are linked with two planets, their primary rulers now being one of the trio of planets that were discovered relatively recently—in astrological terms, at least—namely Uranus, Neptune, and Pluto—with their traditional planetary governors being relegated to secondary-ruler status. The planets are named for Roman deities, apart from the Sun and the Moon, which the ancient Greeks (from whom the Romans derived their pantheon) and Romans nevertheless equated with gods and goddesses.

Although each sign of the zodiac has a ruling planet (and two in the case of Scorpio, Aquarius, and Pisces) that is said to impart its characteristics to those born under that constellation, all of the planets affect us according to both their positions when we were born and when they move into our zodiacal constellations in real time. You can discover which planet was in which house, or area of your life, at the time of your birth by drawing up your birth chart or asking an astrologer to do so. The planets are said to bring out, energize, and direct the potential with which our zodiacal signs endow us at birth. Some are believed to have a more immediate effect than others, however, namely the Sun, Moon, Mercury, Venus, and Mars, which, because they are closest to the Earth and pass through the signs of the zodiac (the ecliptic plane) relatively swiftly, are termed "personal" planets. The "transpersonal," or "middle," planets are Jupiter and Saturn, which are both farther away from the Earth and move more slowly, while the "impersonal," or "outer," planets are the even more distant and sluggish Uranus, Neptune, and Pluto, whose real-time influence is said to be generational.

***Below:** The ancient Greeks personified the Sun as the solar god Helios (the Roman Sol), who was said to drive his horse-drawn chariot across the sky during the day, starting his journey in the East at dawn, and finishing in the West at sunset.*

THE SUN ☉

The Greeks and Romans worshiped the Sun as Helios, Apollo, and Sol Invictus, all male deities, which is why this "planet" is associated with masculinity. The Sun is Leo's ruling planet, and its sigil is said to represent the seed of inspiration or potential contained within the self. The Sun (and Leo's) house is the fifth, which is that of creativity, children, and the things that we enjoy doing in our free time.

It is easy to understand why ancient astrologers associated such traits as

Left: *The U.S. astronaut Neil Armstrong was born on August 5, 1930, making him a Sun-ruled Leo. Was it the Sun that blessed him with the necessary authority, leadership qualities, and determination that together enabled him to command Apollo 11 and win a place in the history books as the first person to set foot on the Moon on July 20, 1969?*

warmth, burning vitality, and a sunny personality with the Sun (one of the personal planets), and why it can represent a significant man—be it a father, husband, boyfriend, or boss—in a person's birth chart. As the star that dominates the sky, and around which all of the planets revolve, it is furthermore not surprising that power, authority, and leadership qualities, or the desire for them, as well as a longing to shine and to be admired as a "star," should be among its attributes. More importantly, perhaps, it is the planet of individuality, identity, and personality, representing as it does the ego, how we feel about ourselves, our outlook on life, and the face that we present to others. It is strongly linked with willpower, self-confidence, and self-esteem, and hence with pride and dignity, along with the self-sufficiency, resilience, and decisiveness of adulthood. The Sun consequently denotes personal integrity, or the ability to remain true to oneself, and suggests that we deal with others in an honorable or generous way. In addition, the Sun is the planet of personal ambition and blesses us with the determination, energy, and creativity that are necessary if we are to make our aims a reality, whether they be to raise a family, build up a business, or bring any sort of visionary project to fruition. It also gives us a joyful appreciation of life, which may manifest itself as playfulness, exuberance, vigor, and a willingness to experiment. More negatively, it can result in someone being egotistical, domineering, and attention-demanding.

Below: *The Sun bestows a sunny nature upon all its children—particularly little Leos, whose ruling "planet" it is—as well as warmth, energy, and a tendency to be somewhat self-centered.*

Above: *In Greek mythology, the Moon goddess Artemis (the Roman Diana) was the twin sister of Apollo, like Helios, a Sun god. A virgin huntress whose weapon was a bow and arrow and whose symbol was a crescent Moon, Artemis was said to have the power to help women in labor to deliver their babies safely.*

THE MOON ☾

Because its phases cause its appearance to change over the course of the approximately twenty-eight days that it takes to orbit the Earth, the Greeks and Romans associated the Moon's cycle of waxing until it becomes full, then waning until it disappears or "dies," followed by its reappearance as the new Moon and its consequent waxing, waning, "death," and "reincarnation," with goddesses of youth and virginity, maturity and motherhood, and old age and death, notably Artemis (the Roman Diana), Selene, and Hecate. As well as representing virgin, mother, and crone goddesses, or the triple goddess, its influence over women's menstrual cycles and the tides of the seas and oceans resulted in it being strongly associated with femininity, female fertility, and reproduction, but also with emotions, partly because bodies of water represent the depths of the unconscious mind in symbolic thought, and partly because the Moon is usually only seen at night, which is why it is also linked with dreams, through which the unconscious expresses itself. The Moon governs Cancer, and its sigil is a crescent Moon, which depicts the bow of the huntress goddess Artemis (Diana). The Moon (and Cancer's) house is the fourth, which is related to parents, the home, and our private lives.

One of the personal planets, the Moon's appearance in an individual's birth chart can signify an important woman—specifically a mother, or mother figure—in the subject's life or how he or she relates to women in general, but is generally interpreted as denoting that person's inner life, soul, unconscious urges, or instinctual reactions. As the symbol of the archetypal mother, however, the Moon nevertheless suggests that our emotions and instincts are strongly affected by our memories of our relationship with our mothers—who may have been "good" or "bad," giving or withholding, interested or disinterested, kind or cruel—when we were young, along with our experiences of growing up in our childhood homes, which we may either seek to recreate or compensate for as adults, depending on whether their atmosphere made us feel happy or miserable when we were small, vulnerable, and impressionable. The Moon can therefore indicate that we crave the emotional security of being loved and cherished, especially if we felt unloved or neglected when we were young, and can also highlight our own maternal feelings or longing to mother others or a particular person, or else to devote our energy to feeding the potential inherent in a "brainchild." It also denotes the importance that we attach to our homes, domestic lives, and the relationships that we have with family members. The Moon furthermore points to the habits or attitudes that were so ingrained in us when we were small that they are now second nature, and our unthinking responses to others or the situations in which we find ourselves, especially when they unsettle us. Because it generates no light of its own, unlike the Sun, whose radiance it subtly reflects, the Moon additionally signifies that we are easily swayed by others, and thus that we are in danger of being gullible or of not knowing our own minds, although the more positive traits of adaptability, openness, and receptiveness, along with empathy and compassion, are also implied. Further gifts of Mother Moon are imagination and innate creativity, both of which can ultimately bring fulfillment should they produce an idea that we find satisfaction in nurturing from conception to fruition. Yet some of the downsides bestowed on us by this "planet" include a tendency to be backward-looking, reactionary, or to live in the past, or a childish or immature attitude. Still more are an overdependence on loved ones for emotional sustenance, which may result in clinginess or neediness; oversensitivity, in turn triggering moodiness when our feelings have been wounded; and a propensity to control those closest to us by means of emotional blackmail, which is usually manifested as guilt-inducing, martyrlike behavior. When under the influence of the Moon, people may also reason or behave irrationally, but this needn't be a negative characteristic, for tapping into the unconscious and acting intuitively, rather than logically, can often have startlingly successful consequences.

MERCURY ☿

Because its rate of orbit around the Sun is the fastest of all of the planets at eighty-eight days, Mercury was named for the winged-sandaled, fleet-footed messenger of the Roman gods (whose counterpart was Hermes in Greece), the son of Jupiter (Zeus) and Maia, and a quick-witted trickster from the moment that he was born, as well as a silver-tongued charmer and an ingenious inventor. This planet's sigil represents the god's staff, the caduceus, and is also the biological symbol for a hermaphrodite. Mercury rules Gemini and Virgo, and is linked with two houses, the third (Gemini's), which is concerned with siblings, communication, travel, learning, and everyday transactions and commerce

***Below:** The Moon gives those under its sway—especially people born under the zodiacal sign of the crab—the desire and ability to conceive, nurture, and bring their creation to fruition, be it a baby or an imaginative concept or project, in other words, a "brainchild."*

(Mercury was the patron deity of Roman merchants), and the sixth (Virgo's), which is mainly associated with work, service, and health (Mercury's snake-entwined caduceus was said to have healing powers, which is why it is often used to represent medicine, too).

Mercury is a personal planet whose appearance in a birth chart indicates how we gather knowledge and then use logic and reason to analyze it. Mercury therefore points to our intellectual ability or cleverness, our schooling, curiosity, and general appetite for learning, along with our capacity for thinking objectively. It also denotes how we communicate our thoughts to others, be it through speech or writing, which, if we use Mercury's articulacy to the full, may be clearly, fluently, and persuasively, yet also critically (and not everyone appreciates their actions being subjected to the scrutiny of a neutrally minded person whose opinions are unclouded by emotions, and who can therefore lack empathy). Relationships with siblings, or brother or sister figures, can be signified, too, when Mercury is highlighted. Further gifts of the fast-moving messenger god include the ability to think on one's feet, dextrousness, versatility, adaptability, and a zest for travel. If this desire to be mentally and physically occupied at all times is frustrated, however, restlessness, unreliability, capriciousness, and pranks may result, and it is no coincidence that the word "mercurial" can mean both liveliness and volatility, or that the word "quicksilver," an alternative name for the element of mercury, can denote unpredictability or slipperiness.

Below: *The planet Mercury's namesake is the Roman messenger god (the Greek Hermes), a winged herald whose staff (the caduceus), sandals, and hat enabled him to flit between the heavens, Earth, and the underworld at great speed.*

Hermes, or Mercury

The cunning and adroitness, the same good humour and ready answer which he gave proof of in the first days of his infancy, were often afterwards and with like success displayed by him—as, for example, when he stole the sceptre of Zeus, Aphrodite's girdle, Poseidon's trident, the sword of Ares, the tongs of Hephaestos, or Apollo's bow and arrows, in each case managing to make up matters, and smooth away the indignation of his victims.... But these and such-like instances of his knavery and cunning do not by any means express the whole character of Hermes [Mercury]; for his skill was also directed frequently to the purposes of useful invention. It was he, for example, who invented Apollo's lyre, as well as that one by which the Theban musician, Amphion, did such wonders; and it was he who taught Palamedes to express words in writing. And, besides, wherever danger that required skill and dexterity as much as courage presented itself, he was always present to assist.

—A.S. Murray

The Manual of Mythology (1882)

***Left:** One of Mercury's gifts to Gemini and Virgo individuals in particular is wanderlust, or the desire to travel far and wide, thereby gaining knowledge from being exposed to new experiences.*

Writing in *Christian Astrology* in 1647, the English astrologer William Lilly summed up Mercury's good qualities as follows: "he represents...a subtil and politick brain, intellect, and cogitation; an excellent disputant or Logician, arguing with learning and discretion, and using much eloquence in his speech, a searcher into all kinds of Mysteries and Learning, sharp and witty...desirous naturally of travel and seeing foraign parts; a man of an unwearied fancy, curious in the search of any occult knowledge; able by his own Genius to produce wonders..." Lilly then went on to warn of the potentially negative characteristics associated with Mercury, however: "A troublesome wit, a kinde of Phrenetick man, his tongue and Pen against every man...a great lyar, boaster, prattler, busybody, false, a tale-carrier...constant in no place or opinion...constant in nothing but idle words and bragging." They may be over four-hundred years old, but these judgments still hold true today.

***Below:** Another characteristic that Mercury bestows on those under its influence is the urge to communicate information, as well as a talent for doing so articulately and intelligently.*

Above: *Those born under the zodiacal signs of Taurus and Libra are ruled by Venus, the planet whose namesake is the seductive Roman goddess of love. They are consequently said to share the sensual, and rather vain, goddess's luxurious tastes, also considering it important to look well groomed and be smartly dressed.*

VENUS ♀

The planet Venus (which takes 225 days to orbit the Sun, and up to five months to travel through each zodiacal sign), which, with the exception of the Moon, shines the brightest in the night sky, is named for the Roman goddess of love, whose Greek equivalent was Aphrodite. The goddess being famous in Roman myth for her vanity, Venus' sigil is believed to depict her hand mirror or necklace, and is now also the biological symbol for femininity. Venus governs Taurus and Libra, and its two houses are the second (that of Taurus), which corresponds to finances and material possessions, and the seventh (Libra's), which indicates how we relate to people whom we consider partners, romantic or otherwise.

Venus, a personal planet, points to the things that bring us happiness in life, particularly the ecstasy that we may experience in the arms of a lover, but also light-hearted friendships and the delight that we find in creative endeavors and artistry, be they music, art, the theater, or simply lovely objects. It is partly because the goddess was associated with commerce and prosperity, and partly because she craved ease and opulence, that Venus bestows a talent for money management, a desire for financial security, and an urge to amass material possessions—especially luxury items—on us,

The Goddess Venus

Venus (Aphrodite), the goddess of love and beauty, was the daughter of Jupiter and Dione. Others say that Venus sprang from the foam of the sea. The zephyr wafted her along the waves to the Isle of Cyprus, where she was received and attired by the Seasons, and then led to the assembly of the gods. All were charmed with her beauty, and each one demanded her for his wife. Jupiter gave her to Vulcan, in gratitude for the service he had rendered in forging thunderbolts. So the most beautiful of the goddesses became the wife of the most ill-favored of gods. Venus possessed an embroidered girdle called Cestus, which had the power of inspiring love. Her favorite birds were swans and doves, and the plants sacred to her were the rose and myrtle.

—Thomas Bulfinch
The Age of Fable (1855)

too, thereby enabling us to live comfortably. Romance and sexual desire are Venus' primary province, however, and when this planet appears in a man's birth chart, it may denote his ideal woman, his anima (or the feminine side of his nature), his relationship with his girlfriend or life partner, or else his rapport with women in general; in a woman's chart, Venus may reveal what it is that she wants and needs in a romantic liaison. Venus otherwise signifies a balanced, benevolent, and soft-hearted personality that longs for harmony, hates unpleasantness, and therefore strives to keep the peace when confronted by hostility or arguments, thus encouraging friendly social interaction (and, indeed, in Roman mythology, even Mars, the aggressive god of war, succumbed to her tenderness and seductive charms). People who are influenced by Venus furthermore don't like to rush, typically have deeply sensual and highly developed esthetic tastes, and believe in indulging themselves and others, as well as in having fun with one another. They also take pride in their appearance and manners and similarly expect others to look well turned-out and to behave graciously. All positives have their flip sides in astrology, however, and less pleasing traits associated with Venus include decadence, promiscuity, narcissism, indolence, extravagance, and jealousy, and may result in someone who, in the seventeenth-century words of the English astrologer William Lilly, is given to "spending his [or her] means in Ale-houses, Taverns, and amongst Scandalous, Loose people, a meen Lazy companion...." It goes without saying that such characteristics can poison the blissfully relaxed relationships on which Venus-influenced people place such store, and can lead to an imbalanced and unfulfilling existence.

Venusian Characteristics

If Venus alone takes the domination of the soul, in an honorable position she makes her subjects pleasant, good, luxurious, eloquent, neat, cheerful, fond of dancing, eager for beauty, haters of evil, lovers of the arts, fond of spectacles, decorous, healthy, dreamers of pleasant dreams, affectionate, beneficent, compassionate, fastidious, easily conciliated, successful, and, in general, charming. In the opposite position she makes them careless, erotic, effeminate, womanish, timid, indifferent, depraved, censorious, insignificant, meriting reproach.

—Ptolemy
Tetrabiblos, second century A.D.

Above: *Greco-Roman mythology tells us that Aphrodite (the Roman Venus) came into being when Ouranos' (Uranos', or, in Rome, Uranus') severed genitals fell into the sea, the goddess then being borne by the waves to Cyprus, where she stepped ashore. She was also worshiped as Anadyomene, or "She Who Came Out of the Sea."*

Left: *In a birth chart, Venus can represent either the subject's dream woman or such Venusian characteristics as charm, friendliness, and indulgence.*

***Above:** Mars may have been the Roman god of war, but the planet that bears his name typically channels the aggression, competitiveness, strength, and stamina that are associated with this deity into less destructive pursuits, notably sporting endeavors.*

MARS ♂

Because the iron oxide on its surface causes Mars to glow red, the color of blood and life, the Romans named this planet for their virile and aggressive warrior god (whose Greek counterpart was Ares). It is therefore appropriate that its astrological sigil represents Mars' shield and spear, and that it today signifies masculinity in biological shorthand. Mars, which circles the Sun in 687 days (and takes between six weeks and eight months to pass through each zodiacal sign), rules Aries, and traditionally also Scorpio. This planet's (and Aries') house is the first, which denotes the self, beginnings, and vitality. Through its ancient link with Scorpio, whose primary planetary governor is now Pluto, Mars also brings its influence to bear on the eighth house, which is associated with sexual relationships in particular.

The position of the personal planet of Mars in a birth chart signifies what we really want to achieve or possess in life, and how single-mindedly and passionately we set about getting it. It is the planet of self-seeking or selfish behavior, for when we are fueled by a Martian urge to charge toward our goals, we don't care whose feelings we trample over in our driving need to reach our targets. Mars is therefore the planet that fills us with a pioneering spirit, energy, determination, and forcefulness when in pursuit of tangible aims, be they triggered by competitiveness, realizing career ambitions, or making a sexual conquest, and this planet infuses us with the stamina required to achieve them, too. When Mars is considered in relation to a man, it can denote a macho mindset or leadership qualities

Ares, or Mars

A son of Zeus and Hera, according to the belief of the Greeks, was originally god of the storm and tempest, and more particularly of the hurricane; but this his natural meaning was lost sight of at an earlier period, and more completely than in the case of most of the other gods, the character in which he appears to us being exclusively that of "god of the turmoil and storms in human affairs," in other words, "god of dreadful war," or more correctly, "of the wild confusion and strife of battle." Of all the upper gods he was the most fierce and terrible, taking pleasure in slaughter and massacre.

—A.S. Murray
The Manual of Mythology (1882)

Mars and Venus

Eris, the personification of fateful strife, was usually by [Mars'] side, Dread and Alarm (Deimos and Phobos) attended on his steps. On the other hand we find him, even in the Iliad *(v. 355 and xxi. 416), where his general character is that of a huge fierce combatant, associated with Aphrodite [Venus], the goddess of love. In the* Odyssey *(viii. 266) the story is told of his secret visit to her, when he was detected by Helios, who informed Hephaestos of the fact, whereupon the latter devised a cunning net, and catching the two together under it exhibited them to the gods of Olympos, and called upon Zeus to bring them to trial. This relation of Ares [Mars] to Aphrodite, who was even worshipped as his proper wife in Thebes, indicates very probably the peace and rest that follow the turmoil of war.*

—A.S. Murray
The Manual of Mythology (1882)

Above: *Mars imbues those under its sway with fighting spirit or a martial mindset.*

that either already exist or are lacking and longed for, while Mars' significance for a woman may indicate her masculine ideal, her animus (or the male side of her personality), her boyfriend or husband. More generally, Mars can suggest that we should either toughen up or that our emotions and actions have veered toward the thoughtless and violent. This planet can therefore empower us by making us strong-willed, assertive, and fearless, or can destroy all that we hold dear by prompting us to behave in a reckless or violent manner.

The Martian Character

Mars alone, given the domination of the soul, in an honorable position makes his subjects noble, commanding, spirited, military, versatile, powerful, venturesome, rash, unruly, indifferent, stubborn, keen, headstrong, contemptuous, tyrannical, active, eagerly angered, with the qualities of leadership. In a position of the opposite kind he makes them savage, insolent, bloodthirsty, makers of disturbances, spendthrifts, loud-mouthed, quick-fisted, impetuous, drunken, rapacious, evil-doers, pitiless, unsettled, mad, haters of their own kin, impious.

—Ptolemy
Tetrabiblos, second century A.D.

Below: *Men under the influence of Mars aren't afraid to rise to a challenge and assert their dominance.*

Above: *As a sky god, the Greek Zeus (or the Roman Jupiter) was said to control the weather, and to manifest his displeasure by hurling bolts of lightning.*

JUPITER ♃

Jupiter, which takes eleven years and 315 days to revolve around the Sun, is the largest visible planet, which is why the Romans named it for their sky god, the ruler of their lesser deities, and the ultimate lawgiver. Jupiter's Greek equivalent was Zeus—the son of Cronos (the Roman Saturn) and Rhea (Ops), and the brother of both Poseidon (Neptune) and Hades (Pluto)—and this "transpersonal," or "middle," planet's sigil describes the Greek letter *zeta,* "Z," Zeus' initial. As the planetary governor of Sagittarius, Jupiter's house is the ninth, which is linked with travel and other ways of broadening one's mind and horizons. Because Jupiter was once the sole ruler of Pisces, this planet also influences the twelfth house, which is concerned with healing and spiritual reflection.

Right: *Jupiter is often depicted holding a scepter, the symbol of his supreme authority over the gods and humans, as well as the weather.*

Zeus, or Jupiter

As the highest god...he was styled the father of gods and men, the ruler and preserver of the world. He was believed to be possessed of every form of power, endued with wisdom, and in his dominion over the human race partial to justice, and with no limit to his goodness and love. Zeus orders the alternation of day and night, the seasons succeed at his command, the winds obey him, now he gathers, now scatters the clouds, and bids the gentle rain fall to fertilize the fields and meadows. He watches over the administration of law and justice in the state, lends majesty to kings, and protects them in the exercise of their sovereignty. He observes attentively the general intercourse and dealings of men—everywhere demanding and rewarding uprightness, truth, faithfulness and kindness; everywhere punishing wrong, falseness, faithlessness, and cruelty. As the eternal father of men, he was believed to be kindly at the call of the poorest and most forsaken. The homeless beggar looked to him as a merciful guardian who punished the heartless, and delighted to reward pity and sympathy.

—A.S. Murray
The Manual of Mythology (1882)

The Jovian Character

If Jupiter alone has the domination of the soul, in honorable positions he makes his subjects magnanimous, generous, god-fearing, honorable, pleasure-loving, kind, magnificent, liberal, just, high-minded, dignified, minding their own business, compassionate, fond of discussion, beneficent, affectionate, with qualities of leadership. If he chances to be in the opposite kind of position, he makes their souls seem similar, to be sure, but with a difference in the direction of greater humility, less conspicuousness, and poorer judgment. For example, instead of magnanimity, he endows them with prodigality; instead of reverence for the gods, with superstition; instead of modesty, with cowardice; instead of dignity, with conceit; instead of kindness, with foolish simplicity; instead of the love of beauty, with love of pleasure; instead of high-mindedness, with stupidity; instead of liberality, with indifference, and the like.

—Ptolemy
Tetrabiblos, second century A.D.

The key word associated with Jupiter is "expansion," be it widening our social circle and making new contacts, traveling farther afield and learning about other cultures, enlarging our knowledge through college, university, or other forms of higher education, or deepening our spirituality, morality, or understanding of the world and our place within it. It is therefore regarded as the planet that has the power to bestow broad-mindedness and an all-embracing, all-encompassing outlook upon us, as well as wisdom, particularly in the fields of religion, ethics, and philosophy. And it is through its association with expansiveness that Jupiter is believed to bring good fortune and prosperity and to create new opportunities by pushing back boundaries, consequently blessing us with optimism, hope, and a "can-do" attitude. As the "Great Benefic," as this planet was once known by astrologers, Jupiter is additionally believed to have healing qualities. Other characteristics that are in the gift of the god Jove, as the Romans also called Jupiter, are joviality and exuberance, generosity and loyalty, and an honorable, just, liberal, or charitable way of judging and dealing with others, particularly those who are less fortunate than we. Certain negative traits are attributed to Jupiter, too, however, including a tendency to exaggerate or tell tall tales, greed and intemperance, and misplaced pride, snobbishness, or imperiousness. Despite its general benevolence, another less desirable effect of Jupiter's influence is that it has the potential to make existing problems far worse by blowing them wide open.

Left: *Jupiter encourages us to educate ourselves and thus to grow in wisdom.*

Below: *Another Jovian gift is the desire to expand our consciousness by opening our minds to all manner of spiritual beliefs.*

Right: *The Romans identified Saturn, their god of agriculture, with Cronos, the Titan father of the Greek gods. It was said that Cronos sought refuge in Italy after his dethronement by Zeus (Jupiter), where he taught humans how to cultivate the land.*

SATURN ♄

"He is the supreamest or highest of all Planets; is placed betwixt Jupiter and the Firmament, he is not very bright or glorious, or doth he twinkle or sparkle, but is of a Pale, Wan or Leaden, Ashy colour slow in motion," as William Lilly, the English astronomer, observed in his work *Christian Astrology* (1647). Indeed, Saturn takes twenty-nine years and 167 days to orbit the Sun, which meant that the average Roman citizen might have been

approaching death the second time that he or she viewed it in the night sky. This is one of the reasons why this planet was named for the Roman god of agriculture and time (whose equivalent in Greece was Cronos, or Kronos), who came to be equated with the "grim reaper," or the personification of death who cuts down humans with his sickle, which Saturn's sigil represents. Another is that Cronos was once the chief of the Greco–Roman gods until deposed by his son Zeus (Jupiter), making this planet's position beyond Jupiter appropriate. Saturn, a "transpersonal," or "middle," planet, rules Capricorn, and also Capricorn's house, the tenth, which is concerned with our long-term goals, particularly our career ambitions, and how we apply ourselves to achieving them. As Aquarius' original ruler, Saturn's influence lingers on in the eleventh house, too, which denotes how we relate to friends and social groups.

Saturn's Dethronement by Jupiter

Jupiter, or Jove (Zeus), though called the father of gods and men, had himself a beginning. Saturn (Cronos) was his father, and Rhea (Ops), his mother. Saturn and Rhea were of the race of Titans, who were the children of Earth and Heaven, which sprang from Chaos... The representations given of Saturn are not very consistent; for on the one hand his reign is said to have been the golden age of innocence and purity, and on the other he is described as a monster who devoured his children. Jupiter, however, escaped this fate, and when grown up espoused Metis (Prudence), who administered a draught to Saturn which caused him to disgorge his children. Jupiter, with his brothers and sisters, now rebelled against their father Saturn and his brothers the Titans; vanquishing them, and imprisoned some of them in Tartarus, inflicting other penalties on others.

—Thomas Bulfinch
The Age of Fable (1855)

Below: *Saturn became known as "Father Time," or the "grim reaper," who, according to traditional belief, uses his sickle—an agricultural implement—to scythe down and harvest the lives of those whose time on Earth is up.*

The Saturnine Character

If Saturn alone is ruler of the soul and dominates Mercury and the Moon, if he has a dignified position with reference to the universe and the angles, he makes his subjects lovers of the body, strong-minded, deep thinkers, austere, of a single purpose, laborious, dictatorial, ready to punish, lovers of property, avaricious, violent, amassing treasure, and jealous; but if his position is the opposite and without dignity, he makes them sordid, petty, mean-spirited, indifferent, mean-minded, malignant, cowardly, diffident, evil-speakers, solitary, tearful, shameless, superstitious; fond of toil, unfeeling, devisers of plots against their friends, gloomy, taking no care of the body.

—Ptolemy

Tetrabiblos, second century A.D.

Just as the mythological Saturn was a devouring, disciplinarian father, so the astrological characteristics associated with this planet include repression and limitation, and sometimes even someone's own father if he was a stern and strict figure who overshadowed that individual's childhood. Indeed, imagine such a person, and you will have a good idea of some typical saturnine traits, which may include a conservative and coldly realistic, unfeeling outlook, as well as a firm determination to keep us on the straight and narrow. However, these need not be negative qualities, for they also indicate a prudent, serious, and mature attitude, especially toward others, along with true commitment and devotion, straightforward ambitions, and the understanding that anything worthwhile has to be patiently worked for, and that no corners can be cut in the process. Saturn can therefore be regarded a wise teacher who slowly and soberly shows us how to live a responsible and productive life, and suggests that we will receive tangible rewards for the sacrifices that we make in so doing. For in return for being self-disciplined, tenacious, and diligent in our careers, for instance, we should eventually earn ourselves financial security, an elevated status, the respect of others, and the satisfaction of knowing that our success has been hard won and is consequently well deserved.

Above: *Saturn's influence can be compared to that of an old-school teacher, or a strict disciplinarian who wants us to make the best of ourselves, even if it doesn't always seem that way.*

Left: *Joan of Arc was a Capricorn whose saturnine commitment to her cause cost her her life.*

URANUS ♅

The planet Uranus was discovered in 1781 by the British astronomer Sir William Herschel, Hershel's achievement being commemorated in Uranus' sigil, which represents the letter "H" bisected by a planetary orb. "Herschel's planet," "Herschell," or "Herschellium," was eventually named for Uranus, a primeval Roman sky god whose Greek counterpart was Ouranos, or Uranos. Emerging from chaos, it is told, "Father Sky" came together with Gaia (Gaea), "Mother Earth," to create the landscape and all plants and living creatures, further fruits of their union including the Titans, whom Uranus treated so cruelly that in the end his Titan son, Saturn (Cronos, or Kronos), urged on by Gaia, castrated him with his sickle and assumed the leadership of the gods himself. Uranus takes eighty-four years to orbit the Sun, and is considered an "impersonal," or "outer," planet. Now Aquarius' primary planetary ruler, Uranus takes precedence over Saturn—a rather paradoxical role reversal, given the outcome of their mythological power struggle—in influencing the eleventh house, that associated with Aquarius, which corresponds to friendships and group activities.

Perhaps it is because the planet Uranus was unknown to the ancients that its astrological associations have next to nothing to do with its namesake deity, which may otherwise have been expected to confer such characteristics as despotism, brutality, and maybe even emasculation, or powerlessness, upon those who fall under its influence. Instead, they are tied up both with the planet's extreme tilt—98 degrees on its axis of spin as

***Below:** Uranus gives Aquarians in particular both a youthful outlook and a way of looking at the world that is fresh, original, and untainted by the prejudices that are often acquired in adulthood.*

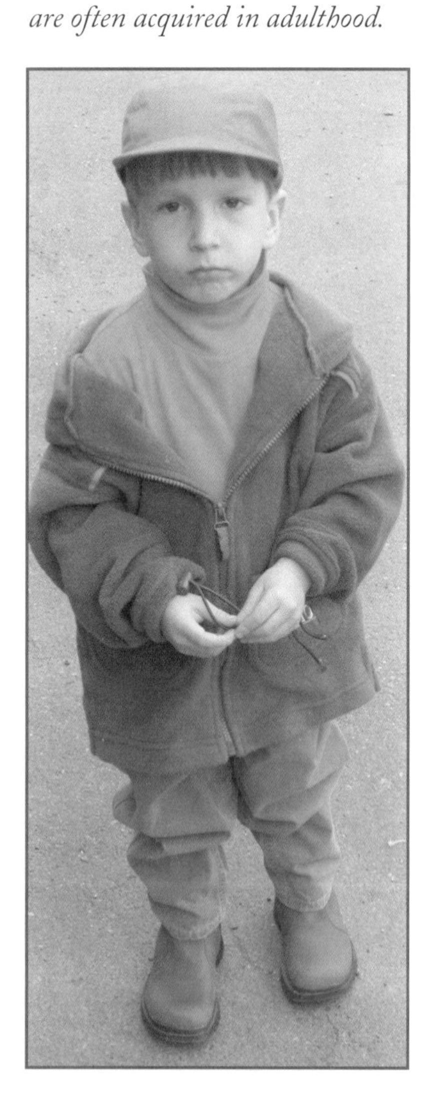

The Titans and the Overthrow of Uranus

The Titans were, like the Olympian deities, twelve in number, and grouped for the most part in pairs: Okeanos and Tethys, Hyperion and Theia, Kreios and Eurybia, Koios and Phoebe, Kronos [Saturn] and Rhea [Ops], Japetos and Themis. Instead of Eurybia we find frequently Mnemosyne.... While Themis, Mnemosyne, and Japetos may be singled out as personifications of a civilizing force...the other Titans appear to represent wild, powerful, and obstructive forces. In keeping with this character we find them rising in rebellion first against their father and afterwards against Zeus [Jupiter].

In the former experiment the result was that Uranos [Uranus], as we learn from the poetic account of the myth, threw them into Tartaros, where he kept them bound. But Gaea [Gaia], his wife, grieving at the hard fate of her offspring, provided the youngest son, Kronos, with a sickle or curved knife, which she had made of stubborn adamant, and told him how and when to wound his father with it irremediably. The enterprise succeeded, the Titans were set free, married their sisters, and begat a numerous family of divine beings, while others of the same class sprang from the blood of the wound of Uranos as it fell to the ground.

—A.S. Murray
The Manual of Mythology (1882)

compared to the Earth's 23 degrees—and its manner of rotation, which, like that of Venus, is clockwise, or retrograde, while that of the rest of the planets is counterclockwise. As a result of these differences, Uranus is linked with innovative, unpredictable, and unconventional ways of thinking and behavior, as well as with rebellion against the norm, so that its energy as the "Great Awakener," as it is sometimes called, can result in sudden, radical, and even revolutionary changes, especially where social systems and values are concerned, when they may have either wonderfully beneficial or disastrously destructive consequences. Indeed, at their most extreme, the effects of being under Uranus' sway may include being an eccentric, "antisocial," or anarchic character, or else a brave and inspired social reformer. Uranus' oddball energy can furthermore trigger the most inventive and unusual of ideas, reflecting its status as the "higher octave" of Mercury, the planet of basic intelligence, but one that lacks Uranus' dynamic, transcendental qualities. Because the Uranian mindset is pioneering, experimental, forward-looking, and determined to transcend conventional boundaries, it follows that it embraces new technology and is inspired by its potential, and that it is ever curious and willing to question established beliefs. There are some significant downsides of having an uncompromisingly willful, logical, and independent, Uranian personality, however, such as forever feeling disconnected from, or at odds with, others.

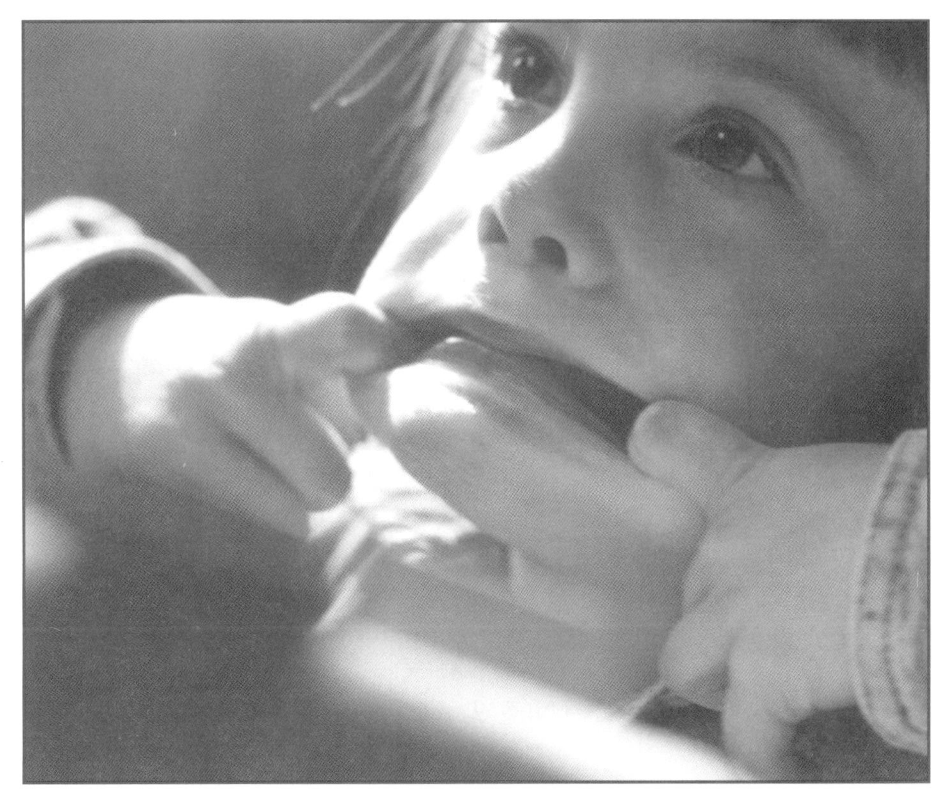

Above: *Uranus enables us to shed any inhibitions and fearlessly challenge authority figures or accepted practices and beliefs.*

Left: *People who were born under zodiacal signs that are governed by more conventional or nonconfrontational ruling planets often brand those under Uranus' sway as being antisocial or rebellious.*

Right: *The influence of Neptune can cause Pisceans in particular to be idealistic daydreamers who seek to escape harsh reality by taking refuge in more agreeable dreams and fantasies.*

Below: *Neptune's symbol is a trident, an implement that Greek fishermen traditionally used to spear fish. When wielded by mighty Neptune, however, it penetrated the earth and even rocks and mountains, thereby causing streams and rivers to spring up, and sometimes also creating devastating floods that overwhelmed the land.*

NEPTUNE ♆

It was not until 1846 that earthlings became aware of Neptune's existence, largely thanks to the German astronomers Johann Galle and Heinrich d'Arrest. Named for the Roman god of the sea (Poseidon in Greek mythology), perhaps because the methane in its atmosphere causes it to appear blue in color, Neptune's sigil symbolizes the trident, a weapon carried by that deity. Appropriately, Neptune is the primary planetary governor of Pisces, the zodiacal sign of the fishes. An "impersonal," or "outer," planet, it takes Neptune 164 years and 292 days to revolve around the Sun and pass through all of the signs of the zodiac, remaining in each for around fourteen years. Neptune's house is also that of Pisces, the twelfth, which relates to our unconscious selves and spirituality.

Neptune was discovered at a time when the Romantic movement was flowering in Europe, a style that encouraged artists, writers, and composers to express their feelings, be they hopeful or fearful, ecstatic or downcast, as well as to pay homage to the glories of the natural world and to celebrate their countries' culture and achievements. This is one of the reasons why astrologers associate Neptune with the emotions, creativity, and an instinctive search for beauty, which is also why it is called the "higher octave" of Venus, the planet that gives us an appreciation of artistry. Neptune's influence is far more profound than that of Venus, however, not least because its namesake god's watery realm is linked with that of the unconscious in symbolic thought, whose workings can appear as confused and mysterious to the rational mind as the constantly changing nature of the oceans

Neptune Becomes Ruler of the Ocean

On the dethronement of Saturn, Jupiter with his brothers Neptune (Poseidon) and Pluto (Dis) divided his dominions. Jupiter's portion was the heavens, Neptune's the ocean, and Pluto's were the realms of the dead. Earth and Olympus were common property.

—Thomas Bulfinch
The Age of Fable (1855)

Neptune's Element

To Poseidon [Neptune] fell the control of the element of water, and he in like manner was conceived as a god, in whose character and actions were reflected the phenomena of that element, whether as the broad navigable sea, or as the cloud which gives fertility to the earth, growth to the grain and vine, or as the fountain which refreshes man, cattle, and horses. A suitable symbol of his power, therefore, was the horse, admirably adapted as it is both for labour and battle, whilst its swift springing movement compares finely with the advance of a foaming wave of the sea.

—A.S. Murray
The Manual of Mythology (1882)

and seas and the myriad strange creatures that dwell within their depths. The Neptunian personality is consequently said to be hard to understand, being nebulous and dreamy, but also, through its connection with the element of water, empathetic, compassionate, and intuitive to the point of having psychic insight. And just as the sea can be calm one moment and turbulent the next, so, under Neptune's influence, we may rapidly switch from feeling composed and content to unstable, muddled, and despairing, a state that we may try to escape by seeking refuge in fantasies and daydreams at best, or mind-altering substances at worst. Yet Neptune's subtle powers can also infuse us with unselfishness and a desire to help others, along with giving us a deep spiritual awareness and an idealistic, if rather imprecise, vision that can enable us to transcend the harsh realities of the real world and pin our hopes on building a better existence, one in which all artificial boundaries have been swept aside and we all live in kindly, happy harmony.

Above: *Neptune, the planet named for the Roman god of the watery realms, is said to have the power to swamp us with stormy or uncontrollable emotions.*

Neptune Rides the Waves

Neptune was the chief of the water deities. The symbol of his power was the trident, or spear with three points, with which he used to shatter rocks, to call forth or subdue storms, to shake the shores and the like. He created the horse and was patron of horse-races. His own horses had brazen hoofs and golden manes. They drew his chariot over the sea, which became smooth before him, while the monsters of the deep gambolled about in his path.

—Thomas Bulfinch
The Age of Fable (1855)

Below: *Because Neptune's element is water, it heightens our caring instincts and enables us to empathize with all living creatures.*

Above: According to Greco–Roman myth, Hades (Pluto) carried Persephone (Proserpina), the daughter of the grain goddess Demeter (Ceres), off to the underworld to be his wife. Zeus (Jupiter) eventually ruled that she should spend half the year (fall and winter) with Hades, and the other half (spring and summer) with her mother.

Below: Pluto is associated with endings and dark despair, but equally with beginnings and joyful hope.

PLUTO ♇

It was the American astronomer Percival Lowell who first suspected the presence of the planet Pluto in our solar system, and when, twenty-five years later, its existence was confirmed by his fellow countryman Clyde Tombaugh in 1930, Pluto's sigil was established as a combination of the letters "P" and "L," partly in Lowell's honor, and partly because they spell out the first two letters of Pluto's name, which is also that of the Roman god of the underworld (alternatively known as Dis, and as Hades in ancient Greece). Pluto, an "impersonal," or "outer," planet, takes 248 years and 183 days to orbit the Sun. As Scorpio's primary ruler, its house is the eighth, which is concerned with intimate relationships, regeneration and transformations, and wealth, particularly that of other people.

The characteristics that astrologists ascribe to the planet Pluto are drawn directly from the tales that Greco–Roman mythology tell of the dark deity that ruled the underworld, the abode of the souls of

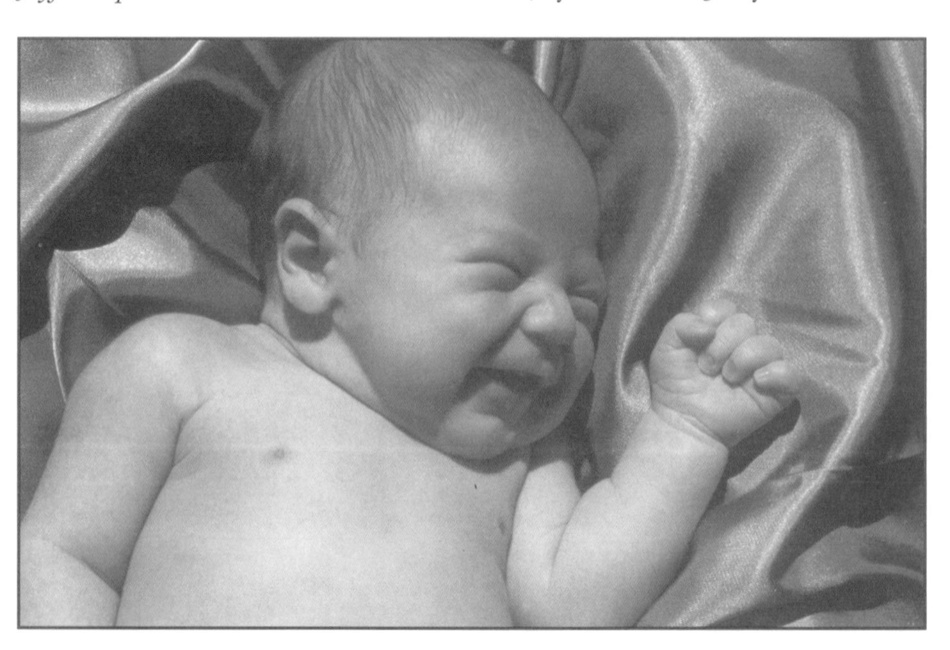

Benevolent, Implacable Pluto

While by virtue of his power of giving fertility to vegetation, of swelling the seed cast into the furrows of the earth, and of yielding treasures of precious metal, he was justly viewed as a benevolent deity and a true friend of man, there was another and very grim side to his character, in which he appears as the implacable, relentless god, whom no cost of sacrifice could persuade to permit any one who had once passed his gates ever to return. For this reason, to die, to go to Hades' [Pluto's] house, to pass out of sight, to be lost in the darkness of the lower world, was looked forward to as the dismal inevitable fate awaiting all men. Yet there must have been some consolation in the belief that the life thus claimed by him had been originally his gift, as were the means of comfort and pleasure thus cut off. In later times, when the benevolent side of his character came more into view, assuring hopes arose concerning a future happy life that robbed death of its terrors.

—A.S. Murray
The Manual of Mythology (1882)

The Entrance to Pluto's Realm

The entrance was guarded by the dog of Hades [Pluto], the dreaded Cerberus, a monster with three heads and a serpent's tail, fawning on those who entered, but showing his horrible teeth to those who tried to pass out. But besides by this gateway, the lower was separated from the upper world by rivers with impetuous torrents, of which the most famous was the Styx, a stream of such terrible aspect that even the highest gods invoked it as a witness of the truth of their oaths.

—A.S. Murray
The Manual of Mythology (1882)

Above: *The mythological Pluto's realm was that of the dead, and when people die, they sometimes leave financial legacies that transform the fortunes of the living, which is why this planet is associated with windfalls.*

those who had died. Not only was this shadowy place invisible and inaccessible to the living, but Pluto himself tended to hold himself aloof from his fellow deities, with the result that this is said to be the planet of mystery and secrecy, one whose intense influence can cause us to feel isolated or alienated from others, to suffer from power complexes, or to have a tendency to hatch plots and plans behind the scenes. Pluto may have the power to depress, yet its influence can bring astounding reversals of fortune, too, for just as Christians believe that we are reborn through death, and the apparently lifeless natural world is rejuvenated as winter gives way to spring, so this planet gives us the necessary endurance and resilience to survive a long period of hardship and to emerge transformed for the better. So not only is Pluto the planet of death and endings, it is that of birth and beginnings, too, compounded by its association with sexual relationships. Similarly, as ruler of the eighth house, Pluto is linked with the money that may enable us to make a fresh start, perhaps as the result of a bequest or legacy. As strange as it may sound, gloomy Pluto can therefore be described as a planet that gives us the hope that however dire our existence, if we can just hold out long enough for a complete metamorphosis to be effected, we may be rewarded by a wonderful, life-changing gift, be it self-reinvention, a baby, or a windfall.

The Elements

For millennia, it was believed that everything in the universe was made up of the four elements—fire, earth, air, and water—in varying degrees. This theory was extended to humans, too, in whom the four elements were thought to take the form of fluids, or "humors," that circulated the body, an imbalance of which could cause specific ailments and personality traits. The element of fire, which supposedly manifested itself as the hot and dry, choleric humor (yellow bile), was said to make someone hot- or bad-tempered; the element of earth's cold and dry humor was black bile, or melancholic, an excess of which could cause a person to be depressed and gloomy; the element of air was equated with the blood and the hot and moist, sanguine humor, which, if dominant, would result in a confident, cheerful, and optimistic personality; and finally, the element of water was said to flow around the body as the cold and moist, phlegmatic humor, which was associated with a stolid and unemotional personality (in contrast to the modern interpretation of water's influence).

Below: *Each sign of the zodiac is associated with part of the human body: Aries with the head; Taurus, the throat; Gemini, the arms; Cancer: the chest; Leo: the heart and back; Virgo, the digestive tract; Libra, the kidneys; Scorpio, the bladder and genitals; Sagittarius, the thighs; Capricorn, the knees; Aquarius, the calves; and Pisces, the feet.*

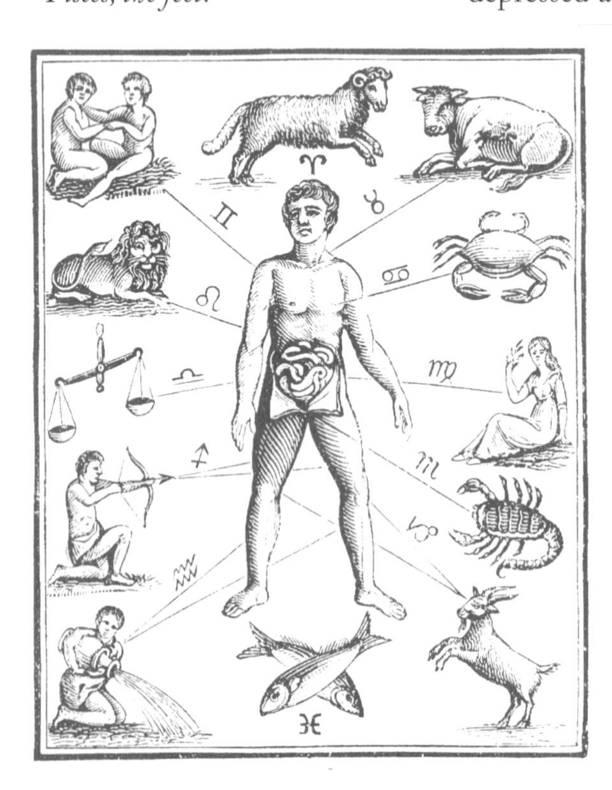

The zodiacal signs were similarly each allocated an element and related characteristics, Aries, Leo, and Sagittarius (all of which have a masculine, active, or

The Seasons, Elements, and Zodiacal Signs

These Signs are again divided many ways; as first, into four quadrants or quarters, answering to the four quarters of the year. The Vernal or Spring quarter, is sanguine, Hot and Moyst, and containes the first three Signs, viz. Aries, Taurus, Gemini. The Estival or Summer quarter is Hot, Dry and Cholerick, and containes the fourth, fifth and sixth Signs, viz. Cancer, Leo, Virgo.

The Autumnal or Harvest quarter is Cold, Dry and Melancholly, and contains the seventh, eighth and ninth Signs, viz. Libra, Scorpio, Sagittarius. The Hyemnal, Brumal or Winter quarter is Cold, Moyst and Phlegmatique, and containes the tenth, eleventh and twelfth Signs, viz. Capricorn, Aquarius, Pisces.

They are again divided in division of the Elements, for some Signs in nature are Fiery, Hot and Dry, viz. Aries, Leo, Sagittarius, and these three Signs constitute the Fiery Triplicity.

Others are Dry, Cold and Earthly [earthy], viz. Taurus, Virgo, Capricorn, and make the Earthly Triplicity.

Others are Aiery [airy], Hot, and Moyst, viz. Gemini, Libra, Aquarius, which make the Aiery Triplicity.

Others are Watry [watery], Cold, and Moyst, viz. Cancer, Scorpio, Pisces, and are called the Watry Triplicity.

—William Lilly
Christian Astrology (1647)

positive, polarity) being equated with fire; Taurus, Virgo, and Capricorn (feminine-, passive-, or negative-polarity signs), with earth; Gemini, Libra, and Aquarius (which share a masculine polarity), with air; and Cancer, Scorpio, and Pisces (all feminine-polarity signs), with water. Because each element influences three signs, these divisions are often called triplicities or trigons. According to astrological belief, the first of the fire, earth, air, and water signs in the zodiacal cycle (Aries, Taurus, Gemini, and Cancer) display the strongest of their element's qualities, which are diluted in the second signs (Leo, Virgo, Libra, and Scorpio), and even more so in the third (Sagittarius, Capricorn, Aquarius, and Pisces). All of the elements are linked with plus points and potential pitfalls, so that whichever sign we were born under, and whichever element therefore has the greatest influence on our thoughts and behavior, we should all strive to counteract the negatives by cultivating the positives associated with other elements, thereby helping us to become more balanced and happier individuals.

THE FIRE SIGNS 

United as they are by the element of fire, those born under the zodiacal signs of Aries, Leo, and Sagittarius are said to have certain characteristics in common. Imagine a fire crackling away merrily in a hearth, its orange flames flickering and springing ever higher as more wood is added, and it is easy to see the connection that the ancient astrologers made between this element and the warm and vibrant, fiery personality. Just as we are drawn to a fire when we are feeling chilly, or gather around this bright focal point, so fiery people are said to be warm-hearted, generous, and magnetic, to relish being the center of attention (notably Sun-governed Leos), and to be stimulated and energized by contact with others, particularly airy individuals, whose ideas act like oxygen on fire, as well as their fire-sign fellows. When their imaginations are fired up, they can be highly creative, and when their enthusiasm has been kindled, their vitality, exuberance, ardor, and passion enlivens those around them. Like fire's unpredictable, leaping flames, Aries, Leo, and Sagittarius individuals are adventurous, outgoing, impulsive, and spontaneous, and often inspirational, experimental trendsetters who are blessed with a masculine polarity's confidence and the courage of their convictions. If a headstrong, fiery character's flame is to burn brightly, he or she needs self-autonomy and freedom of

***Above:** Others are drawn to the warmth and crackling energy that fiery Ariens, Leos, and Sagittarians radiate, and they in turn thrive when given the opportunity to shine in front of admiring crowd.*

action, however, and watery or earthy influences may dampen or suppress a fiery type's high spirits. Along with having a gift for making things happen (and Ariens are spirited initiators), those whose element is fire are furthermore typically honest and optimistic (particularly jovial Sagittarians).

Fire can be dangerous, however, for it can swiftly burn out of control, damaging or consuming everything in its path. In the same way, when fueled by excitement, a fiery temperament can often either become overstimulated and then rashly and unthinkingly overstep certain boundaries, or else a spark of annoyance may rapidly escalate into furious rage. Fiery individuals may therefore lack self-control, and are prone to burnout if they are unable, or unwilling, to rein in their energies. They may be hot-tempered, but their heated outbursts are usually short-lived, and once vented, their fury generally quickly subsides. Further unappealing fiery traits include a tendency to be aggressive and domineering, (particularly Mars-ruled Ariens), arrogant and egotistical (especially Sun-governed Leos), and abrupt and impatient (notably mutable-quadruplicity Sagittarians). Indeed, despite their often heart-warming demonstrativeness, all have a tendency to be the exhibitionists of the zodiac, which others may find tiresome.

Below: *Earth-governed individuals are in their element when participating in such outdoor pursuits as trekking, for feeling the earth beneath their feet grounds them.*

THE EARTH SIGNS 

The earth signs are Taurus, Virgo, and Capricorn, and, as their element suggests, all have fundamentally down-to-earth natures. These are level-headed individuals, who, like their element, are stable and supportive. Even when an earthquake, in the form of personal catastrophe, rocks the very foundations of their existence, their resilience and practical approach generally soon reassert themselves, enabling them to rebuild their world steadily, patiently, and productively, in typically earthy fashion. Those born under earth signs are furthermore logical and straightforward, and prefer to deal with facts rather than waste their time on others' flights of fancy or abstract notions (especially Mercury-governed Virgos), which is why they sometimes find airy types unsettling. Additionally hardworking, loyal, and dependable, they can be relied upon to see a job through to the end, and, once committed, to remain faithful to their friends and loved ones. From this description, it may sound as though sensible, earthy people are rather boring, yet while their constancy and love of routines may make them predictable, it is no coincidence that "earthy" can mean "sensual," or "lusty," and, indeed, Venus-ruled Taureans have a pronounced relish for indulging their senses. All earth-sign characters enjoy spending time outside, too, be it lazing around, hiking, or tending their gardens, for they feel grounded when they are in physical contact with their element. And if you think of the way water seeps into the earth, encouraging growth, it is clear that despite their imperturbable appearance, earthy personalities have a lot going on under the surface, which those whose element is empathetic water have a talent for bringing out.

Some of the disadvantages of having earth as an element include the passiveness that it bestows on its children, a characteristic that is compounded by having a feminine polarity, which means that Taureans, Virgoans, and Capricorneans can be somewhat stolid and inactive, and, because they are naturally prudent and cautious, too, may do little on joyous impulse (which is why they frequently disapprove of spontaneous, fiery individuals) and may rarely take the initiative. They can also be hard-headed materialists (especially saturnine Capricorns) who sometimes take greater pleasure in working hard to accumulate the money and possessions that make them feel secure than in simply having fun, which is why they may seem depressingly upright, serious, and ambitious to playful, air-sign individuals, and miserly to generous, fire-sign people. Another trait that may irritate others is their slow, considered, plodding approach and refusal to be rushed, even if their thoroughness, attention to detail, and tenacity bring concrete results in the end.

THE AIR SIGNS

The zodiacal signs of Gemini, Libra, and Aquarius all have the element of air in common, and because air is associated with the intellect in astrological thought, they are believed to be united in their analytical, logical, and rational way of thinking. These coolly cerebral people are stimulated by ideas, be they those that they think up themselves or those that spring from the minds of creative, fiery characters, artistic, watery individuals, or their ingenious, airy brethren (they often consider practical, earthy types unimaginative and uninspiring, however). Indeed, they themselves tend to come up with the most inventive of concepts, and none more so than groundbreaking, Uranus-governed Aquarians. And just as the air in Earth's atmosphere is both everywhere and moves around freely, so do they, partly because they are constantly in search of new and interesting viewpoints, partly because they are curious about others and enjoy evaluating their personalities, and partly because they are fluent and articulate communicators who feel the urge to impart their news and views to others, maybe because information is transmitted over the airwaves, but in talkative Geminians' case, mainly because they are ruled by Mercury, the

Above: *Taurus, Virgo, and Capricorn people are attracted to earthy pursuits, such as tending their gardens.*

***Right:** Those who come into contact with air-sign people are often captivated by their bright and breezy manner.*

planet named for the Roman messenger god. Sociable, amiable, and easygoing, airy individuals have a charming, playful streak (especially flirty, Venus-ruled Librans) and are great fun to be with, although they soon take off if they feel that their companions have nothing to offer them in the way of intriguing diversions.

The airy traits of blowing hot and cold, fickleness, unreliability, a resistance to being contained, and a horror of being bored can annoy or wound those who were born under more constant, clingy, or patient zodiacal signs, as can, at times, the aloof or breezy manner that is also characteristic of the element of air. Although airy people generally don't mean to irritate or wound, they can lack empathy and emotional depth, and because they don't often need propping up themselves, can't understand why others may occasionally want or require a tangible gesture of devotion, sympathy, or support. When confronted by anger or tears, they may consequently worsen matters by either making themselves scarce or openly speaking their minds in an attempt to clear the air, when their objectivity may be perceived as criticism. Sometimes lacking in direction when their airy element is blowing them this way and that, these impractical types are furthermore prone to wandering around with their heads in the clouds, and don't appreciate being torn from their fascinating fantasies should someone try to encourage them to reconnect with the real world by bringing them back down to earth.

***Below:** Their insecurity-inducing element of water gives Cancer, Scorpio, and Pisces individuals a tendency to tie themselves in knots whenever they feel uncertain or worried.*

THE WATER SIGNS ♒

The element of water (which psychologists associate with the unconscious mind) gives those whose zodiacal signs are Cancer, Scorpio, or Pisces certain shared characteristics, such as profound emotions, genuinely felt compassion, and intuitive insight. Because they also have an introspective, feminine polarity, water-sign individuals often spend much of their time in their personal inner worlds (and none more so than secretive, Plutonian Scorpios), be it contemplating their feelings, daydreaming, or gradually nurturing the germ of a concept to successful fruition. And just as water supports a host of life forms, so the watery mind is teeming—somewhat chaotically—with creative notions, which may nevertheless rarely come to the surface to face the scrutiny of others, partly because sensitive, watery people can't bear the hurt of having a "brainchild" ridiculed or rejected (particularly if they are hypersensitive, Moon-governed crabs), and partly because their nebulous element sometimes makes it hard for them to express themselves. They have no such difficulty understanding others, however, for they are both born listeners and almost psychically attuned to the emotional signals that they pick up from those around them, and because they are sentimental and feel pain so deeply, cannot help but respond with sympathy when someone is distressed, especially if they are altruistic, Neptune-ruled Pisceans. These are kind, giving, and supportive individuals who will sacrifice much for their loved ones if they feel that they are in turn appreciated and cherished.

Cancerians, Scorpios, and Pisceans are often beset by insecurities that blunt, unthinking fiery characters, straightforward, earthy sorts, or objective, airy types may inadvertently trigger, condemning these touchy personalities to agonies of self-doubt and worry. And when they feel wounded, they typically either retreat into themselves or lash out in self-protective retaliation (stinging scorpions most of all), thereby confirming their reputation as being changeable and moody, and bewildering or upsetting the supposed culprits, who may not have appreciated quite how thin-skinned water can make them, and may not be able to grasp exactly why they themselves are deemed to deserve punishment in the form of either the silent treatment or accusatory words. Not only that, but their watery element can endow those born under the signs of the crab, scorpion, and fishes with a tendency to control those close to them by means of sulking and emotional blackmail, and, after a while, others may think it easier to comply than risk being swamped with tears or buffeted by stormy emotions.

Above: *Their loved ones usually consider water-sign people pearls of empathy, intuition, and creativity. The artist Johannes Vermeer (1632–75), a water-ruled Pisces, was renowned for his sensitive, moody paintings.*

Diseases Signified by the Fire Signs

Aries *All Whelks, Pimples in the Face, small Pocks, hare Lips, Ring-worms, Tooth-ach, Head-ach and Baldnesse…*

Leo *Convulsions, paines in the back, trembling or passion of the heart, sore eyes, the yellow-Jaundices…*

Sagittarius *Feavers Pestilentiall, fals from Horses, or hurts from them or four-footed Beasts…*

Fire Signes stir up red choller.

Diseases Signified by the Earth Signs

Taurus *The Kings Evil, sore Throats, Wens, Fluxes of Rheumes falling into the throat, Quinzies…*

Virgo *The Worms, Winde, Chollicke, all Obstructions in the bowels and miseraicks, croking of the Guts…*

Capricorn *All Diseases incident to [the knees], either by Straines or Fractures; it notes Leprosie, the Itch, the Scab…*

Earthly Signs stir up melancholly.

Diseases Signified by the Air Signs

Gemini *All Diseases or infirmities in the Armes, Shoulders, Hands, corrupted Blood, distempered Fancies…*

Libra *Diseases in the Loynes or Hanches; Great Heats in the Back… Surfets by drinking or eating…*

Aquarius *Governeth the Legs, Ancles, and all manner of Infirmities incident to those members…*

Ayery Signes [stir up] Blood.

Diseases Signified by the Water Signs

Cancer *Weak Digestion, cold Stomack, Ptisick, salt Flegms, roten Coughs, dropsicall Humours…*

Scorpio *The Stone in the Secret parts, Fistulaes, or the Pyles… all afflicting the Privy parts either in Man or Woman…*

Pisces *Generally salt Flegms, Scabs, Itch, Borches, Breakings out, Boyles and Ulcers, Colds and moyst diseases…*

Watry Signes [stir up] Spittle.

—William Lilly, *Christian Astrology* (1647)

The Quadruplicities

The three quadruplicities—cardinal, fixed, and mutable—are each associated with a set of characteristics that indicate the innate instincts and motivations that underpin our actions. Also termed the qualities (of life) or modes, the quadruplicities are so called because four zodiacal signs are assigned to each. Although two share a masculine (active, or positive) polarity, and two a feminine (passive, or negative) polarity, the four signs that make up a quadruplicity's group are otherwise dissimilar, not least because each has a different element. It is the ancient link between the Sun's annual cycle and the zodiacal cycle, which starts with Aries in the spring, and then marks out the passing of the four seasons as it progresses, that is believed to have given rise to the concept of the quadruplicities, as described by the English astrologer William Lilly in his work *Christian Astrology* (1647).

Below: *Each of the four seasons is linked with a cardinal-, fixed-, and mutable-quadruplicity sign: spring, with cardinal Aries, fixed Taurus, and mutable Gemini; summer, with cardinal Cancer, fixed Leo, and mutable Virgo; fall, with cardinal Libra, fixed Scorpio, and mutable Sagittarius; and winter, with cardinal Capricorn, fixed Aquarius, and mutable Pisces.*

The Signs again are divided into Moveable [cardinal], Fixed and Common [mutable], Aries, Cancer, Libra, Capricorn are called moveable and Cardinal: moveable, because when the Sun enters into Aries and Libra, the Weather and Season of the Year quickly varies and changes; they are called Cardinal, because when the Sun enters into any of those Signs from that time we denominate the Quarters of the yeer. For from the Sun entering into Aries and Libra the Equinoctial or the Spring and Autumne [fall] arise; from the Sun his entrance into Cancer and Capricorn ariseth the Solstice of Summer and Winter.

The Fixed Signs doe in order follow the Equinoctial and Tropicks; and they are called fixed, for that when Sun enters into them, the season of the year is fixed, and we doe more evidently perceive either Heat or Cold, Moysture or Drinesse. The fixed Signes are these, Taurus, Leo, Scorpio, Aquarius.

Common [mutable] Signes are constitutes between moveable [cardinal] and fixed, and retain a property or nature, pertaking both with the preceding and consequent Sign: and they are Gemini, Virgo, Sagittarius, Pisces. They are called By-corporeal or double bodied, because they represent two Bodies: as Gemini two Twinnes, Pisces two Fishes.

It may be written in idiosyncratic, old-fashioned English, but Lilly's explanation gives us a good understanding of the personal traits imparted by the cardinal-, fixed-, and mutable-quadruplicity signs.

THE CARDINAL SIGNS

The cardinal-quadruplicity signs are Aries (which is masculine and fiery), Cancer (feminine and watery), Libra (masculine and airy), and Capricorn (feminine and earthy). Each cardinal sign heralds the start of a new season, Aries (March 21 to April 20) signaling the beginning of spring, Cancer (June 22 to July 22), that of summer, Libra (September 23 to

October 22), the start of fall, and Capricorn (December 22 to January 19), the onset of winter.

Because their zodiacal signs initiate the seasons, cardinal-quadruplicity people are regarded as self-starters who cope well with change. They are also said to be pioneering, enterprising, and, because they usually take the initiative, to have leadership qualities. These decisive and ambitious, active and go-getting characters are motivated by the desire to achieve their goals as quickly as possible, and they channel all of the energy that they can muster into doing so. Their drive to get ahead can also make them rather self-centered, pushy, and bossy, however, and they typically insist on following their own path in life.

Reflecting the influence of the ruling planets, polarities, and elements associated with their respective zodiacal signs, they tend to take dissimilar approaches when asserting themselves: Arien people do so courageously and forcefully; Cancerian characters, slowly and circumspectly; Libran personalities, tactfully and charmingly; and Capricorn individuals, patiently and deliberately.

THE FIXED SIGNS

The fixed-quadruplicity signs are Taurus (which is feminine and earthy), Leo (masculine and fiery), Scorpio (feminine and watery), and Aquarius (masculine and airy). The reason why each is said to have a "fixed" nature is because its month falls in the middle of a season, when the weather is relatively unchanging: Taurus (April 21 to May 20) in spring, Leo (July 23 to August 22) in summer, Scorpio (October 23 to November 21) in fall, and Aquarius (January 20 to February 18) in winter.

Just as their zodiacal signs hold sway at times when each season and its weather pattern are well established, so fixed-quadruplicity individuals are considered to be capable consolidators who are blessed with remarkable powers of concentration. As well as having stable and loyal personalities, they are furthermore dedicated, determined, and persistent people who hate to give up on anything or anyone to whom they have committed themselves. The downside of having a fixed quadruplicity is that they can be set in their ways, resistant to change, rigid and inflexible, and infuriatingly stubborn or egocentric.

Left: *U.S. politician Samuel Adams (1722–1803) was a Libra. Was it his initiative-bestowing, cardinal quaduplicity that prompted him to instigate the Boston Tea Party in 1773, an act of rebellion that ultimately led to America's declaration of independence from Britain in 1783?*

Below: *The English scientist Charles Darwin (1809–82) was a fixed-sign Aquarius, and it may have been his quadruplicity that made him determined to publish* On the Origin of Species *in 1859, a ground-breaking exposition of the evolutionary process, and then to stick to his beliefs when they were bitterly criticized.*

Below: *Albert Einstein (1879–1955) was a Pisces whose adaptable, mutable quadruplicity enabled him to embrace change. Born in Germany, he lived in Italy as a child, later teaching in Switzerland and Czechoslovakia, eventually moving to the United States in 1933.*

Zodiacal bulls, lions, scorpions, and water-carriers manifest their fixed-quadruplicity characteristics slightly differently: Taureans are steady, but also bull-headed; Leos are constant, yet sometimes egotistical; and although Scorpio people are devoted, they cannot forget a slight; while Aquarians can be both single-minded and dogmatic.

THE MUTABLE SIGNS

The mutable-quadruplicity signs are Gemini (which is masculine and airy), Virgo (feminine and earthy), Sagittarius (masculine and fiery), and Pisces (a feminine, watery sign). "Mutable" means "changeable," and these signs are so named because they prevail at those times of year when the seasons are about to change: Gemini's zodiacal month (May 21 to June 21) coming at the end of spring, Virgo's (August 23 to September 22) occurring when summer is about to give way to fall, Sagittarius' (November 22 to December 21), when winter is on the verge of succeeding fall, and Pisces' month running from February 19 to March 20, when spring is in the winter air.

Mutable-quadruplicity Gemini, Virgo, Sagittarius, and Pisces people are consequently said to be adaptable individuals who are open to change, enjoy variety, and have a visionary's focus on the future. In addition, they are typically sociable, versatile, and cooperative people. Yet they can be so changeable or moody, restless or unstable that it may sometimes seem as though they have split personalities.

Certain aspects of their common mutable quadruplicity are particularly pronounced in those born under the signs of Gemini, Virgo, Sagittarius, and Pisces: Geminis have diverse interests, but tend to be fickle; Virgos are practical problem-solvers who find it hard to make up their minds; Sagittarians are adventurous and unreliable; and Pisceans are flexible, yet emotionally inconstant.

The Polarities

Each zodiacal sign has a polarity, which ancient astrologers described as being either masculine or feminine. Although the words "masculine" and "feminine" still conjure up broadly accurate, if stereotypical, images of the characteristics imparted by the polarities (two opposing sets of attributes), some modern astrologers consider them sexist, and instead prefer to call the masculine polarity "active" or "positive," and the feminine polarity "passive" or "negative." Beginning with masculine-polarity Aries, which is followed by feminine-polarity Taurus, the two polarities alternate through the twelve signs of the zodiac.

The traits with which each polarity is associated, as well as the way in which the two polarities interact with one another, are similar to the yin (masculine, or positive) and yang (feminine, or negative) theory of Chinese Taoist and Confucian belief, namely that everything in the universe consists of these two forces in some measure, and that perfection is achieved when they are equally balanced and thus working in harmony with one another. Similarly, an integrated personality is said to be one in which neither polarity predominates, so that whatever our zodiacal sign's polarity, we should try to develop some of the opposite polarity's qualities.

THE MASCULINE, ACTIVE, OR POSITIVE POLARITY

Aries, Gemini, Leo, Libra, Sagittarius, and Aquarius are all masculine-polarity signs, Aries, Leo, and Sagittarius also being fire signs, and Gemini, Libra, and Aquarius, air signs.

Masculine-polarity individuals are extroverted, active, positive, and energetic types who are typically direct, confident, outgoing, and assertive. These pioneering people tend to act without thinking, behave in a dynamic and uninhibited way, and can be aggressive, forceful, and confrontational, too.

THE FEMININE, PASSIVE, OR NEGATIVE POLARITY

The feminine-polarity signs are Taurus, Cancer, Virgo, Scorpio, Capricorn, and Pisces, of which Taurus, Virgo, and Capricorn are earth signs, and Cancer, Scorpio, and Pisces are water signs.

Feminine-polarity individuals are introverted, passive, negative, and contemplative characters. They consider all of the options before taking action, prefer to work quietly behind the scenes, and have a talent for nurturing, be it others or ideas. Although they are intuitive and receptive, they can be shy, reticent, or withdrawn.

Above: *The Cancerian Helen Keller was born in 1880, deaf and unable to speak. Having a feminine polarity can't have helped her to communicate with others, making her achievement as a teacher and author all the more remarkable.*

Center: *Yin (the white, or "masculine," section of the tai-chi circle) and yang (the black, or "feminine") are depicted in perfect harmony, a state of being to which we should all aspire.*

Left: *The Wright brothers, Wilbur, an Aries born in 1867, and Orville, a Leo born in 1871, were the first people to invent and successfully fly a powered, manned aircraft (in 1903). A pioneering spirit is typically associated with the masculine polarity.*

The Signs of the Zodiac

ARIES (THE RAM) ♈
March 21 to April 20

Ruling planet: Mars
Element: Fire
Polarity: Masculine
Quadruplicity: Cardinal

> *Aries is a Masculine, Diurnall Sign, moveable, Cardinall, Equinoctiall; in nature fiery, hot and dry, cholerick, bestial, luxurious, intemperate and violent: the diurnall house of Mars of the Fiery Triplicity, and of the East.*
>
> —William Lilly
> *Christian Astrology* (1647)

Fueled by their fiery energy, infused with the pioneering spirit of their masculine polarity, filled with a sense of urgency and ambition through their cardinal quadruplicity, and displaying the boldness of Mars, those born under the zodiacal sign of Aries are always on the go, and will ride roughshod over any obstacles in their path to progress. And just as their sign falls at the start of spring, setting another zodiacal year in motion, so Arien people are naturally forceful initiators, and hence have leadership potential. Although these individuals do nothing by halves, and have the power to inspire and enthuse others, they aren't given to pausing to think before throwing themselves headlong into a new venture, and don't readily accept others' advice, either, which means that they sometimes encounter difficulties and dead ends. But because Mars blesses them with fortitude, and their masculine polarity, with a positive outlook, it isn't long before they bounce back and charge off again on a fresh adventure. Those whose zodiacal sign is Aries are warm-hearted, exuberant, and full of vigor, but can also be egotistical, aggressive, and hot-tempered, and their relationships may be tempestuous or short-lived as a result.

Romance
Although outgoing, zestful Ariens are definitely not types whose idea of heaven is a life of cozy, uneventful domesticity, forging a fulfilling bond with a significant someone is important to them. This is partly because Mars' gift to them is a powerful libido, and partly because their

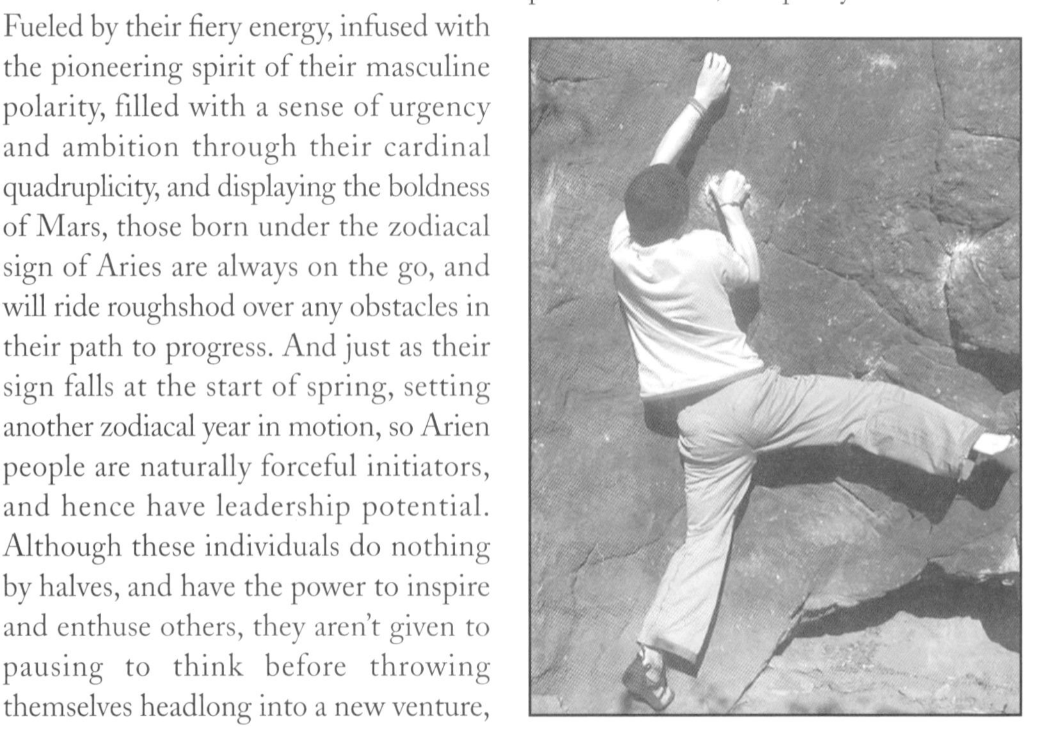

Right: *Aries people cannot resist rising to a challenge, however daunting, or even impossible, it may seem. Although they may fail in their quest because they haven't thought things through or planned properly, their indomitable willpower and extraordinary stamina may equally enable them to succeed.*

element of fire makes them hot-blooded, and spontaneous, too, which is why they often fall head over heels in love at first sight. This same birth influence furthermore typically causes them to feel that being admired and adored is their birthright, and when a lover satisfies this requirement, they respond with a fire sign's impetuous generosity and burning ardor, also injecting excitement into the liaison. There is a danger, however, that as their romance progresses, the passion of its first, exhilarating days inevitably subsides, and their rapport becomes more humdrum, Ariens may start to feel bored, or even tied down, at which point they may either spend more time channeling their formidable energies into pursuing outside interests and seeking out rousing challenges than with their partner, or may increasingly express their frustration by means of belligerent comments or fiery outbursts. Perhaps the key to keeping an Aries lover is to ensure that you engage in plenty of testing activities together.

Left: *Fiery Ariens are passionate lovers who make any romantic encounter unforgettable. Their burning ardor may soon fizzle out if excitement is lacking in their relationship or they feel that their partner is trying to control them, however.*

Friendship

Spending time with an Aries is rarely dull, be it because pushy, cardinal-quadruplicity rams are forever chivvying their friends to participate in stimulating, and typically sporting, pursuits with them (when their Mars-bestowed competitive streak comes to the fore), or because their fiery outspokenness and masculine-polarity lack of inhibition means that they communicate directly, bluntly, and sometimes confrontationally. Indeed, these up-front, assertive individuals like to run their friendships on their own terms, and otherwise need to respect someone's strength of character if they are to consider him or her an equal whose suggestions are worthy of going along with once in a while. They may not have that many good friends, partly because people tend either to love or loathe these loud, brash personalities, and partly because they themselves are so busy packing as much as they can into their lives, but treat those whom they like with great warmth and bonhomie, and are ever ready to ride to their defense if necessary. Don't expect to enjoy long soul-searching sessions or mutually supportive tête-à-têtes with an

Below: *Spirited Aries individuals light up any social gathering. Their confidence and lack of inhibition can excite and inspire others, but may also arouse their competitive instincts, sometimes resulting in heated confrontations.*

Above: A fearless Aries brother will encourage his little sibling to be as daring as he, the result being either exhilaration when she overcomes her fears and triumphs against the odds or howls and floods of tears when she falls flat on her face.

Aries, however, for these characters hardly ever suffer from self-doubt, nor are they that interested in others' emotions, and won't stick around for long if exposed to them.

Family Relationships

Whatever their age or position in the family, those born under the sign of the zodiacal ram know their own minds, are determined to get their own way, and aren't afraid to upset their loved ones in the process. This not to say that they don't care about their relatives—indeed, their element of fire causes them to be warm and demonstrative, and they thrive on the attention that they receive from family members, too—just that having a cardinal quadruplicity usually results in them being self-centered, go-getting characters, while the combined influence of Mars and their masculine polarity makes them assertive and, if their will is thwarted, aggressive. Yet fire gives young Ariens in particular a reckless streak, and Mars, a love of taking risks, so that they frequently have to be prevented from landing themselves in serious trouble, triggering a violent temper tantrum (and older Ariens can be just as hot-headed at times). If you find yourself on the receiving end of a barrage of hurtful accusations being hurled at you in the heat of the moment by an Aries, don't take them too much to heart, however, for going on the attack is simply Mars' way of expressing frustration. And you probably can't help but admire the vital and dynamic Arien spirit.

Aries in the Workplace

Whether or not their position gives them authority over others at work, Mars-governed, cardinal-quadruplicity Aries people are prone to taking the lead and heading determinedly off in a direction of their own choosing, which can make them authoritative bosses and exasperating underlings. These fiery individuals need to be inspired and enthused by a target in order to feel motivated, and become restless, and even destructive, if they have no clear goals to aim for, when their dissatisfaction may manifest itself as a series of hot-tempered explosions. They also lack the patience to slog away at tasks that require attention to detail, are frequently pulled up short for their sketchy planning, and their work is sometimes rushed and careless. Yet when an urgent deadline needs to be met, cardinal-quadruplicity Ariens throw their hearts and souls into doing so, and their confident and enterprising, masculine-polarity approach and fiery vitality can hearten and energize their colleagues. You cannot ignore Ariens in the workplace, and they certainly make things happen, be it for good or bad.

TAURUS (THE BULL) ♉
April 21 to May 20

Ruling planet: Venus
Element: Earth
Polarity: Feminine
Quadruplicity: Fixed

> *Taurus is an Earthly [earthy], Cold, Dry, Melancholy, Feminine, Nocturnal, Fixed, Domestical or Beastial Sign, of the Earthly [earthy] Triplicity, and South, the Night-house of Venus.*
>
> —William Lilly
> *Christian Astrology* (1647)

Because their earthy element makes them matter-of-fact, and their fixed quadruplicity, relatively unchanging, it may seem as though the Taurean personality is sensible and predictable. And indeed it is to a certain extent, yet take Venus, the bull's ruling planet, into account, and Taurus people can surprise others with their self-indulgence, willingness to be coaxed into having fun, and finely honed appreciation of all things artistic. Add a contemplative, feminine polarity to the mix, and additional ingredients that contribute to the Taurean makeup include introspection and thoughtfulness. All in all, don't be fooled by the placid face that Taurus individuals typically present to the world, for if you didn't already appreciate it, you'll gradually come to realize that in the case of Taureans, what you see is not always what you get. That said, there are certain characteristics that may be said to apply to the majority of those born under this sign, such as a balanced, Venusian temperament, an earthy, practical approach to problem-solving, a feminine polarity's prudence, and a fixed quadruplicity's faithfulness, but also stubbornness. Finally, although it may be difficult to fall out with even-tempered, loyal bulls, should their annoyance be aroused, perhaps by persistent pestering or criticism, a rare volcanic eruption may eventually ensue.

Left: *Being ruled by sensual Venus makes it difficult for Taurus individuals to resist titillating their taste buds, which is why it's just as well that their fixed quadruplicity gives them the determination to stick to a diet should they pile on the pounds.*

Romance
The influence that Venus, their planetary governor (whose namesake is the Roman goddess of love), exerts over Taureans, along with their sensuality—a delightful bonus of having an earthy element—together mean that the typical zodiacal bull yearns for a tender

and romantic, physical relationship with an ardent someone. Because their fixed quadruplicity gives them a dislike of change, and earth blesses them with constancy, the astrological indications suggest that once they have found their ideal partner (and their guarded feminine polarity may cause them to take their time in committing themselves), they will remain monogamous, and will expect the same of their beloved. But Taurus is more undemonstrative than fire signs, less gregarious than air signs, and less compassionate and giving than water signs, so that the jealousy that is part and parcel of being ruled by Venus may be aroused if a Taurus individual sees his or her lover responding warmly, flirtatiously, or empathetically to a person whom the bull perceives as being a rival in love. This caution aside, Taureans are generally devoted, supportive, and dependable lovers who will focus on ensuring that their relationship with their sweetheart is harmonious, and that they enjoy a comfortable lifestyle together.

Below: *Although earthy Taureans are hard workers whose fixed quadruplicity blesses them with staying power, it is thanks to indolent, self-indulgent Venus that they like nothing more than lazing around when the pressure's off.*

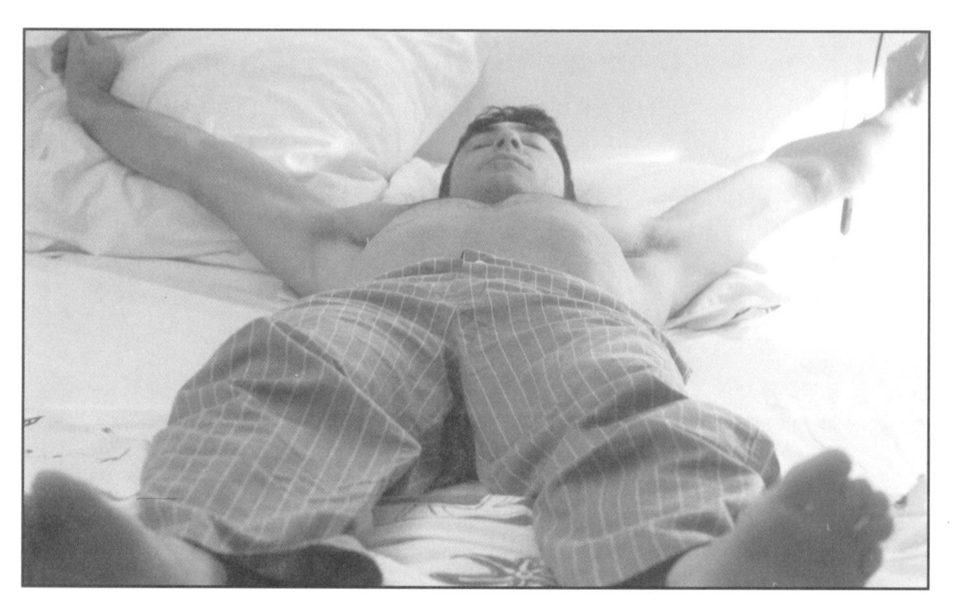

Friendship

Earthy bulls may be responsible and hardworking characters, but they are also children of pleasure-loving Venus, and therefore enjoy treating themselves whenever they can take a break from their family or work commitments. Venus causes them to enjoy other people's company, too, and Taureans consequently relish nothing more than seeing a show or sharing a meal with friends. (Having a gourmet's appreciation of food, and, due to their earthy element and feminine polarity, also being hands-on homebodies, these individuals are often excellent cooks who love to invite friends around for a cozy supper.) Having a fixed quadruplicity means that they are constant friends, too, who are always ready to offer sensible advice or practical support when necessary. Their willingness to help may not stretch to loaning money, however, for financially aware Venus and accumulative earth together make it hard for Taureans to dip into their savings. Although they may value their Taurus friends' many virtues, some people—especially those born under excitement-seeking fire signs—may find them a little too passive, risk-averse, or even downright lazy, for while the combination of their feminine polarity and earth can result in them being cautious realists, Venus' contribution is a tendency to be indolent.

Family Relationships

Home is where the Taurean heart is, partly because zodiacal bulls' feminine polarity is traditionally associated with domesticity, partly because their earthy element causes

them to appreciate the importance of being supported by solid, family foundations, and partly because their fixed quadruplicity blesses them with devotion. Both Venus and earth give these people material values, too, which is why Taurus parents typically work hard to ensure that their children grow up in comfortable surroundings and are well provided for (especially at mealtimes!) Although the routines that they are so fond of, due to the combined influence of their earthy element and fixed quadruplicity, may result in things getting done in a Taurean household, those of their relatives who were born under other signs may find their inflexibility stultifying, and may wish that they were more outgoing, less circumspect, and, on occasions, less obstinate. Yet these individuals are masters of the work–life balance, thanks to Venus, so that while both Taurean parents and children are diligent and conscientious in the workplace or at school, they know how to relax in their time off, be it by puttering around in the kitchen, tending the garden, or simply lounging around.

Taurus in the Workplace

Taurus types are generally those on whom others rely to complete tasks thoroughly and meticulously in the workplace, for not only does their fixed quadruplicity bless them with unshakeable staying power, their earthy element gives them patience and causes them to pay attention to detail. Having a feminine polarity makes Taureans thoughtful, yet also rather unforthcoming, which is one of the reasons why they are often better suited to playing supportive roles than to positions in which they are required to motivate others, which is not to say that they make bad managers. Indeed, Venus' gift to them is a talent for keeping the peace between more inflammable, fiery individuals, while the influence of their fixed quadruplicity enables them to provide easily distracted, airy sorts with direction, and their earthy element helps them to encourage dreamy, watery characters to be more realistic, as well as productive. Steady and resilient Taureans hate to let their coworkers down, yet even if they eventually benefit from it, their colleagues may nevertheless be irritated by their resolutely unhurried, Venusian approach, and may be taken aback when repeated attempts to rush them act on these normally imperturbable people like red rags to a bull or trigger their stubbornness.

Left: *Having an earthy element means that Taurus individuals like to do a job thoroughly and therefore pay scrupulous attention to detail. The Taurean working style may be slow and steady, but is rarely sloppy.*

GEMINI (THE TWINS) ♊
May 21 **to June** 21

Ruling planet: Mercury
Element: Air
Polarity: Masculine
Quaduplicity: Mutable

> *Gemini, it's an aerial [airy], hot, moyst, sanguine, Diurnal, common [mutable] or double-bodied human Sign; the diurnall house of Mercury of the aery [airy] triplicity, Western, Masculine.*
> —William Lilly
> *Christian Astrology* (1647)

Below: *Life with a Geminian lover promises to be an exciting experience, for those born under the sign of the twins are interesting, communicative, and sociable individuals whose catlike curiosity prompts them to explore the world around them.*

The key to understanding the character of someone who was born under the zodiacal sign of the twins is knowing that Geminians like to be occupied at all times, and consequently have a terror of being bored. Ruled by Mercury, the planet named for the Roman messenger god who was said to speed around the world collecting and delivering information, these people furthermore have an intellectually curious and gregarious element in air, an active, masculine polarity, and a variety-loving, mutable quadruplicity. Never happier than when traveling and learning about other cultures, or when swapping ideas with imaginative, well-informed people, if their physical or mental independence is restricted, or their hungry minds are deprived of brain food, they typically display the moodiness that is a characteristic of their mutable quadruplicity. Indeed, although Mercury and air together cause them to be generally easygoing, their mutability can sometimes make it seem as though they have split personalities (and it is not for nothing that Gemini is represented by two individuals). But black Geminian moods rarely last for long, and as soon as an interesting diversion presents itself, all will be sunny again. Even so, their restlessness and airy detachment may give rise to problems in their relationships.

Romance

It is primarily thanks to their positive and dynamic, masculine-polarity mindset, as well as to the love of fun and ready wit that are the gifts of their element of air, that Geminis have no difficulty attracting admirers. Settling down is another matter, though. These airy people can't stand feeling tied down, be it because their partner is overdependent on them or is reluctant to accompany them on their discovery quests, which means that they will typically only commit themselves to someone who is independent, adventurous, and prepared to give them personal space. A further requirement may be that he or she is full of stimulating ideas and suggestions, and is therefore capable of initiating the interesting conversations and supplying the surprises that so delight airy, mutable-quadruplicity characters and prevent their attention from straying. It is also vital that anyone hoping to enjoy a long-term relationship with a Gemini is

Left: *Their airy element and the trickster Mercury together make Geminis playful types who love to tease their nearest and dearest, and in such a charmingly light-hearted way that they are usually forgiven.*

thick-skinned enough to ignore the occasional critical, if well-meant, comment. When all of these criteria on Gemini's ideal-partner checklist have been fulfilled, these individuals' mutable-quadruplicity flexibility and airy amiability will come to the fore, and life with a Gemini lover will certainly never be dull!

Friendship

Airy, Mercury-governed Geminians may be sociable and relish communicating with others, yet these same birth influences can cause them to be rather impersonal, investigative types who quickly move on when their interest in someone has waned, often because they think that they have learned all that there is to know about him or her. Their masculine polarity furthermore makes them extroverts, while their mutable quadruplicity gives them an appetite for change, all of which indicates that, despite their wide social circle, their rapport with their friends is somewhat superficial. Similarly, although their airy liveliness, masculine-polarity energy, and mutable-quadruplicity adaptability attract others to them, they themselves are more concerned with analyzing people's personalities or obtaining information than with giving—or receiving—emotional support. They may therefore typically rapidly switch off, and then flit away, if it seems as though empathy is required of them. Their friends nevertheless treasure their mischievous wit and inventive approach to problem-solving—joint gifts of Mercury and air—along with their positive, masculine-polarity outlook and mutable-quadruplicity flexibility. In short, Geminians may not stick around in an emotional crisis, and may be too busy exploring either the real or intellectual world to maintain regular contact with their friends, but are otherwise always stimulating company.

Family Relationships

Gemini individuals are emphatically not homebodies, and unless an intriguing conversation, informative book, or access to the World Wide Web, for example, gives them the opportunity to satisfy their overpowering urge to explore and learn, they will soon be beset by the restlessness that is so strongly associated with a mutable quadruplicity, and will then shoot out of the house, masculine-polarity style, in search of stimulation. Provided that their close relatives (particularly if they themselves were born under watery, feminine-polarity signs) don't take their

Below: *Airy, masculine-polarity Geminians are lively and outgoing types who rarely stop talking, have a horror of being bored, and hate being cooped up at home with nothing to do.*

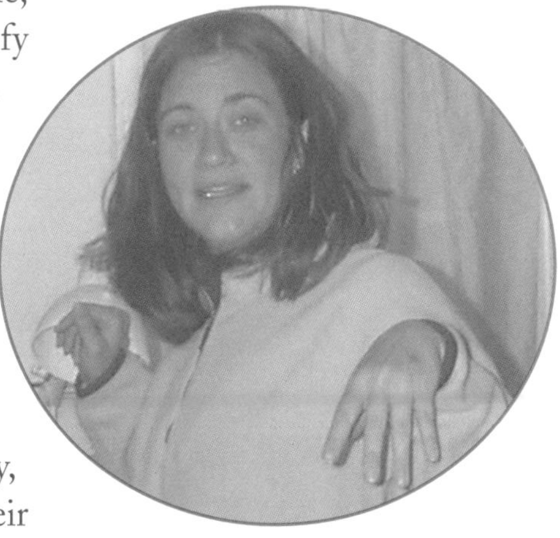

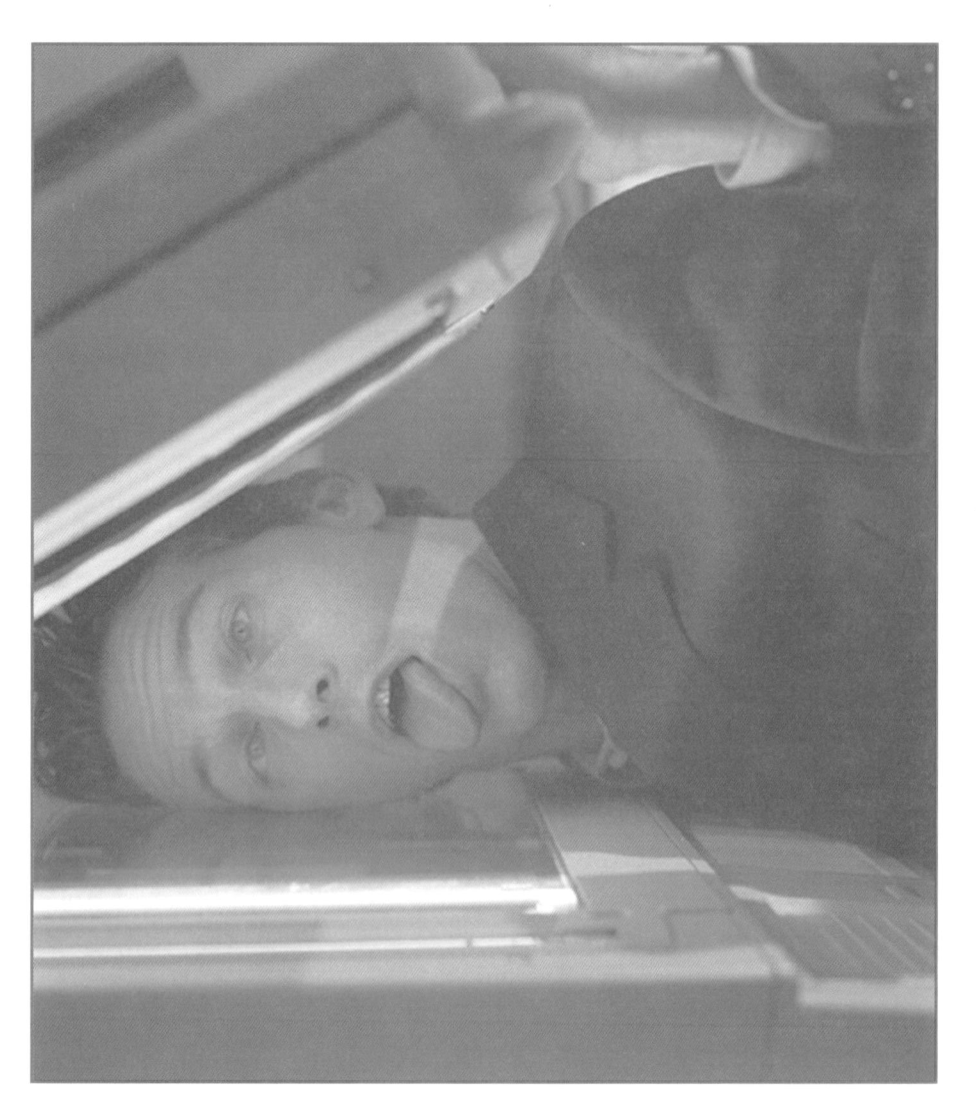

Above: *They may be gifted analysts and incisive thinkers, but airy Gemini individuals like to have fun in the workplace, too, and sometimes resort to practical jokes to liven up a slow working day.*

airy need for freedom as a personal insult or try to restrain them, they will enjoy a relaxed and enlivening relationship with these adaptable, breezy, talkative types. Although they are ever ready to apply their logical, quick-thinking minds to solving family members' problems, airy Gemini people are neither given to emoting nor welcome being exposed to others' raw emotions, which may sometimes make them seem uncaring. This is usually not the case, however: indeed, most Geminians feel great affection for their kinfolk, but, having an dispassionate element in air, find it hard to empathize with confused or heated feelings, and may become impatient, moody, or coolly critical if exposed to them for long.

Gemini in the Workplace

Not only are mutable-quadruplicity Geminians gifted multitaskers, these masculine-polarity people thrive on the challenge of juggling a number of projects at once in the workplace (mainly because both a variety of tasks and keeping busy wards off boredom), and because they are furthermore flexible, are usually ready to take on yet another assignment when asked. These individuals are also logical and independent thinkers, who, thanks to the combined influence of information-gathering Mercury and their intellect-enhancing element of air, have a talent for researching, analyzing, clearly communicating their findings, and then making ingenious, if sometimes impractical, recommendations. This is not to say that Geminians are backroom boffins, for both air and their mutable quadruplicity are associated with sociability, and Mercury gives them a relish of gleaning juicy snippets of news while gossiping around the water-cooler. Typically more interested in ideas than in wielding authority over others, their masculine polarity nevertheless gives them the confidence to do so. Unless they are allowed a certain amount of freedom—of both thought and action—they themselves have a strong aversion to being managed, however, and may become moody and restless if rigidly controlled or restrained.

CANCER (THE CRAB) ♊
June 22 to July 22

Ruling planet: The Moon
Element: Water
Polarity: Feminine
Quadruplicity: Cardinal

> *Cancer is the onely house of the Moon, and is the first Sign of the Watry [watery] or Northern Triplicity, is Watry, Cold, Moyst, Flegmatick, Feminine, Nocturnal, Moveable [cardinal], a Solstice Sign mute and slow of Voyce, Fruitful, Northern.*
>
> —William Lilly
> *Christian Astrology* (1647)

Those born under the zodiacal sign of the crab are extremely giving individuals, partly because the triple dose of responsiveness bestowed on them by their planetary governor, the Moon, their element of water, and their feminine polarity, coupled with the compassion and profound emotions that are also among Moon and water's gifts, cause them to feel others' pain deeply, and consequently to seek to alleviate it. Another reason is that many cultures have for millennia regarded the Moon as a mother goddess, so that those under its influence—be they men or women—are said to have powerful nurturing, as well as creative, or procreative, instincts. This is also why Cancerians are typically so focused on their families (and, if they are parents, especially on their children), and why they tend to assume a stereotypically motherly, or caring, role with regard to their friends and relations, again regardless of their sex. Because they have a self-seeking, cardinal quadruplicity, their interest in others is not entirely unselfish, however, for by lavishing affection on them, they hope to receive a return on their investment, thereby boosting their own sense of well-being. Yet despite their longing for love and approval, their tendency to be clingy, overprotective, and oversensitive can taint their relationships.

Romance

Their feminine polarity may make Cancerians shy, and their reticence may be deepened by their defensive, watery element (for if you don't express yourself, you can't be laughed at or rejected), but when their profound intuition causes them to be sure that the person with whom they have fallen in love feels the same way, their initiating, cardinal

Below: *Caring Cancerians are genuinely concerned about their loved ones' emotional well-being, and will always take the time to listen, which they do with sympathy and understanding.*

quadruplicity may prompt them to overcome their inhibitions and declare their feelings. And as their romance blossoms, Cancer individuals' lovers may be startled to see the transformational effect that being cherished has on them, for it is only when they feel certain that they won't be hurt that they emerge from their shells completely to reveal their true natures, which may be tender and sentimental, gentle and creative. Often driven by their desire to set up home and start a family, when they feel confident of their lover's affection, their cardinal quadruplicity may come to the fore, prompting them to push for a commitment. Yet should their sweetheart be hesitant, or feel unready to settle down, they may become clingy, descend into sulky silences, or resort to tearful accusations. When Cancerians feel secure in their beloved's devotion, however, they make wonderful partners, being sympathetic, protective, and totally dedicated to strengthening their relationship.

__Below:__ Little zodiacal crabs can be shy and insecure, but will blossom, grow in confidence, and emerge from their shells when given unconditional love, unstinting emotional support, and constant reassurance.

Friendship

Although they cannot help but empathize with others, thanks to the combined influence of the Moon and water, and therefore instinctively connect with most people (provided that they are not aggressive or hostile), it may take a while before Cancerian individuals regard someone as being a true enough friend to open up to them. Cancerians are easily upset, and experience may have taught them that many types are often all too willing to take advantage of their soft and compassionate natures before proving themselves woundingly inconsiderate, fickle, or even deliberately hurtful, which is why crabs initially protect themselves with a shield of feminine-polarity, watery reticence. Once someone has proved themselves steadfast or supportive—be it emotionally or practically—and Cancerians' lunar and watery intuition causes them to sense that he or she really cares about them, they typically relax their guard and give of themselves generously. Those who are privileged to count themselves among a Cancer's friends will benefit from the crab's kindness and understanding, but mustn't take their benevolence for granted, for their self-seeking, cardinal quadruplicity can cause them to demand a reward for their emotional outlay.

Family Relationships

Enjoying the unconditional love and emotional support of their families is vital to Cancer individuals' happiness, partly because it is only among their nearest and dearest that hypersensitive crabs feel that it is safe to lower their watery, feminine-polarity defenses and express themselves freely, without fear of their often dreamy notions being hurtfully ridiculed. In addition, Moon and water give them a strong need to nurture others, while their cardinal quadruplicity makes them ambitious on their closest relatives' behalf, so that they will do their utmost to ensure that

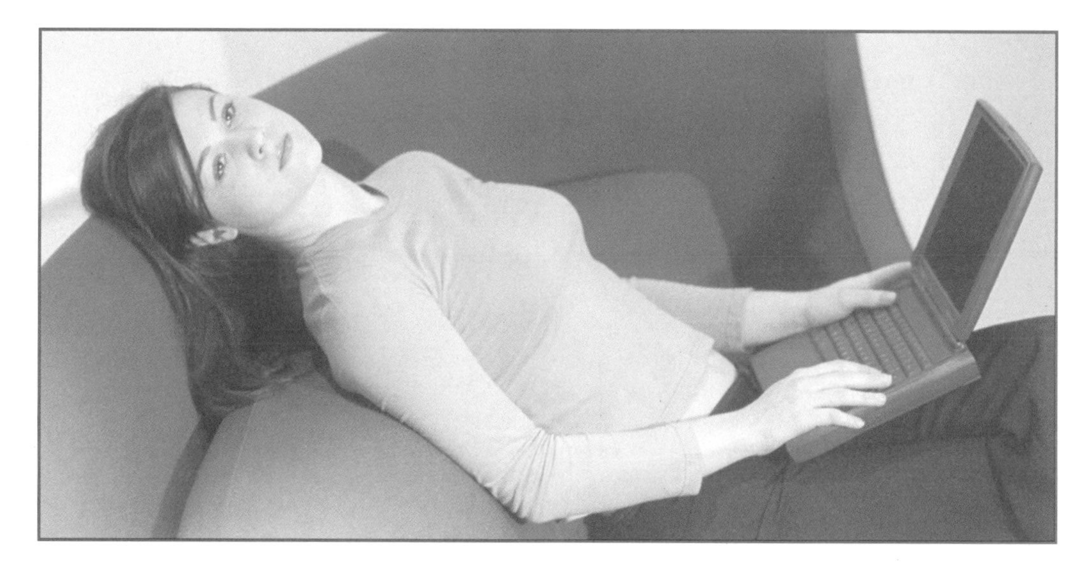

Left: *Although creative Cancer individuals have the potential to dream up the most original and innovative of ideas, they may clam up when wounded by criticism or put under pressure to perform.*

their partners and children in particular fulfill their potential. If their efforts are appreciated, and they are rewarded with grateful hugs and appreciative words, their sense of self-worth will rocket skyward, and they will in turn respond by being even more caring and sympathetic. There is a danger, however, that those of their loved ones who were born under fire or air signs will feel suffocated by their Cancer relation's devoted attention, and will assert their independence by trying to break free of what they perceive as being the crab's fussy control, thereby triggering feelings of rejection, and consequently also the crabbiness that is the downside of having both the Moon and water as birth influences.

Cancer in the Workplace

Because the Moon and water make them so sensitive, Cancer people will typically only be happy, and consequently productive, when working in a harmonious and relaxed environment. Their cardinal quadruplicity apart, all of their birth influences suggest that they tend to internalize the feelings of distress that a fiery or airy colleague's unthinkingly rude or sharply critical comment may arouse in them, until pushed too far, when they may either dissolve into floods of tears or strike back with a vicious verbal nip. If treated with understanding and respect, however, Cancerians may feel increasingly encouraged to overcome their feminine-polarity caution and open up, in the process releasing a torrent of the creative concepts that Mother Moon and Cancer's element of water have together hatched and nurtured before sending their brainchildren out into the wider world. Although they typically prefer to play a supportive role in the workplace (including sympathetically trying to buoy up coworkers when they are feeling down, or taking an interest in fostering an underling's career), their goal-oriented, cardinal quadruplicity gives them leadership potential, as well as the drive that is required if others are to be spurred into action.

Right: Sun-ruled Leos like to take center stage, but they are never more radiant than when in the company of the special person to whom they've chosen to commit themselves wholeheartedly.

LEO (THE LION) ♌
July 23 to August 22

Ruling planet: The Sun
Element: Fire
Polarity: Masculine
Quadruplicity: Fixed

> *Leo is the onely house of the Sun, by nature, Fiery, Hot, Dry, Cholerick, Diurnal, Commanding, Bestial, Barren, of the East and Fiery Triplicity, Masculine.*
>
> —William Lilly
> *Christian Astrology* (1647)

Just as the Sun, their governing planet, dominates both the sky and solar system, and the alpha-male lion—traditionally the king of the beasts—rules his pride, so Leos are said to be commanding individuals who radiate burning energy, qualities that are reinforced by their masculine polarity and fiery element. Leonine people both demand and receive attention, partly because their masculine-polarity dynamism and fiery spirit make them hard to ignore, but also because the Sun infuses them with an effortless air of authority. As long as they receive the respect that they consider their birthright, the combined effect of the Sun and fire will cause them to respond warmly and generously to those around them, furthermore lighting up others' lives with their sunny personalities, exuberance, and creativity. Deeply proud and dignified, zodiacal lions loathe being criticized or made to look stupid, however, nor will they tolerate having their freedom of action restricted, and won't hesitate to roar furiously, explode with anger, or descend into a melodramatic sulk if anyone does so. Yet although Leos have a fixed quadruplicity, their annoyance rarely lasts long, and the benefits of this birth influence include the loyalty and staying power that it bestows on them, particularly when it comes to maintaining personal relationships.

Romance

Having a solar ruler and fiery element gives passionate Leos a craving for attention and approval, which is why zodiacal lions long for a lover who responds to their fiery ardor with equal enthusiasm, who puts their emotional and physical needs first, and applauds their achievements with admiration. Not only do these rather self-centered people want their egos stroked by their beloved, but also boosted by the positive impact that he or she has on others, so that a sweetheart to be proud of—be it on account of that individual's appearance, intellect, or accomplishments—is another requirement. If all of these criteria are fulfilled, and Leos receive the unconditional love that they demand, as well as the stimulation that inspires them, they typically make exciting, imaginative, generous, and demonstrative lovers, mainly thanks to their fiery vitality, creativity, and warm-heartedness. Because their fixed quadruplicity makes them change-resistant, they are usually steadfast ones, too. Yet their quadruplicity can also cause them to be remarkably stubborn should they and their partner disagree, when they may furthermore feel disrespected, and maybe even betrayed. And if a Leo is disappointed in love, tantrums and frequent absences may be the result.

Friendship

Because their element is fire and their polarity is masculine, Leos are sociable and outgoing individuals who love to party, partly because they adore holding court (or, as some would say, showing off) at the center of a group of their admirers—and Sun-ruled Leos need to shine—and partly because their fiery imaginations are stimulated by others. Being active, adventurous, and experimental types, they relish being introduced to new and exciting experiences, or blazing a trail and spontaneously leading the way. They also have a pronounced capacity for indolence, along with extravagant tastes, so that they luxuriate in being wined and dined, and in playing host, too. Unless they perceive someone as being a threat to their authoritative position within their social circle, or their often rather rigid opinions are belligerently challenged, when they may respond with fiery aggression, they are typically warmly affectionate, generous, and benevolent friends. As well as fearlessly standing up for their pals if necessary, the influence that their fixed quadruplicity wields over Leos furthermore means that they tend to stick by their friends through thick and thin, and hate to lose contact with them. If you don't mind deferring to a Sun-governed Leo, he or she should prove a loyal and life-enhancing friend.

Family Relationships

At the time when the theories and principles of astrology were being established, the Sun was regarded as a god whose blazing energy both sustained and encouraged the development of all

__Left:__ Party-animal Leos seize any opportunity to shine, and adore cutting a dash at social gatherings where they are surrounded by stimulating people and the wine and conversation flow freely.

__Below:__ Fiery, masculine-polarity Leos like to burn up their prodigious energy by engaging in challenging, adventurous pursuits, although a beaming leonine smile may soon give way to a temper tantrum if others are reluctant to follow their lead.

life forms. Because they are governed by the Sun, Leos are by extension said to exhibit stereotypically male—even fatherly—traits, whether they are men or women, adults or children. Their confidence-bestowing, masculine polarity, their hot and vital element of fire, and their fixed, or steady and determined, quadruplicity all reinforce their Sun-given characteristics, so that their relations typically depend on Leos in some way, be it to protect and provide for them, to guide or entertain them, or simply to brighten their days with their sunny natures. The double dose of formidable willpower that the Sun and their fixed quadruplicity give them may, however, make Leo parents somewhat authoritarian and leonine children, stubborn or rebellious, which may give rise to conflict, particularly if they share a home with relatives who were also born under a fire sign or have independent air as an element. They may be hot-tempered if their will is thwarted, yet whatever their age or status within the family, most Leos nevertheless display great warmth and commitment toward their loved ones.

Leo in the Workplace

Sun-ruled, fiery Leos have an inborn talent for leading, inspiring, and motivating others, their masculine polarity filling them with drive, and their fixed quadruplicity blessing them with stamina and staying power. Yet these gifts will usually only be advantageous to an employer if a Leo employee is either given a position of authority or is otherwise allowed freedom of action, for although they are generally sunny natured, zodiacal lions both hate being dictated to, and, like their fiery element, refuse to be restricted, while their fixed quadruplicity can make them remarkably stubborn. Indeed, they are not afraid to challenge, or even disobey, their superiors' instructions, either because they are convinced that they know best or simply because they cannot help rebelling. Appealing to Leo underlings' vanity and sense of self-worth by praising their work is often an effective strategy, however, for if they feel that they are respected, and that their contribution is valued, they will typically throw themselves into a task with gusto. And when leonine individuals' imaginations have been ignited, like catherine wheels, they throw out a stream of dazzlingly creative or pioneering ideas, also firing up their colleagues with their high spirits.

***Right:** Although lion cubs are usually little rays of sunshine, they aren't afraid to express their feelings or to defy their parents if they are prevented from getting their own way.*

VIRGO (THE VIRGIN) ♍

August 23 to September 22

Ruling planet: Mercury
Element: Earth
Polarity: Feminine
Quadruplicity: Mutable

> *Virgo it's an earthly [earthy], cold, melancholly, barren, feminine, nocturnail, Southern Sign; the house and exaltation of Mercury, of the earthly triplicity.*
> —William Lilly
> *Christian Astrology* (1647)

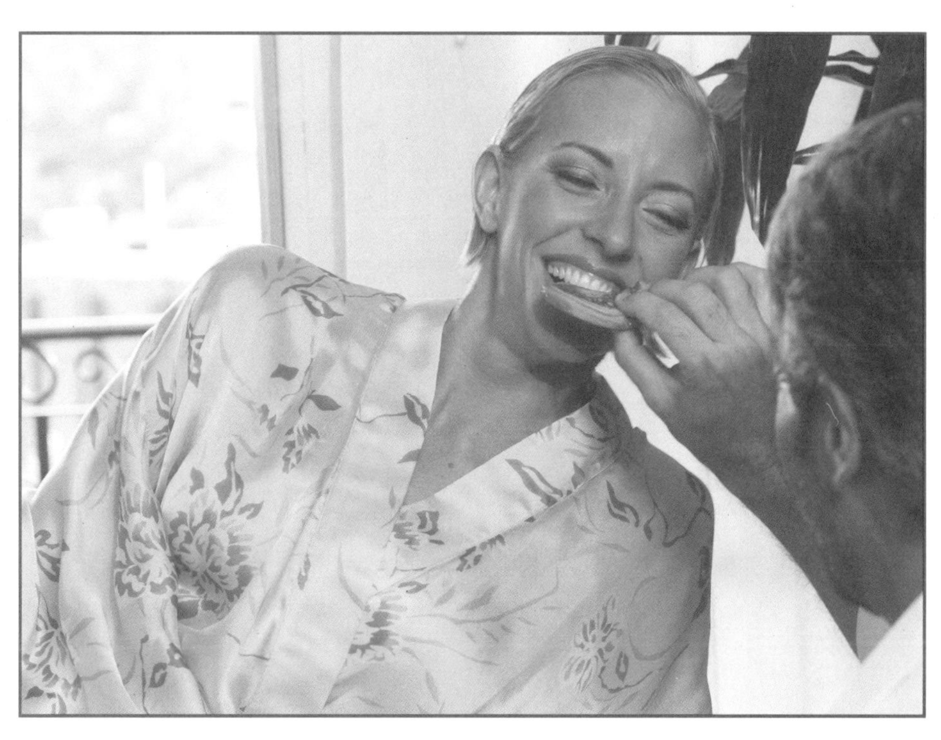

Above: *Their feminine polarity and earthy element together cause Virgo individuals to place great importance on having a well-ordered home, and although their insistence on tidiness may exasperate their loved ones, their earthy sensuality can be deeply endearing.*

Glancing at the astrological influences that contribute to its makeup, the Virgoan character initially seems a mass of contradictions. For on the one hand, there is Mercury, Virgo individuals' ruling planet, which gives them quick wits and the urge to communicate with others, their mutable quadruplicity reinforcing both these characteristics and additionally making them restless and changeable. And on the other, there is the element of earth, which causes them to be steady, straightforward, and stable sorts, and a reticent and introspective, feminine polarity. Perhaps it is these paradoxes that make it hard for those born under other zodiacal signs to understand Virgoans, and why they often worry about how they are perceived. Working through these birth influences backward, however, and expanding on their effects, the essence of the Virgoan personality becomes clearer. A feminine polarity also makes for receptiveness and thoughtfulness; an earthy element, supportiveness; a mutable quadruplicity supplies adaptability and sociability; while Mercury's gift is objectivity. As a result, Virgos can be said to be intelligent people who are open to others' influence, and will do their utmost to help those whom they love or like by giving them realistic, practical, clear-sighted, and well-considered advice, but who may be misinterpreted as being interfering or critical, as well as moody.

Romance

Although their earthy element makes Virgoans sensual people who long for a close and fulfilling connection with a lover, not just anyone will do. Indeed, they can be highly discriminating, for perceptive, neutral Mercury gives them a tendency to see a potential partner's bad, as well as good, points, while their practical element can result in them taking a hard-headed

Above: *Having a sociable, diversity-seeking mutable quadruplicity means that most Virgos have a wide circle of very different friends, and enjoy a change of scenery every so often, too.*

realist's approach to deciding whether they could tolerate these flaws in a lover over the long term. In addition, because their mutable, or variety-loving, quadruplicity can cause them to be attracted to people whose characters are markedly different from theirs, they may find it hard to work out the qualities that they are looking for in a sweetheart. And when they have been smitten by a someone, having a caution-bestowing, feminine polarity may mean that it takes a while before they feel emboldened enough to make a romantic overture. Once in a relationship, however, earthy Virgo individuals typically prove patient, constant, and supportive partners, as well as adaptable ones, thanks to their mutable quadruplicity. Nor should life be dull with a Virgo, for both Mercury and their quadruplicity give them an appetite for travel and stimulating conversation.

Friendship

They may have an introverted, feminine polarity, but this does not mean that Virgos are painfully reticent, nor that they are unsociable, for the union of Mercury and their mutable quadruplicity makes them natural communicators who are interested in others' news and views and enjoy coming into contact and conversing with a diverse range of people. They are therefore likely to have a host of acquaintances, yet there may be only a few individuals whom they regard as being sufficiently faithful or genuinely concerned about their welfare to consider really good friends. Although they enjoy traveling in their free time, when it comes to daily interaction with their friends, these feminine-polarity types take pleasure in a quiet evening of stimulating discussion at home, and if the subject strays to a pal's problem, Virgoans will give serious thought to how to help. Indeed, Mercury, earth, and their mutable quadruplicity together bless them with logical, practical, and analytical brains, so that they will usually come up with a feasible and sensible solution. In neutrally explaining their reasoning, they may, however, inadvertently cause offense by appearing to criticize the decisions or actions that led to their friend's dilemma, thereby upsetting sensitive water-sign people in particular.

Family Relationships

The result of having an introspective, feminine polarity and steady earth among their birth influences is that enjoying a settled and stable home life is important to Virgo individuals of all ages. Although the combined influence of Mercury and their mutable quadruplicity causes them to welcome an occasional change of scenery, they need to have a comfortable, permanent base to which to return, and similarly place great value on maintaining even and constant relationships with their loved ones. Within the family environment, earthy Virgos tend to assume a supportive role, with Virgoan parents taking care of domestic practicalities and otherwise organizing their children's lives, sometimes to annoyance of their independent fire- or air-sign offspring, who may feel that they are being controlled. And whatever their status within the family, their love of routines and insistence on tidiness may exasperate those of their relations who were born under different zodiacal signs (particularly if their element is chaos-tolerant water). They are certainly capable of enlisting the flexibility of their mutable quadruplicity and turning a blind eye to others' mess, but Virgoans find it hard not to try to straighten out disorderly situations, and consequently also feel compelled to give advice, which may not always be appreciated, however.

Virgo in the Workplace

Being both intelligent and practical, thanks to Mercury and their element of earth, and thoughtful and flexible, due to their feminine polarity and mutable quadruplicity, Virgos are typically valuable assets to their employers. These people are usually better suited to hands-on or behind-the-scenes assignments than leading others, partly because their feminine-polarity makes them more passive than active when it comes to motivating their coworkers, and partly because they enjoy work that involves analyzing and developing data and ideas. That said, they are excellent managers whose earthy resilience and staying power set a formidable example, and who support their staff and offer astute advice when guidance is needed. Mercury and their mutable quadruplicity bless them with a gift for communication, too, and although some of their more egotistical or thin-skinned coworkers may not welcome their errors being pointed out, if they accept Virgoans' criticism in the spirit in which it was given, namely helpfully and constructively, they will generally have cause for gratitude. But because Virgo individuals have mutable, mercurial minds, they will soon become bored and restless if they find their work unchallenging or one-dimensional, in which case their normally even-tempered approach may give way to moodiness.

***Left:** As long as their assignments are varied and interesting, earthy, Mercury-governed Virgos are never happier than when methodically working through a pile of paperwork and then communicating their findings to their colleagues.*

LIBRA (THE BALANCE OR SCALES) ♎
September 23 to October 22

Ruling planet: Venus
Element: Air
Polarity: Masculine
Quadruplicity: Cardinal

> *Libra is a Sign aeriall [airy], hot and moyst, Sanguine, Masculine, Moveable [cardinal], Equinoctiall, Cardinall, Humane, Diurnall, of the Aerinall [airy] Triplicity, and Western, the chief House of Venus.*
>
> —William Lilly
> *Christian Astrology* (1647)

The astrological indications suggest that of all of the intelligent, but somewhat dispassionate and emotionally detached, air signs, namely Gemini, Aquarius, and Libra, it is Libra that has the easiest relationships with others. For whereas Gemini and Aquarius' airy independence and self-sufficiency are reinforced by Mercury and Uranus respectively, Libra is governed by indulgent, peaceable Venus, so that those born under this sign are generally more tolerant of others, and more anxious to please and placate, than zodiacal twins or water-carriers. That said, both Venus and their self-seeking, cardinal quadruplicity can make Librans somewhat selfish individuals who are determined to get their own way, and whose masculine polarity gives them the necessary assertiveness to do so, too. But because air blesses them with charm and humor, and, thanks to Venus, these diplomatic people hate to cause offense, they have a talent for bringing others round to their way of thinking in the most engaging and light-hearted of ways. These are furthermore individuals who share Venus' appreciation of artistry, whose element of air infuses them with curiosity, and whose masculine polarity causes them to be uninhibited. All in all, Librans are fun to be with, even if they can sometimes be manipulative.

Romance
Being ruled by Venus, the planet named for the Roman goddess of love, means that Librans are typically born romantics who yearn to be pampered and adored by a dynamic lover who sets their heart racing. Libra is the sign of the balance, and it is also Venus that causes them to long for a romance in which both partners respect one another as equals, and when in an established relationship, to try to smooth over any differences of

Right: *Airy Libras inject an element of fun and laughter into their romantic relationships, which, despite their conciliatory and indulgent, Venusian instincts, are likely to be partnerships of equals.*

opinion so that their rapport with their beloved remains sweet and even. Although there is inevitably a danger that they may end up being overly compliant in their attempts to keep the peace, particularly if their sweetheart was born under a hot-blooded, hot-tempered fire sign, Librans are no doormats. On the contrary, their masculine polarity gives them confidence, their airy element blesses them with intellectual independence, while their cardinal quadruplicity can result in them being rather self-seeking and pushy, making it likely that they will both retain their individuality and discreetly steer their lover in a direction of their own choosing. Issues of control aside, airy, Venusian Librans are generally easygoing, playful types who are set on making a love affair fun.

Above: *It is appearance-conscious Venus that gives Librans the desire to look their best while out on the town, and their element of air that makes them such talkative, fun-loving types.*

Friendship

It is not just because Venus is associated with good times and friendship that fun-loving Librans usually have such a wide circle of playmates. Indeed, having a sociable element in air and an outgoing, masculine polarity causes Librans to be people-persons who delight in the company of others. Their cardinal quadruplicity blesses Libran individuals with initiative, too, so that when it comes to entertaining themselves and their friends, they are rarely short of ideas, and because Venus infuses them with an appreciation of the arts, they have a particular penchant for ushering their friends off to concerts, shows, or exhibitions. (Although they enjoy indulging others, their generosity may not extend to treating them to entrance tickets, however, for Venus also makes them financially prudent.) Born networkers and matchmakers, airy Librans otherwise adore chatting and gossiping, and will try to keep the conversation neutral and light-hearted. And should a fiery person's bluntness upset a sensitive, watery character, for instance, they will quickly step in to try to diffuse the situation with diplomacy and charm, thereby restoring harmony. Their cardinal-quadruplicity self-absorption and airy dislike of being exposed to extreme emotions may nevertheless sometimes result in them seeming selfish and superficial.

Family Relationships

Appropriately enough, given that theirs is the zodiacal sign of the balance, Libran individuals usually have both an energizing and soothing effect on their relatives. Their energy is the joint bequest of their extrovert, masculine polarity and

__Above:__ Their masculine polarity fills little Librans with self-confidence and the spirit of enterprise, but it is due to Venus' influence that they would rather not get their hands dirty while out playing with friends.

go-getting, cardinal quadruplicity, while their dispassionate element of air and laidback Venus, their ruling planet, enable them to interact with their loved ones in a calm and relaxed fashion. Regardless of their age and position within the family, these are furthermore gregarious, pleasure-loving people with a keen esthetic eye, which suggests that they will be proactive in encouraging those closest to them to accompany them to social gatherings, as well as to all sorts of artistic venues. As parents, they will teach their young charges the importance of good manners (a lesson that is usually superfluous if their children are fellow Librans and thus already innately tactful and respectful, however). Family arguments are rarely triggered by Librans either, and when others' hot tempers flare or tears flow, it is typically a Libra who seeks to take the heat out of the situation or to smooth ruffled feathers. Yet at other times they can seem emotionally disengaged and self-interested, mainly due to the influence of their airy element and cardinal quadruplicity.

Libra in the Workplace

Airy, masculine-polarity, Venus-governed Librans are talkative extroverts who like to have fun in the workplace, which suggests that their colleagues will either welcome their enlivening laughter and light-hearted banter or resent being distracted from their work. Self-indulgent Venus can furthermore make Librans lazy at times, yet there is a core of steel running through them, too, for their cardinal quadruplicity fills them with ambition and drive, and because another gift of their ruling planet is financial awareness, these traits may be especially evident when it comes to negotiating a pay rise. Indeed, these individuals are gifted negotiators, as well as mediators, for Venus blesses them with tact and their element of air, with articulacy. Other characteristics bestowed on them by air include a logical and analytical way of thinking, while their cardinal quadruplicity causes them to goal-oriented, which is why Librans often make talented strategists. They are not the most practical of people, however, and can lack staying power when bored, which is why they often rely on their charm to persuade earth-sign coworkers in particular to come to their rescue should they have become bogged down in petty details or their lack of interest in a task have resulted in them falling behind.

SCORPIO (THE SCORPION) ♏
October 23 to November 21

Ruling planet: Pluto; traditionally Mars
Element: Water
Polarity: Feminine
Quadruplicity: Fixed

> *Scorpio is a cold, watry [watery], nocturnal, flegmatick, feminine sign, of the watry Triplicity, fixed and North, the house and joy of Mars, feminine; usually it doth represent subtill, deceitfull men.*
> —William Lilly
> *Christian Astrology* (1647)

Scorpio people's reputation for being "subtle" and "deceitful" has prevailed for centuries, if not millennia, as evidenced by English astrologer William Lilly's summary of the Scorpionic character, which was written long before the discovery of Pluto, now Scorpio's primary ruling planet, in 1930. Today, it is Pluto that is said to make Scorpios subtle, yet rather than deceitful, secretive and enigmatic types that others find difficult to read. Their reticence is deepened by their caution-bestowing, feminine polarity and the shield of reserve that their watery element often prompts them to take refuge behind, for at heart these are profoundly emotional characters who dread having their feelings hurt and who sometimes enlist the aggression of Mars, their secondary planetary ruler, to strike back when they have been wounded. But when buoyed up and supported by the love and affection of their partners, relatives, and friends, they usually feel secure enough to open up and reveal their deeply compassionate and caring side, and because they have a fixed quadruplicity, will display unwavering loyalty and devotion, too. This same birth influence can make them remarkably stubborn, however, and they also find it hard to forgive or forget a slight.

Romance
Single Scorpios long to be in a stable, long-term relationship with someone who cares deeply about them. It is their element of water that gives them such an all-consuming need to love and be loved, not least because it, combined with their introspective and worry-magnifying, feminine polarity, can riddle them with insecurities, while Pluto can cause them to feel depressingly isolated or disconnected

Below: *If others find Scorpios unreadable, it is because they tend to hide their tender, watery feelings and feminine-polarity bashfulness behind a mask of cagey reserve that is often difficult to penetrate.*

from others. Furthermore extremely sensitive types, enamored Scorpios are often so terrified of having their tender hearts injured—or worse still, broken—that it may take an age before they instinctively sense that they won't be ridiculed or rejected and declare their true feelings. When their love is reciprocated, Scorpios make wonderful lovers, for Mars blesses them with passion; water, with kindness and compassion; and their feminine polarity, with thoughtfulness, a potent mixture that Pluto intensifies. And because their quadruplicity is fixed, or constant and unchanging, they are likely to be both monogamous and devoted to their beloved. They may not always be easy to live with, however, for they can display a fixed quadruplicity's obstinacy and inflexibility, and also have a tendency to sink into prolonged silences, thereby frustrating those born under communicative air signs in particular.

***Right:** Young scorpions are sensitive souls who need to feel loved and secure before they deem it safe to drop their guard and interact openly with their loved ones.*

Friendship

Scorpios can be loners, partly because their fixed quadruplicity gives them a dislike of having to make the compromises that are often inherent in friendships; partly because their feminine polarity causes them to be self-contained characters; and partly because, under Pluto's influence, they tend to hold themselves apart from others. And although their watery element infuses them with a longing to receive the affection and emotional support of people who care about them, it also makes them deeply vulnerable to being hurt. This is one of the reasons why Scorpios tend to protect their tender feelings by being unforthcoming, for if you don't expose your soft, inner core, you don't make it a target. It is therefore hard to get to know Scorpio individuals, but when someone has shown persistent kindness or constancy to a zodiacal scorpion, he or she will gradually feel it safe to open up and expose the caring and compassionate soul that lies beneath. Indeed, once Scorpio people have extended the hand of friendship, their fixed quadruplicity gives them the potential to remain loyal for life, that is, unless they feel somehow betrayed, when their pain may prompt them to nurse a lifelong grudge.

Family Relationships

Their families mean the world to zodiacal scorpions, for it is often only when among those who love and support them unconditionally that they feel secure enough to express their usually closely guarded emotions and simply be themselves. Even young Scorpios are giving and sympathetic family members, their element of water—the realm of intuition and the emotions—enabling them instinctively to sense if a loved one is feeling worried or down, when they will seek to provide comfort and reassurance. Scorpio parents furthermore have a profound gift for nurturing their children's emotional well-being, while the siblings of a Scorpio brother or sister will frequently confide in him or her in the knowledge that their secrets will go no farther, thanks to the influence that taciturn Pluto and an unforthcoming, feminine polarity wields over scorpions. Those of their relations who were born under fire or air signs may feel suffocated by the Plutonian intensity of Scorpio's devotion to them, however, and should they try to break free, may be punished by being subjected to the disappointed scorpion's sulkiness or silent treatment, which can be extraordinarily long-lasting. Indeed, while their fixed quadruplicity causes Scorpios to be devoted relations, it can make them stubborn ones, too.

Above: *Scorpios sometimes appear standoffish and unapproachable in the workplace, yet these are actually profoundly empathetic and caring individuals who will always extend a helping hand to a struggling coworker.*

Scorpio in the Workplace

Their coworkers often consider Scorpio people enigmatic personalities, and it is true that zodiacal scorpions typically hold themselves aloof from others, which is partly due to their feminine-polarity reserve and partly the result of having secretive Pluto as a planetary governor. Pluto also causes Scorpios to recognize that knowledge is power, and that this valuable commodity should therefore not be shared indiscriminately, particularly in a cut-throat business environment where no one is to be trusted and everyone has to look out for him- or herself. They may present an inscrutable face to the world, but their element of water blesses Scorpio individuals with deep compassion, and an upset colleague may therefore be surprised and touched when one of their number offers sympathy and understanding. It is this birth influence that is responsible for their remarkable intuition and creativity, too, so that they are frequently a source of original ideas and solutions. Some of their greatest assets are the bequest of their fixed quadruplicity, however, including their determination, formidable concentration, and staying power. Their colleagues may occasionally be infuriated by the inflexibility that is also associated with Scorpio's quadruplicity, though.

Right: *Fiery, masculine-polarity Sagittarians are uninhibited people who act on impulse, enjoy experimenting, and whose optimistic, Jovian outlook brightens the lives of those with whom they come into contact.*

SAGITTARIUS (THE ARCHER) ♐

November 22 to December 21

Ruling planet: Jupiter
Element: Fire
Polarity: Masculine
Quadruplicity: Mutable

> *Sagittarius is of the fiery triplicity, East, in nature fiery, hot, dry, Masculine, Cholericke, Diurnall, Common [mutable], by-corporall or double bodied, the House and Joy of Jupiter.*
>
> —William Lilly
> *Christian Astrology* (1647)

Reading William Lilly's summary of Sagittarius, you may wonder why this English astrologer called the archer "by-corporall" or "double bodied." The answer is that Sagittarius represents the centaur, a mythical, hybrid creature with a man's head, torso, and arms and a horse's body and legs that signifies the fusion of human intellectual potential and raw animal power—or the conscious and unconscious minds—in symbolic thought. The most famous centaur in Greco-Roman mythology was Cheiron (Chiron), who instructed such heroes as Achilles in the arts of healing, hunting, and music, and whom Zeus (Jupiter) placed among the stars as Sagittarius (the Latin for "archer") upon his death. This zodiacal sign's astrological influences underline Sagittarius' mythological character, for its ruling planet, Jupiter, is said to impart knowledge and encourage the expansion of the mind, as well as having healing powers; the element of fire contributes vitality and high animal spirits; a masculine polarity supplies dynamism; and a mutable quadruplicity signifies a complex and changeable nature. Sagittarian people are consequently typically adventurous, energetic types who are eager to broaden their mental and physical horizons, often act on the spur of the moment, and are furthermore adaptable, but can also be moody, especially if others limit their freedom.

Romance

Their fiery element causes Sagittarian people to be hot-blooded and spontaneous, and their masculine polarity, enterprising and outgoing, while Jupiter's all-embracing outlook is reinforced by a mutable quadruplicity's love of variety. As a result, it may take Sagittarians a while before they feel ready to call a halt to their enthusiastic pursuit of anyone who catches their fancy, and instead to contemplate settling down and spending the rest of their lives with just one individual. Their mutable, or changeable, quadruplicity can result in them being restless, and even inconstant, if, fueled by Jupiter's optimism, they make the wrong decision and yoke themselves to a petty minded, clinging partner, for both Jupiter and fire fill Sagittarians with the need to be with a person whom they find intellectually inspiring, who gives them the freedom to act on impulse, and who won't try their limited patience by being jealous and possessive. As long as these criteria are fulfilled, Sagittarians will usually repay their lover's tolerance with fiery passion and their mutable quaduplicity's flexibility, also enlivening their relationship with their masculine-polarity vigor and Jovian, big-picture mentality. In short, life with a Sagittarian will always be stimulating, as well as unpredictable.

Friendship

Having a masculine polarity and mutable quadruplicity suggests that Sagittarian individuals are typically extroverts who have a diverse circle of friends and acquaintances, but that their contact with them will be sporadic rather than steady. It's not that they don't feel affection for their pals (indeed, their fiery element gives them warm hearts, and Jupiter, a benign attitude to others), just that Sagittarians are always on the go, love the new, live for the moment, and are prone to acting spontaneously, which means that their friends may consequently find it hard to pin them down. But when they do, sociable, mutable-quadruplicity Sagittarians shine in the company of their friends, for having a masculine polarity's confidence and a fiery element's relish of being the focus of others' attention gives them a tendency to take center stage and exuberantly regale their audience with tales of their adventurous exploits. This is not to say that Sagittarians are bad listeners, for Jupiter's gifts to them include inclusiveness, the willingness to learn from others, and an interest in discussing wide-ranging issues, particularly those encompassed by philosophy, ethics, and religion. All in all, they usually exert an enlivening and thought-provoking influence over their friends.

__Below:__ Sagittarius individuals are both always on the go and readily distracted, which their friends may not appreciate if they'd been looking forward to the archer's undivided attention and a quiet heart-to-heart.

Below: Fiery Sagittarian youngsters have a tendency to fume, and even blow a fuse, if they are prevented from releasing their pent-up energy by cantering off on a stimulating, outward-bound adventure.

Family Relationships

Although fiery, warm, and demonstrative Sagittarians love their relations, and aren't afraid to say so either, they usually feel bored or suffocated if required to spend long periods of time with them, that is, unless they are engaged in exciting activities together. Their masculine polarity makes them vigorous and outgoing, their fiery element fills them with the spirit of adventure, their mutable quadruplicity gives them an appetite for change, while Jupiter infuses them with the urge to expand their horizons, all of which indicates that Sagittarians won't be home much, and will become restless and frustrated if their freedom of action is curbed. The parents of Sagittarian children may therefore have a tough time restraining these young hot-heads at the same time as ensuring that there is plenty to keep them interested and occupied. Yet although awesome temper tantrums can ensue if their fiery will is thwarted, Sagittarian rages rarely last for long, and they soon revert to their cheery, Jovian selves again. And it is thanks to Jupiter that benevolent Sagittarian parents have a gift for raising their children to take a broad-minded view of the world and its inhabitants, often by exposing them to different cultures and experiences.

Sagittarius in the Workplace

Sagittarian individuals have an invigorating effect on their coworkers, who often find their Jupiter-bestowed, wide-ranging outlook and optimism inspiring, and their fiery enthusiasm infectious. Their masculine polarity makes them confident and enterprising, too, while their mutable quadruplicity gives them versatility and a relish of variety, so that these are dynamic and flexible people who are able to keep a number of projects on the go at the same time. The downsides of working alongside Sagittarians may, however, include their mutable-quadruplicity moodiness and fiery temper, although these characteristics generally only manifest themselves in these normally cheerful and exuberant types when zodiacal archers don't feel mentally challenged, are required to apply themselves to a time-consuming, humdrum task, or are straining at the leash to break free of an authoritarian boss' restraining hand. And when they enjoy increased personal autonomy, perhaps as a result of promotion, Sagittarians have the potential to be outstanding bosses, for Jupiter causes them to treat their staff inclusively and to welcome their ideas and suggestions, while their fiery element and masculine polarity bless them with charisma and the ability to motivate others with their burning energy and pioneering approach. But whatever their status in the workplace, staying power is not a Sagittarian strong point.

CAPRICORN (THE GOAT) ♄
December 22 to January 19

Ruling planet: Saturn
Element: Earth
Polarity: Feminine
Quadruplicity: Cardinal

> *Capricorn is the House of Saturn, and is Nocturnal, Cold, Dry, Melancholly, Earthly [earthy], Feminine, Solsticall, Cardinal, Moveable, Domesticall, Four-footed, Southern; the exaltation of Mars.*
> —William Lilly
> *Christian Astrology* (1647)

Above: *Most young Saturn-ruled Capricorns need no encouragement to study hard, for graduating is often the first major step toward achieving their long-term, cardinal-quadruplicity career goals.*

Their partners, friends, loved ones, and coworkers can generally rely on Capricorn individuals, be it for well-considered and sensible advice, practical support, or simply to behave predictably! Their feminine polarity causes Capricorneans to be both thoughtful and receptive to others' influence, while their earthy element gives them a realistic and constant outlook, as well as material values, as a result of which they are typically steadily supportive types, even if their support manifests itself as the provision of tangible assistance rather than empathy. Then there is Saturn, Capricorn's ruling planet, whose contribution to the personalities of those born under this zodiacal sign is a mature and serious approach to everything that they undertake, along with ambition, a characteristic that is reinforced by their goal-oriented, cardinal quadruplicity. All in all, Capricorneans can be said to be sober and responsible individuals whose self-starting, cardinal quadruplicity drives them forward in their quest to achieve long-term success, whether it be by working hard to scale the career ladder or by ensuring that their loved ones waste no opportunity to fulfill their vocational potential. They may have the best of intentions, but Capricorn people's conservatism and single-mindedness may sometimes alienate those around them, especially those who believe that life should be fun.

Romance
While they are blessed with an earth sign's powerful sensuality, Capricornean individuals do not give their love lightly, or indiscriminately. And although when under the influence of their go-getting, cardinal quadruplicity they are capable of making the first move should they believe that they have found "the one," their feminine polarity may equally make them too shy or cautious to push themselves forward. Earthy, saturnine Capricorns are

Right: *Capricorns are sensible enough to know that taking a vacation will freshen their minds and restore their energy levels, but while lying on the beach, they'll often be thinking about the tasks that await them at home or work.*

unsentimental realists who may long for the comfort of a lover's embrace, but whose priorities are more pragmatic when it comes to identifying their ideal partner. What zodiacal goats really want is someone who will support them in their careers or otherwise make a significant contribution to the realization of a shared vision, such as raising a family to be proud of or earning the respect of the community. These orderly, earthy types feel uncomfortable when exposed to deep or extreme emotions and dislike unpredictability, too, which is why they may shy away from water- and fire-sign people, yet may approve of an air-sign sweetheart's rational mindset and appreciate his or her gift for making useful social or business contacts. Capricorns may demand a lot from a beloved, but will also strive to ensure that he or she is well provided for.

Friendship

Saturn-governed, cardinal-quadruplicity Capricorn individuals may devote most of their time to the furtherance of their careers or life goals, but this doesn't mean that they don't schedule regular relaxation time into their schedules, partly because they are sensible enough to know that recharging their batteries will result in renewed energy and consequently increased productivity. Although they are not that gregarious, and their feminine polarity can cause them to be reserved, zodiacal goats value those whom they regard as good friends, and enjoy engaging in such typically earthy pursuits as hiking in the hills or sharing a satisfying meal together, or perhaps helping each other with home improvements. And it is thanks to their earthy element that level-headed Capricorneans make patient, loyal, and supportive friends. The nature of the advice that they offer is practical and constructive and therefore of great help to their more impractical, air- and water-sign friends, yet their sober, saturnine suggestions may not always be well received by those who were born under fire signs, who may dismiss them as being boringly unimaginative or conservative. But when their Capricorn friend's cardinal quadruplicity comes to the fore, they may be amazed and inspired by the goat's initiative and vision.

Family Relationships

They are not typically stay-at-homes, for their motivating, cardinal quadruplicity generally sends them out into the wider world to make their way in life, but returning to a stable and settled domestic environment is nevertheless important to Capricorns. Perhaps it is because having an orderly, well-run home maintains these earthy, feminine-polarity people's sense of security, or maybe it is because it is one of the few places in which they feel able to relax (even if many Capricorneans' idea of relaxation is preparing for the coming day at work or school). Being practical, earthy types, Capricorns—even children—are prone to structuring their free time around routines, which may exasperate their more spontaneous, fire-sign relatives, yet whatever their zodiacal sign, few of their kin can complain that things don't get done around the house. Saturn-governed Capricorn parents take their role as providers, caregivers, and guiders very seriously, and cherish high, cardinal-quadruplicity ambitions for their children, too, so that they will invariably chivvy their offspring to get their homework done before having fun, and may also encourage them to map out a career plan at a relatively young age. There is, however, a danger that their well-meaning tendency to organize their children and constant, watchful concern may cause them to be regarded, and resented, as controlling disciplinarians.

Capricorn in the Workplace

Saturn-ruled Capricorns' self-discipline and hard-working approach to their jobs often arouse their colleagues' awe and anxiety, for as bosses in particular, they set formidably high standards that few of those born under other signs of the zodiac feel capable of living up to. Although they enjoy their work, and derive great satisfaction from doing it well, go-getting, cardinal-quadruplicity Capricorns generally do not graft as diligently as they do for the sake of it, but to achieve their life's goals, which may be to provide for their families and a comfortable retirement—a practical, earthy aim—or to earn the respect of others for their achievements, which reflects the influence that ambitious Saturn can wield over them. Their ruling planet, element, and feminine polarity may together make Capricorns cautious and prudent realists in the workplace, who will ponder over a decision long and hard before setting the wheels in motion, and will then work doggedly and determinedly toward realizing their goal. They may be primarily preoccupied with achieving their own targets, but Capricorns also make conscientious, dependable, and supportive coworkers, if not very inspirational or light-hearted ones.

Below: *Earthy Capricorns are devoted mothers and fathers who take a hands-on approach to parenting, yet their children may sometimes protest at the goat's Saturn-influenced insistence that they do everything properly, not sloppily.*

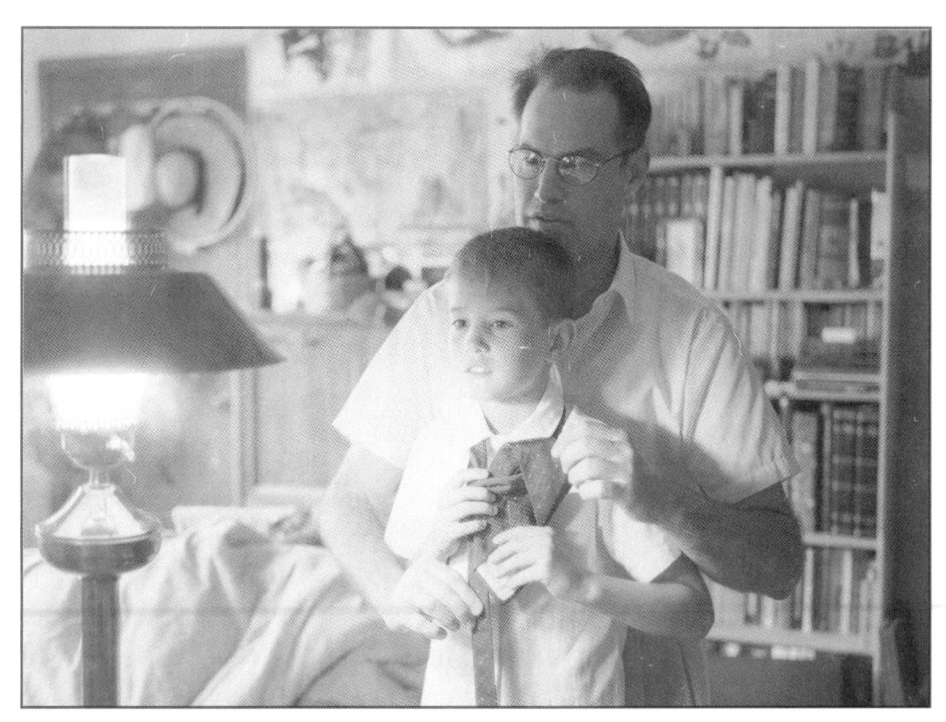

AQUARIUS (THE WATER-CARRIER) ♒
January 20 to February 18

Ruling planet: Uranus; traditionally Saturn
Element: Air
Polarity: Masculine
Quadruplicity: Fixed

> *Aquarius is an aierial [airy], hot and moyst Sign, of the aiery [airy] Triplicity, diurnal, Sanguine, fixed, rational, humane, masculine, the principall house of Saturn, and house wherein he most rejoyceth; Western.*
>
> —William Lilly
> *Christian Astrology* (1647)

Below: *Airy, Uranian Aquarians are intelligent individuals whose cool approach can make them seem emotionally detached. Despite their tendency to flirt and their resistance to being tied down, their fixed quadruplicity gives them the capacity to remain faithful in a relationship.*

Those born under different zodiacal signs usually both treasure and dislike aspects of the Aquarian character. Airy Aquarius individuals' chattiness and cheerfulness attract others to them, although water-sign people may wish that they were less dispassionate and more emotionally expressive, for instance. And while fire-sign personalities may be inspired by the masculine-polarity confidence with which Aquarians communicate their radical, Uranus-inspired notions, they may be infuriated by the coolness with which these analytical, airy types respond to their own imaginative ideas. In addition, although Geminians and Librans share Aquarians' element of air, Gemini's quadruplicity is mutable, or flexible and inconstant, while Libra's is cardinal, or self-centered and ambitious, which suggests that they may appreciate and respect the water-carrier's loyalty and determination, but may be exasperated by the dogmatism that is the joint bequest of Aquarians' fixed quadruplicity and Saturn, their secondary ruling planet. It is therefore fortunate that Uranus-ruled Aquarians neither greatly care what others think of them, nor, thanks to their airy element, require much support, and that their masculine polarity and fixed quadruplicity give them the courage of their convictions. But if they are accepted on their own terms, they typically prove staunch and life-enhancing partners, friends, relations, and colleagues.

Romance
Those who are hoping to enter into, or sustain, a long-term romantic liaison with an Aquarius will be heartened to know that once water-carriers have committed themselves, their fixed, or change-resistant, quadruplicity will usually ensure that they remain faithful, albeit in their own, idiosyncratic way. The difficulty may be extracting such a pledge from them in the first place, for their freedom-seeking element of air gives Aquarians an aversion to being tied down, and when combined with independent-minded, unconventional Uranus, may even result in them initially demanding an open relationship. The key to attracting, and keeping, airy, communicative Aquarius

people's attention is firstly, at least to be interested in, or tolerant of, their inventive, Uranian ideas, and, secondly, to give them as much leeway as they require to investigate whatever it is that intrigues them, be it a person or an abstract concept. It probably goes without saying that possessive or unconfident types will almost certainly suffer agonies of jealousy or insecurity when their lover is an emotionally detached, self-willed Aquarius. Yet if they can only learn to trust their sweetheart, they will reap immeasurable rewards, such as a masculine polarity's positive outlook, a fixed quadruplicity's steadfastness, and constant, stimulating conversation.

Above: *Airy Aquarians are friendly and forthcoming, as well as full of unconventional, Uranus-inspired ideas, making them a delight to be around (as long as the conversation interests them).*

Friendship

Aquarian people frequently puzzle their friends. On the one hand, their element of air makes them sociable, talkative, and fun-loving, and their masculine polarity, outgoing extroverts, while Uranus gives them a fascination with progressive ideas and the potential inherent in new technology, yet should the conversation stray from the abstract into the realm of personal emotions, they are typically off like a shot. But just when you are starting to feel deeply hurt that Aquarius appears to have dropped you because you've been going through a traumatic or life-changing experience and he or she clearly isn't interested in your feelings, the water-carrier may surprise you by calling to suggest a get-together. It may seem paradoxical, but although airy Aquarians find it hard to empathize with their friends, their fixed quadruplicity causes them to be devoted to them, so that they will generally try to maintain contact, even following a disagreement. It is important not to overestimate impersonal Aquarians' capacity for fellow feeling, however, for they are simply not fired up or brought down by their emotions in the same way as their fire- or water-sign friends; instead, their invigorating talent is for encouraging others to think "outside the box."

Family Relationships

Thanks to the influence that Saturn and their fixed quadruplicity exert over them, there is no question that zodiacal water-

Above: Even small Aquarians need to be given the freedom to explore the wider world, and may become mutinous if prevented from following the outgoing, enterprising, and investigative instincts that are the gifts of their masculine polarity, Uranus, and air.

carriers have a responsible and steadfast attitude toward their loved ones, although their family members may not always recognize the depth of Aquarians' concern for them. For their dispassionate, intellect-emphasizing element of air, together with Uranus, their cool, unemotional ruling planet, may cause them to seem rather detached and aloof, and because they can lack empathy, they often genuinely do not know how to respond when confronted by displays of extreme emotion, thereby hurting or disappointing their water-sign relatives in particular. Add a masculine polarity's activeness to the curiosity and desire for freedom that are the joint gifts of air and Uranus, and the result is that Aquarians usually prefer to be out and about investigating the latest pioneering concept to seize their interest to spending some quiet time at home with their nearest and dearest. They may not know how to deal with others' feelings, but fixed-quadruplicity Aquarian people are always there for their loved ones in a crisis, and will usually come up with logical and ingenious solutions to their problems. And their inventiveness, chattiness, and love of fun certainly enliven their relatives' days.

Aquarius in the Workplace

Aquarians are generally well liked in the workplace for their positive and dynamic, masculine-polarity approach and bright and breezy outlook. Air makes them forthcoming and articulate, too, so that they have no difficulty expressing the trailblazing concepts with which Uranus fills their heads. And although more conservative, earthy types may dismiss their Uranian notions as being zany or impractical, their exploratory ruling planet and analytical element usually ensure that they are both based on sound research and backed by the latest findings. It is also from Uranus that Aquarians derive their fascination with new technology, so that they are often the first people whom their colleagues call for help when a piece of equipment is malfunctioning. Yet many of those who work with them consider Aquarius individuals oddballs, partly because their ideas can be so radical or eccentric, partly because their fixed quadruplicity can cause them to be self-opinionated, and partly because they are not that interested in their coworkers' feelings, and can therefore appear somewhat cold or standoffish, despite their undoubted gift for communication. Be they bosses or underlings, their sharp intellects and fixed-quadruplicity tenacity nevertheless arouse others' respect.

Right: Their colleagues may frown on the unconventional Aquarian working style, but zodiacal water-carriers don't give a fig what others think of them, and if a canine companion and floor-level work surface help the ideas to flow, perhaps that's all that matters.

PISCES (THE FISHES) ♓

February 19 to March 20

Ruling planet: Neptune; traditionally Jupiter
Element: Water
Polarity: Feminine
Quadruplicity: Mutable

> *Pisces is of the Watry [watery] Triplicity, Northern, cold Sign, moyst, Flegmatick, feminine, nocturnal, the house of Jupiter, and exaltation of Venus, a Bycorporeal, common [mutable] or double-bodied Sign, an idle, effeminate, sickly Sign, or representing a party of no action.*
>
> —William Lilly
> *Christian Astrology* (1647)

English astrologer William Lilly's rather harsh description of the Piscean personality illustrates how greatly zodiacal fishes are often misunderstood. It is thanks to the emotion-heightening effect of their element of water and the idealism that is the gift of Neptune, their primary ruling planet, that those born under this sign are usually sensitive, compassionate dreamers who can be paralyzed by indecision should they have mixed feelings about someone or something, or be torn between two courses of action. This tendency to be indecisive is exaggerated by their mutable, or changeable, quadruplicity, which may also cause them to go to extremes (and it is no coincidence that depictions of the Piscean fishes frequently portray them swimming off in opposite directions). It doesn't help that the combined influence of a feminine polarity and the inarticulacy-bestowing element of water results in them internalizing their worries in particular, and consequently clamming up, which is one of the reasons why they may appear passive or inert. Apart from being oversensitive at times, unselfish, giving Pisceans typically enjoy profoundly fulfilling relationships with a diverse range of characters, for their mutable quadruplicity gives them an appetite for variety and Jupiter, their secondary planetary governor, blesses them with an all-embracing outlook.

Romance

Pisceans need someone to love. It is not just that zodiacal fishes' element of water is the realm of emotions in symbolic thought, or that Neptune infuses them with the urge to merge mind, body, and soul with a perfect lover. Because they have a feminine polarity, Pisces people can be rather shy and reserved, yet their mutable quadruplicity makes them long to be

Below: *Infused with the Neptunian hope of living happily ever after, and glowing with the joy of having their love requited, their wedding day is a dream come true for Pisceans.*

Right: *Watery Pisces people yearn for a lover who will cherish them, support them, and give them the courage to throw their feminine-polarity caution to the wind and indulge their mutable-quadruplicity love of variety.*

more outgoing and to be introduced to new people and experiences, which they instinctively feel would happen under the emboldening influence of a more confident beloved. Their watery element increases their feminine-polarity caution by causing them to be both extremely vulnerable to being hurt and seething with insecurities, which is why it may take them a while to learn to trust a potential sweetheart before revealing the depths of their feelings for him or her, but once a romantic connection has been established, the floodgates burst open, unleashing a torrent of love. Fire-sign sorts in particular will relish being idealized and adored by Neptune-governed Pisceans, while earthy and airy individuals will welcome their mutable-quadruplicity adaptability. Apart from fellow water-sign people, those born under other zodiacal signs may ultimately find their Piscean lovers' watery clinginess, overdependence, or intense concern for their well-being suffocating, however.

Friendship

Pisces individuals have the potential to make wonderful friends. Their feminine polarity may cause them to be somewhat shy and introverted, but their mutable quadruplicity bestows on them sociable instincts, an enjoyment of change, and the flexibility to accept and adjust to different personalities. And while Jupiter's legacy to Pisceans is a genuine interest in learning from others, Neptune's bequest, reinforced by a watery element's caring and nurturing tendencies, is altruism, so that their friends are often flattered by their questions and touched by their concern. Although Pisceans are predisposed to giving, partly because the combination of Neptune and water heightens their powers of intuition to the extent that their sympathy is instantly aroused when they detect that someone is in pain—be it emotional or physical—which they then cannot help but seek to alleviate, they in turn derive an increased sense of security and self-worth from their pals' attention and support. It is unlikely, however, that many of their friends can match their unselfishness, and because water makes Pisceans touchy and hypersensitive, they may overreact to a thoughtless word or prolonged absence by displaying their watery, mutable-quadruplicity moodiness, thereby baffling, upsetting, or exasperating the supposed culprit.

Family Relationships

It is mainly due to Neptune that Piscean people of all ages visualize, and try to create, an ideal family, one in which no one ever argues, and everyone is so filled with love for each other that they always unselfishly put their relations first. In the real world, however, their relatives may neither share their vision nor be capable of fulfilling it, particularly if they don't have Pisces' watery element or feminine polarity, both of which are associated with caring and domesticity. Although Pisceans set a formidable example by empathizing with, nurturing, and supporting their loved ones, also enlisting their mutable-polarity flexibility to minimize conflicts, their water-bestowed emotional neediness and the supersensitivity that is triggered when they feel unappreciated can result in them becoming moody and withdrawn. If they are parents, there is consequently a danger that those of their children who were born under independence-seeking fire or air signs will resent what they perceive as Pisces' attempts to control them through manipulation or emotional blackmail, and may react angrily or icily, thereby deepening their parent's distress. But as long as Pisceans aren't taken for granted or treated like doormats, they will blossom with contentment and show the best of themselves.

Pisces in the Workplace

Although Piscean people are typically treasured by their colleagues, they can be frustrating individuals to work alongside, too, for zodiacal fishes often display a Neptunian tendency to daydream and a mutable quadruplicity's inconstancy, which means that they can't always be relied upon to remain focused on a task or to meet a crucial deadline. They can also be infuriatingly hesitant, partly because their feminine polarity makes them cautious, and partly because, having a mutable quadruplicity, they are often torn between two equally attractive courses of action. And because their hearts rule their heads, when pushed to make up their minds, they may go with their instincts, which confusing-inducing Neptune may have muddled, leading them into disaster. That said, their Neptunian, watery intuition, coupled with their extraordinary creativity, can result in stellar successes, and the original ideas that flow from their fertile imaginations frequently amaze and inspire others. And when it comes to their people skills, Pisceans are cherished for their flexibility, genuine empathy, and idealistic tendency to think the best of their workmates. If they are bosses, these are furthermore individuals who will unselfishly nurture their underlings' careers.

Above: *Piscean individuals' tendency to drift into a daydream when there is work to be done may irritate their colleagues, yet brilliant, instinctive hunches often swim into their minds while they are somewhere on planet Neptune.*

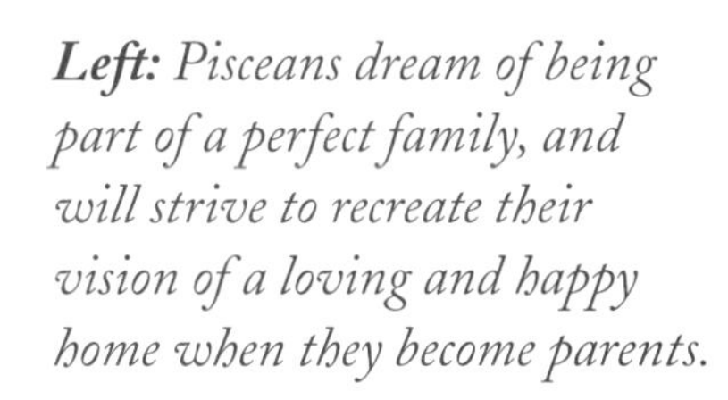

Left: *Pisceans dream of being part of a perfect family, and will strive to recreate their vision of a loving and happy home when they become parents.*

Blood's thicker than water,
and when one's in trouble
Best to seek out a relative's
open arms.

EURIPIDES, *Andromache* (c.426 BC)

FAMILY

"When our relatives are at home, we have to think of all their good points or it would be impossible to endure them," said the Irish writer George Bernard Shaw in *Heartbreak House* (1929). Bear this observation in mind when you read the page that unites your zodiacal sign with that of a close relative with whom you have a fraught relationship, for if you focus on the positives, rather than the negatives, and make a real effort to understand your parent, child, or sibling, you could transform your relationship for the better.

You can't choose your relations, no more than you can change the ruling planets, elements, polarities, and quadruplicities that together influence both your feelings and actions and theirs, and whether you are willing to admit it or not, your rapport with your family members has the power either to light up your life or doom you to spend your days under a dark cloud of rage, resentment, or depression. By giving you an insight into your kin's motivations and needs, and how they may conflict with yours, astrology has the power to provide you with a new perspective on your relationship, and consequently the necessary sympathy or tolerance to make allowances for your parent's controlling tendencies, your child's temper tantrums, or your brother or sister's infuriating behavior. And if you are one of the lucky ones who has always enjoyed an affectionate and relaxed bond with a particular loved one, you may be interested to know why the stars have smiled upon you both. The chances are that you will nod your head with delighted recognition when you read the astrological reasons, but don't be too complacent, for relationships are rarely static, and it may well be that one day you will need to consult the relevant page for advice on how to weather a stormy spell.

ARIES

ARIES

Aries Birth Influences

Ruling planet: Mars
Element: Fire
Polarity: Masculine
Quadruplicity: Cardinal

Because Aries parents and Aries children share an overwhelming love of fun, adventure, and excitement, life in this household will never be dull. Commanding Aries is not known for its willingness to submit to authority, however, or for its patience, and dramatic conflicts may arise when these self-willed children rebel against the boundaries set by their equally headstrong parents.

Parents: Grown-up Ariens love children. And how could they not, enjoying as they do letting off steam by rollicking and romping, exploring the world around them, and testing themselves against new challenges just as much as their offspring? If you are the Arien child of an Arien parent, you no doubt relished your action-packed childhood, but because there is a strong competitive streak in the Aries makeup, there may have been an element of rivalry, on the field of play, at least. Being a bold free-thinker, your Arien parent probably encouraged you to seek out the unusual and follow an unconventional path in life, an approach that may thankfully have accorded with your own inclinations. A clash of wills may have been inevitable when your dominant Aries parent tried to impose his or her will on you, however. You resent what you perceive as being controlled, and your parent no doubt operated on a short fuse whenever you were mutinous. Once the explosion was over, though, you almost certainly instantly kissed and made up.

Don't worry if you find your two Aries children sometimes seem to take sibling rivalry too far. Despite their competitiveness, they are probably very proud of each other.

Children: Arien children are born with the urge to strike out on their own, a character trait that Aries parents respect because they share it. Children often need to be protected from themselves, however, and the young Aries will not react meekly to being restricted. Patient and oblique manipulation is frequently the best way of steering them in the right direction, but if you're a typically impatient and direct Aries parent, you'll probably find that difficult! So stand ready to dispense warm hugs and many words of solace and encouragement if your child's latest bid for independence ends in tears.

Sibling Relationships: If you are an Aries who has an Arien sibling, your childhood years must have resembled a fierce power struggle as you constantly strove to outdo each other and flared up in fury whenever you bore the brunt of the other's bossiness. Competition will probably always permeate your relationship, but being warm-hearted types, you are probably secretly rather proud of your wayward Arien sibling.

Aries Birth Influences

Ruling planet: Mars
Element: Fire
Polarity: Masculine
Quadruplicity: Cardinal

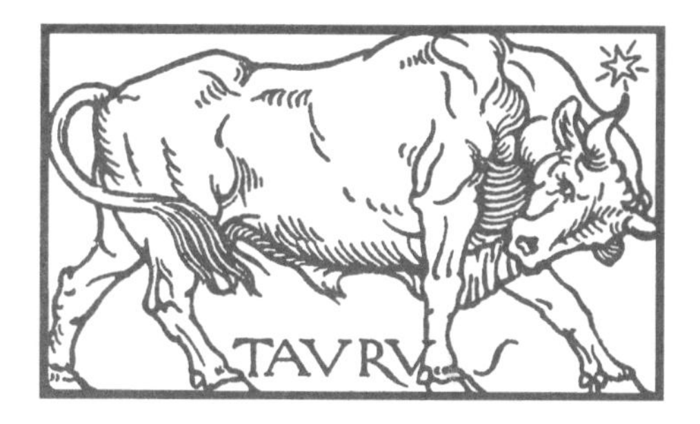

TAURUS
ARIES

Being fundamentally different characters, the occasional flare-up is to be expected between an adventurous Aries parent and steady Taurus child, a cautious Taurus parent and a heedless Aries child, or go-getting Aries and stay-at-home Taurus siblings. Yet this relationship is rooted in mutual affection and devotion.

Parents: If you are an Aries with a Taurus parent, he or she probably drove you to distraction when you were growing up. No doubt your scrupulous Taurean mother insisted that you do your homework when you were itching to play outside, or your protective Taurean father infuriated you by forbidding you to do something that he perceived as being reckless. From an adult perspective, you may now understand that your parent had your best interests at heart, and wasn't your home a warm, well-ordered haven, and couldn't you always rely on your parent's support?

If you are a Taurus with an Arien parent, you probably still shudder at the memory of being chivvied to pack more action into your childhood because it would supposedly be fun, when you were perfectly happy immersing yourself in your hobbies at home. Or maybe your Arien mother's eccentric outlook, or your Arien father's wild ideas, embarrassed your rather conventional younger self. If so, you're today probably quite proud of his of her originality and fearlessness.

Children: Arien parents of Taurus children often despair at their offspring's lack of get up and go and careful, somewhat plodding, approach to life. You've probably learned that it's useless to try to force them to be more daring, however, because pushing them simply makes them dig in their heels, and if you prod them too much, an awesome temper tantrum ensues. Still, thank goodness that you don't have to worry about them endangering themselves with their foolhardy behavior, unlike Taurean parents of Arien children! Indeed, if you are a Taurus parent of an Aries child, you may be never happier than when keeping a watchful eye on your child at home, and no doubt fret about his or her tendency to dash off in hot pursuit of a new enthusiasm. You won't change that, but can instead ground your little Aries in a warm and loving home environment.

Sibling Relationships: If you are a Taurus with an Aries sibling, or vice versa, you may not have been close childhood friends, not least because Taurus was forever home and Aries was always out. Although you may have had your fair share of spats, you probably just got on with your own thing, but woe betide anyone who threatened your sibling, because you would no doubt invariably step in to defend him or her.

Taurus Birth Influences

Ruling planet: Venus
Element: Earth
Polarity: Feminine
Quadruplicity: Fixed

A typical Taurus parent will always make sure that young Aries finishes his or her homework before heading out to play.

Aries Birth Influences

Ruling planet: Mars
Element: Fire
Polarity: Masculine
Quadruplicity: Cardinal

ARIES
GEMINI

Aries Birth Influences

Ruling planet: Mars
Element: Fire
Polarity: Masculine
Quadruplicity: Cardinal

The combination of Aries' active nature and Gemini's inquisitive mind, reinforced by both signs' aversion to humdrum routines, creates a lively and somewhat chaotic household. Cool Gemini's capacity for criticism and short-tempered Aries' impatience are an inflammable mixture, however.

Parents: If you have an Arien parent and are a Gemini, he or she probably exposed you to countless exciting childhood experiences, although you may have wished that you had time to absorb what you had learned before being whisked off on the next adventure. Your rather authoritarian parent's tendency to insist that you obeyed what you considered to be pointless instructions without explaining their importance may have riled you, and may still cause friction today, but you may have always felt secure in his or her fierce love for you.

If you are an Aries with a Gemini parent, he or she no doubt encouraged you to listen respectfully to people's viewpoints and then to make up your mind for yourself. You must have loved growing up in a home in which day-to-day chores were deemed boring, but it probably rankled when your objective parent occasionally found fault with your thoughtless actions. Perhaps by now you understand why you needed to be pulled up short from time to time.

Children: If you are a Gemini who has an Arien child, your offspring's antics must entertain you, and his or her courage must make you proud. But your little Arien may be reckless, and therefore requires controlling. The secret is not to nitpick or demolish his or her self-esteem with wounding words, but to guide through flattery, which you are eminently capable of doing.

You must adore the way that your child charms people of all ages with his or her engaging personality if you have a Gemini child and are an Aries. But patience is not one of your strengths, and your flighty child's lack of staying power and endless questions probably drive you up the wall. Try to keep your temper and make sensible, well-argued suggestions rather than forcing him or her to bend to your will.

Sibling Relationships: If you are an Aries with a Gemini sibling, you must have enjoyed some madcap times as children, with your impish brother or sister always daring you to go one step farther? There were probably lots of rows, too, and if you are the Gemini in this relationship, these may have been triggered by your sibling's bossiness, while your own ambiguous nature no doubt irritated your Arien partner in crime.

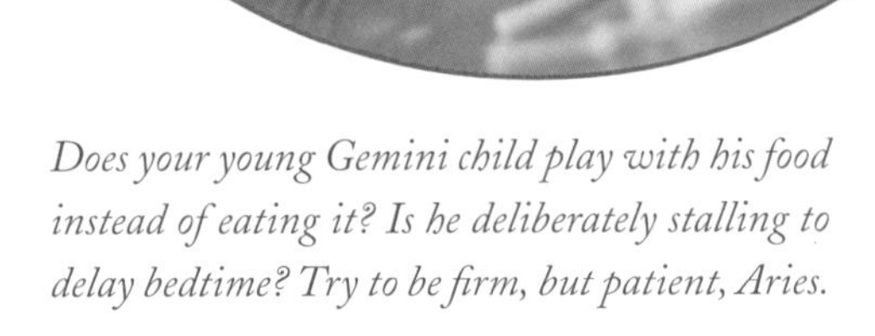

Does your young Gemini child play with his food instead of eating it? Is he deliberately stalling to delay bedtime? Try to be firm, but patient, Aries.

Gemini Birth Influences

Ruling planet: Mercury
Element: Air
Polarity: Masculine
Quadruplicity: Mutable

CANCER
ARIES

While the home is nurturing Cancer's domain, the one place where the crab feels safe enough to emerge from his or her shell completely, adventurous Aries regards it more as a base from which to charge off in search of fresh challenges. Problems may therefore arise if clinging Cancer tries to rein in Aries, or if heedless Aries treats Cancer's haven as a hotel.

Parents: If you are an Aries with a Cancerian parent, you probably remember your childhood as being mainly a pampered time. Cancer is typically patient, exceptionally caring, and blessed with the ability to understand a troubled child's point of view. He or she needs to feel appreciated, however, and young Aries is often too preoccupied with making forays into the wider world to be considerate. And if your Cancer parent feels taken for granted, he or she may retreat into hurt silence until you go out of your way to make amends, so try to be aware of his or her feelings.

If you are the Cancer child of an Aries, you must recall your parent's sudden enthusiasms with amused affection, although they may often have alarmed your younger self. Aries fills his or her children's lives with fun and excitement, but also with tests of courage, which may have frightened you and made you dread not being able to match your impatient father or mother's daring lest you provoked an explosion of frustration.

Children: If you are a Cancer with an Aries child, your active little ram must make you feel both proud and a little sad. Proud of your child's courage, and sad because he or she seems to prefer playing with friends to spending time with you. But aren't you deeply moved by your child's occasional fierce demonstrations of affection?

Your Cancerian child's uncanny ability to sense your moods must amaze you if you are an Aries. Yet you probably wish that he or she ventured out more, and perhaps you worry about your offspring's dependence on you and lack of confidence. Don't try to mold him or her into your intrepid image, however, but instead lavish lots of love on your sensitive crablet.

Sibling Relationships: If you are an enterprising Aries with a home-loving Cancerian sibling, or the other way round, your paths probably didn't cross that much as children, and maybe still don't. But when you do connect, Aries revels in Cancer's interest and cosseting, while Cancer delights in being the focus of dynamic Aries' attention.

Cancer Birth Influences

Ruling planet: The Moon
Element: Water
Polarity: Feminine
Quadruplicity: Cardinal

An Aries parent or older sibling will try to encourage shy young Cancer to be more adventurous and come out of his or her shell.

Aries Birth Influences

Ruling planet: Mars
Element: Fire
Polarity: Masculine
Quadruplicity: Cardinal

ARIES / LEO

Aries Birth Influences

Ruling planet: Mars
Element: Fire
Polarity: Masculine
Quadruplicity: Cardinal

A combination of Aries and Leo siblings is likely to result in a playful household that is often fun—but these headstrong children will also find plenty to fight about.

Leo Birth Influences

Ruling planet: The Sun
Element: Fire
Polarity: Masculine
Quadruplicity: Fixed

A household that contains an Aries and a Leo pairing is likely to be loud, lively, and loving. Chores will be neglected for more stimulating pursuits, and the interaction between parents and children will be direct and involved. But being natural leaders, both Leo and Aries resent being ordered around, making some impassioned spats inevitable.

Parents: If you have an Aries parent and are a Leo, your childhood years probably passed in a whirl of excitement. Aries whisks his or her children off to introduce them to bracing new activities, and although you may have enjoyed these excursions, the lion likes to be idle, so that you must sometimes have longed to be left to laze. Because you are both fire signs who need to exert control over those around you, there must also have been some spectacular clashes of will when your parent tried to force your mutinous younger self to be obedient. You may now need to remind your parent respectfully that, as an adult, you will no longer accept being told what to do.

If you are an Aries with a Leo parent, you must similarly have had some almighty rows, perhaps triggered by your burning desire to head off in a different direction to that laid down by your mother or father. Outbursts over, your parent no doubt then quickly distracted you with a joke and an intriguing proposition, thus restoring the usual sunny atmosphere to your home. Your inventive parent probably ensured that your days were entertaining and instructive, although you would often have rather played with friends than trail around yet another art gallery.

Children: An Aries child's courage and curiosity makes a Leo parent's heart swell with pride, but there may be times when your offspring's capriciousness worries and exasperates you. Keeping him or her safe means teaching your child that acting heedlessly can have terrible consequences, but do not dictate to your headstrong lamb, and instead talk through your concerns reasonably.

Your Leo child's loving nature and cheerfulness must delight you if you are an Aries, even if you gripe at your indolent cub's occasional lack of get up and go. You probably also find his or her tendency to challenge your authority tiring, but secretly revel in your child's self-confidence and fearlessness.

Sibling Relationships: If you are an assertive Aries with a masterful Leo sibling, or the other way round, your jostles for supremacy must have sparked off plenty of squabbles. Your mutual love of fun and games probably overshadowed your arguments, however, and your plucky sibling may remain an inspiring playmate.

VIRGO

ARIES

When all of the family members are in the best of moods, a house in which fiery Aries and practical Virgo live will be both stimulating and remarkably well run. Yet when one's habits irritate the other, the atmosphere can become explosive.

Parents: If you are an Aries, your Virgo parent no doubt ensured that you had plenty to keep you occupied when you were young, although his or her preferred activities may not have coincided with yours. One of Virgo's maxims is "A place for everything and everything in its place," and your parent may therefore have insisted that you tidy your room when you were burning to play outside with your friends. You probably didn't appreciate it then, but, looking back, may now understand why he or she felt it necessary to nag you to do those boring chores or to be careful with your allowance. Don't be too quick to reject your parent's orderly and careful ways.

There may have been times when you felt like the adult in your childhood relationship with your Aries parent if you are a Virgo. While you are the sort of person who finds routines comforting, your spontaneous parent must often have caused you anxiety by telling you to drop everything in order to join him or her in an adventurous excursion. You probably had to keep reminding your parent to keep humdrum appointments, too. Even so, life was no doubt never dull with your Arien parent, and perhaps you now regard his or her courage, initiative, and warmth with great fondness.

Children: Although you may adore your spirited little Aries, he or she must worry you if you are a Virgo. You may especially wish that your child would think before acting. Do not lecture him or her too much, however, because headstrong Aries will simply turn a deaf ear to constant criticism.

If you are the Aries parent of a Virgo child, you are probably astounded by your offspring's quick and logical thought processes. You may, however, find your child's endless fretting about all manner of potential disasters tiresome, but try not to lose your patience and instead calmly reassure him or her.

Sibling Relationships: If you are an Aries with a Virgo sibling, or a Virgo with an Arien brother or sister, you almost certainly bickered your way through childhood. Perfectionist Virgo must have carped on about Aries' rashness and embarrassing fads, while impulsive Aries must have fumed at Virgo's aloofness and control-freak tendencies. Yet you may rather respect these qualities in your sibling now.

Virgo Birth Influences

Ruling planet: Mercury
Element: Earth
Polarity: Feminine
Quadruplicity: Mutable

If you're the Virgo parent of an Aries teenager, try to reach a reasonable compromise over the issue of tidiness so that it doesn't become a constant source of tension between you. Perhaps you can allow some leeway in his or her own domain in exchange for enforcing strict rules elsewhere.

Aries Birth Influences

Ruling planet: Mars
Element: Fire
Polarity: Masculine
Quadruplicity: Cardinal

ARIES

LIBRA

Aries Birth Influences

Ruling planet: Mars
Element: Fire
Polarity: Masculine
Quadruplicity: Cardinal

A Libran child is likely to be a good student, interested in his or her studies. If your Libra sibling was always held up as an example of good behavior at school, Aries, don't let this spoil your self-esteem or cause ongoing tension between you.

Libra Birth Influences

Ruling planet: Venus
Element: Air
Polarity: Masculine
Quadruplicity: Cardinal

It is not just family ties that create a bond between Aries and Libra. Both are united in their need to be occupied, although being more proactive than responsive Libra, Aries is likely to be the driving force. Libra's calming influence on impatient Aries in turn generally ensures that this is a harmonious relationship.

Parents: If you are an Aries with a Libra parent, he or she was no doubt the deviser of plenty of diverting experiences during your childhood. And as hot-headed as you are, easygoing Libra hates conflict, so your disagreements may have been few. Libra believes that mental stimulation is important, and your parent therefore probably encouraged you to take an interest in your school work and to form your own opinions about what you saw and heard. He or she may often have stressed the importance of fairness, however urgent your Arien need to get ahead, and you should learn to take this advice on board, if you haven't already.

Neither of you are homebodies, so you must have explored much together if you are the Libran child of an energetic Aries, whose boredom threshold is as low as yours. Because you like your surroundings to be orderly, but your parent considers household chores tedious, you may continually have been tidying up your chaotic household, however, as well as mollifying others when blunt Aries upset them by speaking his or her mind. Even so, your demonstrative parent's warmth and fierce devotion to you may have made you feel loved.

Children: Although you must find your usually beautifully behaved Libra child's mantra "It's not fair" tiresome if you are an authoritative Aries, don't automatically demand obedience. Even small Librans possess a natural sense of justice and sympathy for others' viewpoints, making explaining the reasoning behind your decisions a far more effective strategy.

If you are a house-proud Libra, you may despair at your boisterous Aries child's untidiness—it must be like clearing up after a mini-tornado! You may nevertheless be proud of your strong-willed child's spirit, but may wish that he or she would let others have their say rather than insisting that they follow the Arien leader.

Sibling Relationships: You are likely to have different interests if you are an arty Libra with an action-oriented Arien sibling, or vice versa, which may be precisely why you find each other interesting. Your relationship may be enhanced by your shared sense of fun, but straightforward Aries may be baffled by airy Libra's changeability, while cool Libra may disapprove of fiery Aries' aggression.

SCORPIO
ARIES

There are bound to be arguments when forceful Aries and iron-willed Scorpio share a home, yet at the core of this relationship lies deep affection and unwavering loyalty. When Aries isn't bringing the scorpion to boiling point, the demonstrative ram warms Scorpio's heart, and in return the caring scorpion provides a constant anchor for restive Aries.

Parents: If you are the Scorpio child of an Aries parent, your childhood may have been tempestuous, but never lacking in love. Your active parent more than likely led the way in adventurous quests, and although you must have enjoyed testing your courage, there may have been times when you would have preferred some solitude. Any conflict between you probably arose from your determination to follow your own path rather than Aries' decree, which must have ignited your hot-tempered parent's anger. Although you may now be devoted to your warm-hearted Arien elder, you may still be nursing a mild sense of grievance.

While the possessive scorpion prizes security, that of the reckless ram is a restless sign. As a headstrong Aries you may have wished for more freedom from your Scorpio parent when you were younger. You probably now recognize that he or she was trying to prevent you from landing yourself in trouble, but may then have hotly resented Scorpio's firm, restraining hand. Being the focus of your devoted parent's attention may nevertheless have made you feel secure and special, even if you sometimes felt rather stifled by the intensity of Scorpio's love.

Children: As the Arien parent of a scorpion, his or her tendency to question your authority probably makes you feel proud, amused, and maddened in equal measure. Scorpio may appear tough, but is actually very sensitive, and can take criticism too personally. Explaining yourself patiently and reasonably will encourage your empathetic child to follow your wishes.

If you are the Scorpio parent of a headstrong young Aries, life must never be dull. You may admire your child's energy and exuberance, but may worry that the Arien streak of impulsiveness will expose him or her to danger. Aries learns from experience, however, so try not to be overprotective.

Sibling Relationships: There must have been fights aplenty if you and your sibling are a self-willed Scorpio and an assertive Aries. Being both bold and brave, you probably felt exhilarated when united in your purpose, though, especially when family loyalty was called into play.

Scorpio Birth Influences

Ruling planet: Pluto; traditionally Mars
Element: Water
Polarity: Feminine
Quadruplicity: Fixed

Scorpio and Aries siblings can grate on each other when each wants to do his or her own thing.

Aries Birth Influences

Ruling planet: Mars
Element: Fire
Polarity: Masculine
Quadruplicity: Cardinal

ARIES
SAGITTARIUS

Aries Birth Influences

Ruling planet: Mars
Element: Fire
Polarity: Masculine
Quadruplicity: Cardinal

♂

When your sunny Sagittarian child gives you a cheeky smile, you probably can't help but join in the fun, especially if you are an adventurous Aries.

Sagittarius Birth Influences

Ruling planet: Jupiter
Element: Fire
Polarity: Masculine
Quadruplicity: Mutable

♃

There are thrills and spills aplenty when these restless, questing fire signs are members of the same family. Neither can sit still for long, both are bored by everyday routine, and their mutual love of fun creates a firm bond. However, disagreements may be sparked off by Aries' bossiness or Sagittarius' fickleness.

Parents: If your parent is an Aries and you were born under the sign of the archer, there can hardly have been a dull moment in your childhood. Aries people are active types who relish challenge, teach by example, and believe in learning through experience. As a result, your parent was probably constantly leading the way in a joint adventure, urging you on to match his or her boldness, while always keeping a protective eye on you. Authoritative, single-minded Aries may not have been pleased when you lost interest in his or her current enthusiasm, however, and you may consequently have had a few fiery arguments.

As the Aries offspring of a Sagittarian parent, your childhood was no doubt filled with merriment and plenty of interesting activities. As well as sharing a child's sense of fun, mutable Sagittarius can be just as fidgety as Aries. With his or her strong nomadic instinct, your outgoing parent may consequently have been forever whisking you off to explore unfamiliar places. Because of this, you may have been less keen on being ushered around umpteen museums, although you may now recognize that Jupiter ruled Sagittarius was trying to broaden your young mind.

Children: If you are the Arien parent of a Sagittarius, your child's pluckiness may remind you of yourself at that age. Your little archer's sense of humor may make you smile, too, but you may find his or her mood swings wearisome. Don't lose your patience when Sagittarius is down, because it won't be long before all is sunshine and laughter again.

Your Aries child's self-certainty must both please and concern you if you are a Sagittarius. While you may delight in his or her confidence, you may wish that your young ram would be more accepting of others' opinions. Don't make an issue of this, however; instead gently present alternative viewpoints.

Sibling Relationships: You probably get along like a house on fire if you are one of a pair of Aries and Sagittarius siblings, even if the ram's domineering tendencies and archer's changeability provoked some explosive spats when you were young. Generally, though, you no doubt match each other in adventurousness, liveliness, and daring, and may treasure your warm and stimulating relationship.

CAPRICORN

ARIES

Both Aries and Capricorn adore their loved ones and would do anything for them, yet personality clashes are inevitable. Daily routines make down-to-earth Capricorn feel secure, but provoke Aries' rebellious spirit. And while progressive Aries needs freedom, conventional Capricorn can be a strict disciplinarian.

Parents: If you are the Capricorn offspring of a fiery Aries, you can't have doubted your parent's fierce love for you. As a reserved Capricorn, you probably felt slightly embarrassed by his or her enthusiastic outpourings of affection, even if they made you feel safe. You may, however, have been alarmed by Aries' adventurousness, and disliked being encouraged to participate in activities that your parent deemed exciting, but your cautious Capricorn self considered dangerous. Yet looking back, you may recognize that Aries would never have put you at risk.

Memories of your childhood may be of continually butting heads with your Capricorn parent if you are an assertive Aries. While you were driven by the urge to follow your own path, Capricorn was no doubt equally determined that you should trot obediently along the route that he or she had mapped out for you. From an adult perspective, you may today realize that Capricorn wanted the best for you, and made great personal sacrifices to ensure that you never went without.

Children: You must worry incessantly if you are the Capricorn parent of a headstrong Aries. You plan every step that you take, while your impulsive young ram tends to rush enthusiastically, but unthinkingly, into everything. Aries resists following orders, so rather than sternly laying down the law, bring your patience and constructiveness into play by calmly explaining why this approach may be doomed to failure.

If you are an Aries parent and your child is a careful Capricorn, you may feel that your roles have been reversed. For instance, when you try to initiate some rough-and-tumble with your kid, Capricorn may back away, announcing that he or she has homework to do. Even so, you are probably impressed by Capricorn's strong-willed determination and unusually mature attitude.

Sibling Relationships: You probably didn't spend much time together if you are a Capricorn who grew up with an Aries sibling, or vice versa, because your interests, goals, and characters are so different. Yet you no doubt knew that your idiosyncratic brother or sister was a force to be reckoned with and was worthy of your respect.

Capricorn Birth Influences

Ruling planet: Saturn
Element: Earth
Polarity: Feminine
Quadruplicity: Cardinal

Your Capricorn daughter's apparent indifference to your motherly adoration may trouble you if you are a passionate Aries, but she probably expresses her affection in different ways.

Aries Birth Influences

Ruling planet: Mars
Element: Fire
Polarity: Masculine
Quadruplicity: Cardinal

ARIES

AQUARIUS

Aries Birth Influences

Ruling planet: Mars
Element: Fire
Polarity: Masculine
Quadruplicity: Cardinal

When Aries and Aquarius are closely related, the family dynamics are often very lively indeed. With the combination of Arien enthusiasm and Aquarian imagination, the household fizzes with a spirit of adventure. Yet while fiery Aries' emotional warmth and airy Aquarius' cool objectivity can be a wonderful blend, it may cause temperatures to reach either boiling or freezing point in the family atmosphere, and fixed Aquarius can be completely unyielding when these two fight.

Parents: As an Aquarian child, you no doubt found your Aries parent both exciting and exasperating. Exciting, because both of you are restless and easily bored, and your parent, who is furthermore a creature of impulse, may have been forever spiriting you off at moment's notice bound for a challenging new experience. You need your own space, however, and were probably sometimes exasperated when Aries insisted on active togetherness when you would have preferred to be left alone to think in peace.

Your childhood can't have been boring if you are the Arien child of an Aquarius. While you are stimulated by the new, Aquarius is an inquisitive explorer, and your trips together were probably fun. Your ruling planet is the action-oriented Mars, and that of Aquarius is technical Uranus, so you may have been less enthused by your parent's tendency to talk while you wanted to find things out for yourself.

As children, your Arien sibling was bound to lead you off on an adventure or two if you are an Aquarius, but did you sometimes resist his or her efforts and provoke a furious response?

Children: Not being one to follow the herd yourself, you must be proud of your Aquarian child's individuality if you are an independent Aries, but may worry that he or she is becoming something of a loner. Don't fret too much: older Aquarians don't generally care what people think of them, and this sign's magnetic personality always attracts friends.

You probably love your young ram's strength of will and fearlessness if you are an Aquarius, yet may wish that Aries wouldn't unleash a furious tantrum whenever that strong will is thwarted. Explain your viewpoint reasonably, but not too coldly, lest your warm-hearted child feels that your love for him or her has cooled.

Sibling Relationships: If you are one of a pair of Aries and Aquarius siblings, your childhood years must have been a mixture of sunshine and tempests. Being both outgoing and adventurous, you no doubt have many exhilarating memories of growing up together, but may equally recall times when headstrong Aries' bossiness and inscrutable Aquarius' objectivity provoked thunder and lightning.

Aquarius Birth Influences

Ruling planet: Uranus; traditionally Saturn
Element: Air
Polarity: Masculine
Quadruplicity: Fixed

PISCES
ARIES

While spontaneous, active Aries infuses the household with fire and energy, empathetic Pisces goes with the flow, at the same time creating a supportive atmosphere. Yet acrimony may arise if selfless Pisces regards Aries as being overly egotistical, or if Aries' burning zest for life is dampened by Pisces' martyrlike tendencies.

Parents: As a Piscean child, you may have struggled to keep up with your human-dynamo Aries parent. The combination of influences from powerful Mars, a masculine (or active) polarity, fiery energy, and a cardinal sign's urgency makes Aries a formidably vigorous person. Your own zodiacal sign is mutable, or adaptable, and your element is water and your polarity, feminine (or passive), making you less hurried and more introspective than energetic, outgoing Aries. Because of this, you may have longed for more periods of solitary reflection.

If you are the Arien offspring of a Pisces, you may have enjoyed an unconventional, but secure, childhood. Pisces' planetary rulers are jovial Jupiter and inclusive Neptune, bestower of the gifts of fantasy, compassion, and altruism, and your good-humored parent probably raised you with imagination, understanding, and total devotion. Yet you may have struggled to break free of your parent's all-enveloping embrace, and may have become impatient when wounded Pisces sank into martyr mode.

Children: Despite being laid-back and nonconfrontational, Pisces, you probably find your Aries child a handful. Headstrong, Mars-ruled Aries was born to battle, and you may find your young ram's resistance to being guided tiring, and may become upset by the fiery tantrums that result whenever Aries' colossal will is thwarted. Draw comfort from your child's equally warm hugs, and don't take his or her heedlessness too personally.

Although your young Pisces' kindness and consideration for others must warm your heart, Aries, you probably worry about his or her lack of self-assurance, being so assertive yourself. This is down to your different polarities, so don't badger your child, but instead build up Pisces' confidence with lots of praise.

Sibling Relationships: In a sibling relationship, bossy Aries generally acts as the ringleader, always steering compliant Pisces into exhilarating temptation. This pair usually has a lot of fun together, but remember, Aries, that your sensitive Piscean sibling may be deeply hurt if you ignore his or her feelings and wishes. And Pisces, don't take Aries' brusqueness as an indication that your sibling doesn't love you.

Pisces Birth Influences

Ruling planet: Neptune; traditionally Jupiter
Element: Water
Polarity: Feminine
Quadruplicity: Mutable

♆ ♃

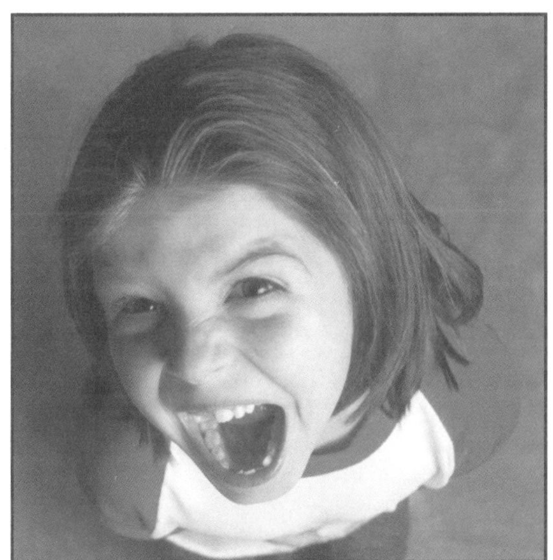

As an easygoing Pisces, you may be quite bewildered when your little Aries unleashes her fiery temper! Giving guidance to such a headstrong, young lady can be difficult, but persevere.

Aries Birth Influences

Ruling planet: Mars
Element: Fire
Polarity: Masculine
Quadruplicity: Cardinal

TAURUS

TAURUS

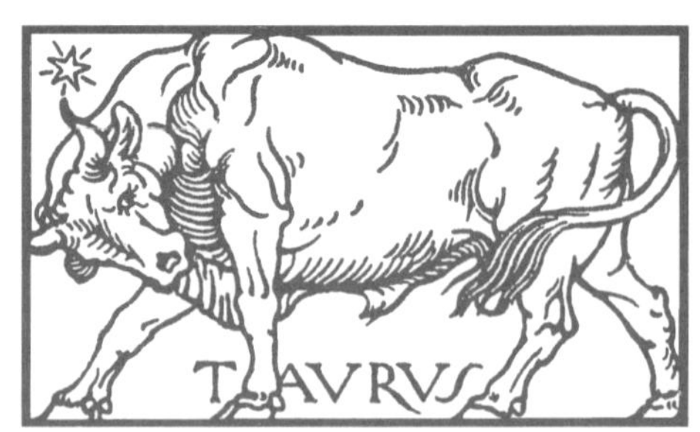

Taurus Birth Influences

Ruling planet: Venus
Element: Earth
Polarity: Feminine
Quadruplicity: Fixed

Unless a volatile fire sign is part of the family mix, the domestic life of a pair of close Taurean relatives is usually quiet, cozy, and regulated. These self-possessed people loathe discord, take their creature comforts very seriously, and find routines soothing. They can, however, be somewhat lazy when off-duty, resulting in an indolent, easygoing, or even inactive household, while their mutual stubbornness may occasionally cause them to lock horns.

Parents: You and your parent are no doubt similar personalities if you were both born under the sign of the bull, and because the archetypal Taurean character is stable, laid-back, and affectionate, your childhood relationship with your elder must have been even, relaxed, and loving. It is both your joint element of earth and Taurus' fixed-sign status that give the two of you a love of constancy and a dislike of change, so that you probably basked in the security of waking up in the morning knowing exactly what your parent had planned for the day. What you may not have appreciated, however, was how expertly your parent managed the household's finances, and how hard he or she worked to ensure that your home looked attractive and that you didn't go without. As an adult, you may now recognize these gifts of your ruling planet, Venus, in yourself, and perhaps have a better understanding of the effort and perseverance that maintaining a comfortable lifestyle requires. Thank your lucky stars that your fixed sign bestows the necessary tenacity upon you, too!

Children: You must be proud of your self-contained calf if you are a grown-up bull. Not only is your child no doubt a sensible young soul who instinctively understands life's realities and rarely makes outlandish demands, but this down-to-earth youngster is also steady and patient, all of which makes raising him or her relatively easy. That said, you may wish that your Taurean charge wasn't so slothful at times, but as you probably know, having the same traits yourself, it's pointless trying to push Taurus individuals, who insist on moving through life at their own pace.

Peaceable Taurean siblings at rest are a truly contented (if unusually inactive) pair.

Sibling Relationships: If you and your sibling are both Taureans, the influence of peace-loving Venus probably ensured that you spent your childhood pursuing your common interests in general harmony, as you may still do today. Even so, there were probably times when a disagreement caused you each to dig in your heels and refuse to give way until your parent stepped in to break the deadlock.

Taurus Birth Influences

Ruling planet: Venus
Element: Earth
Polarity: Feminine
Quadruplicity: Fixed

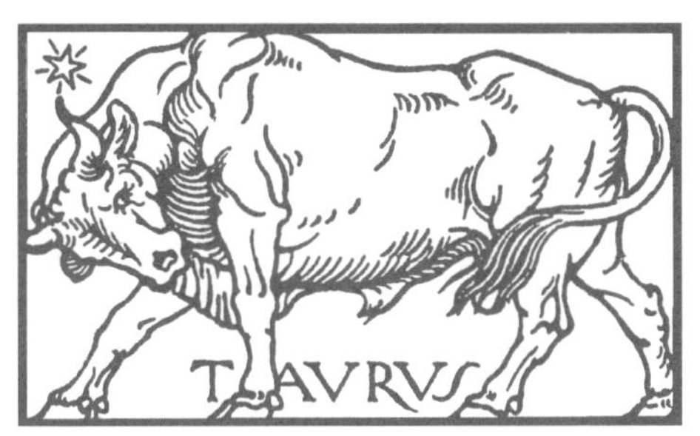

GEMINI
TAURUS

A fundamental difference between earthy, fixed-sign Taurus and the airy, mutable sign of the twins is that the bull considers home a safe haven, while Gemini regards it as a base from which to make forays into the wider world. Although they are both relaxed and affectionate, a family relationship between stay-at-home Taurus and gadabout Gemini may therefore occasionally be rather strained.

Parents: If you are a Gemini who grew up in the care of a Taurus parent, you may have chafed a little under the bull's gentle restraint. Your element of air gives you a desire for freedom of both mind and body, which may have been at odds with earthy Taurus' realistic, practical, and protective temperament. But because the bull is generally lenient, and Gemini adaptable, you probably reached a reasonable compromise.

You may have found your Gemini parent's chaotic approach to running a household unsettling if you are a typical Taurus who likes order and routine. One of Mercury's gifts to Gemini is itchy feet, or a desire to see the world, which may have been another source of worry, as you prefer to stick with what you know. Looking back, however, you probably now realize how much Gemini opened your eyes to different customs or cultures.

Children: Although you must be devoted to your Gemini child, Taurus, the differences inherent in your fixed and mutable quadruplicities may cause you to find his or her restlessness and constant questions rather tiring. It's best to use a diversionary strategy that piques young Gemini's curiosity when trying to steer him or her in the right direction, even if it provokes yet more questions!

If you are the Gemini parent of a Taurus, you probably love your young bull's resilience, but may be baffled by his or her indolence. You may also have discovered that Taurus can be astonishingly obstinate, no matter how skillfully you invoke your powers of persuasion. The only solution may be to enlist your capacity for flexibility and go with the Taurean flow.

Sibling Relationships: Because Taurus is ruled by harmonious Venus, and Gemini by adaptable Mercury, you may not have had many childhood conflicts with your brother or sister if you were born under these signs. However, you probably didn't spend much time together, because information-gathering Gemini was forever roaming while Taurus lazed around at home. No doubt you appreciate your sibling tremendously today, Gemini particularly prizing Taurus' rock-solid supportiveness and Taurus cherishing Gemini's refreshing liveliness.

Gemini Birth Influences

Ruling planet: Mercury
Element: Air
Polarity: Masculine
Quadruplicity: Mutable

A Taurean parent will be an invaluable source of strength and comfort to a restless Gemini, even though their attitudes to life are quite different.

Taurus Birth Influences

Ruling planet: Venus
Element: Earth
Polarity: Feminine
Quadruplicity: Fixed

TAURUS
CANCER

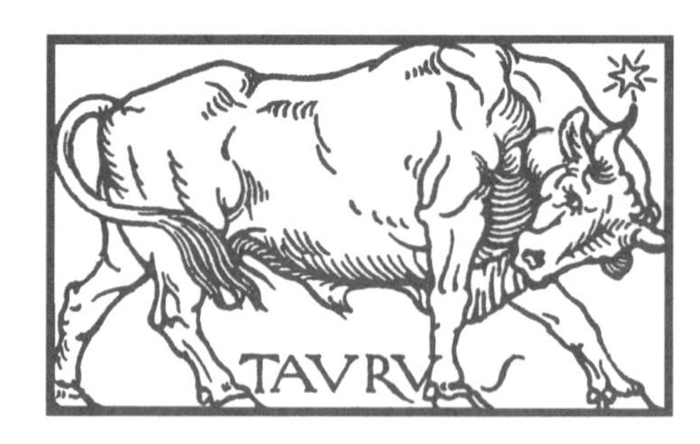

Taurus Birth Influences

Ruling planet: Venus
Element: Earth
Polarity: Feminine
Quadruplicity: Fixed

The family ties that bind Taurus and Cancer together are usually deeply affectionate. The bull's element of earth provides the stability that allows water-sign Cancer's love to flow freely, the caring crab in turn nourishing the bull's emotional welfare. Taurus' bull-headedness and Cancer's moodiness may, however, cause some friction.

Parents: If you are a Cancer, your element of water can sometimes flood you with a sense of insecurity, which is why your childhood self may have regarded your steady Taurus parent as your anchor. The influence of earth makes the bull steady and patient, while that of Venus bestows a mellow temperament and an ability to make money go far. All in all, your dependable parent must have made you feel loved and well looked after, even if Taurus' rather lethargic nature sometimes grated on you.

The combined sway of the maternal Moon and nurturing water over the crab probably meant that your well-being was of overriding importance to your Cancer parent during your childhood years if you are a Taurus. And because the typical Taurus appreciates creature comforts, you must have enjoyed the crab's dedicated care. Even-tempered and straightforward as you are, though, you may have been taken aback by your parent's occasional crabbiness and tendency to retreat into his or her shell.

Children: Your child's uncomplicated, determined outlook must please and astound you if he or she is a Taurus and you are an emotionally complex, sometimes wavering Cancer. You have the bull's fixed quadruplicity to thank for this, but then the downside may be your child's formidable obstinacy. Don't take this bull-like behavior as a personal affront.

Although your heart must warm to the way that your little crab instinctively realizes when you are feeling down and tries to comfort you, you may worry about Cancer's lack of confidence if you are a Taurus. You can't change the influence of water over your child, but are admirably equipped to provide the constant support that makes the crab feel safe and protected.

Sibling Relationships: If you and your sibling are respectively a zodiacal bull and crab, you have probably always got on well. The receptiveness and empathy that are the gifts of the Moon, water, and Cancer's feminine polarity make the crab willing to listen to Taurus, while Taurus' unexcitable temperament stabilizes Cancer's fluctuating feelings. Taurus' stubbornness may, however, provoke some Cancerian tears, while the bull may find the crab's changeability somewhat trying.

Taurus and Cancer make a harmonious combination as siblings, especially when Taurus is the older sibling and behaves protectively toward his or her insecure, vulnerable younger sister or brother.

Cancer Birth Influences

Ruling planet: The Moon
Element: Water
Polarity: Feminine
Quadruplicity: Cardinal

LEO

TAURUS

The fire that is Leo's element creates a warm and lively focal point in any home that contains a lion and bull, Leo's energizing influence in turn being underpinned by the common sense and dependability that are earth's gifts to Taurus. Although tempers may flare if one thwarts the other's will, this is usually a loyal and loving pair within the family context.

Parents: The combination of a parent's natural authority with the influence of the Sun—a ruling planet around which all of the rest in the solar system revolve—makes it likely that your Leo mother or father was a commanding presence in your childhood if you are a Taurus. Yet because Taurus has inherited Venus' easygoing nature, you probably didn't kick against such a warm and benevolent protector. That said, your earthy element causes you to value constancy, and you may have found the impulsive facet of fiery Leo's personality unnerving.

Your childhood memories of your Taurus parent are probably fond if you are a Leo. As a protégé of the Sun, the lion can be lazy and self-indulgent, but always demands the best in life, and in these respects living with the bull must have been satisfying, for Venus infuses similar characteristics in Taurus, along with a talent for managing the money that pays for such expensive tastes. Your fiery nature makes you impatient of routine, however, and you may therefore have rebelled against practical Taurus' household rotas.

Children: If you are the Taurus parent of a lion cub, your child's unwavering belief that he or she is in the right must often prove exasperating. While such strong self-confidence can be an asset, there may be occasions when you have to check little Leo, provoking a fiery explosion of fury. Your element and ruling planet give you exceptional patience and soothing skills, and these are the times to use them!

Although your young bull's self-reliant, placid personality must ease your job as a parent if you are a Leo, you may wish that he or she were less slow to embrace your suggestions. Your fiery element makes you much more impetuous than change-resistant Taurus, so don't provoke a rare, but spectacular, temper tantrum by pushing your youngster too far.

Sibling Relationships: If you and your sibling are a Taurus and Leo, you probably got on well as children, except, perhaps, when imperious Leo treated the bull high-handedly, or when Taurus ignored the attention-seeking lion. Even so, both having fixed signs, your affection for each other may be constant and enduring.

Leo Birth Influences

Ruling planet: The Sun
Element: Fire
Polarity: Masculine
Quadruplicity: Fixed

If your Leo child is prone to fiery tantrums, try encouraging him or her to develop an outlet for frustration in drama or martial arts, Taurus, especially during adolescence.

Taurus Birth Influences

Ruling planet: Venus
Element: Earth
Polarity: Feminine
Quadruplicity: Fixed

TAURUS
VIRGO

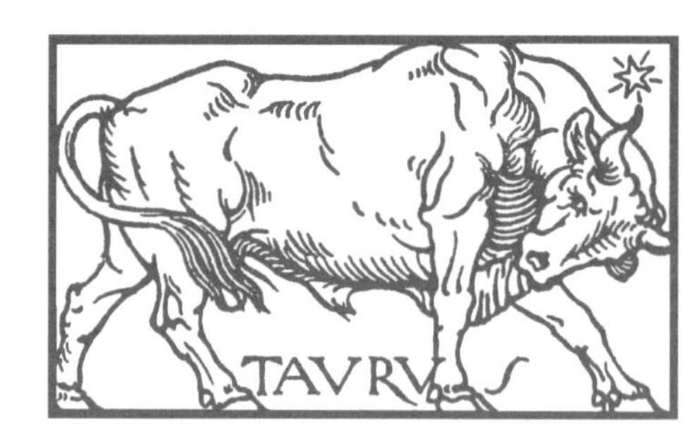

Taurus Birth Influences

Ruling planet: Venus
Element: Earth
Polarity: Feminine
Quadruplicity: Fixed

If you have a Taurus parent, he or she probably values family mealtimes. While you may have spent your adolescence itching to leave the table and do your own thing, Virgo, you may have felt secure in the knowledge that your parent was there for you.

Virgo Birth Influences

Ruling planet: Mercury
Element: Earth
Polarity: Feminine
Quadruplicity: Mutable

Both Taurus and Virgo are earth signs associated with stability, which is why these people generally root themselves in family life and are loyal to their loved ones. Neither Venus-ruled Taurus nor mutable Virgo enjoys conflict either, so that their relationship is usually peaceful. The bull's indolence may nevertheless annoy fast-paced Virgo, while Virgo's fussiness may needle laid-back Taurus.

Parents: Food probably looms large in your childhood memories if you are a Virgo and your parent is a zodiacal bull. Taureans tend to express love in tangible ways, and the influence of his or her element of earth and planetary ruler, the indulgent Venus, makes it likely that your parent was forever encouraging you to tuck into a delicious dish. Although your dependable, steady parent no doubt made you feel loved and secure, because your quadruplicity is mutable, or changeable, and Taurus' is fixed, you may have wished that your parent were a little more spontaneous at times.

If you are a Taurus and your parent is a Virgo, you were probably on the same wavelength when you were growing up. Your two common birth influences—your feminine, or passive, polarity and earthy element—make both of you receptive, practical, and materialistic people. Yet because Virgo's ruling planet is objective Mercury, the messenger of the gods in Roman mythology, you may not have appreciated some of the critical messages that your parent transmitted to you.

Children: Those born under the fixed sign of the bull can be infuriatingly stubborn, which may not be news to you if you are a Virgo and your child is a Taurus, and you may also have learned that the best solution is to rely on your natural flexibility. But doesn't your little bull's loving temperament make up for your occasional difference of opinion?

You are probably proud of your Virgoan child's quick, inquiring mind if you are a Taurus, but may find his or her restlessness wearing. Mercury instills a quest for knowledge in Virgo, and Virgo's mutability makes your child crave variety, while you are a protégé of idle Venus and have a fixed nature. Try to remain patient and focus on providing your child with a stable background.

Sibling Relationships: If you and your sibling are a Taurus and Virgo, your easygoing, down-to-earth similarities probably outweighed your differences when you were young. That said, Virgo may sometimes have been frustrated by Taurus' laziness and resistance to change, while Taurus may have bristled at articulate Virgo's tendency to find fault.

LIBRA
TAURUS

Being the sign of the balance, Libra strives for a balanced home life, which usually suits the bull because the Taurean element of earth similarly imparts a need for stability. Both signs are also ruled by Venus, the planet of harmony, order, and pleasure, so that any household that includes this pair is likely to operate smoothly and agreeably. The bull's rigidity and obstinacy may nevertheless frustrate Libra, Libra's dithering and moodiness in turn sometimes unsettling Taurus.

Parents: Looking back at your childhood, what you may remember the most about your Taurus parent is the sense of security that he or she gave you if you are a Libra. The bull's earthy element no doubt ensured that Taurus established efficient household routines and was a dependable and supportive parent. Because your zodiacal sign is cardinal, or enterprising, and masculine, or active, and Taurus is fixed and feminine, or passive, you may have wished that your parent were more adventurous and outgoing at times, however.

If you are a Taurus, you were probably proud of the positive impact that your charming Libra parent had on others when you were younger. Venus gives you a shared belief in the importance of graciousness and putting others at their ease, the element of air also making Libra a lively conversationalist. Yet this element accounts for Libra's occasional unpredictability, uncertainty, and coolness, too, which you may have found upsetting, partly because you are such a constant person yourself, and partly because your feminine polarity makes you so receptive to others' moods.

Children: Although you must bless your little bull's steadiness if you are a Libra, you may shy away from your child's awesome temper tantrums, however rare they may be. Taurus will not be pushed into doing anything that is contrary to his or her nature, so employ the logical intelligence that is your airy birthright in talking your child round to your point of view.

Your breezy Libra child's low boredom threshold and lack of staying power may exasperate you if you are a fixed-sign Taurus, but then his or her winning ways must melt your heart. Draw on your earthy patience and practicality to keep Libra entertained.

Sibling Relationships: The peaceable influence of Venus probably sweetened your childhood relationship if you are a Taurus and your sibling is a Libra or the other way round, but you may nevertheless have had your disagreements. Given Taurus' fixed temperament and airy Libra's changeability, these are likely to have centered on the bull's stubbornness or Libra's fickleness.

Libra Birth Influences

Ruling planet: Venus
Element: Air
Polarity: Masculine
Quadruplicity: Cardinal

Families with Taurus and Libra members usually make for happy households; the warmth and harmony of this combination tend to be infectious.

Taurus Birth Influences

Ruling planet: Venus
Element: Earth
Polarity: Feminine
Quadruplicity: Fixed

TAURUS
SCORPIO

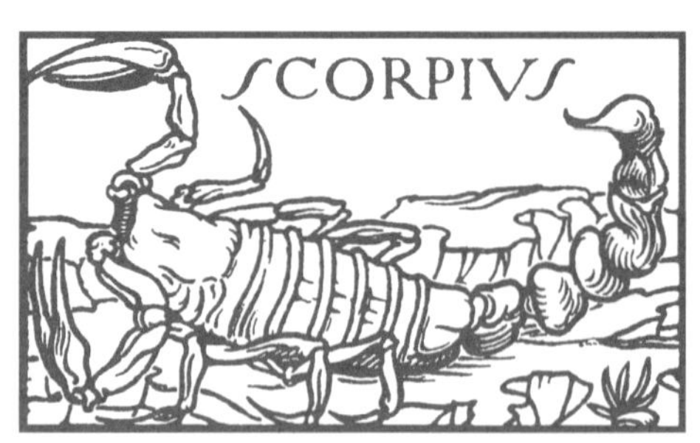

Taurus Birth Influences

Ruling planet: Venus
Element: Earth
Polarity: Feminine
Quadruplicity: Fixed

An easygoing Taurus may find a Scorpio parent's moodiness disturbing. If you are a Scorpio parent, try not to retreat into your own world and leave your child fretting—he or she might worry or take your detachment personally.

Scorpio Birth Influences

Ruling planet: Pluto; traditionally Mars
Element: Water
Polarity: Feminine
Quadruplicity: Fixed

Their families mean the world to Taurus and Scorpio, and they regard their homes as havens. Imperturbable Taurus provides the stability that is so important to Scorpio's mental equilibrium, the understanding scorpion in turn nurturing the bull's emotional well-being. Yet there may be times when Scorpio becomes impatient with Taurus' indolence or lack of imagination, or when the bull is frustrated by Scorpio's inscrutability and volatile temperament.

Parents: Taurus parents are determined to give their children material comforts and steadfast support. This earthy, protective mindset is augmented by the gifts bestowed by Venus, the bull's ruling planet—notably, an indulgent approach and a shrewd way with money. If you are a Scorpio whose element of water occasionally makes you feel insecure, your practical, dependable parent must therefore have exerted a grounding, calming influence on you. That said, the active, excitement-seeking facet of your nature that derives from Mars, your secondary ruling planet, may sometimes cause you to try to break free of the monotony of Taurus' routines.

Living with a Scorpio parent is often like being in a hothouse, such is the intensity of the loving concern that the scorpion showers on loved ones. If you are a Taurus, you must have flourished under Scorpio's tender, loving care and were probably happy to accept the scorpion's gentle direction, partly because Venus gives you a desire for an easy, conflict-free life. Having changeable water as an element and reclusive Pluto as a planetary ruler, Scorpio can appear moody and remote at times, however, which may have troubled you, being a more placid and open person.

Children: You must be grateful for your Taurean child's unflappable nature if you are a Scorpio, because it helps to keep your relationship on an even keel. But because water is a more restless element than earth, you may occasionally wish that your home-loving youngster were a little less idle and rather more adventurous.

If you are an even-tempered Taurus, you may find your baby scorpion's mood swings wearying, but then Scorpio's empathy may compensate for the downside of having water as an element. Try calming troubled waters by explaining that Scorpio is upsetting you, and the chances are that he or she will make amends.

Sibling Relationships: If you and your sibling were born under the family-focused, fixed signs of Taurus and Scorpio, you were probably affectionate and loyal to one another as children. Your mutual stubbornness may have triggered some long-running squabbles, however.

SAGITTARIUS
TAURUS

Thanks to the benevolent influence of Venus and Jupiter, the atmosphere in a Taurean–Sagittarian home is typically relaxed and good-humored. And while the earthy bull ensures that domestic life is regulated by efficient procedures, the fiery archer contributes energy and ideas to the mix. Even so, there will be occasions when Sagittarius becomes impatient with Taurus' lack of spontaneity, and when Sagittarius' restlessness irritates Taurus.

Parents: Your overriding childhood memory of your Taurus parent, if you are a Sagittarius, may be that he or she was always there for you. Having practical earth as an element gives Taureans a preference for hands-on parenting, while Venus makes them easygoing and indulgent. You probably therefore never felt neglected or unloved. As an adventurous person, you may nevertheless sometimes have wished that your parent were more imaginative and a little less devoted to routines.

If you are a Taurus, your Sagittarian parent was probably a wonderful source of wisdom and fun when you were growing up. A Jupiter-ruled, fiery sign, enthusiastic Sagittarius is a humorous, unconventional thinker who believes in combining education with enjoyment, and can often seem more like a friend than an authority figure. Because you were born under a fixed, or unchanging, sign, and your parent under a mutable, or restive, constellation, you may have had difficulty coping with Sagittarius' unpredictability, however.

Children: You must be relieved that your little Taurus is so realistic and sensible if you are his or her Sagittarian parent, not least because these earthy characteristics make it easier to safeguard your child's well-being. You may be trying to prod him or her to be more exploratory, but don't push too hard lest you trigger Taurus' awesome bullheadedness.

If you are a Taurus, what you must particularly love in your Sagittarius child is his or her cheerful nature. What you may find trying, however, is Sagittarius' occasional hot-headedness and low boredom threshold. The best approach is to remain patient and to encourage your child to devise safe ways of entertaining him- or herself!

Sibling Relationships: Although you may not have been bosom buddies as young children—mainly because your energy levels and interests are so different—you no doubt got on well with your sibling if one of you is a Taurus and the other a Sagittarius. Neither of you likes to provoke head-on confrontations, but even so, Taurus' obstinacy and Sagittarius' impulsiveness must have sparked occasional short-lived fights.

Sagittarius Birth Influences

Ruling planet: Jupiter
Element: Fire
Polarity: Masculine
Quadruplicity: Mutable

Did your enthusiastic Sagittarian mother always take you out and about in search of new experiences, even when you preferred to stay home, Taurus? Remember that she has always had your best interests at heart and tried to make life fun and stimulating for you.

Taurus Birth Influences

Ruling planet: Venus
Element: Earth
Polarity: Feminine
Quadruplicity: Fixed

TAURUS

CAPRICORN

Taurus Birth Influences

Ruling planet: Venus
Element: Earth
Polarity: Feminine
Quadruplicity: Fixed

Capricorn and Taurus family members are often found settled comfortably around the dining table. When you were young, Capricorn, you probably enjoyed Taurus' mealtime routines.

Capricorn Birth Influences

Ruling planet: Saturn
Element: Earth
Polarity: Feminine
Quadruplicity: Cardinal

Conflict between Taurus and Capricorn relatives is usually rare, partly because they share the same family values. Fixed-quadruplicity Taurus dislikes change and Saturn-ruled Capricorn is a traditionalist, and their shared feminine polarity and earthy element make them equally thoughtful and supportive. Taurus' laziness may sometimes frustrate cardinal-sign Capricorn, however, while saturnine Capricorn's emphasis on discipline may irritate the more relaxed, Venus-governed Taurus.

Parents: If you are the Capricorn offspring of a Taurus parent, your childhood memories are probably of feeling loved and looked after. Having the same element means that both Taurus and Capricorn derive satisfaction from routines, a comfortable, well-equipped home, and hearty family meals, all of which your parent no doubt supplied, along with a delicious dose of Venusian indulgence. Even so, you may have wished that your parent were less slow in agreeing to let you pursue your more enterprising childhood visions, illustrating the difference between your fixed and cardinal natures.

The zodiacal goat is governed by Saturn, the planet associated with wisdom, which is why you may have admired and respected your Capricorn parent if you are a Taurus. His or her feminine, or receptive, polarity must have made Capricorn ever ready to listen to your worries, and the advice that you received was probably practical and prudent. Yet you may have felt a little burdened by the weight of expectation that your proud parent invested in you, in the hope that you would make a stellar success of your life, or at least make the best of your talents.

Children: There may be many qualities that you admire in your Taurus child if you are a Capricorn, such as his or her tenacity, self-reliance, and patience. That said, little bulls often enjoy being idle, which may offend the cardinal, go-getting side of your own nature. Try to tolerate this Taurean trait, and console yourself with the thought that a rested mind is a productive one!

If you are a Taurus, your Capricorn youngster probably amazes you with his or her mature outlook, discipline, and self-motivation. As you are a protégé of pleasure-loving Venus, however, you may wish that Capricorn would lighten up a bit. If so, rest assured that Capricorn is happiest doing his or her own thing.

Sibling Relationships: Although Taurus and Capricorn generally get along harmoniously, you may remember having a few disagreements if you and your sibling were born under these signs. Was the cause of this friction cardinal Capricorn's impatient pushiness and fixed Taurus' firm resistance to being bossed around, perhaps?

AQUARIUS
TAURUS

As well as compensating for each other's strengths and weaknesses, Taurus and Aquarius relatives generally interact amicably, except when Taurus takes exception to the water-carrier's airy attitude or the bull's earthy realism grates on Aquarius. They may have their occasional differences, but because they are fixed signs, both are typically firmly attached to one another.

Parents: When you were young, you may not have appreciated your Taurus parent quite as much as you do today if you are an Aquarius. You no doubt loved your parent's indulgent and caring nature (the gifts of Venus, Taurus' planetary ruler, and the bull's feminine, or receptive, polarity), but may have wished that he or she were a little more enthusiastic about your unconventional interests, for example. Yet their element of practical earth keeps Taureans' feet firmly on the ground, and you may now marvel at how efficiently your parent ran your household.

If you are a Taurus, you may have struggled to keep up with your Aquarius parent when you were a child. Not only is Aquarius' masculine polarity more dynamic than yours, but this sign's ruling planet is the innovative Uranus, and its element is lively air. That said, life must have been interesting, with your communicative parent introducing you to a variety of ideas in a funny, attention-grabbing way. You may, however, have found Aquarius' eccentricities somewhat embarrassing.

Children: Despite your shared, fixed quadruplicity, which makes you both equally uncompromising at times, if you are an Aquarius, you may wish that your Taurus child were a little less rigidly conformist and a little more curious. You can't change his or her element, but take heart from the knowledge that you are eminently capable of encouraging little Taurus to consider alternative viewpoints.

Being such a down-to-earth person yourself if you are a Taurus, you may fret about your Aquarius child's tendency to daydream. If so, take solace from the possibility that your Uranian-governed youngster may dream up a groundbreaking invention, and, what's more, implement it with the help of Aquarius' pioneering polarity, communicative element, and determined, fixed quadruplicity.

Sibling Relationships: If you and your sibling are respectively a Taurus and an Aquarius, you may have had a harmonious relationship when you were young, even if Aquarius was forever tinkering with gadgets, while Taurus was idly relaxing. It may have seemed as though you inhabited different planets, but your affection for one another was probably never in doubt.

Aquarius Birth Influences

Ruling planet: Uranus; traditionally Saturn
Element: Air
Polarity: Masculine
Quadruplicity: Fixed

♅ ♄

Even though young Taurus and Aquarius siblings are quite different in outlook and temparament, they usually get on well.

Taurus Birth Influences

Ruling planet: Venus
Element: Earth
Polarity: Feminine
Quadruplicity: Fixed

TAURUS
PISCES

Taurus Birth Influences
Ruling planet: Venus
Element: Earth
Polarity: Feminine
Quadruplicity: Fixed

Do not be alarmed, Taurus, if your little Pisces is cheerful one moment, but subdued the next. Your steadfast, indulgent Taurean parenting will provide him with the stability he needs.

Pisces Birth Influences
Ruling planet: Neptune; traditionally Jupiter
Element: Water
Polarity: Feminine
Quadruplicity: Mutable

Combine the Taurean traits of indulgence, practicality, and dedication with Piscean unselfishness, empathy, and adaptability, and the result is usually a harmonious family pairing, enhanced by a shared feminine polarity. Nevertheless, there may be occasions when Taurus' stubbornness or insensitivity upsets Pisces, or the Piscean tendency to slip into self-denying or dreamy mode exasperates the bull.

Parents: If you are a Pisces, you may have regarded your Taurus parent as a rock-solid source of strength and comfort when you were growing up. Their tolerant planetary ruler, sensible, earthy element, and fixed quadruplicity make Taureans laid-back, straightforward, and steadfast, and your parent was probably no exception. Because your own mutable and watery birth influences may sometimes have caused your younger self to feel as though you were drifting helplessly through life, you may have clung to down-to-earth Taurus for security.

Altruistic Neptune, the caring element of water, and a feminine polarity give Pisceans the powerful urge to nurture others and an intuitive insight into their emotions. If you are a Taurus, you may consequently have found your Pisces parent the most understanding and encouraging of people. That said, the moodiness that often besets Pisceans may sometimes have unsettled you, and, because you are a child of hedonistic Venus, you may not have appreciated Pisces' habit of putting family or domestic duties before personal pleasure.

Children: If you are a Pisces who is often overwhelmed by conflicting emotions, you must admire your young bull's self-certainty and fixity of purpose, but may wish that he or she were a little more open to different viewpoints, yours included. If so, you may find that Taurus responds better to some gentle teasing about his or her inflexibility than to your overt disappointment or disapproval.

If you are the Taurus parent of a tender little Pisces, you may worry about your child's seemingly inexplicable mood swings and how easily he or she is influenced by others. You can't change your child's element or quadruplicity, but can provide the love and stability that Pisces craves and needs.

Sibling Relationships: Both Taurus and Pisces shrink from conflict, which is why you probably had an easygoing relationship as children if you and your sibling were born under these zodiacal signs. Even so, down-to-earth Taurus may sometimes have snorted at Pisces' idealism and dreaminess, while sensitive Pisces may have taken offense at the bull's lack of sympathy.

GEMINI
GEMINI

When two Geminis live under one roof, their home is sure to be filled with incessant activity and constant chatter. Having Mercury (whose namesake is the wing-sandaled Roman god of communication) as a ruling planet, freedom-loving air as an element, and an extrovert and mutable nature makes them restless, talkative, and outgoing people who are stimulated by ideas and bored by housework and routines. They generally get on well, but some stability may be lacking.

Parents: If you and your parent are both Geminis, you have probably always understood each other implicitly, which is not to say that you have always agreed with one another, because those born under the dual-natured sign of the twins can sometimes go to opposite extremes. Even so, thanks to your easygoing, logical element and forgiving characters, you could probably talk through your differences reasonably and dispassionately. For you, the plus points of having a Gemini as a parent may have been his or her ability to explain the mysteries of the world to your curious younger self, the excitement of being whisked away on trips on the spur of the moment, and not being forced to do chores around the house. You may, however, have had a scatterbrained mother who was sometimes distracted from caring for you because she was so busy chatting on the phone, or an overly objective father who tended to analyze endlessly where you had gone wrong rather than empathize with your disappointment and comfort you when you suffered a setback.

Children: Your quick-thinking little Gemini's stream of questions and insatiable appetite for knowledge must gladden you if you are his or her Gemini parent, because, as a protégé of Mercury who loves learning yourself, you must appreciate an inquiring mind. If you believe that variety is the spice of life, you must also be pleased that Gemini has such a diverse range of friends. Although you may have been exactly the same when you were young, you may nevertheless worry about your child's low boredom threshold, because your adult perspective tells you that a certain amount of self-discipline and staying power is a vital prerequisite for achieving happiness and success later in life.

Sibling Relationships: Lots of mercurial mischief and verbal sparring no doubt featured in your childhood if you and your sibling are Geminis. Your airy element causes you both to be playful and amiable, while your mutability gives you flexibility, so you probably enjoyed one another's company—unless one of you wasn't in the mood for playing games.

Gemini Birth Influences

Ruling planet: Mercury
Element: Air
Polarity: Masculine
Quadruplicity: Mutable

Gemini siblings will share many a fun playtime and much mischief, but the chaos that sometimes ensues may lead them both into trouble!

Gemini Birth Influences

Ruling planet: Mercury
Element: Air
Polarity: Masculine
Quadruplicity: Mutable

GEMINI

CANCER

Gemini Birth Influences

Ruling planet: Mercury
Element: Air
Polarity: Masculine
Quadruplicity: Mutable

Young Gemini's cute ways and funny comments will always brighten a Cancer parent's day.

Cancer Birth Influences

Ruling planet: The Moon
Element: Water
Polarity: Feminine
Quadruplicity: Cardinal

Having been born under a sign that is associated with the traditionally feminine qualities of nurturing, caring, and domesticity, Cancer's haven is usually the home, unlike intellectual, outgoing, masculine-sign Gemini, who often lives in the mental realm when not exploring the wider world. Gemini and Cancer relatives may therefore not always be on the same wavelength, but nevertheless typically love and respect one another.

Parents: You almost certainly can't complain that your Cancer parent neglected you if you are a Gemini. The combined influence of the Moon, the element of water, and a feminine polarity bestow upon Cancerians an intense urge to foster their loved ones' physical, and especially emotional, well-being. But because your element is freedom-loving air, and your sign is mutable, or restless, you may occasionally have felt smothered by your parent's constant attention.

Gemini's birth influences include the communicative Mercury and air, an element linked with the intellect, which is why it may sometimes have seemed as though you were being raised by a teacher—albeit a cheerful, easygoing one—if you are a Cancer. Gemini can be somewhat impersonal or detached, however, and because your feminine polarity, planetary ruler, and element frequently flood you with a deluge of confusing emotions, there may have been times when you longed for a little more empathy from your parent.

Children: Your Gemini child's funny, observant comments must make you smile if you are a Cancer, and you may be rather in awe of his or her social confidence, too. Yet you may feel a little sad that restive Gemini is so eager to stray from your side. Don't be reproachful, though: just ensure that there are plenty of things to occupy Gemini's mind at home, and that the family atmosphere is happy and supportive.

For one so young, Cancer's astonishing insight and understanding of people's feelings must astound you if you are his or her more dispassionate Gemini parent, although you may be worried by your crablet's insecurity. If so, provide reassurance, at the same time gently encouraging Cancer to be more venturesome.

Sibling Relationships: If you and your sibling are an extrovert Gemini and introvert Cancer, your childhood may have found one of you always on the move and the other opting to stay at home. You can both be moody, but amiable, mutable Gemini's adaptability and considerate, cardinal Cancer's occasional assertiveness probably ensured that yours was a friendly relationship, as well as one of equals.

LEO
GEMINI

Both Gemini and Leo find household chores tedious and prefer to channel their energies into intellectual, creative, or diverting activities, which means that their home is likely to be comfortably chaotic and suffused with a lively atmosphere. Whatever their age, Gemini and Leo are united in their youthful outlook and generally easygoing temperaments, although Gemini's changeability and Leo's assertiveness may occasionally cause friction.

Parents: If you are a Leo, you may feel grateful that you grew up with a liberal Gemini parent. Because Gemini is a sign that is associated with the intellect, your parent was no doubt more interested in encouraging you to explore the world of the mind than making you tidy your room, which probably suited you very well. Yet Mercury-governed, airy Gemini is dispassionate in comparison to Sun-ruled, fiery Leo, and you may therefore have wished that your parent had been more demonstrative in showing his or her love for you.

If you are a Gemini, you probably found your Leo parent fun to be around when you were younger, for the Sun's influence infuses the lion with playfulness, while the gifts of fire include creativity and enthusiasm. That said, Leos tend to consider themselves top cats, and, being a freedom-loving Gemini, you may consequently have considered your parent a little too authoritarian at times.

Children: Your Gemini child's appetite for learning may fill you with pride if you are a Leo, but you may worry about his or her inability to concentrate on a subject for long before becoming bored. This is a manifestation of Gemini's mutable, or restless, side, and the best way of encouraging your youngster to remain focused may be to pique his or her curiosity.

You may find your Leo child a bit of a handful if you are a Gemini, perhaps because he or she is so strong-willed and hates being told what to do. If so, the key to averting a temper tantrum whenever you have to impose your will is to bring your canny negotiating skills into play.

Sibling Relationships: You must have had hours of fun with your sibling if one of you is a Gemini and the other a Leo, and, because you were both born under masculine, or uninhibited, signs, you may have been forever encouraging each other to make mischief. Gemini may have been annoyed by Leo's bossiness, however, while fixed-sign Leo may have been frustrated by mutable Gemini's tendency to abandon a game before the lion was through.

Leo Birth Influences

Ruling planet: The Sun
Element: Fire
Polarity: Masculine
Quadruplicity: Fixed

Gemini children love to learn new things, but don't have a long attention span. You may have to use your gift for inspiring others, Leo, to help him see his project through to the end.

Gemini Birth Influences

Ruling planet: Mercury
Element: Air
Polarity: Masculine
Quadruplicity: Mutable

GEMINI
VIRGO

Gemini Birth Influences

Ruling planet: Mercury
Element: Air
Polarity: Masculine
Quadruplicity: Mutable

As a child, Gemini, you must have felt safe in your Virgo mother's arms. You may have appreciated her advice, too, even if you did not always follow it!

Virgo Birth Influences

Ruling planet: Mercury
Element: Earth
Polarity: Feminine
Quadruplicity: Mutable

Constant dialogue is likely to be the key feature of a relationship between Mercury-governed Gemini and Virgo kin, their mutual love of travel and intellectual pursuits reinforcing the bond between them. Both are mutable, or flexible, signs, but Virgo may nonetheless find living with airy Gemini's inconstancy exasperating, while Gemini may be incapable of sticking to earthy Virgo's routines.

Parents: If you are a Virgo and your parent is a Gemini, you must have found him or her an inspiring teacher when you were growing up. Mercury fills adult Geminians with the urge to pass on all that they have learned about the world and gives young Virgoans an equally strong desire to absorb the details of that wisdom. Because Gemini's element is air, your parent must have been a lively and cheerful presence in your life, although, as your element is the steadier earth, you may sometimes have been rattled by his or her capriciousness.

Virgo's polarity is feminine, or passive, while Gemini's is masculine, or active, which is one of the reasons why your parent's preferred lifestyle may have been a little too settled for your liking if he or she is a Virgo and you are a Gemini. Another is the discrepancy between your airy and earthy elements, as a result of which you may have been impatient with Virgo's regular habits. Yet one of the advantages of having a steady and dependable Virgo parent may have been feeling secure during your childhood years.

Children: If you are a Virgo, the sign that is said to be the counselor of the zodiac, your little Gemini's tendency to ignore your sensible advice and act on a whim may concern you. If so, take heart from the knowledge that intelligent Gemini learns valuable lessons from making mistakes, and try not to find fault constantly with your free-spirited child.

It may seem as though your roles have been reversed if you are the playful Gemini parent of a conscientious Virgo child, illustrating the effect that your different elements have on your personalities. Young Virgos can also be worriers, and if yours tends to fret unnecessarily over mere trifles, try to instill a little of your own optimistic, breezy outlook in him or her.

Sibling Relationships: You and your sibling no doubt shared many interests as children if one of you is a Gemini and the other is a Virgo. Even if Gemini's fancifulness occasionally annoyed Virgo, and Virgo's down-to-earth attitude rankled with Gemini, your relationship was probably always stimulating.

LIBRA
GEMINI

Life is never boring or quiet when a pair of Gemini and Libra relatives are together, and they probably won't be at home much either. These masculine air signs are outgoing and curious, bright and playful, chatty and sociable, with Mercury-ruled Gemini itching to travel and Venus-governed Libra always wanting to see the latest show or exhibition. Mutable Gemini can be aimless and indecisive, and cardinal Libra more go-ahead and pushy, however, which may sometimes cause mild discord between them.

Parents: If you are the Libran child of a Gemini parent, you may have enjoyed an intellectually stimulating childhood, your shared element and Gemini's ruling planet, Mercury, both being associated with intelligence and communication. Your parent may also have whisked you off to a variety of places on vacation, although because yours is a cardinal, goal-oriented sign and Gemini's is more spur-of-the-moment, you may not have seen all that you'd aimed to.

Your Libra parent may have indulged your every childhood whim if you are a Gemini, but this probably had less to do with your powers of persuasion than with the influence of Venus, Libra's compliant, peace-loving governing planet. Gemini being a mutable, restless sign, you may have found sitting through Libra's beloved artistic and cultural performances taxing at times.

Children: You may find it difficult not to spoil your child if you are the Libran parent of a lively and engaging Gemini, but being someone who sets yourself objectives, may be concerned about Gemini's lack of direction in life. If so, try discreetly fostering Gemini's curiosity in his or her favorite subject and chances are that this will develop into an abiding interest or career.

If you are the Gemini parent of a Libra, you may marvel at your child's innate good manners, for which you have Venus to thank. You may be less enamored of the constant cries of "It's not fair!" but are superbly equipped to explain precisely why your little Libra can't always have his or her own way.

Sibling Relationships: Because you were both born under signs that are associated with sociability and mental pursuits, there must have been many areas in which your interests overlapped as children if you or your sibling is a Gemini and the other a Libra. Neither of you enjoy conflict, so your relationship was probably quite amicable, even if Libra was sometimes exasperated by mutable Gemini's inability to make up his or her mind and Gemini found cardinal Libra's purposefulness equally trying.

Libra Birth Influences

Ruling planet: Venus
Element: Air
Polarity: Masculine
Quadruplicity: Cardinal

Gemini and Libra brothers are a sociable pair, but Libra may be irked if something else captures Gemini's attention. Don't worry, Gemini, he won't remain irritated for long.

Gemini Birth Influences

Ruling planet: Mercury
Element: Air
Polarity: Masculine
Quadruplicity: Mutable

GEMINI

SCORPIO

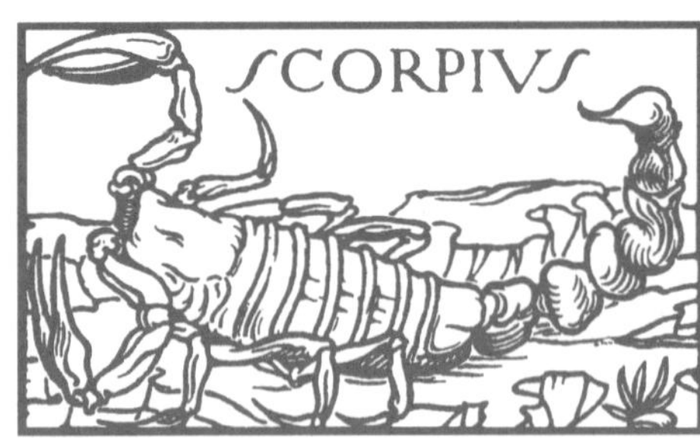

Gemini Birth Influences

Ruling planet: Mercury
Element: Air
Polarity: Masculine
Quadruplicity: Mutable

If you are a Gemini parent, try to respect your little Scorpio's need for privacy. Encourage her to talk to you, but don't make an issue of it.

Scorpio Birth Influences

Ruling planet: Pluto; traditionally Mars
Element: Water
Polarity: Feminine
Quadruplicity: Fixed

Gemini and Scorpio usually have very different characters. As a masculine, mutable air sign whose ruling planet is the communicative Mercury, Gemini is extroverted, logical, talkative, and changeable. Scorpio—a feminine, fixed, water sign governed by mysterious Pluto—is introverted, emotional, reticent, and dislikes change. As a result, these relatives may often be at odds, but may equally exert a beneficial influence on one another.

Parents: Your parent was probably a cheerful presence in your childhood world if he or she is a Gemini and you are a Scorpio. Their airy element makes Geminians lively, agreeable, and fun-loving, which means that they are always on the lookout for playmates, children included. Because both air and Mercury are associated with the intellect, your parent may have invented some ingenious games for you to play together, too. When you were upset, however, you may have longed for more compassion from your somewhat unemotional Geminian parent.

If you are a Gemini, as a child you must have felt secure in the knowledge that your Scorpio parent was always there for you, although there may have been times when you felt a little stifled by the intensity of his or her devotion. That the scorpion is a homebody and you have itchy feet may not have helped, but because you were no doubt an inventive and garrulous youngster, you may have appreciated having such an encouraging and receptive audience in Scorpio.

Children: You must admire your little Gemini's social confidence and quick, inquiring mind if you are a Scorpio, but may be concerned about his or her lack of perseverance and tendency to be easily distracted. These characteristics are probably down to Gemini's mutable quadruplicity, and the best strategy may be to explain to your intelligent child that self-discipline brings its own rewards.

Your privacy-loving, secretive Scorpio child may be something of an enigma to you if you are a sociable and direct Gemini, but then you don't have inscrutable Pluto for a planetary ruler and unfathomable water for an element. Don't try to push your child into opening up, yet also make sure that he or she understands that you are ready to listen should the need arise.

Sibling Relationships: Your paths may not have crossed much as children if one of you is an outgoing Gemini and the other a reserved Scorpio, but because airy Gemini is so affable, and watery Scorpio so empathetic, you must nevertheless have felt real affection for one another.

SAGITTARIUS

GEMINI

A house that is home to a pair of Gemini and Sagittarius relatives reverberates with the sound of conversation punctuated with laughter—that is, when they are in, of course, for these people are not typically homebodies. Despite the occasional spat, perhaps triggered by Sagittarius' headstrong, fiery temperament colliding with airy Gemini's cool objectivity, their relationship is usually affectionate.

Parents: Your childhood was probably packed with interesting experiences if you are a Sagittarius who was raised by a Gemini. Your zodiacal signs are mutable (which means that you both enjoy change) and masculine, or outgoing, and your respective ruling planets and elements can also be complementary. You may consequently have responded appreciatively to airy, Mercury-governed Gemini's penchant for travel and knack of imparting knowledge in the most entertaining of ways. There may, however, have been occasions when you longed for your parent's undivided attention.

If you are a Gemini, you may have benefited from your Sagittarian parent's gift for making learning fun. As a protégé of Jupiter, the planet named for the wise and jovial father of the Roman gods, Sagittarius is a born teacher—the element of fire adding the gift of inspiration—and you may remember having been exposed to countless educational events that whetted your mercurial appetite for learning. But there may also have been times when you found it difficult to share fiery Sagittarius' enthusiasm for a particular subject, provoking a distressing blast of displeasure.

Children: If you are a Sagittarius, although you may take pride in young Gemini's inquiring mind and drollness, you may not like his or her fibs. To avoid being reprimanded, Geminians tend to spin inventive, yet plausible tales. Perhaps the best way of countering this habit is to curb your own fiery temper, thereby removing one of the reasons why your child may resort to telling untruths in the first place.

The influence of fire is often very pronounced in Sagittarian children, which is why your little archer's energy may leave you breathless if you are a Gemini, and is also why he or she is so warm and demonstrative. The downside may be the fury with which Sagittarius reacts to being restrained. If so, let your child's rage play itself out and then offer a distracting diversion.

Sibling Relationships: Geminian and Sagittarian siblings are stimulated by each other's company and rarely stop talking, but if you are a Sagittarius, you may find Gemini's readiness to contradict you annoying, while Sagittarius' thoughtlessness may continue to act as an occasional irritant on Gemini.

Sagittarius Birth Influences

Ruling planet: Jupiter
Element: Fire
Polarity: Masculine
Quadruplicity: Mutable

♃

Gemini and Sagittarius may be forever giggling. But can Gemini also make you see red with a critical comment, Sagittarius?

Gemini Birth Influences

Ruling planet: Mercury
Element: Air
Polarity: Masculine
Quadruplicity: Mutable

GEMINI
CAPRICORN

Gemini Birth Influences

Ruling planet: Mercury
Element: Air
Polarity: Masculine
Quadruplicity: Mutable

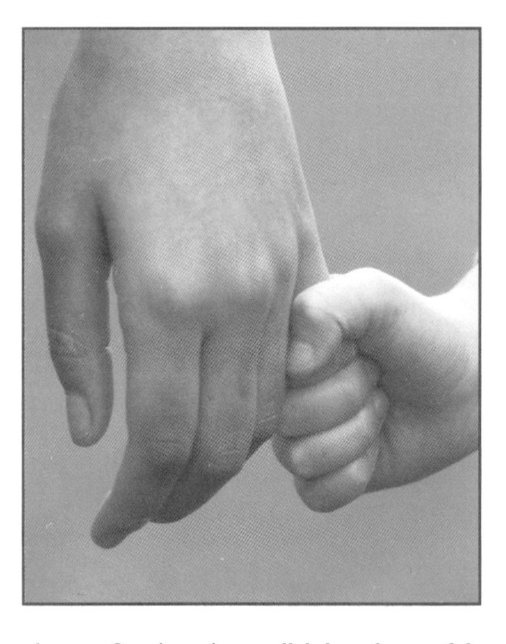

A young Capricorn is so well-behaved most of the time that a Gemini parent shouldn't have to guide him or her with too firm a hand.

Capricorn Birth Influences

Ruling planet: Saturn
Element: Earth
Polarity: Feminine
Quadruplicity: Cardinal

Gemini and Capricorn relatives are typically like night and day. While Gemini is talkative, imaginative, and volatile, Capricorn is reticent, practical, and steady, and whereas Gemini makes split-second decisions, Capricorn is a ponderer. Given their fundamental dissimilarities, they are bound to have their differences, but because airy Gemini is so affable and forgiving, and earthy Capricorn so resilient and loyal, their disagreements are unlikely to undermine their affection for one another.

Parents: If you are a Capricorn, you are governed by Saturn, the planet associated with maturity, and you may therefore have felt as though you were the adult while growing up with your young-at-heart Gemini parent. Airy, mercurial Gemini is forever on the lookout for fun and finds chores and routines depressing, which is why, having been born under an earthy, saturnine sign yourself, you may have been continually trying to impose order on your somewhat chaotic household. Despite this, you probably delighted in your parent's usually cheerful, easygoing nature.

Gemini craves freedom, and if the sign of the twins is yours and you have a Capricorn parent, you may often have felt restricted. It is due to upright Saturn's influence in particular that Capricorns can be rather authoritarian people who believe that nothing worthwhile can be achieved without hard work and patience—a viewpoint that was probably alien to your quick-witted, restless nature. Still, you must have felt safe and loved in dependable, devoted Capricorn's care.

Children: Your chatty, cheery little Gemini must brighten your days if you are a Capricorn, but you probably fret about his or her lack of direction and application. Don't let this keep you awake at night. Mutable Gemini may not share your ambitious, cardinal quadruplicity, but has the intelligence and charm to make a success of life.

If you are the Gemini parent of a Capricorn, you must be thankful that your child is so well behaved, although Capricorn's conscientiousness, organization, and regular habits must be a source of puzzlement to you. Don't worry that all work and no play will have a dulling effect on your child, though, because cardinal Capricorns will always be driven by their enterprising ideas.

Sibling Relationships: If you are one of a Gemini and Capricorn pair of siblings, you probably inhabited different worlds as children, with bubbly, outgoing Gemini flitting in and out of the house while inward-focused Capricorn plotted and prepared for the future. Your sense of humor—Gemini's mischievous, Capricorn's dry—must have created a delicious bond between you, however.

AQUARIUS

GEMINI

****

A house that is home to a Gemini and an Aquarius will almost certainly ring with laughter and buzz with articulate conversation, but will hardly ever rattle as doors are slammed in anger. Both having been born under masculine air signs, Gemini and Aquarius are equally uninhibited, fun-loving, and intelligent, as well as natural communicators whose ruling planets give them a fondness for exploring the world of the mind. Although mutable Gemini can be moody, and fixed-sign Aquarius, obstinate, neither enjoys falling out with one another, which is why their relationship is generally easygoing and affectionate.

Parents: If you are an Aquarius, you may have loved the way that your Gemini parent treated you as an equal when you were growing up and was ever ready to answer your questions. As well as being egalitarian, informative, and communicative, airy, Mercury-ruled Geminians of all ages have a mischievous streak that must have appealed to your own playful nature. But because your sign is fixed, and Gemini's, mutable, you may sometimes have wished that your parent were less changeable.

You were probably a fidgety child if you are a Gemini, and one of the things that you may recall with fondness about your Aquarian parent is his or her talent for capturing your attention with a startlingly anarchic idea. It is Uranus' influence that gives Aquarians a tendency to think "outside the box," which you must have found thrilling in an adult. As a mutable personality, however, you may have been frustrated by Aquarius' settled ways.

Children: Although you must approve of your Gemini child's lively, inquiring mind if you are an Aquarius, you may worry that he or she has the attention span of a gnat and is easily distracted from a task in hand. If so, plunder your reserves of Uranian inventiveness and airy playfulness to lure little Gemini's mind back again.

If you are a Gemini, your Aquarian child's original way of thinking may amaze and impress you, but you may be concerned that he or she will be branded an oddball and will consequently have difficulty making friends. Don't worry about it. Fixed, Uranian Aquarians don't care what others think of them, and their airy charm in any case draws others into their orbit.

Sibling Relationships: Constant chat must have characterized your childhood if you and your sibling are a Gemini and an Aquarius, yet there may have been the occasional squawk of annoyance when Gemini's capriciousness irritated Aquarius or Aquarius' stubbornness exasperated Gemini.

****

Aquarius Birth Influences

Ruling planet: Uranus; traditionally Saturn
Element: Air
Polarity: Masculine
Quadruplicity: Fixed

****

There will be giggles galore when Gemini and Aquarius enjoy playtime time together.

****

Gemini Birth Influences

Ruling planet: Mercury
Element: Air
Polarity: Masculine
Quadruplicity: Mutable

GEMINI

PISCES

Gemini Birth Influences

Ruling planet: Mercury
Element: Air
Polarity: Masculine
Quadruplicity: Mutable

Don't worry if your young Pisces is reticent with other children, Gemini. Be supportive, and encourage her to get to know people at her own pace.

Pisces Birth Influences

Ruling planet: Neptune; traditionally Jupiter
Element: Water
Polarity: Feminine
Quadruplicity: Mutable

Gemini and Pisces relatives usually get on well, partly because their shared mutable quadruplicity causes them to shy away from head-on conflict, and partly because airy Gemini is so genial and watery Pisces, so gentle and caring. That said, Gemini's emotional detachment can upset sensitive Pisces, and independent Gemini may find being the focus of Pisces' unselfish love claustrophobic.

Parents: As a Piscean child, you may have yearned for your Gemini parent's undivided attention. You may not have felt neglected, but because airy Geminians are typically restless social butterflies whose minds rule their hearts, and your watery element can make you feel emotionally insecure, you may have wished that your parent spent more time with you and was more demonstrative in expressing affection. Nevertheless, growing up with enthusiastic, lively Gemini must have been fun.

You may now realize how much your Pisces parent did for you if you are an adult Gemini. Neptune, their ruling planet, gives Pisceans an altruistic urge to sacrifice their own desires for those whom they love. Their element of water also makes them born nurturers, and their feminine polarity causes them to be receptive to others' moods, so your parent was probably always attuned to your needs. As a youngster, however, you may have felt stifled by, and sometimes driven to escape from, your dedicated parent's all-consuming devotion.

Children: If you are a somewhat shy Pisces and your child is a Gemini, your heart must swell with pride whenever you see him or her chatting happily to anyone and everyone. Gemini may be more outgoing, sociable, and communicative than you, but is probably also less compassionate. Because Gemini is logical, the best way to teach your child to consider others' feelings is to discuss the workings of cause and effect with him or her as often as you can.

Your young Pisces' mind may be a mystery to you if you are a Gemini, maybe because you operate rationally and confidently, whereas the Piscean brain seems to be swamped by emotions and self-doubt. Don't expect your child to change—indeed, you could learn a thing or two from his or her Neptunian sensitivity—but try to bolster Pisces' self-confidence.

Sibling Relationships: Gemini may be extroverted and rather superficial, and Pisces, introverted and profound, but one of the gifts bestowed on both you and your sibling by your common quadruplicity is flexibility, which is why you were probably able to learn to accommodate your differences as children.

CANCER

CANCER

Having as they do a responsive and nurturing ruling planet in the Moon, an emotionally sensitive and compassionate element in water, and a feminine polarity, Cancerian relatives are finely attuned to one another's feelings, tend to put each other first, and—it probably goes without saying—love one another deeply. Because they are both cardinal, or go-getting, people however, there will be times when one is single-mindedly set on pursuing a cherished aim in life, which may cause the other to feel shut out.

Parents: If you and your parent are both Cancers, you almost certainly had, and may still have, a very close relationship. Your planetary governor is regarded as the archetypal mother in many cultures' mythologies and sacred beliefs. Because of this, and also because your common polarity is feminine, whether it is your mother or father who shares your sign, Cancer is associated with such traditionally female qualities as intuition, empathy, gentleness, and unselfishness. Your parent's priority must therefore have been providing you with emotional and physical nourishment, be it by showering you with hugs and kisses, comforting and reassuring you when you were upset, or making sure that you were always well fed and clothed. But as you grew up, started to focus on realizing your dreams, cardinal-quadruplicity style, and relied less on your Cancer elder for support, you may have seen a crabbier side of your emotional parent, who may have found your increasing independence painful, and may have expressed his or her heartache with some hurtful comments.

Children: Your Cancerian child's thoughtfulness must gratify you if you are also a crab, but Cancer children haven't yet had their soft and vulnerable shell toughened up by time and experience, and their watery element can make them feel fearful and insecure, which is why he or she may often cling to you in floods of tears. You may have difficulty getting to the bottom of the problem because Cancer's watery element can render weeping crablets confused and inarticulate, but then, being an instinctive type, you can probably guess what's wrong and know that time, attention, and soothing words will calm the emotional storm. But try not to smother your impressionable child with your overwhelming love, and gradually encourage him or her to become more self-sufficient.

Sibling Relationships: Although you and your sibling no doubt loved and understood each other implicitly if you are both Cancers, you may have looked to your non-Cancerian friends for fun and stimulation.

Cancer Birth Influences

Ruling planet: The Moon
Element: Water
Polarity: Feminine
Quadruplicity: Cardinal

A Cancer child will take her time to overcome her shyness. You must learn to help her to stand on her own two feet, Cancer, and not to be overprotective.

Cancer Birth Influences

Ruling planet: The Moon
Element: Water
Polarity: Feminine
Quadruplicity: Cardinal

CANCER
LEO

Cancer Birth Influences

Ruling planet: The Moon
Element: Water
Polarity: Feminine
Quadruplicity: Cardinal

Leo loves being the center of attention, but a Cancer parent should be careful not to fuss over her too much in case she feels driven to break away.

Leo Birth Influences

Ruling planet: The Sun
Element: Fire
Polarity: Masculine
Quadruplicity: Fixed

Watery, Moon-ruled, feminine-polarity Cancerians are usually totally focused on their families, and derive enormous satisfaction from nurturing their loved ones, especially their emotional welfare. Fixed-sign Leos are similarly devoted to their nearest and dearest, but, being ruled by the Sun, and with fire as an element and an uninhibited, masculine polarity, play more of an invigorating role within the family. The kindly and warm-hearted lion usually have a loving relationship, but cautious Cancer's overprotectiveness may cramp the lion's impulsive style, while Leo's need to be independent may wound the sensitive crab.

Parents: If you are a fiery Leo who adores being the center of attention, you must have basked in your dedicated Cancer parent's vigilant care as a child, that is, until you hit adolescence, when you may have felt smothered by the crab's concern, and may have asserted your individuality with open rebellion. But now that you are grown up and are living your own life, you probably feel deep affection for your parent.

You must have vivid memories of your childhood if you are a Cancer and your parent is a Leo. The influence of the Sun manifests itself in Leo as playfulness, as well as authoritativeness, while the gifts of fire include energy and enthusiasm. Because you are very responsive to others' influence, you must have been swept along by your dynamic parent's exuberance. Being more of a worrier than fearless Leo, you may, however, sometimes have longed for more understanding and sympathy from your parent when you felt insecure.

Children: Your little crab's compassion charms you if you are a Leo, but you may be mystified by the tears that spring from seemingly insignificant triggers. The answer lies in intuitive Cancer's empathy and profound emotions, and the best way to calm your distraught crablet is to wrap your arms around your child, listen, and reassure.

Their element of fire is particularly pronounced in lion cubs, which is why you may marvel at your vibrant Leo child's zest for life if you are a more circumspect Cancer. Try not to be too affected by your child's temper tantrums, though: little Leos have a flair for drama, and are easily soothed and distracted with a hug and a promise of fun to come.

Sibling Relationships: If you and your sibling are a crab and a lion, Leo may have been the bossier and Cancer, the more thoughtful. Although shouting and weeping may have featured in your childhood years when you annoyed or upset one another, you probably generally encouraged and supported each other.

VIRGO
CANCER

Sharing a feminine polarity means that having a settled home life is important to both Cancer and Virgo. Cancer's ruling planet and element—the nurturing Moon and compassionate water—usually cause the crab to prioritize their emotional relationship, whereas earthy Virgo is typically more concerned with practicalities. But Mercury-governed Virgo is also more communicative and resilient than reticent, thin-skinned Cancer, so Cancer may take Virgo's fault-finding personally, while Virgo may in turn be frustrated by Cancer's sulky silences.

Parents: If you are a Virgo, the interaction between your feminine polarity, mutable quadruplicity, and mercurial planetary governor may have caused you to be an anxious child, which is why you may often have turned to your empathetic Cancer parent for comfort. A problem shared is a problem halved, as they say, and intuitive, caring Cancer must have been a soothing sustainer. Yet you may sometimes have felt oppressed by Cancer's all-consuming love for you, which, being less emotional, you may have felt unable to reciprocate.

Mercury often manifests itself in Virgo as impartiality, while their mutable quadruplicity and element of earth can make these people overly analytical. If you are a Cancer and your parent is a Virgo, this may have been both advantageous and disadvantageous for you when you were younger. You may have regarded your parent as a mentor whose logical, organized mind helped to keep you focused when feelings clouded your judgment, but may also have wished that Virgo were less neutral.

Children: You must love your little Cancer's sympathetic nature if you are a Virgo, but may worry that he or she is constantly seeking your approval. It is Cancer's unstable, watery element that gives your child a craving for the affirmation of your praise, so build up Cancer's confidence by curbing your critical tendencies.

Although you may marvel at your Virgo youngster's thirst for knowledge, you may find the "I'm bored" refrain rather trying if you are Cancer. Virgo's changeable nature makes your child restless, so draw on that fertile imagination of yours to dream up ways of occupying his or her mind.

Sibling Relationships: You may not have had the smoothest of relationships if you and your sibling are a Cancer and a Virgo. Because Virgo talks straight, there may have been times when a negative comment caused oversensitive Cancer to respond with a nasty nip before scuttling back into his or her shell. But now that you are older, you probably appreciate one another's support.

Virgo Birth Influences

Ruling planet: Mercury
Element: Earth
Polarity: Feminine
Quadruplicity: Mutable

Your young Cancer may prove to be an intuitively expressive musician, Virgo. If she is shy, taking up an instrument can provide an excellent outlet for her emotions.

Cancer Birth Influences

Ruling planet: The Moon
Element: Water
Polarity: Feminine
Quadruplicity: Cardinal

CANCER

LIBRA

Cancer Birth Influences

Ruling planet: The Moon
Element: Water
Polarity: Feminine
Quadruplicity: Cardinal

Family-minded Cancer and diplomatic Libra siblings are likely to share a close bond, even if they have different interests and temperaments.

Libra Birth Influences

Ruling planet: Venus
Element: Air
Polarity: Masculine
Quadruplicity: Cardinal

Watery Cancerians look to their families for the love that makes them feel secure, and derive deep satisfaction from supporting their loved ones. Airy Librans, by contrast, want their relatives to be playmates, and, being ruled by placatory Venus, tend to act as peacemakers. Domestic harmony is vital to feminine-polarity Cancer, but because masculine-polarity Libra may rarely be at home, there is a danger that the crab may feel uncared for, and that Libra may then give crabby Cancer a wide berth.

Parents: If you are a Libra, your Cancer parent may have treated you like a little prince or princess when you were growing up. If you felt as though the crab's world revolved around you, it probably did, as the Moon, a watery element, and a feminine polarity all cause Cancerians to put their children's wishes and needs first. Cancer can be overprotective, however, and because you were born under an independent sign, your urge to escape the crab's caring control may have caused some friction between you.

You may have basked in your Venus-ruled, Libran parent's light-hearted indulgence when you were small if you were a responsive young Cancer. Being so sensitive, you were probably also grateful to Libra for striving to maintain an emotionally balanced atmosphere in your home and trying to lift your spirits whenever you were upset. That said, airy Libra is less empathetic than you, and when you were feeling down, you may have preferred some understanding words and a reassuring cuddle to a joke and a treat.

Children: If you are an art-loving Libra, you may be astonished by your young crab's instinctive grasp of the messages conveyed by a painting or piece of music. It is the joint influence of the Moon and water that makes Cancer so intuitive, but often also insecure. Don't try to analyze why, and just buoy up your child by being there for him or her.

You must be proud of young Libra's good manners and knack for getting along with everyone if you are a Cancer, and can thank Venus and the element of air for these gifts. You may be less thrilled by the selfishness and flightiness that are also part and parcel of the Libran personality. If so, try not to nag or complain too much.

Sibling Relationships: Even if Cancer was always content to stay at home while Libra was out playing with friends, you and your sibling probably had a fond and friendly relationship if you were born under these zodiacal signs.

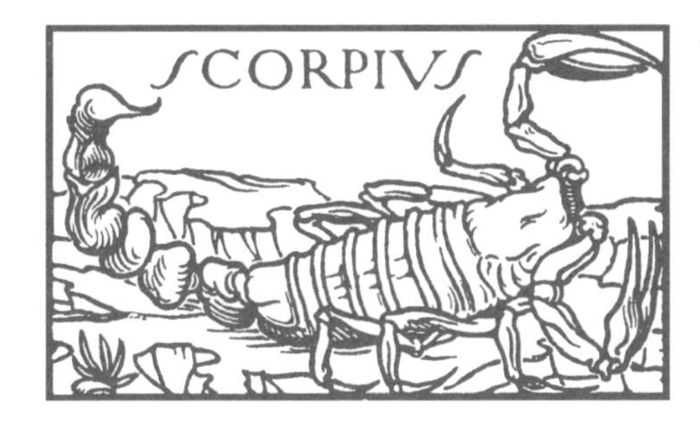

SCORPIO / CANCER

Because they share a feminine polarity and watery element, the lives of most Cancer and Scorpio people revolve around their families, in whom they make an enormous emotional investment. These are therefore usually close-knit relatives, whose bond is strengthened by their empathetic, nurturing natures. This is not to say that their relationship is always sweetness and light. Indeed, Cancer's intrusiveness may result in the scorpion retreating behind a veil of secrecy, while fixed-sign Scorpio's stubbornness can cause the sensitive crab to weep tears of frustration.

Parents: As a young Scorpio, you must have turned to Cancer for encouragement and support. Thanks to the serene Moon, their planetary ruler, and compassionate element, Cancerian parents have a talent for sympathetically fostering their children's well-being. With your receptive polarity, you must have blossomed under his or her gentle guidance. But because your governing planet, Pluto, makes you more reticent than Cancer, you may occasionally have resented and resisted your parent's prompting to divulge what was on your mind.

The intensity of your Plutonian Scorpio parent's devotion to you must have made you feel secure if you are a zodiacal crab. And because Scorpio shares your element, he or she may have instinctively understood and comforted you when you were unable to articulate your childish fears. Yet Scorpio is a fixed, or uncompromising, sign, and yours is cardinal, or go-getting, and you may have been deeply upset by your parent's refusal to allow you to pursue a cherished ambition that he or she dismissed as being a pipe dream.

Children: Your dark governing planet and emotional element may make you prone to the occasional black mood if you are a Scorpio, in which case you may be moved by your little lunar crab's caring concern. The intuitive Moon also makes Cancer impressionable, so try to ensure that your child is exposed to your lighter side, too.

Although you can probably sense how your Scorpio child is feeling, the workings of his or her mind may sometimes be a mystery to you if you are a Cancer. Pluto-ruled, watery scorpions are deep thinkers who need their personal space, so don't push him or her into opening up.

Sibling Relationships: If you and your sibling are a Cancer and a Scorpio—both inward-looking, feminine-polarity, water signs—you may have spent much of your childhood immersed in your own rich, inner worlds, but were no doubt generally receptive to each other's opinions.

Scorpio Birth Influences

Ruling planet: Pluto; traditionally Mars
Element: Water
Polarity: Feminine
Quadruplicity: Fixed

♇ ♂ ≈

Scorpios are often reticent and introspective. If your child is lost in serious thought, Cancer, you can encourage him to reveal all when he's in a more communicative mood.

Cancer Birth Influences

Ruling planet: The Moon
Element: Water
Polarity: Feminine
Quadruplicity: Cardinal

CANCER
SAGITTARIUS

Cancer Birth Influences

Ruling planet: The Moon
Element: Water
Polarity: Feminine
Quadruplicity: Cardinal

A young Sagittarian's lust for life may make a protective Cancer parent quake in his boots! If you are the Cancer parent of a young archer, try to let your child off the reins once in a while, and don't let your worries overwhelm you.

Sagittarius Birth Influences

Ruling planet: Jupiter
Element: Fire
Polarity: Masculine
Quadruplicity: Mutable

Moon-ruled, watery Cancer may be caring and empathetic, while Jupiter-governed, fiery Sagittarius is jovial and warm-hearted, but a fundamental difference between the two is that the feminine-polarity crab is a homebody, while the masculine-polarity archer likes to be constantly on the move. If they can accept their dissimilarities, Cancer will try to be understanding, Sagittarius will be adaptable, and affection will then flow freely between them.

Parents: Most Cancerians yearn to become parents, and, when they do, are fulfilled by raising their children. This is mainly due to the influence of their nurturing element of water and planetary governor, Mother Moon. If you are a fiery Sagittarius who loves being the center of attention, you must have relished being the focal point of your Cancer parent's world, and no doubt flourished under his or her gentle encouragement. But because yours is an adventurous, fiery sign, you may frequently have lost your temper when restrained by protective Cancer.

If you are a receptive Cancer, you must have loved being with your Sagittarius parent when you were growing up. Jupiter makes Sagittarians good-natured guardians, and their fiery element, masculine polarity, and mutable quadruplicity may have blessed you with a generous, fun-loving parent who introduced you to a variety of enjoyable games and educational activities. Feminine-polarity Cancerians are more introverted and privacy-loving than Sagittarians, though, so you may sometimes have wished that your parent were content simply to stay at home.

Children: Although you must adore your little crab's loving nature if you are a Sagittarius, you may be concerned that he or she is too willing to go with the flow. This illustrates the contrast between your own, pioneering polarity and Cancer's cautious one, as well as between your impulsive element of fire and Cancer's responsive, watery element. Don't push the issue, lest you make your sensitive child feel inadequate.

You probably can't help but admire your fearless Sagittarius child's zest for life if you are a Cancer, but no doubt worry incessantly about his or her recklessness. While it is true that their fiery element can make little archers thoughtless and impulsive, you may be heartened to know that these are also children who learn by experience. Don't nag Sagittarius too much because this may prove counterproductive.

Sibling Relationships: If you and your sibling are a Cancer and a Sagittarius, you may each have occasionally provoked the other's tears or fury as children, but may also have benefited from one another's different outlooks and approaches.

CAPRICORN
CANCER

Whatever their age, sex, or family status, Cancers often assume a motherly role in the home, and Capricorns a fatherly one, and not only because Cancer's planetary governor is the Moon, the archetypal mother, while Capricorn's is Saturn, the father many gods in Roman mythology. The element of water makes crabs nurturing, while earth gives goats a no-nonsense attitude, and these "soft" and "hard" characteristics echo traditional gender stereotypes. Both have a supportive, feminine polarity and are ambitious, cardinal signs, so typically strive to foster their relatives' well-being—Cancer's concern being their emotional health and Capricorn's, their material welfare. They will not always welcome one another's help, however.

Parents: As a young Capricorn, you may have particularly liked your Cancerian parent's sympathetic, encouraging way of listening as you formulated your plans for the future. You may, however, have squirmed with embarrassment or suppressed irritation if you felt that your caring, concerned parent was fussing over you too much.

If you are a Cancer, although you may have considered your earthy Capricorn parent a dependable and devoted mainstay during your childhood, you may not have felt as though he or she really understood you. Your goal in life was no doubt simply to be happy and fulfilled, but because Saturn-governed, earthy Capricorns want the best for their children and believe that success can only be achieved through hard work, he or she may have mapped out a homework plan or career path for you that made your heart sink.

Children: If you are a Capricorn, you probably melt when your loving little Cancer gives you a hug, but may wish that he or she were less dreamy. If so, there may come a time when you'll be deeply impressed by the fascinating and original ideas that flow from that creative imagination.

Your Capricorn child's readiness to do his or her chores must amaze and please you if you are a Cancer. Don't worry that Capricorn is too conscientious, though, because earthy, saturnine kids enjoy being productive.

Sibling Relationships: If you and your sibling are a Cancer and Capricorn, you share a self-contained, feminine polarity and driving, cardinal quadruplicity, and so may have spent much of your youth quietly pursuing your separate interests. You probably liked and supported one another, though, even if Capricorn sometimes found watery Cancer's mood swings tiresome, especially during adolescence, and Cancer sighed at earthy Capricorn's lack of fellow feeling.

Capricorn Birth Influences

Ruling planet: Saturn
Element: Earth
Polarity: Feminine
Quadruplicity: Cardinal

As a child, Cancer, did you worry that you would not be able to live up to your Capricorn parent's high expectations? There may have been times when you longed to escape Capricorn's watchful eye and express your creativity.

Cancer Birth Influences

Ruling planet: The Moon
Element: Water
Polarity: Feminine
Quadruplicity: Cardinal

CANCER
AQUARIUS

Cancer Birth Influences

Ruling planet: The Moon
Element: Water
Polarity: Feminine
Quadruplicity: Cardinal

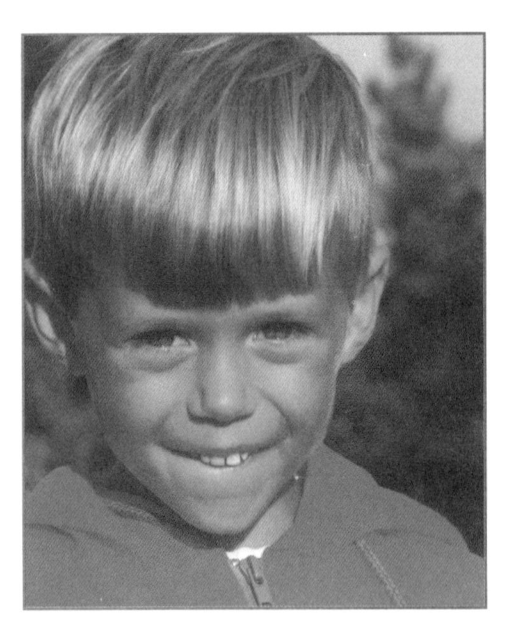

Shy young Cancers love to share their daydreams with Aquarius parents, who encourage them to express their creativity.

Aquarius Birth Influences

Ruling planet: Uranus; traditionally Saturn
Element: Air
Polarity: Masculine
Quadruplicity: Fixed

As long as Cancer gives airy Aquarius space, and Aquarius occasionally cherishes the watery crab, these two will have an agreeable relationship. Both are thoughtful, even if Moon-ruled Cancer's thoughtfulness takes the form of consideration for others and intellectual, Uranian Aquarius is more preoccupied with developing inventive ideas. Their opposite polarities sometimes make it seem as though they inhabit different planets, yet Cancer's innovative, cardinal quadruplicity and Aquarius' steadfast, fixed one can create a strong bond between them.

Parents: If you are an Aquarius, you may now recognize that your Cancer parent's support when you were younger was far greater than you realized at the time. The combination of Cancer's planetary ruler, element, and polarity makes zodiacal crabs compassionate parents who are instinctively attuned to their children's emotions and unobtrusively nurture their well-being. Even so, Cancer's cautiousness and protectiveness may have sometimes rankled with you.

Airy, Uranus-governed Aquarian parents tend to treat their children as equals and encourage them to think for themselves, which may have delighted you when you were younger if you are a cardinal Cancer with a fertile imagination. Indeed, Aquarius may rarely have dismissed your visionary notions as pipe dreams, and no doubt relished discussing them with you. Despite his or her committed, fixed quadruplicity, Aquarius may not have been a touchy-feely type, however, and there may have been occasions when you longed for fewer words and more hugs.

Children: Although your crablet's responsiveness to your suggestions must please you if you are an Aquarius, you may wish that he or she were less impressionable and anxious to receive others' approval. (This illustrates the difference between the intellectual independence that Uranus and air instill in you and the suggestibility and sensitivity that the Moon and water bestow on Cancer.) If this is so, gently try to build up Cancer's confidence.

If you are a Cancer, you may be a little worried that your Aquarius child's nonconformist way of thinking will be frowned on at school. Don't be too concerned: good teachers smile on originality, and, as you well know, cheerful, airy Aquarians are blessed with a charmingly persuasive way with words.

Sibling Relationships: Because Cancer is empathetic, caring, and hates arguing, and Aquarius is easygoing, forgiving, and loyal, your relationship has probably always been rooted in mutual affection if you and your sibling were born under these signs.

PISCES
CANCER

When their shared feminine, or contemplative, polarity, and caring element of water are taken into consideration, along with the crab's nurturing, lunar ruling planet and Pisces' altruistic planetary governor in Neptune, it is unlikely that a pair of empathetic Cancer and Pisces relations will have anything other than a loving relationship. Even so, there may be occasions when cardinal Cancer's ambition causes Pisces to retreat into a world of daydreams, or when mutable Pisces' unpredictability disconcerts the stability-seeking crab.

Parents: You probably felt as though you were the apple of your Cancer parent's eye when you were growing up if you are a Pisces, which must have made you feel safe and secure, as well as boosting your often shaky confidence. The double dose of intuition that the Moon and water bestow on Cancer may have meant that your parent instinctively sensed how you were feeling. You may, however, have wished that cardinal Cancer would ease the pressure that he or she inadvertently put you under by not investing so much faith in your ability to fulfill your potential.

If you are an emotionally vulnerable Cancer, you must have blossomed under your gentle Piscean parent's care when you were small. And because the Moon makes you so impressionable, and your shared watery element causes you to be innately giving, you may have been inspired to emulate Neptune-ruled Pisces' unselfish example. That said, the coming-together of your common watery, or changeable, element and Pisces' mutable, or unstable, quadruplicity may sometimes have caused your parent's moods to fluctuate wildly, leaving you feeling all at sea.

Children: Your little crab's vivid imagination must delight you if you are an equally artistic Pisces, although because you are so compassionate, you may feel real pain when your emotional child dissolves into floods of tears having envisaged a sad scenario. If so, enlist one of the advantages of having a mutable quadruplicity by hitting on a cheering diversion that will distract and hearten you both.

You probably value your Piscean child's considerateness and flexibility on the rare occasions that your views diverge, if you are a Cancer. But if you are slightly concerned by Pisces' dreaminess, draw on your initiating, cardinal quadruplicity to encourage him or her to re-engage with the real world.

Sibling Relationships: Although you may have been naturally attuned to one another as children if you and your sibling are a Cancer and a Pisces, you probably looked to other playmates to provide fun and stimulation.

Pisces Birth Influences

Ruling planet: Neptune; traditionally Jupiter
Element: Water
Polarity: Feminine
Quadruplicity: Mutable

A caring, understanding Cancer parent usually intuitively knows how to make Pisces children feel secure and self-confident.

Cancer Birth Influences

Ruling planet: The Moon
Element: Water
Polarity: Feminine
Quadruplicity: Cardinal

LEO
LEO

Leo Birth Influences
Ruling planet: The Sun
Element: Fire
Polarity: Masculine
Quadruplicity: Fixed

Whatever their ages, Leo people are fearless and uninhibited, set on having fun, and highly creative, but can also be hot-tempered, willful, and stubborn. Although Leo relatives will have exhilarating times together, there will also be a few fiery clashes, particularly between authoritative Leo parents and rebellious leonine children. Yet nursing grudges is not the magnanimous Leo way, and because these two also share a fixed, or loyal, quadruplicity, it won't be long before the thunderclouds clear and all is sunny again.

Parents: If you and your parent are both zodiacal lions, you probably have vivid childhood memories of your Leo elder radiating energy, roaring with laughter, and indolently lazing around, too. Your shared birth influences include the vitalizing Sun, the impulsive element of fire, and an outgoing, masculine polarity, which is why you may have needed no encouragement to follow your vibrant, spontaneous, dynamic parent's lead, or to relax and recharge your batteries when you were all played out. And because the combination of the Sun and fire causes you both to appreciate the new and original, as well as stunning visual spectacles, you may have relished being taken to shows by your culture-loving parent. When you were older, however, you may have challenged your parent's authority, and because Leos expect children to obey their ground rules and will not tolerate disrespect—however lenient and indulgent they may otherwise be—you may recall having some explosive rows.

Leo siblings are often found laughing—when they're not trying to murder each other, of course!

Children: Because the lively element of fire tends to be particularly pronounced in spirited lion cubs, a fixed quadruplicity may not manifest itself in your leonine child as tenacity, but obstinacy, which you may find both amusing and irritating if you are also a Leo. You probably have a sneaking admiration for such stubbornness because you can be exactly the same, but may still find it infuriating if little Leo's defiance is triggered by your insistence that he or she does what you say. Such standoffs are the inevitable result of you both having a strong-minded planetary ruler in the Sun, and perhaps the best strategy in these situations is to draw on your fiery inspiration to think up an exciting distraction that is sure to appeal to your thrill-seeking child.

Sibling Relationships: If you and your sibling are both vigorous, bossy Leos, you may forever have been sparking off one another's burning enthusiasm or hot temper as children, but no doubt felt warm affection for each other deep down.

Leo Birth Influences
Ruling planet: The Sun
Element: Fire
Polarity: Masculine
Quadruplicity: Fixed

VIRGO / LEO

There may be plenty of things that a pair of Leo and Virgo relatives find irritating in one another: Leo's untidiness may drive orderly Virgo up the wall, for example, while Virgo's penny-pinching ways may annoy generous Leo. Yet there may be a strong bond of affection between these two, partly because Leo is so warm and loyal, and partly because Virgo is supportive and flexible.

Parents: If you are a Virgo, your Sun-governed Leo parent was probably a powerful presence in your childhood, perhaps as an authoritative mentor who was also warm-hearted and magnanimous. Because you have a mutable, restless quadruplicity, you may often have been enlivened by Leo's fiery spontaneity, but being a more restrained person yourself, were you sometimes embarrassed by your uninhibited parent's exhibitionist tendencies and hot temper?

When you were young, Leo, it may have seemed as though your Mercury-ruled, Virgo parent was forever criticizing you, particularly for acting recklessly. This illustrates how the impulsive lion's fiery element and outward-bound, masculine polarity can trigger earthy, feminine-sign Virgoans' distress if they fear that their children's rashness will expose them to danger. You may have responded with temper tantrums, but may nevertheless have secretly relished being the focus of your parent's concern.

Children: Little Leos are very image-conscious, and it may be that you find your child's insatiable desire for expensive clothes a trial if you are a financially prudent Virgo. If so, why not offer Leo extra cash for doing household chores? This will make your child feel deliciously grown up, and because Leo has a fixed, tenacious quadruplicity, may even result in a spick-and-span home!

You may think that your earthy, feminine-polarity Virgo child's tidiness is bordering on the obsessive if you are a fiery, outgoing Leo. You can't change this trait because messy surroundings seriously upset Virgos, but try to encourage your child to engage in more creative activities, too.

Sibling Relationships: If you and your sibling are a Leo and a Virgo, the commanding lion no doubt took the lead when you were younger. You may sometimes have been sufficiently enlivened by Leo's fiery energy to play along, if you are a Virgo, but there may also have been times when you resisted becoming involved in a risky escapade. And if you are a Leo, although you may have branded cautious Virgo a killjoy on such occasions, your earthy sibling's level-headedness may frequently have kept you out of trouble.

Virgo Birth Influences

Ruling planet: Mercury
Element: Earth
Polarity: Feminine
Quadruplicity: Mutable

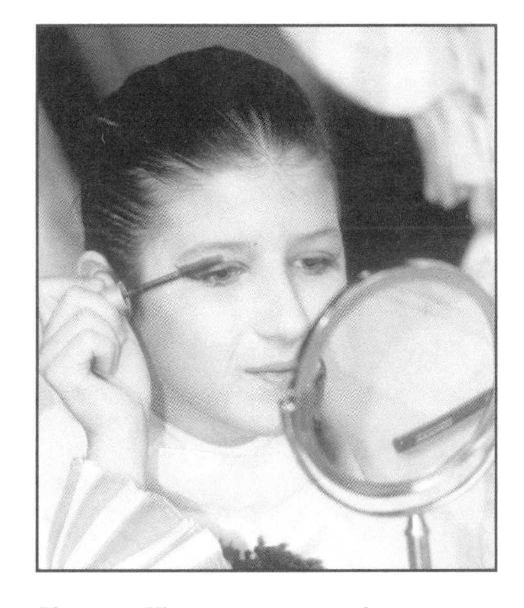

If you are a Virgo, you may worry that your young Leo's obsession with her appearance is distracting her from her homework. Vanity is a leonine trait, but so is pride, so she'll make sure that it gets done.

Leo Birth Influences

Ruling planet: The Sun
Element: Fire
Polarity: Masculine
Quadruplicity: Fixed

LEO
LIBRA

Leo Birth Influences

Ruling planet: The Sun
Element: Fire
Polarity: Masculine
Quadruplicity: Fixed

With so many mutual interests and characteristics, Leos and Libras usually interact well within a family environment. Conflict may, however, arise when Sun-ruled Leo's willfulness offends Venus-governed Libra's balancing instinct, or when Libra's occasional indolence and lack of direction drives decisive Leo to distraction.

Parents: With their unwavering commitment to their families and inherent need for stability, both Libra and Leo have the potential to be loving, encouraging, and supportive parents. If your father is a fiery Leo, and in many respects still a child at heart, he may effortlessly establish a rapport with young people, but his rather authoritative manner probably grates on you if you are a Libra. You expect to be treated as an equal, and this tension is likely to increase as you grow older unless you can convince your parent to respect your airy point of view.

If you're a Leo, your Libra parent's airy, objective approach may have infuriated you when you were an impetuous child, as may his or her insistence on orderliness within the home, but you may now value the constantly available balanced advice and benevolent parental support that you receive from Libra.

A Libra parent values learning and education, and will try to encourage her Leo child to read and to think for herself—no problem for a self-willed Leo!

Children: If you're a Libra, your natural sense of justice ensures that you always take your child's viewpoint into consideration, but don't let your Leo child's strong will get out of control, or you'll pay dearly when your cub enters his or her teenage years. If you're a Leo parent, your Libra child's airy inclination to consider all of the possibilities before reaching a decision may test your patience to its limits. In order to minimize potential conflict, try not to dominate your child, and to give unobtrusive guidance.

Sibling Relationships: Although generally sunny-natured, Leo children have a tendency to throw spectacular tantrums whenever their strong wills are thwarted, behavior that poised young Librans shrink from. Yet Leo's fiery temper is short-lived, and if you are a Libra, you are a born peacemaker. Children born under both of these signs will seek to establish their individuality early in life, and tensions may therefore arise if cardinal Libra perceives Leo's bossiness as being unacceptably dominating. Despite these differences, Libras and Leos are usually playful, good-natured youngsters, and, what's more, are devoted to their siblings, even if they don't always show it.

Libra Birth Influences

Ruling planet: Venus
Element: Air
Polarity: Masculine
Quadruplicity: Cardinal

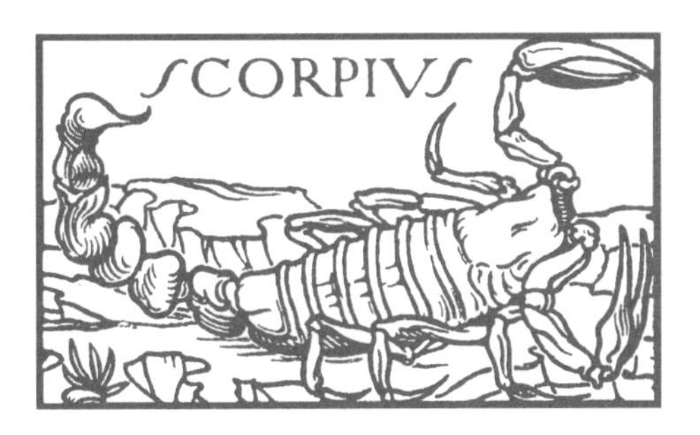

SCORPIO
LEO

Although Leo and Scorpio may have dramatically dissimilar personalities, because they share a fixed quadruplicity, they are united in their devotion to their loved ones, including one another, which is just as well, given that they are equally obstinate. Their relationship is usually affectionate, even if Scorpio's stubborn silences sometimes cause the lion to roar, and if Leo's self-willed behavior often provokes the scorpion into delivering a stinging rebuke.

Parents: When you were a child, your Leo parent was probably your chief entertainer and guide if you are a Scorpio, partly because you have a feminine, or passive, polarity, whereas Leo's is masculine, or active, and partly because the Sun-governed lion is so authoritative. It is thanks to their fiery element that Leos are bursting with *joie de vivre*, and your parent no doubt exerted an enlivening influence on you, too. But because Pluto and water give you a need to reflect, you may have longed for a little more privacy.

If you are a Leo, you probably loved having your Scorpio parent to yourself when you were small, perhaps because no one else made you feel so intensely loved. Having been born under a fire sign, you may have craved attention and approval, and watery, empathetic Scorpio may have instinctively understood your desire to be applauded and was happy to oblige. Yet fiery Leo is fearless, and Scorpio's element and polarity reinforce a parent's protectiveness and caution, so that you may have resisted some of the scorpion's parental restraint.

Children: Your cub's warmth must delight you if you are a Scorpio, but if your child is a typically exuberant, attention-seeking, hot-headed Leo, you may be utterly worn out by bedtime. You have a thoughtful, feminine polarity, so try to encourage Leo to follow your example and direct his or her energy inward once in a while. This way, you'll have a little peace, and Leo may develop a rich inner world.

You may admire your Scorpio child's determination if you are a Leo, but because scorpions have a secretive element and ruling planet, as well as a self-contained polarity, may not always understand what motivates him or her. Pushing Scorpios to open up is generally counterproductive, so give your child space.

Sibling Relationships: If you are one half of a pair of Leo–Scorpio siblings, you may not have been bosom buddies when you were young, but may have respected one another's strength of will, especially after a few fiery explosions from Leo and some biting words from Scorpio.

Scorpio Birth Influences

Ruling planet: Pluto; traditionally Mars
Element: Water
Polarity: Feminine
Quadruplicity: Fixed

Scorpio parents will shower a little Leo with all of the love and attention he longs for.

Leo Birth Influences

Ruling planet: The Sun
Element: Fire
Polarity: Masculine
Quadruplicity: Fixed

LEO
SAGITTARIUS

Leo Birth Influences

Ruling planet: The Sun
Element: Fire
Polarity: Masculine
Quadruplicity: Fixed

A Sagittarius youngster will probably get on with his or her leonine parent exceptionally well. Both are gregarious and believe in open, straightforward communication.

Sagittarius Birth Influences

Ruling planet: Jupiter
Element: Fire
Polarity: Masculine
Quadruplicity: Mutable

It is thanks to their respective ruling planets that sunny Leo and jovial Sagittarius usually enjoy a warm relationship, and because they share a masculine polarity and fiery element, an exciting and dynamic one, too. Despite the mutual understanding and goodwill bestowed on them by these birth influences, their different quadruplicities may sometimes give rise to friction, with fixed-sign Leo's intransigence exasperating flexible Sagittarius, and the mutable archer's moodiness unsettling the slightly more even-tempered lion.

Parents: If you are a Sagittarius and your parent is a Leo, you probably got on like a house on fire during your childhood because your common element and polarity give you the same stimulation-seeking appetites and outgoing inclinations, so perhaps you threw yourself into the imaginative activities that your parent organized. But because commanding Leo expects unquestioning obedience, and you are just as strong-minded, you may have had some fiery rows.

Having the Sun as a planetary governor means that self-assured young Leos are rarely intimidated by age or authority, and if you were one of them, you may have considered your Sagittarian elder more of a friend than a parent. Broad-minded, Jupiter-governed Sagittarius probably didn't mind at all, fire and his or her mutable quadruplicity perhaps manifesting themselves as a tendency to communicate openly and honestly with you, too. Although you may never have felt that Sagittarius talked down to you, you may have disliked the way that your intellectually restless parent often strayed from a subject that you wanted to talk through.

Children: The one thing that may worry you about your otherwise energetic Leo child, if you are a Sagittarius, is the mental laziness that he or she displays at times. Leos have a fixed quadruplicity, which means that they prefer to stick with the familiar, so try to arouse Leo's creativity, but don't push the issue in case you end up with a mutinous cub on your hands.

You may see a lot of yourself in your little Sagittarius if you are a Leo, but may find his or her mood swings trying. Mutable Sagittarius is quickly bored, and can then become fractious or capricious, so keep tedium at bay by devising a variety of diversions—but also look for ways of maintaining Sagittarius' focus.

Sibling Relationships: You and your sibling must have had riotous fun when you were small if you are a Leo and a Sagittarius. Leo's bossiness and Sagittarius' fickleness may have ignited a few temper tantrums, though.

CAPRICORN
LEO

Whatever their relationship, fiery Leo likes to liven things up, and earthy Capricorn to tone them down. While the sunny, masculine-polarity lion is playful and outgoing, the Saturn-ruled, feminine-polarity goat tends to be responsible and thoughtful. Relatives with these star signs can therefore learn valuable lessons from one another, even if friction is sometimes inevitable. That said, their mutual devotion is typically never in doubt.

Parents: Having an earthy element, you may prize stability if you are a Capricorn, and Leo's quadruplicity being fixed, or constant, your leonine parent probably made you feel secure when you were a child. And because Sun-governed, masculine-polarity Leos are confident, while Capricorn children can be quite shy, there may have been times when your fiery parent's uninhibited example encouraged you to overcome your natural trepidation and be more venturesome, but also others when you were reluctant to risk embarrassing yourself.

If you are a Leo, you may frequently have engaged in battles of wills with your Capricorn parent when you were younger, partly because the Sun gives Leo a need to act independently, and partly because fire bestows spontaneity upon you. You may therefore have considered Capricorn's cautious and sober parenting style repressive, but may nevertheless have relished being the focus of the goat's concerned attention.

Children: Your cardinal quadruplicity may fill you with ambition for your bright little cub if you are a Capricorn, and you may therefore worry that leonine laziness will prevent your child from fulfilling his or her career potential. But zodiacal lions generally react badly to overt attempts to control them, so don't push your child too hard to knuckle under, and take heart from the knowledge that when fiery Leos are really enthused, their fixed, or tenacious, quadruplicity comes to the fore.

If you are the Leo parent of a Capricorn child, you may be amazed that he or she has already mapped out a life plan and is taking the first steps toward achieving it by studying conscientiously. If so, you are seeing the combined action of Capricorn's go-getting, cardinal quadruplicity, mature planetary ruler, and patient element of earth. Your child's determination must make you proud, but you may wish that you could encourage Capricorn to be more frisky.

Sibling Relationships: You probably get along if you and your sibling are a Leo and a Capricorn, but may not have spent much time playing together if the lion grew up as an impulsive extrovert and the goat, as a sensible introvert.

Capricorn Birth Influences

Ruling planet: Saturn
Element: Earth
Polarity: Feminine
Quadruplicity: Cardinal

A cautious Capricorn parent should try to accommodate a young Leo's adventurous leanings, which can be obvious from an early age.

Leo Birth Influences

Ruling planet: The Sun
Element: Fire
Polarity: Masculine
Quadruplicity: Fixed

LEO
AQUARIUS

Leo Birth Influences
Ruling planet: The Sun
Element: Fire
Polarity: Masculine
Quadruplicity: Fixed

An Aquarius child would often prefer to play on his or her computer than be dragged along to a cultural event or party. Once there, however, he or she will probably enjoy the stimulation.

Aquarius Birth Influences
Ruling planet: Uranus; traditionally Saturn
Element: Air
Polarity: Masculine
Quadruplicity: Fixed

Sharing as they do a fixed quadruplicity, both Leo and Aquarius are committed to their families, even if airy, dispassionate Aquarius may sometimes flinch at fiery Leo's demonstrativeness, while Leo may misinterpret Aquarius' emotional detachment as a lack of interest or affection. It is thanks to their generally amiable natures that these relatives nonetheless get on well, and are usually enlivened by one another's company.

Parents: If you are an Aquarius, you may appreciate the way that your Leo parent nurtured your mind when you were younger. Having the Sun as a planetary governor and fire as an element means that Leos are creative and value originality, so that your parent may regularly have taken you to plays, events, or exhibitions. And because Uranus and air make you intellectually curious, Leo may have whetted your appetite to learn more. You may, however, have felt uncomfortable on those occasions when Leo's fiery temper manifested itself.

When you were younger, your airy Aquarius parent may have allowed you to treat him or her as an equal if you are a Leo, which no doubt minimized any Sun-bestowed, self-assertive tendencies that you may have had. You may also have responded positively to Uranian Aquarius' encouragement to think for yourself, although there may have been times when you wished that your parent would simply praise your ideas rather than querying your reasoning.

Children: You and your child have a masculine polarity if you are an Aquarius and he or she is a Leo, so you must approve of your little lion's confidence, but may sigh at some of the traits that are part and parcel of having a fiery element. Leo may be hot-tempered and attention-seeking, for example, while you may be cool and collected, in which case enlist the aid of your airy element and inventive planetary governor to calm your child by coming up with a diversion that will stimulate you both.

You may admire your Aquarian child's unconventional thought processes if you are a Leo, even if you do not welcome your objective little water-carrier's questioning of your authority. If so, don't lay down the law, but instead try to explain why you feel that Aquarius will benefit from following your ground rules.

Sibling Relationships: You may have had lots of fun together when you were small if you and your sibling are a Leo and an Aquarius, even if Leo didn't share Aquarius' fascination with gadgets, and Aquarius remained unmoved by Leo's occasionally melodramatic behavior.

PISCES / LEO

Because Sun-ruled, fiery Leo is essentially warm-hearted and generous, and Neptune-governed, watery Pisces is unselfish and caring, relatives born under these signs generally have a mutually supportive rapport. Their respective polarities reinforce their bond, too, with Leo boosting uncertain Pisces' confidence, and Pisces encouraging the impulsive lion to be more thoughtful. Even so, they are bound to have their differences and disagreements.

Parents: If you are a Pisces, there may have been times when Neptune, water, and your mutable quadruplicity made you feel unsure of yourself, and when you therefore looked to your Leo parent for guidance. The Sun, fire, and a fixed quadruplicity together ensure that Leo is self-confident, positive, and steady, so that he or she may have had a fortifying, heartening, and stabilizing influence upon you. Being an intuitive individual, you may sometimes have felt that your indecisiveness tested fiery Leo's patience, however, thereby sending you deeper into the realms of insecurity.

Neptune is associated with self-sacrifice, which is one of the reasons why your Piscean parent may have always put your younger self first if you are a Leo. And because the Sun causes you to be rather self-centered, you must have basked in Pisces' unconditional love. Yet feminine-polarity, mutable Pisces' emotions can swing wildly in a barometerlike response to others' behavior, and your fiery tantrums and heedlessness may frequently have triggered some disconcerting tears.

Children: Leo's sunny nature and self-belief must delight you if you are his or her Pisces parent, but you may frequently wish that your child wouldn't act on impulse, illustrating the contrast between the lion's polarity and element and your own. Proud lion cubs hate to look stupid, so try appealing to your child's dignity by pointing out that being rash can have precisely this effect.

Although the waves of love emanating from your little Pisces may wash over you in the most disarming of ways, you may occasionally find him or her exasperating if you are a Leo. Maybe it is because Pisces is so inconsistent, due to the fishes' mutable quadruplicity, whereas you are constant, thanks to your fixed one, in which case try to inspire your child to stay on track by leading by example.

Sibling Relationships: Leo's vitality and spontaneity and Pisces' delicacy and changeability may have been a recipe for highly charged emotions when you were small if you and your sibling were born under these signs, but an important plus point may have been the profound affection that underpinned your relationship.

Pisces Birth Influences

Ruling planet: Neptune; traditionally Jupiter
Element: Water
Polarity: Feminine
Quadruplicity: Mutable

♆ ♃ ≋

The bond between Leo and Pisces siblings will usually be exceptionally supportive.

Leo Birth Influences

Ruling planet: The Sun
Element: Fire
Polarity: Masculine
Quadruplicity: Fixed

VIRGO
VIRGO

Virgo Birth Influences
Ruling planet: Mercury
Element: Earth
Polarity: Feminine
Quadruplicity: Mutable

There should be no lack of communication between a Virgo parent and child, for whom talking things through comes naturally.

Virgo Birth Influences
Ruling planet: Mercury
Element: Earth
Polarity: Feminine
Quadruplicity: Mutable

Virgo relations rarely find one another annoying, even if their finicky ways exasperate relatives born under other signs. Their shared feminine polarity and planetary governor cause these two to be thoughtful, objective people, their earthy element also making them orderly, and their mutable quadruplicity giving them a need to be constantly occupied, so that their rapport is typically based on their mutual understanding and interests. Their tendency to find fault may sometimes give rise to petty bickering, however.

Parents: If you and your parent are both Virgos, you probably had a close—but not claustrophobic—relationship when you were growing up. The union of the element of earth and a feminine polarity within Virgo senior may have resulted in your parent being someone who was patient, constant, and supportive, while the influence of Mercury and a mutable quadruplicity may have manifested itself as a propensity to deliver mini-lectures on a range of subjects, which you may have soaked up if, like many Virgo juniors, you were all ears and eager for information. But as tidy or organized as you may have been in comparison to your non-Virgoan friends or siblings, there may have been times when your fastidious parent made it clear that you were not quite measuring up to his or her meticulous standards.

Children: The restlessness imparted by a mutable quadruplicity can be particularly pronounced in little zodiacal virgins, as you may already have discovered if you and your child are Virgos. Indeed, your busy schedule may no longer allow you sufficient downtime for boredom to set in, but you may remember being just the same at that age. Their feminine polarity makes young Virgos self-contained individuals, while Mercury's gift is intelligence and a thirst for learning, which means that working on a challenging puzzle or reading an educational book may be the perfect distraction for your twitchy child. Alternatively, try giving him or her a small chore that will transform the appearance of your home. Earthy Virgos of all ages relish shipshape surroundings, and some light polishing or weeding, for example, may therefore be just the thing to divert and gratify your down-to-earth child.

Sibling Relationships: Both Mercury and a mutable quadruplicity are associated with communication, and if you and your sibling are Virgos, your youthful relationship may consequently have resembled an ongoing conversation. Although the occasional squabble may have broken out if one criticized the other, mutable Virgos dislike conflict, so you probably soon reverted to neutral ground.

LIBRA — VIRGO

Virgo and Libra relatives generally operate on an even keel, mainly because both dislike upset. That said, Virgo's realism may sometimes bore Libra, just as Libra's self-indulgence may exasperate Virgo. Even so, each can learn a lot from the other, with Virgo teaching Libra to be more responsible, and Libra instructing Virgo in the importance of relaxation.

Parents: You may have taken your Virgo parent for granted when you were young if you are a Libra, but may now appreciate how hard he or she worked to keep you on track. Having an earthy element and feminine polarity causes Virgos to be both sensible and supportive, whereas airy, cardinal Libras are more impractical and self-centered, which is why your parent may sometimes have seemed tediously straight, and perhaps even a killjoy. But then you may today recognize that you benefited from your parent's astute guidance.

Your inward-looking, feminine polarity and complex, mutable quadruplicity may have made you something of a worrier when you were small if you are a Virgo, and if your parent is a Libra, he or she may have had a unique ability to dispel your fears. A masculine polarity causes Libran individuals to be positive, a cardinal quadruplicity gives them a can-do mindset, while Venus encourages them to take a laid-back approach, all of which may have heartened you. But being a perceptive, Mercury-ruled person, you may frequently have felt that diplomatic Libra was telling you what you wanted to hear rather than the unvarnished truth.

Children: If you are the Venus-governed, Libran parent of an earthy Virgo, you may be a little saddened by your child's tendency to put duty before fun, even if you know that Virgo's conscientiousness will stand him or her in good stead. Try to bring out your child's mercurial and mutable, variety-loving side by arranging plenty of intellectual diversions that you can both enjoy and discuss.

You may find it difficult to be cross with your engaging little Libra if you are his or her Virgo parent, but may wish that fibbing didn't come so naturally to your child. Airy Libra may be trying to fend off censure by being economical with the truth, so try to curb your criticism.

Sibling Relationships: Neither of you are particularly emotional if you and your sibling are a Virgo and a Libra, which is why your relationship may not have been that profound as children. A bonus may have been constant communication and consequent exposure to different viewpoints, however.

Libra Birth Influences

Ruling planet: Venus
Element: Air
Polarity: Masculine
Quadruplicity: Cardinal

A young Virgo can be a worrier sometimes, but fortunately a Libra parent will always be positive and help to put things into perspective.

Virgo Birth Influences

Ruling planet: Mercury
Element: Earth
Polarity: Feminine
Quadruplicity: Mutable

VIRGO
SCORPIO

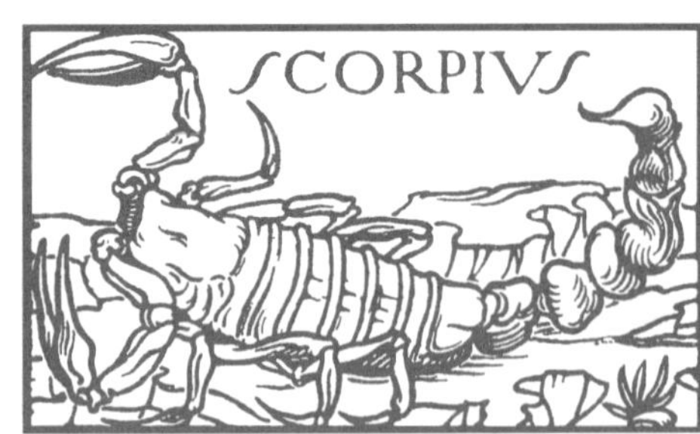

Virgo Birth Influences

Ruling planet: Mercury
Element: Earth
Polarity: Feminine
Quadruplicity: Mutable

Scorpios need stability and security when they are growing up, and a Virgo parent is likely to provide the steady support that they need.

Scorpio Birth Influences

Ruling planet: Pluto; traditionally Mars
Element: Water
Polarity: Feminine
Quadruplicity: Fixed

Having a happy and stable home life is vital to the mental well-being of both Virgo and Scorpio, partly because their shared feminine polarity is traditionally associated with domesticity, and partly because the support of loved ones gives them a much-needed sense of security. With earthy Virgo typically taking care of the practicalities, and watery Scorpio providing emotional backup, they generally interact harmoniously, except when rational, Mercury-governed Virgo hurts Scorpio's feelings, or when Scorpio descends into a dark, Plutonic sulk.

Parents: Having a fixed quadruplicity means that Scorpios dislike change, which is why your earthy, Virgo parent's household routines may have been comforting if you are a Scorpio, even if his or her enjoyment of variety—the legacy of a mutable quadruplicity—sometimes unsettled you. And because the combination of your feminine polarity and element of water no doubt make you introspective and sensitive, you may have been grateful for earthy, mercurial Virgo's rational and sensible counsel whenever you felt particularly confused or anxious.

You, too, can be a worrier if you are a Virgo (again due to your shared polarity, but in your case reinforced by your changeable, mutable quadruplicity), and when you were small, you may have been reassured by your watery, fixed-quadruplicity, Scorpio parent's compassion and unconditional love. Yet your parent may sometimes have been the cause of your angst, for if Pluto-ruled scorpions feel unappreciated, they tend to sink into brooding silence, so that you may have feared that you'd done something wrong, but had no idea what.

Children: You may marvel at your Virgo child's analytical mind if you are his or her instinctive Scorpio parent, but may wish that he or she were a little more empathetic when you are feeling low. Communication is the key to getting through to Virgos, so translate your emotions into words, and you may discover that Virgo is more understanding than you thought.

Scorpio's touchiness and stubbornness may concern you if you are his or her Virgo parent, particularly if you've triggered these traits by trying to steer your child in a certain direction. Respect Scorpio's strength of character, but be more tactful!

Sibling Relationships: If you and your sibling are a Virgo and a Scorpio, Virgo may have been relatively straightforward, and Scorpio, complicated, but you probably liked, and were loyal to, one another. That said, Virgo's restlessness may have disconcerted Scorpio, while Scorpio's secretiveness may have acted as an irritant on Virgo.

SAGITTARIUS

VIRGO

Although their mutable quadruplicity gives Virgo and Sagittarius an appetite for change, these two are otherwise very different. Under the combined sway of Mercury, an earthy element, and a feminine polarity, Virgo may be dispassionate, steady, and introspective, whereas Jupiter, fire, and a masculine polarity may cause Sagittarius to be jovial, spontaneous, and outgoing. Add Virgo's restraint and critical tongue, and Sagittarius' impulsiveness and forthrightness, to a hothouse family environment, and disagreements are inevitable. All in all, it is just as well that their mutable quadruplicity gives them flexibility.

Parents: As a youngster, you may have had mixed feelings about your Virgo parent if you are a Sagittarius. Being expected to adhere to earthy Virgo's routines and tidy ways may frequently have inflamed your fiery impatience, for instance, yet Virgo may have been the person to whom you turned when you needed advice. And if a double dose of Mercury and a mutable quadruplicity gave your parent the urge to travel, your birth influences suggest that you enjoyed exploring the wider world.

You may have been somewhat unsettled by the uninhibited spontaneity of your Sagittarian parent when you were small if you are a Virgo, whose polarity and element may make you far more cautious and even-tempered. But Mercury and your mutable quadruplicity bestow curiosity and intelligence upon you, too, and you may consequently recall occasions when your instructive, Jupiter-governed parent awakened your interest by exposing you to certain educational experiences.

Children: Your sensible Virgo child may give you little cause for concern if you are a Sagittarius, but you may wish that he or she would respond more enthusiastically to your spur-of-the-moment suggestions. Analytical Virgos prefer to ponder all aspects of a proposal before committing themselves, so leave the offer open while encouraging your child to consider the positives rather than the negatives.

You may find little Sagittarius' optimism and zest for life heart-warming if you are a Virgo, yet may worry that his or her recklessness will land your child in real trouble one day. If so, be warned that nagging may prove counterproductive; instead, as neutrally as possible explain the benefits of thinking before acting.

Sibling Relationships: Both Virgo and Sagittarius are communicative signs, and if you and your sibling were born under them, constant chatter may have been a feature of your relationship. Virgo's fault-finding or Sagittarius' brutal honesty may have provoked a few short-lived rows, however.

Sagittarius Birth Influences

Ruling planet: Jupiter
Element: Fire
Polarity: Masculine
Quadruplicity: Mutable

Sagittarius and Virgo siblings are most likely to be found talking—unless they've just had a fight and are in a temporary sulk.

Virgo Birth Influences

Ruling planet: Mercury
Element: Earth
Polarity: Feminine
Quadruplicity: Mutable

VIRGO
CAPRICORN

Virgo Birth Influences

Ruling planet: Mercury
Element: Earth
Polarity: Feminine
Quadruplicity: Mutable

Both Virgo and Capricorn enjoy productive domestic pursuits, and a Virgo parent will enjoy teaching as much as young Capricorn likes to learn.

Capricorn Birth Influences

Ruling planet: Saturn
Element: Earth
Polarity: Feminine
Quadruplicity: Cardinal

A house that is home to a Virgo and a Capricorn is likely to be buzzing with productivity, for these are earthy, practical people who need to be occupied. Being feminine-polarity individuals, these two are usually also self-contained characters, although Virgo keeps the channels of communication open, while Capricorn's powerful sense of responsibility may manifest itself as the urge to keep mutable Virgo on track. Their relationship may seem dull to outsiders, but their mutable and cardinal quadruplicities provide the diversity and drive that lift it above the mundane.

Parents: You may have had a comfortable relationship with your Virgo parent if you are a Capricorn. Because you share a feminine polarity and element of earth, you may have been in tune with Virgo's contemplative mindset, and may also have embraced your parent's routines. Mercury and their mutable quadruplicity make Virgoans both well informed and communicative, and because your own governing planet is associated with learning, you may be grateful for the knowledge that your parent imparted to you, although it may sometimes have been difficult to keep up with Virgo's rapidly changing thought processes.

If you had any quibbles about your Capricorn parent when you were younger, if you are a Virgo, one of them may have been his or her reticence, for protégés of the Roman messenger god are on a constant information-gathering mission, and Saturn's influence can make Capricorn particularly reserved. Another may have been cardinal Capricorn's focus on his or her responsibilities, but then being realistic and perceptive, you may have recognized that your parent's priority was providing for you.

Children: Your Virgo child's inquiring mind must be a source of delight if you are a Capricorn, yet you may be concerned that mutable Virgo's restlessness will hinder your child's progress. If so, don't fret too much because your common earthy element also gives Virgo steadiness.

You may admire Capricorn's concentration if you are his or her Virgo parent, but if you believe that variety is the spice of life, may worry that this ingredient is missing from Capricorn's. Try to pique Capricorn's interest in a new activity once in a while.

Sibling Relationships: You were probably on the same wavelength as children if you and your sibling are a Virgo and a Capricorn, even if you wished that mutable Virgo weren't such a chatterbox if you are a Capricorn, and you took exception to saturnine Capricorn's tendency to tell you to grow up if you are a Virgo.

AQUARIUS

VIRGO

Although Virgo and Aquarius are verbal people, their dispassionate birth influences usually ensure that any arguments are few and far between. Indeed, the only traits that are likely to trigger each other's irritation are feminine-polarity Virgo's negativity and fixed-sign Aquarius' unbending opinions. Both being intelligent individuals, Mercury-ruled Virgo's objectivity and Uranus-governed Aquarius' independence of thought create a natural intellectual bond between them.

Parents: Your earthy, Virgo parent's tendency to organize you may have irked you as a child if you are an airy, freedom-loving Aquarius, but because you are also easygoing, you probably didn't make too much fuss. And anyway, there may have been compensations. If you were a curious youngster, your mercurial parent may have answered your questions readily and knowledgeably, for example.

If you are a Virgo, your mutable quadruplicity may have made you exceptionally restless as a child, particularly when there was nothing to occupy your mind, in which case your airy, Uranian, Aquarius parent may have had a talent for diverting you, perhaps with an ingenious word game. Your parent's erratic behavior may have made you feel rather insecure, however, if, like most earthy Virgos, you prize constancy.

Children: You must approve of the analytical skills that may already be evident in your mutable, mercurial Virgo child if you are an Aquarius, especially if your airy element gives you the same investigative instincts. Yet having a masculine, or extrovert, polarity, you may not understand why more introvert, feminine-polarity Virgo frets over trifles. When Virgo appears glumly preoccupied, encourage your child to talk through his or her fears with you, for it may just be that a combination of attention and logic puts them to rest.

Your little Aquarius' radical ideas may astound you if you are his or her Virgo parent. Astrologers term Uranus, Aquarius' planetary governor, the "higher octave of Mercury," which means that you may be on the same wavelength, but Aquarius thinks more unconventionally than you. In addition, while your earthy element causes you to be realistic, air encourages Aquarius to be anything but. Don't try to suppress Aquarius' inventiveness, yet at the same time, neutrally explain why some of his or her wilder notions may be impractical.

Sibling Relationships: If you and your sibling are a Virgo and an Aquarius, you may have spent much of your childhood talking, usually happily, but sometimes sharply if Virgo was very critical, or Aquarius was too self-opinionated.

Aquarius Birth Influences

Ruling planet: Uranus; traditionally Saturn
Element: Air
Polarity: Masculine
Quadruplicity: Fixed

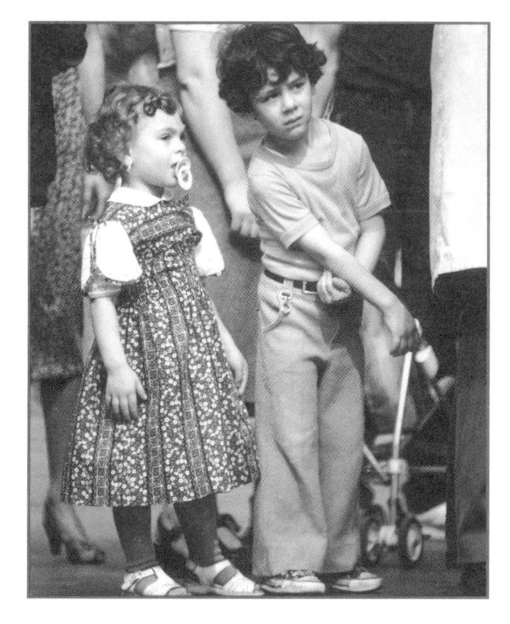

Virgo and Aquarius siblings will spend much of their time talking—occasionally arguing, but usually getting along.

Virgo Birth Influences

Ruling planet: Mercury
Element: Earth
Polarity: Feminine
Quadruplicity: Mutable

VIRGO

PISCES

Virgo Birth Influences

Ruling planet: Mercury
Element: Earth
Polarity: Feminine
Quadruplicity: Mutable

A Pisces parent will be unconditionally loving and supportive of his or her children and will always take an interest in their hobbies and activities.

Pisces Birth Influences

Ruling planet: Neptune; traditionally Jupiter
Element: Water
Polarity: Feminine
Quadruplicity: Mutable

Having a settled home life and supportive relatives is important to both Virgo and Pisces, partly because their shared, feminine polarity can make both somewhat shy and retiring, and partly because earthy Virgo requires stability, and watery Pisces, emotional sustenance. Yet although Virgo is a natural organizer, and Pisces, a born empathizer, Mercury-ruled Virgo may be irritated by Neptune-governed Pisces' disorderly ways, Pisces in turn being disappointed by Virgo's dispassion.

Parents: If you are a Pisces, it may sometimes have seemed as though your house-proud Virgo parent was suffering from obsessive–compulsive syndrome. Whereas Mercury-governed, earthy Virgo was probably both ultratidy and routine-loving, due to the influence of your own planetary ruler and element, you were no doubt comfortable with chaos and couldn't fathom why your messiness upset your feminine-polarity parent so much. You may, however, have commiserated with Virgo's distress, and may also have found your earthy parent's dependability a source of great reassurance.

There may have been times when you felt as though you were the parent, if you are an earthy Virgo, and your watery Pisces elder, the child in your relationship. You may frequently, for instance, have had to remind dreamy Pisces to keep an appointment, or have felt compelled to tidy up after him or her. That said, when a friend was mean to you, your Neptunian parent may have had an uncanny knack of tuning into your feelings and offering you heartfelt sympathy and encouragement.

Children: Although you may be gratified by your Virgo child's intelligence if you are a Pisces, you may wish that he or she were more able to imagine what it must be like to be in someone else's shoes. Your child may lack your profound insight, but not your fellow feeling, so explain that some people are more sensitive than Virgo and should therefore be treated gently.

Your Pisces child's altruism may disarm you if you are a Virgo. Even so, you may be worried by Pisces' gullibility, particularly if his or her playmates appear to be taking advantage of your child's caring nature. Try to instill some of your mercurial objectivity in Pisces, and make sure that you are not too critical.

Sibling Relationships: If Virgo and Pisces are you and your sibling's zodiacal signs, your relationship may generally have been harmonious when you were youngsters, not least because your mutable quadruplicity makes you both adaptable. Virgo's critical tongue and Pisces' absent-mindedness may have acted as irritants, however.

LIBRA
LIBRA

Two outgoing, masculine-polarity, Libra relatives won't be in much, but when they are at home together, conversation and laughter typically reverberate around the house. Sharing Venus as a planetary ruler makes them tolerant and self-indulgent types, while their airy element causes them to be bright, lively, and full of fun. But although their cardinal quadruplicity gives them a pioneering mindset, it also means that they like to have their own way, which, if they weren't such an easygoing duo, would be a potential flashpoint for bitter arguments.

Parents: You probably smile when you look back on your childhood if you are a Libra who grew up in the care of a fellow Libra. Whatever their age or family status, those born under the zodiacal sign of the balance tend to treat others as equals and hate uncomfortable atmospheres, so that you may have regarded Libra senior as more of a friend than a parent, and may rarely have exchanged hot-tempered or angry words with him or her. In addition, the combination of a masculine polarity and the influence of Venus may have resulted in your parent being an energetic culture vulture who frequently whisked you off to museums, movies, design centers, boutique shops, or exhibitions, and because you are both intelligent and communicative, airy people, you may subsequently have had long discussions about what you'd enjoyed seeing or hearing. Yet because air infuses Libras with a craving for personal freedom, and a cardinal quadruplicity can make them somewhat self-centered, you may not have seen as much of your parent as you would have liked.

Children: You may have few complaints about your clever, well-mannered, positive, Libra child if you are also a Libra, although on the occasions when his or her all-or-nothing, cardinal quadruplicity comes to the fore, little Libra may be quite demanding. Still, your shared airy element no doubt bestows a logical mindset upon your child, and Venus adds an abhorrence of unpleasantness, so it may be that he or she will accept your reasoning if you explain why you can't always be indulgent and give him or her everything that her heart desires. You may have to sweeten the pill with a treat, though!

Sibling Relationships: If you and your sibling are both Libras, you may each have had a delightful playmate in the other as youngsters, for Venus and air may together have bestowed an appetite for enjoyment upon the pair of you. Even so, there may have been a little cardinal-quadruplicity rivalry going on, compounded by some airy coolness when a Libran will was thwarted.

Libra Birth Influences
Ruling planet: Venus
Element: Air
Polarity: Masculine
Quadruplicity: Cardinal

If you're the proud Libra parent of a small bundle of Libra joy, you can look forward to a harmonious relationship with your child.

Libra Birth Influences
Ruling planet: Venus
Element: Air
Polarity: Masculine
Quadruplicity: Cardinal

LIBRA
SCORPIO

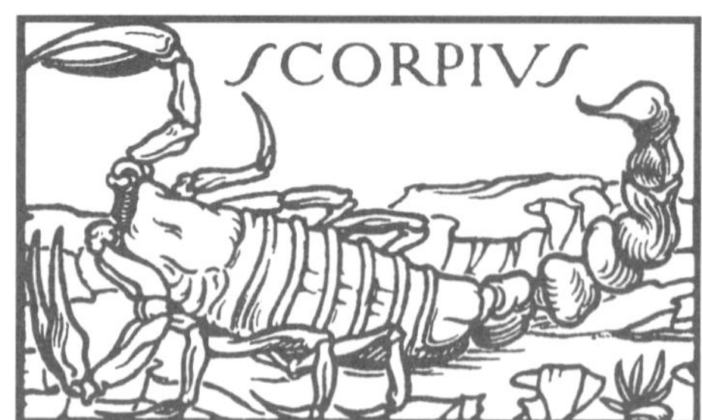

Libra Birth Influences

Ruling planet: Venus
Element: Air
Polarity: Masculine
Quadruplicity: Cardinal

A Libran parent's positive attitude sets a good example for a shy Scorpio child, encouraging him or her to gain self-confidence.

Scorpio Birth Influences

Ruling planet: Pluto; traditionally Mars
Element: Water
Polarity: Feminine
Quadruplicity: Fixed

Airy Libra's flightiness and Plutonian Scorpio's reticence may be irritants, yet relatives born under the signs of the balance and scorpion generally interact harmoniously, not least because Venusian Libra is a peacemaker, while fixed-sign Scorpio is loyal to family members. Indeed, while Libras can be almost impossible to fall out with, Scorpios have such a profound emotional attachment to their loved ones that they tend to regard them in the rosiest of lights.

Parents: You may have been a shy child if you are a feminine-polarity Scorpio, in which case your positive, masculine-polarity, Libran parent may have had a unique ability to boost your confidence. You probably adored being spoiled by your indulgent, Venus-influenced parent, too, but may have wished that he or she spent more time with you if this sign's enterprising, cardinal quadruplicity or gregarious, airy element often sent Libra out and about.

If you are a Venus-ruled Libra and your parent is a Pluto-governed, watery Scorpio, the intensity of his or her love for you may have made your younger self feel simultaneously like a star and suffocated, and especially the latter when your independence-demanding element and outgoing polarity asserted themselves. And although sensitive Scorpio may have retreated into a sulk when you flew out of the house set on having a good time, your airy charm and his or her devotion-bestowing, fixed quadruplicity probably ensured that your relationship was soon back on an even keel.

Children: Your bright, cheerful, talkative little Libra probably lights up your life if you are a Scorpio parent. If Venus and air cause Libra to be self-indulgent and impatient at times, however, try to impart some of your fixed-sign tenacity to your child by explaining why developing self-discipline and staying power is important.

Although you may frequently have difficulty figuring out what's going on in your Scorpio child's mind if you are a communicative Libra, the watery element that contributes to Scorpio's reserve may also manifest itself as empathy and compassion, so don't worry that your enigmatic little scorpion doesn't feel deeply connected to you.

Sibling Relationships: Your childhood rapport with your sibling, if he or she is a Libra and you are a Scorpio or the other way round, was probably based on mutual goodwill, perhaps because Libra's priority was keeping the peace, or maybe because Scorpio was caring. Even so, airy Libra may have been too emotionally detached for Scorpio's liking, while Libra may have been frustrated by Pluto-ruled, watery Scorpio's intense, private personality.

SAGITTARIUS

LIBRA

Whatever their age, Libra and Sagittarius relatives generally gel. Libra's pushy, cardinal quadruplicity and Sagittarius' frank, fiery element may occasionally cause annoyance, but because they usually have such a good time in each other's company, any friction is unlikely to last for long. Otherwise, combine indulgent Venus with jovial Jupiter, add a dash of airy curiosity and a sprinkling of mutable diversity, and bind the mix with a double helping of positive, masculine-polarity energy, and you have a recipe for a loving and lively relationship.

Parents: It would be surprising if you and your Libran parent ever seriously fell out if you are a Sagittarius. You may have a fiery temper and an aversion to being controlled, but airy, Venus-governed Libra is both steeped in charm and a natural peacekeeper, so that he or she may have had a velvet touch when it came to exerting parental authority over you, even if you sometimes resented Libra's cardinal-quadruplicity self-assertiveness.

If you are a Libra, you may have been happy to follow your exuberant Sagittarian parent's lead when you were a youngster. Your shared masculine polarity may have made you as outgoing as him or her, and you may have especially appreciated your fiery parent's generosity in buying you the beautiful things that you had set your heart on. Mutable Sagittarius can be moody, however, which may have unsettled you if you preferred an even atmosphere.

Children: You may suspect your cardinal-quadruplicity, Libran child of manipulating you if you are a Sagittarius, but may not mind if you enjoy spoiling him or her. Another thing that you may take pleasure in about your child is the way that Libra's airy questioning brings out the Jupiterian teacher in you.

You may smile at little Sagittarius' visionary ideas if you are a Libra, but may find the restlessness that is also the gift of a mutable quadruplicity rather trying. If so, start introducing your child to a range of the cultural and intellectual activities that you yourself enjoy, and you'll both be satisfied.

Sibling Relationships: "Anything for an easy life" may have been your motto when you were small if you are a Venusian Libra, which is why you may often have let your fiery Sagittarian sibling's rude comments go. Similarly, you may sometimes have considered your diplomatic Libran sibling hypocritical if you are an outspoken Sagittarius, but being quick to forgive, may not have made an issue of it. And anyway, why squabble when there was so much fun to be had together?

Sagittarius Birth Influences

Ruling planet: Jupiter
Element: Fire
Polarity: Masculine
Quadruplicity: Mutable

Libra and Sagittarius people usually have an easy, relaxed relationship and enjoy each other's company, helping to create a warm, lively atmosphere at family gatherings.

Libra Birth Influences

Ruling planet: Venus
Element: Air
Polarity: Masculine
Quadruplicity: Cardinal

LIBRA
CAPRICORN

Libra Birth Influences

Ruling planet: Venus
Element: Air
Polarity: Masculine
Quadruplicity: Cardinal

Sharing a cardinal quadruplicity, Libra and Capricorn siblings will often be found leading their friends when playing.

Capricorn Birth Influences

Ruling planet: Saturn
Element: Earth
Polarity: Feminine
Quadruplicity: Cardinal

A relationship between Libra and Capricorn family members is usually well balanced, and not just because Libra is said to be the sign of the balance (and anyway, the Libran scales can seesaw dramatically). Apart from their common, ambition-bestowing, cardinal quadruplicity, Libra and Capricorn's birth influences are associated with opposing characteristics, so that when pleasure-loving Venus and sober Saturn, impractical air and realistic earth, and an outgoing, masculine polarity and introspective, feminine one are exposed to one another, the result is usually equalization. And although some dissonance may occur, conciliatory Venus, mature Saturn, and a cardinal quadruplicity's drive may ensure that it is short-lived.

Parents: You may have been exasperated by your airy, Venus-governed, Libran parent's short attention span when you were growing up if you are an earthy, Saturn-ruled Capricorn, yet may not have minded constantly having to give him or her reminders. Indeed, a benefit may have been Libra's lively and cheerful presence, and your parent may also have been someone whose positive, masculine-polarity mindset gave you belief in your capabilities when your own negative, or feminine, polarity filled you with doubts about yourself.

You may have considered your earthy, Capricorn parent a rock of stability when you were young if you are an airy, volatile Libra who had a tendency to go where the wind blew, and often to extremes, particularly when self-indulgent Venus made it difficult for you to resist temptation. Steady Capricorn may always have been there to bring you back down to earth, but while you may have appreciated his or her determination to provide a steady, supportive home, you may frequently have wished that your saturnine parent would ease up once in a while.

Children: Your little Libra's charm and desire to please may make your heart melt if you are a Capricorn, yet you may worry that his or her airy intelligence gives your child a tendency to see—and take—short-cuts. If so, don't be a disciplinarian, and instead explain why hard work and application are often vital.

You may be relieved that your Capricorn child is so well behaved if you are a Libra who hates having to impose discipline. That said, if you fret that Capricorn seems to be trying to grow up too fast, keep things fun!

Sibling Relationships: If you and your sibling are a Libra and a Capricorn, you no doubt got on amicably as children, even if Libra had a wide circle of friends, while Capricorn was happier with his or her own company.

AQUARIUS

LIBRA

Because they have a masculine polarity and an airy element in common, a relationship between Libra and Aquarius family members is typically open, neutral, light-hearted, and easygoing. Yet although both are unemotional, positive types, their different ruling planets and quadruplicities may occasionally arouse annoyance, with independent, Uranus-governed Aquarius standing firm against cardinal Libra's pushiness, and tolerant, Venus-ruled Libra being exasperated by fixed-sign Aquarius' inflexibility and refusal to back down or apologise.

Parents: You may remember your childhood as being a time of exploration if you are an Aquarius with a Libran parent. You both have an inquisitive, airy element and uninhibited, masculine polarity, and Libra is furthermore indulgent, so that he or she may have encouraged you to follow your investigative, Uranian instincts, and may have applauded your enterprising notions. Libra may have been lenient and open-minded, yet may also have had soaring aspirations where you were concerned, which your freedom-seeking, somewhat rebellious side may have resisted, however.

If you are a Libra who was raised by an Aquarius, the memories that spring to mind when you look back on your youth may include your parent's obsession with new technology, a subject that may have bored you when you were under pleasure-loving Venus' sway. Still, you were probably grateful that your parent never talked down to you and shared your youthful outlook.

Children: You may delight in your airy, Libra child's cheerful temperament if you are an Aquarius, even if he or she is a little too money-oriented for your liking. In case you were wondering, it is the influence of Venus that causes Libra to be materialistic, whereas Uranus makes you more interested in abstracts. You may not understand this trait, but is being acquisitive so bad?

As a conciliatory person yourself if you are a Venusian Libra, you may wish that your Aquarian child were more willing to compromise at times. If so, take heart from the knowledge that persistence is also the gift of a fixed quadruplicity. And aren't you proud of Uranian Aquarius' inventive, individualistic mind?

Sibling Relationships: You may not have been that close, but probably communicated constantly as children if you and your sibling are a Libra and an Aquarius, be it swapping ideas or egging one another on in playful mischief. Libra's bossiness may have irked Aquarius, however, while Aquarius' pig-headedness may sometimes have got on Libra's nerves.

Aquarius Birth Influences

Ruling planet: Uranus; traditionally Saturn
Element: Air
Polarity: Masculine
Quadruplicity: Fixed

♅ ♄

An Aquarius child will probably be quite happy to entertain herself and will become absorbed in a world of her own, especially when she is discovering new experiences.

Libra Birth Influences

Ruling planet: Venus
Element: Air
Polarity: Masculine
Quadruplicity: Cardinal

LIBRA

PISCES

Libra Birth Influences

Ruling planet: Venus
Element: Air
Polarity: Masculine
Quadruplicity: Cardinal

A Pisces child is likely to be vulnerable and easily upset, so a Libra parent should always be prepared to offer a comforting cuddle.

Pisces Birth Influences

Ruling planet: Neptune; traditionally Jupiter
Element: Water
Polarity: Feminine
Quadruplicity: Mutable

It is their ruling planets, Venus and Neptune, that ensure that Libra and Pisces generally have an agreeable relationship, with Venus equipping Libra with pacific tendencies, and Neptune giving Pisces unselfish instincts. Having an extroverted, masculine polarity, a lively element in air, and a go-getting, cardinal quadruplicity, Libra is likely to be the more proactive, while a feminine polarity's receptiveness, a watery element's compassion, and a mutable quadruplicity's adaptability indicate that Pisces is happy to play a supportive role. Mild upset may, however, arise due to Libra's dispassionate, self-absorbed nature and Pisces' moodiness and oversensitivity.

Parents: Your childhood memories of your airy, Venus-ruled, Libran parent, if you are a Pisces, may be of an unruffled, indulgent, and positive person who had the magical ability to calm your anxieties and boost your confidence. That said, Libra's masculine polarity and cardinal quadruplicity may have made your parent an outgoing individual with personal ambitions to fulfill, while you may have craved the reassurance of him or her spending more time with you.

You may have the uncomfortable feeling that you sometimes took advantage of your Pisces parent's kindness when you were younger if you are a Libra whose airy charm and cardinal-quadruplicity determination usually result in you getting your own way. Your parent may not have minded, though, for Neptune infuses Pisces individuals with altruism, their watery element causes them to be caring, and their feminine polarity, to be rather passive. Yet being even-tempered yourself, you may often have been unsettled by mutable Pisces' mood swings.

Children: Although you may be proud of your clever, engaging little Libra, you may wish that he or she were more considerate if you are a Pisces. You have an intuitive element, and Libra, a logical one, which is why your child may lack your instinctive empathy. Venusian Libras nevertheless hate to hurt others, so explain that thinking of him- or herself alone often has this effect.

You are probably relieved that your young Pisces is willing to go along with your wishes if you are a Libra, but may be concerned that your trusting child is easily influenced, and upset, by his or her friends. Despite your cautions, this may never change, so always be ready to administer a comforting hug.

Sibling Relationships: Mutual gentleness and affection may have characterized your rapport as children if you and your sibling are a Libra and a Pisces, even if cool Libra was somewhat emotionally detached, and touchy Pisces, anything but.

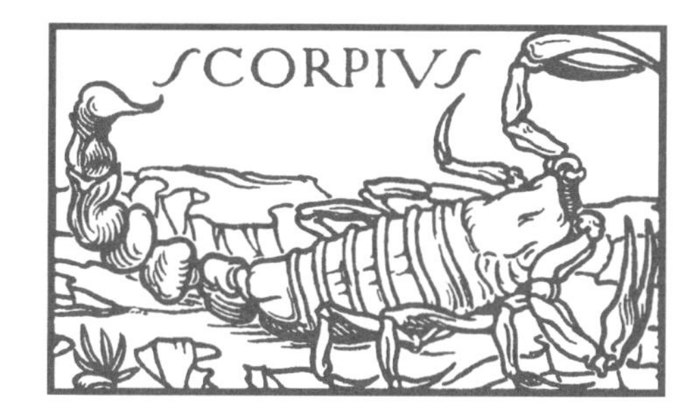

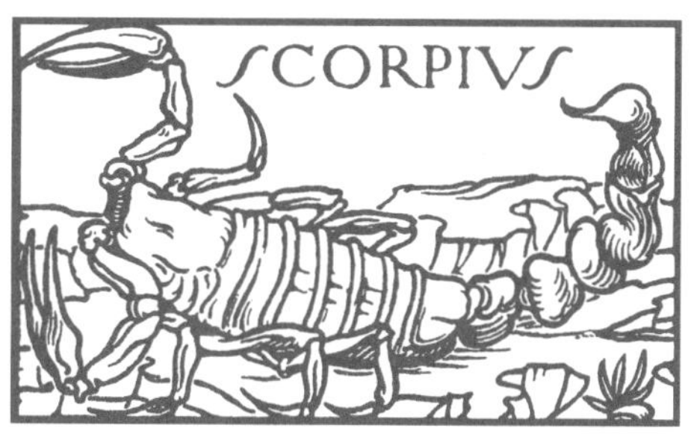

SCORPIO

SCORPIO

Their families usually mean everything to Scorpio individuals, and not just because their fixed quadruplicity makes them such loyal and committed types. Combine a feminine polarity, Pluto, and a watery element, and in scorpions you have people who are naturally reserved and find it difficult to connect with others, although they long for the security and affection inherent in close relationships. And it is in family members, especially if they are fellow Scorpios, that they typically find the love and understanding that they crave. That said, their mutual, fixed-quadruplicity obstinacy may sometimes trigger long-lasting disagreements, and they both tend to be moody.

Parents: You may have had a strong bond with your Scorpio parent when you were small if you are also a zodiacal scorpion, perhaps partly because your personalities are so similar, thanks to your shared birth influences, and partly because the element of water infuses Scorpios with profound intuition, empathy, and compassion. While your parent may have respected your water- and Pluto-bestowed need for privacy, he or she may have sensed when you were bottling up worries, may gently have encouraged you to divulge them, and may then have heartened you by imparting a piece of Plutonian wisdom, namely that no situation is so hopeless that it cannot be transformed for the better. The few occasions when you had a difference of opinion may have been very upsetting, however, for both being fixed-quadruplicity people, it is unlikely that either of you readily backed down.

Children: You must adore your little scorpion's intensely caring nature if you are his or her Scorpio parent, but may fret about the emotional vulnerability that is part and parcel of having a watery element. If your heart aches when Scorpio comes home in tears after a friend's been mean, try not to be too overprotective of him or her—after all, you won't always be there to fight your child's battles. Instead, explain that not everyone in this world is kind, that nasty comments shouldn't be taken too personally, and that whatever happens, you will always remain devoted to him or her. And if you find your Scorpio youngster's stubbornness exasperating, he or she probably feels the same way about your own intransigence!

Sibling Relationships: Although Pluto, water, and your feminine polarity may have caused you to inhabit little worlds of your own if you and your sibling are both Scorpios, your affection for one another is unlikely to have been in doubt, even if you each used silence as a weapon when annoyed with the other's inflexibility.

Scorpio Birth Influences

Ruling planet: Pluto; traditionally Mars
Element: Water
Polarity: Feminine
Quadruplicity: Fixed

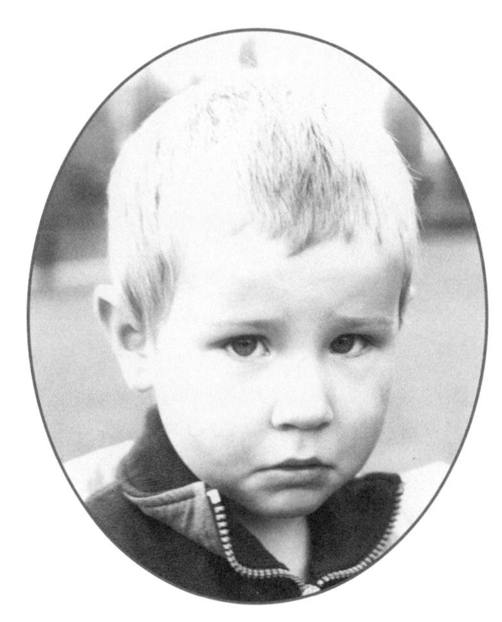

Instead of being overprotective, a Scorpio parent will need to help a wounded Scorpio child to learn how to deal with life's ups and downs.

Scorpio Birth Influences

Ruling planet: Pluto; traditionally Mars
Element: Water
Polarity: Feminine
Quadruplicity: Fixed

SCORPIO
SAGITTARIUS

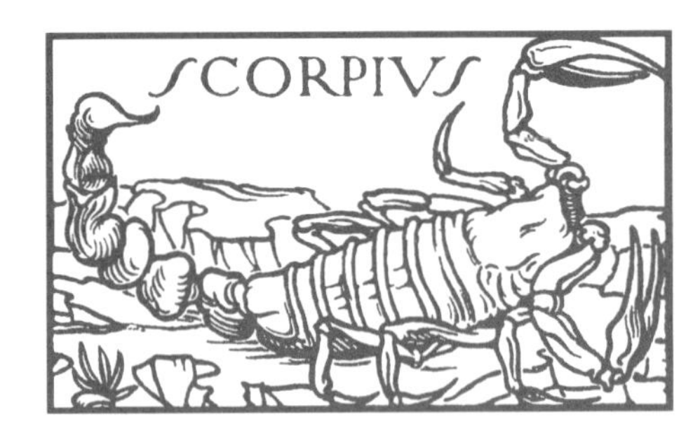

Scorpio Birth Influences

Ruling planet: Pluto; traditionally Mars
Element: Water
Polarity: Feminine
Quadruplicity: Fixed

If you are a Sagittarian parent, you may be exasperated by young Scorpio's moodiness, but your positive personality should help him to bounce back when he's feeling down.

Sagittarius Birth Influences

Ruling planet: Jupiter
Element: Fire
Polarity: Masculine
Quadruplicity: Mutable

Scorpio and Sagittarius relatives are unlikely to enjoy a relaxed relationship, despite their mutual affection and the benevolent influence of Jupiter, Sagittarius' ruling planet. For while watery, fixed-quadruplicity Scorpios are both caring and devoted to their loved ones, they can be possessive and uncompromising, and whereas fiery, mutable-quadruplicity Sagittarians are warm-hearted and easygoing, they may be uncontrollable and erratic. It doesn't help that Pluto, Scorpio's planetary governor, is associated with eruptions, but then a plus point is that it has the power to effect a wonderful transformation in these relations' rapport as the years pass.

Parents: Now that you are an adult, if you are a Sagittarius, you may be touched by your Scorpio parent's empathy, yet it may have been a very different story when you were growing up. Having an adventurous, fiery element and uninhibited, masculine polarity, you may have been forever pulling away from protective Scorpio's restraint, and may have rebelled against his or her inflexibility, too. You may now recognize, however, that your devoted, Scorpio parent had your best interests at heart.

While your fiery, Jupiter-governed, Sagittarius parent may have exerted an energizing and heartening influence over you when you were younger if you are a feminine-polarity Scorpio, you may have found his or her mutable-quadruplicity restlessness distressing. A fixed quadruplicity imbues scorpions with a dislike of change, and water makes them exceptionally sensitive and prone to insecurity, so that there may have been times when your sense of having triggered Sagittarius' impatience or irritation made you feel deeply miserable.

Children: When it manifests itself, you may marvel at your little scorpion's watery intuition if you are a Sagittarius, but because he or she is usually so unforthcoming, may consider your child an enigma. Don't use a direct, masculine-polarity approach to force Scorpio to open up, and instead encourage your child to communicate more with you by boosting his or her confidence with approval and reassurance.

Despite your devotion to your ardent Sagittarian child, you may worry that your young archer's spontaneity and wildness will land him or her in real trouble one day if you are a cautious Scorpio. If so, be warned that nagging may alienate Sagittarius, so try to allow him or her to learn from experience.

Sibling Relationships: If you and your sibling are a Scorpio and a Sagittarius, although you have probably always inhabited different planets, you may nevertheless care deeply about one another, even if it takes a crisis to prove it!

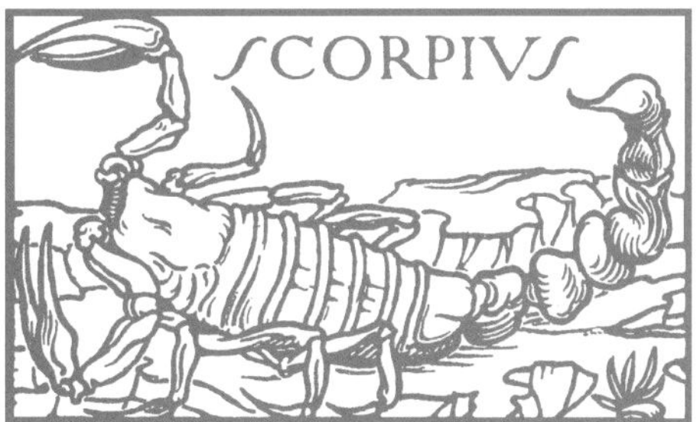

CAPRICORN

SCORPIO

Although Scorpio and Capricorn relatives usually care deeply about one another, it may not always seem so, for they have an undemonstrative, feminine polarity in common, which, in Scorpio's case, is compounded by isolating Pluto and the reticence of a watery element. And it is a cardinal quadruplicity's urge to lead and Saturn's soberness that can cause Capricorn to be demanding and controlling. Fortunately, Scorpio's fixed quadruplicity and Capricorn's earthy element are both associated with dedication, while the combination of slow-moving Saturn and Pluto suggests that this relationship will become more and more affectionate as time goes by.

Parents: When you were small, you may not have had a strong connection with your Scorpio parent if you a Capricorn, be it because enigmatic Pluto made him or her so difficult to read or because earth and Saturn cause you to have a straightforward mindset, and your cardinal quadruplicity can make you rather self-absorbed. As you grew older, however, you may have increasingly recognized the depth of your parent's love for you and how greatly you benefited from Scorpio's empathetic backup.

If you are a Scorpio with a Capricorn parent, you may have considered him or her a dependable anchor who gave your life stability when you were a child, and having a fixed quadruplicity, probably found his or her earthy routines comforting. You may now understand that saturnine Capricorn had your best interests at heart, yet your watery, emotional younger self may have felt misunderstood by dispassionate Capricorn, as well as under too much pressure to fulfill his or her high expectations, which may have aroused your fixed-quadruplicity obstinacy.

Children: You may approve of your fixed-quadruplicity, Scorpio child's tenacity if you are an earthy, Saturn-ruled Capricorn, but may think that he or she needs toughening up if the consequence of having a watery element is oversensitivity. Don't be too stern, though, lest sensitive Scorpio becomes withdrawn and resentful.

Your Capricorn child's mature, saturnine outlook may astound you if you are his or her Scorpio parent, yet because your watery element infuses you with compassion, and earthy, cardinal-quadruplicity Capricorn is both pragmatic and self-interested, you may wish that he or she showed more fellow feeling. You can't change Capricorn's birth influences, so be grateful that earth makes your child so loyal.

Sibling Relationships: Your youthful relationship may have been restrained if you and your sibling are a feminine-polarity Scorpio and Capricorn, yet you no doubt supported one another when necessary, Scorpio, emotionally, and Capricorn, practically.

Capricorn Birth Influences

Ruling planet: Saturn
Element: Earth
Polarity: Feminine
Quadruplicity: Cardinal

Capricorn and Scorpio siblings may not appear to have a close emotional bond, but can nevertheless always count on each other.

Scorpio Birth Influences

Ruling planet: Pluto; traditionally Mars
Element: Water
Polarity: Feminine
Quadruplicity: Fixed

SCORPIO

AQUARIUS

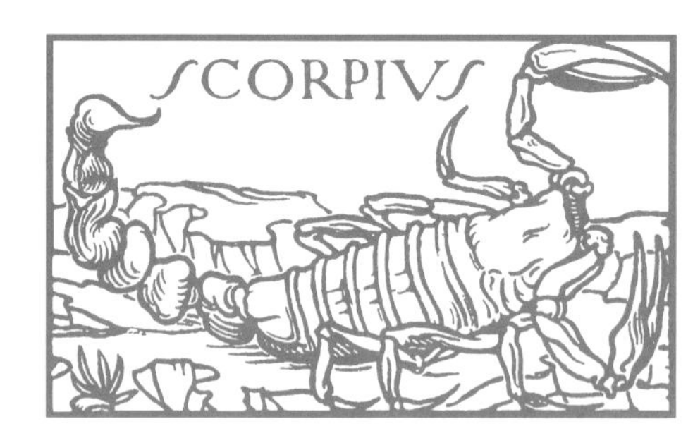

Scorpio Birth Influences

Ruling planet: Pluto; traditionally Mars
Element: Water
Polarity: Feminine
Quadruplicity: Fixed

Having very different personalities, Scorpio and Aquarius siblings may need a diversion to keep them interested and the atmosphere calm.

Aquarius Birth Influences

Ruling planet: Uranus; traditionally Saturn
Element: Air
Polarity: Masculine
Quadruplicity: Fixed

At first sight, it may appear as though watery Scorpio's emotional neediness and powerful attachment to loved ones and airy, impersonal Aquarius' desire for independence may result in these relatives being permanently at odds, yet this generally isn't so, for Scorpio is also empathetic, and Aquarius, tolerant. And although Uranus may cause Aquarius to challenge conventional family values, thereby sometimes hurting sensitive Scorpio, having a fixed quadruplicity in common means that both are fundamentally faithful to one another.

Parents: The combination of uncommunicative Pluto, an inward-looking, feminine polarity, and the inarticulacy that is often a side effect of having a watery element may have made your Scorpio parent more unforthcoming than you would have liked when you were younger if you are a chatty, airy Aquarius, but you probably never doubted the intensity of the fixed-quadruplicity scorpion's devotion to you. Even if having an outgoing, masculine polarity and freedom-seeking, airy element meant that you felt compelled to break away from Scorpio at times, your fixed quadruplicity may always have brought you back again.

Your masculine-polarity, Aquarian parent may have exerted a positive influence over your younger self when your own feminine, or negative, polarity and gloomy Pluto depressed your mood if you are a Scorpio, and you may have appreciated his or her airy, undemanding manner, too. That said, because your element is intuitive water, you may have felt that Aquarius didn't comprehend the depth of your childish fears when you were in the doldrums, or recognize your longing for a hug rather than some blithe words effectively telling you to snap out of it.

Children: Despite your pride in your little scorpion's fixed-quadruplicity willpower, you may be concerned that he or she seems unsociable if you are an Aquarius. If so, it may help to know that zodiacal scorpions prefer to have a few good friends whom they can trust to lots of casual acquaintances, illustrating the difference between Scorpio's self-protective, watery element and your gregarious, airy one.

You may adore your airy, Aquarius child's engaging charm if you are a Scorpio, but not the way in which he or she may dispassionately question your authority. Be assured that this isn't a sign of hostility, just a manifestation of airy, Uranian individuality.

Sibling Relationships: Scorpio being introverted, and Aquarius, extroverted, you may not have been close as children if you and your sibling were born under these signs, yet may still have enjoyed a mutually loyal and affectionate relationship.

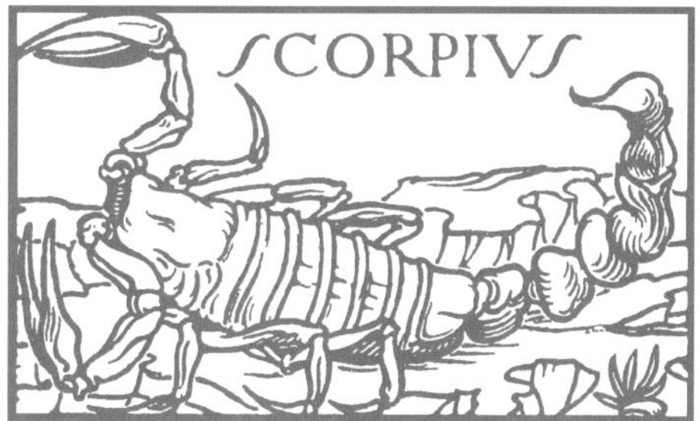

PISCES
SCORPIO

Start with a double dose of watery domesticity, add two introspective, feminine polarities, and then throw Pluto's secrecy and Neptune's dreaminess into the mix, and it is likely that Scorpio and Pisces relatives will spend a lot of time together, but often within their respective inner worlds. Their element of water is associated with both intuition and emotion, which suggests that these two nevertheless have a profound instinctive bond, and if fixed Scorpio's inflexibility and mutable Pisces' restlessness sometimes tests its strength, then these same birth influences can also provide the faithfulness and adaptability that ensure that it remains intact.

Parents: If you are a Pisces and your element of water and feminine polarity riddled you with insecurities and worries as a child, your Scorpio parent may have been the most reassuring and soothing of consolers. Because Scorpio shares your element and polarity, your parent may have implicitly understood your fears and known exactly how to dispel them. Scorpio may have supplied the stability that made you feel safe and secure, too, even if you found your parent's unvarying routines tedious.

You must have adored your Pisces parent when you were young if you are a Scorpio, for Neptune and water together make Pisceans altruistic, compassionate, and loving people who put their children's happiness first. Pisces' Neptunian vagueness and changeable, mutable-quadruplicity moods may have troubled if you yearned for his or her constant attention, however.

Children: Although you may sense when your Scorpio youngster is feeling down if you are a watery, Neptune-governed Pisces, you may wish that your child were more forthcoming about his or her problems so that you could get to the root of the matter, in which case blame the influence of taciturn Pluto. The steadfastness of Scorpio's love for you must lighten your life, though.

Your Neptune-governed, Pisces child's unselfish desire to please must touch you deeply if you are a Scorpio, yet you may be concerned that people could take advantage of this heart-warming trait should Pluto make you suspicious of others' motives. You can't change your child's inborn altruism, and experience will teach Pisces about trustworthiness, so in the meantime be ready to act as a comforter when necessary.

Sibling Relationships: Your relationship may always have been affectionate and mutually supportive if you and your sibling are a Scorpio and a Pisces. That said, fixed-quadruplicity Scorpio's stubbornness may sometimes have upset Pisces, while mutable Pisces' inconsistency may have annoyed Scorpio.

Pisces Birth Influences

Ruling planet: Neptune; traditionally Jupiter
Element: Water
Polarity: Feminine
Quadruplicity: Mutable

♆ ♃ ♒

Scorpio and Pisces relatives are likely to share an extremely close, loving relationship.

Scorpio Birth Influences

Ruling planet: Pluto; traditionally Mars
Element: Water
Polarity: Feminine
Quadruplicity: Fixed

SAGITTARIUS

SAGITTARIUS

Sagittarius Birth Influences

Ruling planet: Jupiter
Element: Fire
Polarity: Masculine
Quadruplicity: Mutable

If you are the Sagittarius parent of a child who shares your star sign, you'll understand his or her sense of adventure. His or her friends and siblings may be less daring, however!

Sagittarius Birth Influences

Ruling planet: Jupiter
Element: Fire
Polarity: Masculine
Quadruplicity: Mutable

Benevolent Jupiter smiles on a pair of Sagittarian relatives and blesses them with a bond that is based on mutual joviality, to which their fiery element adds warmth, their masculine polarity, a positive attitude, and their mutable quadruplicity, adaptability. As a result, these good-natured relations usually get on well, and even if one's fiery rashness or self-assertiveness sometimes causes the other's own hot temper fleetingly to flare, neither likes to quarrel.

Parents: If you are the Sagittarian child of a Sagittarius, your recollection of your childhood may be jam-packed with memories of the diverse activities that you enjoyed together, while your parent's words of Jovian wisdom may still echo in your mind. Because you share a mutable, or restless, quadruplicity, as well as an energetic, masculine polarity and stimulation-seeking, fiery element, your parent's relish of exposing you to all manner of experiences, particularly those that aroused your fiery sense of adventure, may have exhilarated you. And if the influence of Jupiter brought out the teacher in your Sagittarian parent, you may have been fascinated by the knowledge that he or she imparted. Yet because you may have regarded your Sagittarian elder as an equal, and fiery, mutable, zodiacal archers are on the one hand gregarious folk and, on the other, hate being barred from anything, you may have occasionally been infuriated when your parent wouldn't allow you to accompany him or her to a strictly adults-only event.

Children: You no doubt see a lot of your younger self in your Sagittarian child if you are also a zodiacal archer, including, perhaps, the fiery, masculine-polarity recklessness that may have caused your own despairing parents to beg you to think twice before flinging yourself headlong into a potentially hazardous situation. If so, you may know that Jupiter-ruled, Sagittarian youngsters both hope for the best and learn from experience. You could nonetheless limit your little Sagittarius' opportunities to get into trouble by ensuring that you spend as much time together as possible pursuing a wide range of interests that enthuse you both, which shouldn't be a hardship for a variety-loving person like you, especially if you feel like a child at heart and have a cheerful and lively young playmate.

Sibling Relationships: The two of you must have been a high-spirited handful if you and your sibling were both born under the exuberant sign of the archer. You may have been good friends, but given your forceful, fiery natures, some blazing rows may nevertheless have briefly inflamed your relationship.

CAPRICORN

SAGITTARIUS

Whatever their actual age or relationship, it may sometimes seem as though Sagittarius remains a perpetual child, while Capricorn was born mature. For whereas Sagittarius believes that anything is possible, and is furthermore spontaneous, uninhibited, and has a short attention span, Capricorn is realistic, steady, thoughtful, and formidably focused. Yet although Sagittarius may encourage Capricorn both to lighten up and loosen up, and Capricorn may rein in some of Sagittarius' wilder impulses, they may still feel that they have little in common.

Parents: Because Jupiter is associated with wisdom, and Saturn, with learning, your Jovian, Sagittarian parent may have imparted many valuable lessons to your younger self if you are a saturnine Capricorn, although longing for some peace and quiet may be your abiding childhood memory. Your polarity is feminine, or introverted, while Sagittarius' is masculine, or extroverted, and while your cardinal quadruplicity and earthy element may have filled your head with plans for the future that you were doggedly working toward, mutable-quadruplicity, fiery Sagittarius may forever have distracted you by sweeping you off in search of stimulation.

Having as you do a restless, mutable quadruplicity, an unrestrained, fiery element, and an active, masculine polarity if you are a Sagittarius, you may have spent much of your youth trying to break free of your cautious Capricorn parent's control. Fiery people hate being constrained, and Saturn-governed Capricorns can be restrictive, albeit in their children's best interests. Looking back, however, you may now realize how much you depended on earthy, organized Capricorn to keep you on track.

Children: Even if you find your Sagittarian child's warm, positive nature irresistibly appealing if you are a Capricorn, you may worry that he or she is too easily distracted. If so, don't reprove your youngster unless absolutely necessary, and instead line up a variety of activities to keep that restless, mutable mind occupied.

It may amuse and impress you that your child is so sensible if he or she is a Capricorn and you are a Sagittarius, but you may be concerned that fun doesn't seem to feature much in your kid's life. Unlike you, Capricorns are unsettled by excitement, so don't try to push your child into behaving uncharacteristically.

Sibling Relationships: If you and your sibling are a Sagittarius and a Capricorn, thank goodness that the archer is adaptable and easygoing, and the goat, patient and phlegmatic, otherwise you'd have had a disastrous relationship rather than merely a somewhat disengaged one!

Capricorn Birth Influences

Ruling planet: Saturn
Element: Earth
Polarity: Feminine
Quadruplicity: Cardinal

Sagittarius is interested in most things, while Capricorn is willing to share. These siblings usually get on, even if they are rarely on the same planet.

Sagittarius Birth Influences

Ruling planet: Jupiter
Element: Fire
Polarity: Masculine
Quadruplicity: Mutable

SAGITTARIUS
AQUARIUS

Sagittarius Birth Influences

Ruling planet: Jupiter
Element: Fire
Polarity: Masculine
Quadruplicity: Mutable

A Sagittarius parent often behaves as though he or she is the same age as little Aquarius!

Aquarius Birth Influences

Ruling planet: Uranus; traditionally Saturn
Element: Air
Polarity: Masculine
Quadruplicity: Fixed

Jovian Sagittarius may be cheerful, and airy Aquarius, easygoing, but they are unlikely to have a profound emotional bond. These individuals are far more interested in lively, intellectual interaction, mainly due to Sagittarius' mutable quadruplicity and Aquarius' airy element, and tend to treat one another as equals, whatever their relationship. As a result, they may be uninhibited in expressing themselves, and if fixed-quadruplicity Aquarius' stubbornness occasionally infuriates Sagittarius, a fiery outburst may be the result, while mutable-quadruplicity Sagittarius' lack of constancy may sometimes provoke a cool response from Aquarius.

Parents: Airy young Aquarians have a pronounced sense of fun, and if you were once one of them, your exuberant, Sagittarian parent may have been an ideal playmate, despite the age gap. Sagittarius' fiery element and mutable quadruplicity may have caused your parent to be spontaneous, and because Uranus may have sharpened your appetite for experimentation, you no doubt enjoyed the activities to which he or she introduced you. You may have been unsettled by Sagittarius' unpredictability, though, if your fixed quadruplicity gave you a longing for stability.

Your Aquarian parent may have been a source of inspiration to your younger self if you are a Sagittarius, for if your fiery element infused you with a craving for mental stimulation, it may have been thrillingly satisfied by his or her inventive, Uranian notions. Devoted, fixed-quadruplicity Aquarius may also have always been there for you, thereby fulfilling your fiery need for attention, but thanks to his or her airy element, in breeziest of ways, so that you didn't feel suffocated. You may, however, have been impatient with Aquarius' resistance to change when your mutable, or restless, quadruplicity exerted an especially strong influence over you.

Children: You may revel in your Sagittarius child's confidence if you are an Aquarius who shares his or her masculine polarity, yet your fixed quadruplicity may make you wish that your impetuous young archer displayed more staying power.

Your little Aquarius' original ideas may delight you if you are a creative, fiery Sagittarius, even if you aren't so keen on his or her fixed-quadruplicity stubbornness, particularly when you're trying to open your child's eyes to alternative viewpoints.

Sibling Relationships: Sagittarius may have been the more temperamental and impulsive, and airy Aquarius, more dispassionate and steady, if you and your sibling are a zodiacal archer and water-carrier, which may have given rise to a few disagreements. Even so, you probably had an affectionate rapport overall.

PISCES
SAGITTARIUS

It is thanks to their shared, mutable quadruplicity that Sagittarius and Pisces are generally an amicable pair, Sagittarius' Jovian benevolence and fiery warmth and Pisces' Neptunian unselfishness and watery empathy also boding well for their relationship. Their personalities may otherwise be markedly dissimilar, however, and although their differences may strengthen their bond, fiery Sagittarius' need for independence and Pisces' longing for emotional closeness may test it at times.

Parents: Your Sagittarian parent may have been a cheerful and reassuring presence during your childhood if you are a Pisces. For whereas your feminine polarity and watery element may have filled you with doubts and fears—worsened by Neptune's confusing influence—Sagittarius' masculine polarity and fiery element, along with optimistic Jupiter, may have given your parent a gift for dispelling your worries and prompting you to think positively. Even so, your watery, Neptunian intuition may have made you recognize that your timidity often aroused fiery, mutable Sagittarius' impatience.

Having altruistic Neptune as a planetary ruler and a caring element in water, your Pisces parent probably couldn't do enough for you when you were small, which may have gratified you if you are a Sagittarius whose fiery element causes you to enjoy being the center of attention. It may also have given you a craving for freedom, however, and although Pisces may have understood your restlessness, your parent may have been saddened by your urge to break free of his or her protective embrace.

Children: Your little Sagittarius' burning enthusiasm may light up your days if you are a Pisces, yet you may wish that he or she weren't so hot-tempered when being restrained, especially if fiery outbursts send you on a emotional rollercoaster ride. When Sagittarius is on the verge of a tantrum, enlist your mutable quadruplicity by swiftly proposing an activity that will distract your child.

When you've had a tough day, his or her watery compassion may warm your heart if you are the Sagittarian parent of a Pisces child, even if you worry that your youngster is overdependent on you. Having a mutable quadruplicity makes your child sociable, so try broadening Pisces' horizons.

Sibling Relationships: If you and your sibling are a Sagittarius and a Pisces, masculine-polarity Sagittarius may have been more outgoing than homebody, feminine-polarity Pisces, but you may nevertheless have liked and supported one another when you were younger. That said, Sagittarius' outspokenness may sometimes have wounded sensitive Pisces, and Pisces' shyness may have exasperated self-assured Sagittarius.

Pisces Birth Influences

Ruling planet: Neptune; traditionally Jupiter
Element: Water
Polarity: Feminine
Quadruplicity: Mutable

Sagittarius parents should try to help Pisces children to overcome their shyness by encouraging them to meet potential playmates.

Sagittarius Birth Influences

Ruling planet: Jupiter
Element: Fire
Polarity: Masculine
Quadruplicity: Mutable

CAPRICORN

CAPRICORN

Capricorn Birth Influences

Ruling planet: Saturn
Element: Earth
Polarity: Feminine
Quadruplicity: Cardinal

Capricorn siblings usually both look out for each other and are steadily supportive, be they little kids or adult goats.

Capricorn Birth Influences

Ruling planet: Saturn
Element: Earth
Polarity: Feminine
Quadruplicity: Cardinal

A house that is home to a pair of Capricorns is likely to be buzzing with productivity, for thanks to their driving, cardinal quadruplicity and the serious intent with which Saturn, their ruling planet, endows them, these relatives have ambitious plans that they generally pursue with unswerving dedication, even in their spare time. Nor will they neglect their household chores, for their feminine polarity and element of earth may cause them to find comfort in domestic routines. These two may understand and respect one another, yet if their goals differ, may not have a deep emotional connection.

Parents: Your Saturn-ruled, Capricorn parent was almost certainly devoted to you if you were also born under the astrological sign of the goat, and may have expressed his or her love in typically practical, earthy style by ensuring that you were well clothed, fed, and educated, thereby satisfying your own need for stability. Having a feminine polarity in common may have made you and your parent equally contemplative and receptive to one another's opinions, and if your cardinal quadruplicity gave you high aspirations, you may have benefited from your earthy, saturnine, Capricorn elder's realistic and mature advice and steady guidance in setting you on the path toward realizing your dreams. Your dedicated, hard-working parent may furthermore have been a formidable role model, although a downside may have been that you didn't see that much of him or her. And if Capricorn senior cherished the fond hope that you would follow in his or her footsteps when you grew up, you may have found it difficult to break the news if you had alternative ideas in mind.

Children: If you and your child are both Capricorns, you may be delighted that your kid appears blessed with a number of virtues that will stand him or her in good stead in the future, maybe including the diligence that is the gift of Saturn, the patience that is the contribution of earth, and the motivation that comes from having a cardinal quadruplicity. You may, however, be worried that he or she is too unforthcoming, a feminine-polarity trait that you may understand because you share it, too, but that may make it difficult to get to the root of the problem when your Capricorn youngster is clearly worried or preoccupied.

Sibling Relationships: You probably enjoyed an even childhood relationship if you are your sibling are Capricorns, even if your respective focus on your individual interests meant that you weren't that engaged with one another. You have no doubt found that your dependable sibling is always there for you, however.

AQUARIUS
CAPRICORN

Capricorn and Aquarius relatives are unlikely to argue much, for earthy Capricorn is patient and matter of fact, while airy Aquarius is amiable and tolerant. They can be good for one another, too, with Saturn-governed, feminine-polarity Capricorn restraining Aquarius when necessary, and Uranus-ruled, masculine-polarity Aquarius encouraging Capricorn to be more imaginative. Capricorn's bossiness and Aquarius' obstinacy may sometimes sour the atmosphere between them, though.

Parents: Having a fixed quadruplicity may mean that you dislike change if you are an Aquarius, in which case you may happily have gone along with your earthy, Capricorn parent's domestic routines when you were a youngster. You may not have appreciated Capricorn's tendency to bring you back down to earth when you took off on an exploratory flight of fancy, however, yet, looking back, may now recognize that your feminine-polarity parent's caution was justified.

Being raised by an Aquarian parent must have been an enlivening experience if you are a Capricorn. Whereas your feminine polarity, planetary ruler, and earthy element may have caused you to be a rather cautious, reserved, and sensible child, Aquarius' corresponding birth influences may have resulted in your parent being positive, lively, and bursting with novel suggestions, thereby boosting your confidence and broadening your mind. Yet there may have been times when Saturn made you wish that your parent were less eccentric.

Children: Although you may have few concerns about your level-headed, Capricorn child, one of them may be that he or she is a little too unadventurous for your liking if you are a free-thinking, outgoing Aquarius. If so, you may be relieved to know that your child is indeed a self-starter, just that this cardinal characteristic is disguised by prudent Saturn, steady earth, and a passive, feminine polarity.

Your little Aquarius' airy cheerfulness must charm you, and his or her fixed-quadruplicity loyalty, gratify you if you are an earthy Capricorn. Even so, you may worry that your Aquarian youngster's Uranian ideas are verging on the anarchic, and that your child's unconventional approach will cause difficulties for him or her at school, and eventually, work. Don't suppress Aquarius' originality, and instead appeal to his or her airy logic by explaining why it is sometimes necessary to conform.

Sibling Relationships: You and your sibling may have had a good-natured childhood relationship if you are a Capricorn and an Aquarius, but both being self-willed, may nonetheless have disagreed occasionally.

Aquarius Birth Influences

Ruling planet: Uranus; traditionally Saturn
Element: Air
Polarity: Masculine
Quadruplicity: Fixed

♅ ♄

An Aquarius child may soon show signs of rebelling against a cautious, Capricorn parent.

Capricorn Birth Influences

Ruling planet: Saturn
Element: Earth
Polarity: Feminine
Quadruplicity: Cardinal

♄ 

CAPRICORN
PISCES

Capricorn Birth Influences

Ruling planet: Saturn
Element: Earth
Polarity: Feminine
Quadruplicity: Cardinal

Pisces parents are typically caring, empathetic, and emotionally supportive. Little Capricorns are likely to thrive when bathed in Pisces' unconditional love.

Pisces Birth Influences

Ruling planet: Neptune; traditionally Jupiter
Element: Water
Polarity: Feminine
Quadruplicity: Mutable

Sharing as they do a feminine, or inward-looking, polarity, it is important to a pair of Capricorn and Pisces relatives that they have a happy home, and thankfully they usually do. Being a realist, earthy Capricorn may take care of practicalities, while watery Pisces' forte is providing emotional support. Tension may, however, be generated by their respective ruling planets and quadruplicities, for while saturnine, cardinal Capricorn may be a disciplinarian with high expectations, Neptunian, mutable Pisces may be a dreamer who lacks constancy.

Parents: If you are a Pisces, what you may have appreciated the most about your Capricorn parent is the sense of stability that he or she gave your younger self. If your mutable quadruplicity and watery element caused you to feel emotionally unsettled, earthy, Saturn-governed Capricorn's steady devotion may have kept you on an even keel, for example. Yet you may have disliked the pressure that Capricorn put you under to aim for a conventional career and material success, when your Neptune-inspired dreams may have been of making a selfless contribution to the world.

Although you may have adored your kind and caring Pisces parent if you are a Capricorn, you were probably a straightforward, earthy youngster, in which case you may have been exasperated by his or her Neptunian vagueness and watery absent-mindedness. Still, if your feminine polarity made you rather shy at school, it may have been wonderful to come home to someone so loving, whose gentle interest encouraged you to open up, and who listened with sympathy.

Children: You may be awestruck by your young Capricorn's sensible, earthy nature and Saturn-bestowed sense of duty if you are a Pisces, yet may wish that your child were less self-centered. But then only fellow Pisceans share your exceptional unselfishness and compassion, and at least Capricorn isn't as thin-skinned as you.

There may be many qualities that you admire in your little Pisces if you are a Capricorn, such as his or her mutable-quadruplicity flexibility, although you may be less enamored of the changeability that is also associated with this birth influence. If so, enlist your earthy patience, and when he or she wavers, encourage Pisces to stick with an activity or decision.

Sibling Relationships: Even if your childhood relationship was generally good-natured if you and your sibling are a Capricorn and a Pisces, Capricorn's insensitivity may occasionally have reduced Pisces to tears, while Pisces' tendency to go to emotional extremes may have annoyed Capricorn.

AQUARIUS
AQUARIUS

The wonderful thing about a relationship between two Aquarian family members is that they usually genuinely like, and are interested in, each other, although they would be unusual if they made emotional demands of one another or displayed their affection overtly, for these airy types are both independent and dispassionate. Indeed, thanks to the interaction of their element and ruling planet, their bond is strongly intellectual, and because they share a masculine polarity, also open and uninhibited. And the glue that holds them together is typically their committed, fixed quadruplicity, which may, however, also make them equally unyielding when their opinions or wishes conflict.

Parents: If you and your parent were both born under the sign of the water-carrier, you may have regarded your elder as more of a friend than an authority figure when you were young, and not just because Uranian, Aquarian individuals of all ages have an aversion to playing conventional family roles. Your masculine polarity may have caused you both to be extroverts, and your airy element, communicative, which suggests that your rapport was probably founded on the no-holds-barred conversations that you had with one another, fueled, no doubt, by the enterprising influence that Uranus exerted over you both. Your airy parent may generally have been easygoing, yet there may nonetheless have been times when you were irritated by his or her adamant, fixed-quadruplicity refusal to let you behave exactly as you pleased.

Children: You must delight in your little Aquarius' airy curiosity and inventive, Uranian way of thinking, as well as in the confidence with which your child expresses him- or herself, if you are a free-thinking Aquarius, too. You may furthermore enjoy introducing little Aquarius to your own pet theories or interests, and may even be inspired when your child asks a question that sends you off on a voyage of exploration and discovery together. But you may be less enthused by the fixed-quadruplicity obstinacy that Aquarius junior may display when you don't see eye to eye.

Sibling Relationships: If you and your sibling are both Aquarians, the only occasions when your cheerful, childhood chatter may have given way to cool silence is if a disagreement triggered your joint, fixed-quadruplicity stubbornness. In addition, because you may both have had a Uranian fascination with all things mechanical and technical, you may often have squabbled about whose turn it was to play with the newest gadget to enter your household. Otherwise, your relationship was almost certainly friendly and mutually stimulating.

Aquarius Birth Influences
Ruling planet: Uranus; traditionally Saturn
Element: Air
Polarity: Masculine
Quadruplicity: Fixed

Aquarius siblings should get along well—as long as they are willing to share their toys!

Aquarius Birth Influences
Ruling planet: Uranus; traditionally Saturn
Element: Air
Polarity: Masculine
Quadruplicity: Fixed

AQUARIUS
PISCES

Aquarius Birth Influences

Ruling planet: Uranus; traditionally Saturn
Element: Air
Polarity: Masculine
Quadruplicity: Fixed

When your Pisces child seems worried or bewildered, encourage her to think positively, Aquarius.

Pisces Birth Influences

Ruling planet: Neptune; traditionally Jupiter
Element: Water
Polarity: Feminine
Quadruplicity: Mutable

They may be dissimilar, but that doesn't mean that Aquarius and Pisces relatives often clash. Indeed, given that Aquarius may be calm and constant, and Pisces, gentle and adaptable, they are likely to have an easy, affectionate bond. And while masculine-polarity, Uranus-governed Aquarius may inject energy into their relationship, feminine-polarity, Neptune-ruled Pisces may be instinctively supportive. Airy Aquarius' need for independence and watery Pisces' longing for closeness may occasionally give rise to friction, however.

Parents: The problem with having a changeable, mutable quadruplicity, an emotion-heightening element in water, and muddling Neptune as a planetary ruler is that you may often have felt moody, anxious, and confused as a child if you are a Pisces. If so, your Aquarian parent's fixed-quadruplicity steadiness and airy way of talking through your worries and logically laying them to rest, as well as his or her positive, masculine-polarity outlook, may have soothed and stabilized you. But you may have been disappointed that airy Aquarius wasn't more demonstrative.

You were probably a talkative child if you are an airy Aquarius, and no doubt bursting with ingenious, Uranian ideas, too, in which case you may have had a receptive and sympathetic audience in your watery, Piscean parent. Looking back, you may now realize how much Neptune-governed Pisces sacrificed for you, yet at the time may have felt stifled by your parent's devotion, and may consequently have felt compelled to assert your independence.

Children: As a Neptunian idealist, if you are a Pisces, you may be delighted that your Aquarian child has such progressive—even revolutionary—notions should the influence of Uranus be especially pronounced in him or her. You may find Aquarius' fixed-quaduplicity stubbornness painful, though, if your own instincts are mutable, or flexible, and it upsets you when you disagree.

You may be intrigued by the mysterious workings of your little Pisces' mind if you are a curious, airy Aquarius and may be deeply impressed by the astonishing intuition that is the joint gift of Neptune and water. But you may wish that Pisces weren't so insecure and clingy, particularly if you can't quite understand why your child craves your reassurance so much.

Sibling Relationships: You may have enjoyed a good-natured rapport with your sibling if one of you is an Aquarius and the other, a Pisces, even if it seemed as though you inhabited different planets, one logical, the other anything but!

PISCES

PISCES

Their families mean everything to Pisces individuals, for it is typically only when they are sure that they are loved and cherished that they feel secure enough to discard the feminine-polarity mantle of reserve that they typically don to protect their watery, sensitive feelings before venturing out into the wider world. Being both so gentle and caring, two watery, Piscean relatives blossom when they are together, the influence of unifying Neptune often causing them to feel as one, and their mutable quadruplicity enabling them to adapt to one another's fluctuating moods. The only problem may be that their mutable quaduplicity also gives each a craving for variety that the other may not be able to satisfy.

Pisces Birth Influences

Ruling planet: Neptune; traditionally Jupiter
Element: Water
Polarity: Feminine
Quadruplicity: Mutable

♆ ♃ ≈

Parents: If you are the Pisces child of a Piscean parent, he or she may have been the one to whom you instinctively turned for comfort and reassurance when you were young, particularly when Neptune and water had swamped you with feelings of confusion and insecurity. And it may only have been with Pisces that you felt able to let down your feminine-polarity guard and pour out your hurt or worries, safe in the knowledge that your parent would respond with compassionate concern. Indeed, there may have been many occasions when Pisces raised your spirits by sharing a nugget of a transcendental, Neptunian wisdom with you, which may have remained with you to this day. But because your parent may have been so selflessly focused on you, and your mutable quadruplicity may have given you an appetite for change, Pisces may sometimes have retreated into wounded silence when you opted to spend time with a playmate rather than with him or her, in turn making you feel guilty.

A loving and compassionate Pisces parent is superbly equipped to soothe a needy Pisces baby who requires constant reassurance.

Children: Although you may treasure your little Pisces' kindness and thoughtfulness if you are also a Pisces, it may trouble you that your child is so easily upset, not least because the combination of Neptune and water may result in you sharing his or her pain. You probably know that thin-skinned Pisceans never really toughen up as they grow older, so draw on your own experience to advise your child how best to rise above other people's meanness or lack of consideration.

Sibling Relationships: If you and your sibling are fellow Pisceans, Neptune and water may have blessed you with a profoundly intuitive and mutually supportive connection. Tears may nevertheless have been shed should one of you have felt rejected when the other went off alone to play with friends.

Pisces Birth Influences

Ruling planet: Neptune; traditionally Jupiter
Element: Water
Polarity: Feminine
Quadruplicity: Mutable

The only way to have a friend
is to be one.

Ralph Waldo Emerson, *"Friendship," Essays: First Series* (1841)

FRIENDS

When you consider that we can't choose our relatives or colleagues, and that the spell that love casts over us often causes us to view our lovers through a rosy mist of infatuation, a friendship is one of the few relationships that we clear-sightedly enter into. Or do we?

Locate the page that discusses you and your friend's respective birth influences, and how you consequently relate to one another, and the astrological assessment of your rapport may make it spookily apparent that many of the qualities that you like in one another are plus points bestowed on your friendship by your ruling planets, elements, polarities, or quadruplicities, and that your affinity with one another may therefore have been predestined. And should many of the positive observations on that page indeed ring true, you'd be wise to take the potential pitfalls that follow seriously. Friendships are all too easily broken when the cement that results from sharing a passionate attraction, a blood tie, or a contractual obligation is lacking, and frequently to the long-term detriment of both sides. So if you enjoy your friend's company, remember that to be forewarned is to be forearmed, and be prepared to ride out your differences when the going gets tough, as it almost inevitably will. Show the page in question to your friend, too, for as the American writer Elbert Hubbard sagely commented in *The Note Book* (1927), "Your friend is the man [or woman] who knows all about you, and still likes you." As well as following your guiding principle, try to exercise mutual tolerance and respect, and in years to come, you'll no doubt both be laughing at the doom-and-gloom scenario painted at the end of your common page, and will be continuing to revel in your life-enhancing friendship, whatever your compatibility rating.

ARIES / ARIES

Aries Birth Influences

Ruling planet: Mars
Element: Fire
Polarity: Masculine
Quadruplicity: Cardinal

When two strong-minded zodiacal rams come together in a social context, a fiery battle of wills is likely to ensue. Both are equally matched, so the resulting standoff will either end in a decisive parting of the ways or a deepening friendship based on mutual respect.

Plus points: Due to the feeling of rivalry that each triggers in the other, when Aries meets Aries for the first time, the encounter should be spectacular to watch, particularly if both are of the same sex. The potent combination of the Arien independent outlook, the tendency to regard themselves as leaders, and aggression causes each to consider the other a threat to his or her position among their circle of friends, and they will therefore instinctively try to outdo each other. Because neither will ever concede, this futile attempt at dominance will either end in one taking off in search of more congenial company or the situation being totally diffused with a dose of hearty Arien laughter and each offering the other the warm hand of friendship.

If you are an Aries, you are unlikely to be inseparable from your Aries friend—you are both too absorbed in your own interests, too much in need of fresh experiences, and ultimately too alike. Although there may be the occasional flare-up between the hot-tempered pair of you, you are both types who readily forgive and forget, as long as there is good will on both sides. Your respect for each other's dynamic qualities, love of adventure, and shared sense of humor will otherwise imbue your friendship with fun and understanding, and your relationship will become increasingly relaxed and affectionate as time goes by.

Two Aries can sometimes behave like a pair of drama queens when they're together.

Potential pitfalls: Huge difficulties will arise in a friendship between Aries and Aries if one—or both—persists in trying to command or master the other. No Aries will ever trot placidly at someone else's heel, and if you are an Aries who is constantly trying to force your fiery Arien friend to follow your lead or to acknowledge your superiority, be warned that a blazing, head-on confrontation will almost certainly result, and that your relationship will consequently be reduced to cinders.

Guiding principle: Understand your similarities, accept your equality, and you'll enjoy some riotous, heart-warming times together.

Aries Birth Influences

Ruling planet: Mars
Element: Fire
Polarity: Masculine
Quadruplicity: Cardinal

Compatibility:       

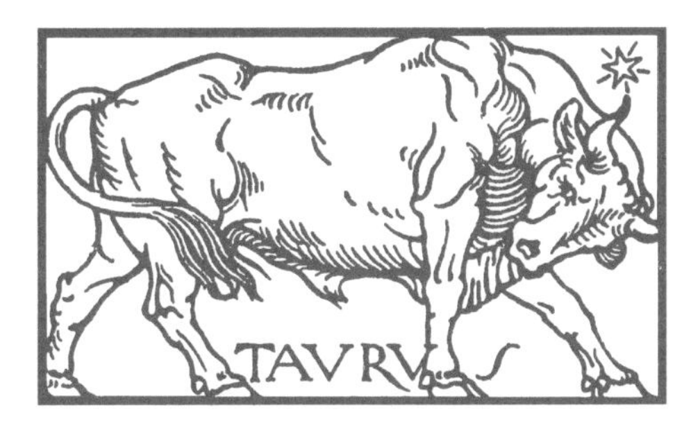

TAURUS

ARIES

Because Taureans prefer to relax, and Ariens to throw themselves headfirst into challenging activities, the paths of these two zodiacal signs will not often cross during their free time. Both are warm-hearted and loyal souls, however, so any friendship between them is likely to last for life.

Plus Points: Both Aries and Taurus are genuinely interested in others, so if ever-probing Aries persists in breaching Taurus' wall of self-contained reticence, he or she will become increasingly intent on getting to know that person better. If you are a Taurus, you will probably be simultaneously attracted and slightly alarmed by Aries' forthrightness and impulsiveness, and will take the time to assess his or her character thoroughly before committing yourself to a friendship with this pushy and dominating person.

When Taurus and Aries do become friends, their very different strengths will enrich their relationship. If you are an Aries, you may, for example, on the spur of the moment suggest going on vacation together to a far-flung destination. If you are Aries' home-loving, Taurean friend, you may initially reject the prospect as being too scary, but once you finally come round to the idea, you'll no doubt take over the practical planning of your vacation, and will do so far more meticulously than your impatient, big-picture friend could ever do. Warm-hearted Aries and steady Taurus make faithful friends, too, being always there for each other and ready to console and comfort the other in times of trouble.

Potential Pitfalls: Aries cannot stand inertia, while Taurus has couch-potato tendencies, which means that if you are an Aries, you'll often make forays away from your slow-moving friend in search of new and exciting people and ventures. Taurus may then feel neglected, and perhaps even jealous, but, on the other hand, resents your attempts to bully him or her into joining in the fun. And if you are a stoical zodiacal bull, it takes a lot of goading to make you lose your temper, but then the ram has a talent to do just this, and, being hot-tempered, will react in kind when you finally explode with fury. Another potential flashpoint may be ignited when straight-talking Aries offends well-mannered, Venus-ruled Taurus with an impetuous, rude comment.

Guiding Principle: Recognize that the other person's strengths are ones that you yourself sorely lack, and enhance your friendship by valuing them.

Compatibility: ☺ ☺ ☺ ☺ ☺ ☺ ☺ ☹ ☹ ☹

Taurus Birth Influences

Ruling planet: Venus
Element: Earth
Polarity: Feminine
Quadruplicity: Fixed

Did your Arien childhood friend lead you into all kinds of fun and adventure, Taurus?

Aries Birth Influences

Ruling planet: Mars
Element: Fire
Polarity: Masculine
Quadruplicity: Cardinal

ARIES
GEMINI

Aries Birth Influences
Ruling planet: Mars
Element: Fire
Polarity: Masculine
Quadruplicity: Cardinal

The conversation will never dry up when Aries and Gemini become friends, be it in the form of quick-fire banter or heated debates. Cardinal Aries may find airy Gemini's tendency to vacillate frustrating, however, while Gemini may resent the Arien propensity to demand and dominate.

Plus Points: Both Aries and Gemini thrive on social interaction, self-centered Aries being energized by an interested audience, and Gemini relishing the opportunity to learn more about what makes Aries tick. Neither are shy, but then neither are they indiscriminate when it comes to forming friendships, partly because emotional neediness is not part of the Gemini makeup, and partly because Aries won't waste time on people whom he or she doesn't consider sufficiently interesting. And in the case of this pairing, each has abundant supplies of what the other values in a friend.

If you are an Aries, you no doubt find your Gemini friend's quick-witted repartee, infectious sense of humor, and mischievous tendency to egg you on a source of delight. If you are a Gemini, you probably likewise revel in your Arien friend's talent for creating, or searching out, fun, and relish hearing what the adventurous ram's been up to during his or her frequent absences. Although your relationship will not be claustrophobically close, you may both be deeply fond of one another, and will give each other practical, if not emotional, support when necessary.

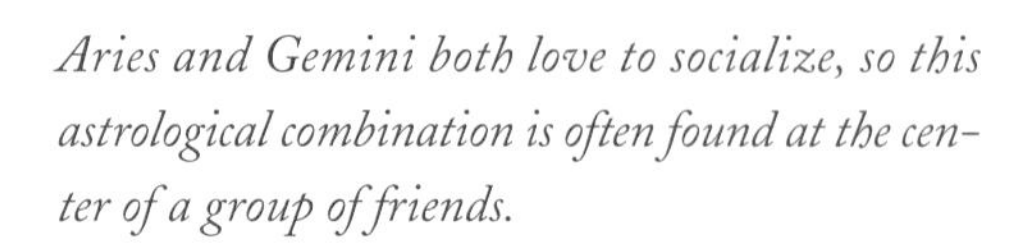

Aries and Gemini both love to socialize, so this astrological combination is often found at the center of a group of friends.

Potential Pitfalls: Problems may arise between Aries and Gemini friends if Aries demands more from Gemini than Gemini is willing to give. Being born under the two-dimensional sign of the twins, Gemini does not share the single-minded Arien approach, preferring to keep his or her options open and to explore all possibilities to rushing headlong into anything. If you are the Arien in this friendship, you therefore cannot help but annoy your friend by chivvying him or her into following your dynamic lead, and may be baffled when this strategy prompts mercurial Gemini to vanish into thin air. Fortunately, both of you keep your relationship fresh by pursuing your own interests, which means that neither of you feel neglected or threatened by your nonexclusive friendship. Aries may, however, be offended when subjected to Gemini's cool, analytical scrutiny, while Gemini may find being pressurized by hot-headed Aries to behave just as impulsively hard to tolerate.

Guiding Principle: Focus on your shared love of laughter and diversion, but don't take each other's criticism too personally.

Compatibility: ☺ ☺ ☺ ☺ ☺ ☺ ☺ ☹ ☹ ☹

Gemini Birth Influences
Ruling planet: Mercury
Element: Air
Polarity: Masculine
Quadruplicity: Mutable

CANCER
ARIES

Energetic Aries injects a dose of excitement into serene Cancer's life, while Cancer exerts a steadying influence on wayward Aries. If the headstrong ram butts Cancer too hard, however, the defensive crab will retaliate by extending a pincerlike claw and administering a painful nip.

Plus Points: One of the qualities that both Aries and Cancer value the most in a friend is loyalty, which augurs well for a friendship between the ram and the crab because both are guaranteed to come to the other's aid in times of trouble. If you are a protective Aries, you will defend your sensitive Cancerian friend to the hilt from verbal sticks and stones, while if you are a compassionate Cancer, you are no doubt always ready to offer a sympathetic ear whenever your Arien friend feels misunderstood or hard done by. During the good times, Cancer is usually invigorated by Aries' boldness and vitality, while Aries treasures Cancer's thoughtfulness and enjoys being fussed over and mothered after a tough day on the battlefield. Fiery Aries also appreciates watery Cancer's artistic leanings, while cautious Cancer admires Aries' enterprising spirit, although neither would go so far as to try to emulate their friend.

Potential Pitfalls: Cancer invests a huge amount of emotional energy in those for whom he or she feels deep affection, which means that this friendship may founder if Aries takes Cancer for granted or treats the crab insensitively. So be warned, Aries, that Cancer may feel betrayed if you abandon him or her for prolonged periods in pursuit of your latest enthusiasm, and that a careless critical comment may send the touchy crab into a seemingly endless sulk. And if you push Cancer too far, your friend may try to prevent you from upsetting him or her even more by striking out at you with astounding viciousness. As for you, Cancer, beware of smothering your Arien friend's feelings for you by demanding more than the active, free-spirited ram can ever provide. You may feel happiest when your friendship is drifting along calmly, yet Aries hates being static and will always urge you to be more adventurous. Similarly, expecting your friend to be as empathetic as you are is simply unrealistic, while clinging too tightly, or too long, to Aries for emotional support will drive the impatient, frequently self-centered ram away.

Guiding Principle: Don't let the differences in your respective personalities threaten your bond, but be grateful for the refreshing, complementary qualities that your friend brings to your relationship.

Compatibility: ☺ ☺ ☺ ☺ ☺ ☹ ☹ ☹ ☹ ☹

Cancer Birth Influences
Ruling planet: The Moon
Element: Water
Polarity: Feminine
Quadruplicity: Cardinal

Aries loves to party, so, Cancer, why not let your Arien friend liven up your life a little and persuade you to go out more?

Aries Birth Influences
Ruling planet: Mars
Element: Fire
Polarity: Masculine
Quadruplicity: Cardinal

ARIES

LEO

Aries Birth Influences

Ruling planet: Mars
Element: Fire
Polarity: Masculine
Quadruplicity: Cardinal

Make the most of your friendship, Leo and Aries, by going out together and indulging your mutual love of fun, parties, and dancing.

Leo Birth Influences

Ruling planet: The Sun
Element: Fire
Polarity: Masculine
Quadruplicity: Fixed

When Aries and Leo become friends, theirs will often be a life-long attachment based on mutual respect and delight in each other's invigorating company. Although their relationship is not stiflingly close, it is underpinned by a reservoir of warm affection and steadfast loyalty and features thrilling high points punctuated by a few fiery disagreements.

Plus Points: When it comes to enjoying themselves, Aries and Leo have very similar tastes. Both relish parties, for instance, outgoing Aries being stimulated by different personalities, and regal Leo adoring holding court at the center of a group of admirers. If you are a sociable Aries with an equally gregarious leonine friend, the pair of you will set out to have a good time, and will still be partying when those with less stamina have fallen by the wayside. If you are a sometimes languid Leo, it won't take long for Aries' infectious enthusiasm and audaciousness to energize you and arouse your sense of fun, while if you are an Aries, you may admire the lion's imperiousness, tolerance, and quick imagination. On a more profound level, you may each appreciate the other's direct, optimistic nature and staunch support, particularly in times of trouble.

Potential Pitfalls: Being both self-assertive, commanding types, Aries may bristle when he or she first meets Leo, who is used to lording it over others and whose hackles may similarly rise in response to a perceived threat to the lion's position. Having sized each other up, they will usually recognize a kindred brave spirit, typically then diffusing the stand-off with an injection of humor, yet the potential for the occasional intense battle of will remains. If you are an Aries, you may respect Leo's mental strength, but may be irritated by the air of pomposity that sometimes surrounds your dignified friend, while his or her tendency to be dogmatic may rattle your progressive nature. On such occasions, you may ridicule the proud lion or try to prod him or her into following your lead, no doubt thereby provoking a mighty roar of displeasure. And if you are a Leo, you may approve of Aries' independence of thought and love of action, but may hate it when the ram's attention wanders from you and may be infuriated when he or she doesn't treat you with the deference that you believe you deserve.

Guiding Principle: The hallmark of your friendship is warmth and fun, so take pleasure in carousing together rather than confronting each other over relatively trifling character differences.

Compatibility:       

VIRGO
ARIES

When vigorous Aries and hard-working Virgo become friends, their paths may not cross that often, but when they do get together, the encounter is always interesting. As long as Aries accepts Virgo's criticism as being well meant, and Virgo loosens up and becomes less uptight in Aries' company, this should be an enduring relationship.

Plus Points: Both Aries and Virgo are people-oriented signs of the zodiac that enjoy interacting with others. If you are an excitement-seeking Aries, coming into contact with new people energizes you, your Virgo friend similarly being stimulated by the cut and thrust of verbal exchanges. A fun-loving pair, not only do you both enjoy parties and other social occasions, but find plenty to talk about when you are alone together. If you are a complex Virgo, you probably find your Arien friend's straightforward view of the world refreshing, and may even feel surprisingly liberated on the rare occasions that the assertive ram persuades you to forget your inhibitions and act spontaneously. And if you are a single-minded Aries, Virgo's informed, well-argued advice may provide you with plenty of useful food for thought. You may find your friend a little more reserved than you'd like, but may know that if you are ever in need of practical help, you can always rely on Virgo, while Virgo can in turn depend on your loyalty and staunch support in times of crisis.

Potential Pitfalls: The same qualities that enrich a friendship between Aries and Virgo can sometimes sour their relationship. Conventional and prudent Virgo often views your adventurousness as extreme behavior, Aries, and sometimes finds your fire and passion threatening, especially when you are trying to involve him or her in something that your friend considers a foolhardy venture. Don't try to push him or her into matching your boldness and exuberance, however, because this will only drive Virgo away. As for you, Virgo, it's important to understand that although your element, earth, makes you a grounded and stable individual, hot-headed Aries is ruled by the element of fire, so that taking an all-consuming approach is therefore as natural to your friend as breathing. There's no point in constantly trying to point out the error of the Arien way because that will only make your friend defensive, and consequently even more aggressive and determined to follow his or her preferred path.

Guiding Principle: Learn from each other's different attitudes and methods, but remain true to your own natures.

Compatibility:     ☺    ☹ ☹

Virgo Birth Influences

Ruling planet: Mercury
Element: Earth
Polarity: Feminine
Quadruplicity: Mutable

Don't strain your friendship with an Aries by bearing grudges or sulking, Virgo, because he or she might overreact—or may even be too busy to notice!

Aries Birth Influences

Ruling planet: Mars
Element: Fire
Polarity: Masculine
Quadruplicity: Cardinal

♂ 

ARIES
LIBRA

Aries Birth Influences

Ruling planet: Mars
Element: Fire
Polarity: Masculine
Quadruplicity: Cardinal

Your Libra friend is an excellent communicator and will always be there for you—as long as you don't give your bluntness or fiery temper free rein, Aries.

Libra Birth Influences

Ruling planet: Venus
Element: Air
Polarity: Masculine
Quadruplicity: Cardinal

Because Aries and Libra are both gregarious signs, they are usually surrounded by a host of different personalities, but can nevertheless strike up a mutually appreciative and supportive friendship. Yet direct Aries may regard Libra's non-confrontational approach as hypocritical, while Aries' bluntness may grate on the more diplomatic, subtle Libra.

Plus Points: This zodiacal pair is stimulated and energized by social interaction, not least with each other. If you are an excitement-seeking Aries, you are no doubt forever leading the way in your quest for fresh experiences and may appreciate adaptable Libra's willingness to go along with you. You may also be a little in awe of your friend's talent for communicating easily and fluently with almost anyone, as well as of his or her Venusian interest in the arts and entertainment, which adds an extra dimension to your life. Aries can learn much from Libra, as can you, airy Libra, from the determined ram, such as speedily reaching a decision and then sticking to it rather than being swayed by different opinions and consequently blowing this way and that. Aries' emotional warmth also enlivens the somewhat dispassionate Libra, who in turn isn't afraid to direct a cooling blast of reason in Aries' direction if his or her enthusiasm becomes overheated.

Potential Pitfalls: Although it is difficult to fall out with dovelike Libra, your friend's preference for pacifying over confronting may occasionally anger you if you are a hawkish Aries. This may be especially so when you are arguing with a third person and feel that Libra should be giving you unconditional support and not undermining your position by acknowledging the validity of the other's point of view. Being an honest and direct character, you may also find your friend's tendency to greet someone enthusiastically when you know that Libra dislikes him or her two-faced. And if you are a Libra, you may equally recoil from the way in which forthright Aries impulsively speaks his or her mind without having considered the hurtful impact that such brutal candidness can have. You probably find Aries' pushiness somewhat tiring, too, and may wish that your fiery friend would try to control his or her quick temper because it is you who has to pick up the pieces in the aftermath of an Arien explosion.

Guiding Principle: Appreciate the positive influence that your friend has on your nature and don't become hung up on what you consider to be his or her negative qualities.

Compatibility:        ☹ ☹ ☹

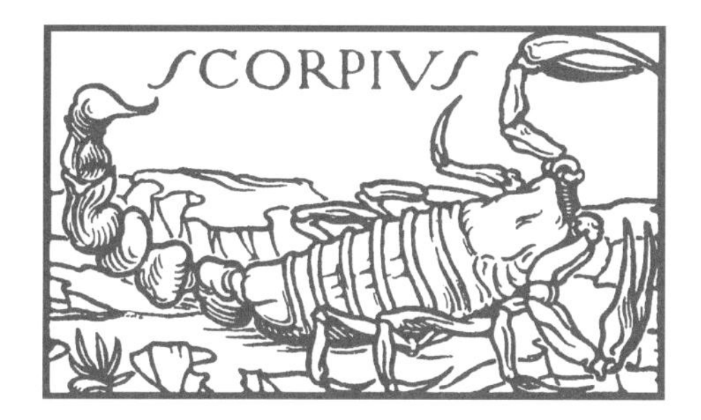

SCORPIO

ARIES

A friendship between Mars-influenced Aries and Scorpio is likely to be based on a love of action, and being both competitive and determined characters, they will spur each other on to attempt ever greater feats of daring. The fiery ram's sociability and touchy scorpion's self-containment may, however, cause friction.

Plus Points: When these fellow warriors first encounter one another, neither Aries nor Scorpio can resist the challenge of testing the other's mettle in a battle of wills. Because they are both formidably resolute, the result will typically be deadlock, but not lacking in mutual respect. If you are an energetic Aries, your friendship with Scorpio will usually be action-packed, be it focused on a sporting activity or a joint venture that channels your shared competitiveness positively. You may value your friend's talent for stimulating your interest with new and original ideas, and may also be grateful for his or her sympathetic ear when you're feeling discouraged. As for you, Scorpio, you may be invigorated by the ram's boundless enthusiasm and enterprising approach to life, and may bask in the warmth that your spontaneous friend exudes.

Potential Pitfalls: As long as both of these headstrong people are moving in the same direction, their friendship should remain strong. Yet disaster may strike if domineering Aries tries to browbeat Scorpio into following the ram's lead, for strong-willed Scorpio will not submit to anyone. And if your obstinacy causes fiery Aries to discharge a volley of wounding words in your direction, Scorpio, your friend's fury will be short-lived, but may mark a turning point in your relationship. With water as your element, you are far more sensitive than your flammable friend, and even if you decide to overlook his or her outburst, you may sheath yourself in a protective coat of steely armor, which the open ram may interpret as shutting him or her out, further provoking Arien frustration. Be warned, Aries, that if you then goad Scorpio into opening up, your friend may respond by lashing out with a vicious sting that spells the death of your friendship. Another potential pitfall lies in the contrast between reserved Scorpio's possessiveness and gregarious Aries' tendency to rove between friends. You will never succeed in changing restless, stimulation-seeking Aries, Scorpio, and may even drive your friend away if you try.

Guiding Principle: Ensure the survival of your friendship by neither taking your elemental differences to heart nor letting the other become the target of your aggression.

Compatibility: ☺ ☺ ☺ ☺ ☹ ☹ ☹ ☹ ☹ ☹

Scorpio Birth Influences

Ruling planet: Pluto; traditionally Mars
Element: Water
Polarity: Feminine
Quadruplicity: Fixed

Did you befriend Scorpio on the track, Aries, believing her to be a supportive training companion and worthy adversary? You may be surprised if Scorpio doesn't agree with your techniques, but try not to fall out about it.

Aries Birth Influences

Ruling planet: Mars
Element: Fire
Polarity: Masculine
Quadruplicity: Cardinal

ARIES
SAGITTARIUS

Aries Birth Influences

Ruling planet: Mars
Element: Fire
Polarity: Masculine
Quadruplicity: Cardinal

Sagittarius' and Aries' warmth and enterprising outlook give them a strong rapport. Both being intent on making their individual ways in the world, they may be the best of friends, but not necessarily the closest. When they do get together, however, their encounters are usually amiable, joyful, and even thrilling.

Plus Points: Both Aries and Sagittarius relish interacting with others, so it is more than likely that this fun-loving pair first met at a social gathering. If you are a Sagittarius, your attention may have been caught by the dynamic ram's vigor, and as an Aries, you were no doubt drawn to the infectious sound of the jovial archer's laughter. As open, honest, and enthusiastic as you both are, it probably wasn't long before you struck up a firm friendship. The qualities that you value in each other are again probably common to you both, notably a positive attitude, a desire for fresh, stimulating experiences, and a resistance to being restricted. The camaraderie formed between curious, imaginative Sagittarius and fearless, determined Aries, coupled with both signs' burning energy and love of risk-taking therefore exhilarates them both, and their friendship may be further enlivened by a hint of healthy competition.

Potential Pitfalls: Aries regards Sagittarius as an equal, but may revert to the ram's natural martial mode in the heat of an exciting moment and start ordering the archer around. If you are a Sagittarius, you will not be bossed around by anyone, and being a fire sign like Aries—albeit a more volatile one—may consequently startle the ram with an outburst of fiery displeasure. What's more, you are adept at aiming arrows of hurtful sarcasm at Aries, causing the wounded ram to question your affection. Because you soon cool down and, like Aries, are a generous and forgiving type, your friendship has the potential to survive such heated crises. Nevertheless, the archer's occasional moodiness may puzzle and unsettle you if you are a straightforward Aries, and although you may try to be sporting, you may resent being the butt of Sagittarius' jokes and may respond by trying to assert yourself again. It is a vicious cycle that may seriously weaken your friendship.

Aries, did you meet your Sagittarian friend at a party? Your similarities make you a lively pair, but be careful of your competitive streak!

Sagittarius Birth Influences

Ruling planet: Jupiter
Element: Fire
Polarity: Masculine
Quadruplicity: Mutable

Guiding Principle: Ignore your minor differences, don't let yourself become stuck in a destructive battle of wills, and instead revel in the enlivening effect that you have on one another.

Compatibility: 

CAPRICORN

ARIES

* *

Fiery Aries is an extrovert, while calm Capricorn is more inward-looking, and it may therefore initially appear as though these zodiacal signs have little in common. Yet although they may not hit it off immediately, this pair shares a powerful strength of purpose and may consequently forge a strong friendship.

Plus Points: If you are an Aries, a speculative conversation with Capricorn may have sparked your interest in your friend rather than his or her behavior. Capricorn is a steady, work-focused personality, and while this description doesn't really apply to impetuous, excitement-seeking Aries, you can certainly be inspired by the same vision, not least because you have a pioneering spirit and cannot resist a challenge. Indeed, it's their purposefulness that usually causes this plucky and determined pair to form a powerful bond. You may sometimes feel the need to quash some of Aries' wilder ideas if you are a sensible Capricorn, but otherwise admire your friend's winning enthusiasm, single-mindedness, and fearlessness. Similarly, if you are an Aries, you may wish that Capricorn were less uptight, more willing to take chances, and would follow your lead, but nevertheless respect the goat's integrity and ambition. This friendship of very different equals has a light-hearted side too, with Aries being disarmed by Capricorn's wacky sense of humor and the pushy ram sometimes succeeding in persuading Capricorn to live a little.

Potential Pitfalls: Gregarious Aries finds pleasure in surrounding him- or herself with a variety of stimulating people. Reserved Capricorn, by contrast, is something of a loner, who tends to regard socializing as an opportunity for networking rather than relaxation. As a result, if you are a serious and solitary goat, you may condemn fun-loving Aries as being frivolous, while your sociable Aries friend may in turn find your earnest approach tiresome and restricting. You are no doubt constantly on the search for enlivening experiences if you are a spontaneous Aries, and if an element of risk is involved, so much the better. Being furthermore a headstrong, generous type, you probably resent circumspect Capricorn's attempts to urge you to be more cautious, and may bristle when the prudent goat scolds you for wasting your time and money on diverting trifles. Aries won't fundamentally change, Capricorn, so try to lighten up once in a while.

Guiding Principle: Accept that your friend's personal qualities balance and complement your own, and learn to welcome, rather than reject, the influence that you have on one another.

Compatibility:       

Capricorn Birth Influences

Ruling planet: Saturn
Element: Earth
Polarity: Feminine
Quadruplicity: Cardinal

* *

If you are an Aries, you may feel like disconnecting your Capricorn friend's business line and dragging him out on an adventure weekend. Capricorn, it won't hurt you to have some fun for a change.

* *

Aries Birth Influences

Ruling planet: Mars
Element: Fire
Polarity: Masculine
Quadruplicity: Cardinal

ARIES
AQUARIUS

Aries Birth Influences

Ruling planet: Mars
Element: Fire
Polarity: Masculine
Quadruplicity: Cardinal

It is often their mutual desire to be surrounded by a variety of people that makes Aries and Aquarius the best of friends. Neither the element of fire nor that of air can tolerate being restricted—including to one another's company—but when they do come together, audacious Aries ignites the water-carrier's innate adventurousness, while innovative Aquarius' ideas stimulate the ram's love of challenge. There is, however, a danger that this friendship may flare up or burn out.

Plus Points: If you are a roving Aries, you are unlikely to have a claustrophobically close relationship with your equally restless Aquarian friend. Both of you are far too intent on experiencing what the big, wide world has to offer to limit yourself to an exclusive, one-on-one friendship. Not only do you accept each other's need for independence, but neither of you feel neglected or resentful when the other flits across the room to talk to someone else. As an Aries, you may also be stimulated by your Aquarian friend's quick, exploratory mind and unconventional Uranian ideas. And Aquarius, being a positive person, you in turn no doubt appreciate Aries' enthusiastic, can-do attitude and talent for firing up the impulsive, fun-loving side of your personality.

Aries and Aquarius companions enjoy exploring new places. However, Aries' tendency to take the lead may infuriate independent Aquarius.

Potential Pitfalls: Two significant pitfalls may cool this warm friendship. The first hinges on Aries' powerful urge to lead. It's important to understand, Aries, that Aquarius is both an independent thinker and an innovator, and is therefore not a person who will passively go along with your wishes. What's more, your resolutely democratic Aquarian friend may come to regard your bossy approach as being dictatorial, and, being someone who demands complete freedom of thought and action, may disappear if you try to dominate him or her too aggressively. The second concerns you, Aquarius. You may not realize it, but you sometimes appear aloof when you shift into observation mode. Because Aries is such an open character, your friend may mistake this mental disengagement as a withdrawal of affection, resulting in the fiery ram confronting you with a heated display of emotion. This confrontation may provoke you into speaking coolly from the head rather than warmly from the heart, which Aries may take very poorly indeed.

Aquarius Birth Influences

Ruling planet: Uranus; traditionally Saturn
Element: Air
Polarity: Masculine
Quadruplicity: Fixed

Guiding Principle: Feed each other's zest for life, make light of your differences, and your friendship will continue to flourish.

Compatibility: ☺ ☺ ☺ ☺ ☺ ☺ ☺ ☺ ☹ ☹

PISCES
ARIES

Intuitive, compassionate Pisces supports Aries when the reckless ram has run into trouble, while loyal Aries returns the favor by staunchly defending Pisces against bullies. Yet this friendship may cool if altruistic Pisces is offended by Aries' selfishness, or if direct Aries becomes irritated by Pisces' erratic approach to life.

Plus Points: The ruling planets of both Aries and Pisces endow them with a positive outlook, Mars manifesting itself in Aries as burning self-confidence, with Pisces receiving its hopeful idealism from Neptune and its optimism from Jupiter. If you were born under the sign of the fishes and are fundamentally sympathetic to your Arien friend, you probably find his or her self-certainty and fiery energy both emboldening and enlivening, and your feminine, or passive, polarity makes you particularly receptive to Aries' masculine, or active, influence. If you are an Aries, you may sometimes be astonished by your Piscean friend's uncanny ability to know what you are thinking before you even open your mouth. Although you are an expressive personality, your emotions are not always written all over your face, and it is the combination of Neptune's psychic gifts and the element of water's intuition that makes Pisces a mind-reader, as well as an unselfish and deeply empathetic friend.

Potential Pitfalls: Their birth influences may draw Aries and Pisces together, but there is an equal danger that they may drive these friends apart. Mars-ruled, cardinal Aries is both single-minded and goal-oriented, which, as a Pisces, you may perceive as being utterly selfish for, due to the Neptune effect, you tend to put others' wants and needs before your own. Being more introverted, you may also sometimes recoil from the heat of your fiery friend's aggression and may feel injured when impulsive Aries neglects you while chasing after his or her latest enthusiasm. And what may really annoy you about mutable Pisces, if you are an uncomplicated Aries, is your friend's inconsistency or moodiness. When you are bored, you can certainly be just as restless, but you stick by your decisions, and may therefore become infuriated by your friend's lack of direction or changeability. Put this down to his or her mutable quadruplicity, and just be grateful for the flexibility that is also its gift.

Guiding Principle: Understand that your respective qualities balance each other, that they bring a valuable dimension to your lives, and that regarding them as faults may destroy your friendship.

Compatibility: ☺ ☺ ☺ ☺ ☺ ☹ ☹ ☹ ☹ ☹

Pisces Birth Influences

Ruling planet: Neptune; traditionally Jupiter
Element: Water
Polarity: Feminine
Quadruplicity: Mutable

You may remember your Piscean childhood friend as someone who would share anything with you, Aries. In return, you were probably his schoolyard guardian and staunch defender.

Aries Birth Influences

Ruling planet: Mars
Element: Fire
Polarity: Masculine
Quadruplicity: Cardinal

TAURUS
TAURUS

Taurus Birth Influences

Ruling planet: Venus
Element: Earth
Polarity: Feminine
Quadruplicity: Fixed

Taureans like to visit a gallery or see a show just as much as spending a cozy night in, and if one of you has cooked up some tasty treats, it might be hard to leave the house!

Taurus Birth Influences

Ruling planet: Venus
Element: Earth
Polarity: Feminine
Quadruplicity: Fixed

A friendship between two Taureans is likely to be steady and enduring, based on mutual understanding and supportiveness, with a shared relish of food and the great outdoors providing especially strong common interests. Yet because they are both rather unadventurous and set in their ways, their relationship may lack a frisson of enlivening unpredictability.

Plus Points: As a Taurus, you may value your Taurean friend greatly, and not just because you are on the same wavelength. Being both governed by artistic, pleasure-loving, but also money-minded, Venus, you probably enjoy getting together to visit art galleries and theaters, to go on outings to shop for new clothes, or to savor delicious dinners at each other's homes. It is from Venus, too, that you derive your harmonious characters, meaning that you no doubt rarely fall out. It is your joint element of earth that sends you out adventuring, hiking, or otherwise enjoying the natural world together, or that causes you to pool your formidable practical talents in furtherance of a constructive project. And because Taurus is a fixed sign, you may be united in your loyalty to one another, and may know that you can always rely on your steadfast friend to be there for you.

Potential Pitfalls: Those born under the sign of the bull have a feminine polarity, which means that you two Taureans tend to react rather than initiate. Thanks to Venus, you have an appetite for fun, but the combination of your passive polarity, your fixed, or rigid, quadruplicity, and your sensible, earthy element results in personalities from which the spark of spontaneity is sometimes missing. As fond as you are of your friend, you may therefore find him or her a little boring and predictable, and may therefore be drawn to more lively characters. You may consequently stray from your fellow bull's side in social situations only to be surprised by his or her dour reaction. But, as a Taurus yourself, wouldn't you also be disgruntled by the sight of your friend laughing delightedly at someone else's witty comments when you'd expected to have Taurus' undivided attention? Those under the protection of Venus are sociable, but can be rather possessive friends, so don't let this become an issue. Also beware of becoming entrenched in minor disagreements, lest your mutual obstinacy ultimately drives you apart.

Guiding Principle: Cherish the comfortable times that you spend together and your instinctive understanding of one another, but do not let outside influences or differing viewpoints jeopardize your friendship.

Compatibility:        

GEMINI

TAURUS

A friendship between even-tempered Taurus and easygoing Gemini is usually mutually beneficial, with the down-to-earth bull keeping flighty Gemini in touch with reality, and bright and breezy Gemini injecting a dose of unpredictability into Taurus' settled life. That said, mutable Gemini's erratic moods may leave fixed-sign Taurus struggling to keep up, while Taurus' prudence may irk Gemini.

Plus Points: If you are a Taurus, your feminine, or passive, polarity and element of earth may make you more reserved and self-contained than Gemini, who was born under a masculine, or active, extrovert, air sign. The influence of your ruling planet, Venus, however, means that you enjoy interacting with others just as much as your sociable friend. Yet while the air that is inquisitive Gemini's element fills him or her with the urge to discover what makes people tick, you simply enjoy the pleasure of relaxing in the company of congenial friends—another Venusian trait—and may find adaptable Gemini both interesting and easy to get along with. If you are a Gemini, the qualities that you no doubt appreciate in your earthy Taurean friend include his or her supportiveness, practical outlook, and steadfast loyalty, especially when you are in need of a helping hand. You've probably been the lucky beneficiary of Taurus' love of food and cozy domesticity, too, returning the favor by sharing with the more sedentary bull all that you have learned on your travels.

Potential Pitfalls: Steady Taurus has a stabilizing influence on volatile Gemini, and if you were born under the restless sign of the twins, you may often appreciate spending some downtime recharging your batteries in comfortable companionship with the undemanding bull. But because your quadruplicity is mutable, you may not be able to give your friend your undivided attention for long before itching to fly away in search of a change. Similarly, you may wish that Taurus were less cautious when you are in a madcap, frivolous mood. Gemini's ruling planet, Mercury, is Roman mythology's trickster figure, and if you are a sensible Taurus, Venus may have endowed you with a sense of fun, yet you may feel safer when your feet are firmly on the ground. Being bull-headed, you may also stoutly resist Gemini's attempts to persuade you to strike out along an unknown path. Gemini's willingness to leave you behind can be hurtful, but don't take it too personally.

Guiding Principle: Regard your differences positively, and don't get into a sniping match about characteristics that you can't fundamentally change.

Compatibility:       

Gemini Birth Influences

Ruling planet: Mercury
Element: Air
Polarity: Masculine
Quadruplicity: Mutable

If you are a Taurus, you're more likely to keep your feet on the ground than your airy Gemini friend.

Taurus Birth Influences

Ruling planet: Venus
Element: Earth
Polarity: Feminine
Quadruplicity: Fixed

TAURUS
CANCER

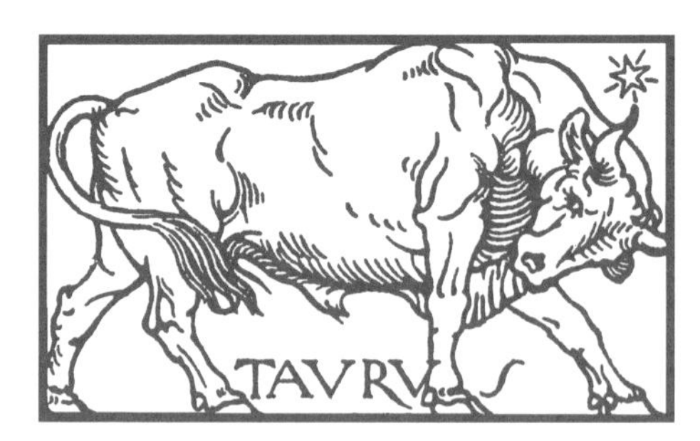

Taurus Birth Influences

Ruling planet: Venus
Element: Earth
Polarity: Feminine
Quadruplicity: Fixed

Taurus and Cancer friends are affectionate and loyal, always supportive and protective of one another.

Cancer Birth Influences

Ruling planet: The Moon
Element: Water
Polarity: Feminine
Quadruplicity: Cardinal

Because they both enjoy the warm companionship of a relaxed evening in, a friendship between Taurus and Cancer is unlikely to revolve around a dizzy social whirl or to feature any rip-roaring escapades. Their bond is instead based on profound mutual support and affection, with the bull giving Cancer practical assistance and the crab supplying Taurus with empathetic encouragement.

Plus Points: Not only are Taurus and Cancer both kind-hearted souls, they are deeply loyal to those whom they consider true friends. Although this relationship may have developed slowly—partly because sensitive Cancer is wary of opening up, and partly because Taurus takes time to decide whether someone is a worthy intimate—once established, it is likely to last a lifetime. If you are a zodiacal crab, what you may especially value in Taurus is the dependability that comes from having been born under a fixed sign, the practicality that the element of earth bestows, and, because you are probably hopeless with money, the canny investment advice that financially astute, Venus-ruled Taurus gives you. If you are a Taurus, you may in turn be grateful to have such a sympathetic, caring friend in Cancer, whose element of water and guardian planet, the Moon, causes the crab to sense others' emotions, and provide comfort and solace when necessary. Being a food-lover, you may also relish the satisfying meals that nurturing Cancer cooks up for you.

Potential Pitfalls: Due to their shared feminine polarity, Taurus and Cancer can be somewhat passive characters who react rather than initiate. But Cancer has a cardinal quadruplicity, and so responds positively to change, whereas fixed-sign Taurus is set in his or her ways and is happy to remain so. If you are Taurus' Cancerian friend, you may therefore wish that the bull were a little more willing to sample new experiences, even if it only means going to a different restaurant once in a while. Perhaps your only gripe with Cancer, if you are a Taurus, is his or her inexplicable mood swings, in that your friend may have a confusing tendency to laugh along with you one moment and clam up the next. Was it something you said? Quite possibly: water's influence makes Cancer both changeable and hypersensitive, and maybe you unwittingly hurt your friend's feelings with an unconsidered remark.

Guiding Principle: Maintain your admirably supportive habits, but consider adding a new dimension to your friendship by occasionally venturing into pastures new.

Compatibility:       

LEO — TAURUS

There may be a few occasions when the bull's bullheadedness and the lion's pride means that it is not so much a question of seeing eye to eye as trying to stare each other down. But enthusiastic Leo's sunny nature and steady Taurus's affability generally keep this friendship on an even keel. Both being fixed signs, Taurus and Leo are typically loyal friends to one another.

Leo Birth Influences

Ruling planet: The Sun
Element: Fire
Polarity: Masculine
Quadruplicity: Fixed

Plus Points: Venus and the Sun both being associated with joyfulness, pleasure, and self-indulgence, it is the influence of their respective ruling planets that gives Taurus and Leo an agreeable common bond. If you are a Taurus, Venus also instills an appreciation of artistry and luxury in you, while your feminine polarity makes you receptive to the influence of others. This is why you may respond so positively to the creativity, love of the high life, and initiative that are the gifts of Leo's solar ruler and masculine polarity. But even the most vigorous Leo sometimes enjoys nothing more than lazing around in congenial company, and if this is true of you, Leo, you no doubt value your Taurean friend's equal capacity for indolence, as well as his or her sensual relish of savoring fine food in comfortable surroundings. Because your element is fire, while that of Taurus is earth, you may also invigorate matter-of-fact Taurus with your imaginative flair, he or she in turn keeping your feet on the ground when necessary.

When Taurus and Leo disagree, neither readily backs down. If you are the lion, remember that you won't change the bull's mind by roaring any louder.

Potential Pitfalls: If you are a Leo, the combination of your planetary ruler and masculine polarity makes you a somewhat dominating personality, as well as someone who expects others to fall in with your wishes, not because you are a control freak, but because you tend to think that you know best. It is difficult for anyone to fall out with peaceable Taurus, on whom Venus bestows an abhorrence of arguments, while earth adds remarkable patience, but if you are a sensible bull, you may not allow Leo to lead you in a direction that you consider imprudent or even irresponsible. You may consequently dig in your heels and refuse to budge from your position, ignoring Leo's furious roars of displeasure. Your zodiacal signs are both fixed, so neither of you is likely to concede defeat.

Taurus Birth Influences

Ruling planet: Venus
Element: Earth
Polarity: Feminine
Quadruplicity: Fixed

Guiding Principle: Prize your friend's life-enhancing qualities, and should your mutual obstinacy cast a cloud over your relationship, try to agree to disagree.

Compatibility:        

TAURUS / VIRGO

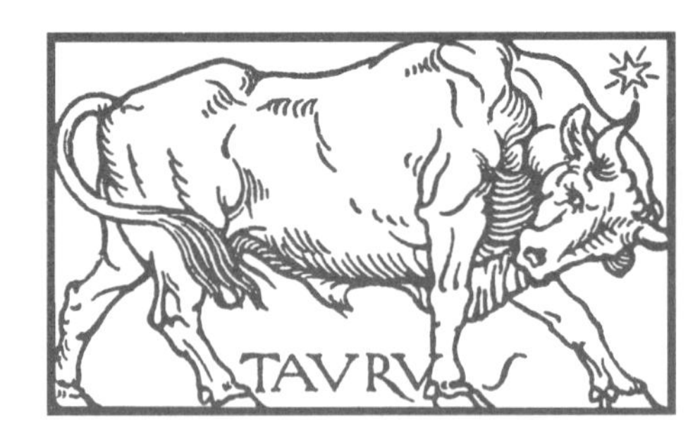

Taurus Birth Influences

Ruling planet: Venus
Element: Earth
Polarity: Feminine
Quadruplicity: Fixed

Although they will not always like the qualities that contribute to the strength of their friendship, fixed-sign Taurus may have a steadying influence on mutable, restless Virgo, while analytical Virgo can offer the bull insightful, if sometimes painful, advice. And not only does their joint element of earth make them deeply loyal to one another, it provides the common ground on which their enduring friendship is firmly based.

Plus Points: Being down-to-earth people, Taurus and Virgo have a mutual understanding that is as sensible and realistic as it is straightforward. Both of you may also enjoy spending time together in natural surroundings, but if you are Taurus' Virgoan friend, it may be you who causes the pair of you to venture farther afield. This is partly because the bull's fixed nature gives him or her a preference for sticking to familiar places, and partly because Mercury, your fleet-footed planetary ruler, endows you with a love of travel. It may have been Taurus who introduced you to the joys of eating well, however, the bull having been blessed with the discerning palate of self-indulgent Venus. If you are an even-tempered, rather lazy Taurus, you in turn must appreciate mutable Virgo's adaptable, easygoing nature, as well as be stimulated by the conversations that you have with your mercurial-minded, well-informed friend. You both must be grateful for the practical help and support that you earthy people give one another when necessary, too.

It may take a while to entice your Taurean friend out on an expedition, but don't give up, Virgo. When you do succeed, Taurus is an amiable companion.

Potential Pitfalls: If you are a mutable, Mercury-ruled Virgo, your birth influences make you a quick-thinking, intellectually curious person who delights in variety, which is why you may sometimes find the bull's slow, stolid, and settled style irksome. Yet while fixed Taurus may take time to consider new ideas before accepting them or rejecting them out of hand, do not dismiss the value of this approach. Indeed, there may have been times when your friend has had a stabilizing effect on your restlessness and has made you realize that things are fine as they stand. No one likes being criticized, especially Taurus, and if you are a zodiacal bull, you probably wish that communicative Virgo would spare you his or her thoughts on your supposed faults. Try to understand that your perceptive friend is trying to help, not hurt you, and don't feel personally attacked.

Guiding Principle: Be tolerant of each other's character quirks, and if this proves difficult, consider how much poorer your life would be without your steadfast friend.

Virgo Birth Influences

Ruling planet: Mercury
Element: Earth
Polarity: Feminine
Quadruplicity: Mutable

Compatibility:       

LIBRA
TAURUS

The planetary guardian of both Taurus and Libra is Venus, the Roman goddess associated with the pleasures of the senses, giving these friends a natural bond that is deepened by the distress that discord arouses in both. And while cardinal, air-sign Libra supplies their relationship with initiative and ideas, fixed, earthy Taurus provides continuity and stability. As long as these elements remain balanced, their friendship should be happy and enduring.

Plus Points: Having gregarious air as an element and an impatient, cardinal quadruplicity makes Libra a social butterfly. If you were born under this sign, encountering Taurus for the first time as you flitted from person to person may have stopped you in your tracks. What was it about Taurus that captured your attention? Perhaps it was his or her courtesy and appreciation of the arts, qualities to which you are drawn because Venus has bequeathed them to you, too. Or maybe it was his or her steadiness and willingness to listen—the respective gifts of the element of earth and a feminine polarity. Whatever it was, you have probably come to value the earthy bull's practical, pragmatic outlook, which counterbalances your own tendency to drift around with your head in the clouds. If you are Libra's Taurean friend, it may equally be your Venusian similarities and the fundamental differences in your characters that account for your liking of him or her. Libra's masculine, or active, polarity and airy element may make your cardinal friend more outgoing, inquisitive, and pioneering than you, and you may therefore find the interest and excitement that Libra brings to your rather settled world especially, and surprisingly, enjoyable.

Potential Pitfalls: Although the influence of Venus means that this pair rarely falls out, they may not always get along swimmingly. What may particularly irritate you about sedate Taurus, if you are an airy, restless Libra, is your friend's preference for cozy nights in and the astonishing stubbornness that he or she can sometimes display. If you are a fixed-sign Taurus, you may in turn be hurt by what you perceive to be Libra's fickleness, maybe because you expect friends to demonstrate their loyalty quite overtly, by sticking closely to each other's sides. Rather than giving up on one another, try giving a little!

Guiding Principle: Minimize the pitfalls inherent in the conjunction of your birth influences and gain maximum mutual satisfaction from your friendship by taking turns in deciding how to spend your time together.

Compatibility: ☺ ☺ ☺ ☺ ☺ ☺ ☺ ☹ ☹ ☹

Libra Birth Influences
Ruling planet: Venus
Element: Air
Polarity: Masculine
Quadruplicity: Cardinal

If you are a Taurus, you may be wounded by what you perceive to be a snub from your Libran friend. Yet she is probably not being malicious and may just need some space.

Taurus Birth Influences
Ruling planet: Venus
Element: Earth
Polarity: Feminine
Quadruplicity: Fixed

TAURUS
SCORPIO

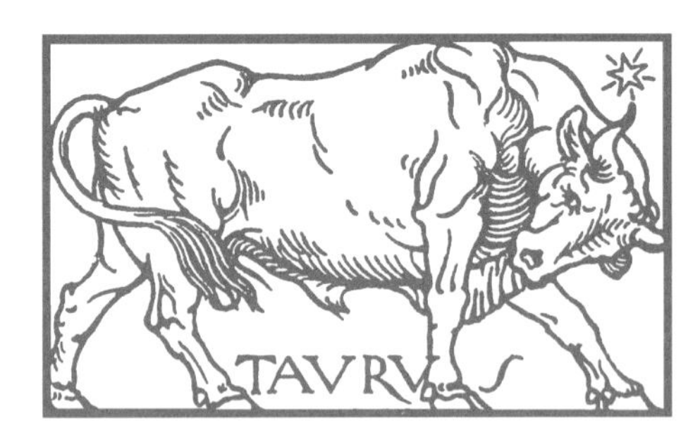

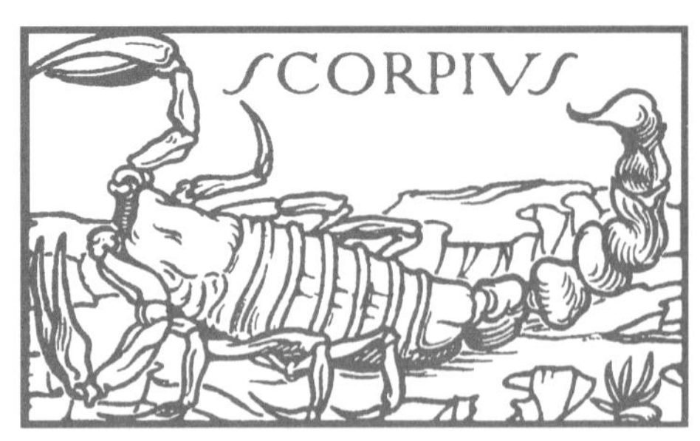

Taurus Birth Influences
Ruling planet: Venus
Element: Earth
Polarity: Feminine
Quadruplicity: Fixed

If your scorpion friend appears to be sulking, Taurus, you may have offended her somehow. You will have to use all of your Venusian charm and earthy patience to win her round again.

Scorpio Birth Influences
Ruling planet: Pluto; traditionally Mars
Element: Water
Polarity: Feminine
Quadruplicity: Fixed

Their shared fixed-sign status, as well as the earthy bull's constancy and the watery scorpion's empathy, usually ensure that Taurus and Scorpio are the most faithful of friends, although their relationship is more likely to be characterized by understated mutual backing than tempestuous times or fizz and frolics. This is partly because both are feminine, or passive, signs and partly because their ruling planets, Venus and Pluto respectively, endow Taurus with a desire for harmony and Scorpio with a dislike of frivolity.

Plus Points: If you are a Scorpio, the combination of your fixed quadruplicity, protective element of water, inward-looking feminine polarity, and intense planetary ruler make you something of a loner who prizes your privacy. You may not commit yourself to friendship lightly, but when you do, it is typically for life. What persuaded you that Taurus was worth sacrificing your solitude for? Maybe it was his or her steadiness and readiness to offer you practical advice—gifts of the element of earth that counterbalance your own element's changeability and tendency to follow your heart rather than your head. Venus-ruled Taurus probably encourages you to relax and have fun once in a while, too, but then you also have much to offer your friend. Indeed, if you are the scorpion's Taurean friend, there must have been many occasions when you were feeling down and Scorpio's willingness to listen to your problems and to empathize with your feelings raised your spirits. You have Scorpio's receptive feminine polarity and sympathetic element of water to thank for that. An invaluable bonus may be that the scorpion would never betray your confidence.

Potential Pitfalls: Although both Taurus and Scorpio can be possessive friends, the greatest threat to their friendship in this respect lies in the scorpion's sensitivity. Because you are so single-minded in your devotion to those whom you care for, if you are a Scorpio, you no doubt expect them to be equally dedicated to you. If you are a Taurus, your loyalty may not be in doubt, but fun-loving Venus exerts a sociable influence over you, along with a susceptibility to charm, both of which may cause you temporarily to divert your attention from the scorpion to a captivating someone, which your friend may take as a personal insult. A brooding, gloomy Scorpio may then severely test your renowned Taurean stoicism and your friend may find further reason to question your fidelity as a result.

Guiding Principle: Appreciate the support that you give one another, and try to be tolerant when the outside world intrudes on your relationship.

Compatibility:      

SAGITTARIUS
TAURUS

A friendship between the zodiacal bull and archer can be joyous, provided that pleasure-loving, indulgent Venus predominates in Taurus, and jolly, generous Jupiter, in Sagittarius. Mutual resentment may arise if the stolidity and inflexibility of the earthy, fixed bull and spontaneity and changeability of the fiery, mutable archer conflict.

Plus Points: There must be times when you really look forward to being in the soothing company of your Taurean friend if you are a busy Sagittarius. Whereas all of your birth influences suggest that you are an active, outgoing person, the combined influence that gentle Venus, a feminine polarity, steady earth, and a fixed quadruplicity wield over Taurus may make your friend someone who enjoys pampering people, particularly by plying them with food and drink. Taurus is also receptive to the needs of others, offering them practical support and unwavering devotion. You must therefore feel that you can always rely on your friend, be it for comfort or help.

If you are a Taurus, you in turn must value your friendship with kindly Sagittarius, maybe because he or she is so interesting and invigorating. Being ruled by Jupiter, the archer is probably cheeringly positive and endearingly understanding, and being in contact with Sagittarius' fiery element may inspire you and warm your heart. Because you are more of a homebody, you no doubt also relish hearing about everything that lively Sagittarius has heard, seen, and done since you last met. Because articulacy is one of the qualities bestowed by the archer's mutable quadruplicity, and humor is the bequest of Jupiter, his or her storytelling must have you in gales of laughter.

Potential Pitfalls: When Taurus and Sagittarius gel, they are the most affectionate of friends, but won't always feel wildly enthusiastic about one other. Thanks to earth, Venus, and a passive polarity, fixed Taurus' idea of having a good time is to laze around doing very little, which you may find incredibly frustrating if you are a Sagittarius whose mutability, fieriness, and masculine polarity give you a desire to be always on the move and to act on the spur of the moment. But then your occasional restlessness, quick temper, and lack of constancy can equally upset and disappoint the steady, placid, and dependable bull.

Guiding Principle: Don't demand more than your friend can give, and instead bring out the best in one another by focusing on doing things that you both enjoy.

Compatibility: ☺ ☺ ☺ ☺ ☺ ☹ ☹ ☹ ☹ ☹

Sagittarius Birth Influences
Ruling planet: Jupiter
Element: Fire
Polarity: Masculine
Quadruplicity: Mutable

If you are a Sagittarius, your Taurus friend's tendency to lie back and relax when you want to leap up and canter off somewhere may infuriate you.

Taurus Birth Influences
Ruling planet: Venus
Element: Earth
Polarity: Feminine
Quadruplicity: Fixed

TAURUS
CAPRICORN

Taurus Birth Influences

Ruling planet: Venus
Element: Earth
Polarity: Feminine
Quadruplicity: Fixed

Your Taurean friend may not share your interest in your work, Capricorn, and may become bored if you dwell on it in conversation.

Capricorn Birth Influences

Ruling planet: Saturn
Element: Earth
Polarity: Feminine
Quadruplicity: Cardinal

Taurus and Capricorn may not see as much of each other as they would like—often due to Capricorn's workaholic tendencies—but these earthy, loyal, and supportive friends typically enjoy relaxing together. That said, although the input of their respective ruling planets, Venus and Saturn, should enrich their friendship, it could equally result in divisive differences.

Plus Points: Because Taurus and Capricorn both have earth as their element, their friendship is usually based on solid common ground, notably their straightforward outlook and enjoyment of such simple sensual pleasures as sharing a mouth-watering meal. If you are a Capricorn, the combination of your driving, goal-oriented quadruplicity and Saturn, your serious planetary guardian, probably means that you rarely switch your focus from work to play, but relish Taurus' restful companionship when you do. Having been born under indulgent Venus' guardianship, the easygoing bull may encourage you to unwind and have a bit of fun, and, having a feminine polarity, may be a sympathetic listener who is always ready to offer practical advice.

Capricorn's polarity is also feminine, making your friend similarly receptive to your viewpoint if you are a Taurus, and because this zodiacal sign's quadruplicity is cardinal, you may often be surprised by the bold suggestions that he or she makes when discussing your quandaries. They are not ill considered, however, because the influence of Saturn means that Capricorn is thoughtful and responsible, and as a fellow earthy person, someone who is as pragmatic and realistic as you are. You may admire, and perhaps be inspired by, Capricorn's ambition, too, but may nevertheless believe that your friend works too hard.

Potential Pitfalls: The importance that cardinal Capricorn attaches to getting ahead in life can become obsessive, which can sometimes result in you finding the company of your single-minded friend boring if you are a Venus-ruled Taurus. Although you may be trying your utmost to broaden Capricorn's horizons by gently encouraging him or her to share your interest in the arts, this strategy may not be working. If you are a Capricorn, you may consider your Taurean friend to be frivolous in this respect, and may also disapprove of his or her tendency to fritter away valuable free time by lazing around rather than being productive, but maybe you should consider recharging your batteries in the same way once in a while.

Guiding Principle: True friends are hard to find, so keep yours by exercising patience and tolerance whenever your different approaches conflict.

Compatibility:      

AQUARIUS

TAURUS

A friendship between Taurus and Aquarius is likely to last for life, not least because both have fixed quadruplicities and hate to give up on anything or anyone. Taurus provides the easygoing companionship that Aquarius finds relaxing, Aquarius in turn shaking up the bull's steady existence in the most enjoyable of ways. Yet their respective elements, earth and air, may sometimes prove a source of mutual irritation.

Plus Points: What you may appreciate the most about Taurus, if you are an Aquarius, is his or her reliability and willingness to lend a sympathetic ear. Having a feminine, or receptive, polarity, Taurus probably responds thoughtfully to your own masculine, more expressive, polarity, and, because the bull's ruling planet is the peaceable Venus, he or she may generally agree with you rather than challenge your opinions. And if it is advice that you are seeking, Taurus' counsel is no doubt sensible because the bull's element is practical earth. Add to the mix a bon viveur's sensual tastes, and in Taurus you may have a friend who is both indulgent and unfailingly supportive.

You must consider Aquarius a breath of fresh air if you are his or her Taurean friend. Your different polarities indicate that Aquarius is more outgoing, which, when coupled with his or her gregarious, airy element, means that you may frequently find yourself in a roomful of strangers having a great time. Although you may not be able to get a word in edgewise in a one-on-one situation with talkative Aquarius, you probably don't mind because your Uranus-ruled friend has such interesting—even radical—ideas to share with you.

Potential Pitfalls: Taurus may be a placid personality, and Aquarius somewhat emotionally detached, but this doesn't mean that their friendship is immune from the occasional flash of temper. If you are an Aquarius, both air and Uranus have given you the gifts of curiosity, an interest in the new, and a desire to experiment, none of which may suit the matter-of-fact, change-resistant bull, who can be unbelievably stubborn if pushed too hard. But then you may similarly be exasperated by Taurus' inertia, limited imagination, and tendency to bring you abruptly back down to earth when you are reveling in a flight of fancy.

Guiding Principle: Don't engage in the futile exercise of trying to mold your friend in your own image; simply enjoy each other's company instead.

Compatibility:       

Aquarius Birth Influences

Ruling planet: Uranus; traditionally Saturn
Element: Air
Polarity: Masculine
Quadruplicity: Fixed

If you are a Taurus with a fun-seeking Aquarian companion, you may find that you have been talked out of the house and into a club before you know what's hit you!

Taurus Birth Influences

Ruling planet: Venus
Element: Earth
Polarity: Feminine
Quadruplicity: Fixed

TAURUS
PISCES

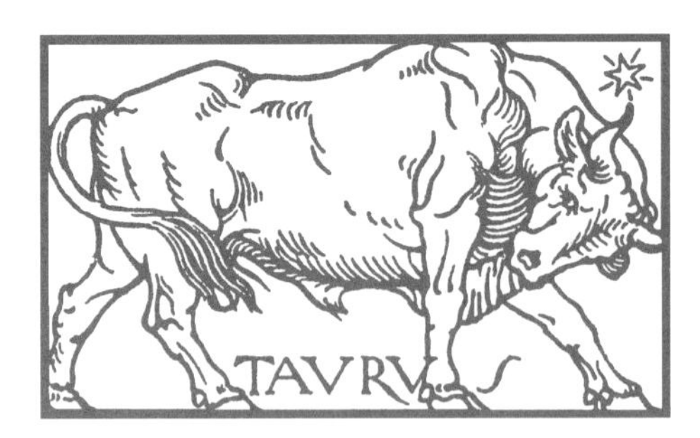

Taurus Birth Influences

Ruling planet: Venus
Element: Earth
Polarity: Feminine
Quadruplicity: Fixed

Taurus and Pisces are both feminine-polarity, or responsive, people who generally react positively to one another, partly because their interests are similar, due to the influence of their planetary rulers, and partly because each provides the support that the other needs, Taurus offering a practical, earthy outlook, while Pisces supplies insight and empathy. Their different quadruplicities may occasionally sour their mutual fondness, however.

Plus Points: If you are a Pisces and your friend is a Taurus, you probably find him or her easy to get along with. Not only do your respective ruling planets, Venus and Neptune, endow each of you with good-natured personalities, you may both be attracted to the beauty inherent in artistic creations. You must also be grateful for Taurus' steadiness, the gift of both the element of earth and a fixed quadruplicity that stabilizes you when you are being tossed this way and that by your own emotional element of water and restless quadruplicity. And if you are totally confused about how best to proceed when faced with a problem, he or she is no doubt ever ready to offer you sensible advice and practical help until you find your way again.

Pisces' spooky ability to detect when you are feeling down, despite the brave face that you may have been hiding behind, must amaze you if you are a Taurus. You have the joint input of Neptune and water to thank for Pisces' ultrasensitive, almost psychic streak, as well as for the compassionate and selfless way in which your friend puts your problems first. Indeed, Pisces must be someone whom you believe would never knowingly hurt you, and what better quality could you ask for in a friend than that?

You may be baffled as to why your Piscean friend became upset and then quietly slipped away if you are a Taurus. Did you close your ears to sensitive Pisces instead of listening?

Potential Pitfalls: Although it is unlikely to end your friendship, be warned that there may be tension between you at times. Fixed-sign Taureans often stick obstinately to their opinions, which may distress you if you are a mutable Pisces, particularly if those opinions go against your altruistic, Neptunian desire to make the world a better place. If you are a straightforward, rather materialistic Taurus, you in turn may not understand why Pisces, who often has difficulty expressing his or her emotions, sometimes becomes so upset with you. You may also be irritated by your friend's tendency to be swayed by others' viewpoints.

Guiding Principle: Mutual tolerance and respect are the keys to keeping your friendship happy and harmonious.

Compatibility: ☺ ☺ ☺ ☺ ☺ ☺ ☺ ☹ ☹ ☹

Pisces Birth Influences

Ruling planet: Neptune; traditionally Jupiter
Element: Water
Polarity: Feminine
Quadruplicity: Mutable

GEMINI — GEMINI

It is unlikely that two Gemini friends will spend much time together, but they usually have a great time when they do. Their ruling planet, element, polarity, and quadruplicity make this pair the most curious, interesting, outgoing, and communicative of people, which means that their idea of fun is debating all manner of issues, and in this they are equally matched. Neither really needs the other, however, and their shared restlessness and love of variety may eventually result in them seeing each other less and less, and ultimately perhaps never at all.

Gemini Birth Influences

Ruling planet: Mercury
Element: Air
Polarity: Masculine
Quadruplicity: Mutable

Plus Points: What you may especially like about your Gemini friend, if you yourself are also a Gemini, is his or her uncomplicated personality and the fun that you have together. Not only is your shared governing planet named for Mercury, the trickster of Roman mythology, but your joint element of air and changeable quadruplicity may cause you to be rather unemotional types who hate being clung to, crave freedom, and are stimulated by change. As a result, you no doubt understand each other's need for independence and are probably grateful that your friend doesn't demand more of your attention than you are willing, or able, to give. Yet when your paths do converge, you must experience a jolt of delight in finding yourself again in the presence of someone who is as assertive, analytical, articulate, and well-traveled as you.

If you and your friend are Geminis, there are probably times when you can't get a word in edgewise and feel like screaming! You'll have your turn eventually, so try to be patient.

Potential Pitfalls: Your mutual desire to communicate your opinions is so urgent that each of you may find it difficult to get a word in edgewise when the other is in full flow. And because your shared polarity is masculine, or competitive, and you are easily bored, and can be moody, it may be that if one succeeds in dominating the conversation, the other may feel unenthused and resentful, and may take off in search of a more congenial diversion. A one-off occurrence like this won't necessarily cause a rift in your friendship because easygoing Gemini rarely nurses grudges, but if it becomes the norm, each of you may soon feel that the other has little to offer in the way of stimulation.

Guiding Principle: You may both lead busy lives, but make sure that you regularly schedule times to get together lest you eventually drift apart. And remember that Geminis do not welcome being relegated to listener status, and must be allowed to have their say in every conversation!

Compatibility: ☺ ☺ ☺ ☺ ☺ ☺ ☺ ☺ ☹ ☹

Gemini Birth Influences

Ruling planet: Mercury
Element: Air
Polarity: Masculine
Quadruplicity: Mutable

GEMINI
CANCER

Gemini Birth Influences

Ruling planet: Mercury
Element: Air
Polarity: Masculine
Quadruplicity: Mutable

Few zodiacal signs are as mentally stimulating as Gemini, and few are as caring as Cancer, so that each has the potential to be a life-enhancing friend to the other. The feminine-polarity, lunar-ruled, and water-influenced crab responds instinctively to masculine-polarity, mercurial, airy Gemini, who is in turn fascinated by Cancer's hidden depths. Both can be moody and changeable, however, a tendency that may prove an alienating factor in their friendship.

Plus Points: You must cherish your Gemini friend's ability to make you laugh, if you are a Cancer, as well as the interesting nuggets of information that he or she shares with you when you are together. Both Mercury and the element of air inject a mischievous streak and relish of gossip into Gemini's personality, and you may also value Gemini's objective viewpoint and neutral advice when emotions have clouded your judgment. Being more extrovert and sociable than you, he or she may have introduced you to a host of strangers, too, some of whom may since have become good friends. It is again the combination of Mercury and air that makes you so curious about people, if you are a Gemini, which means that you may find your Cancerian friend's inscrutability, or the sense that he or she is holding something back, irresistibly intriguing. Cancer's introverted, feminine polarity, and the sensitivity that is imparted by a lunar planetary ruler and water, can cause your friend to withhold his or her true feelings for fear of being mocked, attacked, or rejected. Yet the same birth influences make Cancer a thoughtful, empathetic, and compassionate friend, and perhaps the one to whom you turn for sympathy and comfort on the rare occasions when you are feeling down.

Gemini, you may find that your considerate, deep Cancer friend isn't as lively and outgoing as you are. Perhaps she feels that you don't care as much as she does about your friendship. Make sure that you don't inadvertently slight her.

Potential Pitfalls: Not only do Geminians lack Cancerians' emotional depth, but they can quickly become bored if a conversation fails to push their intellectual buttons. If you are a Cancer with an inexhaustible capacity for listening, you may consequently feel profoundly hurt if Gemini does a disappearing act when you are telling him or her about your difficult day. But then you can also be crabby at times, which impatient Gemini may similarly find both inexplicable and hard to deal with.

Guiding Principle: The pleasure that you derive from being with your friend far outweighs the annoyance that you occasionally trigger in one another, so try to focus on each other's good points and to overlook any perceived character flaws.

Cancer Birth Influences

Ruling planet: The Moon
Element: Water
Polarity: Feminine
Quadruplicity: Cardinal

Compatibility:       

LEO — GEMINI

If a friendship between a Gemini and a Leo had to be summed up in a single word, it would be "fun." A mutable, variety-loving, people-oriented sign, Gemini's liveliness is complemented by fiery Leo's impulsiveness and zest for life, and both find each other's company stimulating. That said, airy Gemini's tendency to blow hot and cold may annoy the fixed-sign lion, while Gemini may sometimes find Leo's self-obsession trying.

Plus Points: Just as air is warmed by fire, and fire is energized by air, so Gemini and Leo friends have an enlivening influence on one another. Having been born under masculine, or outgoing, signs, neither are shrinking violets and both thrive on social interaction. If you are a Leo, you may particularly appreciate Gemini's mischievous sense of humor, and you must roar with laughter at some of the witty observations that your insightful, quick-thinking, Mercury-ruled friend makes about others. Similarly, if you are a Gemini, you may respond positively to the double dose of warmth and vitality that Leo's solar governor and fiery element bestow upon your friend. You may also have cause to be grateful to Leo for his or her generosity or loyalty on those occasions when you have found yourself in a fix, just as Leo may value your analytical mind and astute advice when a knotty problem presents itself.

Potential Pitfalls: Gemini and Leo may have differences of opinion, but these probably don't seriously threaten their affection for one another, partly because Gemini is an adaptable person who quickly forgives and forgets, and partly because Leo's fiery flare-ups are generally short lived. Even so, certain aspects of the other's character may rankle with each. If you are a Leo, you are predisposed to building stable, committed relationships, and may consequently dislike the way in which Gemini breezes in and out of your life, as well as the changeability that is the hallmark of a mutable sign. But it may be that Gemini's occasional moodiness or absences are triggered by Leo's arrogance—the downside of having a friend whose planetary ruler is the Sun. And although the Sun may be the center of our solar system, you may find your friend's apparent assumption that the world revolves around him or her irritating if you are a Gemini.

Guiding Principle: Your lives would be the poorer if you were no longer friends, so focus on the positive, not the negative, aspects of your relationship.

Compatibility: ☺ ☺ ☺ ☺ ☺ ☺ ☺ ☺ ☹ ☹

Leo Birth Influences

Ruling planet: The Sun
Element: Fire
Polarity: Masculine
Quadruplicity: Fixed

Your Gemini friend's witty observations will keep you entertained if you are a Leo, while your love of company and warm personality will appeal to her gregarious nature.

Gemini Birth Influences

Ruling planet: Mercury
Element: Air
Polarity: Masculine
Quadruplicity: Mutable

GEMINI
VIRGO

Gemini Birth Influences

Ruling planet: Mercury
Element: Air
Polarity: Masculine
Quadruplicity: Mutable

You may well have found your ideal travel companion in Virgo if you are a Gemini, and when you are together in an unfamiliar place, are probably glad of your earthy friend's practical mind.

Virgo Birth Influences

Ruling planet: Mercury
Element: Earth
Polarity: Feminine
Quadruplicity: Mutable

Both signs being ruled by communicative Mercury, a friendship between Gemini and Virgo is typically founded on their mutual love of discussion and debate, and they may also be enthusiastic travel companions. Their shared mutable quadruplicity adds another level of understanding to their relationship, which is not, however, likely to be squabble-free, especially when Gemini's airiness is at variance with Virgo's earthiness.

Plus Points: You must find your Gemini friend amusing company if you are a Virgo. The element of air endows Gemini with a playful personality, and because your polarity is feminine, or receptive, and your friend's is masculine, or outgoing, you no doubt find Gemini's breezy influence refreshing. You probably have to smile at some of his or her ingenious ideas, too, which Gemini puts forward with persuasive fluency, even if your realistic, earthy side tells you that they are utterly unfeasible. And if you are a Gemini, you must look forward to getting together with Virgo, perhaps because the discussions that you have with your friend are so stimulating. It is thanks to both Mercury and your changeable nature that you two are gifted conversationalists who think on your feet, share an objective, analytical way of looking at things, and relish the cut and thrust of verbal banter. You may also have cause to be grateful for the prudent advice and practical support that your earthy, Virgoan friend is always ready to offer you.

Potential Pitfalls: Gemini and Virgo are both mutable signs, but the element of earth tends to stabilize Virgo's restlessness, while that of air can make Gemini even more volatile and difficult to pin down. If you are a sensible, steady Virgo, there may consequently be times when Gemini's happy-go-lucky, unreliable nature infuriates you, so much so that you cannot hold your tongue and find yourself unleashing a barrage of criticism. Your response to this disagreeable carping, if you are a Gemini, may be to put as much distance between you and your disapproving friend as possible, perhaps temporarily, but eventually maybe for good. This is not the only reason why you may sometimes consider Virgo a killjoy: as a child of the air, you can't stand having your freedom of thought or action constrained by routine, humdrum matters, and may resent Virgo's attempts to organize you or bring you down to earth.

Guiding Principle: Try to laugh off your differences if they threaten to sour your friendship, and never stop talking to one another!

Compatibility:       

LIBRA
GEMINI

The rapport between Gemini and Libra friends is typically based on their mutual enjoyment of stimulating conversation and appetite for fun, partly because they were both born under masculine, or extrovert, signs and partly because their element is the lively, intellectual air. Despite being congenial types who generally shy away from confrontation, both may find certain facets of one another's character trying at times: Libra can sometimes be unsettled by mutable Gemini's mood swings, for example, and Gemini, irritated by Libra's meddlesome ways.

Plus Points: If you are Gemini and Libra friends, your shared birth influences probably not only brought you together, but may now give you an innate understanding and appreciation of one another's personalities. Having a masculine polarity makes you both uninhibited, which is just as well because one of the gifts of your airy element is your delight in openly discussing all manner of subjects with someone who is as confident, articulate, and intelligent as you, and you are certainly evenly matched in this respect. Mercury, the planet named for the Roman messenger god, endows Gemini with the urge to gather and disseminate information, and if you are a Libra, you may consequently regard your friend as an inexhaustible source of knowledge—and gossip. And because Libra's planetary ruler is the sensual, refined Venus, your interest may in turn be aroused by your friend's enthusiasm for the arts if you are a Gemini. Another common bond between you may be your love of parties, as well as your usually light-hearted, positive outlook.

Potential Pitfalls: Gemini is a mutable-quadruplicity sign, which, if you are a Venus-governed Libra, means that you may occasionally be troubled by your friend's tendency to be bright and breezy one moment, and glum and gloomy the next. Illustrating one of the reasons why Libra is called the sign of the balance, you may instinctively strive to restore equilibrium when Gemini's temper veers to a disgruntled extreme—which your friend may not appreciate. Indeed, if you are a Gemini who is feeling temporarily out of sorts, you may feel that interfering Libra is intruding on your personal space. Another aspect of your Libran friend's personality that may sometimes grate on you is the pushy impatience that comes from having a cardinal quadruplicity.

Guiding Principle: Keep talking, but respect each other's privacy and don't let the occasional off-day cast a cloud over your friendship.

Compatibility: ☺ ☺ ☺ ☺ ☺ ☺ ☺ ☺ ☹ ☹

Libra Birth Influences

Ruling planet: Venus
Element: Air
Polarity: Masculine
Quadruplicity: Cardinal

Gemini and Libra companions share a love of fun, but has a silly game ever ended in cross words? Gemini's mood swings can be startling, Libra, so try not to crowd your friend.

Gemini Birth Influences

Ruling planet: Mercury
Element: Air
Polarity: Masculine
Quadruplicity: Mutable

GEMINI

SCORPIO

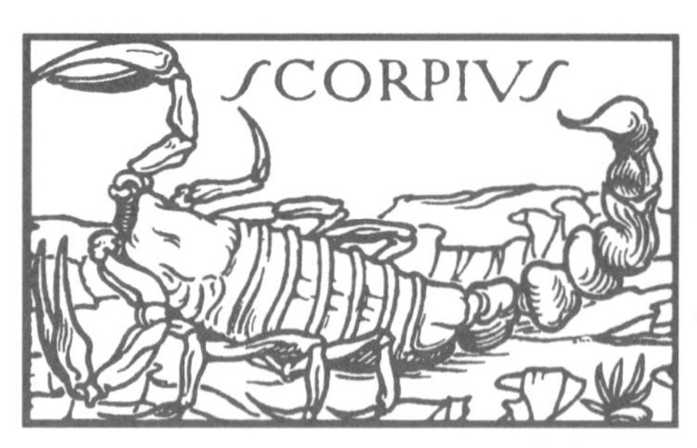

Gemini Birth Influences

Ruling planet: Mercury
Element: Air
Polarity: Masculine
Quadruplicity: Mutable

If you are a steady Scorpio, you may feel that you are running a different race from your lively Gemini friend. Do you become irritated when he persists in trying to make you open up?

Scorpio Birth Influences

Ruling planet: Pluto; traditionally Mars
Element: Water
Polarity: Feminine
Quadruplicity: Fixed

♇ ♂ ♒

Gemini often being flighty and fickle, and Scorpio steady and selective, there has to be something special between these two friends, or they would never have forged a bond in the first place. Although secretive, Pluto-ruled Scorpio can be something of a closed book, an enigmatic personality keeps inquisitive Gemini interested. And while Scorpio may consider airy Gemini superficial, even the most serious scorpion can't help but lighten up under fun-loving Gemini's influence.

Plus Points: The scorpion's ruling planet is the slow-moving Pluto, named for the dark god of the Roman underworld, while Gemini's is the speedy Mercury, whose fleet-footed Roman namesake is said to have flown through the air that is also this sign's element. These mythological images convey the fundamental dissimilarity between Scorpio and Gemini friends, which is compounded by their respective elements, polarities, and quadruplicities. Yet if you are a feminine-polarity Scorpio, you probably cannot help but respond affectionately to the assurance with which masculine-polarity Gemini may try to win you round to some of his or her outrageous flights of fancy. Your cheerful friend's wit must also make you laugh, and you may have great respect for Gemini's quick intellect, too. If you are a Gemini who likes nothing better than a stimulating conversation, you may welcome the startling emotional insights that your water-ruled, Scorpio friend contributes to your discussions. Not only that, but when you need a confidant, you may particularly appreciate fixed-sign Scorpio's steadfast friendship, as well as his or her ability to keep a secret.

Potential Pitfalls: Gemini's birth influences can make those born under this sign socially promiscuous people, a trait that you may find hurtful if you are a sensitive Scorpio who chooses friends carefully and then remains devoted to them. Indeed, it may seem as though you are the one doing all of the giving, while Gemini does all of the taking, in your relationship, which may ultimately cause you to simmer with suppressed anger. The combination of Pluto and water gives Scorpio a tendency to brood over perceived slights and to become increasingly uncommunicative in the process, which you may find both baffling and tiresome if you are a Gemini who believes in talking things through and rarely bears a grudge.

Guiding Principle: Your friend adds a unique contribution to your life, so don't let a mutually negative attitude to your differences drive you apart, and instead try to understand and accommodate them.

Compatibility: ☺ ☺ ☺ ☺ ☺ ☹ ☹ ☹ ☹ ☹

SAGITTARIUS
GEMINI

Both having been born under mutable signs, Gemini and Sagittarius friends probably don't see that much of each other—their love of variety is too great—but usually have a great time when they do. With fiery Sagittarius thriving on excitement, airy Gemini ever ready to have fun, and both of their ruling planets being associated with the quest for knowledge, theirs is likely to be a lively and stimulating relationship. That said, Gemini may sometimes be too detached for Sagittarius' liking, while Sagittarius' self-regard may not always suit Gemini.

Plus Points: There must never be a dull moment when you're in the company of your Gemini friend if you are a Sagittarius, as exposure to the banal makes both of you fidgety. Because the influence of Mercury gives Gemini sharp wits and a silver tongue, and Jupiter's gift to you is wide-ranging interests, you must enjoy the all-embracing conversations that your articulate friend initiates to keep boredom at bay. In addition, your shared masculine polarity means that you are both outgoing and uninhibited, and because your own fiery element causes you to be an impulsive, thrill-seeking type, you may appreciate airy Gemini's willingness to seek out merriment with you. Similarly, if you are a Gemini, you may find being with fiery Sagittarius an enlivening experience, maybe because your friend's original—even eccentric—ideas are so intriguing, or because his or her optimistic outlook and boundless energy are so infectious. You may also bask in the warmth of fiery Sagittarius' affectionate personality, and may value your friend's generosity of spirit.

Potential Pitfalls: One of the problems with you both having a mutable, or restless, nature is that if one of you gets on his or her hobbyhorse—Mercury-governed Gemini perhaps chattering on about a recent vacation, or Jupiter-ruled Sagittarius musing on the latest complementary therapy—the other's mind may soon start to wander. If Gemini's brain is not engaged, he or she may try to steer the conversation in a different direction, which you may find infuriating if you are a fiery Sagittarius who likes to have an audience, so much so that you may snap aggressively at Gemini. And if you are an airy Gemini, you may take exception to your friend's occasional heated outbursts. But you are an objective person, so consider the possibility that Sagittarius' annoyance is justified.

Guiding Principle: Try to listen to one another with patience and respect—it's a small price to pay for such an invigorating friendship.

Compatibility: ☺ ☺ ☺ ☺ ☺ ☺ ☹ ☹ ☹ ☹

Sagittarius Birth Influences

Ruling planet: Jupiter
Element: Fire
Polarity: Masculine
Quadruplicity: Mutable

Whenever Gemini and Sagittarius friends meet up, they are likely to head for the nearest party, where they will dance until they drop!

Gemini Birth Influences

Ruling planet: Mercury
Element: Air
Polarity: Masculine
Quadruplicity: Mutable

GEMINI
CAPRICORN

Gemini Birth Influences

Ruling planet: Mercury
Element: Air
Polarity: Masculine
Quadruplicity: Mutable

If you are a Gemini with a problem, you'll appreciate meeting up with your Capricorn friend for some sensible advice over a cup of coffee.

Capricorn Birth Influences

Ruling planet: Saturn
Element: Earth
Polarity: Feminine
Quadruplicity: Cardinal

A friendship between Gemini and Capricorn is generally less of a meeting of minds than an attraction of opposites. Airy, masculine-polarity Gemini's playfulness and social confidence add sparkle to earthy, feminine-polarity Capricorn's sedate existence, while saturnine Capricorn encourages mercurial Gemini to slow down and give some serious thought to life's practicalities. These two can learn a lot from one another, but that is not to say that they won't have their disagreements.

Plus Points: What you may particularly value about your Gemini friend, if you are a Capricorn, is his or her ability to make you relax. If you are typical of your zodiacal sign, the combined influence of Saturn and your cardinal quadruplicity may cause your primary focus in life to be your career. Your earthy element gives you a straightforward mindset, while your feminine polarity tends to make you rather reserved. Gemini, by contrast, is lively and outgoing, bent on having fun, loves playing with ideas and words, and likes nothing better than rubbing shoulders with a wide variety of people. Once Gemini's persuasive tongue has worked its magic and you've reluctantly agreed to accompany your friend to a social event, you may be surprised to find yourself having a good time, and may perhaps even be pleased by the useful contacts that you have made.

If you are a Gemini, teasingly chivvying earnest Capricorn to lighten up must be an entertaining pastime, but there is no doubt a thread of real fondness running through your mischievous banter, for you must know that you have a true friend in Capricorn. Being a changeable and flighty character yourself, you must especially appreciate Capricorn's earthy constancy and readiness to provide practical help when you find yourself in a jam or dilemma. In short, Capricorn is probably someone on whom you can always depend.

Potential Pitfalls: Gemini's moody mutability may try your patience if you are a steady Capricorn, and the childish contrariness that is the hallmark of the zodiacal twins may also offend your mature, saturnine nature. Don't be tempted to lecture your friend, however, because this will almost certainly drive Gemini away. And Gemini, you may sometimes find your friend's soberness, predictability, and tendency to offer bracing advice tedious, but try to curb your impatience and be grateful for the stabilizing influence that Capricorn has on you.

Guiding Principle: Don't let your differing outlooks cloud your affection for one another, and consider following your friend's example once in a while.

Compatibility: ☺ ☺ ☺ ☺ ☹ ☹ ☹ ☹ ☹ ☹       

AQUARIUS

GEMINI

Although airy Gemini and Aquarius are inspired by each other's wit and wisdom, and can debate, discuss, and laugh with one another for hours on end, they are unlikely to be the closest of friends. This is partly because their joint element of air makes them both gregarious, with a wide circle of acquaintances, and partly because the same birth influence causes them to be somewhat emotionally detached, so that they prefer superficial contact to more profound involvement. That said, fixed-sign Aquarius may be a steadfast friend to mutable Gemini, who may return the favor by adapting to Aquarius' sometimes uncompromising ways.

Plus Points: Both Gemini and Aquarius are air signs, which means that these friends are bright and breezy, talkative types who are stimulated by social interaction. They also share a masculine polarity, making them unafraid to speak their minds. What you may especially like about Gemini, if you are an Aquarius, is that he or she is an articulate, well-informed, and objective sparring partner with whom you can argue about all manner of subjects safe in the knowledge that your neutral friend won't become upset, hold anything against you or take it personally. And when it comes to gaining new knowledge, communicative, Mercury-ruled Gemini is the magpie of the zodiac, so you may frequently come away from your get-togethers musing over some fascinating snippets of information.

If you are a Gemini, your mutable quadruplicity probably gives you an appetite for the new, and one of the qualities that you may particularly treasure in your Aquarian friend is the unpredictability of his or her views. The source of his or her ability to surprise is Uranus—the planet associated with inventiveness and innovation—which is why Aquarius' radical ideas may often resonate so strongly with you. There may be nothing unpredictable about Aquarius' habits, but then you may know from experience that the water-carrier's fixed quadruplicity can make him or her a reliable friend.

Potential Pitfalls: Mild friction between mutable Gemini and fixed-sign Aquarius may arise as Gemini is typically far more restless, moody, and inconstant than Aquarius, while Aquarius may sometimes be too stubborn and unyielding for Gemini's taste. But because Gemini is flexible, and Aquarius won't easily give up on a friend, these dissimilarities shouldn't threaten their friendship.

Guiding Principle: Keep talking!

Compatibility: ☺ ☺ ☺ ☺ ☺ ☺ ☺ ☹ ☹ ☹

Aquarius Birth Influences

Ruling planet: Uranus; traditionally Saturn
Element: Air
Polarity: Masculine
Quadruplicity: Fixed

Good communication is the foundation of a Gemini–Aquarius friendship. Stay away from touchy subjects, though, Gemini, because Aquarius can be astonishingly stubborn.

Gemini Birth Influences

Ruling planet: Mercury
Element: Air
Polarity: Masculine
Quadruplicity: Mutable

GEMINI
PISCES

Gemini Birth Influences

Ruling planet: Mercury
Element: Air
Polarity: Masculine
Quadruplicity: Mutable

If you're a typically sociable Gemini, don't forget to pick up the phone and call your more introverted Pisces friend every so often.

Pisces Birth Influences

Ruling planet: Neptune; traditionally Jupiter
Element: Water
Polarity: Feminine
Quadruplicity: Mutable

Although Gemini and Pisces friends are not usually on the same wavelength, they have the potential to get a lot out of their relationship, not least affection. Airy, masculine-polarity Gemini gives inward-looking Pisces the confidence to venture out into the wider world, for example, while watery, feminine-polarity Pisces encourages outgoing Gemini to be more introspective. Yet these two are such inherently dissimilar personalities that contact between them may be limited, and then a meeting of minds, rare.

Plus Points: Being rather shy yourself if you are a Pisces, you may envy Gemini's self-assurance and talent for getting along with almost anyone. These combined gifts of an active polarity and gregarious, airy element contrast with your own passive polarity and insecurity-inducing element of water. A result of Gemini's cheerful chivvying, however, you may now be starting to enjoy having fun with Gemini's other friends. Due to the dual influence of your ruling planet, Neptune, and water, you may often find yourself so deluged with conflicting emotions that you are paralyzed by indecision. At these times, you may be grateful for airy, Mercury-governed Gemini's perceptive and impartial advice.

If you are an inquisitive Gemini, you may find Pisces something of an enigma, fueling your interest in discovering more about the personality that lies beneath the gentle, dreamy face that he or she presents to the world. In the course of your investigation, you may have been intrigued to learn that Neptune-ruled Pisces is extraordinarily idealistic or spiritual, and this may generate many interesting discussions. You must also appreciate your friend's readiness to lend a sympathetic ear when you are going through a bad patch, for which you have Pisces' feminine polarity, compassionate element, and altruistic planetary ruler to thank.

Potential Pitfalls: Extroverted, variety-loving Gemini is so readily diverted by the new that months may pass before he or she calls Pisces to suggest meeting up, which you may find hurtful if you are a thin-skinned Pisces. If so, try not to take Gemini's neglect personally. If you are a Gemini, you may be mystified by Pisces' changeable emotions, but then your mutable sign can make you moody, too, so don't take off in search of more congenial company should Pisces become tearful, and instead stay and talk things through.

Guiding Principle: True friendship is all about give and take, so try to take an interest in each other's views and listen in the spirit of understanding.

Compatibility:       

CANCER
CANCER

A friendship between two people who are both Cancers is unlikely to be action-packed or superficial, for the feminine-polarity crab is typically quiet and introspective, and, due to the influence of his or her lunar planetary governor and watery element, deeply empathetic. These are therefore almost certainly friends who turn to one other for sympathy and emotional support whenever they are feeling down, but who may not see that much of each other otherwise, often because their cardinal quadruplicity gives them a compulsion to focus on achieving their life's goals.

Plus Points: You must value your relationship immensely if you and your friend are zodiacal crabs, especially if you spend most of your time responding to the demands and needs of those whose star signs are different. After a stressful day of being at the beck and call of your Aries boss or taking care of your children, you must be truly grateful to be able to pour out your heart to someone who listens to you with understanding and offers you sincere commiserations and encouragement. It is the combination of the Moon and water that has blessed you both with intuitive, giving, and nurturing natures. Because you have an inward-looking, feminine polarity, however, you may internalize your emotions, maybe partly because they fill you with confusion and partly because sharing them makes you feel vulnerable. Your friend may therefore be one of the few people whose emotional radar can detect your inner turmoil, and whom you can trust not to wound you with his or her indifference, impatience, or criticism.

Potential Pitfalls: One of the downsides of having a watery element is Cancerians' tendency either to have difficulty expressing their feelings or to clam up, and it may be that although one of you can sense that the other is unhappy, you can't fathom why, or if you are feeling miserable, you may wish to spare your friend your problems. This may create a barrier of silence between you that may either become unbreachable or result in the dam breaking and both of you being swamped with painfully raw emotions, so keep the channels of communication open, but be alert to each other's need for privacy. And don't feel hurt if your friend occasionally gives priority to his or her family or work commitments; no doubt you do the same at times under the driving influence of your cardinal quadruplicity.

Guiding Principle: Carry on caring for one another!

Compatibility: ☺ ☺ ☺ ☺ ☺ ☺ ☺ ☺ ☹ ☹

Cancer Birth Influences

Ruling planet: The Moon
Element: Water
Polarity: Feminine
Quadruplicity: Cardinal

Two Cancer friends will share a deep, trusting bond.

Cancer Birth Influences

Ruling planet: The Moon
Element: Water
Polarity: Feminine
Quadruplicity: Cardinal

CANCER
LEO

Cancer Birth Influences

Ruling planet: The Moon
Element: Water
Polarity: Feminine
Quadruplicity: Cardinal

Loyal Leo and caring Cancer may form a lifelong friendship during childhood.

Leo Birth Influences

Ruling planet: The Sun
Element: Fire
Polarity: Masculine
Quadruplicity: Fixed

Cancer and Leo each have the potential to supply what the other requires in a friend. Fiery Leo likes to take center stage, and the lunar crab is usually more than happy to applaud from the sidelines, for instance, while exposure to solar Leo's sunny nature boosts watery, emotional Cancer's occasionally somber spirits. Cardinal Cancer's enterprising ideas are also a hit with Leo, whose fixed quadruplicity makes the loyal lion a friend on whom Cancer can rely. Leo's egotism and fiery temper may nonetheless alienate the sensitive crab, and the lion may lose patience with Cancer's moodiness.

Plus Points: If you are a Leo, your masculine polarity, fiery element, and commanding planetary ruler may manifest themselves in you as a desire to surround yourself with people who respond to you with enthusiasm and respect, which is why you may welcome Cancer's company. Having the Moon as a planetary governor and a feminine polarity causes the crab to be susceptible to others' influence, as well as gentle and uncompetitive, so you may really shine in your friend's presence. It is mainly due to Cancer's watery element that your friend is so touchingly compassionate, and you may furthermore be inspired by the cardinal crab's surprisingly ambitious way of thinking.

Leo is a masculine sign, and Cancer a feminine one, which, if you are a Cancer, may not only mean that the lion is more outgoing than you, but also has a more positive mindset. Because your watery element can fill you with doubts and worries, you must be grateful to have such an upbeat friend in Leo, whose own element and ruling planet infuse him or her with an infectiously vital, life-affirming outlook. Because you can frequently feel insecure, you may also cherish the leonine characteristics of constancy and dependability, bestowed on your friend by his or her fixed quadruplicity.

Potential Pitfalls: Nurturing Cancer is one of life's givers, but the crab needs to see a return on the emotional outlay that he or she invests in friends. If you are a fiery Leo, you may therefore find that Cancer becomes sulky and withdrawn if he or she regards your impulsiveness as thoughtlessness or your self-absorption as selfishness. Crabby Cancerians sometimes resort to emotional blackmail, but be warned, if you are a crab, that Leos can't stand being manipulated, and that you may consequently ignite an explosion so devastating that it all but destroys your friendship.

Guiding Principle: Enjoy being together, but don't take one another for granted.

Compatibility:       

VIRGO
CANCER

Rather than rip-roaring, the type of friendship enjoyed by Cancer and Virgo is generally quiet and settled, partly because they share a reserved feminine polarity and partly because receiving each other's support is more important to them than hitting the nightspots. Virgo appreciates having a caring and responsive friend in Moon-governed, watery Cancer, while Cancer in turn values earthy Virgo's down-to-earth advice and steadfastness. That said, there are traits in each that may annoy the other, but usually not enough to prompt a parting of the ways.

Plus Points: One of the joys of having a Cancerian friend, if you are a Virgo, may be his or her capacity for listening. Like yours, Cancer's polarity is feminine, or receptive, but having an intuitive ruling planet and sensitive element causes him or her to be far more attuned to others' emotions than you, as well as more empathetic. And because your ruling planet, Mercury, makes you verbally expressive, and you are usually assured of a sympathetic audience in Cancer, he or she may be the one to whom you turn when you need to pour out your woes. Cancer's element being secretive water, you furthermore probably know that your friend would never betray your confidence.

If you are a Cancer, the Moon and your watery element can make you hypersensitive to the moods of those around you, in which case you may feel as though you are on an emotional rollercoaster at times, and may consequently find Virgo's company a welcome antidote. Because your friend's planetary governor is Mercury, and his or her element is earth, the vibes that you instinctively pick up from Virgo are no doubt intelligent, sensible, and steady, so that being with him or her probably has a calming, stabilizing effect on you.

Potential Pitfalls: Once watery, emotionally vulnerable Cancerians have lowered their defenses and taken their friends into their hearts, they expect these privileged few to treat them with gentleness and compassion. If you are a Virgo with a neutral mindset, however, you may sometimes hurt Cancer by objectively pointing out that your friend has behaved inadvisably, which the touchy crab may take as a personal insult. But then you may be equally offended if you feel that you are being punished for your helpfulness by either affronted silence or irrational crabbiness.

Guiding Principle: Your friendship means a lot to you both, so ward off the danger of inadvertently alienating one another by communicating openly, but tactfully.

Compatibility: ☺ ☺ ☺ ☺ ☺ ☺ ☺ ☺ ☹ ☹

Virgo Birth Influences

Ruling planet: Mercury
Element: Earth
Polarity: Feminine
Quadruplicity: Mutable

If you're a steady Virgo, you'll appreciate your Cancer friend's caring nature, and you won't worry if he's sometimes moody or withdrawn.

Cancer Birth Influences

Ruling planet: The Moon
Element: Water
Polarity: Feminine
Quadruplicity: Cardinal

CANCER
LIBRA

Cancer Birth Influences
Ruling planet: The Moon
Element: Water
Polarity: Feminine
Quadruplicity: Cardinal

Do you wish that Cancer would stop hiding and come out to party more often if you are a Libra? Try to take the time to find out what you have in common with your friend.

Libra Birth Influences
Ruling planet: Venus
Element: Air
Polarity: Masculine
Quadruplicity: Cardinal

Although a pair of Cancer and Libra friends may feel real affection for one another, they probably won't spend that much time together. Part of the reason for this may be that they have very different preferences when it comes to having a good time—Cancer savoring a quiet evening in, while Libra parties the night away, perhaps. Their relationship may also be somewhat superficial, mainly because emotionally vulnerable Cancerians tend to keep their feelings close to their chest, while tactful Librans hate causing offense, which means that neither may be completely open with the other.

Plus Points: Having the sensitive Moon as a planetary ruler, a caring element in water, and a receptive, feminine polarity may result in your Cancer friend being someone who instinctively senses when you are feeling down—however bravely you laugh off your problems—and offers you a helping hand, which you must appreciate if you are a Libra. The same birth influences no doubt make Cancer gentle and nonconfrontational, qualities that you may particularly value if Venus, your peaceable planetary governor, causes you to shrink from heated arguments.

If you are a Cancer, the combination of the Moon, water, and a passive polarity may make you highly responsive to the moods of those around you, which is why being in Libra's company may usually be such a pleasure. Not only does Libra dislike making waves (which suits you very well if being exposed to aggression wreaks mayhem on your emotions), but your airy friend's infectious good nature, playfulness, and chattiness must encourage you to relax, brush aside some of your inhibitions, and join in the fun.

Potential Pitfalls: Cancer can be a homebody who likes nothing better than whiling away the hours with a heart-to-heart conversation, and this may eventually bore you to tears if you are an airy, masculine-polarity, gadabout Libra. Similarly, if you are a Cancer, although you may quite enjoy being taken to the occasional enlivening party by Libra, you may lack your friend's social confidence and probably prefer more intimate get-togethers. As a result, your paths may not cross that frequently. Another barrier to a close friendship may be watery Cancer's reticence and Venusian Libra's diplomacy, which, if you are a Cancer, may cause you to keep your true feelings to yourself, and, if you are a Libra, to mask yours under a layer of discretion.

Guiding Principle: Make time for one another, and try to discover more about your friend when you are together.

Compatibility: ☺ ☺ ☺ ☺ ☺ ☺ ☹ ☹ ☹ ☹

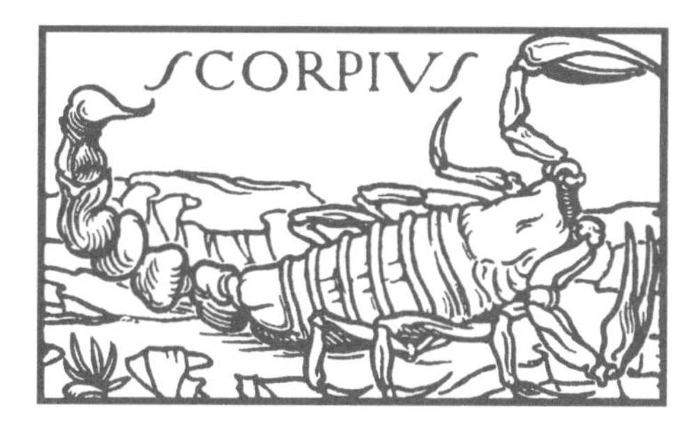

SCORPIO
CANCER

Guarded, Pluto-ruled Scorpio can be something of a closed book to people born under other signs, but cardinal Cancer has a rare ability to encourage the scorpion to open up, thereby initiating a friendship that is likely to last a lifetime. This is partly because fixed-sign scorpions rarely give up on anyone who has won their affection, but mainly because Scorpio and Cancer's shared element of water causes them to understand that friendship is as much about giving as taking. There may be times, however, when each finds it difficult to reach out to the other.

Plus Points: If you are a Scorpio, your Cancer friend is probably one of the few people whom you trust enough to talk to openly and honestly. Due to the combined influence of mysterious Pluto, an introverted, feminine polarity, and a sensitive, watery element, you may be a reserved person who does not like to broadcast your emotions and opinions to all and sundry. Because your Cancer friend shares your polarity and element, and is also ruled by the intuitive Moon, he or she is probably just as thoughtful and private as you, as well as being exceptionally insightful and empathetic. You may consequently feel secure in the knowledge that discreet, caring Cancer will not abuse your friendship.

If you are a Cancer, you may similarly sense that Scorpio would never betray your confidence, which you no doubt consider a vital quality in a friend. It is your shared element of water, perhaps compounded by personal experience, that also gives you both an innate awareness of the emotional devastation that fickleness, unkindness, or being the subject of idle gossip can wreak on sensitive souls, especially on thin-skinned, Moon-ruled crabs. Scorpio has a fixed quadruplicity, so you may be deeply grateful for his or her loyalty and reliability, too.

Potential Pitfalls: Scorpio's fixed quadruplicity and solitary ruling planet together indicate that the scorpion is more of a loner and more possessive than you, and if you are a less discriminating crab, you may sometimes feel torn between seeing Scorpio or another friend. If you are a Scorpio, you may then resent having to compete with others for the crab's attention. Don't punish Cancer by retreating behind a wall of wounded silence because zodiacal crabs often react to being hurt by becoming equally withholding, and where there is no communication, there may eventually be no friendship.

Guiding Principle: Maintain your solid friendship by making time for one another, but don't demand an exclusive relationship.

Compatibility:       

Scorpio Birth Influences

Ruling planet: Pluto; traditionally Mars
Element: Water
Polarity: Feminine
Quadruplicity: Fixed

♇ ♂

Cancer and Scorpio are well-suited companions who enjoy a deep mutual trust and respect that they rarely experience with other friends.

Cancer Birth Influences

Ruling planet: The Moon
Element: Water
Polarity: Feminine
Quadruplicity: Cardinal

CANCER
SAGITTARIUS

Cancer Birth Influences

Ruling planet: The Moon
Element: Water
Polarity: Feminine
Quadruplicity: Cardinal

Sagittarius' vibrant enthusiasm must really lift your spirits if you are a Cancer, but do you occasionally wish that she'd sit down and listen to you more?

Sagittarius Birth Influences

Ruling planet: Jupiter
Element: Fire
Polarity: Masculine
Quadruplicity: Mutable

A friendship between feminine-polarity Cancer and masculine-polarity Sagittarius typically stands or falls on Cancer's ability to be assertive enough to hold the archer's interest, and on Sagittarius' capacity to give the crab sufficient time and attention. These provisos aside, Moon-governed, watery Cancer and Jupiter-ruled, fiery Sagittarius are usually affectionate buddies who cool one another down or warm one another up when necessary, and generally have plenty to talk about.

Plus Points: You were probably under the influence of your variety-seeking, mutable quadruplicity when you first got to know Cancer, if you are a Sagittarius whose fiery element often sends you on a search for stimulation. Having been born under a feminine, lunar sign, your friend is probably not someone who demands attention, but what you must really appreciate about Cancer is the way that he or she listens to you empathetically and offers insightful advice. Thanks to the creative crab's cardinal quadruplicity, you may also be inspired by the urgency with which your friend puts forward his or her visionary ideas.

Because the Moon, your watery element, and feminine polarity make you so responsive to the vibes that others radiate, you must enjoy spending time with Sagittarius if you are a zodiacal crab. Being exposed to negativity can particularly upset you, but Sagittarius is normally jovial, bursting with *joie de vivre*, and thrillingly uninhibited, for which you can thank Jupiter, the element of fire, and your friend's masculine polarity. After some gentle probing, you may also have discovered Sagittarius' philosophical side (the bequest of Jupiter), and this may often give you much food for thought.

Potential Pitfalls: Not only can Cancerians' passiveness bore sensation-seeking Sagittarians at times, but their unstable, watery element can sometimes throw crabs into emotional turmoil, when they may clutch at friends to keep them on an even keel. If you are a fiery, mutable Sagittarius, there may consequently be occasions when you resent being tugged from the excitement of the real world to be confronted with a maelstrom of confused Cancerian emotions. Your Sagittarius friend's lack of interest in how you are feeling will not go unnoticed if you are an intuitive Cancer, and you may express your hurt by withdrawing into your shell or criticizing a Sagittarian weak spot, neither of which will endear you to your friend.

Guiding Principle: Ensure that your friendship remains relaxed—that way, you'll bring out the best in each other.

Compatibility:       

CAPRICORN
CANCER

That neither Cancer nor Capricorn is particularly comfortable amid large social gatherings is largely down to their common feminine, or reserved, polarity. The influence of their respective ruling planets and elements also makes them tend to value strong friendships over superficial acquaintanceships. It may take time, but once they have gained one another's trust, they are likely to remain friends for life, with Moon-governed, watery Cancer offering Capricorn a sympathetic ear, and Saturn-ruled, earthy Capricorn providing Cancer with sensible advice.

Plus Points: If you are a typical, cardinal Capricorn whose focus is on getting ahead in your career, you may dislike wasting your precious free time on people from whom you gain little. The exception is no doubt your Cancer friend, whose lunar governor and element of water give crabs a double dose of intuition, empathy, and compassion. Your friend may therefore instinctively detect when something is on your mind, encourage you to open up, and then listen attentively. That may often be enough to make you feel better, but Cancer may sometimes come up with imaginative solutions to your problems, too. All in all, if you spend most of your waking hours thinking about work, you must appreciate having such a caring friend.

Those born under the sign of the zodiacal crab can be both impressionable and thin-skinned, and if you are one of them, you may sometimes feel overwhelmed by impulsive, fiery personalities or be hurt when stood up by unreliable, airy individuals. This is why you may be thankful that your earthy, Capricorn friend is so steady and dependable. Indeed, it may mean a lot to you that predictable Capricorn never sends you into emotional turmoil by springing nasty surprises on you, and has the ability to stabilize your often fluctuating moods with his or her calm, straightforward outlook and helpful, practical suggestions.

Potential Pitfalls: Cancer and Capricorn share a cardinal quadruplicity, which means that both are goal-driven people, even if their aims in life—be they personal or professional—don't overlap. They may consequently not see much of one another, and, having an introverted, feminine polarity, may not be that inspired or enlivened by each other when they do. If you are a realistic Capricorn, you may sometimes be irritated by lunar Cancer's dreaminess, and if you are a Cancer, you may occasionally find saturnine Capricorn's sober mindset dispiriting.

Guiding Principle: Try to be as tolerant as possible of what you perceive to be your friend's negative traits.

Compatibility: ☺ ☺ ☺ ☺ ☺ ☺ ☹ ☹ ☹ ☹

Capricorn Birth Influences

Ruling planet: Saturn
Element: Earth
Polarity: Feminine
Quadruplicity: Cardinal

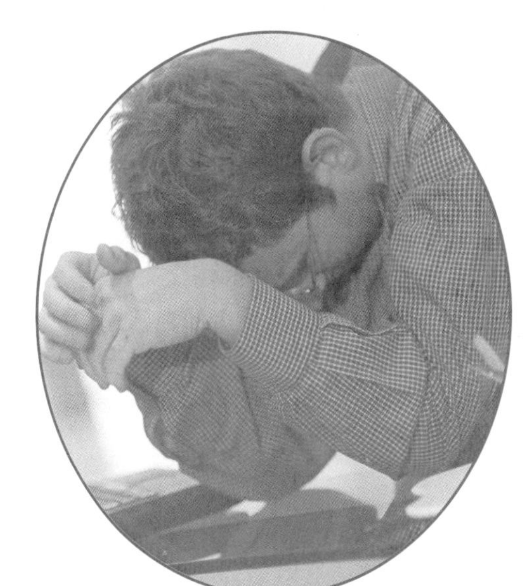

When the stresses and strains of work are getting to you, Capricorn, remember that you've got a compassionate friend in Cancer, who has the power to soothe your troubled mind.

Cancer Birth Influences

Ruling planet: The Moon
Element: Water
Polarity: Feminine
Quadruplicity: Cardinal

CANCER
AQUARIUS

Cancer Birth Influences
Ruling planet: The Moon
Element: Water
Polarity: Feminine
Quadruplicity: Cardinal

Aquarius, take some time out from the whirl of your social life to pick up the phone and call Cancer, or else your friend may feel neglected.

Aquarius Birth Influences
Ruling planet: Uranus; traditionally Saturn
Element: Air
Polarity: Masculine
Quadruplicity: Fixed

If they take a leaf out of one another's book occasionally, Cancer and Aquarius friends have the potential to broaden each other's horizons, but unless they make a concerted effort to hook up, they may otherwise not spend much time together. This is partly because watery, feminine-polarity Cancer enjoys intimate, one-on-one sessions, while airy, masculine-polarity Aquarius prefers larger gatherings, but also because their characters are typically like night and day. Nevertheless, given Cancer's empathetic, kindly nature and fixed-sign Aquarius' tendency to remain faithful to good friends, it is unlikely that their relationship will ever peter out completely.

Plus Points: What you may find particularly touching about your Cancer friend, if you are an Aquarius, is his or her habit of enquiring about your welfare when you meet, and genuine concern should you be going through a difficult phase. It is the union of the nurturing Moon and empathetic water that causes Cancer to be a caring and sympathetic individual who will always try to soothe a troubled mind. When you have steered the conversation away from personal matters into what you may consider the safer waters of abstract concepts, you may also be startled by the ambitious, original ideas that surface from the depths of the cardinal crab's intuitive brain.

If you are a zodiacal crab, your feminine polarity and lunar planetary governor may make you very receptive to others' influence, and you therefore probably find Aquarius an enlivening person to be with. It may be that Aquarius is more sociable and outgoing than you, and therefore introduces you to a variety of interesting personalities, for example, or perhaps you are impressed by the fluency and persuasiveness with which your airy, Uranus-ruled friend puts forward his or her ideas and opinions, however radical. When you find yourself in a fix, you may be grateful for your resourceful friend's recommendations, but may especially appreciate his or her loyalty.

Potential Pitfalls: If you are an Aquarius, although there must be occasions when you need to pour out your heart to someone as understanding as the crab, your feelings rarely get the better of you, which is why you may find Cancer's emotion-led way of thinking tiresome at times. Similarly, if you are a Cancer who has invested time and effort in buoying up your friend, you may be hurt that Aquarius doesn't reciprocate so intensely when your own mood needs a boost.

Guiding Principle: Try to be patient and forgiving when your friend's idiosyncrasies annoy or disappoint you.

Compatibility: ☺ ☺ ☺ ☺ ☹ ☹ ☹ ☹ ☹ ☹

PISCES
CANCER

Sharing as they do an introverted, feminine polarity, Cancer and Pisces may not have the most exciting of relationships, but typically offer one another qualities that they both consider far more important in a friend than stimulation, namely sympathy and support. In fact, Cancer's driving, cardinal quadruplicity and Pisces' restless, mutable one can pep up their friendship, but what these two really cherish is their innate understanding of one another and the emotional closeness that they increasingly develop under the influence of their joint watery element and their congruent planetary rulers, the Moon and Neptune.

Plus Points: You may feel as though your Cancer friend is one of the few who is on the same wavelength as you if you are a Pisces, and that you can pour out your heart to him or her without fear of being ridiculed. Your watery element and feminine polarity may sometimes cause you to withdraw into yourself, be it as a self-protective measure when someone has hurt you or to shut out the outside world in order to think deep thoughts, a tendency that Cancer probably respects because he or she does the same. And because Moon-ruled Cancer is so sympathetic, it must be easy to open up to your friend, either to reveal the source of your unhappiness or to let the crab in on your dreams.

If you are a Cancer who spends most of your time looking after, and worrying about, your family, or having your caring nature taken advantage of by egotistical colleagues in the workplace, enjoying a few quiet hours with your empathetic Pisces friend must be a welcome antidote. Not only may you sense that he or she has your emotional welfare at heart, but experience may tell you that Neptune-governed Pisces is utterly unselfish and will try his or her utmost to buoy you up, which is often all that is required to boost your mood.

Potential Pitfalls: Neither Cancer nor Pisces will knowingly upset a loved one unless they have been so wounded that their pain prompts them to lash out in retaliation, which is unlikely to happen in a friendship that is as supportive as theirs. If you are a Pisces, you may, however, dislike Cancer's pushiness on those occasions when his or her self-seeking, cardinal quadruplicity comes to the fore, while you may sometimes be unsettled by mutable Pisces' inconstancy if you are a Cancer.

Guiding Principle: Give each other as much as you take from one another.

Compatibility: ☺ ☺ ☺ ☺ ☺ ☺ ☺ ☺ ☹ ☹

Pisces Birth Influences

Ruling planet: Neptune; traditionally Jupiter
Element: Water
Polarity: Feminine
Quadruplicity: Mutable

Pisces and Cancer share many caring and sympathetic qualities, including being good listeners. As friends, this pair will make the time to talk and prop one another up.

Cancer Birth Influences

Ruling planet: The Moon
Element: Water
Polarity: Feminine
Quadruplicity: Cardinal

LEO / LEO

Leo Birth Influences

Ruling planet: The Sun
Element: Fire
Polarity: Masculine
Quadruplicity: Fixed

Masculine-polarity, Sun-ruled Leos are dynamic, self-confident people who know that they have a magnetic aura that draws others to them and adore being at the center of an admiring crowd. Because they have a fiery element, they also seek the stimulation of being with people who ignite their imagination, which other creative, enthusiastic lions certainly do. As long as they defer to one another occasionally, a friendship between two Leos is therefore one of ebullient equals. Imagine a pair of lions or lionesses playfully fighting, all the while roaring delightedly, and you have the image of a typical leonine relationship. Should the play fight turn serious and one try to gain domination, however, you can no doubt picture the bloodcurdling snarls and flying fur.

Plus Points: You must have a special liking for your Leo friend if you are also a zodiacal lion, perhaps because he or she is as exuberant, big-hearted, impulsive, and generous as you, thanks to your shared element of fire. This same birth influence, when combined with that of the powerful Sun, also injects an energizing frisson of danger into your relationship that you may rarely experience when with a more passive person like a Cancer or Taurus. But you probably find the sense of competition that may be simmering below the surface of your relationship exciting, and in any case, may have too much fun with Leo to risk causing your friendship to come to an explosive end by engaging in an egotistical power struggle. As time goes by, your common fixed, or change-resistant, quadruplicity will almost certainly make you both increasingly fond of one another, so that the prospect of sparking off an irrevocable parting of the ways may be unthinkable.

If your friend is a Leo like you, you'll no doubt have lots of fun together—but take care that you don't become too competitive.

Potential Pitfalls: If you and your Leo friend manage to suppress your solar-fueled urge to assert your authority over one another from the start, your friendship looks set to endure. There may be a few fiery outbursts of annoyance along the way if one of you feels that the other is failing to accord the imperial lion due respect, but being perpetually angry is not a natural leonine condition, and if there is goodwill on both sides, you will soon be laughing uproariously together again. Leo's pride will not tolerate being persistently challenged or sidelined, however, and if this happens, a devastating showdown may result.

Guiding Principle: Step into the background and let your friend shine once in a while.

Compatibility:       

Leo Birth Influences

Ruling planet: The Sun
Element: Fire
Polarity: Masculine
Quadruplicity: Fixed

VIRGO

LEO

As contradictory as it may sound, Leo and Virgo may be good friends, but may not always like one another very much. For example, while fixed-sign Leo will stand loyally by Virgo in a crisis, and earthy Virgo will always be ready to offer the lion practical assistance, fiery, Sun-ruled Leo's attention-seeking ways and colossal self-esteem may irritate Virgo beyond endurance at times, while objective, Mercury-governed Virgo's criticism may infuriate admiration-demanding Leo. When they aren't raising one another's blood pressure, however, they often benefit from each other's influence, and can have plenty of fun, too.

Plus Points: If you are a Virgo, your feminine polarity may make you rather shy and lacking in confidence, which is why spending time with your Leo friend may often exhilarate you. Fiery, masculine-polarity, Sun-ruled Leo is probably so exuberant, extroverted, and self-assured that you may be swept along on a tide of leonine energy into situations that you wouldn't have believed you would enjoy—standing in the spotlight and singing a duet with your friend in a karaoke bar, perhaps. Because fixed-quadruplicity Leos hate to lose contact with their friends, you may also appreciate the effort that the lion makes to stay in touch with you.

Although you may prefer—and, indeed, expect, given your commanding planetary governor—to hear only good things about yourself if you are a Leo, there may be occasions when you recognize that you need the advice of someone who has your best interests at heart, but who is also realistic and perceptive. This is when you may steel yourself to turn to your Virgo friend for a dose of bracing medicine. When all is sunny in your world, however, there must be other qualities that you like in mutable Virgo, such as his or her flexibility when you insist on doing things your way.

Potential Pitfalls: Fiery Leo may be an exceptionally enlivening friend, but if you are a Virgo, your element of earth, feminine polarity, and planetary ruler may cause you to be a sensible and thoughtful observer, and the lion's behavior may sometimes seem reckless, melodramatic, or just plain juvenile. And if you are a Leo who longs for adulation and craves like-minded playmates, Virgo's reproving words or refusal to join in the fun may be a complete turnoff.

Guiding Principle: When you annoy one another, try to switch your negative thoughts to positive ones, and remember that your differences make you friends.

Compatibility:        ☹ ☹ ☹

Virgo Birth Influences

Ruling planet: Mercury
Element: Earth
Polarity: Feminine
Quadruplicity: Mutable

Virgo should find a loyal companion in Leo, whose sunny disposition and energetic antics will bring some much-needed fun into Virgo's quiet life.

Leo Birth Influences

Ruling planet: The Sun
Element: Fire
Polarity: Masculine
Quadruplicity: Fixed

LEO
LIBRA

Leo Birth Influences

Ruling planet: The Sun
Element: Fire
Polarity: Masculine
Quadruplicity: Fixed

With their positive, outgoing characters, Leo and Libra make a dynamic duo whose magnetism draws others into their stellar orbit. One-on-one, they are united by their mutual interests, although neutral and receptive Libra and egotistical Leo can sometimes get on each other's nerves.

Plus Points: Any friendship between Leo and Libra will not be of the reclusive, exclusive variety, and if you two were born under these signs, you will instead find yourselves at the center of a vibrant social circle. Extroverts with an upbeat, can-do attitude to life, both airy Libra and fiery Leo thrive when surrounded by others. Venusian Libra adores bringing people together for some flirtatious fun, while attention-seeking Leo relishes an admiring audience. And when Leo's exuberance threatens to spiral out of control, Libra's moderating influence will usually restore a harmonious balance.

Along with respect, one of the foundations of an enduring friendship is common interests, which Libra and Leo have in abundance. Apart from their innate sociability, both are blessed with a sophisticated esthetic eye, and these lovers of the arts and entertainment will happily spend hours in each other's company at parties, galleries, or movie theaters. If you're a Libra, you probably admire and encourage fiery Leo's boldness and creativity, while your friend basks delightedly in your indulgent approval. If you're a Leo, you'll respond to Libra's Venusian hedonism.

Leo, don't be upset by Libra's unbiased comments. Remember that your Libra friend is only trying to offer you advice, and doesn't mean to be hurtful.

Potential Pitfalls: Leo admires Libra's discerning eye—especially when it smiles on Leo—but feels attacked when criticized. So Leo, when your airy, objective Libra friend offers you some well-meaning advice, you may explode and then sulkily retreat to lick your wounds. Your affectionate nature won't allow you to remain miffed for long, however, and, in any case, your discord-hating friend will try to smooth over any rift in your relationship. If you're a Libra, a more diplomatic soul, you may take offense at the self-centered lion's arrogant attitude, and unless your friend controls these tendencies, may coolly withdraw the hand of friendship, leaving Leo feeling hurt and bewildered.

Libra Birth Influences

Ruling planet: Venus
Element: Air
Polarity: Masculine
Quadruplicity: Cardinal

Guiding Principle: Celebrate your shared love of life, and don't take your differences too personally.

Compatibility:        

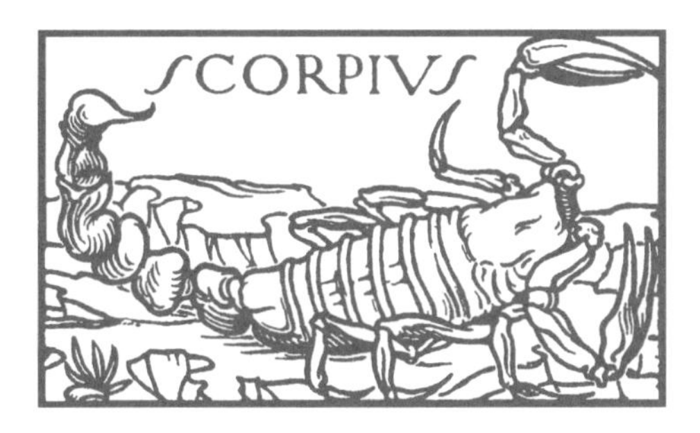

SCORPIO

LEO

Having a fixed quadruplicity in common, Leo and Scorpio each fulfill the other's main requirement in a friend: faithfulness. As long as this is evident, they will both try to overlook one another's perceived failings, which, in Scorpio's case, may be Leo's social promiscuity, and, in Leo's, Scorpio's impenetrable reserve. Each adds a new dimension to the other's life, too, with Leo encouraging Scorpio to adopt a more positive attitude, and Scorpio teaching the lion to be more considerate.

Plus Points: Sun-ruled, masculine-polarity Leo may exude such a potent aura of sunny self-assurance that spending time with him or her may rapidly lift both your spirits and confidence if you are a Scorpio whose own, Plutonian planetary governor, watery element, and feminine polarity can together sometimes cause you to feel disconnected, down, and doubtful. Leo's warm-hearted generosity—be it in trying to jolly you along or in splashing out on a meal or theater tickets for the pair of you—may also make you feel as though you are important to your leonine friend, thereby giving you a ego-boost.

If you are a Leo, you may similarly be flattered to have Scorpio's friendship. It may not have escaped your notice that, unlike you, Pluto-governed Scorpio doesn't enjoy socializing for the sake of it, and has a small circle of close friends rather than lots of superficial acquaintances, in which case being a member of the charmed circle may make you feel valued and privileged. In addition, on those rare occasions when you feel the need to talk to someone in confidence, you probably know that you'll have an empathetic listener in watery Scorpio, and can trust him or her never to broadcast your problems or secrets.

Potential Pitfalls: It may sometimes appear as though you have a one-way friendship with Leo if you a Scorpio, perhaps when you've arranged a date that Leo cancels at the last minute because an irresistible opportunity has presented itself, or when he or she forgets that you are there when playing to the crowd, for which blame the lion's spontaneous, attention-seeking element. But be warned, Leo, that when sensitive scorpions feel slighted, they are unlikely to forgive and forget, and that you may be punished with the silent treatment for a crime that you weren't aware of committing. Avoid this happening by trying to be alert to your friend's feelings and occasionally putting them first.

Guiding Principle: Try to regard your differences sympathetically.

Compatibility: ☺ ☺ ☺ ☺ ☺ ☹ ☹ ☹ ☹ ☹

Scorpio Birth Influences

Ruling planet: Pluto; traditionally Mars
Element: Water
Polarity: Feminine
Quadruplicity: Fixed

♇ ♂ ♒

If Leo has said something careless and hurt Scorpio's feelings, the friendship may be difficult to mend.

Leo Birth Influences

Ruling planet: The Sun
Element: Fire
Polarity: Masculine
Quadruplicity: Fixed

LEO
SAGITTARIUS

Leo Birth Influences

Ruling planet: The Sun
Element: Fire
Polarity: Masculine
Quadruplicity: Fixed

Although Sun-ruled, fixed-sign Leo's commanding air and firmly held opinions may occasionally irritate Sagittarius, and the Jupiter-governed, mutable archer's honesty and inclusiveness may sometimes cause the lion to feel disrespected, these two usually have far too much fun together to consider terminating their friendship. It is thanks to their shared element of fire and masculine polarity that Leo and Sagittarius are equally enthusiastic, spontaneous, and determined to enjoy themselves, which is why they typically have a mutually invigorating rapport.

Plus Points: On the rare occasions when you find yourself at a loose end and itch for some enlivening company, if you are a Sagittarius, it may be Leo whom you call first to see if he or she is free. What you probably particularly like about your friend is the lion's relish of excitement, creativity, and confidence, which is not that surprising, given that your shared fiery element and masculine polarity bestow the same traits upon you, too. But having the Sun as a ruling planet no doubt gives Leo an extra-playful edge, as well as a truly warm and generous personality, so that your friend may be both stimulating company and a pleasure to be with.

If you are a Leo, the fiery element that you and your Sagittarian friend have in common may make you both impulsive, but because the archer has a mutable quadruplicity, his or her unpredictable views may really keep you on your toes, and often in the most challenging of ways—and fearless Leos certainly love a challenge. The same birth influence may bestow adaptability on your friend, while Jupiter may cause him or her to seize on your more inspired ideas and give them a whole new dimension, thereby sending your ego soaring, too.

Leo and Sagittarius people are typically spontaneous and lively, so they're virtually unstoppable when they get together!

Potential Pitfalls: There may be times when you are riled by the aura of arrogant self-certainty that the authoritative lion exudes if you are a Sagittarius who is both more open-minded and less egotistical than Leo. Not only that, but your friend may reject outright the validity of your wider perspective when you're discussing social issues, for example, which you may find incredibly frustrating. And if you are a Leo, you may consider Sagittarius' refusal to fall in line with your beliefs a betrayal of trust, and may then become equally heated. When this happens, quickly change the subject!

Sagittarius Birth Influences

Ruling planet: Jupiter
Element: Fire
Polarity: Masculine
Quadruplicity: Mutable

♃

Guiding Principle: Never forget that you are life-enhancing equals, and that each of you therefore deserves the other's understanding when you disagree.

Compatibility:        

CAPRICORN
LEO

Because Leo is so extroverted and exuberant, and Capricorn so introverted and career-minded, it may seem to outsiders as though this is a rather mismatched pair of friends, with the lion providing the driving force and Capricorn giving little in return. They would be wrong, however. It is true that saturnine, feminine-polarity Capricorn finds Sun-ruled, masculine-polarity Leo cheerful and invigorating company, but off the social stage and behind the scenes, the earthy goat gives the lion sensible counsel, and, having a cardinal quadruplicity, sometimes a much-needed push when Leo's laziness manifests itself.

Capricorn Birth Influences

Ruling planet: Saturn
Element: Earth
Polarity: Feminine
Quadruplicity: Cardinal

Plus Points: The quality that you may especially prize in your Leo friend, if you are a Capricorn, is the loyalty that is the gift of a fixed quadruplicity, so that although you may not see one another that often, you may sense that Leo would never let your friendship peter out. When you are together, you probably find yourself basking in the warmth of the lion's sunny personality, and may often be given much food for thought in the form of fiery Leo's trendsetting ideas. All in all, being with Leo may be an energizing experience, and a welcome change from slaving away in the office or at home.

Feminine-polarity Capricorn may be reserved, but that's no doubt fine with you if you are a Leo who adores being the center of attention, because rather than competing with you, your friend may be content to sit back and listen. This doesn't mean that Capricorn is a wishy-washy type—on the contrary, a cardinal quadruplicity equals forcefulness, while having Saturn as a planetary governor may make your friend serious and resolute. As a result, you may deeply respect your friend, and may therefore be willing to countenance taking earthy Capricorn's no-nonsense advice every so often.

Capricorn and Leo will probably form an enduring friendship, despite the differences in their personalities. It helps that Capricorn often prefers to sit back and listen, while Leo enjoys performing in front of people.

Potential Pitfalls: Leo is almost certainly more sociable and outgoing than you, if you are a Capricorn, and you may consequently wish that your friend weren't so eager to drag you off to a party when you'd prefer to relax *à deux*. But every cloud has a silver lining, and you may have made a number of useful contacts through Leo. And if you are a Leo, your greatest gripe about down-to-earth Capricorn may be that his or her realistic mindset doesn't fire your imagination, but perhaps that doesn't matter too much in view of the goat's steadfast friendship.

Guiding Principle: Follow your friend's example once in a while.

Compatibility: ☺ ☺ ☺ ☺ ☺ ☺ ☺ ☹ ☹ ☹

Leo Birth Influences

Ruling planet: The Sun
Element: Fire
Polarity: Masculine
Quadruplicity: Fixed

LEO
AQUARIUS

Leo Birth Influences
Ruling planet: The Sun
Element: Fire
Polarity: Masculine
Quadruplicity: Fixed

A friendship between Leo and Aquarius is typically more casual and superficial than intimate and deep, partly because both of these extroverted, masculine-polarity people enjoy being surrounded by a crowd, and partly because a Sun-governed Leo can be rather self-centered, and airy Aquarius, somewhat detached. Although they may consequently not have a profound emotional connection, they are certainly interested in each other's ideas, and, sharing as they do a fixed, or faithful, quadruplicity, are likely to remain in touch with one another.

Plus Points: If you are an Aquarius, the dual action of Uranus, your trailblazing planetary ruler, and your intellectual element of air may give you an insatiable appetite for all things unusual and inventive, and you may therefore respond appreciatively to the creative workings of your fiery Leo friend's mind. Not only that, but your common masculine polarity may make your friend as positive and enterprising as you, so that you may have many mutually inspiring discussions during which the pair of you take an innovative concept and radically develop it. You may also be invigorated by Leo's burning energy and spontaneity, as well as grateful that your friend is generally so good-humored.

Having a fiery element means that zodiacal lions have an all-consuming need for stimulation, which is why, if you are a Leo, you may look forward to conversing with your Aquarian friend, whose unconventional, Uranus-influenced views may deliver an electrifying jolt. You may admire airy Aquarius' articulacy, too, and may find his or her bright-and-breezy outlook refreshing, especially if, like most Sun-ruled, masculine-polarity Leos, you are neither pessimistic nor introspective. All in all, you probably relish lively Aquarius' quirkiness and sense of fun.

A teenage Leo–Aquarius pair will probably enjoy experimenting and hanging out together, but their bond may not be that deep.

Potential Pitfalls: The Sun can bestow an arrogantly self-certain manner on Leos, and if you are an egalitarian Aquarius, there may be occasions when Uranus compels you to challenge what you perceive to be the lion's pompous posturing. If you are a fiery Leo who expects loyalty and approval from your friends, you may then respond to Aquarius' cool and objective criticism with annoyance. Another potential flashpoint lies in your joint fixed quadruplicity, which may endow you both with equally firmly held views, and when these are diametrically opposed, a stubborn standoff may ensue, with Leo simmering with suppressed rage, and Aquarius exuding an air of icy aloofness. If this happens regularly, steer clear of contentious subjects!

Aquarius Birth Influences
Ruling planet: Uranus; traditionally Saturn
Element: Air
Polarity: Masculine
Quadruplicity: Fixed

Guiding Principle: Agree to disagree, and don't take your differences personally.

Compatibility: ☺ ☺ ☺ ☺ ☺ ☺ ☹ ☹ ☹ ☹

PISCES
LEO

Leo and Pisces are typically total opposites, which means that their dissimilarities will either enrich or blight one another's lives. Masculine-polarity Leo's lack of inhibition may invigorate Pisces, for example, but may equally prove overpowering, while feminine-polarity Pisces' introspection may intrigue or irk the lion. But if something clicks between them, their respective quadruplicities may ensure that they become—and remain—good friends, with Leo demonstrating steadfast loyalty, and Pisces, effortless adaptability.

Plus Points: With the exception of your mutable quadruplicity, all of your birth influences point toward you being an inward-looking individual if you are a Pisces, who is nevertheless highly receptive to, and deeply affected by, the vibes that other people give out. As a result, you probably cannot help but be enlivened by your Leo friend's fiery energy and infectious enthusiasm, as well as being cheered by his or her sunny nature. And because that mutable quadruplicity may make you itch for a change once in a while, you may enjoy Leo's tendency to act on impulse, too.

Center stage is Sun-ruled Leo's natural habitat, and if you are a zodiacal lion, you must relish the appreciative response that you receive from your kind, amenable Pisces friend when airing your opinions or telling an anecdote. And when your pride has been wounded and you are in need of a sympathetic ear, you may instinctively turn to Neptune-governed, watery Pisces in the knowledge that he or she will listen to you empathetically and will then take your side, thereby giving you the ego-boost that restores your exuberance.

Potential Pitfalls: If you are a Pisces, your psychic planetary ruler and intuitive element of water may give you the insight to see through the brash face that Leo presents to the world to the warm heart that lies within, but such is the lion's fiery dynamism that the flames may rarely subside sufficiently for you to catch a glimpse of your friend's softer side. As a result, keeping up with Leo may not only drain you, but may give you little in the way of emotional nourishment. Your main problem with Pisces, if you are a Leo, may be the passiveness bestowed on your friend by a feminine polarity, compounded by the subtleness of Neptune and the reticence of water. You may consequently find Pisces less than stimulating company, and zodiacal lions adore being challenged and surprised.

Guiding Principle: Don't demand more of one another than you are each capable of giving, and learn to appreciate your differences.

Compatibility:        

Pisces Birth Influences

Ruling planet: Neptune; traditionally Jupiter
Element: Water
Polarity: Feminine
Quadruplicity: Mutable

Although Pisces and Leo aren't temperamentally similar, once they've bonded, they may become faithful friends.

Leo Birth Influences

Ruling planet: The Sun
Element: Fire
Polarity: Masculine
Quadruplicity: Fixed

VIRGO
VIRGO

Virgo Birth Influences
Ruling planet: Mercury
Element: Earth
Polarity: Feminine
Quadruplicity: Mutable

A friendship between two Virgos is likely to revolve around conversation, which they both enjoy.

Virgo Birth Influences
Ruling planet: Mercury
Element: Earth
Polarity: Feminine
Quadruplicity: Mutable

Two Virgo individuals usually get along well, not least because each fulfills an important Virgoan requirement in a friend, namely that he or she should be a good conversationalist and a fount of information. It is the combination of communicative, perceptive Mercury and a mutable quadruplicity that gives articulate Virgos an interest in intellectual matters, their shared feminine polarity furthermore causing them to be thoughtful, and their earthy element, level-headed. Yet these birth influences may also make each prone to pointing out the error of the other's ways on a regular basis, and then to make practical recommendations, which may not always be appreciated.

Plus Points: If you are a Virgo and your friend is, too, you no doubt enjoy the meeting of minds that may often characterize your get-togethers. An astrological analysis suggests that you are both self-contained people who nevertheless welcome the chance to swap opinions on all manner of subjects, and to dissect them in minute detail, demonstrating how your planetary governor and mutable quadruplicity manifest themselves and interact. Another common trait may be your down-to-earth resilience, which means that you probably don't have to tiptoe around one another worrying that your objective or realistic viewpoint will trigger tears or tantrums, as they would if either of you were born under a water or fire sign. And another advantage of being a pair of mutable Virgo friends is the adaptability that smoothes the course of any friendship.

Potential Pitfalls: Human nature being what it is, you may each think that you are being helpful in neutrally assessing where your friend may have gone wrong when he or she is in a fix, but may resent being at the receiving end of your fellow Virgo's fault-finding yourself. Not only that, but if your introspective, feminine polarity kicks in, you may consequently spend sleepless nights fretting about whether your friend was justified in highlighting your supposed character flaws or mistakes. If so, try not to obsess too much because it is likely that your earthy, Mercury-ruled friend's comments were intended to offer a straightforward solution rather than immerse you in a crisis of confidence. More generally, your mutual quadruplicity may cause you to welcome variety, and because your Virgo friend's temperament may be so similar to yours, you may not find him or her that invigorating or intriguing.

Guiding Principle: Don't take one another's constructive criticism as a personal attack, but recognize that it is given in the spirit of friendship.

Compatibility:       

LIBRA / VIRGO

Virgo and Libra possess characteristics that, on the one hand, may prove beneficial to each, but, on the other, may act as mutual irritants. Virgo's realistic outlook and matter-of-fact advice may either give Libra a much-needed reality check or may trigger yawns of boredom. And while Venus-governed, airy Libra may inject some fun into Virgo's responsible existence, Virgo may come to regard pleasure-loving Libra as being shallow and fickle. But then it is not as though they spend every waking hour together, and neither bears unreasonable grudges, so it is the positives, rather than the negatives, that typically prevail in their friendship.

Plus Points: Because Virgo's planetary ruler is Mercury, named for the information-gathering Roman messenger god, and this sign's quadruplicity is mutable, or changeable, your Virgo friend may frequently excite your interest and curiosity if you are an airy Libra. Indeed, when you get together, you may spend a lot of time on neutral territory as you discuss all manner of subjects, and if the conversation strays into practical matters, may occasionally receive a vital wake-up call from your earthy friend, perhaps regarding an unavoidable obligation or deadline that you've pushed to the back of your mind.

What may particularly attract you to Libra, if you are a Virgo, is the positive, can-do attitude that comes from having a masculine polarity and cardinal quadruplicity, maybe because your own polarity and quadruplicity sometimes make you feel negative and uncertain. In addition, the intelligence bestowed on Libra by the element of air may give you an intellectual affinity with your friend, while the indulgence that is the gift of Venus may be delightfully relaxing. All in all, being with Libra may be a simultaneously heartening, enlivening, and enjoyable experience.

Potential Pitfalls: Virgo is nothing if not objective and realistic, which you may sometimes find depressing if you are a Libra who looks to your friends for some light-hearted diversion, ego-stroking flattery, and the chance to liberate yourself from the grinding, day-to-day demands of your family or employer. And if you are a sometimes insecure Virgo, you may wish that your Libran friend would be a little more empathetic on those rare occasions when you feel emboldened enough to open up and divulge your innermost concerns. If so, both of you would do well to remember that true friendship is all about give and take.

Guiding Principle: Understand that your personalities complement one another, and that accommodating your differences will enhance both of your lives.

Compatibility:        

Libra Birth Influences

Ruling planet: Venus
Element: Air
Polarity: Masculine
Quadruplicity: Cardinal

Thanks to Virgo's practical skills and Libra's curiosity, these friends can explore and learn a lot together.

Virgo Birth Influences

Ruling planet: Mercury
Element: Earth
Polarity: Feminine
Quadruplicity: Mutable

VIRGO
SCORPIO

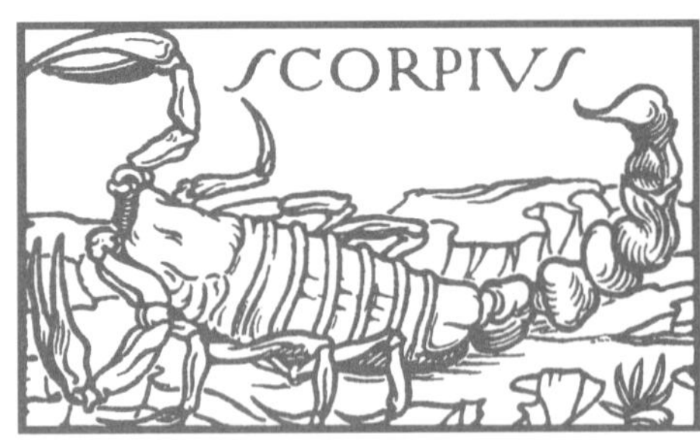

Virgo Birth Influences

Ruling planet: Mercury
Element: Earth
Polarity: Feminine
Quadruplicity: Mutable

If Virgo becomes too critical of a Scorpio, the scorpion may take offense and become agressive.

Scorpio Birth Influences

Ruling planet: Pluto; traditionally Mars
Element: Water
Polarity: Feminine
Quadruplicity: Fixed

If mutable, earthy Virgo weren't so adaptable and loyal, and fixed-sign, watery Scorpio, so steadfast and empathetic, a friendship between these two would probably have been doomed from the outset. But if you're reading this page to discover how your respective birth influences affect your relationship with your Virgo or Scorpio friend, the chances are that they are balanced in your friendship's favor, even if Mercury-governed Virgo's objective viewpoint can upset sensitive Scorpio, and Pluto-ruled Scorpio's reticence can frustrate more forthcoming Virgo.

Plus Points: If you are a typical Scorpio, you may not extend the hand of friendship lightly, partly because your watery element, feminine polarity, and planetary ruler cause you to operate on a profound, rather than superficial, level, and partly because your fixed quadruplicity makes you something of a loner. Yet your Virgo friend may have many qualities that encourage you to think that he or she is worthy of your time and attention, and that also make a positive contribution to your life. It may be that you appreciate earthy, mutable Virgo's patience and flexibility, for instance, but perhaps it is your intelligent, mercurial friend's reasoned observations that you really value when you're in need of astute advice.

When fixed-sign scorpions consider people friends, they generally stick to them through thick and thin, for which you may be grateful if you are Scorpio's Virgo friend. Your constant, earthy element is ranged against your unstable, mutable quadruplicity, while your feminine polarity may make you prone to bottling up this internal conflict, a state of affairs that watery Scorpio may instinctively understand. And by offering you his or her tacit support, Scorpio's sympathetic stance may hearten you to unburden yourself, a cathartic experience for Virgos.

Potential Pitfalls: Although you may often reap the benefits of Virgo's impartial advice, you may occasionally regard his or her counsel as a personal attack if you are a touchy Scorpio, and may then feel so hurt that you lash out, demonstrating the effect that Mars, your aggressive secondary planetary governor, wields over you. But Scorpio is not as articulate as you, if you are a Virgo, so that your friend's unaccountably vicious reaction to your helpfulness may cause you to respond with cold criticism, thus setting a vicious cycle in motion.

Guiding Principle: Each of the astrological factors that makes you good friends has a downside that you should avoid dwelling on, otherwise negativity may poison a relationship that is mutually affirming.

Compatibility: ☺ ☺ ☺ ☺ ☺ ☺ ☺ ☹ ☹ ☹

SAGITTARIUS
VIRGO

Mercury-governed, earthy Virgo's intelligence and supportiveness, and Jupiter-ruled, fiery Sagittarius' positive way of thinking and generosity of spirit bode well for a long-lasting friendship, particularly when the communicativeness bestowed on them both by their mutual quadruplicity is taken into account. That said, these same birth influences, along with their opposite polarities, may prove irritants, with mercurial Virgo's nitpicking in particular frustrating jovial Sagittarius, and Sagittarius' lack of inhibition arousing restrained Virgo's disapproval.

Plus Points: You can probably depend on your Virgo friend for some interesting conversation if you are a Sagittarius whose expansive planetary governor causes you to relish speculating and philosophizing on the meaning of life, the universe, and everything. Not only is Virgo ruled by Mercury, but your friend's polarity is feminine, or deep-thinking, and you are both blessed with the analytical instincts of mutable-quadruplicity individuals. There may also have been occasions when earthy, level-headed Virgo has kept you on track when your fiery element has tempted you to take a reckless step, for which, looking back, you may be grateful.

Getting together with Sagittarius may generally be a cheering experience if you are an introverted Virgo. It is thanks to Jupiter, a masculine polarity, and the element of fire that Sagittarius usually looks on the bright side and doesn't waste time agonizing about the potentially negative consequences of branching out in a different direction, thereby perhaps giving you the confidence to do exactly that. Sharing a mutable quadruplicity means that you both enjoy variety, too, and because your fiery friend is more spontaneous, you may often find that his or her spur-of-the-moment decision sweeps you away on a tide of Sagittarian enthusiasm into a surprisingly entertaining situation.

Potential Pitfalls: Although you may respect Virgo's reasoning, and may recognize that the advice that you receive from him or her is sensible, your friend's objective, matter-of-fact, and cautious mindset may sometimes bore you if you are an adventurous Sagittarius. Even worse, you may bristle at Virgo's well-meaning tendency to point out your supposed failings, for no one likes to feel that they have been judged and found wanting, least of all fiery, somewhat egotistical Sagittarians. And you in turn may frequently be exasperated by Sagittarius' aggressive self-certainty if you are a Virgo, especially if you suspect that your friend's stance is born of instinct or arrogance rather than logic.

Guiding Principle: Agree to disagree when your differences threaten your friendship.

Compatibility: ☺ ☺ ☺ ☺ ☺ ☺ ☹ ☹ ☹ ☹

Sagittarius Birth Influences

Ruling planet: Jupiter
Element: Fire
Polarity: Masculine
Quadruplicity: Mutable

Impetuous Sagittarius may need a grounding influence to keep her out of trouble, which a Virgo friend can provide. Virgo should in turn enjoy her fiery friend's sense of fun.

Virgo Birth Influences

Ruling planet: Mercury
Element: Earth
Polarity: Feminine
Quadruplicity: Mutable

VIRGO
CAPRICORN

Virgo Birth Influences

Ruling planet: Mercury
Element: Earth
Polarity: Feminine
Quadruplicity: Mutable

Because they share the same level-headed, contemplative attitude, thanks to their common element of earth and feminine polarity, a friendship between Virgo and Capricorn may be less than stimulating. As a result, neither mutable Virgo, who relishes diversity, nor cardinal Capricorn, who is dedicated to getting ahead in life, may feel inclined to spend much time together, even if they generally enjoy an agreeable meeting of minds when they do. That said, they are typically mutually supportive individuals, with Mercury-governed Virgo offering Capricorn objective advice, and Saturn-ruled Capricorn's mature outlook strengthening Virgo's resolve. In short, they are probably well disposed toward one another, but not bosom buddies.

When Virgo and Capricorn share certain interests, they may remain companionable for a lifetime, following their favorite sport, for example. They're unlikely to be very close, though.

Plus Points: There may be many qualities that you admire in your Virgo friend if you are a Capricorn, such as the speed at which his or her mercurial mind operates and the articulacy and adaptability of an individual born under a mutable sign, maybe because the influence of Saturn causes you take your time in formulating and expressing your opinions, as well as to stick to your tried-and-trusted ways. Nevertheless, your common element and polarity may give you and Virgo an innate understanding, and you may also welcome Virgo's perceptive, neutral viewpoint, perhaps when discussing the next step that you should take in furthering your career.

If you are a Virgo, you no doubt respect your Capricorn friend. Like you, he or she may be a down-to-earth realist and a person who does not take decisions lightly, but Saturn may infuse Capricorn with a serious sense of responsibility that you find formidable, maybe because you recognize this trait as being a virtue, but don't share it to the same degree. As a child of Mercury, you may consequently give Capricorn's sober counsel serious consideration, and, after analyzing it thoroughly, as is your wont, may come to the conclusion that following it will bring tangible rewards that outweigh the sacrifice required.

Potential Pitfalls: Your free time is no doubt limited if you are a busy, dutiful Capricorn, and when you schedule an evening with Virgo, you may expect your friend to give you his or her full attention. Yet there may be occasions when voluble Virgo can't resist returning the banter of a lively someone, causing you to feel left out. But then if you are a mutable Virgo, cardinal Capricorn's driving ambition may make it seem as though your friend has a tediously one-track mind.

Guiding Principle: Mutual tolerance is the key to keeping your friendship alive.

Compatibility: ☺ ☺ ☺ ☺ ☺ ☹ ☹ ☹ ☹ ☹

Capricorn Birth Influences

Ruling planet: Saturn
Element: Earth
Polarity: Feminine
Quadruplicity: Cardinal

AQUARIUS

VIRGO

Virgo having Mercury as a planetary governor and a mutable quadruplicity, and Aquarius, an airy element and Uranus as a ruler, bodes well for their friendship, for while Virgo enjoys garnering knowledge and is open to new ideas, Aquarius is both garrulous and the source of radically inventive concepts. Their common enjoyment of discussion is generally the glue that holds them together, although feminine-polarity Virgo is also supportive, and fixed-sign Aquarius, loyal. That said, Virgo's earthy realism may irritate Aquarius, just as Aquarius' uncompromising views may annoy objective Virgo.

Plus Points: Being an airy, gregarious individual if you are an Aquarius, you may tend to flit from person to person at social gatherings, seeking inspiration and quickly moving on if someone's small talk bores you. If so, Virgo may be one of the few who really engages your attention. It is Mercury that makes your friend intelligent and quick-thinking, and his or her mutable quadruplicity that enables him or her to go along with you when you change the subject, so that your conversations may be both stimulating and wide ranging. And because Virgo is a feminine-polarity, earthy zodiacal sign, your friend may also be agreeably receptive to your unusual notions, as well as a patient listener who is ever ready to offer helpful advice.

What you may especially like about airy, masculine-polarity Aquarius if you are a feminine-polarity Virgo who can sometimes feel negative and put-upon, is your friend's cheerful, positive attitude and the minimal emotional demands that he or she makes of you. When you get together, it may seem as though you are on a purely intellectual plane, which probably suits a clever, dispassionate, Mercury-ruled individual like you. And because Uranus bestows the most unconventional of opinions on Aquarius, the diversity-loving, mutable-quadruplicity facet of your character may delight in hearing his or her alternative viewpoints. You may benefit from Aquarius' fixed quadruplicity, too, which may make your friend endearingly faithful.

Potential Pitfalls: If you are an Aquarius, Uranus may cause you to challenge accepted beliefs, and although Virgo may understand your reasoning, your earthy friend may often dismiss your ideas as impractical, if ingenious. As a result, you may come to consider your friend unimaginative, but then if you are a Virgo, you may wish that Aquarius weren't so adamant that his or her pipe dreams could change the world.

Guiding Principle: Don't let an intellectual disagreement over a theoretical issue mar your real-life relationship.

Compatibility:        

Aquarius Birth Influences

Ruling planet: Uranus; traditionally Saturn
Element: Air
Polarity: Masculine
Quadruplicity: Fixed

♅ ♄

Aquarius and Virgo acquaintances may bond over a shared interest or joint project, which should keep them happy, for a while, at least.

Virgo Birth Influences

Ruling planet: Mercury
Element: Earth
Polarity: Feminine
Quadruplicity: Mutable

VIRGO / PISCES

Virgo Birth Influences

Ruling planet: Mercury
Element: Earth
Polarity: Feminine
Quadruplicity: Mutable

It is frequently their shared, mutable quadruplicity that brings—and keeps—Virgo and Pisces friends together, on the one hand making them sociable and appreciative of diversity, and, on the other, flexible enough to accommodate their differences, which, apart from their feminine-polarity thoughtfulness, may be considerable. Comparing and contrasting their planetary governors and elements, for instance, Mercury and earth may give Virgo an objective, practical mindset, while Neptune and water may infuse Pisces with an otherworldly, intuitive outlook, "hard" and "soft" characteristics that may prove either mutually alienating or supportive.

Plus Points: Virgo may be the first person to whom you turn for advice when you are in a fix, but quickly need to reach a decision, if you are a Pisces. Whereas Neptune and water can cloud your judgment with conflicting emotions, Mercury and earth bestow an analytical, rational, and realistic approach to problem-solving on Virgo, and because you have a feminine polarity in common, you probably know that your friend will give a lot of thought to your predicament. You may also enjoy discussing your Neptunian spiritual beliefs with interested, open-minded, mercurial Virgo.

It may seem to you as though Pisces has a heart of gold if you are a Virgo. The coming-together of Neptune and water in your friend no doubt manifests itself as unselfishness and compassion, so that when things are going badly for you, Pisces may always be willing to cancel his or her plans to lend you a sympathetic ear. Indeed, Pisces may instinctively understand that letting it all out is often exactly what a communicative Virgo with a feminine-polarity tendency to worry needs in order to feel more positive.

If Virgo provides solid, practical help or advice, and Pisces, unstinting emotional support, this friendship may be important to both parties.

Potential Pitfalls: Mercurial, earthy Virgo may be prone to seeing the world in black and white, which you may sometimes find frustrating if you are a Pisces whose own planetary ruler and element may color your viewpoint so that you discern a subtle spectrum of shades of gray, particularly where human emotions are concerned. As a result, you may consider Virgo to lack empathy, and because you are far more sensitive than your friend, may be hurt by his or her resolutely matter-of-fact manner. But then if you are a Virgo, you may equally be exasperated by what you perceive to be Pisces' wooly, irrational thought processes, as well as by your friend's touchiness when you helpfully try to set him or her straight.

Guiding Principle: Try not to dwell on one another's less appealing traits.

Compatibility: ☺ ☺ ☺ ☺ ☺ ☺ ☹ ☹ ☹ ☹

Pisces Birth Influences

Ruling planet: Neptune; traditionally Jupiter
Element: Water
Polarity: Feminine
Quadruplicity: Mutable

LIBRA
LIBRA

Two Libran friends generally get along swimmingly, and if they don't have the most profound of relationships, this typically suits each very well. Combine self-indulgent Venus with a pushy, cardinal quadruplicity, frivolous element of air, and an extrovert, masculine polarity, and you have a pair of individuals who are set on having a good time and hate to be constrained or brought down by a friend's neediness or confused emotions. They may therefore enjoy one another's lively, undemanding company, but won't necessarily stick together should one suddenly be beset by problems or a more enticing character appear on the scene.

Plus Points: If you and your friend are Libras, you probably interact easily, but perhaps superficially, which may be a welcome relief if you spend your days surrounded by people whose fragile egos require boosting or whose ruffled feathers need smoothing. You may each be Venus-influenced pleasure-givers and peacemakers who loathe unpleasantness and instinctively try to diffuse a heated situation, but your airy element causes you to be rather unemotional types who would rather operate on a strictly intellectual basis and prefer to get more out of a get-together with a friend than you yourself are forced to give. Your fellow Libra may therefore be the ideal companion for a night on the town, being someone who is as easygoing and communicative as you, as well as a confident and energetic self-starter, thanks to your shared masculine polarity and cardinal quadruplicity.

Potential Pitfalls: None of your birth influences suggests that you are committed creatures if you and your friend are both Libras, except, perhaps, to the serious business of furthering your own ambitions, due to your driving, cardinal quadruplicity. And while airy Libras rarely suffer emotional crises, life may inflict a hard knock once in a while, which the practical or empathetic support of a friend may go some way to alleviating. Yet airy Libras often find it hard to muster mundane advice or genuine compassion, and if you are a temporarily crushed Libra, you may feel that your friend is merely going through the motions when he or she commiserates with you, while silently wishing that you would snap out of it and lighten up. But then if you find yourself dealing with an unusually downcast Libra, you may similarly be gripped by boredom, and may soon flit away to have fun with a more light-hearted or hedonistic playmate.

Guiding Principle: Mutual entertainment may be beneficial, but loyalty is invaluable.

Compatibility: ☺ ☺ ☺ ☺ ☺ ☺ ☹ ☹ ☹ ☹

Libra Birth Influences

Ruling planet: Venus
Element: Air
Polarity: Masculine
Quadruplicity: Cardinal

If you're a Libra who enjoys a relaxing evening out after work, or a stimulating show or play, a fellow Libra makes a great companion.

Libra Birth Influences

Ruling planet: Venus
Element: Air
Polarity: Masculine
Quadruplicity: Cardinal

LIBRA
SCORPIO

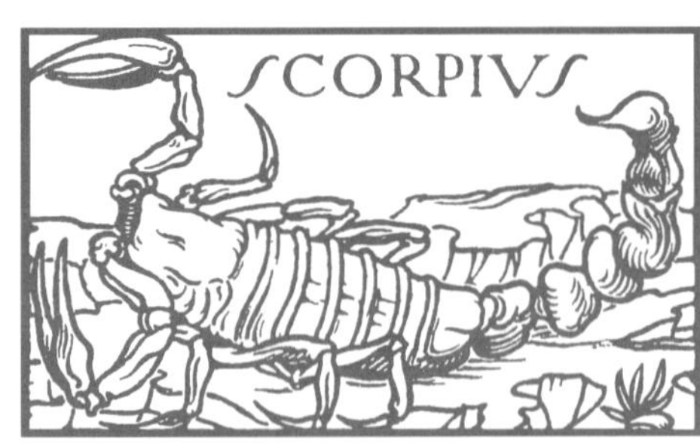

Libra Birth Influences

Ruling planet: Venus
Element: Air
Polarity: Masculine
Quadruplicity: Cardinal

A Libra may find it hard to understand her Scorpio friend sometimes, as Scorpio can be quite shuttered. This makes it difficult for them to become close friends.

Scorpio Birth Influences

Ruling planet: Pluto; traditionally Mars
Element: Water
Polarity: Feminine
Quadruplicity: Fixed

Easygoing, diplomatic Libra, and empathetic, loyal Scorpio have the potential to be good friends, and, indeed, often are, but are nevertheless unlikely to be bosom buddies, or to spend that much time together. For whereas airy, masculine-polarity, Venus-ruled Libra is sociable, outgoing, and inclined to hedonism, watery, feminine-polarity, Pluto-governed Scorpio is reserved, introspective, and tends toward the austere, and while Libra enjoys an impersonal meeting of minds, Scorpio longs for a profound emotional connection. In short, here are two people who may find it difficult to relate to one another.

Plus Points: Being essentially a private and discriminating individual if you are a Scorpio, you probably prefer your own company to that of people who don't repay the emotional commitment that you invest in friends, but may make an exception for Libra. Venus may bestow both a desire to please and an appetite for pleasure on your friend, air and a masculine polarity also making him or her a rational, positive thinker. As a result, you may find Libra soothing and relaxing to be with, as well as a cheeringly constructive problem-solver when dark emotions have clouded your judgment.

Your Scorpio friend may be something of an enigma to you if you are a Libra, which is hardly surprising when you take his or her inward-looking, feminine polarity, self-protective element of water, and secretive planetary governor into account. But because your own airy element may cause you to be curious; your masculine polarity, to be uninhibited; indulgent Venus, to relish seducing others into having fun with you; and your cardinal quadruplicity, to rise to a challenge, your game plan may be to encourage Scorpio to open up and loosen up. And should he or she occasionally do so, you may be amazed by the depth of Scorpio's compassion and faithfulness (gifts of water and a fixed quadruplicity), so that you look at your friend in a new, more affectionate, light.

Potential Pitfalls: Your watery element may bless you with intuition and curse you with touchiness if you are a Scorpio, and you may consequently conclude that cardinal-quadruplicity, airy Libra is both selfish and uninterested in your feelings, despite your friend's polite inquiries into your well-being. You may find Libra's detachment wounding, but then if you are a Libra, you may find coaxing candidness out of Scorpio such hard work that you've given up trying.

Guiding Principle: Appreciate one another for who you are, and don't demand the impossible from your friend.

Compatibility: ☺ ☺ ☺ ☹ ☹ ☹ ☹ ☹ ☹ ☹

SAGITTARIUS
LIBRA

Airy Libra and fiery Sagittarius may not have that profound a relationship, but then neither generally needs propping up, nor is clinginess welcome in a friend. What they typically do have, however, is a wonderful time together. Having a masculine polarity in common, both are extroverts who, thanks to Libra's airy element and Sagittarius' mutable quadruplicity, enjoy conversing with one another and are always ready to welcome someone new into their circle. Libra's impatient, cardinal quadruplicity blends well with Sagittarius' impulsive, fiery element, too, while their respective planetary governors ensure that they have a mutually tolerant rapport.

Plus Points: Your mutable restlessness and fiery spontaneity may often cause you to make an inspired suggestion on the spur of the moment if you are a Sagittarius, and what you may particularly like about your masculine-polarity, cardinal-quadruplicity, Libran friend is his or her enthusiastic response. The influence of Venus may make Libra an art-lover, and his or her airy element, a persuasive charmer, so that your friend may similarly introduce you to all manner of cultural pursuits that satisfy your fiery creativity and feed your appetite for variety. All in all, Libra may be one of your favorite playmates.

Your Jupiter-ruled, masculine-polarity, Sagittarian friend may have a positive outlook that accords agreeably with your own if you are a Libra. Venus probably also infuses you with an abhorrence of uncomfortable atmospheres, and because Sagittarius' mutable quadruplicity may bestow a tendency to avoid conflict on him or her, too, you probably feel as though you are usually on the same, congenial wavelength. And if your airy element gives you an interest in intellectual matters, you may be fascinated by Jovian Sagittarius' religious or philosophical beliefs, even if you consider them a little eccentric (not that you'd ever say so, of course, being a diplomatic child of Venus).

Potential Pitfalls: Although airy Libra is kind, and fiery Sagittarius warm-hearted, neither of you is naturally empathetic, and you can both be somewhat selfish, too, which suggests that should one of you suddenly find that circumstances have sent you spiraling into a rare emotional crisis, the other may not drop everything to support you. Under normal conditions, you may sometimes be annoyed by cardinal-quadruplicity Libra's pushiness if you are a Sagittarius, while fiery Sagittarius' brusqueness may occasionally affront your delicate sensibilities if you are a Libra.

Guiding Principle: Be there for one another in the bad times, as well as the good.

Compatibility: ☺ ☺ ☺ ☺ ☺ ☺ ☺ ☺ ☺ ☹

Sagittarius Birth Influences

Ruling planet: Jupiter
Element: Fire
Polarity: Masculine
Quadruplicity: Mutable

Outgoing Sagittarius will find a lively and fun-loving friend in Libra. Both being independent by nature, neither is likely to lean too hard on the other for emotional support.

Libra Birth Influences

Ruling planet: Venus
Element: Air
Polarity: Masculine
Quadruplicity: Cardinal

LIBRA
CAPRICORN

Libra Birth Influences

Ruling planet: Venus
Element: Air
Polarity: Masculine
Quadruplicity: Cardinal

A serious Capricorn may find him- or herself having some rare fun with outgoing Libra.

Capricorn Birth Influences

Ruling planet: Saturn
Element: Earth
Polarity: Feminine
Quadruplicity: Cardinal

It is their common cardinal quadruplicity that generally attracts Libra and Capricorn to one another and provides a bond that helps these two very different personalities to remain friends. For whereas Libra is extroverted, Capricorn is introverted; Venus-governed Libra can be hedonistic, but Saturn-ruled Capricorn tends to be self-denying; and while airy Libra is volatile and impractical, earthy Capricorn is steady and sensible. Yet because each recognizes and respects the initiative, ambition, and forcefulness that their shared cardinal quadruplicity bestows on them both, they have the potential to forge a relationship that is rooted in respect.

Plus Points: Your masculine-polarity, airy, Libran friend may possess certain qualities that you rather envy if you are a feminine-polarity, earthy Capricorn, such as the confidence and charm with which he or she negotiates social situations that may make you feel uncomfortable. Yet with easygoing Libra by your side, you may find yourself relaxing and perhaps even enjoying yourself, especially if the influence of benevolent Venus has blessed Libra with a gift for networking and matchmaking and your friend is consequently busy introducing you to useful business contacts or even an attractive someone. And when spending time with your communicative friend, you may be pleased to find that he or she shares your cardinal-quadruplicity determination to move onward and upward in life.

If you are an airy Libra, dealing with practicalities may bore you to tears, which is why you may appreciate having such a mature and responsible friend in earthy, saturnine Capricorn. Indeed, he or she may be flattered when you ask for advice, be it on how best to proceed in furthering your career or which investments will yield the best return, particularly if Venus has given you an interest in making your money work for you. You also probably know that, having a feminine polarity, Capricorn will give the matter considerable thought.

Potential Pitfalls: Airy Libra may be such a sociable person that you have difficulty pinning him or her down for a get-together if you are a Capricorn, and if others are present, you may be disgruntled if your friend flits away to enjoy some light-hearted banter with someone else. Although you may not mean to annoy Capricorn if you are a kindly, Venusian Libra, you may sometimes find your friend's earthy, saturnine company a little dreary, and may wish that he or she would lighten up and simply have fun.

Guiding Principle: Follow your friend's example once in a while.

Compatibility: ☺ ☺ ☺ ☺ ☺ ☹ ☹ ☹ ☹ ☹

AQUARIUS

LIBRA

It may sound contradictory, but although they generally like each other a lot, Libra and Aquarius friends may neither see one another that often nor enjoy an intimate heart-to-heart when they do. The key to this paradox lies primarily in their common masculine polarity and element of air, which cause them to be outgoing, sociable people who each have a wide circle of acquaintances with whom they prefer to have a no-strings-attached relationship. In addition, pleasure-loving, Venus-governed Libra desires a playmate, and Uranus-ruled Aquarius, a sounding board off whom to bounce experimental ideas. Each usually fulfills the other's requirements, although a cardinal quadruplicity can make Libra self-seeking, and a fixed one may result in Aquarius being egocentric, thus providing further reasons why they may not be that close.

Plus Points: You're probably always pleased to see your Libra friend if you are an Aquarius, maybe because a conversation of the abstract sort that you enjoy is usually guaranteed, but perhaps mainly because he or she shares your positive outlook and makes few emotional demands of you. The airy element that bestows intelligence upon each of you may also infuse you both with playfulness, and because Venus blesses Libra with a heightened appetite for fun and a talent for networking, your friend may lead you into all sorts of entertaining situations or introduce you to a variety of friends.

If you are a Libra, you may enjoy the sense of being with an equal when you are with Aquarius, be it because your friend is as confident and gregarious as you or because you are on the same intellectual wavelength. Not only that, but Uranus may prompt Aquarius to come up with the most inventive notions, especially regarding social issues, which you may find delightfully intriguing. And because Aquarius' quadruplicity is fixed, you may be flattered by your friend's tendency to keep in touch.

Potential Pitfalls: One of the few things that may irritate you about Libra, if you are an Aquarius, is your friend's self-absorption and cardinal-quadruplicity driving ambition. But then you may consider your fixed-quadruplicity Aquarian friend self-opinionated and inflexible if you are a Libra. A word of advice to both of you talkative types: don't monopolize the conversation, particularly if it's about yourself!

Guiding Principle: Remember that friendship is a two-way process.

Compatibility: ☺ ☺ ☺ ☺ ☺ ☺ ☺ ☹ ☹ ☹

Aquarius Birth Influences

Ruling planet: Uranus; traditionally Saturn
Element: Air
Polarity: Masculine
Quadruplicity: Fixed

Aquarius and Libra are likely to enjoy a casual, fun-filled friendship. Both are outgoing, sociable, and prefer a large group of friends to a small circle of closer confidants.

Libra Birth Influences

Ruling planet: Venus
Element: Air
Polarity: Masculine
Quadruplicity: Cardinal

LIBRA
PISCES

Libra Birth Influences

Ruling planet: Venus
Element: Air
Polarity: Masculine
Quadruplicity: Cardinal

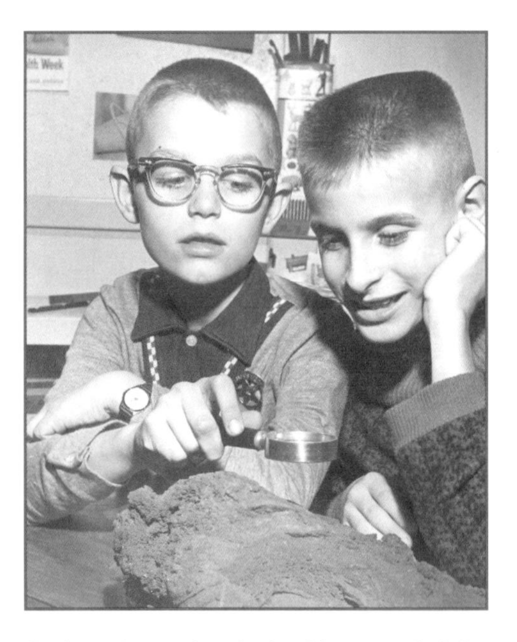

Reticent, but variety-loving Pisces may find that a positive, cardinal-quadruplicity Libra friend introduces him to new ideas and experiences.

Pisces Birth Influences

Ruling planet: Neptune; traditionally Jupiter
Element: Water
Polarity: Feminine
Quadruplicity: Mutable

Libra and Pisces friends are usually a mutually sympathetic pair, with masculine-polarity, airy Libra reassuring and cheering sometimes shy and negative, feminine-polarity Pisces, and watery, Neptune-governed Pisces offering Libra attention and compassion. They are similar in some respects, too, for Venus and Neptune endow them both with delicacy in their dealings and an abhorrence of conflict that is reinforced by Libra's airy element and Pisces' mutable quadruplicity. Yet there may be occasions when Libra's self-interest and coolness hurt selfless, insecure Pisces, and when Pisces' confused feelings estrange rational, unempathetic Libra.

Plus Points: Your airy, Venus-ruled, Libra friend may be a calm and kindly presence in your life if you are a Pisces, which you must appreciate if your feminine polarity, combined with your watery element and planetary ruler, cause you to be ultrasensitive to overpowering characters, when your mutable, changeable quadruplicity may send you from one emotional extreme to the other. Indeed, it is not for nothing that the sign of Libra is called the balance, and your even-tempered, tolerant, Venusian friend may have a soothing influence on you, as well as a heartening one, thanks to his or her bright and breezy, airy element and positive, masculine polarity.

Your Pisces friend may be someone to whom you turn when you require a favor if you are a Libra, for not only are watery, Neptunian, Pisces people blessed with caring natures, but they typically put others' needs first. At other times, your airy curiosity may be aroused by the aura of mystery that surrounds your reticent friend, and because you may find it hard to resist a challenge, due to your questing, cardinal quadruplicity, may make it your mission to discover more about enigmatic Pisces. And perhaps you've already ascertained that Neptune-governed Pisces is a deeply spiritual person.

Potential Pitfalls: Having a self-centered, cardinal quadruplicity, a self-indulgent planetary ruler, an outgoing, masculine polarity, and an unemotional, airy element may mean that Libra is often more interested in having a good time than in propping you up when you are feeling down if you are a Pisces, which may cut your vulnerable heart to the quick. But then because Pisces finds it difficult to express his or her feelings or to ask for help, you may simply not notice your friend's dejection if you are a less intuitive Libra who rarely intends to hurt, or else may believe that having fun is the best antidote.

Guiding Principle: Communicate openly, honestly, and, above all, considerately.

Compatibility: ☺ ☺ ☺ ☺ ☺ ☺ ☹ ☹ ☹ ☹

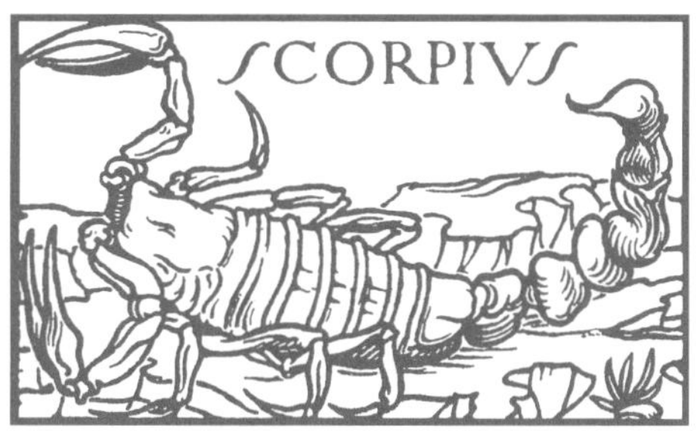

SCORPIO
SCORPIO

Having identical birth influences, including the intuitive, empathetic element of water, two Scorpio friends usually instinctively understand one another, which is just as well, given that those born under the sign of the scorpion can be highly reticent, private individuals, due to the interaction of self-protective water, secretive Pluto, and an introspective, feminine polarity. Despite being on the same, somewhat guarded, wavelength, these watery friends generally care deeply about one another and will go out of their way to provide emotional support when necessary, unless one feels slighted or betrayed by the other, in which case their common, fixed, or uncompromising, quadruplicity may create an aggrieved distance between them that can't be bridged.

Plus Points: If you are a Scorpio who prefers your own company to mixing with casual acquaintances, you may have a handful of very good friends with whom you enjoy spending time, your fellow scorpion no doubt included. Your joint feminine polarity may cause you to be somewhat shy, which is why you may be relieved that Scorpio's preference, like yours, is for quiet, one-on-one get-togethers during which you can catch up with one another's news and views. You may also be grateful that although your watery element makes Scorpio someone who doesn't pry, he or she may nevertheless detect when you are feeling down and may then display the sensitivity and compassion that encourages you to open up and share your troubles, which is often a comfort for Pluto-ruled Scorpios who tend to feel emotionally disconnected or isolated. And because you have a fixed quadruplicity in common, Scorpio is probably as loyal to you as you are to your friend.

Potential Pitfalls: They may hide it well, but Scorpios can be extremely thin-skinned, and furthermore require constancy from their friends. Neither of you would intentionally injure your friend by being uncaring or fickle, but it may be that a misunderstanding results in one of you believing that the other has behaved in a deliberately hurtful fashion—perhaps if he or she has stood you up for what you consider a trivial reason. If this happens, the upset scorpion may either punish the other with silence or, if the Mars effect bestowed by your secondary planetary ruler kicks in, may go on the attack, in turn wounding the other. And when two scorpions are both seething with resentment, this may become a permanent state of affairs.

Guiding Principle: Don't let hypersensitivity ruin your relationship.

Compatibility: ☺ ☺ ☺ ☺ ☺ ☺ ☹ ☹ ☹ ☹

Scorpio Birth Influences

Ruling planet: Pluto; traditionally Mars
Element: Water
Polarity: Feminine
Quadruplicity: Fixed

Two Scorpio friends should find in one another a sympathetic, understanding listener to whom they can open up, despite their customary reticence.

Scorpio Birth Influences

Ruling planet: Pluto; traditionally Mars
Element: Water
Polarity: Feminine
Quadruplicity: Fixed

SCORPIO — SAGITTARIUS

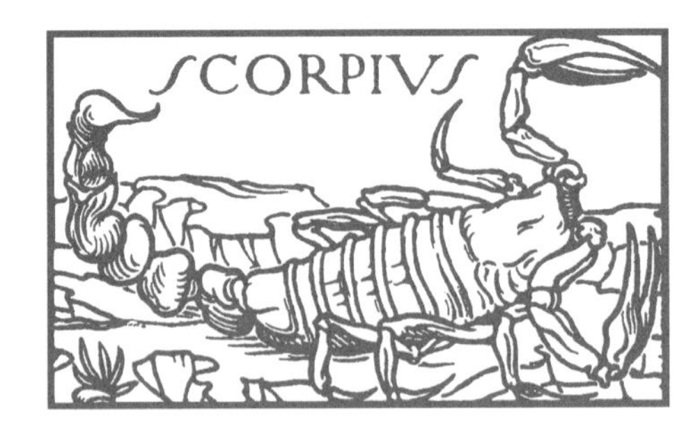

Scorpio Birth Influences

Ruling planet: Pluto; traditionally Mars
Element: Water
Polarity: Feminine
Quadruplicity: Fixed

Sagittarius isn't given to diplomacy and can be honest to the point of hurtfulness, a trait that does not bode well for a friendship with sensitive Scorpio.

Sagittarius Birth Influences

Ruling planet: Jupiter
Element: Fire
Polarity: Masculine
Quadruplicity: Mutable

♃

Communication may be a major stumbling block in a friendship between Scorpio and Sagittarius individuals, for while the Plutonian scorpion can be reticent to the point of speechlessness and is highly sensitive, Jovian Sagittarius is typically both outspoken and thoughtless. Nor are Scorpios renowned for their flexibility, or archers for their patience, but then Scorpio's loyalty and Sagittarius' adaptability may compensate for these friendship-threatening traits. Yet once they have established a connection, Scorpio may benefit from Sagittarius' warmth and cheerfulness, and Sagittarius, from Scorpio's caring, sympathetic character.

Plus Points: There may be times when Scorpio is so unforthcoming that you are overcome with exasperation if you are a Sagittarius, yet if your attention-seeking, fiery element comes to the fore, you are probably pleased to have an audience in the scorpion. In addition, because your ruling planet is good-natured, expansive Jupiter, you may enjoy encouraging Scorpio to open up and reveal some of the thoughts that are swimming around that introspective, feminine-polarity brain. Indeed, your glimpses into enigmatic Scorpio's psyche may have convinced you that the watery, fixed-quadruplicity scorpion is a profoundly empathetic and faithful friend.

Your fiery, masculine-polarity Sagittarius friend no doubt has an enlivening influence on you if you are a more passive, watery, feminine-polarity Scorpio, and you may find his or her Jovian optimism cheering if Pluto sometimes infuses you with gloom, and may be grateful for the mutable archer's willingness to accommodate your rather settled ways. You are both creative thinkers, too, thanks to your respective elements, and Sagittarius' bright ideas—which your mutable-quadruplicity friend may quickly forget about—may frequently inspire your own dreamy, artistic side, giving you plenty to muse upon after you have parted company.

Potential Pitfalls: Despite your relish for taking center stage, you may also be a gregarious person who seeks the stimulation of others' viewpoints if you are a fiery Sagittarius, and may consequently soon lose interest in Scorpio when your friend is particularly reserved. And if you are a touchy, watery Scorpio, you may be hurt when it is obvious that Sagittarius' mind is wandering, and, depending on whether Pluto or Mars asserts itself, may then either retreat into wounded silence or deliver a stinging rebuke, neither of which is likely to endear you to your friend, and may even provoke a brutally honest response that makes matters worse.

Guiding Principle: Maintain an open, but tactful, two-way connection.

Compatibility: ☺ ☺ ☺ ☺ ☺ ☹ ☹ ☹ ☹ ☹

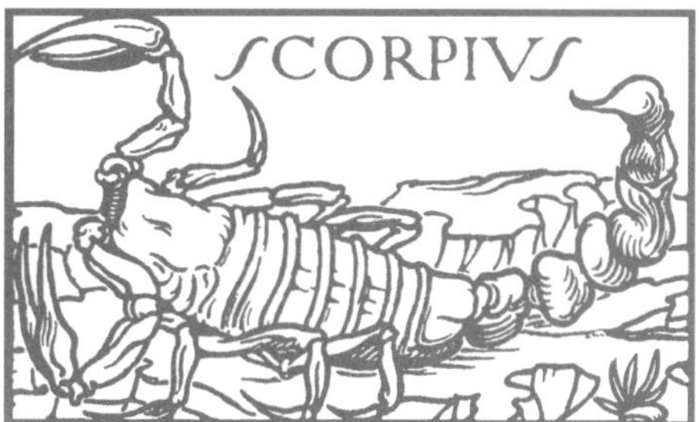

CAPRICORN
SCORPIO

Their families or careers may demand most of their time, but it is unlikely that a Scorpio and a Capricorn would let their friendship lapse, partly because Scorpio's fixed quadruplicity and Capricorn's earthy element are both associated with loyalty, and partly because each contributes something to the other's life. Pluto-ruled, watery Scorpio may be a sympathetic confidant who would never betray Capricorn's confidences, for instance, while Saturn-governed, earthy Capricorn may give Scorpio welcome practical advice. Yet because they share an introspective, feminine polarity, and Scorpio is particularly reticent, while cardinal-quadruplicity Capricorn is self-interested, they may not form that strong a bond.

Plus Points: The combination of a receptive, feminine polarity and compassionate element of water often causes zodiacal scorpions to be empathetic listeners, the influence of guarded Pluto, their ruling planet, also making them excellent keepers of secrets. If you are a feminine-polarity Capricorn with a tendency to worry, you may consequently regard your Scorpio friend as someone with whom you can share your work or domestic problems safe in the knowledge that the scorpion would never divulge them to a third party. That perceptive, creative Scorpionic mind may often come up with some excellent solutions, too.

Your element of water and feminine polarity may make you feel a little insecure and lacking in self-confidence if you are a Scorpio, and you may therefore value earthy Capricorn's steady friendship if it seems to demonstrate that you are worth sticking with, and in any case, having a fixed quadruplicity no doubt means that you warm to friends who return your faithfulness. Indeed, considering how driven cardinal Capricorn is to fulfill his or her responsibilities, you may be touched that your friend regularly takes time out of his or her hectic schedule to spend a few hours with you, and may also be grateful for a dose of prudent, Saturn-inspired, Capricornean guidance when you are in a dilemma and aren't thinking straight.

Potential Pitfalls: Although you may be rather reserved if you are Capricorn, Scorpio may be triply so, for not only does the scorpion share your feminine polarity, but Pluto and water's additional influence may sometimes result in your friend being infuriatingly unforthcoming, giving you the feeling that you are wasting your precious free time on him or her. And Scorpio, you may feel hurt if you sense that cardinal Capricorn's mind is preoccupied and that you don't have his or her full attention.

Guiding Principle: Be patient with one another.

Compatibility: ☺ ☺ ☺ ☺ ☺ ☺ ☺ ☹ ☹ ☹

Capricorn Birth Influences

Ruling planet: Saturn
Element: Earth
Polarity: Feminine
Quadruplicity: Cardinal

If Capricorn and Scorpio get to know one another well enough to bond, their friendship is likely to endure, and they'll make a point of finding time to spend together.

Scorpio Birth Influences

Ruling planet: Pluto; traditionally Mars
Element: Water
Polarity: Feminine
Quadruplicity: Fixed

SCORPIO
AQUARIUS

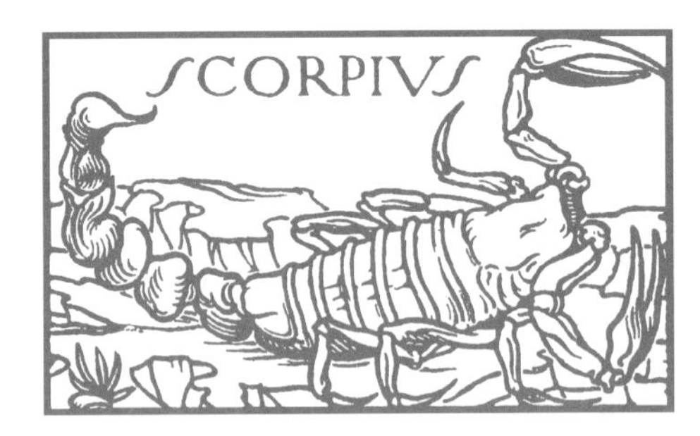

Scorpio Birth Influences

Ruling planet: Pluto; traditionally Mars
Element: Water
Polarity: Feminine
Quadruplicity: Fixed

Given that Scorpios are generally unforthcoming, and that Aquarians enjoy conversing, it may seem as though it would require a miracle for a zodiacal scorpion and water-carrier to become friends. In fact, the catalyst is often a connection between Scorpio's Plutonian, transformational tendencies, and Aquarius' Uranian, or revolutionary leanings, and once a bond has been established, their mutual fixed, or loyal, quadruplicity may ensure that it is never broken. Nevertheless, watery Scorpio's touchiness may test Aquarius' patience, while Scorpio's sensitive feelings may be hurt by airy, egocentric Aquarius' lack of empathy.

Plus Points: Inquisitive, airy Aquarians cannot resist trying to discover what makes other people tick, and if you are one of their number, your Scorpio friend may never cease to arouse your curiosity. Combine a feminine polarity's introversion with a watery element's self-protective reticence, and then add a dose of Plutonian caginess, and Scorpio may be a tough nut to crack, yet you must have succeeded to some extent, otherwise you would not be friends. You may still not fully understand Scorpio—which may be part of his or her continuing attraction—but may suspect that your Pluto-governed friend has sympathy with your nonconformist, Uranian views, and may be in no doubt of the watery, compassionate scorpion's kindness.

It is not just because you have a feminine, or passive, polarity and your friend's is masculine, or active, that you may enjoy the enlivening effect that Aquarius has on you if you are a Scorpio. Aquarius may come up with all manner of inventive ideas that strike a chord with both your water-bestowed instincts and Plutonian taste for reinvention. And because airy Aquarius is easygoing, seems genuinely interested in your opinions, and may already have proved a faithful friend, you may find yourself relaxing your guard and opening up when you're together, which may be a refreshing relief if you are usually suspicious of people's motives.

Breezy Aquarius loves to talk about her ideas, and may either be entertaining company or too impersonal for empathetic Scorpio.

Potential Pitfalls: Their elements of water and air cause Scorpio and Aquarius to be respectively "feeling" and "thinking" types, which may give rise to misunderstandings. If you are an Aquarius, you may not realize how deeply a breezy comment of a personal nature may wound emotionally vulnerable Scorpio, who may not be able to accept that Aquarius didn't mean to be hurtful.

Guiding Principle: Don't let your dissimilarities create a gulf between you.

Compatibility: ☺ ☺ ☺ ☺ ☺ ☺ ☹ ☹ ☹ ☹

Aquarius Birth Influences

Ruling planet: Uranus; traditionally Saturn
Element: Air
Polarity: Masculine
Quadruplicity: Fixed

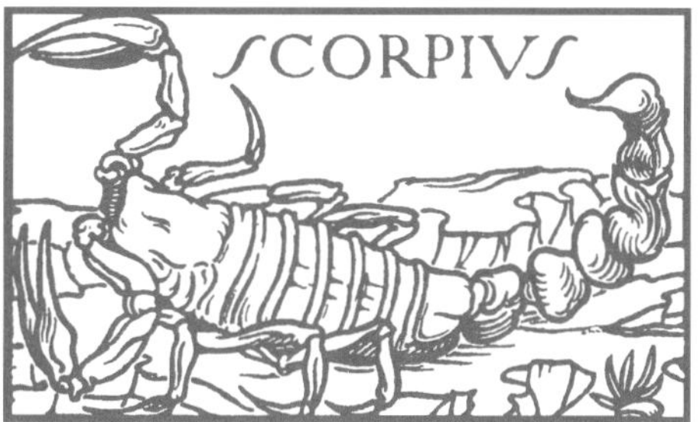

PISCES
SCORPIO

That Scorpio and Pisces friends instinctively empathize with one another is down to their shared watery element, which makes them equally intuitive and sympathetic, especially when they sense the other's genuine goodwill. And despite having been born under cautious, feminine-polarity signs, Pluto-governed Scorpio may drop his or her guard when with ultracompassionate, Neptune-ruled Pisces, Pisces' faith in Scorpio in turn being boosted by the scorpion's loyalty-bestowing, fixed quadruplicity. Mutable Pisces' mood swings may unsettle sensitive Scorpio, however, just as Scorpio's obstinacy may distress flexible Pisces.

Plus Points: When you have suffered a setback, if you are a Pisces, and the interaction of confusion-inducing Neptune and water and your inhibited, feminine polarity have resulted in you feeling bewildered and withdrawn, your Scorpio friend may be one of the few whom you trust enough to open up to. Indeed, if your watery element in particular makes it hard for you to express your emotions, you may be profoundly thankful that Scorpio, a fellow feminine-polarity, watery person, seems to understand you implicitly, and that Pluto gives him or her a gift for keeping your secrets. Because Scorpio's quadruplicity is fixed, you probably know that you can rely on your friend to stick with you, too.

Although Neptunian, watery Pisces' almost psychic insight into your thoughts may be disconcerting for a resolutely private person like you if you are a Scorpio, it may come as a relief to have someone with whom you can share your hopes and fears without worrying that they will be laughed at or dismissed. Not only that, but due to the combination of a feminine polarity, visionary Neptune, and gentle water, your idealistic, caring friend's reaction may either lift your spirits or soothe your troubled soul. Mutable-quaduplicity Pisces' adaptability may be a blessing, too, if, having a fixed quadruplicity yourself, you are rather set in your ways.

Potential Pitfalls: As far as you are concerned, if you are mutable Pisces with an accepting, Neptunian nature, one of the downsides of Scorpio's fixed quadruplicity may be your friend's refusal to countenance alternative viewpoints, and if the aggression of Mars, the scorpion's secondary ruling planet, comes to the fore, you may be devastated by his or her uncompromising vehemence. And regardless of whether it was your rigidity that threw Pisces into emotional turmoil, you may find your mutable friend's moodiness upsetting if you are a thin-skinned Scorpio.

Guiding Principle: Don't let your personal differences get you down.

Compatibility: ☺ ☺ ☺ ☺ ☺ ☺ ☺ ☹ ☹ ☹

Pisces Birth Influences
Ruling planet: Neptune; traditionally Jupiter
Element: Water
Polarity: Feminine
Quadruplicity: Mutable

Pisces and Scorpio are likely to forge a deep connection with one another. Their instinctive companionship often transcends the need for words.

Scorpio Birth Influences
Ruling planet: Pluto; traditionally Mars
Element: Water
Polarity: Feminine
Quadruplicity: Fixed

SAGITTARIUS
SAGITTARIUS

Sagittarius Birth Influences
Ruling planet: Jupiter
Element: Fire
Polarity: Masculine
Quadruplicity: Mutable

If you're an intrepid Sagittarius, you'll enjoy spending time with a fellow adventurous archer.

Sagittarius Birth Influences
Ruling planet: Jupiter
Element: Fire
Polarity: Masculine
Quadruplicity: Mutable

Two outgoing, thrill-seeking, Sagittarian friends are generally so busy pursuing their personal quests to experience all that the world has to offer that they may not see much of one another. Nevertheless, they typically have a rumbustious time when they do. No quiet homebodies they, their enterprising, masculine polarity and vital, fiery element send them out and about, spurring one another on and often trying to outdo each other, too. Not that their relationship is entirely superficial, however, for their mutable quadruplicity is associated with the intellect and communication, while Jupiter, their ruling planet, gives them an interest in life's big questions, so that they'll also have plenty of wide-ranging discussions. Yet because they are so similar, and, sharing a mutable quadruplicity, crave variety, they'll soon be going their separate ways again—temporarily, at least.

Plus Points: If you and your friend were both born under the sign of the archer, you must relish the sense of being with an equal, especially if your joint, masculine polarity causes each of you to be as confident as the other. Not only that, but because Jupiter's gift to the pair of you is an optimistic, "can-do" outlook, and your common, mutable quadruplicity gives you an appetite for change, as well as flexibility, there may be few activities that either of you dislikes sampling together, so you have plenty of scope for stimulation. Indeed, thanks to your fiery element, it is probably your shared adventurousness, reinforced by your warmth and exuberance, that creates such a natural rapport between you, so that after being apart, you may quickly pick up where you left off, namely having fun.

Potential Pitfalls: The biggest potential pitfall that may threaten a friendship between two mutable-quadruplicity, Sagittarian individuals is a prolonged period of togetherness—perhaps on vacation—when they may quickly become bored, and consequently ratty, with one another, and some aggressive words said in the heat of the moment may trigger a series of fiery explosions. Fortunately, these will generally be short-lived, and because neither of you tend to nurse grudges, will soon be forgotten. And while you may be generous types, having a fiery element and mutable quadruplicity in common may mean that neither of you is that empathetic or dependable, so that should one of you be burdened by work or domestic problems, the other may not have sufficient interest or patience to provide steady emotional or practical support.

Guiding Principle: Be there for each other in both good times and bad.

Compatibility: ☺ ☺ ☺ ☺ ☺ ☺ ☺ ☺ ☹ ☹

CAPRICORN

SAGITTARIUS

It may take years before Sagittarius and Capricorn regard themselves as friends rather than acquaintances, for restless, mutable-quadruplicity Sagittarius may not stay around long enough to break down feminine-polarity Capricorn's reserve, while mature, Saturn-ruled Capricorn may initially regard fiery Sagittarius' impulsive behavior as childish. When they get to know one another better, however, they may come to appreciate certain of the other's qualities, Capricorn perhaps being cheered by Jovian, masculine-polarity Sagittarius' optimism, and Sagittarius maybe relying on earthy Capricorn's dependability. Nonetheless, they may never be close, partly because fiery, mutable Sagittarius craves diversity and excitement, and partly because earthy, cardinal Capricorn takes his or her responsibilities so seriously.

Plus Points: The interaction of Saturn, your element of earth, and your feminine polarity may result in you being a sober, steady introvert if you are a Capricorn, while your driving, cardinal quadruplicity may cause you to be set on achieving your goals in life, yet you wouldn't be human if you didn't feel the need to relax once in a while. And because mutable-quadruplicity, masculine-polarity Sagittarius is probably more sociable and outgoing than you, your friend may introduce you to a variety of people, which, despite your relative shyness, you'll appreciate. On a more personal level, you may welcome Sagittarius' Jovian way of looking on the bright side when you are feeling disheartened by life's obstacles and pitfalls.

If you are a Sagittarius, your earthy, Saturn-governed, Capricorn friend may be someone to whom you turn if you require prudent advice or practical support should you find yourself in a mess due to your mutable-quadruplicity tendency to live for the moment rather than plan for the future. Indeed, when you are forced to face facts, you may be grateful for your earthy friend's realistic outlook and the loyalty that he or she shows in helping you to get back on track. You may also be startled to discover that your friend is less unimaginative than you first thought, especially when your fiery attention is grabbed by one of Capricorn's bright ideas.

Potential Pitfalls: You may not approve of fiery, masculine-polarity Sagittarius' spontaneity and thoughtlessness if you are a sensible, cautious Capricorn, but then you may think that the earthy, feminine-polarity goat is a stick in the mud if you are a Sagittarius, and possibly even a killjoy if repressive Saturn's influence over your friend is particularly strong.

Guiding Principle: Adopt "tolerance" and "patience" as your watchwords.

Compatibility: ☺ ☺ ☺ ☺ ☹ ☹ ☹ ☹ ☹ ☹

Capricorn Birth Influences

Ruling planet: Saturn
Element: Earth
Polarity: Feminine
Quadruplicity: Cardinal

Capricorn and Sagittarius are like night and day, but then opposites not only attract—they can be good for one another, too.

Sagittarius Birth Influences

Ruling planet: Jupiter
Element: Fire
Polarity: Masculine
Quadruplicity: Mutable

SAGITTARIUS
AQUARIUS

Sagittarius Birth Influences
Ruling planet: Jupiter
Element: Fire
Polarity: Masculine
Quadruplicity: Mutable

Sagittarius, restrain yourself if you notice that Aquarius is irritated, or you'll risk your friendship.

Aquarius Birth Influences
Ruling planet: Uranus; traditionally Saturn
Element: Air
Polarity: Masculine
Quadruplicity: Fixed

The astrological indications suggest that Sagittarius and Aquarius have a mutually stimulating friendship, although not a particularly close one, but then both have an aversion to stifling relationships, the archer's element, fire, being associated with independence, and the water-carrier's, air, with freedom. Indeed, it is in the realm of the intellect that these two find common ground, for Sagittarius' mutable quadruplicity and Aquarius' airy element make each as bright and communicative as the other, and while airy, Uranus-governed, Aquarius is curious and inventive, fiery, Jupiter-ruled Sagittarius is creative and visionary. Add their dynamic, masculine polarity to the mix, and this lively duo probably never stops talking, even if mutable-quadruplicity Sagittarius' inconstancy can exasperate fixed Aquarius, and Aquarius' dogmatism sometimes sparks Sagittarius' fiery annoyance.

Plus Points: You may relish the unpredictable if you are an Aquarian child of unconventional Uranus, which is why you may delight in the company of Sagittarius, whose mutable quadruplicity may cause your friend to be changeable, and element of fire, impulsive, so that you may never know what to expect when you get together. Most of all, however, you may enjoy the conversations that you have with your friend, for Sagittarius may have a broad-minded, Jovian outlook that enables him or her to embrace your own, radical, Uranian theories with fiery gusto. And a further benefit of Sagittarius' fiery element may be his or her warmth and generosity.

You no doubt have a wide circle of friends if you are a sociable, mutable Sagittarius who revels in diversity, yet Aquarius may be the one whose trailblazing, Uranian mindset really kindles your fiery, trendsetting imagination. Your joint, masculine polarity may furthermore result in Aquarius being as outgoing and confident as you, so that he or she may rarely trigger your impatience by balking at some of your more adventurous, fiery suggestions. Perhaps best of all, as far as you are concerned, fixed-quadruplicity, airy Aquarius may be someone who makes a point of staying in touch, but doesn't make tiresome emotional demands of you.

Potential Pitfalls: Your respective quadruplicities may have a positive effect on your relationship, in that adaptable Sagittarius may be willing to accommodate Aquarius' rather rigid ways, and Aquarius may remain a faithful friend to sometimes fickle Sagittarius. Yet there may be times when constant Aquarius is irritated by Sagittarius' fluctuating views, and when flexible Sagittarius is infuriated by Aquarius' obstinacy.

Guiding Principle: Quickly change the subject when you disagree!

Compatibility: ☺ ☺ ☺ ☺ ☺ ☺ ☺ ☹ ☹ ☹

PISCES
SAGITTARIUS

Although Sagittarius may be extroverted and forceful, and Pisces, introverted and gentle, their birth influences suggest that these two can become good friends, and not just because Sagittarius is warm-hearted and Pisces, caring. For while Jupiter, Sagittarius' ruling planet (and traditionally also that of Pisces), is regarded as being benevolent, and Neptune, Pisces' planetary governor, is considered altruistic, their shared, mutable quadruplicity furthermore blesses each with the gifts of sociability and adaptability. That said, fiery, unthinking Sagittarius may sometimes hurt thin-skinned Pisces' feelings, while watery, vulnerable Pisces may occasionally crave more emotional support than impatient Sagittarius can give.

Pisces Birth Influences
Ruling planet: Neptune; traditionally Jupiter
Element: Water
Polarity: Feminine
Quadruplicity: Mutable

♆ ♃

Plus Points: You may often come away from a get-together with Sagittarius flushed with excitement if you are a Pisces, such is the enlivening effect that your friend's exuberant, fiery element and uninhibited, masculine polarity may have on your own responsive nature. Indeed, being with Sagittarius may be a heartening experience, for your friend's Jovian optimism, fiery zest for life, and the positive outlook that is typical of a masculine polarity may lift your spirits when Neptune, your watery element, and your feminine polarity have left you feeling confused and down. Because fiery Sagittarius is so spontaneous, you may enjoy being led into new situations by your confident, vibrant friend, too.

If you are a fiery, masculine-polarity Sagittarius who spends your days energetically pursuing your interests, searching for stimulation, or enthusing your family and workmates, spending some downtime with watery, empathetic Pisces may both soothe you and recharge your batteries. A double dose of watery, Neptunian intuition and the fellow feeling of another mutable-quadruplicity person may in addition cause Pisces to have a spooky insight into your emotions, so that when you are feeling dissatisfied or on edge, your compassionate friend's concern may be enough to raise your fiery, attention-appreciating morale.

To keep your friendship solid, Sagittarius, remember to be there for Pisces when she is feeling down, and not just when she's in a good mood.

Potential Pitfalls: The interaction between Neptune, water, and your feminine polarity may result in you being hypersensitive if you are a Pisces, and there may consequently be times when a tactless remark made by fiery Sagittarius triggers all of your insecurities. And when this happens, and Pisces either bursts into tears or sinks into wounded silence, you may lack the understanding and staying power required to boost your friend's fragile ego if you are a Sagittarius.

Guiding Principle: Give and take; forgive and forget.

Compatibility: ☺ ☺ ☺ ☺ ☺ ☺ ☹ ☹ ☹ ☹

Sagittarius Birth Influences
Ruling planet: Jupiter
Element: Fire
Polarity: Masculine
Quadruplicity: Mutable

♃ 

CAPRICORN
CAPRICORN

Capricorn Birth Influences

Ruling planet: Saturn
Element: Earth
Polarity: Feminine
Quadruplicity: Cardinal

Dedicated as they both generally are to achieving their personal or professional goals, due to their driving, cardinal quadruplicity, a pair of Capricorn friends may not have a lot of free time to spend with one another, but when they do, may feel as though they are kindred spirits. And indeed they are in many respects, for their feminine polarity may make them reserved, just as Saturn, their ruling planet, may cause them to be sober and sensible types, and earth, their element, constant. They may consequently enjoy an undemonstrative, yet staunch, friendship that adds an extra dimension to their lives, even if neither is always aware of the other's feelings.

Capricorns take their careers and family life seriously and may not have much time for an active social life. Still, they'll appreciate the steady friendship of a fellow Capricorn.

Plus Points: Given that your mutual preoccupation with your career or family responsibilities may take up most of your waking hours if you and your friend are both cardinal-quadruplicity Capricorns, you probably don't see that much of one another, but may genuinely enjoy your get-togethers. It may be that you are grateful that your friend doesn't demand that you act out of character by insisting that you hit the nightspots together or pours out his or her emotions in excruciatingly discomforting detail and then expects you to respond empathetically, for instance, or it may be that you appreciate your fellow Capricorn's mature, saturnine advice or earthy, practical suggestions when you are pondering over a dilemma in typically measured, feminine-polarity style. Either way, because you share a constant, earthy element, and may furthermore have a Saturn-bestowed sense of obligation toward one another, each of you probably knows from experience that the other can be depended upon.

Potential Pitfalls: Looking at your shared birth influences, it is unlikely that either of you rather driven, cardinal-quadruplicity, Capricornean characters would prioritize hanging out or having fun with your friend over your responsibilities, but, even so, you would probably drop everything to prop up the other in a crisis. The typical, practical Capricornean style is to quietly offer a few down-to-earth suggestions or lend him or her whatever money you could spare, and in any case, your saturnine, earthy friend may appear a realistic, resilient fatalist who dislikes being fussed over. Nevertheless, go the extra mile in times of trouble, and you may find that it reaps dividends in terms of loyalty, even if you never find yourself in a similar situation.

Guiding Principle: To paraphrase President Kennedy, ask not what your friend can do for you, but what you can do for your friend.

Capricorn Birth Influences

Ruling planet: Saturn
Element: Earth
Polarity: Feminine
Quadruplicity: Cardinal

Compatibility:       

AQUARIUS
CAPRICORN

The lack of opportunity to spend time in one another's company may mean that it takes a while before a Capricorn–Aquarius acquaintanceship deepens into friendship, but because earthy Capricorn is constant, and fixed-quadruplicity Aquarius, loyal, they are likely to remain part of one another's social circle thereafter. They may not have the closest of bonds, however, partly because feminine-polarity Capricorn may be reserved, and partly because airy Aquarius can be impersonal, yet may nevertheless be genuinely interested in each other's ideas, even if Saturn-ruled Capricorns are sometimes too conventional for Aquarius, and Capricorn considers Uranus-governed Aquarius' notions eccentric or impractical.

Plus Points: You may especially value earthy Capricorn's dependability if you are a fixed-quadruplicity Aquarius who likes to maintain regular contact with your friends. Indeed, although cardinal-quadruplicity Capricorn's workaholic tendencies may result in your friend enjoying precious little leisure, responsible Saturn may ensure that he or she at least returns your calls. And when you do get together, your airy curiosity may be piqued by a glimpse of cardinal-quadruplicity forcefulness lying beneath the phlegmatic front that your feminine-polarity friend presents to the world, triggering an investigative, Uranian urge to probe deeper into Capricorn's personality.

If you are a cardinal-quadruplicity Capricorn, you may not spend enough time relaxing, and two of the benefits of having a friend in Aquarius may be the water-carrier's Uranus-bestowed offbeat personality and airy communicativeness, which may cause him or her to talk you into experimenting and trying new, fun things. As well as being a fount of quirky knowledge, having a positive, or masculine, polarity, may give Aquarius a talent for boosting your confidence when your own, feminine, polarity has filled you with worries or doubts.

Potential Pitfalls: Although earthy Capricorn may be patient, and airy Aquarius, easygoing, each of you may occasionally be irritated by the other's firmly held views, for once you have made up your minds, neither of you readily countenances alternative opinions. Earthy Capricorn may be very conventional, so that you may be annoyed, if you are an Aquarius, when you make a pioneering proposal and your friend looks at you as though you were mad, for instance, just as you, if you are a Capricorn, may be exasperated should fixed-quadruplicity Aquarius refuse to accept that you may be right in pointing out that he or she is being unrealistic.

Guiding Principle: Shrug off your differences.

Compatibility: ☺ ☺ ☺ ☺ ☺ ☹ ☹ ☹ ☹ ☹

Aquarius Birth Influences

Ruling planet: Uranus; traditionally Saturn
Element: Air
Polarity: Masculine
Quadruplicity: Fixed

To avoid dwelling on your differences, Aquarius and Capricorn, try taking on a challenge together.

Capricorn Birth Influences

Ruling planet: Saturn
Element: Earth
Polarity: Feminine
Quadruplicity: Cardinal

CAPRICORN
PISCES

Capricorn Birth Influences

Ruling planet: Saturn
Element: Earth
Polarity: Feminine
Quadruplicity: Cardinal

Perhaps it is because they have a passive, feminine polarity in common that Capricorn and Pisces individuals typically enjoy a mutually supportive relationship rather than a rip-roaring one. Or maybe it is because mutable Pisces is adaptable enough to follow cardinal Capricorn's lead, while sober Saturn exerts a restraining influence over the goat. Either way, these friends are generally happiest when quietly catching up with one another, with earthy Capricorn often giving dreamy Pisces sensible advice, and watery Pisces offering Capricorn kindness in return. That said, Saturn-governed Capricorn may be a little too unimaginative for Pisces, while Neptune-ruled Pisces' otherworldly fantasies may exasperate the goat.

Shy, insecure Pisces appreciates steady Capricorn's dependable personality, while Capricorn may value gentle Pisces' kindness.

Plus Points: If you are a Pisces whose watery element and mutable quadruplicity sometimes flood you with insecurity and send your emotions swinging back and forth, you may be grateful to have such a constant and even-tempered friend in earthy Capricorn. And when confusion-inducing Neptune has paralyzed you with indecision, level-headed Capricorn may help you to think straight, too. In addition, you may know from experience that your responsible friend keeps his or her promises, which is why you may turn to saturnine Capricorn when you are in need of practical assistance.

There may be few people in your circle who show such goodwill toward you as Pisces if you are a cardinal-quadruplicity Capricorn, especially if working toward achieving your ambitions gives you little time to cultivate friendships. As well as being willing to fit in with your busy schedule, mutable Pisces may be blessed with compassion, thanks to Neptune and water, which may cause your friend instinctively to sympathize with, and soothe, you when you are making frustratingly slow progress.

Potential Pitfalls: It is when the conversation strays from personal matters that you and your friend may encounter some pitfalls if one of you is a Capricorn and the other, a Pisces. For whereas Saturn-ruled, earthy Capricorn has a sober and straightforward outlook, Neptune-governed, watery Pisces may be an idealistic daydreamer, so that your respective views on society, for example, may irritate each of you so much that Pisces has to blink back tears of frustration and you both sink into feminine-polarity silence. Should this happen, try to change the subject to a less contentious one in order to remain on good terms.

Guiding Principle: Don't let your dissimilar outlooks drive a wedge between you.

Compatibility: ☺ ☺ ☺ ☺ ☺ ☺ ☹ ☹ ☹ ☹

Pisces Birth Influences

Ruling planet: Neptune; traditionally Jupiter
Element: Water
Polarity: Feminine
Quadruplicity: Mutable

♆ ♃

AQUARIUS / AQUARIUS

Being forced to listen to someone's emotional outpourings or being trapped in a humdrum conversation are both nightmare scenarios for Aquarius people, which is why they usually relish one another's company so much. For thanks to their element of air and Uranus, their ruling planet, these confident, masculine-polarity individuals are curious and communicative characters who are fascinated by unconventional ideas and are furthermore experimental thinkers. That they are "thinking" rather than "feeling" types generally works to their advantage, as does sharing a loyalty-bestowing, fixed quadruplicity, although this birth influence can also make them somewhat stubborn, so that should they disagree, neither may be willing to back down and break the deadlock.

Plus Points: Apart from being relieved that your Aquarian friend doesn't emote or subject you to tedious sagas about his or her work or domestic life, if you are also an airy, rather impersonal, Aquarius, you must really enjoy your discussions. Your inquisitive minds and quick intellects are the gifts of your airy element, reinforced by the investigative instincts of Uranus, your planetary governor, which also fills you both with radical notions—particularly regarding social or technological issues—that others may think zany or eccentric, but whose possibilities for the future excite you fellow Aquarians. Having a masculine polarity in common may also mean that each of you is as uninhibited as the other in expressing your views, with the result that you may both delight in your direct interaction. And another bonus may be that your joint, fixed quadruplicity prompts you to have regular contact.

Potential Pitfalls: It shouldn't seriously threaten your friendship, yet there is nevertheless a danger that your fixed-quadruplicity obstinacy may cool the atmosphere between you should you have a difference of opinion, for both of you somewhat self-opinionated Aquarians have a tendency to stick firmly to your guns when your beliefs are challenged. Otherwise, your mutual, airy detachment may never cause you to feel that close to one another, so that your connection may remain resolutely superficial, which needn't be a pitfall, it is true, although there may be times when a domestic crisis gives even relatively unemotional Aquarians a longing to cry on a sympathetic and supportive someone's shoulder. And it is again your airy element, fueled by your outgoing and energetic masculine polarity, that may make each of you so gregarious that you have difficulty fitting one another into your busy social schedules.

Guiding Principle: Should you have a standoff, agree to disagree and move on.

Compatibility:       

Aquarius Birth Influences

Ruling planet: Uranus; traditionally Saturn
Element: Air
Polarity: Masculine
Quadruplicity: Fixed

Aquarius, don't let a disagreement with your fellow Aquarian threaten your wonderful friendship. Change the subject to a less contentious one.

Aquarius Birth Influences

Ruling planet: Uranus; traditionally Saturn
Element: Air
Polarity: Masculine
Quadruplicity: Fixed

AQUARIUS

PISCES

Aquarius Birth Influences

Ruling planet: Uranus; traditionally Saturn
Element: Air
Polarity: Masculine
Quadruplicity: Fixed

Although Aquarius and Pisces may like one another, it is doubtful whether they will ever be bosom buddies, partly because airy, Aquarian individuals can be impersonal, and partly because watery, Pisces people tend to protect their sensitive feelings beneath a layer of feminine-polarity reticence. These characteristics may work to their mutual advantage, however, for Aquarius may be intrigued by the air of mystery that surrounds Neptune-governed Pisces, while Pisces may welcome having a friend whose detachment keeps emotional turmoil at bay. In addition, while airy Aquarius may both hearten and stabilize Pisces when necessary, watery, mutable Pisces may prove an empathetic and adaptable friend to Aquarius.

Aquarius and Pisces often enjoy an easygoing friendship, but not an especially cozy or profound one.

Plus Points: Spending time with Aquarius may be an invigorating experience if you are a Pisces, particularly if your mutable quadruplicity blesses you with an enjoyment of diversity, as well as a smidgeon of the intellectual curiosity that is so pronounced in the airy water-carrier. Because your feminine polarity may cause you to be more restrained than uninhibited, masculine-polarity Aquarius, your airy, articulate friend may lead your conversations into original, Uranian territory, where your humanitarian, Neptunian instincts may find common ground with his or her interest in social issues, for example. You may also be pleased that Aquarius makes an effort to keep in touch with you, especially if his or her fixed-quadruplicity loyalty and positive, masculine-polarity attitude together boost your self-confidence.

You may appreciate having such a kindly and flexible friend in Pisces if you are an Aquarius, and may be touched and soothed by his or her watery compassion when you've had a frustrating day. Not being one to need much buoying up, however, you may be far more concerned with trying to get to the bottom of those unfathomable Piscean depths, for while your airy element infuses you with inquisitiveness, your masculine polarity may make you rise to the challenge of breaking down your friend's reserve and discovering more about his or her personality. And what an intriguing one it may be, given that Pisces' birth influences include a complex, mutable quadruplicity and a planet associated with spirituality.

Pisces Birth Influences

Ruling planet: Neptune; traditionally Jupiter
Element: Water
Polarity: Feminine
Quadruplicity: Mutable

Potential Pitfalls: There is a real danger that you may feel hurt and rejected by the aloofness that airy Aquarius may sometimes display if you are a touchy Pisces, and that you may find watery Pisces' craving for closeness suffocating if you are an Aquarius.

Guiding Principle: Aim for a relaxed, but not too casual, relationship.

Compatibility: ☺ ☺ ☺ ☺ ☺ ☹ ☹ ☹ ☹ ☹

PISCES
PISCES

* *

For many Piscean friends, being together is like spending time in a refreshing oasis after enduring a grueling period in a lonely, emotional desert, for having selfless, Neptunian personalities, being surrounded by demanding, self-centered, or inconsiderate people who were born under other zodiacal signs can be punishing and upsetting for these sensitive souls. Indeed, watery Pisceans are both empathetic and caring, and are furthermore blessed with a profound insight that enables them to reach out to their feminine-polarity fellows when they sense their unspoken distress. As a result, their get-togethers may resemble mutual therapy sessions, aided in part by their common, mutable quadruplicity, which may give them flexibility, yet also a craving for change that may result in them inadvertently wounding each other.

Plus Points: If you are a Pisces and your friend is one, too, the astrological indications suggest that you are bosom buddies. For while you may usually feel the need to hold back your feelings in both watery, self-protective style and reticent, feminine-polarity fashion when dealing with individuals who do not share your birth influences, you may have an intuitive, watery connection with your fellow Pisces that gives you an instinctive belief that he or she understands, and has sympathy with, you. And experience may have confirmed your conviction, for there may have been many occasions when unselfish, Neptune-governed Pisces has canceled his or her plans in order to nurse and support you through an emotional crisis. Similarly, you may revel in the feel-good factor when the tables have been turned and it is down to you to offer compassion and support, which you are eminently capable of supplying, not least because your dual-natured, mutable quadruplicity enables you to give as well as take.

Potential Pitfalls: When one of you Pisces friends is feeling unhappy, he or she may demand the other's exclusive time and attention, which could prove problematic in practical terms, however gladly well-meaning Pisces comes to the rescue. Add your joint, mutable quadruplicity to the mix, however, and the result of such intensive togetherness may be that neither of you passive, feminine-polarity individuals may be able to fulfill your longing to be diverted from the despondency into which you have both sunk, so that whoever is first tempted to break away by a cheerful someone may leave the other in a deep, feminine-polarity sulk, and may well feel guilty about it, too.

Guiding Principle: Accept that you both have your own lives to lead.

Compatibility: ☺ ☺ ☺ ☺ ☺ ☺ ☺ ☺ ☹ ☹

Pisces Birth Influences

Ruling planet: Neptune; traditionally Jupiter
Element: Water
Polarity: Feminine
Quadruplicity: Mutable

♆ ♃ ♒

* *

The bond between two Pisces friends should be both supportive and enduring.

* *

Pisces Birth Influences
Ruling planet: Neptune; traditionally Jupiter
Element: Water
Polarity: Feminine
Quadruplicity: Mutable

We must resemble each other a little in order to understand each other, but we must be a little different to love each other.

Paul Géraldy, *L'Homme et L'Amour* (1951)

ROMANCE

Whether your romance is in its early, heady days, or you and your beloved have been together for years, reading an astrological analysis of how your respective zodiacal signs relate to one another can give you an invaluable insight into your compatibility and consequently the nature of your future together.

Turn to the page that links your star signs, and you will discover the plus points that augur well for a long and loving romance, for these reveal the characteristics that attracted you to one another in the first place, as well as the qualities that you most value in each other. But the course of true love rarely runs smoothly, and you will almost certainly encounter some rocky patches in your relationship that you can do nothing about due to a conflict of birth influences. Or can you? Indeed you can. Being alerted to the potential pitfalls that threaten your romance will empower you to take positive steps to counteract the negative effect that the coming-together of your ruling planets, elements, polarities, and quadruplicities may ultimately have on your feelings for one another, thereby enabling you to rise above your problems and strengthening your bond as a couple. And be the number of hearts at the bottom of the page a gloom-inducing two or an exhilarating nine, remember that if you both keep your guiding principle at the forefront of your minds, you and your sweetheart have the potential to score the perfect ten. For if, after a while, it seems as though you are star-crossed lovers, remember that where there is love, there is always hope, and that if you are both determined to work at overcoming your astrological differences, in the words of the Italian poet Dante (1262–1321), yours may truly be "The love that moves the Sun and the other stars" (*The Divine Comedy*).

ARIES
ARIES

Aries Birth Influences
Ruling planet: Mars
Element: Fire
Polarity: Masculine
Quadruplicity: Cardinal

The passion will be intense when two Ariens meet, but if one tries to dominate the other, he or she will soon find that it takes two to tango.

Aries Birth Influences
Ruling planet: Mars
Element: Fire
Polarity: Masculine
Quadruplicity: Cardinal

The sparks of attraction between two red-hot Ariens can ignite an inferno of passion, but mutual understanding is the key to whether the flames of love burn brightly for years to come or whether it all ends abruptly, in a dramatic display of fireworks.

Plus Points: A fun, exciting, and passionate love life is vital to lusty Aries, and who better to provide the stimulation that the ram craves than a star mate born under the same sign? When Aries meets Aries, the attraction can be instant, each being drawn to the other's charisma, adventurousness, and directness. These uninhibited, Mars-ruled people are not ones to repress their powerful sexual appetites—self-denial is not in the Arien vocabulary—so the relationship may quickly become intimate, but not necessarily permanent. There is so much that Aries wants to experience and do in life that it may take a while before he or she is ready to settle down, yet when that time comes, a fellow Arien is often just the partner to provide the warmth and loyalty, but also the spontaneity and thrills, that will keep the wayward ram at home.

A shared, all-consuming ambition is usually the superglue that keeps cardinal Aries and Aries together, perhaps a visionary project into which they can channel their formidable focus and energies, be it a joint business venture or raising a family together.

Potential Pitfalls: If two impulsive Aries people commit their lives to one another on the spur of the moment, these two headstrong zodiacal rams may soon be either locking horns or charging away from each other in opposite directions. Aries can be a dominating personality, which is why it is vital that both partners respect each other's interests and treat one another as equals. So if you're an Aries who's in a relationship with another Aries, try not to explode with jealousy if your partner switches his or her attention to someone else or becomes enthusiastic about a project that doesn't involve you. After all, you sometimes do exactly the same. Don't try to control your partner's life either—you won't tolerate anyone treating you like a doormat, so why should your fellow adventurer through life?

Guiding Principle: It's your individual differences that add spice to your lives together, so don't let them become bones of contention, and instead enjoy them.

Compatibility: ♥♥♥♥♥♥♥♡♡♡

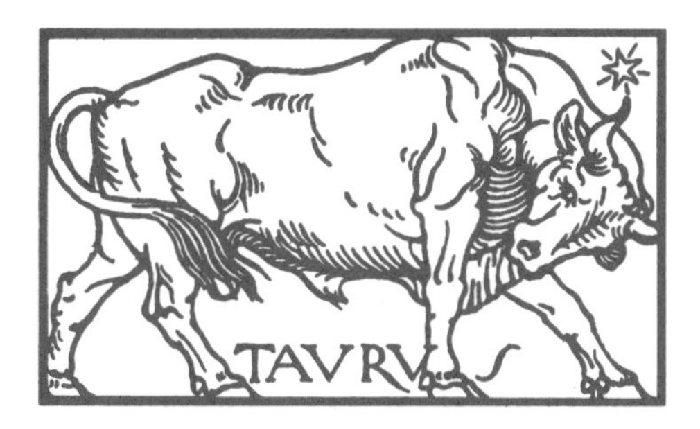

TAURUS

ARIES

Aries is from Mars, and Taurus from Venus, but when on planet Earth, fiery Aries inflames the bull's passion, while earthy Taurus grounds the impetuous ram. Although very dissimilar, these lovers can complement each other wonderfully if they work at accommodating their differences.

Plus Points: When Aries meets Taurus, each is instantly attracted by the other's sex appeal, level-headed Taurus being fascinated by Aries' dynamism and charisma, and curious Aries being drawn to the intriguing air of reserve and sensuality that Taurus exudes. Because both are passionate by nature, they will share a powerful bond if their relationship becomes intimate.

If you are a home-centered, money-conscious Taurus, you will appreciate Aries' driving, entrepreneurial spirit and earning power, for example, while your impatient partner will gratefully accede to your desire to run your lives, and, if necessary, regulate your joint finances, carefully and efficiently. The outside world can often be a lonely, hostile place if you are an Aries, and you will be buoyed up by your Taurean partner's loyalty and warm-hearted, patient support, in turn offering him or her an infusion of fun and spontaneity that keeps your romance fresh.

Potential Pitfalls: Apart from their shared pleasure in bedroom pursuits, Aries and Taurus often have little in common. If you are a questing ram, you may require constant stimulation and relish new experiences, and may soon become frustrated by the earthy bull's stolid, home-loving, routine-based personality. And if you are a practical Taurus, you may eventually find the Arien tendency of charging off on what you perceive to be yet another hare-brained scheme infuriating, especially if it upsets your plans.

If you are a typically possessive Taurean, you may be stabbed with red-hot pangs of jealousy if you mistake your Aries partner's intense interest in someone for flirtation. If you are an Aries who was simply investigating an unusual character, Taurus's overreaction will, no doubt, mystify you, but then you may similarly not recognize the stubborn bull's refusal to be bossed around, and will be deeply shocked should he or she explode when pushed too far. Either way, if each of you shows contrition and tries hard to understand how the other ticks, you'll be back on the track toward a happy future together.

Guiding Principle: Compromise! Aries, don't try to control or change Taurus, and Taurus, give Aries the space to roam.

Compatibility: ♥♥♥♥♥♥♡♡♡♡

Taurus Birth Influences

Ruling planet: Venus
Element: Earth
Polarity: Feminine
Quadruplicity: Fixed

For a Taurus–Aries couple, the physical side of their relationship is the key to their happiness.

Aries Birth Influences

Ruling planet: Mars
Element: Fire
Polarity: Masculine
Quadruplicity: Cardinal

ARIES
GEMINI

Aries Birth Influences

Ruling planet: Mars
Element: Fire
Polarity: Masculine
Quadruplicity: Cardinal

If you're part of a Gemini–Aries couple, don't stay home too much or allow boredom to set in. Keep moving, and make your romance fun!

Gemini Birth Influences

Ruling planet: Mercury
Element: Air
Polarity: Masculine
Quadruplicity: Mutable

Excitement forms the bedrock of a relationship between fiery Aries and volatile Gemini, but Gemini may find Aries' single-minded, controlling tendencies suffocating, while Aries may become infuriated by Gemini's indecisiveness.

Plus Points: Aries and Gemini are very similar in their fundamental needs and approach to life. Being easily bored, both are in constant search of stimulation, loathe being dictated to, and find the predictable stifling, for example. When they meet, they will therefore instantly recognize a kindred free spirit and will be drawn to one another. If you are a curious Gemini, you'll be attracted by the independent, can-do Arien attitude, and will want to know more about that person, in turn captivating Aries with your humor, charm, and wide-ranging way of thinking. And if you are a typical go-getting Aries who loves the thrill of the chase and the object of your pursuit is Gemini, his or her tendency to keep you guessing by blowing hot and cold will inflame your ardor. Both enlivening and affectionate people, Aries and Gemini share a positive outlook that should result in a relationship that fizzes with fun and enthusiasm, especially if adaptable Gemini is willing to make allowances for the resolute Arien way.

Potential Pitfalls: Aries is a straightforward character who makes snap decisions and then charges toward his or her goal with unwavering focus and determination. Gemini, by contrast, prefers to gather as much information as possible and to weigh up the pros and cons carefully before making a commitment, and may therefore exasperate Aries by seeming to dither and procrastinate. If you are an undecided Gemini, you may respond to assertive Aries' attempts to push you into making up your mind either by delivering a devastating tongue-lashing or by walking out on your domineering partner—perhaps for good. And if you are an Aries, it is vital that you give your Gemini lover the time and space in which to explore the wider world. Don't immediately conclude that if he or she suddenly becomes interested in someone else's opinions, or gives you less attention than you feel you deserve, you have grounds for jealousy either. Airy Gemini finds intensity a turn-off just as much as fiery Aries resents not being treated as the most important person in Gemini's life.

Guiding Principle: Revel in each other's adventurous qualities, treat one another with understanding, and be warned that becoming embroiled in a power struggle will end in disaster.

Compatibility: ♥ ♥ ♥ ♥ ♥ ♥ ♡ ♡ ♡ ♡

CANCER

ARIES

A relationship between fiery Aries and watery Cancer can test both partners to their limits. Demonstrative Aries is progressive and daring, while reserved Cancer is backward-looking and cautious; short-tempered Aries is emotionally robust, while brooding Cancer is easily wounded. But if there is a true meeting of the hearts, this warm, ambitious pair can overcome their differences.

Plus Points: It is often said that opposites attract, and if you are a somewhat self-preoccupied Aries, you will immediately be hooked by Cancer's empathetic nature and will become increasingly determined to penetrate the shell of this rather private individual so that you can learn more about him or her. If you are a romantic Cancer, you in turn will be flattered by the dynamic ram's interest in you, also being attracted to his or her fearlessness, a masculine-polarity quality that you admire in others perhaps because you are such a feminine-polarity worrier yourself. There's every indication that a whirlwind romance will ensue, too, not least because impetuous Aries is an all-or-nothing personality and nurturing Cancer's life mission is to establish a loving home with a protective mate. And when this relationship becomes long term, both deeply value what they have built together.

Potential Pitfalls: The very characteristics that often draw Aries and Cancer together can drive them apart. A rash word from blunt Aries can cut sensitive Cancer to the quick, and the crab will then typically retreat into his or her shell to nurse the festering wound. If you are a straightforward Aries, you will probably be puzzled by Cancer's silent treatment, and if you then probe too deeply for the reason, may be stunned by your lover's hurtful response. And if you are an emotionally needy, home-loving Cancer, you may misinterpret the Arien drive to explore the wider world as neglect and a withdrawal of affection. Either way, your watery predisposition to dwell on ancient grievances and the ram's natural urge to put the past behind him or her and instead look ahead to the future can act like a bucket of icy-cold water on the flames of Aries' passion. As for you, fiery Aries, unless you control your impatience and exercise a little tact in your relationship with Cancer, your impetuousness may drive a permanent wedge between you.

Guiding Principle: Don't let your dissimilar outlooks and approaches become insurmountable bones of contention, but instead recognize their life- and love-enhancing qualities and try to be tolerant.

Compatibility: ♥ ♥ ♥ ♥ ♡ ♡ ♡ ♡ ♡ ♡

Cancer Birth Influences

Ruling planet: The Moon
Element: Water
Polarity: Feminine
Quadruplicity: Cardinal

When Aries ignores her Cancer partner and lavishes her attention on someone else, Cancer's feelings will be deeply hurt. Don't push your luck, Aries, and don't cling too tightly, Cancer.

Aries Birth Influences

Ruling planet: Mars
Element: Fire
Polarity: Masculine
Quadruplicity: Cardinal

ARIES / LEO

Aries Birth Influences

Ruling planet: Mars
Element: Fire
Polarity: Masculine
Quadruplicity: Cardinal

A romance between these two fire signs ignites a burning passion that is hard to quench. Both being warm-hearted, direct, and loyal, neither plays fast and loose with the other's feelings, these outgoing characters instead being fueled by their shared exuberance. There may, however, be the occasional heated argument if the regal lion tries to command the independent ram, or if pushy Aries takes advantage of Leo's easygoing nature.

Plus Points: While party-animal Leo enjoys nothing more than having a good time in others' company, Aries is constantly searching for a stimulating someone, and when Aries is drawn into Leo's orbit, there is usually an instant spark of attraction. Both recognize that they are equally matched in terms of their fearlessness, confidence, and charisma, and if you are an Aries, Leo's humor and laid-back charm will work its spell on you, while romantic Leo will be enthralled by your swashbuckling aura. Your courtship will be a magical time, with Aries ensuring that it is full of adventure and Leo staging candlelit suppers as a prelude to passion, and because neither of you can tolerate a humdrum lifestyle, your relationship is likely to continue in this thrilling vein. Although retaining your individuality is important to you both, Leo and Aries are open and faithful personalities who find each other's independence exhilarating rather than threatening.

If you are a Leo, life may never have felt better since you fell in love with dynamic Aries. Your partnership should remain strong unless one of you tries to dominate the other.

Potential Pitfalls: Both Leo and Aries prefer leading to following, creating a potential flashpoint. If you are an essentially good-natured and rather lazy Leo, you may choose to overlook Aries' assertiveness, but if pushed too far, will knock the ram back in line with a powerful swipe of your paw. And if you are an impetuous, active Aries, there may be times when the indolent lion's refusal to follow your lead causes you to explode with pent-up fury. Because neither Aries nor Leo readily admits to being at fault, or backs down easily, your rows are likely to be spectacularly fiery, but then the making-up will be memorable! If you are to remain an item, also remember, Aries, as you are dashing off to fight new battles, that a Leo in love will not tolerate being neglected for long, and, Leo, try not to mastermind your Arien lover's plans of action.

Guiding Principle: Restrict your urge to lead to the wider world, respect one another as equals, and revel in the love and excitement that your partner brings to your life.

Leo Birth Influences

Ruling planet: The Sun
Element: Fire
Polarity: Masculine
Quadruplicity: Fixed

Compatibility: 

VIRGO
ARIES

Because each has an inborn ability to drive the other to distraction, both partners will have to be very tolerant individuals if a relationship between fiery Aries and down-to-earth Virgo is to work. Yet if Aries and Virgo are truly committed to one another, love can conquer all.

Plus Points: When Aries meets Virgo, the initial attraction may be mutual. If you are an independent Aries, you may find Virgo's air of calm self-sufficiency alluring, and, mindful of the expression "still waters run deep," may be overtaken by the urge to dive into those waters to explore his or her personality in greater depth. And if you are an idealistic Virgo—particularly if you are female—Aries' dashing and chivalrous nature may lead you to believe that your knight in shining armor has just cantered onto the scene. Aries' blunt and forthright approach appeals to Virgo's strong dislike of pretentiousness, too, while humor-loving Aries is captivated by Virgo's razor-sharp wit.

Potential Pitfalls: After the first rosy glow of romance has faded, many potential pitfalls may wreck this love affair. If you are a perfectionist Virgo, you would rather remain single than yoke yourself to a partner who doesn't measure up to your demanding standards, and Aries may fail your test. While you set great store on planning, reckless Aries scares you by charging ahead without considering the consequences of his or her impulsive actions; you like to weigh up every aspect of an issue before coming to a reasoned conclusion, but bossy Aries may try to browbeat you into quick agreement; you need a tidy, orderly life, yet hasty, heedless Aries leaves a trail of chaos in his or her wake.

If you are an Aries, you may also find Virgo infuriating. You probably can't stand the way that objective Virgo coldly harps on about your past mistakes and criticizes your disorganized methods and belief in following your gut instinct. Not only that, but when you are raring to hit the nightspots, Virgo may turn killjoy and insist that you both spend the evening at home. You may also resent the attention that mutable Virgo lavishes on his or her friends, and as a result may feel unappreciated and neglected.

Guiding Principle: Your essential characters will never change, so give each other plenty of space, try to turn a blind eye to the traits that you each perceive as being faults in the other, and instead focus on your love for one another.

Compatibility: ♥ ♥ ♥ ♡ ♡ ♡ ♡ ♡ ♡ ♡

Virgo Birth Influences

Ruling planet: Mercury
Element: Earth
Polarity: Feminine
Quadruplicity: Mutable

Virgo won't like it if Aries' idea of domestic harmony doesn't include doing the dishes.

Aries Birth Influences

Ruling planet: Mars
Element: Fire
Polarity: Masculine
Quadruplicity: Cardinal

ARIES
LIBRA

Aries Birth Influences

Ruling planet: Mars
Element: Fire
Polarity: Masculine
Quadruplicity: Cardinal

Mars and Venus in perfect harmony? If you want the ideal relationship, it is important that Aries makes concessions to Libra, and that Libra toughens up a little.

Libra Birth Influences

Ruling planet: Venus
Element: Air
Polarity: Masculine
Quadruplicity: Cardinal

Aries is ruled by Mars, and Libra, by Venus, planets named for the Roman deities of war and love. And just as the warrior Mars softened in the arms of seductive Venus, so accommodating Libra can tame the aggressive ram, Aries in turn firing up dreamy Libra. Outspoken Aries may offend Libra's delicate feelings, however, and vacillating Libra may exasperate decisive Aries.

Plus Points: When Aries and Libra are drawn together, the attraction is one of opposites. While fiery and intense Aries is beguiled by Libra's cool, airy charm and sophistication, Libra's romantic heart flutters wildly when he or she is the sole focus of charismatic Aries' ardent attention. If you are a Venus-ruled Libra, you may be longing for a soulmate to adore and stand up for you, and may therefore find Aries' passion, determination, and fearlessness an irresistible combination. A single-minded, go-getting ram's life can often be stressful and lonely, and if you are such an Aries, Libra's indulgence and thoughtfulness may soothe and relax you, and you may also admire your peace-making lover's ability to take the heat out of antagonistic situations. Neither of you can stand dishonesty either, making yours a sincere and trusting relationship.

Potential Pitfalls: If you are an adaptable, conciliatory Libra who loathes discord, you will do your utmost to iron out any differences between you and hot-tempered Aries. Although you may usually be successful, the danger of this approach is that in appeasing assertive Aries, you will end up suppressing your own inclinations, which does not make for a happy Libra. Being a rather self-absorbed soul, you may also be wounded by the self-centered ram's lack of consideration for your feelings and may mistake his or her unthinking tactlessness for deliberate rudeness. And if you are a bossy Aries who resists being deflected from your chosen course, you may become infuriated by what you perceive as diplomatic Libra's attempts to manipulate you, hold you back, or gain the upper hand. While you make up your mind quickly and then immediately swing into action, airy Libra's tendency to weigh up the pros and cons carefully before deciding on a course of action—and occasional inability to reach a decision at all—may also sorely test your limited capacity for patience.

Guiding Principle: Rather than taking offense, try to see the merits of your very different viewpoints, and remember that an equal balance of air and fire fuels the flames of passion.

Compatibility:    

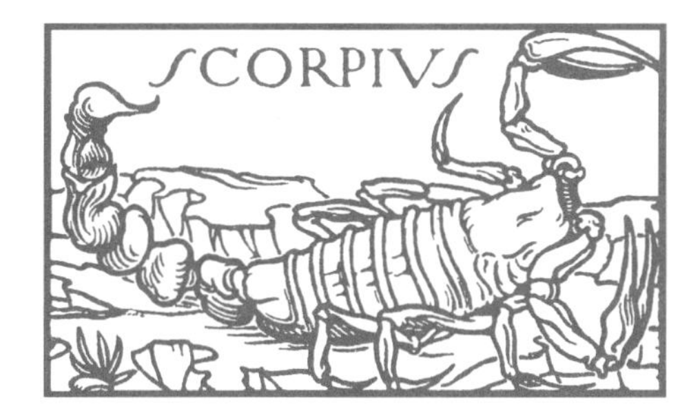

SCORPIO
ARIES

Because Aries and Scorpio are both ruled by Mars, albeit to different degrees, their mutual attraction lies in their fearlessness and determination. Yet these shared characteristics can result in spectacular confrontations between the fiery ram and jealous scorpion, whose primary planetary ruler is secretive Pluto, and the passion in this relationship can easily turn from love to loathing.

Plus Points: On meeting Scorpio, Mars-governed Aries may instantly be drawn to the powerful sexual magnetism exuded by someone as focused, ambitious, and determined as him- or herself, with Scorpio similarly responding to Aries' spirit and driving energy. As an Aries, you may also be tantalized by the feeling that Scorpio is holding something back, and may make it your mission to breach Scorpio's defenses and discover the sensuality that you are sure lies within. If you are an unattached Scorpio, your life's purpose is no doubt to find "the one," that perfect someone who loves as deeply and as devotedly as you, and you may recognize these qualities in the warm and demonstrative ram. Because you are similar in certain respects, not least in demanding unconditional love and loyalty from a lover, the ingredients that make an exciting and enduring relationship are certainly at hand.

Potential Pitfalls: The course of true love is rarely smooth, and unless both Aries and Scorpio are willing to make difficult compromises, their relationship may hit the rocks. If you are the Aries partner in this love affair, you need to feel in control, yet equally independent Scorpio refuses to be steered or driven. You are also frank and loathe emotional games, yet Scorpio can be withholding and enigmatic, which may cause you to lose patience and unleash a fiery blast of frustration. Aries' hot temper, and the hurtful accusations that your outspoken lover may sometimes hurl at you, may pierce your heart if you are a sensitive Scorpio. Although you are deeply empathetic, you find it hard to forgive and forget, and may express your pain either by being just as aggressive as Aries, or, because water is your element, exuding icy coldness. To add insult to injury, the Arien tendency to seek out others for stimulation and diversion often may arouse your jealousy, your possessiveness in turn making the freedom-loving ram feel trapped.

Guiding Principle: When your lover annoys or wounds you, articulate your feelings candidly and dispassionately. Try to understand the other's viewpoint and to moderate your behavior accordingly.

Compatibility: ♥♥♥♡♡♡♡♡♡♡

Scorpio Birth Influences

Ruling planet: Pluto; traditionally Mars
Element: Water
Polarity: Feminine
Quadruplicity: Fixed

Aries and Scorpio make a challenging match. If you are an open Aries, you may quickly come to resent your Scorpio lover's secretive side. Unless you can reach a compromise, you may be headed for an acrimonious split.

Aries Birth Influences

Ruling planet: Mars
Element: Fire
Polarity: Masculine
Quadruplicity: Cardinal

ARIES / SAGITTARIUS

Aries Birth Influences

Ruling planet: Mars
Element: Fire
Polarity: Masculine
Quadruplicity: Cardinal

A confrontation between Sagittarius and Aries lovers will be hot, but their anger should burn out quickly as both are forgiving and optimistic. Making up afterward is the fun part!

Sagittarius Birth Influences

Ruling planet: Jupiter
Element: Fire
Polarity: Masculine
Quadruplicity: Mutable

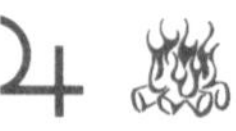

A romance between these two fire signs can ignite an exciting and fervent relationship, for these well-matched lovers usually understand each other very well. However, should domineering Aries try to control independent Sagittarius, or the archer's variableness frustrate the straightforward ram, there may be moments of frustration.

Plus Points: Aries and Sagittarius will probably have been brought together by their shared adventurousness. It is primarily this that will keep their relationship both lively and alive, for neither will settle for a humdrum love life. If you are an open and assertive Aries, you may be attracted by the Sagittarian traits of cheerfulness, self-confidence, and enthusiasm because they mirror your own approach to the world. Similarly, if you are a Sagittarius, you may be enthused by Aries' honesty, energy, and optimism because you, too, are blessed with these qualities. Neither of you are passive, inward-looking types, and Aries' zest for the new and his or her tendency to push against boundaries, coupled with Sagittarius' need to keep on the move with a spirit of discovery, is a heady combination.

Potential Pitfalls: Due to the influence of Mars, Aries likes to lead others in the direction of his or her choosing. But Sagittarius' guardian planet is Jupiter, the father of the Roman gods and follower of his own path. And while Aries and Sagittarius' joint element is fire, the difference is that Aries is a cardinal, or self-assertive, sign, while Sagittarius is mutable, or variable. If you are the Sagittarius in this relationship, you may therefore not only fight back if Aries tries to push you too far, but may even escape the controlling ram if you feel boxed in. So Aries, try to suppress your dominance, and when your views or preferences conflict, allow freedom-loving Sagittarius the independence that you yourself demand. The same mutability makes Sagittarius' moods changeable, which may confuse you if you are a steadfast Aries. This will sometimes lead to you reacting with exasperation, only to provoke an even more hot-tempered response from Sagittarius. But neither of you have slow-burning temperaments, nor are you prone to sulking, so the fireworks will soon subside. Indeed, the occasional fiery row can supply that extra injection of excitement that you both relish in a relationship.

Guiding Principle: Keep the flames of passion burning brightly by ensuring that your relationship remains stimulating and good-humored, and by respecting one another as equals.

Compatibility: ♥♥♥♥♥♥♥♥♡♡

CAPRICORN

ARIES

The combination of Aries' fieriness and Capricorn's earthiness creates a relationship that is both passionate and rooted in reality. Aries' impulsiveness may grate on cautious Capricorn, however, while the fun-loving ram may be frustrated by the goat's gravity. Yet if both of these resolute, cardinal signs are determined to make their relationship work, it will.

Plus Points: Capricorn is a rather reticent individual, but if you are an Aries, you may have been drawn up short on your first meeting when he or she made an offbeat, humorous, and deeply intriguing comment. Being a questing Aries who adores a challenge, you may have become increasingly fixated on melting the goat's reserve and discovering the true personality lying beneath Capricorn's cool, self-contained exterior. As a result, you may have found that your lover's steely will and purposefulness match your own, which you may find incredibly stimulating, as you may the goat's earthy sensuality. If you are the Capricorn in this relationship, your attention may initially have been captured by Aries' self-certainty and obvious ambition, qualities that appeal to you because you are looking for a partner who is both as go-getting and set on success as you. You are no doubt also invigorated by the dynamic ram's liveliness, find his or her optimism endearing, and, having been born under an earthy sign, cannot help but respond when exposed to the heat of Aries' passion.

Potential Pitfalls: Over time, you may find it difficult to overlook certain Arien traits if you are a prudent Capricorn. Hot-headed Aries is impetuous, while you prefer to consider issues coolly, unhurriedly, and in detail before reaching a reasoned decision. You believe that a relationship needs to be built up slowly, steadily, and devotedly, but the ram dashes off in pursuit of a sudden diversion and then expects to be welcomed back with open arms. And because you are a possessive person, Aries' insistence on personal freedom may cause you to become suspicious and insecure, depressed and withdrawn. You may find it difficult to understand this state of mind if you are an open and demonstrative Aries. Indeed, being an impatient ram, you may feel that Capricorn is holding you back, stifling your burning need for independence, and generally spoiling your fun.

Guiding Principle: Laugh off your differences, set your powerful sights on achieving shared goals, and your romance will remain fresh, loving, and mutually supportive.

Compatibility: ♥♥♥♥♥♥♡♡♡♡

Capricorn Birth Influences

Ruling planet: Saturn
Element: Earth
Polarity: Feminine
Quadruplicity: Cardinal

If you are an Aries, you will no doubt rise to the challenge of breaching Capricorn's cool exterior in search of the passionate person underneath. If you succeed, be careful not to appear too inconstant lest he or she retreats from you for good.

Aries Birth Influences

Ruling planet: Mars
Element: Fire
Polarity: Masculine
Quadruplicity: Cardinal

ARIES
AQUARIUS

Aries Birth Influences

Ruling planet: Mars
Element: Fire
Polarity: Masculine
Quadruplicity: Cardinal

Sociable, charismatic, and forward-looking—a description that applies as much to Aries as to Aquarius. Because of this, a romance between these two positive people may be based on mutual understanding. Airy Aquarius provides fiery Aries with invigorating oxygen, but the heat of Aries' passion may suffocate free-spirited Aquarius, while Aries' ardor may be dampened by the water-carrier's coolness and detachment.

Plus Points: You may have been irresistibly drawn to friendly, funny, original Aquarius if you are a stimulation-seeking, hot-blooded Aries. On striking up a conversation, you were no doubt thrilled to discover that this talkative stranger shares your spontaneity and adventurous mindset, and even enjoys traveling as much as you. Although you may have gotten along extremely well, you probably felt that airy Aquarius was holding something of him- or herself back, inflaming your desire to conquer the water-carrier's heart. Aries' vitality, warmth, and self-confidence are in any case a heady cocktail, and if you are an unpretentious Aquarius, you may also have been attracted by the direct ram's total lack of airs and graces. As you got to know Aries better, you may furthermore have been relieved to realize that this person is just as independent as you, so that while you choose to be together, your focus on outside interests enables you both to retain your individuality.

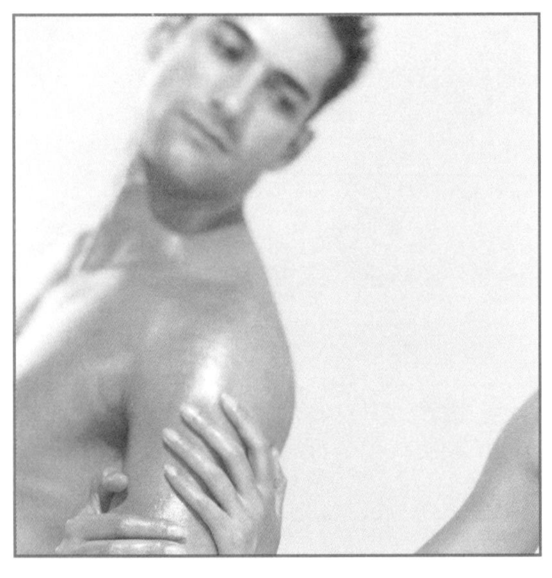

A fiery Aries may find him- or herself wounded once too often by the apparent indifference of an oblivious Aquarian lover, in which case this relationship is likely to burn out.

Potential Pitfalls: Neither Aries nor Aquarius are typically jealous or possessive personalities, partly because they are both so busy pursuing their own interests. Yet, being governed by commanding Mars, Aries may try to lead Aquarius, and if there is one thing that the water-carrier demands, it is personal freedom. If you are an Aquarius, your airy element injects a breath of fresh air into your relationship with Aries, but if you don't like the ram's forceful ways, you may become desperate for some breathing space and time apart. The Arien element is fire, which, if you were born under this sign, endows you with intense animal passion—something your more cool, cerebral Aquarian lover may find somewhat stifling. Your ardent feelings may consequently be wounded by what you perceive to be the water-carrier's apparent indifference to you, and you may feel that your partner is not prepared to put enough effort into the relationship.

Aquarius Birth Influences

Ruling planet: Uranus; traditionally Saturn
Element: Air
Polarity: Masculine
Quadruplicity: Fixed

Guiding Principle: Try to keep your romance healthy by understanding that your lover needs just as much freedom as you, and by communicating openly and honestly with one another when problems arise.

Compatibility: ♥♥♥♥♡♡♡♡♡♡

PISCES
ARIES

Dashing Aries arouses the sentimental Piscean's sense of romance, while Pisces' more passive qualities of selflessness and devotion stroke the ram's fiery ego. Yet independent Aries may start to feel trapped if Pisces becomes too clingy, while sensitive Pisces may be wounded by Aries' inattentiveness and brutal honesty.

Plus Points: If you are a Pisces under the influence of Neptune, particularly if you are a woman, you may have spent many hours daydreaming about your ideal lover, whom you may have imagined as being positive, protective, romantic, and, of course, devoted to you. When Aries entered your life, you may have been dazzled by the zealous ram's confidence, courage, and charisma, causing you to believe that your fantasy had come true. As an Aries, you may sometimes find life as a soldier of Mars tough and rather lonely, in which case empathetic Pisces' loving, supportive sympathy acts on your battle-weary soul like a soothing balm. Yours is a cardinal sign, but Pisces is mutable, indicating that his or her ability to adapt to your moods, as well as willingness to go along with some of your adventurous suggestions, are other qualities that you appreciate in your lover.

Potential Pitfalls: A relationship between Aries and Pisces certainly won't be all hearts and roses. Being a fire sign, Aries can be somewhat self-centered and thoughtless, while if you are a Pisces, your element of water endows you with great emotional depth, but also makes you extremely sensitive and vulnerable to feelings of insecurity. You are seeking a soulmate, someone who feels as deeply about you as you do about him or her, with whom you can share everything that life has to offer. You may therefore be profoundly hurt by the ram's tendency to disappear suddenly in hot pursuit of an irresistible challenge and by his or her apparent lack of consideration for your feelings. As an idealist, you may have put Aries on a lofty pedestal, a position that attention-loving Aries relishes, yet may find difficult to live up to. Indeed, if you are an action-oriented, freedom-loving Aries, you may come to feel as though you are being swamped by the intensity of Pisces' feelings and expectations, and may express your frustration with searing candor, thus adding insult to injury.

Guiding Principle: Learn to love your differences rather than perceiving them as a threat to your relationship or individuality.

Compatibility: ♥♥♥♥♡♡♡♡♡♡

Pisces Birth Influences

Ruling planet: Neptune; traditionally Jupiter
Element: Water
Polarity: Feminine
Quadruplicity: Mutable

Aries' dramatic, romantic gestures leave a dreamy Pisces weak at the knees, but there's no knowing how long the magic will last, especially if Aries is distracted by a tempting challenge.

Aries Birth Influences

Ruling planet: Mars
Element: Fire
Polarity: Masculine
Quadruplicity: Cardinal

TAURUS / TAURUS

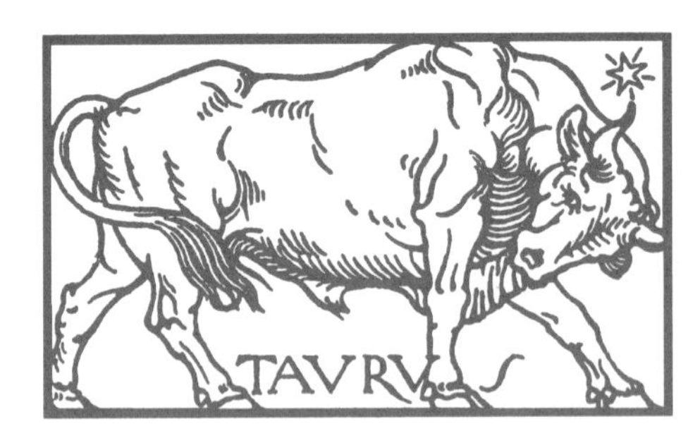

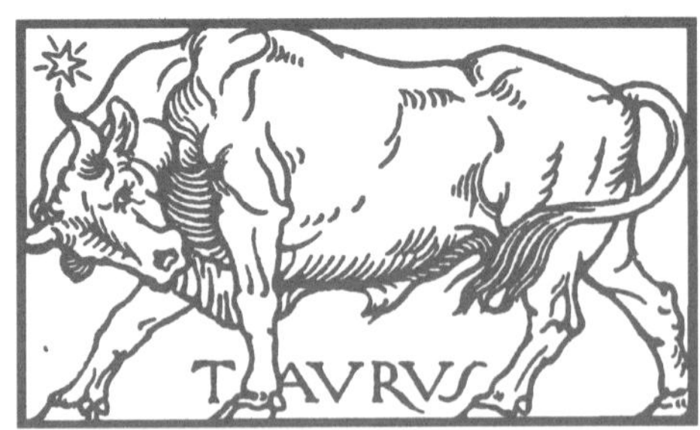

Taurus Birth Influences

Ruling planet: Venus
Element: Earth
Polarity: Feminine
Quadruplicity: Fixed

The double dose of Venusian romance, the restraint of a feminine polarity, the stability and sensuality of the element of earth, and a fixed sign's staying power all bode well for a loving and lasting liaison between two Taureans. Their possessiveness and obstinacy may sometimes throw a wrench in the works, but should not cause this steadfast pair's love affair to grind to a halt.

Plus Points: As children of your ruling planet, Venus, if you were both born under the sign of the bull, your romance with your Taurean lover may have begun with a teasing exchange of flirtatious comments. More significantly, perhaps, you detected an undercurrent of warm sincerity beneath the banter, and, after a few dates, were probably left in no doubt of this calm person's kindness, reliability, and stable temperament. Taurus is not a person who generally enjoys a string of one-night stands or whirlwind romances with more flighty types, and instead longs for a steady, affectionate partner with whom to create a secure and affluent atmosphere of domestic bliss. It may therefore seem as though you have found "the one" in your even-tempered fellow bull, and you no doubt respond strongly to his or her powerful sex appeal, the gift of the Taurean element of earth. The feeling is almost certainly mutual, and because the influence of Venus bestows on you both an abhorrence of discord, an appreciation of the finer things in life, and a materialistic outlook, your relationship looks set to remain harmonious, as well as rich in more ways than one.

If you and your partner are both Taureans, yours is likely to be a steady, kind, and supportive relationship. Take care that jealousy doesn't get in the way of such a mutually satisfying union.

Potential Pitfalls: Jealousy and stubbornness are the greatest threats to two bulls' desire to live happily ever after. Taureans can be very possessive, so be warned that if an attractive third party homes in on you and you respond with playful coquetry, you may soon see your lover glowering with suppressed fury. But because once committed, fixed-sign Taureans generally stay committed, and because you often react in exactly the same way when the roles are reversed, each of you understands, deep down, that's there's no real cause for concern. However, a more serious rift in your romance may arise if you disagree about something that is fundamental to your joint future because, being intractable, neither of you readily backs down.

Guiding Principle: Make a joke of your jealous tendencies, be prepared to give way occasionally when you disagree, and otherwise just appreciate one another.

Taurus Birth Influences

Ruling planet: Venus
Element: Earth
Polarity: Feminine
Quadruplicity: Fixed

Compatibility:

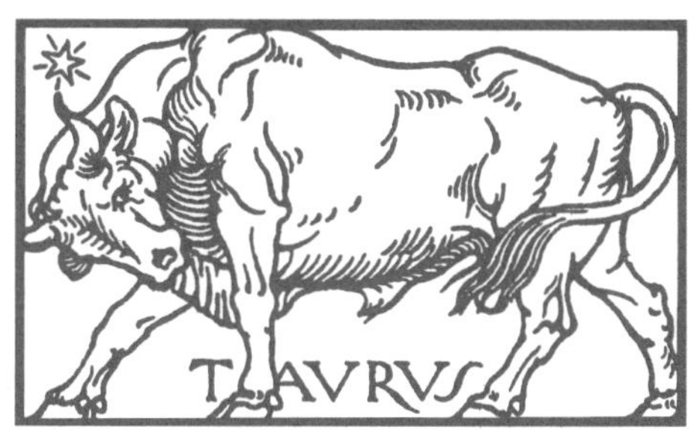

GEMINI
TAURUS

Not only does a romance between Taurus and Gemini unite their feminine and masculine polarities, but the bull's earthiness grounds flighty Gemini, while the twins' breeziness enlivens placid Taurus. Yet because fixed-sign Taurus can be unmoving and inflexible, and mutable Gemini thrives on novelty and change, these sweethearts may eventually find themselves heading in different directions.

Plus Points: Opposites often attract, and, as a Taurus, this may be the reason why you find Gemini alluring, or, if your birth sign is that of the twins, the bull, endearing. Indeed, just like yin and yang, the contrasting qualities that your polarities bestow on you have the potential to merge into a perfect whole, passive, inward-looking Taurus being invigorated by active, outgoing Gemini's animation, and Gemini being drawn into Taurus' nurturing, supportive embrace. If you are a restless Gemini who is longing to put down roots, the steady stability that is the gift of the element of earth no doubt deepens Taurus' appeal. And because your earthy element endows you with a rather sober and unquestioning temperament if you are a Taurus, you must be captivated by airy Gemini's playfulness, as well as flattered by his or her obvious curiosity about you. Venus, your ruling planet, also gives you a weakness for charmers, and as a protégé of Mercury, Gemini's silver tongue therefore probably melts your defenses.

Potential Pitfalls: Over the longer term, the biggest stumbling block in the path of Taurus and Gemini's love may be the bull's constancy and the twins' changeability. Although these traits may initially have seemed appealing in the rose-tinted haze of the early days of your affair, they may later become infuriating. While the earthy bull prefers an unpredictable, routine existence, being a mutable sign, Gemini, you crave variety and may feel so stifled by the bull's unvarying habits that you may not be able to stop yourself from flitting off for the occasional breath of fresh air. If you are a steadfast Taurus, you may consequently start to question Gemini's commitment to your relationship, and if Gemini's tendency to flirt arouses your jealousy, you may not be able to contain your fury. Yet expressing your feelings with such uncharacteristic forcefulness may not be a bad thing, particularly if it shocks Gemini into curbing his or her wandering ways.

Guiding Principle: Gemini, employ your flexibility by adapting to the Taurean way, and, Taurus, try to accommodate Gemini's need for diversion.

Compatibility: ♥♥♥♥♡♡♡♡♡♡

Gemini Birth Influences
Ruling planet: Mercury
Element: Air
Polarity: Masculine
Quadruplicity: Mutable

Gemini knows how to woo, and you probably can't help feeling flattered if you are a Taurus. Be wary of Gemini's wandering eye, though!

Taurus Birth Influences
Ruling planet: Venus
Element: Earth
Polarity: Feminine
Quadruplicity: Fixed

TAURUS
CANCER

Taurus Birth Influences
Ruling planet: Venus
Element: Earth
Polarity: Feminine
Quadruplicity: Fixed

Venus is the planet of sensual love, while the Moon is the realm of deep emotions, making a liaison between Taurus and Cancer amorous and tender. Add Taurus' stability and Cancer's caring to the mix, and you have a relationship that is both passionate and supportive. Straightforward Taurus may not understand the crab's moodiness, however, while sensitive Cancer may be hurt by the bull's lack of empathy.

Plus Points: Even though Taurus and Cancer share a feminine, or passive, polarity, Cancer is a cardinal, or initiating, sign, indicating that a romance between the bull and the crab may have begun with Cancer making the first move. Your emotional vulnerability makes you rather circumspect if you are a crab, but your lunar longing for a fulfilling relationship and intuition that Taurus was the one for you may have prompted you to overcome your inhibitions. What attracted you to Taurus? Well, it may initially have been the bull's earthy animal magnetism and the gentle sense of fun and kindness that are the gifts of Venus. And you must now bask in the sense of security that your sweetheart's steadiness brings to your life. If you are Cancer's Taurus beloved, you may similarly have been waiting for the right person to settle down with, an undemanding someone with whom to share a life of snug domesticity. In Cancer, you must feel that you have found a partner who is both loving and nurturing—characteristics triply reinforced by the crab's ruling planet, element, and polarity—yet, having a cardinal quadruplicity, is also someone who is as ambitious as you in planning your future together.

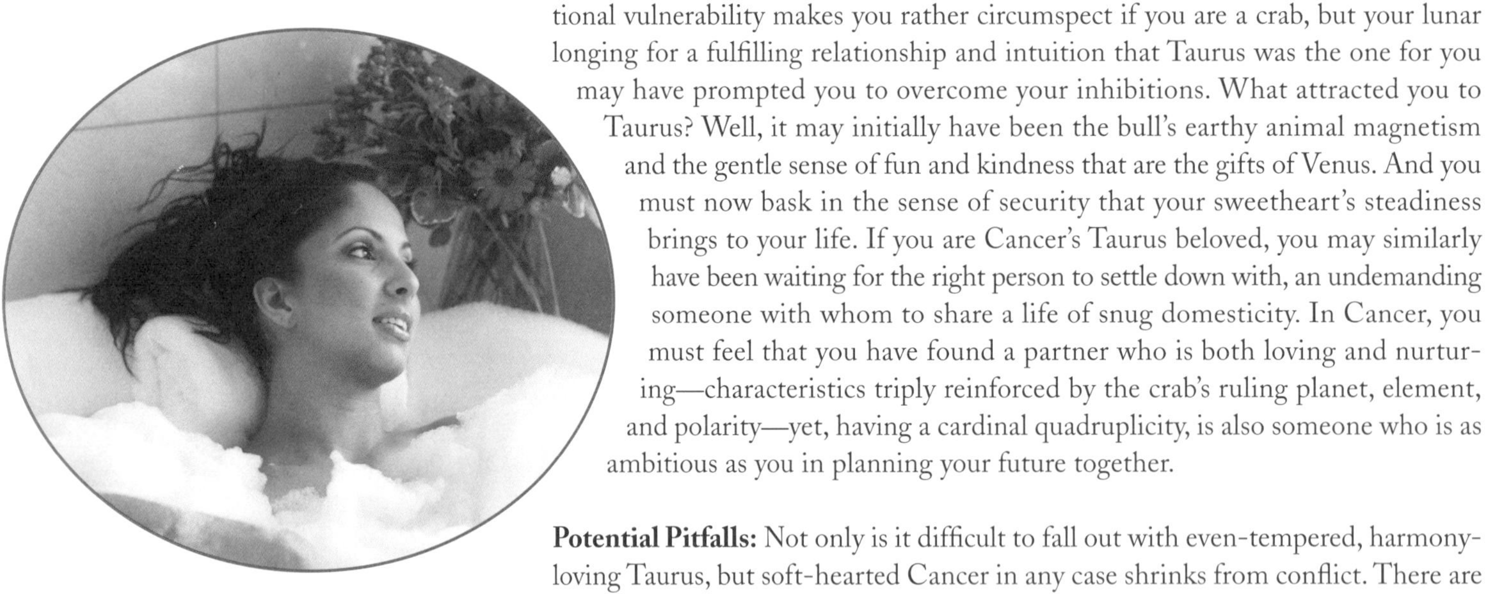

A Taurus–Cancer couple will be blessed with a sensual and loving relationship. Your favorite romantic evenings may well be those that you spend together at home.

Potential Pitfalls: Not only is it difficult to fall out with even-tempered, harmony-loving Taurus, but soft-hearted Cancer in any case shrinks from conflict. There are nevertheless some aspects of each other's characters that may cast a tiny cloud over their relationship. If you are a cardinal Cancer, you are probably more enterprising and amenable to change than fixed Taurus, while the combination of your other birth influences can make you oversensitive. You may consequently withdraw into your shell if you take offense at Taurus' stubborn refusal to countenance a lifestyle adjustment. And if you are an uncomplicated Taurus, you may be bewildered by the crab's touchiness, yet may be reluctant to probe into the cause, thereby giving Cancer the impression that you don't care about his or her feelings.

Cancer Birth Influences
Ruling planet: The Moon
Element: Water
Polarity: Feminine
Quadruplicity: Cardinal

Guiding Principle: Be tolerant of your minor personal differences and focus on building a contented life together.

Compatibility: 

LEO — TAURUS

The bull and lion's birth influences augur well for a romance between them. Taurus' element of earth and feminine, or passive, polarity stabilize and support spontaneous Leo, whose fiery element and masculine, or active, polarity in turn stimulate and animate the stolid bull. Although both Venus and the Sun endow Taurus and Leo with good-natured, pleasure-loving personalities, neither of these fixed-sign people will back down easily should they disagree.

Plus Points: The Sun bestows a sunny, playful disposition on Leo, while Venus' gifts to her Taurean children include an easygoing temperament and an enjoyment of fun, qualities that appeal to the lion. If you are a Leo, you must also be attracted by Taurus' courtesy, quiet confidence, and indulgence of your whims. Being rather self-centered, the qualities that you demand in your partner include unquestioning love and fidelity, and, as a fixed sign like yourself, your steadfast Taurean lover probably doesn't disappoint on this score. Even more appealing is the double dose of earthy, Venusian sensuality that ignites your fiery passion.

If you were born under the sign of the bull, you may have been irresistibly drawn to the laughter, warmth, and energy generated by Leo when you first entered the lion's orbit. Your feminine polarity means that you absorb and mirror others' moods, and fiery Leo must therefore have a warming and enlivening influence upon you. Both Venus and your earthy element make you value tangible, or material, expressions of affection, and you must consequently relish the tokens of love that the generous lion showers upon you. No doubt you are also grateful for Leo's tendency to be as lazy as you at times!

Potential Pitfalls: The main pitfall in a relationship between Taurus and Leo lies in the stubbornness that their fixed-sign status can trigger in them both. The flashpoint for you, if you are a Leo, may be the bull's jealousy. Your element of fire causes you to crave the excitement of social contact, and if you become too enthusiastic about a certain someone, possessive Taurus may feel threatened, which may eventually infuriate you. And if you are a prudent Taurus who prizes stability, you may be further unsettled by the lion's hot-headed impulsiveness and tendency to spend money as if there were no tomorrow.

Guiding Principle: Revel in the joy that your lover brings to your life, and when you disagree, try to flick your fixed-sign switch from obdurate obstinacy to loving loyalty.

Compatibility: ♥♥♥♥♥♥♥♡♡♡

Leo Birth Influences
Ruling planet: The Sun
Element: Fire
Polarity: Masculine
Quadruplicity: Fixed

A Leo–Taurus couple should enjoy an affectionate, playful relationship.

Taurus Birth Influences
Ruling planet: Venus
Element: Earth
Polarity: Feminine
Quadruplicity: Fixed

♀ 

TAURUS / VIRGO

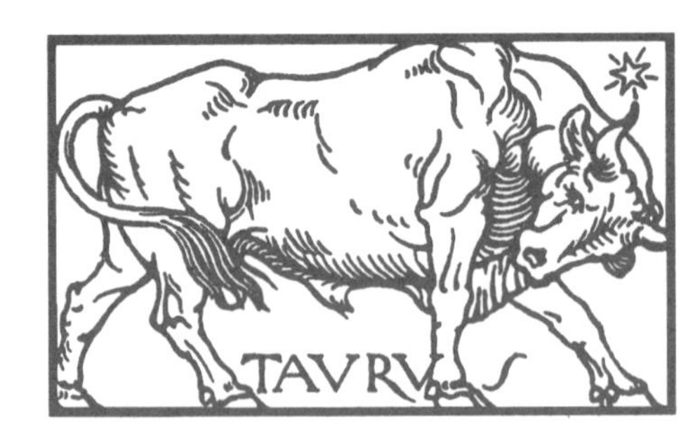

Taurus Birth Influences

Ruling planet: Venus
Element: Earth
Polarity: Feminine
Quadruplicity: Fixed

Their shared polarity and element promise Taurus and Virgo a romance that is tender, sensual, and committed. The pairing of Venus and Mercury also means that indulgent Taurus encourages Virgo to relax and savor life's pleasures, while communicative Virgo gives the Taurean mind food for thought. Their respective quadruplicities may cause friction, however, as fixed Taurus is wary of change, which is exactly what mutable Virgo thrives on.

Plus Points: Their feminine polarity makes both Taurus and Virgo receptive individuals, and when they first meet, the signals that they receive from one another may arouse their desire to get to know each other better. What may have caused your interest in Taurus to deepen into love, if you are a voluble Virgo, is his or her willingness to listen to you and rock-solid dependability, which you probably value because you yourself can be so changeable. Despite being as sensible as you, having indolent, hedonistic Venus as a ruling planet accounts for the bull's relish of a leisurely meal enjoyed in comfortable surroundings, and you may consequently be learning to appreciate the pleasure to be had in slowing down, switching off the busy brain that Mercury has bestowed on you, and giving rein to your senses. If you are a Taurus, the qualities that you may especially prize in Virgo include his or her ability to adapt to your settled ways and the intellectual curiosity that opens your eyes to various viewpoints, for which you have both Virgo's planetary ruler and mutability to thank. Finally, because both Taurus and Virgo's element is earth, you not only understand each other's physical needs, but know how to satisfy them, which augurs well for that side of your relationship!

If you are an earthy Taurus, you share your element with your Virgo lover, suggesting that yours will be a sensuous and satisfying relationship.

Potential Pitfalls: Because Taurus is ruled by peace-loving Venus, and Virgo is a mutable sign that avoids confrontation, neither of you are types to pick an argument for the sake of it. Aspects of your lover's character may nevertheless start to irritate you so much over time that you may not be able to hold your tongue. And if you are a Virgo, it may be precisely your critical tongue that may hurt and anger Taurus, while if you are a bull, your refusal to compromise may infuriate flexible Virgo.

Virgo Birth Influences

Ruling planet: Mercury
Element: Earth
Polarity: Feminine
Quadruplicity: Mutable

Guiding Principle: Be grateful for the fresh dimension that you bring to each other's lives, and if problems arise, talk through your differences calmly, reasonably, and with an open mind and a positive attitude.

Compatibility: ♥♥♥♥♥♥♥♡♡♡

LIBRA
TAURUS

* *

Venus, the Roman goddess of love and planetary ruler of both Taurus and Libra, smiles indulgently on a romance between this pleasure-loving pair, while the union of the bull's feminine and Libra's masculine polarity also augurs well for their future together. But is it truly a match made in heaven? Will airy Libra prove too flighty for earthy Taurus, or will rigid Taurus make breezy Libra feel trapped?

Plus Points: Your shared Venusian traits and interests, which include a good-humored nature and an appreciation of all things artistic, may have brought you together if you are a Taurean–Libran couple. Attraction having deepened into love, there may now be a number of qualities that each of you adores in the other that are not in the gift of your ruling planet. What you may especially prize in Taurus, if you are a Libra, is his or her supportiveness and dependability—both characteristics of the element of earth that ground and hold you steady when your own element, air, causes you to feel rootless and insecure. And if it is unswerving commitment that you want from a partner, fixed-sign Taurus won't disappoint. If you are a Taurus, you have probably discovered that Libra has the ability to invigorate you in the most charming of ways. With an enterprising, cardinal quadruplicity and the lively element of air as birth influences, Libra may constantly come up with fresh ideas about how to spend your time together. You may go along with them simply to indulge your lover initially, but may be pleasantly surprised by how much you are enjoying yourself. All in all, you must find Libra a breath of fresh air, and perhaps you wonder how you did without your enlivening partner before you met.

Potential Pitfalls: Despite the blessing of Venus, a romance between Taurus and Libra is unlikely to be problem-free. The bull can be a possessive, inflexible, and lethargic personality, which you may find suffocating, constricting, and even boring if you are a capricious Libra who likes to go where the wind blows. As for you, Taurus, you may be upset by the curious interest that flirty Libra shows in people whom you regard as rivals in love. This flirtatious behavior is due to the combination of air and the influence of Venus and is usually guileless, but may nevertheless arouse your jealousy.

Guiding Principle: Don't strive to change the person with whom you fell in love, but instead try to understand, and make allowances for, your different quirks and needs.

Compatibility: ♥♥♥♥♥♥♡♡♡♡

Libra Birth Influences

Ruling planet: Venus
Element: Air
Polarity: Masculine
Quadruplicity: Cardinal

* *

At times, Taurus can be a couch potato, which may frustrate active Libra, but then the dependable bull makes up for this irritating trait in other ways.

* *

Taurus Birth Influences

Ruling planet: Venus
Element: Earth
Polarity: Feminine
Quadruplicity: Fixed

TAURUS
SCORPIO

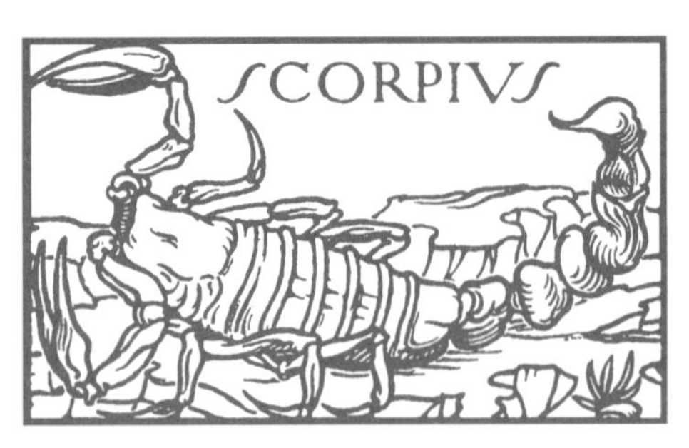

Taurus Birth Influences

Ruling planet: Venus
Element: Earth
Polarity: Feminine
Quadruplicity: Fixed

Because Taurus and Scorpio are fixed signs, both generally remain committed once attraction has blossomed into love. The earthy, Venus-ruled bull anchors and softens sometimes insecure and intense Scorpio, the empathetic scorpion in turn giving the bull emotional backup and total devotion. Taurus' matter-of-fact outlook may wound touchy Scorpio, however, while Scorpio's emotional complexity may mystify straightforward Taurus.

Plus Points: Both Taurus and Scorpio take affairs of the heart extremely seriously, largely because Taurus' planetary guardian is the Roman goddess of love and Scorpio's element is water, the realm of emotions. And once Cupid's arrow has hit its mark, these fixed signs will strive to stick together through thick and thin. What you must especially cherish in Taurus, if you are a Scorpio, is his or her supportiveness and dependability—gifts of the element of earth that make you feel loved, protected, and secure. You probably respond ardently to the bull's earthy sensuality and Venusian sense of fun, too, not least because one of your ruling planets is Mars, the warrior god who enjoyed many an erotic encounter with pleasure-seeking Venus. If you are a Taurus, you, too, must feel as though you are being swept away by a tidal wave of passion whenever you snatch an intimate moment with the intensely sexy scorpion. That may not be all that you are thankful for in your lover, however, for when a loved one is feeling down, Scorpio's watery element and feminine polarity manifest themselves as deep compassion and the desire to comfort.

Your secretiveness may make you clam up at times if you are a Scorpio, jeopardizing a steady, supportive relationship with Taurus.

Potential Pitfalls: The biggest potential pitfalls that Taurus and Scorpio face in their relationship stem from their shared feminine polarity and fixed quadruplicity, which make them very responsive to others' moods, but also inflexible. Yet sensitivity is not a typical Taurean trait, and if you are an uncomplicated bull, you may be flummoxed by Scorpio's occasional moodiness and secretiveness— the bequests of water and Pluto, the dark, mysterious god of the underworld who is the scorpion's primary planetary ruler. If you are a Scorpio and Taurus pushes you too hard either to snap out of it or to open up without really trying to understand you, you may feel so hurt or irritated that you may withdraw farther into yourself or else deliver the fatal sting that ends your relationship.

Guiding Principle: Be patient with one another and focus on offering each other unconditional love, as well as emotional and practical support.

Compatibility: ♥♥♥♥♥♥♥♥♡♡

Scorpio Birth Influences

Ruling planet: Pluto; traditionally Mars
Element: Water
Polarity: Feminine
Quadruplicity: Fixed

SAGITTARIUS

TAURUS

The early days of a romance between Taurus and Sagittarius are usually scintillating. Good-natured, Venus-ruled Taurus charms the archer, while the bull basks in the aura of enlivening energy that cheerful, warm-hearted Sagittarius exudes. But the earthy, fixed-sign bull's rigidity may soon make the fiery, spontaneous archer feel trapped, while changeable Sagittarius' inconstancy may distress steady Taurus.

Plus Points: It was probably their planetary rulers, respectively laid-back Venus and jovial Jupiter, that provided the initial spark of attraction between Taurus and Sagittarius. The Sagittarian polarity is masculine, or active, and if you are a good-humored, confident archer, you may have been captivated by the easygoing bull's relaxed demeanor and willingness to follow your lead in having fun when you first met, as well as being tantalized by his or her powerful sensuality. Taurus is a feminine, or receptive, sign, and if it is yours, you no doubt quickly found yourself responding to charismatic Sagittarius' optimism and infectious wit. You were probably flattered by the interest that this vital person showed in you, too. Indeed, because the archer's element is fire, your lover's vitality and passion must still invigorate and seduce you, and if you are a Sagittarius, you must equally relish Taurus' earthy physicality.

Potential Pitfalls: The greatest threat to an enduring romance between Taurus and Sagittarius lurks in their different elements and quadruplicities. The stabilizing influence of earth makes Taurus a creature of habit, while that of a fixed quadruplicity means that the bull stubbornly resists changing his or her settled ways. You may eventually find this behavior stifling if you are a Sagittarius, partly because your fiery element endows you with a delight in being impulsive, and partly because your mutable quadruplicity gives you a thirst for new experiences. That said, your birth influences also include flexibility and an aversion to arguments, which, if used positively, could prevent your relationship from descending into the doldrums. If you are a Taurus, you may similarly have to muster all of your Venusian reserves of serenity and indulgence if you are to remain together. Your lover's capriciousness and tendency to seek stimulation elsewhere may injure your feelings and activate your possessiveness, but be warned that your reaction may drive freedom-loving Sagittarius away.

Guiding Principles: Don't attempt to change each other, but instead try to be tolerant and adaptable in accommodating your different approaches to life. Do this, and you should move forward into the future together, rather than separately.

Compatibility: ♥♥♥♥♡♡♡♡♡♡

Sagittarius Birth Influences

Ruling planet: Jupiter
Element: Fire
Polarity: Masculine
Quadruplicity: Mutable

Exuberant Sagittarius is always looking for fun, which makes life more interesting for a somewhat staid Taurus.

Taurus Birth Influences

Ruling planet: Venus
Element: Earth
Polarity: Feminine
Quadruplicity: Fixed

TAURUS
CAPRICORN

Taurus Birth Influences
Ruling planet: Venus
Element: Earth
Polarity: Feminine
Quadruplicity: Fixed

Taurus and Capricorn both value commitment, making a serious relationship between these two a near certainty.

Capricorn Birth Influences
Ruling planet: Saturn
Element: Earth
Polarity: Feminine
Quadruplicity: Cardinal

Both receptive, feminine-polarity signs, romantic, Venus-ruled Taurus melts Capricorn's reserve, while serious, Saturn-governed Capricorn provides the steady commitment that Taurus longs for. Although their shared element of supportive earth creates an especially strong bond between them, fixed Taurus' obstinacy and cardinal Capricorn's forcefulness may occasionally cast a shadow over their relationship.

Plus Points: Their common birth influences indicate that neither Taurus nor Capricorn give their hearts unthinkingly, but because Capricorn has a go-getting, cardinal quadruplicity, it is likely that he or she initiated their romance. If you are that Capricorn, whose saturnine planetary ruler endows you with a sincere, mature, and prudent outlook, you may have recognized in Taurus precisely the qualities that you are looking for in a lifelong partner. These may include the loyalty, practicality, and sensuality that are the gifts of earth, making you well matched because earth is also your element; the focus and dedication of a fixed quadruplicity; the restraint, but also responsiveness, of a feminine polarity; and, as a real bonus, the easygoing indulgence and tenderness that are the bequests of Venus.

Capricorn may similarly appear to meet many of the requirements on your ideal-partner checklist if you are a Taurus. Venus, your ruling planet, may have been the Roman goddess of love, but she was associated with hard-headed materialism, too, as is your and Capricorn's earthy element, which also instills in you both a desire to establish a comfortable, financially secure home base. You may therefore feel certain that Capricorn will not only commit him- or herself wholeheartedly to you, but, being ambitious and hard-working, as well as enterprising and driven, will make a considerable contribution to your future together. You must also find your lover's dry sense of humor a delight.

Potential Pitfalls: A relationship between Taurus and Capricorn may become tense if the characteristics bestowed by pleasure-loving Venus are particularly pronounced in Taurus, or those of austere Saturn are prominent in Capricorn. If this is the case and you are a sometimes self-indulgent Taurus, you may end up accusing Capricorn of being a killjoy, which Capricorn may counter by taking you to task for your alleged frivolity. But be warned, Capricorn, that if you try to coerce Taurus into living life your way, you may activate your lover's stubborn, fixed quadruplicity.

Guiding Principle: Don't risk all that you have going for you as couple by harping on about each other's supposed character flaws, but instead try to see them as virtues.

Compatibility: ♥♥♥♥♥♥♥♥♡♡

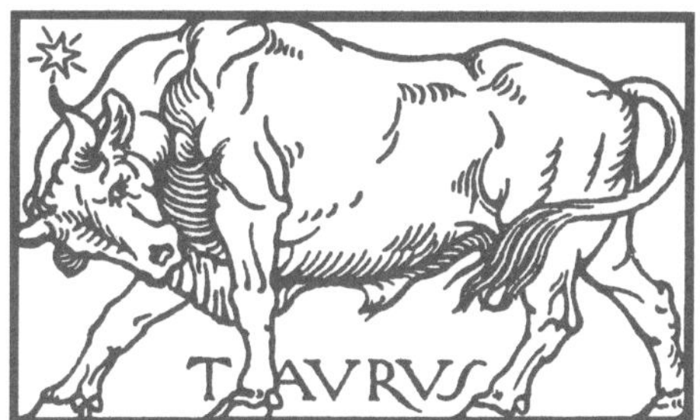

AQUARIUS

TAURUS

Taurus and Aquarius are such contrasting personalities that the early days of a romance between them are often exhilarating, with the Venus-ruled bull awakening Aquarius' sensuality and Uranus-governed Aquarius introducing Taurus to his or her anarchic, Uranian way of thinking. This honeymoon period may not last for long, however, particularly if earthy Taurus' possessiveness and inflexibility increasingly arouse airy Aquarius' desire for freedom, or if capricious Aquarius lets steady Taurus down once too often.

Plus Points: The Aquarian polarity being masculine, or uninhibited, and the Taurean being feminine, or receptive, it is likely that Aquarius was the driving force behind these two becoming an item. If you are that Aquarius, your airy element makes you curious, communicative, and something of a flirt, and your interest in Taurus may have been aroused by the Venus-influenced bull's gently teasing response. And as you got to know earthy Taurus better, you may have found his or her common sense and steadfastness both stabilizing and soothing. With your lover's encouragement, you may also have discovered the pleasure that can be derived from indulging your senses, be it by listening to music or titillating your taste buds.

If you are a Taurus, the romantic, Venusian facet of your character that makes you so susceptible to charmers was probably captivated by Aquarius when you first met. It is thanks to his or her element of air that your sweetheart is so people-oriented, playful, and fun to be with, as well as a gifted communicator of the highly original ideas that are the bequest of Uranus. Because you share a fixed quadruplicity, you no doubt also approve of the dogged determination with which Aquarius often pursues a vision, perhaps because you feel that this augurs well for a long-lasting love affair.

Potential Pitfalls: Taurus is a realistic, down-to-earth person who needs to feel rooted in a relationship, while Aquarius has a tendency to build castles in the air and requires his or her personal space. They may therefore have different expectations of each other. If you are an earthy Taurus who demands solid commitment from a partner, you may be bitterly disappointed by airy Aquarius' breeziness, coolness, and unreliability. Equally, if you are an Aquarius, you may find Taurus' love of routines, lack of imagination, and jealousy suffocating.

Guiding Principle: Taurus and Aquarius are fixed, or faithful, signs, so if you both want your relationship to endure, it will, provided that you each work hard at understanding and accommodating the other's needs.

Compatibility: ♥♥♥♥♡♡♡♡♡♡

Aquarius Birth Influences

Ruling planet: Uranus; traditionally Saturn
Element: Air
Polarity: Masculine
Quadruplicity: Fixed

If your partner is an Aquarius, he or she is probably an inveterate charmer—if not an outright flirt—whether in a business or social context. As a steady Taurus, you may find his or her flirtations hurtful at times, however harmless they may be.

Taurus Birth Influences

Ruling planet: Venus
Element: Earth
Polarity: Feminine
Quadruplicity: Fixed

TAURUS

PISCES

Taurus Birth Influences

Ruling planet: Venus
Element: Earth
Polarity: Feminine
Quadruplicity: Fixed

A Taurus and Pisces couple may well be soulmates. If you are a sensitive Pisces, you probably appreciate Taurus' romantic ways and feel supported by his loyal nature.

Pisces Birth Influences

Ruling planet: Neptune; traditionally Jupiter
Element: Water
Polarity: Feminine
Quadruplicity: Mutable

♆ ♃

Pisces longs for a soulmate, and Taurus for a steady partner, and the astrological indications suggest that each may find what they are searching for in the other. Not only are the planets that rule these signs associated with similar characteristics, but the Taurean element is supportive earth and that of Pisces is nurturing water. And although Taurus is a fixed sign and Pisces is mutable, that could work to their advantage.

Plus Points: Taurus is governed by Venus, the Roman goddess linked with graciousness and all things artistic, and Pisces by Neptune, the "higher octave" of Venus, which means that Taurus and Pisces are kindred spirits in many respects. If you are a Pisces, you may value Taurus' good manners, for example, and may also delight in viewing paintings or listening to music together. It is the influence of both Neptune and your emotional element of water that makes you such a sensitive, sometimes insecure person, which is why you may respond so ardently to Taurus' kindly, stable, and loyal temperament—the gifts of Venus and earth.

Your shared interests may have brought you and Pisces together, if you are a Taurus, but you may only now be discovering that your sweetheart has extraordinary hidden depths. You were both born under feminine, or receptive, signs, but it is the combination of Neptune and water that causes Pisces to be so profoundly compassionate, as well as loving and giving, sometimes to the point of self-sacrifice. It may also be that gentle, yet occasionally confused and vulnerable Pisces has aroused your desire to cherish your beloved by supplying him or her with constant affection and a comfortable lifestyle.

Potential Pitfalls: Earthy Taurus is a realistic and straightforward person, as well as someone who is happier dealing with tangibles than abstracts, which you may find a little disappointing if you are a more idealistic, complex, and spiritual Pisces. But then an upset Pisces may not be able to articulate the maelstrom of emotions that are swirling around within, which may perplex you if you are a Taurus. Thankfully, your fixed quadruplicity provides the staying power that will enable you to stick with Pisces no matter what, Pisces' mutability in turn helping him or her to adapt to your more inflexible traits.

Guiding Principle: Love each other for what you are, and if your differences start to threaten your relationship, enlist the spirit of compromise in talking them through and finding a solution.

Compatibility: ♥♥♥♥♥♥♥♥♡♡

GEMINI
GEMINI

It is all too easy for two Geminis to fall in love with one another, and not just because they understand each other so well. The combined influence of Mercury, the element of air, a positive polarity, and a mutable quadruplicity makes them highly curious, uninhibited, and communicative people who generally find in each other the intellectual stimulation that they seek. Neither can bear to be tied down either, and they consequently tend to make few demands of one another. But will this be the sort of relationship in which they drift in and out of each other's lives rather than sticking together over the long term?

Gemini Birth Influences
Ruling planet: Mercury
Element: Air
Polarity: Masculine
Quadruplicity: Mutable

Plus Points: Gemini is a zodiacal sign that is predominantly associated with the intellect, so if you and your partner were both born under this constellation, you may have instantly experienced a meeting of minds when you first encountered one another, and may have spent your first exhilarating hours together animatedly exchanging opinions or swapping stories of everything that you have seen and done on your travels. Even now, there's probably no shortage of things to talk about, and in your fellow Gemini you may have found your ideal traveling companion through the journey of life. You no doubt both adore going to parties, too, and because neither of you are possessive types, you probably don't mind if your beloved becomes engrossed in conversation with an interesting someone—indeed, you know that you'll reap the benefits later, when Gemini regales you with all that was said.

A romance between two Geminis may ebb and flow like the tide. Their airy nature may gently pull them apart, but curiosity will probably draw them together again.

Potential Pitfalls: Roman mythology tells us that Mercury, the god for whom Gemini's ruling planet was named, was incorrigibly inquisitive, and it may be that after an intense initial probing of your lover's personality, you think that you have discovered all that there is to know about him or her. Although it is indeed likely that each of you will flit off to explore other people's psyches—and those born under mutable signs thrive on change—you will no doubt find your way back to each other again, partly because you know that you are unlikely to be greeted with sulks and recriminations, and partly because you have so much fun together. Your future as a couple promises to be chaotic and unconventional, but then life will always be interesting, and that is usually enough for Gemini.

Guiding Principle: Ensure that you regularly spend time together—even if it's only on vacation—otherwise, being active, enquiring, and independent Geminis, your paths may rarely cross and you may find yourselves friends rather than lovers.

Compatibility: ♥♥♥♥♥♥♡♡♡♡

Gemini Birth Influences
Ruling planet: Mercury
Element: Air
Polarity: Masculine
Quadruplicity: Mutable

GEMINI
CANCER

Gemini Birth Influences
Ruling planet: Mercury
Element: Air
Polarity: Masculine
Quadruplicity: Mutable

Fun-loving, flighty Gemini can upset sensitive Cancer without even realizing it. Be careful, Gemini! And Cancer, try to lighten up sometimes.

Cancer Birth Influences
Ruling planet: The Moon
Element: Water
Polarity: Feminine
Quadruplicity: Cardinal

At first sight, the astrological prognosis for an enduring romance between Gemini and Cancer does not look particularly promising. Gemini's birth influences include the objective Mercury and the rather superficial element of air, which contrast with Cancer's profoundly emotional ruling planet, the Moon, and deeply sensitive element of water. Yet being a feminine, cardinal sign, the crab responds positively to the confidence of Gemini's masculine polarity, and can furthermore be quite assertive, while mutable Gemini is adaptable. The relationship could consequently work if there is enough give and take on both sides.

Plus Points: Your watery element can make you feel somewhat insecure if you are a Cancer, and one of the things that you must appreciate about persuasive Gemini is his or her talent for reassuring you. Gemini's winning way with words is the gift of Mercury, while his or her masculine polarity's contribution is boldness, and that of air is curiosity. Being a highly responsive person, you probably cannot resist this enlivening combination, and may often find yourself being carried along on a wave of Geminian enthusiasm into situations that you never dreamed of enjoying.

If you are a Gemini, you in turn must relish bringing a breath of fresh air into Cancer's life in return for all of the nurturing that the caring crab lavishes upon you. His or her lunar ruler, element of water, and feminine polarity cause Cancer to focus on your emotional well-being, and you must find your sweetheart's intuition and empathy startlingly touching.

Potential Pitfalls: Gemini may broaden your horizons if you are a Cancer, but you are not naturally experimental, and the experience may therefore sometimes prove unnerving. Mutable Gemini can also be moody, which may upset you greatly, as may his or her airy flirtiness and lack of understanding when you burst into tears. If you are an analytical, articulate Gemini, you may simply not be able to comprehend why Cancer is so distressed, not least because the element of water makes it difficult for the crab to express his or her feelings. And because you feel uncomfortable in emotionally charged atmospheres, it may not be long before you take off in search of freedom and fun, thereby wounding Cancer even more.

Guiding Principle: When your relationship hits a rocky patch, try to accept, and make allowances for, each other's viewpoint. After all, it was no doubt the very differences in your personalities that attracted you to one another in the first place.

Compatibility:   

LEO
GEMINI

Their energy, spontaneity, and playfulness create an exhilarating bond between Gemini and Leo, and because both are masculine, or uninhibited, signs, their relationship is likely to be full of excitement. Yet although Gemini's easygoing personality complements Leo's sunny nature, the twins' emotional coolness may sometimes frustrate the lion, Gemini in turn finding Leo's domineering tendencies a turn-off at times.

Plus Points: Both Gemini and Leo crave an invigorating partner to be proud of, and each generally fulfills these criteria. If you are a fiery Leo who is stimulated by others, you must find airy Gemini's liveliness and cheerful sense of humor highly infectious. You may also marvel at your persuasive, Mercury-governed lover's ability to talk almost anyone around to his or her point of view, not least you, the zodiacal lion being particularly susceptible to Gemini's fluent flattery.

If you are a mutable Gemini who is quickly bored and relishes change, you may respond enthusiastically to Leo's creativity and impulsiveness—both enlivening gifts of the element of fire—as well as to the Sun-ruled lion's love of experimentation, which matches your own curiosity. You were both born under gregarious signs, and it no doubt warms your heart to see how effortlessly charismatic Leo attracts a crowd of admirers when you are with others. In short, life together is rarely dull.

Potential Pitfalls: Gemini and Leo share a masculine polarity, which means that both are initiators rather than followers. When they are of the same mind, theirs is typically a harmonious partnership of equals, but problems may arise if they rub each other up the wrong way. Having the Sun as a planetary ruler and a fixed quadruplicity makes Leo a commanding personality who expects unconditional love and unwavering commitment, which may irk you if you are a Gemini who needs to retain a certain amount of freedom within a relationship. Another potential pitfall is logical Gemini's cool objectivity. The fiery lion takes perceived criticism badly, and may react explosively to analytical Gemini's tendency to point out where Leo may have made a mistake. If you are a Leo, you may also feel wounded by Gemini's restlessness and occasional moodiness, which may lead you to question whether Gemini feels as strongly about you as you do about him or her.

Guiding Principle: Each of you expresses your love for the other in contrasting ways, so try to be tolerant of your differences and otherwise concentrate on enjoying life together.

Compatibility: ♥♥♥♥♥♥♥♡♡♡

Leo Birth Influences

Ruling planet: The Sun
Element: Fire
Polarity: Masculine
Quadruplicity: Fixed

Leo and Gemini love to travel and experiment with new experiences, so this couple is likely to make the most of vacation time.

Gemini Birth Influences

Ruling planet: Mercury
Element: Air
Polarity: Masculine
Quadruplicity: Mutable

GEMINI / VIRGO

Gemini Birth Influences

Ruling planet: Mercury
Element: Air
Polarity: Masculine
Quadruplicity: Mutable

An airy Gemini and earthy Virgo may enjoy spending a few hours together outdoors, and relish the feeling of freedom that it brings, but if outgoing Gemini pulls too hard, the connection could break.

Virgo Birth Influences

Ruling planet: Mercury
Element: Earth
Polarity: Feminine
Quadruplicity: Mutable

Gemini and Virgo share the same mercurial ruling planet and mutable quadruplicity, which means that they have much in common, such as their communicativeness and relish of variety. Difficulties may arise when their respective elements and polarities conflict, however, with airy Gemini's eccentricities provoking cautious Virgo's criticism, and earthy Virgo's organizational instincts dampening freedom-loving Gemini's spirit.

Plus Points: If you and your sweetheart are a Gemini and a Virgo, the qualities that you must treasure in one another are probably those associated with Mercury, your mutual planetary ruler that was named for the fleet-footed, quick-thinking Roman messenger god. These may include your enjoyment of travel, inquisitive minds, and ability to express your thoughts articulately and interestingly, with the result that conversation rarely dries up when you are together. Both Gemini and Virgo are mutable signs, too, so you may also be able to add flexibility and an aversion to arguments to the list of your lover's good points. Their airy element makes lively, congenial Geminians fun to be around, and you may therefore find your Gemini lover invigorating company if you are a sometimes serious Virgo. And if you are a Gemini whose head is often in the clouds, you no doubt in turn appreciate earthy Virgo's practical streak and willingness to take care of such prosaic details as ensuring that your travel documents are all in place before setting off on vacation.

Potential Pitfalls: Although their different elements and polarities can often benefit a relationship between Gemini and Virgo, they can sometimes cause friction, too. Gemini's polarity is masculine, or extroverted, and Virgo's is feminine, or introverted, which means that Gemini's tendency to act uninhibitedly may worry you if you are a sensible Virgo, while Virgo may be too introspective for your liking if you are a breezy Gemini. Flexible you may both be, but like a rubber band that is stretched to its limit, if that flexibility is tested too far, your relationship may reach breaking point. Virgo, do your best to rein in your tendency to criticize and nag Gemini, and as for you, Gemini, you'd do well to follow Virgo's down-to-earth advice once in a while.

Guiding Principle: A love affair is like an ongoing conversation, so keep your relationship living and loving by talking to one another, but don't forget to listen with respect and, if necessary, to enlist your innate adaptability.

Compatibility: ♥♥♥♥♥♡♡♡♡♡

LIBRA
GEMINI

The message from the stars is that a romance between Gemini and Libra promises to be relaxed and happy. Both being air signs, each can admittedly be flighty, but this tendency is typically reined in by the fun that they have together and their ability to accept each other's fickle ways. That said, cardinal Libra's insistence on setting mutual goals may occasionally trigger a moody reaction from mutable Gemini.

Plus Points: Their shared masculine polarity and element of air give Gemini and Libra many common characteristics, not least an outgoing and sociable nature. In addition, their respective ruling planets reinforce many of the traits associated with their airy element. The influence of Mercury makes Gemini doubly quick-witted and loquacious, so if you are a Libra, you may be particularly susceptible to your silver-tongued sweetheart's scintillatingly seductive way with words. Venus similarly contributes an extra dose of playfulness and indulgence to Libra's personality, which is why, if you are a Gemini, you may find your Libran lover so delightful. Add Gemini's mutable and Libra's cardinal quadruplicity to the mix, and you have a pair that never seems to stand still and communicates constantly.

Potential Pitfalls: Gemini and Libra may find each other exhilarating company, but because neither are particularly grounded or tenacious people, there is a risk that if their relationship switches from lively to volatile, both will take off in opposite directions. If you are a cardinal Libra, there may come a stage when you try to push Gemini into making a binding commitment to your relationship, which your beloved may see as an attempt to curtail his or her freedom. And when mutable Geminians feel that they are being controlled or restricted, they often either become cranky and temperamental or simply disappear altogether. Equally, although Libra is the sign of the balance, disappointment in love can cause the scales to tip heavily in one direction, so that if you are a Gemini, you may then see normally peaceable Libra's assertive side come to the fore. Both of you have tolerant signs, however, and if you are truly in love and there is enough give and take on both sides, you should be able to smooth over such a blip in your relationship before it becomes an unbridgeable rift.

Guiding Principle: Keep the channels of communication open, be prepared to compromise when you differ, and otherwise savor the sparkle that you bring to one another's lives.

Compatibility: ♥♥♥♥♥♥♥♡♡♡

Libra Birth Influences

Ruling planet: Venus
Element: Air
Polarity: Masculine
Quadruplicity: Cardinal

If you are a Libra, you may find yourself seduced by Gemini's sweet talk. Allow yourself a momentary distraction from your goals and prepare to be dazzled!

Gemini Birth Influences

Ruling planet: Mercury
Element: Air
Polarity: Masculine
Quadruplicity: Mutable

GEMINI
SCORPIO

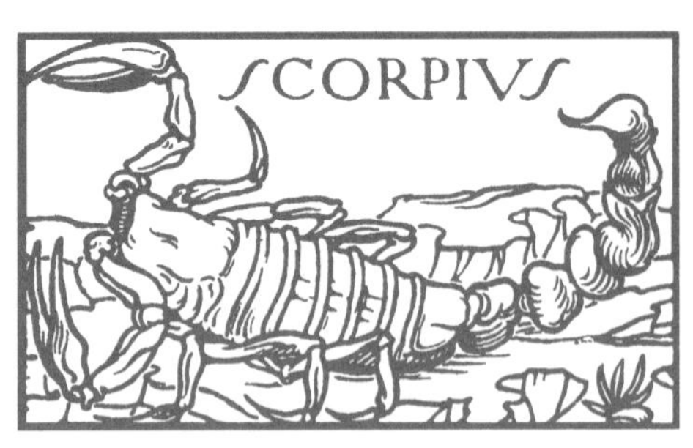

Gemini Birth Influences

Ruling planet: Mercury
Element: Air
Polarity: Masculine
Quadruplicity: Mutable

When your Scorpio lover retreats within herself, your inquisitiveness may lead you to her side, Gemini, where you will probably try to charm her into opening up. But be warned that she may not appreciate this intrusion!

Scorpio Birth Influences

Ruling planet: Pluto; traditionally Mars
Element: Water
Polarity: Feminine
Quadruplicity: Fixed

Opposites are said to attract, which is why Gemini and Scorpio are often drawn to one another so powerfully, with curious, airy Gemini longing to explore secretive, watery Scorpio's hidden depths, and serious Scorpio relaxing and opening up in the company of cheerful, chatty Gemini. But will Scorpio come to regard Gemini as flighty and fickle, or will Gemini feel stifled by Scorpio's possessiveness?

Plus Points: Feminine-polarity scorpions are deeply receptive to others' influence, which is one of the reasons why live-wire, masculine-polarity Gemini may have made such an impact on you when you first met if you are a Scorpio. Gemini's airy element makes your beloved an enlivening, light-hearted charmer, with his or her mercurial ruling planet and mutable quadruplicity reinforcing the Geminian talent for wooing with words. You are probably powerless to resist! Gemini is also highly adaptable, which you must appreciate, having been born under a fixed sign yourself. Inquisitiveness, and particularly the desire to understand the workings of people's minds, is another quality associated with air, while Pluto, Scorpio's ruling planet, compels scorpions to protect their vulnerable emotional core with a shield of secrecy. If you are a Gemini, you may therefore have been seized by the compulsion to penetrate the scorpion's reserve and get to know the person within, and part of your lover's attraction for you may be that you still find him or her an intriguing enigma. You may also be startled and touched by Scorpio's powers of intuition, caring nature, and compassion, all gifts of the element of water.

Potential Pitfalls: Gemini and Scorpio may have to face, and pass, many tests if their romance is to endure. Having been born under a mutable air sign, Gemini can be restless and detached, while fixed, watery Scorpio can be clinging and needy. If you are a Scorpio, Gemini's repeated tendency to flit from your side to talk to a diverting someone may arouse your jealousy, and you may be tormented by fears that your sweetheart is, or will be, unfaithful. Scorpio is more emotional than rational Gemini, but has difficulty articulating his or her feelings, which is why, if you are a Gemini, you may be baffled by what you perceive as being your lover's overreaction to a few harmless conversations. In short, with Scorpio demanding steadfastness, and Gemini freedom, the result may be a rocky relationship.

Guiding Principle: When you don't see eye-to-eye, try to communicate honestly and dispassionately, but, above all, lovingly with one another.

Compatibility: ♥♥♥♥♡♡♡♡♡♡

SAGITTARIUS
GEMINI

When things are good between Gemini and Sagittarius sweethearts, they are very, very good, but when they are bad, they can be explosive. Both signs are masculine and mutable, which indicates that their relationship will center on activities that both enjoy. These activities may include travel and intellectual pursuits, as Mercury's bequest to Gemini is a desire to explore the physical world, and Jupiter's to Sagittarius, the urge to investigate the world of the mind. But will airy Gemini's emotional detachment ignite fiery Sagittarius' anger, or will independent Gemini be prepared to give Sagittarius the attention that the archer craves?

Plus Points: Gemini and Sagittarius' shared birth influences mean that they are generally on the same wavelength: neither are shy or retiring, both relish diversity, and both are sociable, for example. If you are a Sagittarius, you may therefore feel that you have found your soulmate in Gemini, who is probably as confident—and as restless—as you, and whose airy liveliness and ingenious ideas may kindle your fiery enthusiasm. Jupiter's influence may have given you a special affinity with spiritual or philosophical matters, and because Gemini is ruled by Mercury, the planet associated with learning and communication, you must also enjoy the thought-provoking discussions that you have with your objective lover.

If you are a Gemini, there are no doubt similarly many qualities that you cherish in Sagittarius, such as his or her jovial optimism and wide-ranging vision, and the spontaneity, originality, and generosity that the element of fire bestows on Sagittarians. And if, like most Geminis, wanderlust is in your blood, you must appreciate adventurous Sagittarius' unflagging willingness to embark on a new journey with you.

Potential Pitfalls: Both Gemini and Sagittarius require space in which to pursue their individual interests, which isn't generally a problem because each understands and respects the other's needs. That said, airy Gemini can sometimes seem cool and aloof when preoccupied, which may rankle with you if you are a fiery Sagittarius who hates to feel ignored. And if you are a Gemini who has been at the receiving end of a hot-headed outburst, you may fail to understand the logic of the accusations hurled at you, and may then make matters worse by unleashing that acerbic tongue of yours. Thankfully, Sagittarius' fury is usually short-lived, and neither of you enjoys conflict or bears grudges.

Guiding Principle: You are both adaptable and forgiving people, so draw on these gifts and focus on finding common ground should discord threaten your romance.

Compatibility: ♥♥♥♥♥♥♥♡♡♡

Sagittarius Birth Influences

Ruling planet: Jupiter
Element: Fire
Polarity: Masculine
Quadruplicity: Mutable

If you are a Sagittarius, your Gemini lover's apparent coldness may light the fuse of your fiery temper at times. If you explode, you will probably soon be forgiven, but try to avoid doing so or you may receive a biting rebuke yourself.

Gemini Birth Influences

Ruling planet: Mercury
Element: Air
Polarity: Masculine
Quadruplicity: Mutable

GEMINI
CAPRICORN

Gemini Birth Influences

Ruling planet: Mercury
Element: Air
Polarity: Masculine
Quadruplicity: Mutable

It is said that love will always find a way to make a relationship work, but while this may hold true for Gemini and Capricorn, that way will almost certainly be strewn with testing hurdles. Capricorn is self-controlled, sober, constant, and ambitious, while Gemini is uninhibited, light-hearted, flighty, and lives for the moment. But these lovers can be good for one another, with Capricorn bringing stability to Gemini's life and Gemini infusing Capricorn's world with fun and laughter. As long as each feels real love for the other, the rewards of staying together promise to be more than worth the effort.

Gemini and Capricorn have very different temperaments, but as long as there is real love between them, and they both are willing to make an effort, a happy relationship is possible.

Plus Points: Life before Gemini may have seemed somewhat one-dimensional if you are a Capricorn to whom the stars have bequeathed a hefty dose of ambition to forge an upward career path. The influence of Saturn makes you serious and focused on your goal, that of earth makes you steadfast, and that of your cardinal quadruplicity, forceful and driven. But your feminine polarity also causes you to be highly receptive to the personalities of those with whom you come into contact, and your reserve may have been melted by masculine-sign Gemini, whose lack of inhibition, mercurial intelligence, airy congeniality, and flexibility you may find fascinating, endearing, and, above all, enlivening.

If you are a Gemini, the contribution to your makeup of both Mercury and your element of air is a tendency to be ruled by your head rather than your heart, which is why Capricorn may appear to be the one for you. Indeed, you no doubt know that your sweetheart has an iron will, is determined to make a success of him- or herself, and is unquestionably committed to your relationship, and logic may tell you that this person is therefore an ideal partner. It must also be a relief to have an earthy, reliable sweetheart who takes care of the practicalities that you find so tedious.

Potential Pitfalls: Saturn is associated with sobriety, steadiness, and dedication, which is why Gemini's flirtiness, moodiness, and inconstancy may try your patience to its limits if you are a Capricorn. But then if you are a freedom-loving, fun-seeking Gemini, Capricorn's possessiveness and dark frowns of disapproval may ultimately make you feel that your individuality will be stifled if you remain with such a killjoy.

Guiding Principle: Give and take, don't be too quick to condemn what you perceive as being your partner's faults, and when the going gets tough, try not to give up on one another.

Compatibility: ♥♥♥♡♡♡♡♡♡♡

Capricorn Birth Influences

Ruling planet: Saturn
Element: Earth
Polarity: Feminine
Quadruplicity: Cardinal

AQUARIUS
GEMINI

Sharing as they do a masculine, outgoing polarity and airy element, a romance between Gemini and Aquarius is unlikely to be static or clingy. Add intelligent, travel-loving Mercury and experimental, unpredictable Uranus—Mercury's "higher octave"—to the mix, and you have a relationship that many people would consider highly unconventional. Despite their mutual need for independence, the indications are that these two will stay together, not least because mutable Gemini is adaptable and fixed-sign Aquarius is loyal.

Plus Points: Gemini and Aquarius are kindred spirits in many respects. Both having been born under masculine air signs, they are typically extroverted, easygoing, and playful people whose heads rule their hearts and who instinctively like one another. The additional influence of Mercury makes Gemini doubly perceptive and communicative, and if you are an Aquarius, one of the reasons why you may relish spending time with your lover is the stimulating discussions that he or she sets in motion. Although you may find the moodiness that is the bequest of a mutable quadruplicity irritating at times, this is probably more than made up for by Gemini's willingness to give you the space within your relationship that is as vital to you as the air that you breathe.

If you are an airy Gemini, you may thank your lucky stars that in Aquarius you have a sweetheart who encourages you to develop and indulge your own interests rather than trying to curtail your independence. Even more appealing may be the intriguing way in which the Aquarian mind operates: like you, your lover is no doubt curious and clever, and, because Aquarius is ruled by Uranus, he or she may furthermore have a tendency to come up with inventive, radical, or even anarchic ideas that surprise and delight you. The conversation must rarely falter when you are together, and must give you much to think about.

Potential Pitfalls: Gemini is a mutable sign, while Aquarius is fixed, which means that there will be times when Gemini is itching for a change, perhaps of scenery, or maybe of décor or image, but Aquarius, who can be remarkably stubborn, prefers to stay put or keep things as they are. Gemini is flexible, however, and the key to finding a compromise lies in talking.

Guiding Principle: Keep your relationship fresh by continuing to enjoy your individual pursuits, but make sure that you regularly communicate with one another lest you start to drift apart.

Compatibility: ♥♥♥♥♥♥♥♥♡♡

Aquarius Birth Influences

Ruling planet: Uranus; traditionally Saturn
Element: Air
Polarity: Masculine
Quadruplicity: Fixed

As Gemini and Aquarius both enjoy having fun, their relationship should be full of joy and laughter.

Gemini Birth Influences

Ruling planet: Mercury
Element: Air
Polarity: Masculine
Quadruplicity: Mutable

GEMINI

PISCES

Gemini Birth Influences
Ruling planet: Mercury
Element: Air
Polarity: Masculine
Quadruplicity: Mutable

Pisces sometimes seems to live in a world of her own, and her curious Gemini lover may have a fascinating time trying to understand her.

Pisces Birth Influences
Ruling planet: Neptune; traditionally Jupiter
Element: Water
Polarity: Feminine
Quadruplicity: Mutable

While Gemini wants a lover who is a playmate, Pisces yearns for a sweetheart who is a soulmate, and while Gemini needs to retain independence of thought and action within a relationship, Pisces longs for a seamless union of body, mind, and spirit. The prognosis therefore does not look good for an enduring romance between these two, but that is not to say that they are totally incompatible. Indeed, airy, masculine-polarity Gemini has an enlivening, confidence-boosting influence on Pisces, and watery, feminine-polarity Pisces encourages Gemini to be more reflective.

Plus Points: If you are a Gemini, your planetary governor, Mercury, and airy element make you curious about the working of people's minds, which is why you may find your Pisces lover so intriguing. It is subtle Neptune that infuses the Piscean personality with dreaminess, and the enigmatic element of water that gives Pisceans the appearance of inhabiting a world of their own. When compounded by an introspective polarity, Pisces may exude an aura of beguiling mystery that must make you itch to explore your sweetheart's hidden depths. The fast pace set by your ruling planet may also mean that you operate on nervous energy for much of the time, which is why you may welcome the opportunity to slow down, relax, and really think in the company of soothing Pisces.

There must be many qualities that you adore in Gemini if you are a Pisces. Both Neptune and water can make you feel confused and unable to express your feelings at times, and you consequently probably admire mercurial Gemini's clarity of thought and airy articulacy, and may be flattered by this silver-tongued charmer's attention. Having an airy element, kindly Gemini no doubt rarely puts you under pressure, which you must appreciate, along with the positive, "can-do" attitude that masculine-polarity Gemini projects.

Potential Pitfalls: Although Gemini and Pisces share a mutable quadruplicity, this may manifest itself in them in different ways. Airy Gemini is often restless unless surrounded by a variety of people, and you may be wounded by his or her tendency to flit from your side with complete disregard for your feelings if you are a sensitive Pisces. And if you are a more dispassionate Gemini, you may eventually find emotional Pisces' moodiness tiresome, especially if you are starting to feel smothered by the love that he or she lavishes on you.

Guiding Principle: Don't try to change your lover into a mirror image of yourself and respect one another's personal space.

Compatibility: ♥♥♥♥♡♡♡♡♡♡

CANCER
CANCER

When these Cancerian sweethearts were born, among Mother Moon's gifts to each were supersensitivity and intuition. Their watery element reinforces these traits, and also floods them with empathy and profound emotions, and their feminine polarity makes them receptive and thoughtful. They are consequently typically deeply loving and caring people who instinctively support one another and usually dream the same dreams. Yet their shared cardinal quadruplicity gives them ambition, drive, and surprising forcefulness, given that they are otherwise such gentle personalities, and disagreements may arise should one of these lover's goals differ from the other's.

Cancer Birth Influences

Ruling planet: The Moon
Element: Water
Polarity: Feminine
Quadruplicity: Cardinal

Plus Points: What you may each treasure in the other, if you and your beloved are both zodiacal crabs, is how you are instinctively attuned to one another's moods. The influence of your ruling planet, the Moon, and your element of water gives you a double dose of emotional insight and fellow feeling, so that when one of you is upset, the other may sense this distress without a word having been spoken. Because your joint polarity is feminine, you must both be good listeners and must give serious thought to how best to console or reassure your loved one. But one of the problems of having a watery element may be that you are so acutely affected by other people's emotions that you in turn feel their pain, so that you may not be able to think clearly enough to do anything other than envelop your unhappy lover in a warm, empathetic hug. That is often more than enough to soothe and comfort, however.

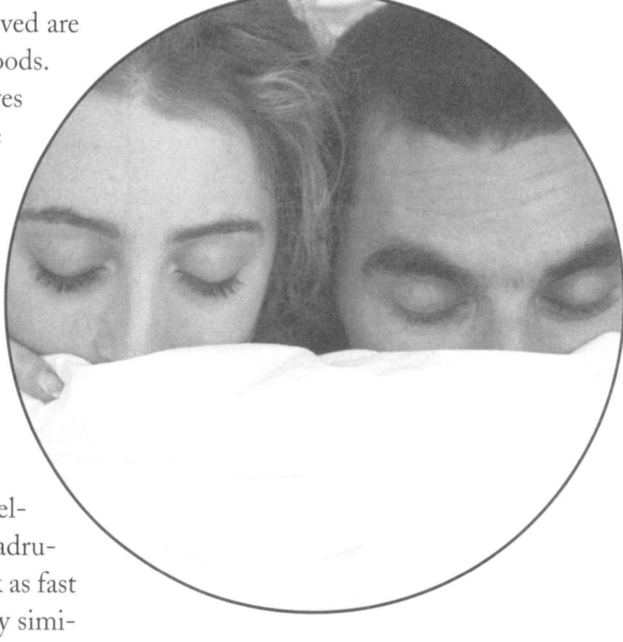

Two Cancer lovers should understand each other implicitly and find comfort in their relationship.

Potential Pitfalls: Most of Cancer's birth influences are associated with feeling, nurturing, and giving, the exception being your go-getting, cardinal quadruplicity, which may fill you with the urge to set yourself targets and then work as fast and determinedly as you can to achieve them. Your aims in life are probably similar, and may center on creating a comfortable home and filling it with children or pets to love and cherish, in which case you will both pour your energy into making your vision come true. But should one of you be inspired by a dream that doesn't especially enthuse the other—maybe your partner wants to train as a counselor and you fear that this work would have a detrimental effect on his or her emotional health—unusually pithy words may result.

Cancer Birth Influences

Ruling planet: The Moon
Element: Water
Polarity: Feminine
Quadruplicity: Cardinal

Guiding Principle: Be there for one another, but try to ensure that you both retain your individuality.

Compatibility: ♥♥♥♥♥♥♥♡♡♡

CANCER
LEO

Cancer Birth Influences

Ruling planet: The Moon
Element: Water
Polarity: Feminine
Quadruplicity: Cardinal

☾ ≈

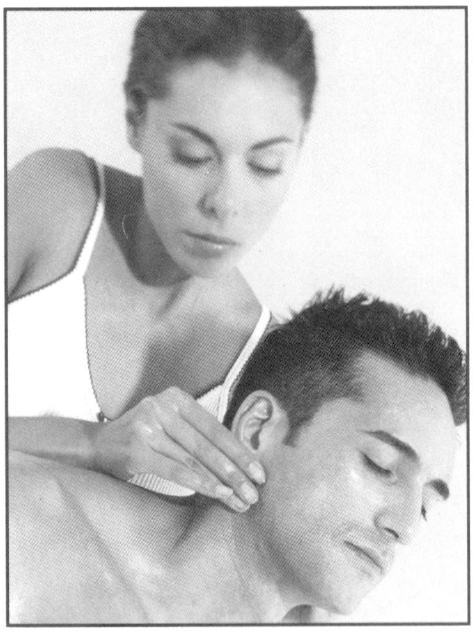

A caring Cancer lover will provide Leo with the attention and affection that he or she thrives on.

Leo Birth Influences

Ruling planet: The Sun
Element: Fire
Polarity: Masculine
Quadruplicity: Fixed

Many cultures have considered the Sun, Leo's ruling planet, to be a god burning with vitality, and the Moon, Cancer's planetary governor, a serene, life-giving goddess. These gender distinctions are reinforced by the lion's masculine polarity and fiery, outgoing element, and the crab's feminine polarity and introspective element of water. Whatever their actual sex, Leos are therefore said to possess conventionally male characteristics, and Cancers traditionally female traits, so that the lion is authoritative, extroverted, and impulsive, while Cancer is sensitive, introverted, and cautious. These personalities will either click—and because fixed-sign Leo is loyal, and cardinal Cancer, determined, and should then stay together—or will soon realize that they are incompatible.

Plus Points: Being constantly driven by your search for excitement can be a tiring business if you are a Leo, and you may therefore love being in Cancer's soothing, sympathetic company. Those born under the sign of the crab are nurturing and empathetic, and it must be a relief to be able to unburden yourself to such a caring and compassionate confidant. Another Cancerian quality that you may find especially endearing is your sweetheart's uncanny ability to anticipate your every need, for which you may have the intuitive Moon and element of water to thank.

If you are a Cancer, your constantly shifting, watery element may often make you feel insecure and in need of love and reassurance, and also highly receptive to others' influence, which is why you may delight in your leonine lover. Having the Sun as a planetary ruler imbues Leo with confidence and warmth, qualities reinforced by the lion's uninhibited polarity and fervor-bestowing element. Because Leo's fixed quadruplicity also makes him or her a committed type, it may seem as though you have found your perfect partner, someone who will stick with you, love and protect you, and will generally brighten your life.

Potential Pitfalls: If you are a spontaneous, stimulation-seeking Leo, there is a danger that you will ultimately find quiet, self-contained Cancer uninspiring and too emotionally needy, while if you are a Cancer, you may be wounded by Leo's heedless tendency to forget that you exist when enthused by his or her latest passion. A word of advice: try not to make unrealistic demands of one another.

Guiding Principle: Dissimilar you may be, but your differences can complement one another beautifully, so try to regard them positively should your relationship hit a rocky patch.

Compatibility: ♥♥♥♥♥♥♥♡♡♡

VIRGO
CANCER

Because they share a feminine, or passive, polarity, Cancer and Virgo are usually rather introverted people, which is not to say that they inhabit worlds of their own and don't interact with one another, because they certainly do. Indeed, communicative, Mercury-ruled Virgo is adept at drawing reserved Cancer out of his or her shell, while the Moon-governed, nurturing crab enjoys making a fuss of Virgo. Although logical Virgo may be mystified by Cancer's touchiness, and mutable Virgo's restlessness can make Cancer jumpy, they each love the overall sense of security that the other gives them.

Plus Points: If you are a typical Virgo, the combination of your inward-looking polarity, busy, mercurial mind, and mutable quadruplicity has probably made you a born worrier, and you must therefore appreciate having an empathetic listener in the crab, whose sweet Cancerian compassion must boost your spirits. And if you are thinking of settling down with your sweetheart, it may already be clear that Cancer would make a caring and supportive partner or parent, so that together you could create a haven of a home.

There may be a number of qualities that you cherish in Virgo if you are a zodiacal crab, perhaps because they counter the influence of your unstable element of water. You may sometimes find yourself so confused by conflicting emotions that you can't reach a decision, for example, when you may appreciate Virgo's rational or practical approach to problem-solving. Your earthy lover's settled habits and reliability may make you feel secure, too, and you may have come to regard Virgo as being your anchor in life. Yet there must also be times when you are grateful that he or she is so adaptable.

Potential Pitfalls: As a child of Mercury, you are no doubt a talkative type if you are a Virgo, and may therefore be frustrated by Cancer's occasional moody reticence. At times like these, Cancer needs to be left alone, but because you are curious, you may try to needle the crab into telling you what he or she is thinking about, whereupon you may be startled by an uncharacteristically snappy response. But then objective Virgo can be coolly critical, which may wound you if you are a Cancer, and you may also dislike feeling on edge whenever the nervous energy of your lover's changeable nature comes to the fore.

Guiding Principle: Draw strength from one another, but be sure to respect each other's feelings.

Compatibility: ♥♥♥♥♥♥♥♡♡♡

Virgo Birth Influences

Ruling planet: Mercury
Element: Earth
Polarity: Feminine
Quadruplicity: Mutable

A Cancer–Virgo couple can make supportive and committed parents.

Cancer Birth Influences

Ruling planet: The Moon
Element: Water
Polarity: Feminine
Quadruplicity: Cardinal

CANCER
LIBRA

Cancer Birth Influences

Ruling planet: The Moon
Element: Water
Polarity: Feminine
Quadruplicity: Cardinal

Even though Libra basks in the attention of a tender lover, and Cancer is typically deeply caring, this couple should give each other some space in case Libra feels suffocated.

Libra Birth Influences

Ruling planet: Venus
Element: Air
Polarity: Masculine
Quadruplicity: Cardinal

The sympathetic interaction between their planets bodes well for a romance between Cancer and Libra, for each, in its own way, is indulgent and giving. Their shared cardinal quadruplicity also makes this couple all-or-nothing types, so that they will usually strive to ensure that their liaison is happy and long-lasting. But because watery Cancerian introverts can be emotionally needy, and airy Libran extroverts need to remain free agents to some extent, Libra may occasionally resist being clung to by Cancer, while Cancer may sometimes feel neglected by Libra.

Plus Points: Venus, your ruling planet, was named for the Roman goddess of love and beauty, which is why you may be a romantic who dreams of enjoying the adoring attentions of a tender lover if you are a Libra. And it may seem as though your dream has come true if your significant other is a crab, and someone who unconsciously anticipates your every need, has your welfare at heart, and is happy to defer to your desires. If so, be grateful to the Moon, which bathes Cancer in intuition, his or her watery element, which infuses your lover with sensitivity and understanding, and the crab's feminine polarity, which makes your sweetheart so receptive.

You probably dread the pain of being in emotional turmoil if you are a Cancer, which is why you may be so glad that your lover was born under the easygoing sign of the scales. If he or she is a typical Libra, the element of air and a masculine polarity cause your beloved to be cheerful and positive, while the peace-loving influence of Venus may mean that he or she abhors unpleasantness and will always try to smooth troubled Cancerian waters. As well as helping to keep your mood tranquil and even, airy, playful Libra must fill your life with fun and laughter.

Potential Pitfalls: When self-contained Cancerians fall in love, they do so wholeheartedly, in the expectation that their powerful feelings will be reciprocated and that they will remain the focus of their partner's life. There may consequently be times when you feel suffocated by Cancer's craving for closeness if you are lively, outgoing Libra, and may flit off for a breath of fresh air, thereby prompting you to fear that Libra has withdrawn his or her love, if you are a Cancer, and causing you to become crabby and despondent.

Guiding Principle: Treat one another considerately and, above all, keep the channels of communication open.

Compatibility: 

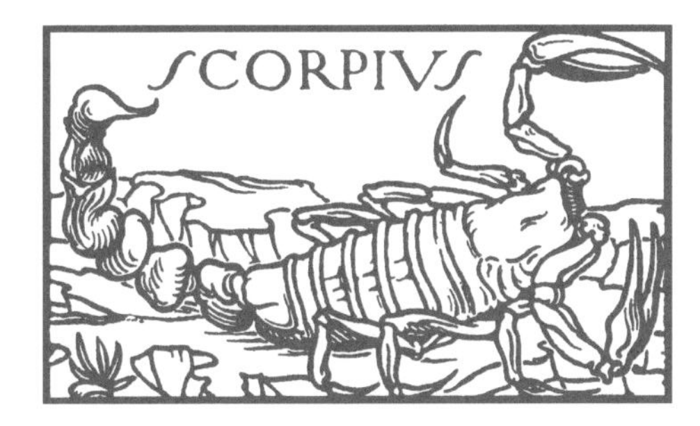

SCORPIO

CANCER

Sharing as they do a feminine, introverted polarity and an emotional element in water, Cancer and Scorpio are both self-contained people who nevertheless yearn for the support and security of being in a loving relationship. Their courtship may progress at a snail's pace as they take time to gain one another's trust, but when each is certain of the other's affection, the floodgates may then burst open, releasing an outpouring of love. Although Moon-ruled Cancer is a little more sensitive than Pluto-governed Scorpio, and may become depressed if the scorpion is overly secretive, while possessive Scorpio's jealousy may be aroused if the impressionable crab develops an innocent liking for an attractive someone, these two have the potential to remain life-long lovers.

Plus Points: If you are a Cancer, your planetary ruler, the susceptible Moon, makes you especially receptive to others' influence, which is why you may be so powerfully drawn to Scorpio's smoldering intensity. The Moon also redoubles your watery intuitiveness, so that although Plutonian Scorpio may be a silent, mysterious type, you probably sense that your lover is as empathetic and caring as you, and will not only look after you, but, having a fixed polarity, will stick by you through thick and thin.

You may be thanking your lucky stars that your beloved is a crab if you are a scorpion, perhaps because you instinctively understand that he or she would never trifle with your emotions, and, having a cardinal quadruplicity, is set on making you happy. Having a watery element may furthermore cause you to need to spend time alone occasionally, while Pluto gives you a tendency to internalize your feelings, traits with which Cancer may sympathize. All in all, in Cancer, you may believe that you have found someone with whom you can connect without the need for words, a true soulmate.

Potential Pitfalls: Compassionate Cancer may respect your need for privacy if you are a Scorpio, but be warned that if your reticence is prolonged or frequent, the crab may feel shut out, and may worry that your love for him or her has waned. And Cancer, remember that Scorpio is not immune from the insecurity inherent in your common watery element either, and that the scorpion may therefore become darkly suspicious if you pay too much attention to someone whom your sweetheart considers to be a rival for your affection.

Guiding Principle: Don't let unfounded fears cast a shadow over your romance.

Compatibility: ♥♥♥♥♥♥♥♥♥♡

Scorpio Birth Influences

Ruling planet: Pluto; traditionally Mars
Element: Water
Polarity: Feminine
Quadruplicity: Fixed

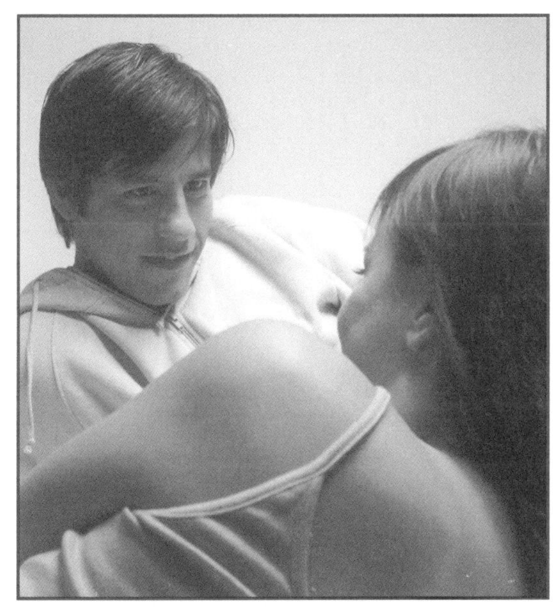

To avoid misunderstandings and maintain a happy relationship, both Scorpio and Cancer should give each other plenty of reassurance.

Cancer Birth Influences

Ruling planet: The Moon
Element: Water
Polarity: Feminine
Quadruplicity: Cardinal

CANCER
SAGITTARIUS

Cancer Birth Influences

Ruling planet: The Moon
Element: Water
Polarity: Feminine
Quadruplicity: Cardinal

Cancer and Sagittarius lovers may be passionately attracted to one another at first, but Sagittarius needs space, which can hurt Cancer deeply.

Sagittarius Birth Influences

Ruling planet: Jupiter
Element: Fire
Polarity: Masculine
Quadruplicity: Mutable

The early days of any romance are always exciting, and if the lovers in question are a Cancer and a Sagittarius, there is the additional thrill of the attraction of opposites. While Moon-ruled, feminine-polarity Cancer may be quiet and self-contained, Jupiter-governed, masculine-polarity Sagittarius is expansive and outgoing, and while watery Cancer is exhilarated by the fiery archer's burning enthusiasm, Sagittarius is soothed when awash in the crab's love. But will this relationship endure over time, as cardinal Cancer increasingly demands commitment from free-spirited Sagittarius, and mutable Sagittarius' incorrigible inconstancy injures the vulnerable crab time and time again?

Plus Points: If you are a Sagittarius, spending time with Cancer must be like stepping into a little oasis of calm amid a frenzy of activity. All of your birth influences indicate that you are an outward-focused person who relishes variety and rarely stands still, and if most of your life is taken up with energetic exploration, getting together with Cancer must be a refreshing change, and maybe also an ego-boost. The Moon, Cancer's planetary ruler, a feminine polarity, and water together make the crab a thoughtful individual who is instinctively attuned to your feelings and derives joy from giving, making you feel like the most important person in the world.

Having been born under a lunar, feminine, watery sign may have given you a tendency to feel shy and unsure of yourself, if you are a Cancer, and to long for a lover who will give you the confidence to venture out of your shell. If so, you may be over the Moon to have a Sagittarian sweetheart. It is Jupiter, their ruling planet, that causes Sagittarians to be kind-hearted, positive thinkers, their fiery element that endows them with infectious vitality, and their masculine polarity that gives them their dynamism, all three also bestowing self-assurance on zodiacal archers. You must now be blossoming under Sagittarius' warm encouragement, as well as delightedly sampling all manner of new experiences.

Potential Pitfalls: Some fundamental problems may soon become evident in a relationship between Cancer and Sagittarius. If you are a cardinal Cancer, your aim may be set up home and have a family together, but Sagittarius may seem in no rush to settle down, for instance. And if you are a fiery, mutable Sagittarius, you may often feel compelled to break free of Cancer's clinging embrace in order to reclaim your liberty, thereby playing havoc with the sensitive crab's emotions.

Guiding Principle: The key to happiness lies in respecting each other's individuality.

Compatibility: ♥♥♥♥♡♡♡♡♡♡

CAPRICORN
CANCER

Cancer and Capricorn share a feminine polarity, as well as a cardinal quadruplicity, which means that both are thoughtful individuals who are set on making their dreams come true. In Cancer's case, these may be family-focused, while Capricorn's visions are more likely to center on career or other accomplishments, but such complementary long-term goals can give backbone to a love affair. And when watery Cancer's empathy and caring and earthy Capricorn's common sense and loyalty are added to the mix, the prognosis for an enduring relationship is good. Yet touchy Cancer may sometimes feel neglected by preoccupied Capricorn, and no-nonsense Capricorn may occasionally find the crab's clinginess cloying.

Plus Points: You may have fallen in love with Cancer, but there probably isn't a romantic bone in your body if you are a Capricorn, so that the qualities that you find endearing in the crab may concern the support that he or she gives you. Having been born under feminine-polarity signs, you may both internalize your worries, and it is thanks to the intuitive Moon and empathetic element of water that your Cancer sweetheart may instinctively sense when you are feeling down and may offer you heartfelt sympathy and understanding. Whatever your lover's sex, you may also feel that Cancer is a born homemaker who would preside over your domestic life, freeing you to forge ahead with other things.

If you are a Cancer, it is your insecurity-inducing, watery element that may make you yearn for a life partner who won't inflict emotional pain on you, and on whom you can rely to take care of practicalities. It may consequently seem as though constant, down-to-earth Capricorn is the one for you, particularly if you hope to have a family. Indeed, not only may cardinal Capricorn be as ambitious as you, but you can't have failed to have noticed the tenacious, committed, hard-working influence of Saturn on your beloved, giving you reason to believe that this is a person who will be a conscientious provider.

Potential Pitfalls: Moon-governed, watery Cancer craves the reassurance of a loving word, comforting embrace, or tender gesture at times, which you may simply not comprehend if you are an undemonstrative Capricorn. And if you are a Cancer, there may be times when you fear that you come second to Capricorn's job, which may cause you to hurl tearful, and perhaps unjust, accusations at your mystified lover.

Guiding Principle: Recognize that you express your love for one another in different, but no less sincere, ways.

Compatibility: ♥♥♥♥♥♥♥♡♡♡

Capricorn Birth Influences
Ruling planet: Saturn
Element: Earth
Polarity: Feminine
Quadruplicity: Cardinal

For workaholic Capricorns, getting up early in the morning is not a problem, but don't forget to give Cancer a loving kiss and hug before you go.

Cancer Birth Influences
Ruling planet: The Moon
Element: Water
Polarity: Feminine
Quadruplicity: Cardinal

CANCER
AQUARIUS

Cancer Birth Influences

Ruling planet: The Moon
Element: Water
Polarity: Feminine
Quadruplicity: Cardinal

Cancer and Aquarius may be initially attracted to one another, but a long-term relationship won't be a case of living happily ever after unless each partner is willing to compromise.

Aquarius Birth Influences

Ruling planet: Uranus; traditionally Saturn
Element: Air
Polarity: Masculine
Quadruplicity: Fixed

The astrological portents suggest that Cancer and Aquarius may feel very differently about one another after some months or years of togetherness than they did in the early days of their romance. To start with, impressionable, Moon-ruled Cancer may be bowled over by airy, masculine-polarity Aquarius' breezy confidence and charm, while the water-carrier may be swept away by the waves of affection emanating from the watery crab. Yet it may not be long before sensitive Cancer is wounded by Aquarius' lack of consideration, or liberty-loving Aquarius feels dragged down by the clinging crab.

Plus Points: Having a responsive, feminine polarity, receptive planetary governor, and empathetic element may have resulted in Cancer being a listener *par excellence*, and you may therefore revel in the crab's company if you are an Aquarius. Your own element and polarity probably cause you to be a talkative extrovert who loves to share the radical ideas that are the bequest of Uranus, your own ruling planet, in which case having such a sympathetic audience may make you feel ten feet tall. And because you may prefer to inhabit the world of the intellect, you may be relieved that Cancer appears so willing to take care of domestic or personal matters for you, too.

If you are a Cancer, you may feel immensely flattered that such a lively, charming, and invigorating person as Aquarius has chosen you to be his or her sweetheart. Your birth influences may fill you with shyness and anxiety at times, but when you have withdrawn into your shell, cheerful, self-assured Aquarius probably has a unique ability to coax you back out again. There may also be occasions when you are grateful for the loyalty that the fixed-quadruplicity water-carrier demonstrates when you are feeling insecure.

Potential Pitfalls: Although your airy element may make you easygoing if you are an Aquarius, it also gives you a need to retain freedom of thought and action within a relationship, and you may consequently eventually feel suffocated by the lunar, watery crab's yearning for constant emotional and physical closeness. And if you are a Cancer, you may be deeply hurt by Aquarius' detachment, frequent absences, and the way that he or she seems either oblivious to, or unconcerned by, your suffering, and simply behaves as though nothing is wrong.

Guiding Principle: Don't take each other's love for granted, and try to understand and support one another.

Compatibility: ♥♥♥♡♡♡♡♡♡♡

PISCES — CANCER

When Cancer and Pisces fall in love, it could truly be a match made in heaven. Not only do they share a feminine, or thoughtful, polarity and a profoundly emotional element in water, making them instinctively attuned to one another, but the Moon and Neptune—their respective ruling planets—endow each with similar characteristics, too, notably intuition, creativity, and kindness. And although the influence of their different quadruplicities may occasionally make their romance a little tense, cardinal Cancer's ambition and mutable Pisces' adaptability can together strengthen their relationship.

Plus Points: Neither Cancer nor Pisces feels completely happy or fulfilled unless they have the comfort and support of a special someone who understands them, loves them unconditionally, and does not trifle with their affections. If you are a Pisces, you may therefore believe that you have found your soulmate in Cancer, who, due to your joint watery element and the additional influence of the crab's lunar governor, may be as giving, sensitive, and vulnerable as you when it comes to affairs of the heart, and probably even more so. You may consequently bask in the loving concern that Cancer shows for you, may be grateful that you can communicate with one another without the need for words, and, above all, may feel a deep sense of relief at the realization that your sweetheart would not betray your trust.

If you are a Cancer, you may similarly regard Pisces as being your ideal lover. Not only may he or she display the empathy and compassion that you crave when buffeted by stormy emotions, but Neptune may give Pisces a dreamy, idealistic mindset and a gift for seeing beauty in the mundane that you may find endearing and inspiring. And because you have an inward-looking, feminine polarity in common, as well as a privacy-seeking element, you may also appreciate Pisces' ability to sense when you need to be alone.

Potential Pitfalls: Because Cancer has a cardinal quadruplicity, he or she may tend to take the lead in your relationship if you are a Pisces, but this may not be a problem if you are willing to be flexible and to sacrifice your personal freedom on the altar of love. And if you are a Cancer, you may sometimes be unnerved by mutable Pisces' restlessness, but may understand that this has nothing to do with the way that he or she feels about you.

Guiding Principle: Carry on caring for one another!

Compatibility: ♥♥♥♥♥♥♥♥♥♡

Pisces Birth Influences

Ruling planet: Neptune; traditionally Jupiter
Element: Water
Polarity: Feminine
Quadruplicity: Mutable

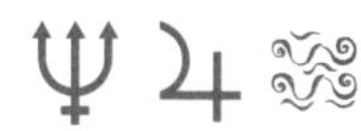

Pisces and Cancer: if you believe that you are soulmates, the stars suggest that this may indeed be so.

Cancer Birth Influences

Ruling planet: The Moon
Element: Water
Polarity: Feminine
Quadruplicity: Cardinal

LEO
LEO

Leo Birth Influences
Ruling planet: The Sun
Element: Fire
Polarity: Masculine
Quadruplicity: Fixed

The Sun, their ruling planet, smiles radiantly on a romance between two zodiacal felines, who, when things are going well, purr loudly with delight as they take turns to stroke each other's egos. Their solar governor, fiery element, and masculine, or active, polarity together make them a passionate pair of lovers who are equally matched in their playful warmth, vibrant love of life, and dynamic energy. And once a spark of attraction has set love ablaze, their loyal, fixed quadruplicity will usually keep it burning brightly, that is, as long as each is careful to pay sufficient attention to the other and is prepared to take a back seat every so often.

Plus Points: If you are a Leo with a leonine lover, you must each be enthused by the other's vital, spontaneous, and fearless spirit, not least because these gifts of your shared planetary ruler, element of fire, and masculine polarity mean that your hearts beat as one, to the same invigorating beat. No doubt you have a lot of fun partying together and egging each other on in your mutual quest for excitement, but because even the most vigorous lions need to unwind every so often, you may also enjoy spending lazy hours relaxing in one another's company, perhaps at the theater or the movies, where you can indulge your mutual love of drama. You may both similarly appreciate the power of a grand romantic gesture, too, and, being generous, devil-may-care types who adore seeing a beloved face light up with joy, must relish showering one another with spectacularly expensive gifts.

A relationship between two Leos will almost certainly be warm, spontaneous, and passionate, giving both lions plenty to laugh about.

Potential Pitfalls: The main potential pitfall lurking in the path of true leonine love—and it is a big one—lies in the proud, and rather egotistical, lion's need to take center stage. You will therefore each have to make an effort to ensure that your lover receives co-star billing in your joint romantic production and step out of the limelight occasionally, otherwise one of you will become increasingly resentful at having been relegated to playing a bit part, or supporting role, in your love affair. Although you have a fixed, or steadfast, quadruplicity in common, which means that it will take a lot before either of you gives up on the other, be warned that all Leos crave adoration, and will assert themselves with roars of displeasure if they feel neglected.

Leo Birth Influences
Ruling planet: The Sun
Element: Fire
Polarity: Masculine
Quadruplicity: Fixed

Guiding Principle: Treat your lover as you yourself expect to be treated, that is, with tenderness, consideration, and respect.

Compatibility: ♥♥♥♥♥♥♥♡♡♡

VIRGO / LEO

On paper, Leo and Virgo appear a wonderfully complementary pair if you believe that balance is important in a love affair. To start with, uninhibited, masculine-polarity Leo gives inhibited, feminine-polarity Virgo confidence, while earthy Virgo encourages fiery, spontaneous Leo to be more thoughtful and pragmatic. Secondly, steadfast, fixed-sign Leo stabilizes mutable, moody Virgo, Virgo in turn teaching Leo a thing or two about flexibility. And thirdly, the Sun-ruled lion energizes dispassionate, Mercury-governed Virgo, who returns the favor by pressing Leo to think analytically. In practice, however, each may irritate the other to such an extent that parting may come as a relief.

Plus Points: You may have certain characteristics in common if you are a Virgo and your beloved is a Leo, such as the resilience and constancy that are the gifts of the lion's solar ruler and fixed polarity and your own earthy element. As a result, you are unlikely to be oversensitive types who flee the scene of an argument rather than staying and resolving your differences, which augurs well for a long-lasting relationship. And Leo may also have many other qualities that you find attractive, including warmth, fearlessness, and loyalty. Here is a passionate person who wears their heart on their sleeve and whose vitality is infectious, a combination that you may find irresistible.

If you are a Leo, it may be important to you that your lover is someone who you are proud to show off, in which case you may be thrilled to witness the effect that Mercury-ruled Virgo's articulacy and intelligence has on others. Having been born under a fixed, or uncompromising, sign, you may also appreciate Virgo's adaptability, as well as the love of variety and restlessness that correspond to your own stimulation-seeking and impulsive nature. In short, Virgo may be an individual you respect, who is willing to follow your lead, and, what's more, keeps up with you.

Potential Pitfalls: Sun-governed, self-centered Leos demand admiration from their partners and consider criticism a betrayal, but if you are an objective Virgo, you may find it difficult to hold your tongue if you think that your leonine lover is being pompous, rash, or recklessly extravagant. And if you are a Leo, earthy, sensible Virgo may exert a disapproving, deadening influence upon you that you may eventually find insufferable.

Guiding Principle: Try to follow each other's example once in a while, or at least to tolerate your idiosyncrasies.

Compatibility: ♥♥♥♥♥♡♡♡♡♡

Virgo Birth Influences

Ruling planet: Mercury
Element: Earth
Polarity: Feminine
Quadruplicity: Mutable

A relationship between Virgo and Leo will stay on the right track if both partners make an equal effort.

Leo Birth Influences

Ruling planet: The Sun
Element: Fire
Polarity: Masculine
Quadruplicity: Fixed

☉ 

LEO
LIBRA

Leo Birth Influences

Ruling planet: The Sun
Element: Fire
Polarity: Masculine
Quadruplicity: Fixed

The combination of airy Libra and fiery Leo fans the flames of passion, but a stiff blast of cold air can extinguish the flames of love, while a raging fire can consume the oxygen that sustains a relationship.

Plus Points: There are many reasons why a romantic union between Leo and Libra appears to be a match made in heaven, not least the interests that they share. Both have a connoisseur's keenly developed appreciation of beauty, and both are magnetically drawn to creative and artistic pursuits. Leo's gregarious, fun-loving nature is perfectly complemented by Venusian Libra's sociable, networking inclinations, Sun-ruled Leo exuding warmth and bonhomie, while charming Libra adeptly puts others at ease. All in all, these extroverts are people-people, and make a dazzling couple at any social event.

Romance is as important to Libra as it is to Leo, although for slightly different reasons. Libra adores being made to feel loved and special amid roses and candlelight, while if you are a fiery Leo, you relish the drama of staging the ultimate romantic gesture. Libra yearns for a soulmate, and for a relationship based on mutual respect and equality, while Leo longs for a partner who will make the proud lion the envy of others, and who will supply a constant source of unconditional love and home comforts in which to bask contentedly. And once they have found their ideal life partner, fixed-quadruplicity Leo and cardinal Libra will commit themselves wholeheartedly to their relationship.

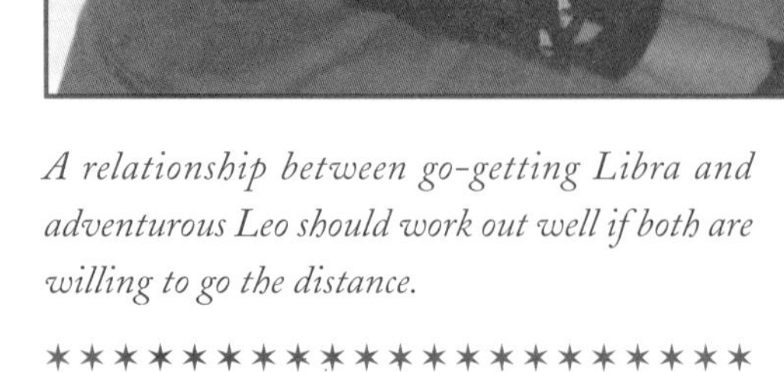

A relationship between go-getting Libra and adventurous Leo should work out well if both are willing to go the distance.

Potential Pitfalls: As promising as a Leo–Libra partnership may initially seem, there are, however, some potential pitfalls in a relationship in which one partner (Leo) is ruled by the heart, and the other (Libra) is ruled by the head. If you're a Venusian Libra and believe that both partners should put equal effort into the relationship, you may come to resent solar Leo's potentially selfish or lazy tendencies. If you are a Leo, you may feel frustrated, undermined, or even devastated by cool-headed Libra's objective criticism or perceived indifference (which can seem especially pronounced in Libra men).

Guiding Principle: Keep your relationship burning brightly by respecting your differences and practicing the art of compromise.

Libra Birth Influences

Ruling planet: Venus
Element: Air
Polarity: Masculine
Quadruplicity: Cardinal

Compatibility: 

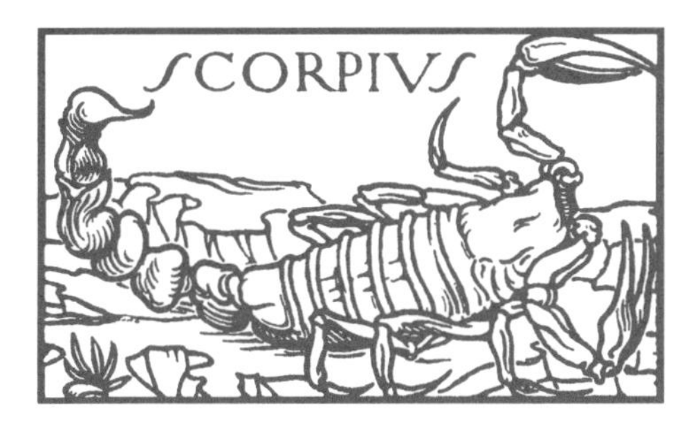

SCORPIO
LEO

Leo and Scorpio share a fixed quadruplicity, which means that they are capable of remaining loyal to one another for life, but the question is, will the bond of love that initially unites these two very different personalities eventually be replaced by the shackles of obligation? Will sunny Leo continue to brighten Scorpio's life, or will the scorpion's suspicious mind cast a cloud over their relationship? And will fiery Leo carry on warming the cockles of Scorpio's heart, or leave it a scorched and arid wasteland?

Plus Points: If you are a zodiacal scorpion, the combination of your feminine, or receptive, polarity and "feeling" element of water may cause you to be deeply responsive to the energy emanated by others, in which case the blazing vigor that Leo radiates may have a huge impact on you. Add the life-affirming vitality imparted by the lion's solar ruler and masculine, or positive, polarity to the all-consuming passion of a fiery element, and the result may be someone who elates and enlivens you, as well as making you feel hotly desired.

You may revel in your ability to lift sometimes gloomy, Pluto-governed Scorpio's mood if you are a Leo, perhaps because the Sun and fire give you a generous nature or because you enjoy the transformational effect that your sunny personality has on others. In return, your steadfast Scorpio sweetheart no doubt provides the tender cherishing and unconditional love that you crave. And because fiery Leos adore being the center of attention, you must relish the way that intense, devoted Scorpio's world seems to revolve around you.

Potential Pitfalls: Outgoing Leo may be far more of a people-person than you, if you are a reserved Scorpio, and may also be very susceptible to flattery, so that if you see your sweetheart responding warmly to an attractive someone's honeyed words, you may be stricken with jealousy. It is due to your element that you are so emotionally vulnerable, while the double dose of reticence that water and Pluto bestow on you may make you unable to articulate your fears. And if you are a fiery Leo who lacks the scorpion's intuitive empathy, you may become impatient with Scorpio's moping and may explode, thus pushing your lover into self-defensive attack mode. Be warned that if this state of affairs continues, Scorpio may nurse grudge after grudge, driving Leo to seek affection and appreciation elsewhere.

Guiding Principle: Try to treat one another with sympathy and understanding.

Compatibility: ♥♥♥♥♡♡♡♡♡♡

Scorpio Birth Influences

Ruling planet: Pluto; traditionally Mars
Element: Water
Polarity: Feminine
Quadruplicity: Fixed

While Scorpio loves to stay home, Leo longs to go out. Take it in turns to go along with your lover.

Leo Birth Influences

Ruling planet: The Sun
Element: Fire
Polarity: Masculine
Quadruplicity: Fixed

LEO — SAGITTARIUS

Leo Birth Influences

Ruling planet: The Sun
Element: Fire
Polarity: Masculine
Quadruplicity: Fixed

If Leo and Sagittarius lovers sometimes fight, they tend to make up quickly. Neither harbors grudges, and both far prefer to have fun.

Sagittarius Birth Influences

Ruling planet: Jupiter
Element: Fire
Polarity: Masculine
Quadruplicity: Mutable

Combine the burning energy and lack of inhibition of two fiery, masculine-polarity signs with Sun-governed Leo's blazing ardor and Jupiter-ruled Sagittarius' boundless optimism, and you have two lovers who entertain and inspire one another, and a relationship that will never stagnate. Their different quadruplicities have a vital role to play in a romance between the lion and the archer, too, with fixed Leo supplying commitment, and mutable Sagittarius, adaptability, although stubbornness and flightiness may be less constructive parts of the package.

Plus Points: You no doubt have a horror of being bored if you are a Sagittarius, which is why you may be blessing your lucky stars that your leonine lover shares your stimulation-seeking, fiery element and masculine, or dynamic, polarity. Having another flaming birth influence in the Sun, Leo's dazzling ideas may instantly ignite the touch paper that fires your imagination, and because you are both spontaneous, energetic types, you may waste no time putting them into action. You may also be grateful for the stability that fixed-quadruplicity Leo brings to your life if, like many Sagittarians, you yourself are rather changeable.

It probably goes without saying that you adore your Sagittarian sweetheart's exuberant, extrovert character if you are a like-minded Leo who shares the archer's element and polarity. Jupiter, Sagittarius' governing planet, may infuse your beloved with other qualities that delight you as well, such as a positive outlook and wide-ranging vision. And because your own commanding planetary ruler gives you an instinctive tendency to lead the way in a relationship, you may appreciate mutable Sagittarius' generally easygoing flexibility and willingness to go along with you.

Potential Pitfalls: One of the downsides of Leo's fixed quadruplicity, if you are a Sagittarius who has to deal with it, is obstinacy, and although you may usually opt for the course of least resistance and accede to the lion's unyielding will, you may dislike feeling as though you are being controlled, and your pent-up frustration may eventually burst forth. Alternatively, your mutable quadruplicity may kick in, and you may abandon the unbending lion and take off for a while. You may perceive this as unfaithfulness if you are a Leo who furthermore hates to be ignored, so that you may unleash the full force of your anger when Sagittarius returns. You both have fiery tempers, which means that you may have some heated arguments, but at least you each quickly forgive and forget.

Guiding Principle: Give one another both freedom and respect.

Compatibility: ♥♥♥♥♥♥♥♡♡♡

CAPRICORN
LEO

Adventurous Leo and cautious Capricorn can be good for one another, particularly if they have a common focus, such as raising a family, when Leo's committed, fixed quadruplicity and Capricorn's driven, cardinal one can be highly complementary. That is not to say that their love affair will be all plain sailing, however, with prudent, earthy Capricorn constantly trying to curb the fiery lion's spur-of-the-moment extravagance, and Sun-ruled Leo forever urging Saturn-governed Capricorn to lighten up and live a little.

Plus Points: If you are a Capricorn, the combination of serious Saturn and your cardinal quadruplicity may impel you to spend your days working as hard as you can to attain your ultimate goal, which is why you may be grateful to have such an enlivening and loyal lover in Leo. Even the most industrious of Capricorns needs to relax once in a while, and because your polarity is feminine, or responsive, you probably can't resist the dynamic, masculine-polarity lion when he or she decrees that you need a break and sweeps you off to play. And a wonderful bonus may be the fiery leonine passion that arouses your own earthy sensuality.

Sun-ruled Leos are renowned for their self-esteem, and if you are one of their number, you may consider it vital that your sweetheart is someone whom you admire and who reflects well on you. And Capricorn may have plenty of qualities that make your heart swell with pride, such as phenomenal determination, ambition, and the patience that your own fiery nature lacks. Being a magnanimous sort, you may be willing to overlook many minor failings in your partner as long as he or she remains devoted and faithful to you, and steady Capricorn probably gives you no cause for concern on that score.

Potential Pitfalls: Although you may find fiery Leo's enthusiasm and energy invigorating if you are a more passive, earthy Capricorn, your lover's spontaneity may sometimes irritate you: if you're putting money aside for your future together and Leo impetuously splashes out on an expensive designer suit, for instance. Your cardinal and fixed quadruplicities may also give rise to tension, with you powering toward a distant objective, and Leo being happy with the here and now. Similarly, if you are an attention-seeking, fun-loving Leo, you may resent the way that you often seem to come second to Capricorn's work, and may sometimes find your lover's practical mindset tedious and uninspiring.

Guiding Principle: Mutual tolerance is the key to lasting love.

Compatibility: ♥♥♥♥♥♥♡♡♡♡

Capricorn Birth Influences
Ruling planet: Saturn
Element: Earth
Polarity: Feminine
Quadruplicity: Cardinal

If you're a busy Capricorn, make sure that you don't leave Leo feeling neglected. A treat or surprise always goes down well with lions.

Leo Birth Influences
Ruling planet: The Sun
Element: Fire
Polarity: Masculine
Quadruplicity: Fixed

LEO
AQUARIUS

Leo Birth Influences
Ruling planet: The Sun
Element: Fire
Polarity: Masculine
Quadruplicity: Fixed

Leo and Aquarius have plenty to build their romance on, but detached, objective Aquarius should try not to hurt the proud lion's feelings.

Aquarius Birth Influences
Ruling planet: Uranus; traditionally Saturn
Element: Air
Polarity: Masculine
Quadruplicity: Fixed

Although fiery, passionate Leo may be a little disappointed that airy, intellectual Aquarius is incorrigibly unromantic, and Aquarius may have scant sympathy with the lion's craving for attention and respect, these two can enjoy the happiest and most rewarding of relationships. Sun-governed Leo is genial, and airy Aquarius, affable; the fiery lion seeks stimulation, which nonconformist, Uranus-ruled Aquarius supplies, inventive Aquarius in turn admiring Leo's creativity. As long as they give one another space, the prognosis looks good, not least because they share a positive, masculine polarity, and a fixed, or loyal, quadruplicity.

Plus Points: You may have a horror of being clung to and of acrimonious, emotion-charged scenes if you an independent, rather impersonal, airy Aquarius, and may consequently be relieved that your Leo lover is generally sunny-natured, and, thanks to your mutual masculine polarity, as assertive and outgoing as you. You may have many other qualities in common, too, such as playfulness and gregariousness, so that you probably have lots of fun together in the company of your friends. And another joy of having a Leo for a lover may be his or her invigoratingly experimental way of thinking, which may chime with your own trailblazing thought processes.

If you are a typical Leo, you must love surprises, which is why you no doubt delight in your Aquarian sweetheart, whose revolutionary planetary governor may make him or her an apparently inexhaustible source of ingenious ideas. Having the self-regarding Sun as a planetary ruler may mean that you can only commit yourself to someone whom you consider worthy of your devotion, and you may therefore feel that charming, dynamic, and original Aquarius more than fulfills this criterion.

Potential Pitfalls: Their joint fixed quadruplicity may give Leo and Aquarius staying power, which bodes well for an enduring relationship, but can also trigger stubbornness in both when they disagree. When this happens, you may be exposed to fiery Leo's explosive temper, Aquarius, while you may be further enraged by airy Aquarius' coolly rational response, Leo. But then the lion's fury is usually short-lived, and Aquarius fortunately doesn't nurse grudges. Yet a more serious problem may continue to simmer on the back burner if domineering Leo tries to limit Aquarius's liberty, or if freedom-loving Aquarius doesn't give Leo the time and approval that the proud lion demands.

Guiding Principle: Maintain your individuality, but try to work at being a couple.

Compatibility: ♥♥♥♥♥♥♥♡♡♡

PISCES / LEO

When first smitten by one another, Leo and Pisces may feel as though they are in seventh heaven. Idealistic, Neptunian Pisces people tend to put their lovers on pedestals, and self-regarding, Sun-governed Leos adore being adored; watery Pisces is sentimental, and fiery Leo, romantic; and while fixed-sign Leo is constant, mutable Pisces is adaptable. Many more positive correspondences could be added to the compatibility list, but also some mismatches, such as Leo's hot temper and Pisces' moodiness, which is why these lovebirds' initial euphoria may not last long.

Pisces Birth Influences

Ruling planet: Neptune; traditionally Jupiter
Element: Water
Polarity: Feminine
Quadruplicity: Mutable

Plus Points: If you are a Pisces, you may have dreamed of having a sweetheart who lavishes love on you, protects you when you are feeling vulnerable, and who will remain faithful to you, and it may therefore seem as though you have found "the one" in Leo. Having the Sun as a planetary ruler and fire as an element may cause Leo to be passionate, generous, and demonstrative, his or her masculine, or confidence-bestowing, polarity and fixed quadruplicity furthermore making the lion a fearless champion and loyal lover. In short, Leo may give you the security that you crave.

Just as the Sun is the center of the solar system, so its leonine protégés expect to be the focus of their lovers' worlds, which is why you may be so gratified by feminine-polarity Pisces' dependence on you for his or her happiness if you are a member of the worldwide pride of zodiacal lions. The combination of Neptune and water may also manifest itself in Pisces as an intuitive understanding of your feelings and an unselfish desire to put your needs first, in addition to which, the fishes' mutable quadruplicity may enable your lover to accommodate your rather inflexible ways.

Leo and Pisces lovers should express their feelings warmly and kindly to avoid misunderstandings or minor problems growing out of proportion.

Potential Pitfalls: Because you may be hypersensitive to others' moods, and are easily wounded by inconsiderate behavior if you are a Pisces, you may sometimes shrink from Leo when he or she is in the grip of fiery fury, or when the honest lion unwittingly hurts your feelings with a disparaging, throwaway comment. And if you are a robust Leo, you may be taken aback by Pisces' lack of emotional resilience, especially if the confusing influence of Neptune renders your lover inarticulate, or that of his or her mutable quadruplicity morose one minute, and merry the next.

Guiding Principle: Try to be understanding, and, above all, forgiving, should you inadvertently upset or annoy one another.

Compatibility: ♥♥♥♥♥♡♡♡♡♡

Leo Birth Influences

Ruling planet: The Sun
Element: Fire
Polarity: Masculine
Quadruplicity: Fixed

VIRGO
VIRGO

Virgo Birth Influences
Ruling planet: Mercury
Element: Earth
Polarity: Feminine
Quadruplicity: Mutable

With the right chemistry, the tender embrace of your Virgo lover's arms will feel like heaven, especially if you, too, are an earthy Virgo, who delights in home comforts.

Virgo Birth Influences
Ruling planet: Mercury
Element: Earth
Polarity: Feminine
Quadruplicity: Mutable

After the first flush of infatuation has faded, an affair between two Virgos can go either way: either they will drive one another to distraction with their critical ways, or they will remain on the same wavelength and live happily ever after. It mainly depends on their personal chemistry—that vital, yet indefinable, magic ingredient—but also on the balance of their shared birth influences, for if the element of earth makes one overly routine-loving and a mutable quadruplicity bestows a craving for variety on the other, for example, they may increasingly come to resent each other. And when Virgos are discontented, they find it difficult to hold their carping tongues.

Plus Points: If you and your beloved are both Virgos, your likes, dislikes, and foibles will inevitably vary because no two individuals are identical. Because your planetary ruler, element, polarity, and quadruplicity are the same, however, certain keywords may describe you both: Mercury's chattiness, perhaps? A down-to-earth approach to life? The supportiveness that is the gift of a feminine polarity? Or the flexibility that is the hallmark of a mutable sign? If so, you and your sweetheart probably have a profound natural affinity, one that will enable you to keep the channels of communication open, to plan your future together realistically, to be there for one another, and, what's more, to be accommodating when you are slightly out of sync. The double dose of sensuality with which your joint element of earth blesses the pair of you suggests that your romance will be deeply fulfilling, too.

Potential Pitfalls: Both partners having a planetary governor in Mercury and a feminine polarity, earthy element, and mutable quadruplicity does not always augur well for an enduringly happy liaison, particularly if one or more astrological agent is particularly pronounced in either partner. It may be, for instance, that Mercury has infected your lover with the travel bug, whereas you are earthier and prefer the comforts of home. If this is the case, and love, along with your shared adaptability-giving quadruplicity, enables you both to make concessions, you may be able to reach a satisfactory compromise. Otherwise, you may find that your mutual dissatisfaction with this imperfect situation causes you each to start giving vent to your irritation through excessive fault-finding, so that your relationship may eventually be marred by constant bickering.

Guiding Principle: When you are affronted by your lover's perceived faults, try to keep your annoyance to yourself.

Compatibility: ♥♥♥♥♥♥♥♡♡♡

LIBRA / VIRGO

As long as Virgo and Libra are willing to sacrifice some of their individual preferences on the altar of commitment, they have the potential to make an exceptionally affectionate couple. This may be a tall order, however, particularly if Libra is hedonistic and Virgo, more sensible. Having a cardinal, or pushy, quadruplicity and a masculine, or active, polarity means that Libra is likely to take the lead, with mutable, feminine-polarity Virgo providing vital support, making them a good team. In addition, the coming-together of Mercury, a mutable quadruplicity, and an airy element in the relationship suggests that there'll always be plenty to discuss, but not always romance-enhancing subjects.

Plus Points: Life is often a serious business for introverted, hard-working Virgos, and if you are one of them, a wonderful benefit of having a Libran lover may be the magically relaxing effect that he or she has on you. It may be, for instance, that Libra's charming chivvying frequently persuades you to down tools in order to attend a party or concert, the balance's element of air no doubt making your beloved sociable, and Venus infusing him or her with an appreciation of the arts. And because your mutable quadruplicity may give you an appetite for change, you may not mind being whisked away to play one bit.

With the exception of laid-back Venus, all of your birth influences may fill you with the need to conduct a love affair on your own terms if you are a Libra. This is one reason why you may rejoice in your Virgo sweetheart, who may usually be willing to go along with you, thanks to a receptive, feminine polarity and flexible, mutable quadruplicity. But you may also be grateful that your earthy Virgo lover is prone to taking care of certain practical matters that, having been born under an air sign, probably bore you to tears.

Potential Pitfalls: Although Virgo is communicative, and Libra, talkative, their very different way with words may cause friction to arise between these lovers. Straightforward Virgo may occasionally shock you by commenting on your self-indulgence if you are a Venus-ruled Libra whose head is often in the clouds and who dislikes being brought back down to earth by cold reality. And if you are a perceptive, Mercury-governed Virgo, you may sometimes be irritated by Libra's honeyed tone, which you may interpret as being calculated to deceive or manipulate.

Guiding Principle: Strive to strike a balance between openness and diplomacy when conveying your point of view to your partner.

Compatibility: ♥♥♥♥♥♥♡♡♡♡

Libra Birth Influences

Ruling planet: Venus
Element: Air
Polarity: Masculine
Quadruplicity: Cardinal

When Libra leads you out for fun and games, Virgo, you may find yourself enjoying a breath of fresh air.

Virgo Birth Influences

Ruling planet: Mercury
Element: Earth
Polarity: Feminine
Quadruplicity: Mutable

VIRGO
SCORPIO

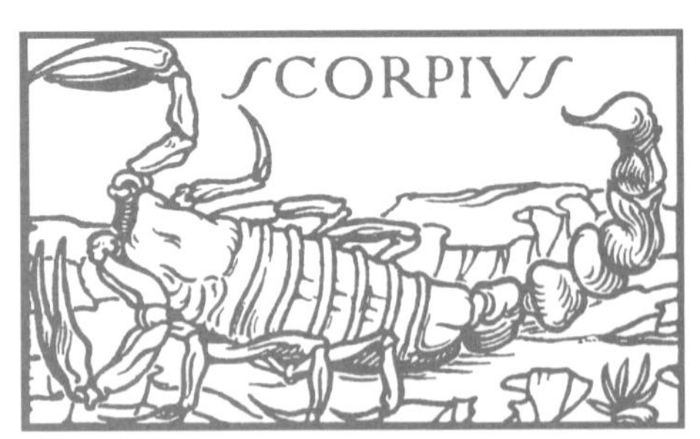

Virgo Birth Influences

Ruling planet: Mercury
Element: Earth
Polarity: Feminine
Quadruplicity: Mutable

Earthy Virgo can quickly calm a troubled Scorpio by creating a sensual atmosphere.

Scorpio Birth Influences

Ruling planet: Pluto; traditionally Mars
Element: Water
Polarity: Feminine
Quadruplicity: Fixed

Virgo and Scorpio are in many respects ideal for one another. Both being rather introverted, feminine-polarity individuals, it may take time for each to open up to the other, but curious, Mercury-ruled Virgo's interest in enigmatic, Pluto-governed Scorpio, and watery Scorpio's sensitivity to, and empathy with, Virgo's feelings usually do the trick. And when they have established a romantic connection, the combination of Virgo's earthy element and Scorpio's fixed quadruplicity typically ensures that they remain committed to one another. Their day-to-day relationship may not always be plain sailing, however, for critical Virgo may frequently injure touchy Scorpio, while Scorpio's reticence may frustrate Virgo.

Plus Points: Your Virgo lover may be blessed with many traits that you admire if you are a Scorpio, such as astuteness, articulacy, and adaptability, all joint gifts of Mercury and a mutable quadruplicity that you don't possess to a highly developed degree yourself. Indeed, there may be times when your ruling planet and element of water cause you to feel so overwhelmed by dark emotions that you can't think straight, when you may be grateful for Virgo's logical assessment of the situation and constructive advice. Earthy Virgo's loyalty may also mean the world to you if, like most watery scorpions, you are terrified of having your heart broken.

Scorpio's instinctive insight and unconditional backing may amaze and touch you if you are his or her Virgoan sweetheart, in which case give thanks to the scorpion's intuitive, compassionate element of water and your shared feminine polarity, which manifests itself in Scorpio as an urge to provide emotional support, whereas your tendency is to offer practical assistance. You may also be fascinated by the mysterious workings of the Pluto-influenced scorpion's mind, and the icing on the cake may be the powerful sensual response that the intensity of Scorpio's love arouses in you.

Potential Pitfalls: If you are a Scorpio, your watery element may often make you feel vulnerable and insecure, and there may consequently be occasions when you take a neutral comment from objective Virgo as a devastating criticism of your personality. And when zodiacal scorpions are wounded, they are apt to withdraw deep within themselves to brood in sullen silence, which may first baffle, then worry, and ultimately anger you if you are a Virgo who has no idea what you're supposed to have done wrong.

Guiding Principle: Keep the channels of communication open, but try to negotiate them delicately.

Compatibility: ♥♥♥♥♥♥♥♥♡♡

SAGITTARIUS
VIRGO

Provided that neat, earthy Virgo doesn't carp on about fiery Sagittarius' untidiness, and Sagittarius' bluntness doesn't offend fastidious Virgo, there is usually plenty to keep these lovers interested in one another. Despite Virgo's sensuality and Sagittarius' passion, their relationship is likely to be more intellectual than emotional, thanks to their respective ruling planets. And while masculine-polarity Sagittarius is more outgoing than feminine-polarity Virgo, they share a restless, mutable quadruplicity, so that the archer may bring Mercury-governed Virgo's enjoyment of travel to the fore, Virgo in turn taking care of the crucial practicalities that Sagittarius finds a turn-off.

Plus Points: If you are a Sagittarius and your partner is a Virgo, your joint mutable quadruplicity may give you certain common characteristics, such as flexibility, a tendency to think analytically, and the urge to communicate, all of which Mercury heightens in Virgo. As a result, you may be grateful that your lover is so adaptable, as well as enjoying the stimulating conversations that you have with him or her. In addition, Virgo's element of earth and feminine polarity may make your beloved patient, organized, and thoughtful, suggesting that his or her steady, day-to-day support gives your life the structure and stability that may otherwise be lacking.

You may have felt your personality blooming, if you are a Virgo, ever since you and Sagittarius became an item. Their masculine, or positive, polarity, fiery element, and Jupiter together make Sagittarians confident, warm, and expansive people whose vitality enlivens those around them, especially receptive, feminine-polarity individuals like you. Sagittarius may also broaden your horizons, perhaps even literally if your lover's spontaneity and your mutual love of variety have triggered your latent wanderlust.

Potential Pitfalls: Although Virgos may welcome a change once a while, their mutability may be rooted in reality by their mundane element of earth. Your fiery nature may therefore instinctively kick against Virgo's orderliness and routines if you are an impulsive Sagittarius, causing Virgo to take you to task for your slapdash ways and you to respond unthinkingly aggressively. Similarly, if you are a Virgo, you may be deeply irritated by Jovian Sagittarius' tendency to consider life's small—but to you, essential—details unimportant, and may regard your sweetheart's outbursts as childish, illogical, or both.

Guiding Principle: Rather than dismissing your lover's more critical observations outright, ask yourself whether he or she may be right.

Compatibility: ♥♥♥♥♥♥♥♡♡♡

Sagittarius Birth Influences

Ruling planet: Jupiter
Element: Fire
Polarity: Masculine
Quadruplicity: Mutable

Virgo and Sagittarius love to go on vacation together, even if Virgo has to organize everything!

Virgo Birth Influences

Ruling planet: Mercury
Element: Earth
Polarity: Feminine
Quadruplicity: Mutable

VIRGO
CAPRICORN

Virgo Birth Influences

Ruling planet: Mercury
Element: Earth
Polarity: Feminine
Quadruplicity: Mutable

A Virgo and Capricorn couple will support each other through thick and thin. If Capricorn is headed for stellar success, she will want her Virgo partner to share it with her every step of the way.

Capricorn Birth Influences

Ruling planet: Saturn
Element: Earth
Polarity: Feminine
Quadruplicity: Cardinal

When Virgo and Capricorn become an item, their liaison typically proves the most stable of matches. Each has an earthy element and feminine polarity, which means that a practical, thoughtful mindset is common to both. While mutable Virgo can be changeable, saturnine, cardinal-quadruplicity Capricorn has phenomenal patience and drive, and communicative, variety-loving Virgo relieves the monotony of Capricorn's often sober existence. This therefore has the potential to be a partnership in every sense, but there is a danger that Virgo's restlessness or Capricorn's ambition may cast a shadow over their relationship.

Plus Points: Preoccupied as you may be with your goals if you are a Capricorn, you may bless the day that you met Virgo. Two are said to be stronger than one, and as you work steadily toward achieving prosperity, it may be wonderful to have supportive Virgo by your side, perhaps because he or she shares your sensible, down-to-earth views (and, as a bonus, your earthy sensuality) and feminine-polarity tendency to consider all of the options before taking action, so that you usually operate on the same wavelength. Mercury-governed, mutable Virgo's willingness to accommodate your hard-working, saturnine ways may also be a boon, and your lover's enjoyment of diversity may add a refreshing dimension to your life, too.

Feminine-polarity people can feel insecure, and if you are a Virgo, the additional input of Mercury and your mutable quadruplicity may sometimes cause you to feel that you are facing too many choices and can't decide between them. On occasions like these, Saturn-ruled Capricorn may offer the temperate advice that restores your sense of balance and gives you renewed purpose. What you may appreciate the most, however, is the rock-solid dependability bestowed on Capricorn by Saturn and earth, and his or her unwavering devotion to you. Indeed, cardinal Capricorn is probably set on going places, and it may be clear that your sweetheart's intention is that you should share in his or her life's journey and success.

Potential Pitfalls: Virgo's mutability may occasionally manifest itself in your beloved as edgy dissatisfaction, which you may find baffling, and ultimately annoying, if you are a straight-as-a-die Capricorn. And the reason for your discontentment, if you are a Virgo, may be that there are times when you'd rather live for the moment than focus on the distant future, yet Capricorn's dependable, but plodding, ways don't easily allow for such spontaneity, however temporary.

Guiding Principle: Try to give, as well as take.

Compatibility: ♥♥♥♥♥♥♥♥♡♡

AQUARIUS
VIRGO

Eight (or nine) birth influences come into play when Virgo and Aquarius get together as a couple, and while none is associated with sentimentality, three in particular—Mercury, air, and a mutable quadruplicity—are linked with the intellect, suggesting that a romance between these two is more likely to be a meeting of minds than of hearts. This pair can be good for one another, with practical, earthy Virgo keeping airy Aquarius grounded, and masculine-polarity Aquarius boosting feminine-polarity Virgo's confidence. Yet Virgo may be too down to earth for trailblazing, Uranus-governed Aquarius, while mutable Virgo's flexibility may be tested to its limits by fixed-sign Aquarius' intransigence.

Plus Points: If you are an airy Aquarius, your main requirement in a lover may be that he or she should be your intellectual equal, someone with whom you can hold a constant conversation, and bright and communicative, Mercury-ruled, mutable Virgo may live up to your expectations, and, having a pensive, feminine polarity, may also gratify you by giving serious thought to your notions. In addition, because your element of air may make you quite flighty and impractical, you may be grateful that earthy Virgo is so steady and sensible, maybe because your beloved gives you prudent advice, or perhaps because he or she takes care of the chores that you find mind-numbingly tedious.

It may similarly be important to you that the person with whom you hope to spend many happy years is both intelligent and thought-provoking if you are a Virgo, in which case Aquarius may not disappoint. Indeed, if your mutable quadruplicity gives you a love of surprises, you may be thrilled by Uranian Aquarius' unpredictable thought processes, and fascinated by his or her technical knowledge. And if your feminine polarity sometimes causes you to bottle up your worries, then masculine-polarity Aquarius may have a unique ability to persuade you to disclose them, and then to encourage you to adopt a more positive outlook.

Potential Pitfalls: Virgo may be interested in your revolutionary concepts if you are an Aquarius, but he or she is probably a matter-of-fact, analytical individual who is apt to pick holes in them, which you will ultimately find tiresome, not to say disloyal. And Aquarius' fixed quadruplicity may likewise weary you if you are a Virgo, for it may make your lover refuse to accept that you have a point when you have a difference of opinion.

Guiding Principle: Don't let criticism or stubbornness drive a wedge between you.

Compatibility: ♥♥♥♥♥♥♡♡♡♡

Aquarius Birth Influences

Ruling planet: Uranus; traditionally Saturn
Element: Air
Polarity: Masculine
Quadruplicity: Fixed

The flighty antics of your airy Aquarius partner may make you tremble if you are a more grounded, earthy Virgo, but Aquarius needs you around to pick up the pieces after taking a tumble.

Virgo Birth Influences

Ruling planet: Mercury
Element: Earth
Polarity: Feminine
Quadruplicity: Mutable

VIRGO

PISCES

Virgo Birth Influences

Ruling planet: Mercury
Element: Earth
Polarity: Feminine
Quadruplicity: Mutable

Although they share a self-contained, feminine polarity and flexible, mutable quadruplicity, the influence of their respective ruling planets and elements is such that most Virgo and Pisces individuals are radically different. The combination of Mercury and earth makes the typical Virgo rational and realistic, for instance, whereas that of Neptune and water causes Pisces to be intuitive and dreamy. As a result, their relationship is likely to be either marred by their mutual lack of understanding or, alternatively, enriched by their dissimilarities.

Plus Points: The qualities that you may appreciate the most in your Virgoan sweetheart, if you are a Pisces, are the patience and dependability that are the gifts of an earthy element. Indeed, if the interaction of all of your birth influences often makes you feel confused and insecure, he or she may be the rock to whom you cling for stability, and on whom you may rely for practical, day-to-day support. A further bonus may be the adaptability that enables your mutable-quadruplicity Virgo lover to accommodate your mood swings and quirks.

If you are a perceptive, mercurial Virgo, you are probably in no doubt of the depth of Pisces' love for you. While the element of water may heighten your beloved's emotions, it is Neptune who may be responsible for your lover's profound altruism. It may therefore seem as though empathetic Pisces is dedicated to bringing you happiness, a selfless aim that may be aided by his or her adjustability, a mutable-quadruplicity trait. All in all, knowing that there is someone in this world who will always put you first must be a wonderful feeling.

Beware of your sharp tongue, Virgo, for if Pisces takes your comments personally, you may be faced with someone deeply hurt. Your relationship could ultimately end up being a rocky one, too.

Potential Pitfalls: Objective, straight-talking Virgo may have a tendency to tell it like it is, and because Neptune and your element of water may make you doubly sensitive if you are a Pisces, there may consequently be occasions when your lover inadvertently shatters your self-confidence or trust with an observation that you take as a hurtful criticism. Not only is Pisces far less emotionally robust than you, Virgo, but tears may render him or her totally inarticulate, so that you may have no inkling of what has triggered them, and still less of an idea of how to stem them. If you really wish to weather these potential storms and remain a couple, it is vital that Pisces tries to develop a thicker skin and keep a sense of proportion, and that Virgo works on controlling his or her urge to analyze and criticize and on being more compassionate.

Pisces Birth Influences

Ruling planet: Neptune; traditionally Jupiter
Element: Water
Polarity: Feminine
Quadruplicity: Mutable

♆ ♃

Guiding Principle: Be tolerant of one another, and be careful not to let the feminine-polarity negativity that is latent in you both poison your relationship.

Compatibility: ♥♥♥♥♥♡♡♡♡♡

LIBRA
LIBRA

One thing can almost be guaranteed about a romance between two Libra lovers, that there will be few arguments, for not only are those born under the sign of the balance said to be the diplomats of the zodiac, but their ruling planet is Venus, named for the Roman goddess of love and harmony. Having an outgoing, masculine polarity and communicative, airy element makes these two a lively and sociable—but also somewhat emotionally detached—pair, so that while it may be fun-filled, their relationship is likely to be somewhat superficial. And because both have a cardinal, or self-seeking, quadruplicity, there is a danger that neither will be able to satisfy the other's Venusian craving for adoration.

Libra Birth Influences

Ruling planet: Venus
Element: Air
Polarity: Masculine
Quadruplicity: Cardinal

Plus Points: It may seem as though you are soulmates if you and your sweetheart are both Libras, perhaps because you are so similar, thanks to your common birth influences, or maybe because you have such a good time together and rarely, if ever, fall out. While your masculine polarity may make you both positive, confident people, it is your element of air that causes you to be a bright, gregarious, and talkative couple. No homebodies you, but when you are alone together, the conversation is probably constant, and punctuated with laughter. In addition, Venus, your shared planetary governor, may infuse each of you with an appreciation of entertainment and the arts, a tolerant attitude, and an abhorrence of arguments. Add to all of these plus points a common cardinal, or ambition-bestowing, quadruplicity, and it may be that you are both driven by the same goal, perhaps to enjoy a comfortable life together.

Your relationship may stay evenly balanced if you are two Libras, but there is a chance that you will demand too much adoration from one another. Ensure that your egos don't get in the way of love.

Potential Pitfalls: It is, however, the cardinal side of your natures that may end up marring your romance, for its effect may result in you both being somewhat self-absorbed characters who require instant gratification, which, in the Venusian realm of pleasure and romance, usually means wanting to be perpetually indulged, loved unconditionally, and preferably put on a pedestal and worshiped. This is a tough expectation for any rational, unemotional, airy Libra to live up to, however, and you may consequently each end up suspecting that your sweetheart is not totally devoted to you. This needn't be an insurmountable problem, however, because your airy element again gives each of you a need for freedom, so just imagine how suffocated you'd feel if your lover were an ultraclingy or jealously possessive person.

Libra Birth Influences

Ruling planet: Venus
Element: Air
Polarity: Masculine
Quadruplicity: Cardinal

Guiding Principle: Don't make unrealistic demands of one another.

Compatibility: ♥♥♥♥♥♥♥♡♡♡

LIBRA
SCORPIO

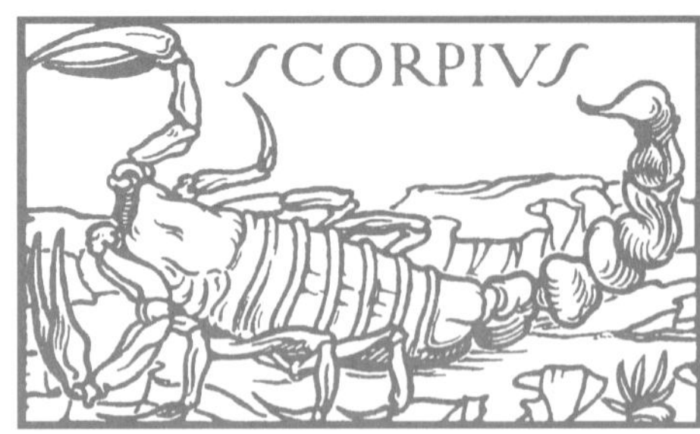

Libra Birth Influences

Ruling planet: Venus
Element: Air
Polarity: Masculine
Quadruplicity: Cardinal

If jealous Scorpio's green eyes get the better of her, you may need to dig deep to find enough patience to deal with the situation, Libra.

Scorpio Birth Influences

Ruling planet: Pluto; traditionally Mars
Element: Water
Polarity: Feminine
Quadruplicity: Fixed

Although Libra and Scorpio can have a beneficial effect on one another, with Libra encouraging the serious scorpion to lighten up, and Scorpio providing the constant devotion that romantic Libra craves, staying together may be a tall order. For while Venusian, cardinal-quadruplicity Libra can be frivolous and self-serving, and, having a masculine polarity and airy element, may be rather unthinking and unfeeling, Plutonian, fixed-sign Scorpio is typically intense and self-disciplined, as well as introspective and deeply emotional, thanks to a feminine polarity and watery element. There is consequently a real risk that Scorpio will come to regard his or her Libra lover as superficial and uncaring, and that Libra will eventually consider Scorpio a jealous jailer.

Plus Points: If you are a Scorpio who is often beset by a Plutonian and feminine, or negative, polarity's tendency to brood suspiciously, you may envy the way that your airy, Libran lover takes everything at face value, and, due to his or her masculine polarity, usually retains a positive attitude. Not only does Venus, their planetary governor, bless those born under the sign of the balance with an appreciation of the arts, but these airy, articulate *bon viveurs* can be very persuasive, so that you may often be seduced into accompanying Libra to an event that, you may be surprised to find, arouses your watery creativity. In short, charming Libra may exert a calming, relaxing, and stimulating influence over you.

There is no doubt a sentimental, Venusian side to your character that adores being adored if you are a Libra, which is why you may appreciate being the focus of your watery, fixed-quadruplicity, Scorpio sweetheart's powerful and unswerving passion. Having a go-getting, cardinal quadruplicity and intellectual element in air, perhaps you have already figured out exactly where you are headed in life, too, and because Scorpio's polarity and element are more passive than yours, may be satisfied that your lover is willing to go along with you.

Potential Pitfalls: You may be hurt by Venus-ruled, airy Libra's self-indulgent, breezy outlook if you are a Scorpio, particularly when you are in Pluto's grip and are feeling down. Indeed, Libra probably lacks your empathy, and may have little patience when you withdraw into yourself. And if you are a Libra, you may dislike being disapproved of when your airy element sends you off gallivanting, and may soon start to feel suffocated by Scorpio's possessiveness.

Guiding Principle: Work at being a committed couple, but retain your individuality.

Compatibility: ♥♥♥♥♥♥♡♡♡♡

SAGITTARIUS
LIBRA

They may have only one birth influence in common—the masculine polarity that makes both confident and outgoing—but the remaining six give Libra and Sagittarius similar characteristics, and often an irresistible mutual attraction. Libra's airy element and Sagittarius' mutable quadruplicity cause both to be verbal, intellectual types, for example, while Venus bestows a pleasure-loving attitude on Libra that often clicks with Sagittarius' fiery zest for life. Meanwhile, Jupiter blesses Sagittarius with an optimistic, expansive outlook that complements Libra's cardinal-quadruplicity, can-do attitude. Perhaps the worst that could be said is that fiery Sagittarius may feel that airy Libra lacks passion, and that tactful, Venusian Libra may be offended by Sagittarius' brutal honesty.

Plus Points: Tolerance, a clever mind, and an appetite for enjoyment may be high on your list of ideal qualities in a lover if you are a Sagittarius, in which case you may rejoice in having a Libran beloved. Because your element is fire, you may have a horror of being constrained, which Libra may well understand because his or her element of air is associated with independence, as well as with the intellect, thus satisfying your mutable-quadruplicity desire for a bright, communicative partner. In addition, air and Venus may together manifest themselves in Libra as hedonism and indulgence, which may complement your own fiery, sensation-seeking tendencies and Jupiter-inspired inclusiveness.

You may be both excited and relieved to have a Sagittarian sweetheart if you are a Libra. Excited, because Sagittarius' fiery spontaneity and enthusiasm, positive, jovial mindset, and dynamism may encourage you to shake off what few inhibitions you have to join your lover in some spur-of-the-moment fun. And relieved, because Sagittarius won't make too many emotional demands of you or sit sulking at home when you are out on the town because he or she is just as much of a free and gregarious spirit as you, thanks mainly to a mutable quadruplicity.

Potential Pitfalls: Libra's cardinal quadruplicity can cause those born under this sign to put themselves first, which may not always please you if you are a sometimes egotistical Sagittarius who may also feel disgruntled if airy Libra's mind seems to be elsewhere when you're sharing an intimate moment. As for you, Libra, your delicate, peaceable, Venusian side may sometimes shrink from fiery Sagittarius' bluntness and hot temper, and you may also find your mutable lover's restlessness tiring.

Guiding Principle: Give one another space, but don't let yourselves drift apart.

Compatibility: ♥♥♥♥♥♥♥♥♡♡

Sagittarius Birth Influences

Ruling planet: Jupiter
Element: Fire
Polarity: Masculine
Quadruplicity: Mutable

Sagittarius and Libra lovers share an optimism and lust for life that will hold them together, but Libra may become exhausted when Sagittarius leaps up and heads off yet again.

Libra Birth Influences

Ruling planet: Venus
Element: Air
Polarity: Masculine
Quadruplicity: Cardinal

LIBRA
CAPRICORN

Libra Birth Influences

Ruling planet: Venus
Element: Air
Polarity: Masculine
Quadruplicity: Cardinal

Libra and Capricorn may intimidate others with their ambition and drive. They can make a great match, with fun-loving Libra enlivening Capricorn, and the goat in turn providing his or her airy companion with stability.

Capricorn Birth Influences

Ruling planet: Saturn
Element: Earth
Polarity: Feminine
Quadruplicity: Cardinal

A glance at Libra and Capricorn's birth influences may set the alarm bells ringing, for while Venus, air, and a masculine polarity may make Libra people self-indulgent, frivolous, and outgoing, Saturn, earth, and a feminine polarity may cause Capricorn to be temperate, sensible, and reserved. They may therefore have a beneficial influence on one another, with Libra persuading Capricorn to take time out from work to play once in a while, and Capricorn curbing some of Libra's flightier instincts, but it is more likely that mutual disapproval may take its toll on their relationship. The saving grace, however, may be their shared cardinal quadruplicity, which may give both a pressing desire to improve their status in life, and a recognition that each can help the other to achieve their joint goal.

Plus Points: If you are a rather introspective, feminine-polarity Capricorn who is uncomfortable making inconsequential small talk, you must admire your airy, Libran lover's persuasive way with words, and may chuckle when you see others succumb to his or her charm. You may also be grateful that Venus-governed Libra can be remarkably tolerant of your Saturn-bestowed workaholic tendencies, yet what must really arouse your affection and respect is Libra's driving ambition, which may be disguised under a honeyed veneer, but may be obvious to you because you share it, too. Here, you may feel, is someone whose social skills and positive, masculine-polarity outlook will help you to get ahead in life.

Like your Capricorn lover, your aim may be to better yourself if you are a cardinal-quadruplicity Libra, and, as a child of Venus, maybe you yearn to live in luxury and to surround yourself with beautiful, expensive possessions. It may be clear to you that Capricorn has what it takes to be a financial success, and that together you make a complementary team, with your earthy sweetheart no doubt contributing the steadiness and resilience that you lack. In addition, a wonderful bonus may be Capricorn's earthy sensuality.

Potential Pitfalls: Extroverted, gregarious Librans like nothing better than a party at which they can flit from person to person, which may be your idea of hell if you are an inward-looking Capricorn with a much more reserved personality. And if you are a fun-loving Libra, you may weary of Capricorn's restraint, and may even find spending time alone with your down-to-earth lover dull.

Guiding Principle: Remain focused on your common vision, give and take, and allow one another a certain amount of freedom.

Compatibility:   ♥♥♥♥♥♥♡♡♡♡

AQUARIUS

LIBRA

Libra and Aquarius people often make ideal partners. Sharing as they do a masculine polarity and element of air, both are positive, bright and breezy, communicative individuals who typically give one another the space that each needs in order to stay contented. And while Venus enables Libra to accommodate Uranus-governed Aquarius' eccentricities, fixed-quadruplicity Aquarius responds by remaining loyal to Libra. Yet Aquarius' uncompromising views may sometimes test Libra's tolerance severely, and resolutely independent Aquarius may resist being manipulated or chivvied along by pushy, cardinal-quadruplicity Libra.

Plus Points: With Uranus and air—both of which are associated with the intellect—among your birth influences if you are an Aquarius, it is unlikely that you are ruled by your emotions or that you have a real rapport with those who are, which is why you may feel so comfortable with your equally airy Libran lover. Although you no doubt enjoy the creature comforts provided by sensual, Venus-ruled Libra, you may primarily value your meeting of minds, and may revel in the enthusiasm with which your masculine-polarity, cardinal-quadruplicity sweetheart usually greets the inventive theories that emanate from that trailblazing, Uranian mind of yours.

If you are a Libra, the combination of air and your pioneering, cardinal quadruplicity may manifest itself in you as an urge to forge your own way in life, which is not to say that you're a loner—far from it—merely that following in someone else's wake is not your style. You may therefore be grateful that your Aquarian beloved is just as independent as you, yet, due to his or her fixed quadruplicity, seems committed to your relationship. When alone together, you may have lots to talk about as well, for Aquarius is nothing if not an original thinker, and your cardinal quadruplicity probably fills your own head with ambitious ideas.

Potential Pitfalls: Librans can be rather self-centered, and once they have set their hearts on a goal, they are likely to pursue it with single-minded determination, which may annoy you if you are an Aquarius who figures largely in Libra's progressive plans, but, having a fixed quadruplicity, would prefer to leave things as they are. You may find Aquarius infuriatingly stubborn in such circumstances if you are a Libra, and may soon start to resent having to fit in with a lover who always does exactly what he or she pleases.

Guiding Principle: Try to think of yourselves as a couple, as well as individuals, and to give and take in equal measure.

Compatibility: ♥♥♥♥♥♥♥♥♡♡

Aquarius Birth Influences

Ruling planet: Uranus; traditionally Saturn
Element: Air
Polarity: Masculine
Quadruplicity: Fixed

If you are an Aquarius, being so independent yourself, you are not the type to be jealous of your Libra partner, but may sometimes wish that she were less of a free agent and more loyal to you.

Libra Birth Influences

Ruling planet: Venus
Element: Air
Polarity: Masculine
Quadruplicity: Cardinal

LIBRA
PISCES

Libra Birth Influences

Ruling planet: Venus
Element: Air
Polarity: Masculine
Quadruplicity: Cardinal

Influenced by Venus and Neptune, Libra and Pisces lovers may enjoy an especially tender and harmonious relationship.

Pisces Birth Influences

Ruling planet: Neptune; traditionally Jupiter
Element: Water
Polarity: Feminine
Quadruplicity: Mutable

When you consider that Venus, Libra's ruling planet, was named for the Roman goddess of love, Neptune, Pisces' governing planet, is the "higher octave of Venus," and that airy Libra is easygoing and watery Pisces, compassionate, these lovers appear made for one another. In addition, masculine-polarity, cardinal-quadruplicity Libra may boost feminine-polarity, mutable-quadruplicity Pisces' confidence and resolve, Pisces returning the favor by being supportive and flexible. Yet Libra's detachment may sometimes wound clingy, oversensitive Pisces, and Pisces' moodiness and reticence may test Libra's staying power.

Plus Points: Before you met Libra, if you are a watery, Neptune-ruled Pisces, you may have been longing for a soulmate, in which case the arrival of Libra in your life may have seemed like a dream come true. The effect that your respective planetary governors has on each of you may result in you being a pair of lovebirds who are in instinctive harmony, with Libra's Venus-bestowed gentleness and indulgence arousing your own, Neptunian tenderness. Thanks to Libra's positive, masculine polarity, the breeziness that comes from having air as an element, and the initiative that is the gift of a cardinal quadruplicity, your lover may also have a talent for raising your spirits and giving you purpose when the confusing interaction of your birth influences have left you feeling negative and muddled.

Watery, Neptunian Pisces' deep and unselfish love for you must both gratify and satisfy you if you are a Venusian Libra, whose cardinal quadruplicity may make you rather self-centered. You may also be reaping one of the major benefits of having a sweetheart with a mutable quadruplicity, namely adaptability. Indeed, it must be wonderful to have a partner who not only puts you first, but hates it just as much as you when rare disagreements sour your romance, who shares your appreciation of the arts, and tries to see beauty in everything, thereby demonstrating the close affinity between Venus and Neptune.

Potential Pitfalls: Airy Libra is almost certainly not as sensitive as you if you are a watery Pisces, and is no doubt more outgoing, too, so that there may be times when your lover inadvertently upsets you by flitting off when you are feeling emotionally fragile. And if dejected, neglected Pisces regularly becomes tearful and uncommunicative, you may eventually lack the patience to spend hours devoting yourself to coaxing a smile out of your lover if you are a Libra.

Guiding Principle: Try to find a happy medium between closeness and independence.

Compatibility: ♥♥♥♥♥♥♥♡♡♡

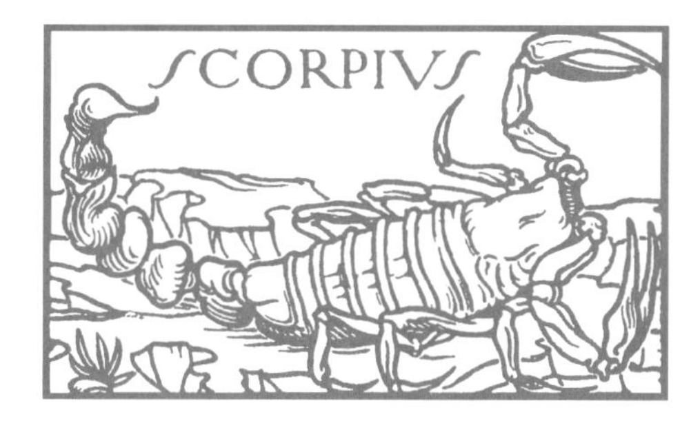

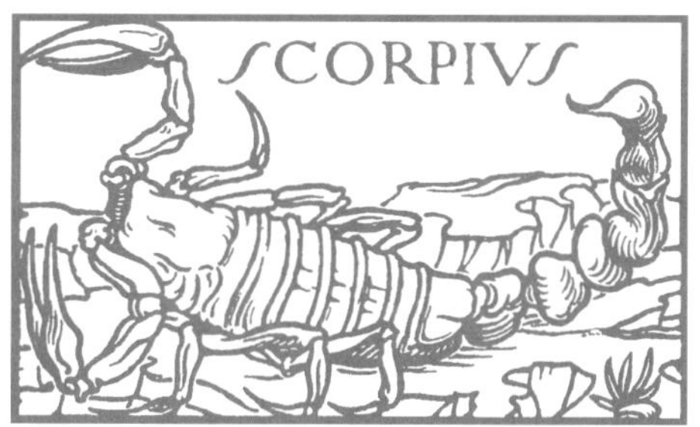

SCORPIO
SCORPIO

Trust is vital to the success of a Scorpio–Scorpio romance, for only then will a pair of self-protective scorpions throw caution to the wind, open up their hearts to one another, and live happily, empathetically, and ardently ever after. But should this crucial ingredient be missing, their feminine-polarity reserve may never be fully breached; their suspicious, Plutonian minds may increase their watery insecurity; and their fixed-quadruplicity inflexibility may make it difficult for them to change their negative mindsets, so that both may end up feeling isolated and miserable.

Plus Points: Assuming that you and your Scorpio sweetheart have progressed to the stage in your relationship where you are both certain that your love for one another is true, then you are probably in seventh heaven if you are also a zodiacal scorpion. While your shared primary planetary ruler and feminine polarity may cause you both to be wary and unforthcoming, initially at least, in your dealings with others, now that you have found someone who clearly cares deeply about you, you may have deemed it safe to drop your guard and unleash the pent-up torrent of love bestowed on you by your emotional, watery element. Having your passion reciprocated must be blissful, as must having a lover who understands you so well and sympathizes with you, and, because you share a fixed, or constant, quadruplicity, whom you also believe will remain faithful to you.

Potential Pitfalls: If you are a Scorpio whose beloved is a fellow scorpion, it may be that your powerful, watery intuition gives you the distinct sense that your Pluto-governed lover is holding something back or is not being entirely honest with you. If so, rather than shrug off your hunch or calmly confront Scorpio, the interaction of your constrained, feminine polarity, distrustful Pluto, and your anxiety-inducing element of water may make you worry that he or she is cheating on you and to look for evidence of infidelity. In fact, feminine-polarity Scorpio may simply be preoccupied with nothing more sinister than a work problem, but won't fail to notice, and be wounded by, the way that you have simultaneously withdrawn into yourself while watching him or her like a hawk. And because you both share a fixed, or unchanging, quadruplicity, once set, it may be hard to break this pattern of mistrust, resentment, and mutual alienation.

Guiding Principle: Try not to keep secrets from one another or to jump to false conclusions.

Compatibility: ♥♥♥♥♥♥♥♡♡♡

Scorpio Birth Influences

Ruling planet: Pluto; traditionally Mars
Element: Water
Polarity: Feminine
Quadruplicity: Fixed

Any secrecy in a Scorpio–Scorpio romance could spell the end of your relationship. Without trust, you have nothing, so treat your lover as you would want to be treated yourself.

Scorpio Birth Influences

Ruling planet: Pluto; traditionally Mars
Element: Water
Polarity: Feminine
Quadruplicity: Fixed

SCORPIO
SAGITTARIUS

Scorpio Birth Influences

Ruling planet: Pluto; traditionally Mars
Element: Water
Polarity: Feminine
Quadruplicity: Fixed

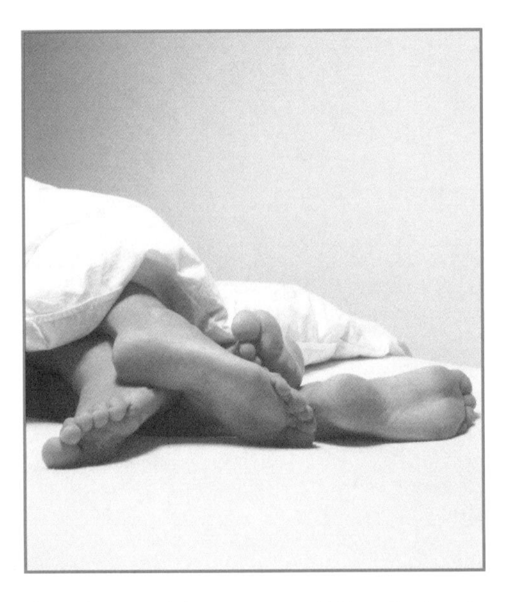

Opposites are said to attract, and if fiery Sagittarius and intensely ardent Scorpio bring out the best in each other, this could be a passionate, though perhaps turbulent, love affair.

Sagittarius Birth Influences

Ruling planet: Jupiter
Element: Fire
Polarity: Masculine
Quadruplicity: Mutable

Scorpio and Sagittarius lovers could hardly be more different. For a start, whereas Scorpio's primary planetary ruler is Pluto, named for the dark and enigmatic Roman god of the underworld, Sagittarius' is Jupiter, the planet that the Romans associated with their fatherly, benevolent, sky god. Scorpio's element is furthermore sensitive water, while Sagittarius' is thoughtless fire; Scorpio's feminine polarity equals introversion, and Sagittarius' masculine polarity, extroversion; and, finally, their fixed quadrupicity causes zodiacal scorpions to be constant, in contrast to Sagittarius' restlessness-bestowing, mutable quadruplicity. If love brings out the best of their birth influences, all should be well, but there is otherwise a real danger that this pair's initial attraction will turn into mutual aversion.

Plus Points: It is your fiery element that makes you hot-blooded if you are a Sagittarius, and it may consequently seem as though you have hit the jackpot in getting together with your Scorpio lover, within whom the passion of Mars may be amplified by the intensity of Pluto. Scorpio's passive, feminine polarity, emotionally giving element of water, and fixed quadruplicity may result in your lover being totally focused on you, too, which you may find highly gratifying if your attention-demanding element gives you an appetite for adoration.

Although your physical compatibility must be a bonus if you are a Scorpio whose beloved is a Sagittarius, you may value your fiery sweetheart's warmth and vitality even more. Indeed, if isolating Pluto, insecurity-inducing water, and your constrained, feminine polarity together frequently have a negative effect on you, being exposed to Sagittarius' jovial optimism, fiery energy, and masculine-polarity confidence may send your spirits soaring. You are probably grateful for Sagittarius' adaptability, too, the gift of his or her mutable quadruplicity.

Potential Pitfalls: Scorpios can be fearsomely possessive, which may not suit you at all if you are an outgoing, variety-loving Sagittarius who hates to feel tied down. Patience is not one of your strong points either, so that when you are confronted by a brooding Scorpio whose jealousy has been aroused by an innocent conversation that you had with an attractive someone, you may not feel inclined to stick around to suffer more of the silent treatment. And if you are a Scorpio, you may feel hurt that your lover tends to put distance between you rather than reassuring you that your fears are groundless, and may conclude that Sagittarius no longer cares for you.

Guiding Principle: Neither suffocate nor neglect one another.

Compatibility: ♥♥♥♥♡♡♡♡♡♡

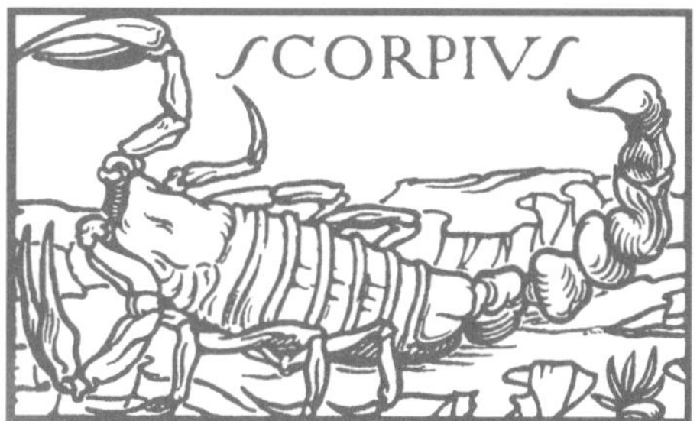

CAPRICORN

SCORPIO

Scorpio and Capricorn's courtship is likely to be prolonged, for their shared, feminine polarity can make both rather cautious and reserved, and Scorpio may be triply so, due to the extra input of unforthcoming Pluto and self-protective water. Yet once they have established a romantic connection, the astrological omens look good for an enduring relationship. Watery, fixed-quadruplicity Scorpio's emotional support and unwavering commitment may fuel the saturnine goat's own devotion, for instance, Scorpio in turn reveling in the security that comes from having such a dependable and aspirational partner in earthy, cardinal-quadruplicity Capricorn. Some excitement may be lacking from their liaison, it is true, but then neither typically sets great store by that.

Plus Points: If you are a Capricorn, your long-term goal may be material success, thanks to the interaction of ambitious Saturn and your driving, cardinal quadruplicity, in which case you may have found your perfect other half in Scorpio. This may be partly because your lover's fixed quadruplicity provides great staying power, and partly because the Pluto-governed scorpion understands that transforming one's fortunes is something that can't be accomplished overnight. As a result, your sweetheart may be willing to put up with your long working hours, and because Scorpio has an empathetic element in water, may listen sympathetically to your woes when you've suffered a setback.

Your watery element may have a tendency to cast you adrift on a sea of emotions if you are a Scorpio, and usually pessimistic ones, which is one of the downsides of having a dark and gloomy planetary ruler and feminine, or negative, polarity. You may therefore consider your steady, earthy Capricorn beloved a rock of stability, and someone whose logical outlook has the power to dispel your more irrational fears. You may also be grateful for Saturn-ruled, cardinal Capricorn's sense of responsibility and determination to ensure that your life together is comfortable, and a thrilling bonus may be the earthy sensuality that matches your own passion.

Potential Pitfalls: Watery Scorpio can be oversensitive, while you are a straightforward type if you are an earthy Capricorn. There is therefore a danger that expressing the truth as you see it may injure Scorpio's feelings if your lover believes that you are criticizing him or her. And if you are a Scorpio, there may be occasions when you feel that hardworking Capricorn cares more about his or her career than you.

Guiding Principle: Remain focused on your future as a couple.

Compatibility: ♥♥♥♥♥♥♥♥♡♡

Capricorn Birth Influences

Ruling planet: Saturn
Element: Earth
Polarity: Feminine
Quadruplicity: Cardinal

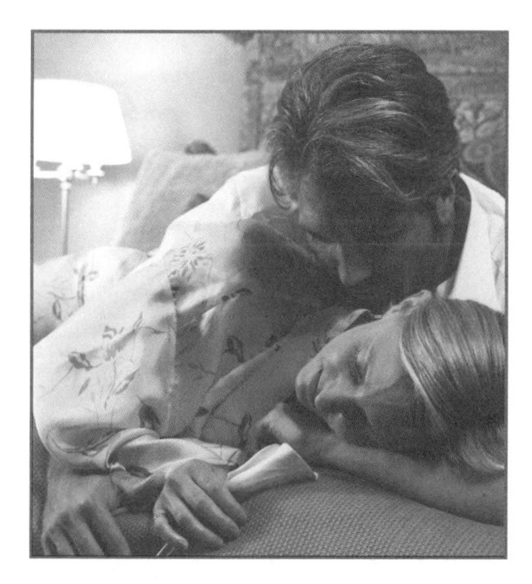

You probably treat your beloved Scorpio with respect, Capricorn, and are no doubt glad of the unwavering commitment that you receive in return. If you can maintain this equilibrium, your relationship looks set to last.

Scorpio Birth Influences

Ruling planet: Pluto; traditionally Mars
Element: Water
Polarity: Feminine
Quadruplicity: Fixed

SCORPIO

AQUARIUS

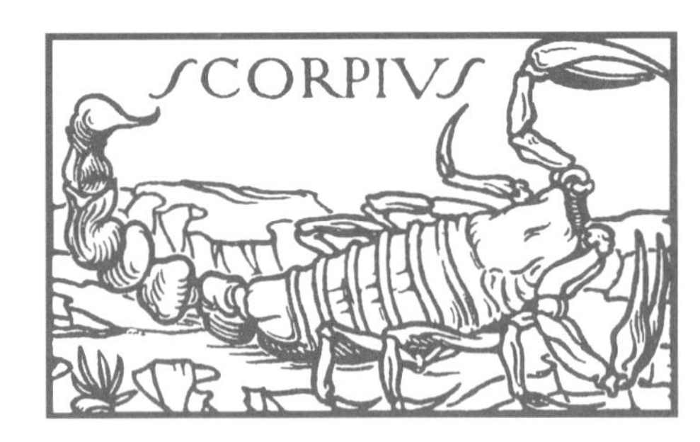

Scorpio Birth Influences
Ruling planet: Pluto; traditionally Mars
Element: Water
Polarity: Feminine
Quadruplicity: Fixed

When you start to feel the daggers of Scorpio's resentful glare, Aquarius, then it is perhaps time that you paid more attention to her. But Scorpio, try not to swamp Aquarius with emotion.

Aquarius Birth Influences
Ruling planet: Uranus; traditionally Saturn
Element: Air
Polarity: Masculine
Quadruplicity: Fixed

Their common fixed, or constant, quadruplicity may be the magic ingredient that keeps a pair of Scorpio and Aquarius lovers together forever; that, and the aura of mystery that Plutonian, feminine-polarity Scorpio exudes, which may never lose its power to intrigue curious, airy Aquarius, and the intuitive way in which watery Scorpio understands that masculine-polarity Aquarius' thoughtlessness is not intended to hurt. Even so, airy, communicative Aquarius may be frustrated by Scorpio's reticence, while watery, sensitive Scorpio may end up feeling dissatisfied, and even alienated, by the water-carrier's emotional detachment.

Plus Points: If you are a typical Aquarius, your element of air may cause you to be primarily interested in others' minds, while the influence of Uranus, your ruling planet, may give you an affinity for those who think unconventionally. If so, your Scorpio lover may be a never-ending source of fascination, for as well as being shrouded in a cloak of feminine-polarity reserve that you can't help wanting to penetrate, you may occasionally succeed in catching a glimpse of a strange, profoundly deep, process of metamorphosis at work, in which case you've seen interaction of the scorpion's unfathomable element of water and transformational Pluto. You no doubt also appreciate the caring and emotional support that are characteristics of Scorpio's watery element, along with the faithfulness that, as the gift of a fixed quadruplicity, may match yours.

You may consider your Aquarius sweetheart's positive, masculine-polarity outlook and airy calm wonderful qualities if you are a Scorpio whose watery element can send you bouncing back and forth between emotional extremes. And you may be particularly grateful for Aquarius' talent for drawing you out of yourself and distracting you from Pluto's gloom-inducing influence, be it by encouraging you to talk or by sharing his or her oddball, Uranian ideas. Above all, however, you may thank your lucky stars that fixed-quadruplicity Aquarius is loyal to you.

Potential Pitfalls: Watery Scorpio may make emotional demands that you are incapable of fulfilling if you are an airy, impersonal Aquarius, a failing that may disappoint you if you are a watery Scorpio who longs for a meeting of hearts rather than of intellects. A conflict between controlling water and freedom-seeking air may further arouse Scorpio's possessive instincts, which may have a suffocating effect on Aquarius, thereby increasing the distance between you.

Guiding Principle: Don't expect the impossible of one another.

Compatibility: ♥♥♥♥♥♡♡♡♡♡

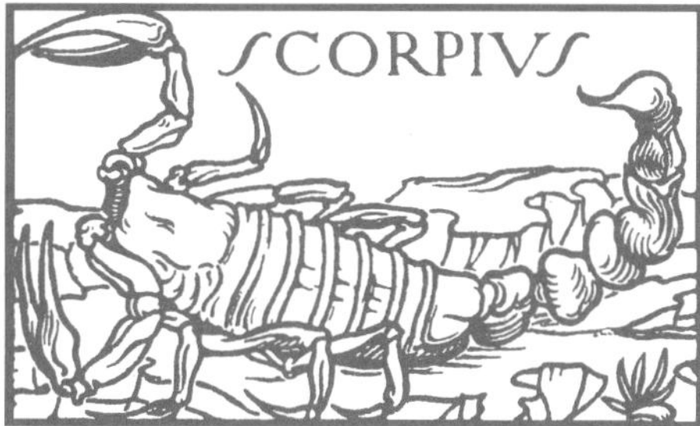

PISCES
SCORPIO

Despite their joint feminine, or reserved, polarity, the transcendental love that Scorpio and Pisces may feel for one another has the power to enable them to cast off their inherent caution and blossom spectacularly. Why? Well, the answer lies primarily in their mutual element of water, which infuses each with profound emotions and overwhelming joy when their feelings are reciprocated. A few blips may occur in this relationship as a consequence of Pluto-ruled Scorpio's secretiveness and Neptunian Pisces' desire for them to be as one, or fixed-quadruplicity Scorpio's dislike of change and mutable Pisces' appetite for variety, but given their mutual sympathy, their differences are unlikely to be disastrous.

Pisces Birth Influences

Ruling planet: Neptune; traditionally Jupiter
Element: Water
Polarity: Feminine
Quadruplicity: Mutable

Plus Points: You may have been in seventh heaven ever since the day that you and Scorpio revealed your tenderness for one another if you are a Pisces, for your element of water may bless Scorpio with as caring and compassionate a nature as yours, while the combination of intense Pluto and ardent Mars may make the scorpion the most passionate of lovers. And because Scorpio's quadruplicity is fixed, or constant, his or her unwavering devotion to you may steady and reassure you when your own, mutable quadruplicity fills you with restlessness.

You may be intuitive, if you are a Scorpio, yet your Pisces sweetheart may be doubly so, for not only does he or she share your watery element, but the additional input of Neptune may result in an intuition that is verging on the psychic, an additional gift of Neptune no doubt being total unselfishness. As a naturally taciturn child of Pluto, your heart may therefore melt when you realize that sympathetic Pisces seems to understand you without words needing to be spoken, and would furthermore do anything to make you happy, aided by his or her adaptability-bestowing, mutable quadruplicity.

A watery pairing of Scorpio and Pisces lovers can be blissfully supportive. Thanks to their mutual tenderness and empathy, any emotional storms are quickly quieted.

Potential Pitfalls: Among the few things that may slightly disappoint you about Scorpio, if you are a Pisces, may be the inflexibility that comes from having a fixed quadruplicity, particularly if it manifests itself as an insistence on staying put when you are experiencing a mutable-quadruplicity desire for a change of scene. And if you are a Scorpio, a minor quibble that you may have with Pisces is his or her need to be included, or at least be told about, every aspect of your life, when it may be hard for you to overcome your Plutonian urge to keep some details to yourself.

Guiding Principle: Keep on empathizing with one another!

Compatibility: ♥♥♥♥♥♥♥♥♡♡

Scorpio Birth Influences

Ruling planet: Pluto; traditionally Mars
Element: Water
Polarity: Feminine
Quadruplicity: Fixed

SAGITTARIUS
SAGITTARIUS

Sagittarius Birth Influences
Ruling planet: Jupiter
Element: Fire
Polarity: Masculine
Quadruplicity: Mutable

One thing's for sure: when two energetic, exuberant, variety-loving Sagittarian individuals fall for one another, their love life will never be dull, for all of their birth influences are associated with burning vitality and rampant restlessness. Indeed, they typically begin their romance fired up by their spontaneous element and fueled by the boundless optimism of Jupiter and the vigor of their masculine polarity, but the question is, will the effect that their mutable, or changeable, quadruplicity has on each enable them to adapt to the changing dynamics within their relationship, or will they end up seeking the excitement that they crave elsewhere?

There is probably never a dull moment if you and your partner are both Sagittarians. Remember to spend some quality time together, away from the whirl of your individual social lives.

Plus Points: When you first met, if you and your lover were both born under the sign of Sagittarius, you probably both felt an instant attraction, and, having an impetuous, fiery element in common, it may not have been long before you became an item. The characteristics that you no doubt love about one another the most include the confidence that comes of having a masculine, or uninhibited, polarity; the broad-mindedness and willingness to try anything that is the gift of Jupiter; the appetite for change that is part and parcel of having a mutable quadruplicity; and, of course, the passion and spontaneity bestowed by a fiery element. It may therefore seem as though you are perfectly matched, and that with your fellow Sagittarius by your side, your future looks thrilling.

Potential Pitfalls: There is definitely a danger that the flames that feed your mutual infatuation may gradually flicker, die down, and eventually be reduced to embers if you and your beloved are both zodiacal archers, although not as a result of the effect of loyal, magnanimous Jupiter. No, the warning signals lie firstly in your mutual, fiery need for stimulation, for after an intense period of getting to know one another, your personalities may no longer hold any surprises, at which point your outgoing, masculine polarity and diversity-seeking, mutable quadruplicity may come to the fore. This may be the crux of your relationship, for if you are willing to follow first one's lead, and then the other's—and your mutable quadruplicity suggests that you are each capable of being flexible—being exposed to new experiences by leap-frogging in this way may satisfy your fiery impulsiveness and mutable desire for change. If you head off in different directions, however, be warned that there will be plenty of alluring people in your respective paths.

Sagittarius Birth Influences
Ruling planet: Jupiter
Element: Fire
Polarity: Masculine
Quadruplicity: Mutable

Guiding Principle: Resist the urge to stray by planning electrifying activities together.

Compatibility: ♥♥♥♥♥♥♥♡♡♡

CAPRICORN
SAGITTARIUS

Sagittarius and Capricorn would be guaranteed a long and satisfying future together if only the archer had more staying power and the goat were more flexible, but unfortunately it is the earthy goat who is blessed with constancy, and the mutable-quadruplicity archer who is the adaptable one (although these characteristics can still work to their mutual advantage). The main stumbling block in a relationship between these two is that fiery, mutable Sagittarius hates to feel tied down and thrives on variety, whereas earthy Capricorn prizes stability and is single-minded. It doesn't help that Sagittarius' polarity is masculine, or active, while Capricorn's is feminine, or passive, nor that the Jupiter-ruled archer thinks big and the Saturn-governed goat can be limiting. Still, where there is love, there is always a way, and plenty of long-standing Sagittarius–Capricorn couples would attest to that!

Plus Points: The combined influence of sober Saturn, sensible earth, and an ambitious, cardinal quadruplicity may focus you on the serious business of getting ahead in life if you are a Capricorn, yet even hard-working goats need to relax once in a while, and your fiery, enthusiastic, Sagittarian lover may have a rare ability to encourage you to release some of your inhibitions, let your hair down, and simply enjoy yourself. The qualities that you may treasure the most in your Sagittarian beloved, however, may be Jupiter's optimism and a masculine polarity's positive attitude, which may boost your confidence when severe Saturn and your own feminine, or negative, polarity have depressed you and sapped your self-belief.

As for you, Sagittarius, the Capricornian characteristics that you may especially appreciate are your earthy sweetheart's patience and dependability, which may mean that he or she is always waiting for you when you've been swept away by a spontaneous impulse and are consequently late for your date. And another thrilling bonus of having an earthy lover may be the sensuality that arouses your own fiery passion. But it is Capricorn's cardinal quadruplicity that may give you a direct connection with your beloved, for penetrate that feminine-polarity reserve, and you may find that he or she is bursting with bright, aspirational ideas that ignite your interest.

Potential Pitfalls: After a honeymoon period, mutable-quadruplicity Sagittarius may prove too unpredictable for earthy, steady Capricorn, while the archer may conclude that Capricorn cannot provide the excitement and space that are vital to the happiness of any Sagittarius.

Guiding Principle: Work on taking a leaf out of one another's book.

Compatibility: ♥ ♥ ♥ ♡ ♡ ♡ ♡ ♡ ♡ ♡

Capricorn Birth Influences

Ruling planet: Saturn
Element: Earth
Polarity: Feminine
Quadruplicity: Cardinal

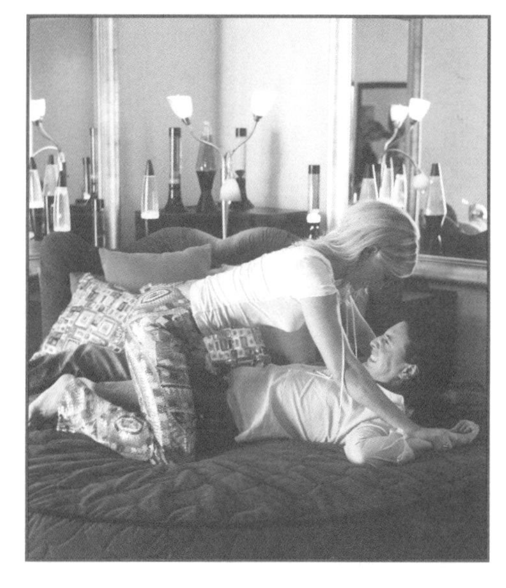

If you persist in trying to pin Sagittarius down, Capricorn, you may find yourself alone. And Sagittarius, try to consider the effect that your fiery actions may have on your earthy partner.

Sagittarius Birth Influences

Ruling planet: Jupiter
Element: Fire
Polarity: Masculine
Quadruplicity: Mutable

SAGITTARIUS
AQUARIUS

Sagittarius Birth Influences

Ruling planet: Jupiter
Element: Fire
Polarity: Masculine
Quadruplicity: Mutable

Once Aquarius and Sagittarius have struck a balance between independence and companionship, they should be in step for the rest of their lives.

Aquarius Birth Influences

Ruling planet: Uranus; traditionally Saturn
Element: Air
Polarity: Masculine
Quadruplicity: Fixed

A love affair between Sagittarius and Aquarius may appear unconventional to outsiders, yet these two definitely have a strong affinity, even if it isn't that romantic and the only birth influence that they have in common is their extrovert, masculine polarity. Looking closer, broad-minded Sagittarius has no trouble embracing Aquarius' radical ideas, and just as the fiery archer resists being controlled, so the airy water-carrier demands freedom. And while Sagittarius is adaptable, Aquarius repays the favor with loyalty. All of this should be enough to keep these two together, as long as they make an effort to devote time to one another.

Plus Points: Once you have found someone with whom you believe you can spend the rest of your life, your fixed quadruplicity may fill you with faithfulness if you are an Aquarius, and your Sagittarian lover may certainly seem worth hanging on to. Having an airy element and pioneering, masculine polarity, liberty of both thought and deed may be vital to you, which Sagittarius may understand because he or she is probably the same, and is also blessed with the easygoing attitude that is the gift of a mutable quadruplicity, as is an interest in intellectual matters that may match your own, air-bestowed appetites. Indeed, best of all may be the positive response that you receive when you air your inventive, Uranus-inspired theories, which Jupiter-governed, fiery Aquarius may not only accept, but creatively expand.

If you are a Sagittarius, you may similarly be grateful that your Aquarian sweetheart doesn't try to change or restrict you, and what may really thrill you is the way in which he or she satisfies your fiery need for stimulation. For while your mutable quadruplicity may give you a craving for variety, so Uranus-ruled Aquarius may supply a never-ending stream of unpredictable notions and suggestions, thereby firing up the enthusiasm that is a characteristic of your element. The correspondence between your quadruplicity and Aquarius' element in particular may also enrich your liaison, in that you may both be sociable, analytical, and communicative types, so that after an evening spent with friends, you may have great fun dissecting their characters.

Potential Pitfalls: Although airy Aquarius can be emotionally detached, and fiery Sagittarius, attention-seeking, these characteristics shouldn't threaten your relationship. Be warned, however, that indulging your mutual taste for freedom may diminish your sense of togetherness.

Guiding Principle: Retain your individuality, but also ensure that you remain a committed couple.

Compatibility: ♥♥♥♥♥♥♥♥♡♡

PISCES

SAGITTARIUS

Before Neptune was discovered, Jupiter ruled Pisces, as well as Sagittarius, and not only does the planet associated with optimism continue to influence the Piscean personality, but Neptune's contribution is idealism. At the outset of their romance, it is therefore likely that Sagittarius and Pisces wholeheartedly believe that they will live happily ever after, and that their joint, diversity-loving, mutable quadruplicity will prompt them to find their differences refreshing. Yet it may not be long before fiery, masculine-polarity Sagittarius feels suffocated by watery, feminine-polarity Pisces' clinginess or sensitive Pisces is wounded by Sagittarius' craving for freedom, ultimately spelling the end of their affection for one another.

Plus Points: If you are a Neptune-governed Pisces who has spent your life looking for the perfect partner, it may seem as though your search has come to an end now that you've met your Sagittarian sweetheart. Like you, Jupiter-ruled Sagittarius may tend to look on the bright side, and when the interaction of confusion-inducing Neptune and your insecurity-bestowing, watery element have caused you to withdraw into yourself in typical feminine-polarity fashion, your beloved may have a talent for enlisting his or her masculine, or positive, polarity and fiery warmth to draw you out again. Having as you do a mutable quadruplicity in common, you may also be grateful that Sagittarius shares your enjoyment of change.

It is your fiery element that may make you relish receiving attention and admiration if you are a Sagittarius, in which case you may revel in watery Pisces' adoration and may be gratified by his or her Neptunian propensity to think the best of you. And because spontaneous fire and your uninhibited, masculine polarity may give you the urge to do exactly as you please, you may be delighted that Pisces usually gladly goes along with you, for which you have unselfish Neptune, your lover's giving element and passive polarity, and a mutable-quadruplicity's flexibility to thank.

Potential Pitfalls: You may have sympathy with your Sagittarian lover's restlessness if you are a Pisces, for your shared mutable quadruplicity may have the same effect on you, but may be hurt when your watery intuition tells you that your fiery lover is burning to spend some time apart from you. Indeed, Neptunian, watery Pisces' longing for constant togetherness may become increasingly unbearable if you are a fiery, independent Sagittarius who cannot stand feeling tied down.

Guiding Principle: Try to tread the fine line between being a couple and retaining your individuality.

Compatibility: ♥♥♥♥♥♡♡♡♡♡

Pisces Birth Influences

Ruling planet: Neptune; traditionally Jupiter
Element: Water
Polarity: Feminine
Quadruplicity: Mutable

If you are a Pisces, are you anxious when your Sagittarian lover does not come home at the expected time? For your relationship to last, you should not expect her to give you her undivided attention for long. And Sagittarius, try to take Pisces' sensitive feelings into consideration.

Sagittarius Birth Influences

Ruling planet: Jupiter
Element: Fire
Polarity: Masculine
Quadruplicity: Mutable

CAPRICORN
CAPRICORN

Capricorn Birth Influences
Ruling planet: Saturn
Element: Earth
Polarity: Feminine
Quadruplicity: Cardinal

Unless they were also born under the sign of the zodiacal goat, friends of a Capricorn couple may think that this pair's bond is more like a working relationship than a love affair, and in some respects, they'd be right, for these individuals are united in their cardinal-quadruplicity ambition to better themselves, while Saturn gives them the conviction that there are no short-cuts to success, and that hard work is required if they are to attain their common aim. Yet however goal-oriented or status-conscious they may be, sharing an earthy element and a feminine polarity makes a stable domestic life important to them both, and behind closed doors, a double dose of earthy sensuality may belie the undemonstrative front that they present to outsiders.

Plus Points: If you and your Capricorn lover have dated people with different star signs who made impossible demands of you, you may both be thrilled and relieved to have fallen in love with one another. You must be on the same sensible, saturnine wavelength for a start, and may not only tolerate, but approve of, each other's cardinal-quadruplicity, go-getting attitude, knowing that you are each striving to ensure that you will enjoy a comfortable, financially secure future together. And whereas you may know from experience that a masculine-polarity partner has little patience with your cautious, thoughtful approach, your feminine-polarity, Capricorn beloved may be just as prudent as you, and, thanks to your mutual element of earth, equally patient and dependable, too. A wonderful bonus may furthermore be your physical compatibility, another gift to you both from your earthy element that may bless you with some magical moments that put a new spring in your step and make you eager to tackle anything that the day throws at you.

Capricorns can be serious souls, but there is probably a strongly sensual side to their relationship, which, with their mutual sincerity, can make for a deeply fulfilling life together.

Potential Pitfalls: The inevitable danger, if you are two Capricorns who have jobs or make an active contribution to your community, is that you may both devote so many hours to your work that time together falls by the wayside. That's not all, either: because your feminine polarity may result in you being inward-looking types who lack the intuition associated with the element of water, for instance, when you are bottling up your worries, your sweetheart may have no inkling that anything is troubling you. (Remember the saying, "A problem shared is a problem halved?")

Guiding Principle: Safeguard your happiness by scheduling regular downtime together and keeping the channels of communication open.

Compatibility: ♥♥♥♥♥♥♥♥♡♡

Capricorn Birth Influences
Ruling planet: Saturn
Element: Earth
Polarity: Feminine
Quadruplicity: Cardinal

AQUARIUS

CAPRICORN

A glance at their respective birth influences suggests that Capricorn and Aquarius couldn't be more different, and consequently ill-suited, yet a closer examination suggests that this need not be the case. It may be true that Saturn-ruled, cardinal-quadruplicity Capricorn is career-minded, but then airy Aquarius needs to retain a certain amount of independence, and neither is emotionally needy, so that each may willingly allow the other the space that they need to pursue their individual priorities, while also remaining mutually faithful, thanks to the combination of Saturn, earth, and Aquarius' fixed quadruplicity. And although masculine-polarity, Uranus-ruled Aquarius may be more enterprising than cautious, feminine-polarity Capricorn, that can work to their advantage, too.

Plus Points: One of the best things about having an earthy Capricorn for a lover, if you are a somewhat scatter-brained, airy Aquarius, may be that you can depend on him on her, be it to wait patiently for you when you've lost track of time and are running late for your date, or to take care of practicalities when your head is in the clouds. Other benefits may include Capricorn's mature, Saturn-bestowed view of your relationship, earthy trust, and cardinal-quadruplicity preoccupation with his or her own goals, as a result of which your sweetheart may be happy to give you the freedom of action that is so vital to your sense of well-being.

If you are a Capricorn whose beloved is an Aquarius, you may similarly be grateful that your lover doesn't complain of feeling neglected when you've put in extra hours at work. On the contrary, your sweetheart's airy, Uranian curiosity about your long-term plans may give you a warm glow, and you may also appreciate Aquarius' analytical way of thinking and unorthodox suggestions when a stumbling block has slowed your progress. And because Aquarius has a masculine, or positive, polarity, he or she may often boost your confidence when your feminine polarity has made you feel especially inhibited or negative.

Potential Pitfalls: Apart from the danger that you may end up having more of a platonic friendship than a romance if your focus on your separate interests means that you see little of one another, there may be a fundamental character clash to overcome. It may be that saturnine Capricorn's natural conservatism is at odds with Uranus-ruled Aquarius' unconventional mindset, for instance, or perhaps that feminine-polarity Capricorn is too retiring for outgoing Aquarius.

Guiding Principle: Remain free agents, but not at the expense of your togetherness.

Compatibility: ♥♥♥♥♥♥♡♡♡♡

Aquarius Birth Influences

Ruling planet: Uranus; traditionally Saturn
Element: Air
Polarity: Masculine
Quadruplicity: Fixed

♅ ♄

Your Capricorn lover is probably steady, loyal, and independent, all of which you may love if you are an airy Aquarius who needs a great deal of freedom, but appreciates practical support.

Capricorn Birth Influences

Ruling planet: Saturn
Element: Earth
Polarity: Feminine
Quadruplicity: Cardinal

CAPRICORN
PISCES

Capricorn Birth Influences

Ruling planet: Saturn
Element: Earth
Polarity: Feminine
Quadruplicity: Cardinal

If you are an unforthcoming Capricorn, you may be relieved that Pisces understands you implicitly, without you having to articulate your needs. But Pisces probably needs reassurance once in a while, so don't forget to ask how he or she is feeling.

Pisces Birth Influences

Ruling planet: Neptune; traditionally Jupiter
Element: Water
Polarity: Feminine
Quadruplicity: Mutable

Capricorn and Pisces may each see the devoted lover that they have been looking for in the other, if not the ideal soulmate that exists only in their dreams. While Saturn-ruled, earthy Capricorn is committed and constant, Neptune-governed, watery Pisces is empathetic and loving, and whereas cardinal-quadruplicity Capricorn gives them a mutual target to aim for, mutable-quadruplicity Pisces is eminently capable of adapting to Capricorn's down-to-earth ways. Their common feminine polarity may cause them to be reticent, however, so that both may bottle up their dissatisfaction should Capricorn's matter-of-fact view of their relationship upset sentimental Pisces, or Pisces' mood swings unsettle even-tempered Capricorn.

Plus Points: Above all, you may be thankful for the sense of stability that you may have been reveling in ever since you met your Capricorn lover if you are a Pisces whose watery element and mutable quadruplicity may make you feel insecure and a helpless victim of your fluctuating emotions. It is the joint influence of earth and Saturn that may result in Capricorn being loyal and dependable, and, thanks to your sweetheart's ambitious, cardinal quadruplicity, he or she may already have mapped out your future together, thereby giving you the belief that you will enjoy lifelong happiness. And if you have experienced earthy Capricorn's sensuality, you may feel that your beloved feels as close to you as you do to him or her.

If you are a feminine-polarity Capricorn, you may find it hard to open up to others, with the exception, no doubt, of your Piscean lover. Not only does Pisces share your polarity, but a double dose of Neptunian and watery intuition may give him or her an almost spooky insight into your feelings, as well as an endearing gift for comforting you when you've had a tough day. Perhaps best of all, if your cardinal quadruplicity fills you with the urge to dedicate yourself to achieving demanding life goals, Neptunian, mutable-quadruplicity Pisces may appear willing to set aside his or her own aspirations in order to support you.

Potential Pitfalls: However much you may appreciate Capricorn's steadiness and reliability if you are a Pisces, you may be deeply disappointed that making tender gestures is alien to his or her nature. But then if you are an unsentimental Capricorn, you may be irritated by what you perceive to be Pisces' obsession with romance, and may dislike the morose silences into which your sweetheart descends if you've supposedly neglected his or her feelings.

Guiding Principle: Tactfully explain your needs to one another.

Compatibility: ♥♥♥♥♥♥♥♡♡♡

AQUARIUS
AQUARIUS

The astrological prognosis for an Aquarius–Aquarius romance is very promising indeed. "Romance" is perhaps the wrong word to use to describe the liaison between two Aquarius lovers, however, for a meeting of minds is typically more important to these Uranus-ruled, airy individuals than fiery passion, an earthy, sensual attachment, or a watery, emotional bond. Even so, these lovers are likely to remain true to one another precisely because they find each other so unpredictable, interesting, and challenging. Yet there is nevertheless a danger that they may not think of themselves as a couple, and it follows that when both consider themselves free agents, plenty of tempting opportunities to stray may present themselves.

Aquarius Birth Influences
Ruling planet: Uranus; traditionally Saturn
Element: Air
Polarity: Masculine
Quadruplicity: Fixed

Plus Points: If you are an Aquarius who has hooked up with a fellow Aquarius, you may be thanking your lucky stars. You may have a fixed, or faithful, quadruplicity, but may know from experience that you find neediness, possessiveness, or dullness a complete turn-off in a lover. This is why you may be so relieved that your Aquarian sweetheart both demands and allows you freedom of thought and action, thanks to your joint, airy element, which may also bless each of you with an intellectual curiosity that Uranus, your common ruling planet, excites and fulfills in equal measure by infusing you both with radical notions that your masculine polarity makes you unafraid to express. As airy, talkative individuals, you may be constantly swapping invigorating ideas that others may consider shocking, as they may your supposedly unconventional relationship, but then neither of you cares about others' opinions, do you?

Inquisitive Aquarians may recoil from the constraints of conventional romantic relationships, but two Aquarians may understand one another well enough to live together happily ever after.

Potential Pitfalls: Although your shared fixed quadruplicity may make you Aquarian lovers loyal to each other, it may also cause you to be equally strong-willed, so that if you have a difference of opinion, neither of you may be willing to concede that the other has a valid point, causing a rare breakdown in communication between you. And if you each consequently feel the need to put space between you and follow your airy, sociable instincts, there is a risk that one—or both—of you may encounter a stranger who intrigues or inspires you enough to want to get to know him or her better. Should you give way to this urge, be warned that the distance between you may increase to an unbridgeable extent.

Aquarius Birth Influences
Ruling planet: Uranus; traditionally Saturn
Element: Air
Polarity: Masculine
Quadruplicity: Fixed

Guiding Principle: Should a fascinating someone attract your attention, ask yourself this: could he or she be as unfailingly tolerant and stimulating as Aquarius?

Compatibility: ♥♥♥♥♥♥♥♥♡♡

AQUARIUS
PISCES

Aquarius Birth Influences

Ruling planet: Uranus; traditionally Saturn
Element: Air
Polarity: Masculine
Quadruplicity: Fixed

Aquarius, don't let an intriguing stranger turn your head. Remember that your Pisces lover has hidden depths that you've yet to plumb.

Pisces Birth Influences

Ruling planet: Neptune; traditionally Jupiter
Element: Water
Polarity: Feminine
Quadruplicity: Mutable

Highlight a few of the characteristics associated with Aquarius and Pisces' respective birth influences, and their future as a happy couple may seem questionable. For whereas the element of air and Uranus are said to cause Aquarians to be aloof and self-willed, that of water and Neptune supposedly make Pisceans emotional and altruistic, and while Aquarius' polarity and quadruplicity are linked with extroversion and steadfastness, Pisces' polarity and quadruplicity indicate introversion and instability. These dissimilarities may cause Aquarius and Pisces to fall out of love with one another, yet may equally hold their relationship together, not least because faithful Aquarius can boost Pisces' sometimes fragile confidence, and flexible Pisces can accommodate Aquarius' uncompromising ways.

Plus Points: You may admire your Aquarian sweetheart's resolutely independent, Uranian mindset if you are a Pisces whose watery element may give you a tendency to empathize with everyone you talk to. Your ruling planet may also confuse your thoughts, while your quadruplicity is mutable, or changeable. Encouraged, perhaps, by airy Aquarius' playful teasing and masculine-polarity assurance, you may be even be taking a leaf out of your beloved's book and bravely overcoming your feminine-polarity shyness in order to stand up for the humane, Neptune-bestowed ideals that you believe in. Best of all, however, fixed-quadruplicity Aquarius' unwavering loyalty may result in you feeling valued and secure.

Uranus and your airy element may together make you try to probe deeper into people's personalities if you are an Aquarius, and if your lover is a Pisces, he or she may be an endless source of fascination. First, there may be that feminine-polarity reserve to penetrate, then you may discover his or her compassion and spiritual streak, and just when you think that you have got his or her measure, Pisces' mutable quadruplicity may kick in to change the picture completely. And on a day-to-day level, you may particularly appreciate Pisces' unselfishness and understanding.

Potential Pitfalls: The biggest threats to your relationship may lurk firstly in airy Aquarius' need to remain a free agent and watery Pisces' craving for togetherness, and, secondly, in Aquarius' urge to communicate and Pisces' reticence. If you feel that you are drifting apart, enlist the aid of your different quadruplicities and show constancy, if you are an Aquarius, and adaptability, if you are a Pisces.

Guiding Principle: Be grateful for one another's life-enhancing traits (and try to turn a blind eye to the rest!)

Compatibility: ♥♥♥♥♥♥♡♡♡♡

PISCES / PISCES

The greatest pain that emotionally vulnerable Pisces people can experience is the anguish inflicted when those whom they love and trust the most hurt them, and this is why they may find everlasting happiness in the arms of someone who is as unselfish and caring as they, namely a fellow Piscean. It is their element of water that makes them so sensitive and giving, and Neptune, their ruling planet, that blesses them with altruism and the urge to merge with one another completely. These birth influences also enable them to understand, and empathize with, the natural reticence that their feminine polarity bestows on them both, as well as the complexity that is part and parcel of having a mutable quadruplicity. There may be few downsides of a Pisces–Pisces romance, yet one may be the mutable-quadruplicity appetite for variety that a passive, feminine-polarity lover may not be able to satisfy.

Plus Points: Although the double dose of intuition that is the gift of water and Neptune may have given you the sense that Pisces felt as strongly about you as you did about him or her if you are also a Pisces, it may have taken some time before you and your sweetheart both felt sufficiently sure that you wouldn't be rejected before overcoming that feminine-polarity reserve of yours and revealing the depth of your feelings for one another. And now that you are a couple, you may have found nirvana, for if you have been accustomed to endlessly giving while former lovers did nothing but take, it may be blissful to be with someone who puts your needs and desires first and invariably sympathizes with you, and so instinctively that you needn't struggle to translate your confused thoughts into words, again thanks to Neptune and water. And because one of the advantages of having a mutable quadruplicity is flexibility, you may take it in turns to support each other as necessary, so that you both find joy in helping one another.

Potential Pitfalls: The main pitfall to watch out for if you are a pair of Pisceans is that when the restlessness that is an aspect of your joint mutable quadruplicity comes to the fore in one of you, your responsive, feminine-polarity other half may be unsettled, but may still be unable to come up with an enterprising way of fulfilling that yearning for change.

Guiding Principle: Add spice to your romance by spending time with friends who were born under different zodiacal signs.

Compatibility: ♥♥♥♥♥♥♥♥♥♡

Pisces Birth Influences

Ruling planet: Neptune; traditionally Jupiter
Element: Water
Polarity: Feminine
Quadruplicity: Mutable

A Piscean couple can give each other the tenderness that they crave. Both having kind and caring natures, neither would hurt the other.

Pisces Birth Influences

Ruling planet: Neptune; traditionally Jupiter
Element: Water
Polarity: Feminine
Quadruplicity: Mutable

A man of humanity is one who, in seeking to establish himself, finds a foothold for others and who, desiring attainment for himself, helps others to attain.

CONFUCIUS, *Analects* (SIXTH CENTURY BC)

WORK

"All persons are puzzles until at last we find in some word or act the key to the man, to the woman; straightaway all their past words and actions lie in light before us," noted Ralph Waldo Emerson in his *Journals* (published in 1842). And which people could be more puzzling than those whom you hardly know, having been thrown together simply because you were hired by the same firm?

Yet we often spend more time in the company of our colleagues than with our friends and loved ones, and how we interact with our bosses and workmates can furthermore determine how well we do in our careers, with which our sense of worth and achievement, as well as our earning power—all vital to our well-being—are inextricably linked. Turn to the pages that provide an astrological prognosis of how you are likely get on with those complex characters with whom you have to deal on a daily basis, and you may find the key that gives you a short-cut to improving your rapport with them, and consequently your happiness in the workplace. The benefits of discovering more about the characteristics imparted by your respective planetary governors, elements, polarities, and quadruplicities, and how they either connect or conflict with one another, may not be limited to you personally either. For be it your relationship with your superior or coworker that you wish to understand in more detail, knowing how your respective strengths and weaknesses complement or compensate for one another will give you the power to change your company's fortunes for the better in a small, but not insignificant, way. Above all, you may come to appreciate that you are all individuals with very human vulnerabilities and fears, as well as hopes and aspirations, and thus to learn to have sympathy with your fellow workers, whatever their status.

ARIES

ARIES

Aries Birth Influences
Ruling planet: Mars
Element: Fire
Polarity: Masculine
Quadruplicity: Cardinal

Mars-ruled Aries people regard themselves as natural leaders, but there is rarely room to accommodate two such self-convinced egos in a confined working environment, making conflict inevitable. And when these two willful rams butt heads in the workplace, sparks will fly!

Your Boss: If you have an Arien boss, your coworkers probably consider him or her an inspiring, dynamic director, whose off-the-wall hunches prove either brilliant successes or disastrous failures, but who is always an energizing presence. Never happier than when firing off orders to set his or her latest big idea in motion, or when working against the clock to meet a deadline, the Aries boss is a demanding employer who expects unquestioning loyalty and unstinting hard work. This is usually given, too, except by you, a supposedly "subordinate" fellow Arien who knows that your ideas are more innovative, that you'd martial your troops better, and that you are altogether far more worthy of the job.

A wise and mature Aries boss will recognize your shared qualities, value your innovative, cardinal-quadruplicity way of thinking, and cut you as much slack as you need to explore your preferred avenues and do things your own way. Being a natural dictator of the working world, it is, however, far more likely that he or she instead insists that you toe the line, and because neither blind obedience nor stolid endurance comes naturally to you, it may not be long before there is a fiery and damaging explosion.

There will be intense competition when two Ariens are working together on the same team, as they both want to be the leader and not a follower.

Aries and Aries in the Workplace: Unless Ariens are leading the charge toward the realization of their own goals, they are not suited to being team players. They rebel against the rules and restrictions imposed on them by corporate hierarchies, cannot stand having to perform detailed or methodical tasks, and are forever pushing the boundaries. If you and a coworker were both born under this zodiacal sign, it is likely that you understand each other's direct way of thinking, share a low boredom threshold, and frequently relieve your frustration by deliberately provoking an argument between yourselves. Rather than being comrades-in-Aries, however, your relationship is more likely to be based either on one-upmanship—not least because competing with a worthy, masculine-polarity rival peps up your working life considerably—or outright hostility because you each believe that the other is a formidable adversary in the dog-eat-dog world of work.

Aries Birth Influences
Ruling planet: Mars
Element: Fire
Polarity: Masculine
Quadruplicity: Cardinal

TAURUS
ARIES

Aries generates original and ambitious ideas, while Taurus' detail-focused, methodical approach is capable of translating them into reality. This complementary astrological partnership therefore has the potential to make an extremely successful team, as long as Taurus' caution and Aries' impatience don't drive them apart.

Taurus Birth Influences

Ruling planet: Venus
Element: Earth
Polarity: Feminine
Quadruplicity: Fixed

Your Boss: Life is never dull if you are a Taurus with an Aries boss. He'll be constantly barking orders at you to set the wheels in motion to make his latest groundbreaking concept a market leader, and will then wave you away when you try to get him to discuss specifics. Accounting for every cent certainly doesn't interest him, nor does putting together a structured business plan, so it's just as well that he has a financially astute, efficient, and organized Taurean to rely upon. Being a loyal and accommodating type, you will do your utmost to whip his sketchy ideas into feasible shape, but will not be rushed or dictated to, which may sometimes cause him to explode with frustration. Ultimately, however, he admires your meticulousness, and values your rock-solid work.

If you are an Aries with a Taurus boss, you probably feel like a hyperactive ram straining at the leash to escape her firm hand, be it to follow your powerful instincts or to take charge of your workmates yourself. Her caution infuriates you, as does her insistence that you follow procedure and research your reports carefully and thoroughly. You do, however, respect her judgment—even if she seems to take forever to reach a decision—and are quite impressed by her passion on the rare occasions that she blows a fuse (who would have thought that she had it in her?).

Aries and Taurus in the Workplace: If Aries doesn't push things too far in his or her merciless teasing of Taurus in the hope of provoking a spectacular reaction, these two should make highly effective workmates. One's strengths are the other's weaknesses, so that while fiery Aries brings ideas, energy, and enthusiasm to the workplace, earthy Taurus supplies vital organizational backup, staying power, and, if necessary, a steadying or restraining influence. If you are a Taurus, you may be content to follow cardinal Aries' lead if, after careful consideration, you think that he or she's heading in the right direction, but probably find the Mars-ruled ram's attempts to boss you around irksome. As for you, Aries, you may joke about Taurus' slow and painstaking ways, but know that you can depend on him to meet a deadline and to save your bacon by pointing out any careless mistakes that you've made in your rush to finish the job. All in all, you need each other.

As long as Aries and Taurus work at being understanding and respecting each other's strengths, these two should make a successful team.

Aries Birth Influences

Ruling planet: Mars
Element: Fire
Polarity: Masculine
Quadruplicity: Cardinal

ARIES
GEMINI

Aries Birth Influences

Ruling planet: Mars
Element: Fire
Polarity: Masculine
Quadruplicity: Cardinal

Aries and Gemini's independent mindsets may lead to conflict if either wields authority over the other in the workplace. Issues of control aside, their respective talents make them a potentially successful team, with Aries bringing energy and single-mindedness to any joint enterprise, and Gemini contributing research skills and salesmanship.

Your Boss: Neither Aries nor Gemini responds well to being ordered around, nor do they value office protocols or hierarchies, similarities that may result in a character clash if one is the boss and the other his or her subordinate. If you are a free-thinking Gemini, you may resent your Mars-ruled Aries boss's tendency to order you to fall into line and support her strategies unquestioningly, particularly when you believe your logical, subtle way of working to be more effective than her impulsive, all-out approach. Yet you probably rather admire her decisiveness and energy, partly because you recognize that speed is often vital in the workplace.

You must find your Gemini boss maddening if you are an Aries. While you are raring to go, your vacillating senior insists on holding endless consultation meetings to consider all sides of an issue, only to lose interest and move on to something new just as you thought that you were about to be sent off into action. You may find his charm disarming, however, and may respect his silver-tongued ability to diffuse a heated disagreement between coworkers by using humor and the sweet voice of reason.

If you are an easily bored Aries whose Gemini boss sets up endless meetings, ward off feelings of frustration by contributing your innovative ideas to group discussions, for Gemini is nothing if not open-minded.

Aries and Gemini in the Workplace: When they are working in harmony, Aries and Gemini complement each other extremely well. Whereas Mercury-governed Gemini tends to be an ideas person, go-getting Aries is focused and goal-oriented, so that while Gemini excels at information-gathering, Aries' talent lies in formulating bold plans of action based on Gemini's data and ensuring that they are carried through. Indeed, if one of your weaknesses as a mutable Gemini is a lack of staying power, steadfastness is one of your Arien colleague's strengths; if you are an Aries who finds it hard to deviate from your preferred course, your Gemini workmate is highly adaptable; and if fiery Aries is sometimes brutally direct, airy Gemini is a great persuader. Although both relish a challenging, fast-paced, fun-packed working atmosphere, Aries may condemn Gemini's love of gossip as being frivolous or even disloyal, Gemini in turn often giving Aries the cold shoulder if he or she perceives the ram's natural assertiveness as being domineering.

Gemini Birth Influences

Ruling planet: Mercury
Element: Air
Polarity: Masculine
Quadruplicity: Mutable

CANCER
ARIES

Assertive, energizing Aries and supportive, calming Cancer together have the makings of a dream team in the workplace, as long as Moon-ruled Cancer does not take offense at Aries' brusqueness and pushiness and Mars-governed Aries does not treat charitable Cancer like a doormat.

Your Boss: If you are an Aries with a Cancerian boss, you are no doubt impatiently awaiting the day when you can step into his shoes and wow everyone with your own superior talent for leadership. That day has not yet arrived, however, and in the meantime you must be chafing under Cancer's control a little, maybe not because you don't respect your boss, but because you dislike being an underling. Although you probably wish that feminine-polarity Cancer would take more risks and shared your enthusiasm for time-saving technology, you may appreciate his watery willingness to let you pursue a hunch once in a while. You may also have learned from experience that cardinal Cancer's tolerance cannot be equated with timidity, and that he will give you a painful dressing-down if you insist on pushing his patience too far.

If you are a Cancer who works for an Aries boss, you may regard her with a mixture of admiration and despair. You probably admire her fearlessness and decisiveness, and are often enthused by her idealism, but sometimes worry that she is recklessly chasing a pipe dream, and that all of the tasks that she has piled on your shoulders will consequently be in vain. And while you may understand that tact and patience are not fiery Arien qualities, you may sometimes be deeply hurt when she makes a critical throwaway comment, fails to thank you for your hard work, or simply doesn't notice when you are feeling down. Don't take these things personally.

Aries and Cancer in the Workplace: The Arien contribution to the working environment is impetus and energy, while Cancer supplies diligence and caution. This character combination can be remarkably effective when both are working in happy unison, but may also be a source of conflict. If go-getting Aries becomes so fired up by an exciting project that he or she starts treating Cancer like a personal slave, for example, the distressed crab may withdraw the conscientious support that Aries so relies on. And if Cancer continually tries to correct the ram's hastiness and tendency to ignore vital details, impatient Aries will explode with frustrated fury. Yet Aries quickly forgives and forgets, and empathetic Cancer generally understands that Aries' behavior is thoughtless rather than vindictive.

Cancer Birth Influences

Ruling planet: The Moon
Element: Water
Polarity: Feminine
Quadruplicity: Cardinal

Do you feel that your Arien boss pushes you around, Cancer? At least his bark is worse than his bite, and he'll defend you to the hilt in front of his own boss.

Aries Birth Influences

Ruling planet: Mars
Element: Fire
Polarity: Masculine
Quadruplicity: Cardinal

ARIES / LEO

Aries Birth Influences

Ruling planet: Mars
Element: Fire
Polarity: Masculine
Quadruplicity: Cardinal

Friction is almost inevitable when dominating Aries works alongside authoritative Leo, often resulting in incandescent detonations. Yet if each manages to channel his or her impulse to lead into the job in hand rather than into head-to-head conflicts, Aries' initiative and energy and Leo's imagination and talent for organization are a dynamic combination.

Your Boss: If you are a Sun-governed Leo with an Aries boss, the only way that you will respect her is if she in turn respects you. Although you may be impressed by her focus and drive, you are probably convinced that you would motivate your colleagues better if you were in her shoes. If you dislike her impulsiveness and loathe having to take orders from her, you have your pride, and will ensure that she cannot complain about the quality of your work. If she is shrewd, your boss will recognize your susceptibility to flattery and will occasionally defer to your judgment and praise your achievements warmly, but you are more likely to find that the abrupt ram ruffles, rather than strokes, your magnificent mane.

As a Mars-ruled Aries, you are no doubt itching to push aside your leonine boss and take his place yourself, but nevertheless admire his effortless air of supremacy and bask in the golden glow of approval that he beams in your direction when you've pleased him. Woe betide you if you've cut corners in your haste to complete a tedious task, however, or if you argue against his decisions, because the imperious lion will not tolerate what he perceives to be either slovenliness or insubordination. A wise Leo boss—and many are—will understand your cardinal-quadruplicity need to take the initiative and will let you take charge of your pet project, as long as you accept his overall control.

A Leo boss usually inspires and motivates his team members. He'll demand hard work, but appreciates your efforts when you apply yourself, Aries.

Aries and Leo in the Workplace: Provided that neither Aries nor Leo intrudes on the other's area of expertise or tries to force the ram or lion to bend to his or her will—in any case an exercise in futility given that this fiery zodiacal pair are equally independent and resistant to control—they should make a spectacularly competent team. When truly enthused, both put their all into working toward a common vision, your strength as an Aries being single-minded resourcefulness, with your contribution being creative flair and expert planning if you are a Leo. There may be some short-lived flare-ups along the way, but when this forceful duo is united, their exuberance, resilience, and determination make things happen.

Leo Birth Influences

Ruling planet: The Sun
Element: Fire
Polarity: Masculine
Quadruplicity: Fixed

VIRGO

ARIES

Because fiery Aries is burning to lead others toward collective goals and grounded Virgo is happy to beaver away in an essential behind-the-scenes role, this working relationship can be remarkably successful. Action-oriented, masculine-polarity Aries must beware of hassling prudent, feminine-polarity Virgo to act hastily, however, while perfectionist Virgo should not cramp the ram's visionary style.

Your Boss: If you are an Aries whose boss is a Virgo, you almost certainly find him frustrating to work for. Not only may he seem incapable of recognizing the brilliant simplicity and audacious daring of your proposals, he may always be admonishing you for being too rash and for not having thought your ideas through carefully enough. Still, at least you share the same hands-on approach and straight-forward outlook, and you certainly can't accuse him of being unfair or dictatorial, or of delegating tedious tasks to others while he himself lazes around. And when you do occasionally meet his high standards, Mercury-ruled Virgo usually eloquently acknowledges the quality of your performance, which makes you feel deservedly proud.

As a cool, collected, and rational Virgo, your impulsive Aries boss must sometimes test your patience to its limits. Being a quick-thinking person, you may frequently be fired up by her progressive ideas, but may find her lack of attention to detail irksome, and may wish that she would give you more notice before handing you an urgent assignment if you believe that if a job is to be done well, it cannot be rushed. You may have learned that your demonstrative boss prizes allegiance, and may worry that she misinterprets your reserve, objectivity, and public-spirited tendency to point out where she might be going wrong as disloyalty. If so, take heart from direct Aries' praise: she may be abrupt and unpolished, but is rarely dishonest.

Aries and Virgo in the Workplace: If you are an impatient, big-picture Aries, you'd be advised not to make fun of earthy Virgo's thoroughness because the joke may backfire on you. Your colleague understands that planning and research are important, and is furthermore capable of fluently demolishing your argument if you push him or her too far. And Virgo, try not to feel superior to your pushy, cardinal-quadruplicity Aries coworker. Deep down, you know that he or she makes an invaluable contribution to the team in terms of providing initiative and motivating others. If you each respect each other's talents and viewpoints, you'll interact extremely effectively, and will both feel rewarded by your joint success.

Virgo Birth Influences

Ruling planet: Mercury
Element: Earth
Polarity: Feminine
Quadruplicity: Mutable

If your boss is a critical Virgo, make the most of the times that he praises your Arien efforts. Don't take his nitpicking personally, Aries: he just can't help noticing every imperfection.

Aries Birth Influences

Ruling planet: Mars
Element: Fire
Polarity: Masculine
Quadruplicity: Cardinal

ARIES / LIBRA

Aries Birth Influences

Ruling planet: Mars
Element: Fire
Polarity: Masculine
Quadruplicity: Cardinal

Does your Arien boss sometimes overreact, Libra? His fiery outbursts usually don't last long, so try not to worry about annoying him.

Libra Birth Influences

Ruling planet: Venus
Element: Air
Polarity: Masculine
Quadruplicity: Cardinal

Being progressive, cardinal personalities, Aries and Libra are generally on the same wavelength in the workplace. And when this lively pair is working together as equals, each provides what the other lacks, fiery Aries supplying raw enthusiasm and determination, and airy Libra adding imagination and charm.

Your Boss: If you are a Libra with an Aries boss, you are probably motivated by his certainty and zeal, particularly when your airy interest has been piqued by his latest innovative goal. Being a balanced person, you may often feel the need to persuade him to tone down some of his more extreme ideas, however, which you usually manage to do tactfully, but may sometimes feel injured on the rare occasions when he accuses you of negative thinking and directs a blast of searing anger in your direction. But his fiery fury never lasts for long and should not be taken personally, and he is always warmly appreciative when pleased with your performance.

Although your airy Libran boss's tendency to vacillate may cause steam to shoot out of your ears if you are a purposeful Aries, she seems to know exactly which buttons to push to calm you down. Having observed her employing similar Venusian methods with others, you may recognize that she is a master of flattery and ego-stroking, but when she applauds your own strengths, you feel that her praise is no more than you deserve. Even so, because you are an impatient type who is always eager to swing into action, you probably wish that she would make decisions quickly rather than first consulting as many members of staff as possible, and also that she was less insistent on thorough research. As a child of Mars, you probably cannot help feeling that you would make a more effective team leader.

Aries and Libra in the Workplace: Aries and Libra typically interact happily and effectively as colleagues. Neither are sticklers for office conventions, and both need to be stimulated by their work, similarities that create an instant rapport. If you are an Aries, you may value Libra's ingenuity, flexibility, and talent for smoothing the feathers that you have ruffled by being overly brusque or bossy—unless you have offended Libra, when you may be chilled by your normally good-natured workmate's cool response. And if you are a Libra who can be paralyzed by indecision when faced with a bewildering array of options, you must frequently be relieved when resolute Aries decrees a course of action. Forceful Aries no doubt nudges you back on track when you switch your attention to an intriguing diversion, too, but then you have a moderating influence on the impulsive ram.

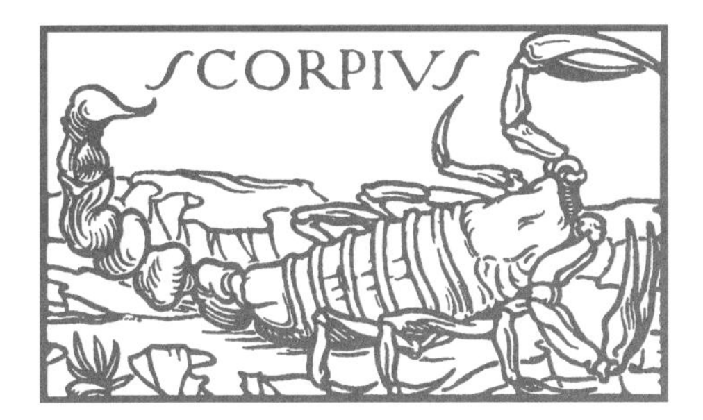

SCORPIO

ARIES

When they share the same vision, Aries and Scorpio work resolutely together like military comrades to achieve their purpose, and the greater the challenge, the more single-minded they become. The combination of Aries' fire and Scorpio's intensity is potent, but the Pluto-ruled scorpion's secretiveness may inflame the direct ram, while Aries' high-handedness can antagonize touchy, watery Scorpio.

Your Boss: If you are a Scorpio under the command of an Arien boss, you probably admire her sense of purpose and ambition because you share these qualities yourself. And when you recognize that her orders will make an important contribution to your company's success, you are happy to carry them out. You will not, however, put up with being ordered around as a matter of course, particularly if you think that hasty Aries has made a flawed decision. For overbearing behavior only makes you resentful and mutinous. You may consequently bear the brunt of the ram's rage, but at least this is short-lived, and, unlike you, Aries does not bear grudges.

You must consider your Scorpio boss something of an enigma if you are a direct, masculine-polarity Aries. Not one to hold anything back yourself, he, by contrast, is a guarded, feminine-polarity person who operates on a need-to-know basis, never straying into the realms of gossip and never letting you in on company secrets. Despite being a closed book in some respects, he issues instructions clearly and authoritatively, understands that you need to be fired up if you are to perform at your best, and acknowledges your loyalty. All in all, you may respect him, even if you don't understand him, but would feel more comfortable and motivated if you weren't kept in the dark so much.

Aries and Scorpio in the Workplace: As long as Aries grasps that trying to boss Scorpio around will result in him or her either being frozen out or subjected to a stinging verbal put-down, these two should make a very efficient team. If you are a Scorpio, you share your Arien colleague's conviction and courage because Mars wields influence over you both, but bring a fixed quadruplicity's focus and discipline to your partnership that Aries often lacks. Your contribution, if you are an Aries, is limitless enthusiasm and an injection of friendly competition that forces your sometimes serious and taciturn workmate to lighten up. You may, however, feel that while you are putting your heart and soul into a project, Scorpio is withholding something of him- or herself. On the other hand, Scorpio may consider Aries excitable and rash.

Scorpio Birth Influences

Ruling planet: Pluto; traditionally Mars
Element: Water
Polarity: Feminine
Quadruplicity: Fixed

You may resent your Scorpio coworker for not seeming as enthusiastic about a project as you, especially if you've been working hard on it, Aries, but Scorpio is a less demonstrative person.

Aries Birth Influences

Ruling planet: Mars
Element: Fire
Polarity: Masculine
Quadruplicity: Cardinal

ARIES
SAGITTARIUS

Aries Birth Influences

Ruling planet: Mars
Element: Fire
Polarity: Masculine
Quadruplicity: Cardinal

Is your Arien coworker sometimes too competitive, Sagittarius? If so, laugh it off, and Aries will soon simmer down.

Sagittarius Birth Influences

Ruling planet: Jupiter
Element: Fire
Polarity: Masculine
Quadruplicity: Mutable

As long as they give each other the freedom to do things their own way, Aries and Sagittarius typically interact enthusiastically, dynamically, and happily in the workplace. But if Mars-ruled Aries is too rigid and authoritarian, or mutable Sagittarius too changeable, sparks will fly between this fiery pair.

Your Boss: You probably have no trouble keeping up with your impulsive Aries boss if you are a visionary Sagittarius. He may be a dynamic, big-picture person, but so are you, and you are just as optimistic and hard-working when galvanized by an ambitious idea. Although you are generally on the same wavelength, friction may arise if you feel that Aries is trying to force you to work in a regimented manner or if he barks orders at you. If you are to sustain your interest in a project, you need to be able to turn your attention to something different every so often, and if focused Aries insists that you remain as disciplined as he, fiery conflict is almost inevitable. Having a freedom-seeking element, you will not stick around for long if required to slave under a dictator. Instead, you crave sufficient autonomy to try out your own methods and ideas.

If you are an Aries with a Sagittarian boss, you probably can't help but like and respect her, even if her mutability and lack of staying power infuriate you. You no doubt appreciate her jovial, upbeat personality, her liveliness, and her inspired ideas, all of which click with your own positive, energetic, and progressive nature. What may drive you to distraction, however, is her tendency to fire you up into action mode, raring to head for a goal that she has set in driving, cardinal-quadruplicity style, only for her to lose interest and switch you to another assignment. That having been said, she typically lightens things up with a disarming joke, which may mollify you, and because Aries is a sign associated with beginnings, you are in any case always stimulated by new challenges.

Aries and Sagittarius in the Workplace: There is sometimes an undercurrent of rivalry in a working relationship between Aries and Sagittarius, both being confident, competitive characters who resist being pushed around and aren't afraid to speak their minds. But amiable Sagittarius generally diffuses Aries' aggression with humor, and the ram in any case usually regards the enlivening archer as a fellow independent spirit. When working in unison, the single-minded determination of Aries and the curiosity and versatility of Sagittarius make a winning team.

CAPRICORN
ARIES

A successful working alliance between enterprising, vigorous Aries and pragmatic, meticulous Capricorn is something to behold. Both of these cardinal signs are driven by their ambition and are equally set on achieving their goals. Yet Capricorn's down-to-earth realism may cramp Aries' fiery, inspirational style, while the ram's reckless approach may irritate the careful goat.

Your Boss: Having a personal rapport with your Aries boss may be less important to you than fulfilling the tasks that she gives you if you are a conscientious Capricorn. She is, after all, your boss, and you have a high regard for her position, as well as her single-mindedness and direct manner. Being a methodical planner, you may wish that she were less hasty, both in making snap decisions and in setting ridiculously tight deadlines—in your opinion, if a job is worth doing, it's worth doing well, and that takes time. You may also find her impulsiveness and predilection for taking risks more unsettling than motivating.

Although your Capricorn boss's capacity for hard work, practical management skills, and saturnine air of authority may command your respect if you are an Aries, you probably find him a hard and uninspiring taskmaster. It's not that you are lazy, just that you need to be enthused by a project if you are to give it your all, and serious Capricorn's well-considered words may rarely fire up your imagination. He no doubt also insists that you pay attention to detail, but try as you might, you are soon overcome by boredom. Capricorn is a good judge of character, however, and although he may frequently reprimand you, he will generally try to give you assignments that arouse your appetite for challenge and draw the best out of you.

Aries and Capricorn in the Workplace: The fact that the adventurous ram and steady goat are like night and day can make them a winning working combination. Every business needs both innovators and regulators, and while Aries supplies initiative, Capricorn provides practical backup. If you are a realistic Capricorn whose feet are planted firmly on the ground, you may be constantly trying to prevent impetuous Aries from racing off in pursuit of an imaginative, but unviable, vision. Nevertheless, you will do your utmost to make your coworker's more sensible concepts a reality. And despite sometimes being frustrated by what you regard as Capricorn's pessimism, Aries, you probably have to concede that the earthy goat's talent for organization and staying power bring the right results.

Capricorn Birth Influences

Ruling planet: Saturn
Element: Earth
Polarity: Feminine
Quadruplicity: Cardinal

When Aries and Capricorn are united, they make an awesome team. Aries is an inspired initiator, Capricorn is a gifted organizer, and their common cardinal quadruplicity supplies tremendous drive.

Aries Birth Influences

Ruling planet: Mars
Element: Fire
Polarity: Masculine
Quadruplicity: Cardinal

ARIES AQUARIUS

Aries Birth Influences

Ruling planet: Mars
Element: Fire
Polarity: Masculine
Quadruplicity: Cardinal

If you are an Aries, your enthusiasm for a task may not always be shared by your more objective Aquarian coworker. But then maybe you should stop and listen to some cool advice.

Aquarius Birth Influences

Ruling planet: Uranus; traditionally Saturn
Element: Air
Polarity: Masculine
Quadruplicity: Fixed

This zodiacal pairing is well-suited in the workplace, largely because Aries and Aquarius' interests and approaches are so similar. Both are enterprising, positive, and thrive on challenge and change, and both relish functioning as part of a team. But while airy Aquarius works in a logical way, fiery Aries is an instinct-driven person, which means that disagreements may arise if Aquarius believes that the ram is behaving thoughtlessly and Aries thinks that the water-carrier is being unnecessarily obstructive or pedantic.

Your Boss: Although your Mars-ruled Aries boss's dictatorial style may sometimes grate on you if you are an Aquarius who believes that all people are created equal and should be treated as such, you probably don't take her commanding manner that personally, grasping as you do that she is focused on getting results, and quickly. Indeed, because your mind needs to be constantly occupied if you are to be happy at work, you no doubt enjoy the fast, cardinal-quadruplicity pace that she sets for her team. However, her pioneering, martial nature probably doesn't embrace new technology, which, as a protégé of Uranus who knows that technology promises to achieve astonishing breakthroughs, may disappoint and frustrate you.

If you are an Aries whose boss is an Aquarius, you probably find him friendly enough, but may not really understand what makes him tick. There are times when you have direct and constructive conversation, yet on other occasions he may seem detached and inscrutable, which, being such an open personality yourself, may puzzle you. Nevertheless, you are no doubt enthused by his original, progressive concepts, and also appreciate having your ideas solicited and considered by your egalitarian boss, even if he then tends to deflate your ego a little by reasonably explaining why he thinks them unworkable.

Aries and Aquarius in the Workplace: As colleagues, Aries and Aquarius generally have a great deal of respect for one another, maybe because the headstrong ram soon learns that the stubborn water-carrier will not be pushed around, Aquarius recognizes that Aries has enormous determination, and both are focused on making progress. If you are an Aries, you may, however, be irritated by what you regard as Aquarius' lack of interest in a project that is of burning interest to you, when, in fact, your airy colleague's busy mind may simply be elsewhere. And if you are the Aquarian member of this team, you may wish that enthusiastic, cardinal Aries would listen to the cool voice of reason before rushing headlong down a path that you know leads to a dead end.

PISCES

ARIES

If Aries and Pisces are both truly inspired by their work, they have the potential to make a happy and effective team, unorthodox Pisces dreaming up the most creative of ideas, and active Aries providing the energy and determination that can make them a reality. Yet straightforward Aries may be infuriated by Pisces' chaotic approach, and sensitive, watery Pisces may find Aries' fiery outbursts and commanding style intolerable.

Your Boss: If you are a watery Pisces who needs to feel understood and appreciated at work, you may feel that your Arien boss undervalues your input. The trouble is, being a cardinal sign, Aries is often too intent on forging ahead with the next task to take the time to praise your contribution to the previous one. In addition, as a blunt protégé of forthright Mars, he may have told you in no uncertain terms that he finds your lack of organization and fluid time-keeping unacceptable, in the process perhaps causing you to dissolve into tears. In fact, he probably does regard you highly, not least on account of the qualities that are the gift of your ruling planet, Neptune, notably your idealistic concepts, your consideration for your colleagues, and your considerable talent for negotiation when only communicating empathetically can save the day.

As a direct and decisive Aries, your appetite for challenge and pursuing new goals may be aroused by the innovative, forward-looking ideas that your Piscean boss generates. However, you may also find your vague, vacillating manager frustrating to work for. You like to be given a clear mission statement, but may find her instructions confusing. This is probably because Neptune and the Piscean element of water have endowed your boss with a double dose of intuition, and she may not quite realize that while she easily absorbs subtle messages, you do not deal in ambiguities. You may also be maddened by her changeability, especially when you have committed your heart and soul to a project, only for her to appear to lose interest. You may dislike having to put up with this aspect of Pisces' mutability, but her flexibility may make up for it.

Aries and Pisces in the Workplace: As long as impatient Aries tries to control his or her hot temper and respects Pisces' original mindset and supportiveness, and sensitive Pisces learns to develop a thicker skin and shrugs off Aries' bossiness and tactlessness, these two can work quite well together. Just concentrate on your shared objectives and don't let your different temperaments and working methods become issues of personal contention.

Pisces Birth Influences

Ruling planet: Neptune; traditionally Jupiter
Element: Water
Polarity: Feminine
Quadruplicity: Mutable

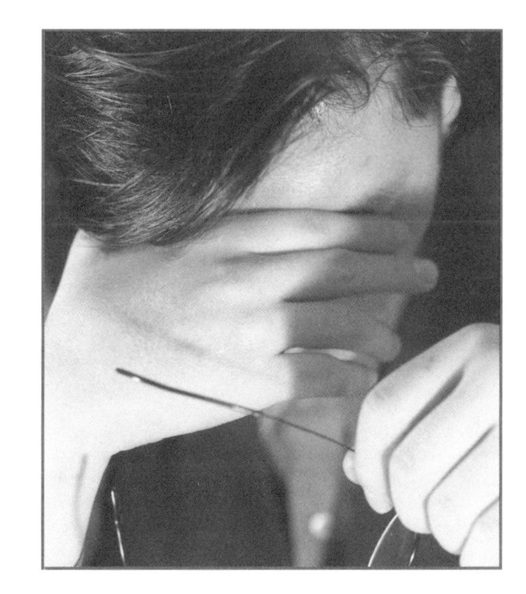

Your outspoken Arien boss may sometimes really get you down if you are a sensitive Pisces. You need to learn to let his or her comments wash over you if you are to be content at work.

Aries Birth Influences

Ruling planet: Mars
Element: Fire
Polarity: Masculine
Quadruplicity: Cardinal

TAURUS
TAURUS

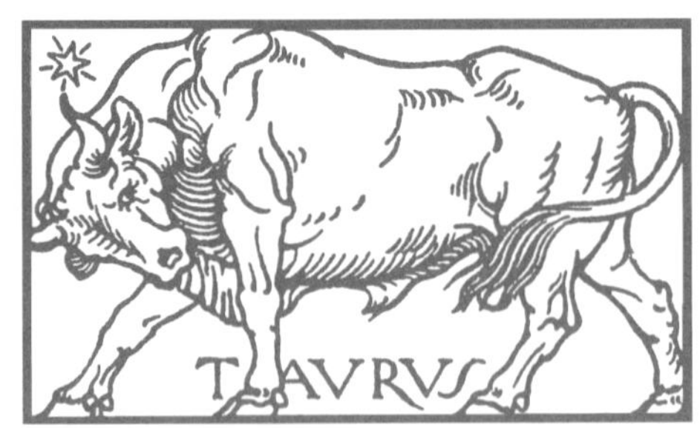

Taurus Birth Influences

Ruling planet: Venus
Element: Earth
Polarity: Feminine
Quadruplicity: Fixed

Although two Taureans usually work together at a steady pace, if one of you needs something done quickly, the other may refuse to speed up, thereby annoying you. Remember that you'd probably be exactly the same in his shoes!

Taurus Birth Influences

Ruling planet: Venus
Element: Earth
Polarity: Feminine
Quadruplicity: Fixed

The combination of Venus' financial acumen, earth's practicality and talent for organization, and a fixed sign's diligence makes Taurus an asset in the workplace. Although they are conscientious team players with similar outlooks and methods, a working relationship between two Taureans can't usually be described as being an inspirational meeting of the minds, however.

Your Boss: What you probably appreciate the most about your boss, if you are both Taureans, is his consistency. Having been born under the sign of the bull, you feel comfortable when you know what to expect from those around you and when your life is regulated by routines, but are unsettled by unpredictability and sudden changes. The stability imparted by the Taurean element of earth, compounded by the steadiness of a fixed quadruplicity, indicates that your senior presides over a well-ordered, smooth-running workplace, and that his overall management style therefore suits you. Yet because you are both hands-on people, you may wish that your boss would give you practical control of certain projects rather than retaining responsibility for them himself. After all, you know that you are just as budget-conscious, methodical, hard-working, and tenacious as he is. Try to avoid letting any such niggles get under your skin.

Taurus and Taurus in the Workplace: The influence of a reactive, passive polarity gives Taureans a preference for working behind the scenes. (Because of this, they often realize the imaginative concepts generated by colleagues whose astrological birth influences are more active and questing.) As a result, you may not find your fellow Taurus coworker the most enlivening of people, but then that's probably neither here nor there as far as you are concerned—after all, work is about producing results, not partying. And you must certainly be grateful to be working alongside someone who, like you, is calm, realistic, and capable, someone you can rely on not to let you down. There are nevertheless two shared characteristics that you may find exasperating in one another. One is the Taurean refusal to be rushed. Working to different deadlines under time pressure, you may need to hurry the other along, only to be frustrated by Taurus' insistence on taking things slow and steady. The other is your stubbornness, or being children of a fixed sign, on the rare occasions when you have a difference of opinion, you each tend to stick resolutely to your guns. Yet because your planetary ruler is the amicable Venus, the upshot may merely be that you agree to disagree.

GEMINI

TAURUS

The Taurean and Geminian approaches to working life could hardly be more different. Imaginative, quick-thinking Gemini is a fount of novel ideas, but often lacks the perseverance to bring them to fruition. Realistic, steady Taurus, by contrast, is happiest when dealing with mundane practicalities and can be relied upon to see any job through to completion.

Your Boss: The stamina, patience, and tenacity of your Taurean boss must be a source of wonder to you if you are an airy Gemini. These are the qualities of both a fixed quadruplicity and the element of earth, which furthermore endows Taurus with a practical outlook and preference for a stable working environment. You probably can't deny that she gets results, but because Gemini thrives on variety and change, you may find the regime over which she presides rather slow, boring, and constraining. Still, like Gemini people, Taureans are nonconfrontational types who don't let emotions interfere with business. Being very adaptable, you probably get along with her rather well, despite your differences.

But if the tables are turned and you are a Taurus with a Gemini boss, you may find your working life disturbingly unpredictable. Gemini is mutable, or changeable, while Taurus is fixed, or unchanging, meaning that you may find it difficult to deal with Gemini's inconstancy, and may initially be resistant to assimilating the flurry of pioneering concepts that he generates. It probably doesn't help that Gemini is ruled by mentally adroit, fast-moving Mercury, while your guardian planet is the more indolent Venus. However, Gemini is a friendly, forgiving, and flexible person, who is generally willing to let you work in your own, more methodical way, as well as at your own, more leisurely pace, as long as you contribute your share of work.

Taurus and Gemini in the Workplace: If you are a Taurus, one of the few things that probably annoys you about your Gemini workmate is his or her tendency to waltz off, leaving you to soldier on with a joint project. Try to understand that Gemini isn't deliberately taking advantage of your conscientiousness, it's just that he or she has a low boredom threshold and doesn't share your recognition of the importance of detail. If you are a Gemini, you may find Taurus' working methods routine and unimaginative, but your colleague's even temper, reliability, and staying power have probably earned your respect.

Gemini Birth Influences

Ruling planet: Mercury
Element: Air
Polarity: Masculine
Quadruplicity: Mutable

Your unhurried attitude to your pace of work may get you into trouble with a mercurial Gemini boss, Taurus, but he or she probably appreciates your attention to detail and thoroughness.

Taurus Birth Influences

Ruling planet: Venus
Element: Earth
Polarity: Feminine
Quadruplicity: Fixed

TAURUS
CANCER

Taurus Birth Influences

Ruling planet: Venus
Element: Earth
Polarity: Feminine
Quadruplicity: Fixed

Taurus and Cancer's shared feminine polarity makes them naturally supportive individuals who are receptive to other people's ideas. Watery Cancer is the more creative and empathetic of the pair, but often lacks the earthy bull's solid practicality and unswerving determination. Together they make a fine team, although the crab's touchiness may bemuse even the most placid of bulls, and straightforward Taurus' occasional tactlessness may distress sensitive Cancer.

Your Boss: You probably respond well to your composed Taurus boss if you were born under the zodiacal sign of the crab. Your lunar ruler, watery element, and passive polarity make you hypersensitive to the emotions that are flying around your working environment, and those that you pick up from the bull are probably generally positive and steadying. The Taurean element of earth makes her a patient and practical person, who, having been born under a fixed sign, is furthermore quite predictable, while Venus injects a touch of relaxed indulgence, so that you know where you stand and can rely on her goodwill should you somehow overstep the mark a little. Because Cancer is a go-getting, cardinal sign, you may, however, be impatient with her tendency to reach decisions extremely slowly and ponderously.

If you are a Taurus working under a Cancerian senior, you must be grateful for his sympathetic words of support when things are going badly at work or you are having problems at home. But you are not a person who likes to dump your emotional baggage on others, so how could he have known that you were worried? The answer lies in Cancer's emotional radar, which soon detects signals that a member of his staff is disturbed, prompting him to reach out to soothe a troubled mind. That said, you may be confused by his sporadic tendency to shut his door to brood over a relatively insignificant setback. This is due to the cranky influence that the changeable element of water wields over him, and, as you've no doubt discovered, his mood will soon become more upbeat.

If something is getting you down, Taurus, you may be surprised when your Cancerian boss appears by your desk and asks if everything's okay. You will find her a supportive listener should you feel a rare need to unburden yourself.

Taurus and Cancer in the Workplace: You probably like and value your coworker if one of you is a steady Taurus and the other a thoughtful Cancer. Down-to-earth Taurus can be a little unimaginative and inert, but Cancer's lunar, aqueous, and cardinal birth influences bring ideas and enterprise to your partnership. Taurus in turn supplies staying power, a shrewd financial awareness, and a calming influence, even if the realistic bull's honesty upsets thin-skinned Cancer at times.

Cancer Birth Influences

Ruling planet: The Moon
Element: Water
Polarity: Feminine
Quadruplicity: Cardinal

LEO
TAURUS

A working relationship between Taurus and Leo is often productive and harmonious. Being a feminine, or passive sign, Taurus is receptive to the ideas that creative Leo (whose polarity is masculine, or active) generates, the fiery lion in return benefiting from the down-to-earth bull's steadying, level-headed influence. Should their vision differ, however, their common, fixed quadruplicity can cause each to be as inflexible as the other.

Your Boss: Even though regal Leos tend to believe that leadership should be theirs by right—their ruling planet is, after all, the Sun around which other planets revolve—you probably respect your Taurus boss if you are a zodiacal lion. Like yours, Taurus is a fixed sign, and you probably can't fault his determination and staying power, and while the Sun gives you a cheerful temperament, the sway that Venus wields over Taurus makes your boss an instinctively nonconfrontational type. Although your character clashes may consequently be few, you probably wish that Taurus were more imaginative and less cautious, which illustrates the difference between the fiery lion's spontaneous approach and the earthy bull's practical, routine-based outlook.

You probably consider your Leo boss a charismatic, inspiring, and energizing person to work for if you are a Taurus, but may long for her to slow down a little in order to give you more time to absorb and methodically think through her brainwaves, knowing from experience that they are either brilliant or completely unworkable. Big-picture Leo is generally not interested in detail, whereas Taurus believes that if an innovative concept is to be realized, mundane practicalities have to be painstakingly pondered, and that effective strategies can only be implemented after diligent research. Your respective elements of impatient fire and patient earth may be at odds here, but at least magnanimous, Sun-ruled Leo is generous in her praise when your careful work contributes to a stellar success.

Taurus and Leo in the Workplace: Both having fixed quadruplicities, Taurus and Leo are equally determined when striving to attain a common goal, and will work tenaciously, and in tandem, too, as long as they are in fundamental agreement. If this is the case and you are a Leo, you inject inspiration, impetus, and vitality into your partnership, your realistic Taurus colleague returning the favor by tempering your occasional rashness with his or her reasoned, sensible point of view. But if Taurus regards the fiery lion as being reckless, or Leo brands the earthy bull pedantic, the stubborn standoff could last for weeks.

Leo Birth Influences

Ruling planet: The Sun
Element: Fire
Polarity: Masculine
Quadruplicity: Fixed

The lion and the bull can both be stubborn. You may be frustrated by your Taurean colleague's rigid ways if you are a Leo who feels that you could breathe life into a foundering project.

Taurus Birth Influences

Ruling planet: Venus
Element: Earth
Polarity: Feminine
Quadruplicity: Fixed

TAURUS
VIRGO

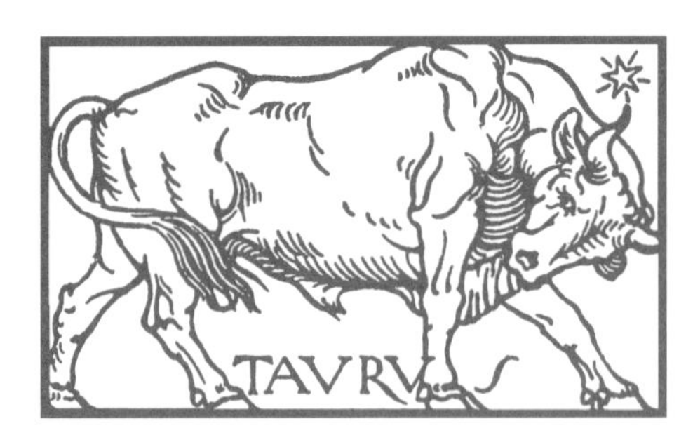

Taurus Birth Influences

Ruling planet: Venus
Element: Earth
Polarity: Feminine
Quadruplicity: Fixed

As long as they don't have a fundamental clash of opinion, when Taurus may shift into obstinate mode and Virgo may become sharply critical, this zodiacal pairing usually interacts harmoniously and productively at work. Their common element of earth and feminine, passive polarity give them a preference for working on practical projects behind the scenes, with fixed-sign Taurus providing staying power and mutable Virgo, adaptability.

Your Boss: The qualities that you like in your Taurean boss, if you are a Virgo, are probably those that your shared element of earth also bestows on you, notably a realistic outlook and a belief that even brilliant ideas will only succeed if they are rooted in firm foundations and backed up with thorough research and a stable support system. Yet the combination of your ruling planet, Mercury, and mutable quadruplicity gives you an analytical, speedy mind and impressive multitasking skills, while Venus-ruled Taurus is less at home in the realm of concepts and, being a fixed sign, prefers to see a task through to the end before embarking on another. You may consequently find the Taurean approach a little too slow, rigid, and one-dimensional for your liking.

Your Virgo boss may sometimes make you feel nervous if you are a Taurus, not because he is short-tempered or aggressive, but because you worry that you may not be able to meet this perfectionist's dauntingly high standards. Virgo's mercurial, mutable mind also operates at lightning speed, and because you are a child of leisurely Venus who prefers to fix your sights on completing one job at a time, you may have difficulty following his seemingly erratic thought processes. Having been born under an earth sign like you, your boss will value your reliability and steady, methodical working style, however, as well as the determined and tenacious way in which you approach any project.

Do you sometimes feel as though your Virgoan boss is marking off your qualities on a checklist? You may fear that your steady Taurean pace is too slow for mercurial Virgo, but be assured that he values your tenacity. Taureans shouldn't ever be paranoid!

Taurus and Virgo in the Workplace: Being straightforward, earthy people whose focus is on doing their work efficiently, neither Taurus nor Virgo has much time for the maneuverings of office politics. Instead, they prefer a working atmosphere that hums along happily, partly because Taurus is ruled by peaceable Venus and partly because mutable Virgo prefers to side-step confrontation. They therefore generally get along well in the workplace, not least because if you are a flexible Virgo, you are able to work around Taurus' rather unvarying habits. If you are a Taurus, you may nevertheless dislike Virgo's tendency to nit-pick, but then your stubbornness probably tests your colleague's patience, too.

Virgo Birth Influences

Ruling planet: Mercury
Element: Earth
Polarity: Feminine
Quadruplicity: Mutable

LIBRA

TAURUS

Although Venus, their shared planetary ruler, endows both Taurus and Libra with goodwill and the desire to work together amicably, their other birth influences may occasionally disrupt their usually harmonious relationship. Disagreements may arise when the bull's fixed, or somewhat static, nature conflicts with Libra's cardinal, or go-getting, approach. Their differences aside, airy Libra typically supplies information and ideas, which earthy Taurus diligently transforms into workable reality.

Your Boss: There are probably certain things on which you and your boss agree if she is a Taurus and you are a Libra, notably those that are associated with Venus, such as the importance of managing budgets efficiently and of keeping the peace when all hell threatens to break loose between hostile associates. You may also be impressed by the powerful concentration and determination that fixed-sign Taurus demonstrates, perhaps because your restless element of air often causes your attention to stray from a task in hand. But having been born under a masculine, or active, cardinal sign, you may find the slow and steady pace at which feminine, or passive, earthy Taurus works uninspiring and sometimes frustrating.

If you are a Taurus whose boss is a Libra, the friendly influence of Venus no doubt ensures that you get along well together. You may also appreciate the clarity and fluency with which he issues instructions, his airy element making him both a born communicator and a person who thinks logically and lucidly. Certain aspects of his character may rattle you, however, including the impatience and sense of urgency that his cardinal quadruplicity can bring to the fore. You may find this difficult to deal with because your earthy element makes you someone who is naturally patient and likes to do a job thoroughly and well, which inevitably takes time.

Taurus and Libra in the Workplace: Taurus and Libra are generally a good team, partly on account of their easygoing temperaments and partly because each has strengths that compensate for the other's weaknesses. If you are a Libra, you may be more innovative and imaginative than Taurus, but then the bull displays the staying power and willingness to pay attention to detail that you frequently lack. And if you are a Taurus, you may be more realistic and practical than airy Libra, but when you find yourselves in a corner, Libra is probably the more adaptable and persuasive of the two of you. His or her chattiness may get on your nerves, however, just as your bullheadedness may annoy Libra.

Libra Birth Influences

Ruling planet: Venus
Element: Air
Polarity: Masculine
Quadruplicity: Cardinal

Does it irritate you, Taurus, when your Libran boss comes tearing over to your desk and demands that you stop what you're doing and immediately start something new?

Taurus Birth Influences

Ruling planet: Venus
Element: Earth
Polarity: Feminine
Quadruplicity: Fixed

TAURUS

SCORPIO

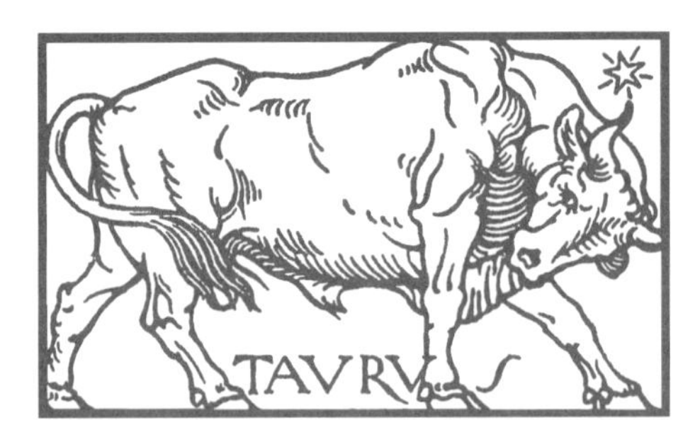

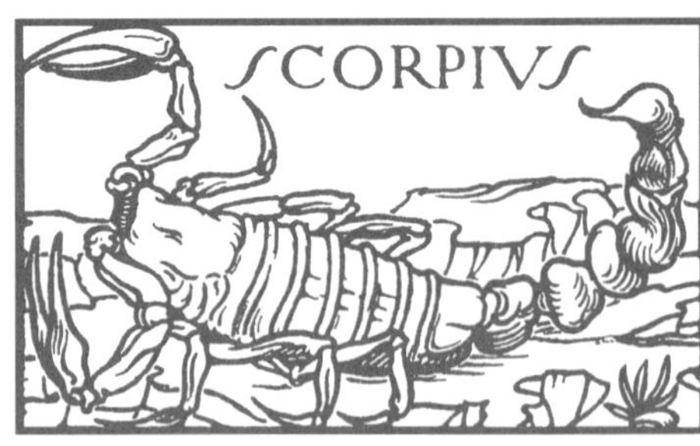

Taurus Birth Influences

Ruling planet: Venus
Element: Earth
Polarity: Feminine
Quadruplicity: Fixed

Scorpio's moodiness will probably exasperate you if you are a good-natured Taurus. If this is the case, stay out of his or her way for a while.

Scorpio Birth Influences

Ruling planet: Pluto; traditionally Mars
Element: Water
Polarity: Feminine
Quadruplicity: Fixed

♇ ♂

As long as they are in agreement, Taurus and Scorpio will concentrate on achieving a mutual goal with equal tenacity and determination because both were born under fixed signs. Although their shared feminine, or receptive, polarity makes them good listeners, earthy Taurus is more patient and good-natured with others than watery, moody Scorpio, but then the scorpion is more intuitive and inventive. Overall, these colleagues typically have a high regard for one another.

Your Boss: You are unlikely to have many complaints about your boss if he is a Taurus and you are a Scorpio. Having Venus as his planetary ruler means that he goes out of his way to ensure that his domain is a resentment-free zone, while his element of earth gives him a tendency to offer sensible, practical solutions to any work-related problems. Because your own element of water makes you a more emotional type, you may nevertheless wish that he showed more sympathy when things are going badly for you, but then you probably cannot fault his kindliness. As a fellow fixed sign, you may also understand that it's important to remain focused on the job in hand, particularly if you're the boss!

You must respect your boss if she is a Scorpio and you are a zodiacal bull, but may nevertheless find her disconcerting. You no doubt appreciate her formidable resolve, staying power, and the value that she places on loyalty because your fixed sign confers these qualities upon you, too. You may also be somewhat in awe of her astonishing insight, particularly into your own character, understanding and compassion being the gift of her watery element. This birth influence can often make her touchy and withdrawn, however, and that of Mars, her secondary ruling planet, sometimes manifests itself as naked aggression, all of which may leave you feeling puzzled and unsettled. At times like these, it's best to keep your head down and continue with your work until her mood undergoes a sea change and brightens again.

Taurus and Scorpio in the Workplace: It is not simply because they both take their work seriously that Taurus and Scorpio usually have a harmonious working relationship. If you are a bull, your even temper, patience, and diligence make you hard to fall out with, while if you are a scorpion, your imagination and empathy elicits a positive response from your Taurus colleague. Even so, Taurus' stolid pragmatism may exasperate creative Scorpio, Scorpio's changeability and Plutonian secretiveness in turn irritating the straightforward bull.

SAGITTARIUS

TAURUS

Provided that their working circumstances give them the leeway to deliver results at their own speed, and that their respective talents are fully utilized, Taurus and Sagittarius complement one another very effectively. Venus and Jupiter usually ensure that their association is harmonious, but conflict between their earthy and fiery elements and fixed and mutable quadruplicities may occasionally cast a cloud of resentment over their working relationship.

Your Boss: You may not find your boss very inspiring if you are a Sagittarius and she is a Taurus, but you probably have to admit that the bull's painstaking methods eventually get results. It's not just your ruling planet, Jupiter, the boss of the gods in Roman mythology, that makes you itch to do your own thing instead of following Taurus' lead. Sagittarius is a mutable, or restless, sign, whose element is progressive fire and whose polarity is masculine, or active, while Taurus is fixed, or rigid, earthy, or constant, and feminine, or passive. No wonder that you are sometimes frustrated by Taurus' rather plodding approach, but then maybe the influence of indulgent Venus means that she sometimes allows you the freedom of action that gives you such a buzz.

There are probably many things that you like about your Sagittarian boss if you are a Taurus, such as his confidence, disarming wit, and inclusive treatment of his staff—all gifts of Jupiter that arouse a positive response in the feminine-polarity, Venusian side of your character. At the same time, the part of you that is earthy and fixed may quiver with annoyance when he cheerily tells you to drop whatever it is that you're doing in order to kick-start his latest big idea. His tendency to do this is due to Sagittarius' innovative, variety-loving mutability and the enthusiastic spontaneity of the element of fire, which are often at odds with your realistic outlook and dislike of change, particularly if it means having to abandon a task before you've completed it. Even so, his evident faith in you must give you satisfaction.

Taurus and Sagittarius in the Workplace: Taurus and Sagittarius' contributions to the workplace are very different, but equally important. While earthy Taurus is a sensible, detail-oriented person with a fixed sign's remarkable staying power, fiery Sagittarius is a vital, creative character with a flair for communication and negotiation. Although both are usually tolerant types, you may find Taurus' stubbornness and slowness frustrating if you are a Sagittarius, while Sagittarius' impulsiveness and changeability may unnerve you if you are a Taurus.

Sagittarius Birth Influences

Ruling planet: Jupiter
Element: Fire
Polarity: Masculine
Quadruplicity: Mutable

As long as you're not in the middle of something else, Taurus, you are probably pleased when your Sagittarian boss comes over to talk to you. You appreciate that he doesn't distance himself from you and that he is so good humored.

Taurus Birth Influences

Ruling planet: Venus
Element: Earth
Polarity: Feminine
Quadruplicity: Fixed

TAURUS
CAPRICORN

Taurus Birth Influences

Ruling planet: Venus
Element: Earth
Polarity: Feminine
Quadruplicity: Fixed

Sharing as they do a feminine, passive polarity and practical, earthy element, Taurus and Capricorn may not be the most innovative or imaginative of workplace pairings, but can rely on each other to do a job meticulously and thoroughly. With such a similar approach, they seldom disagree, although cardinal Capricorn's personal ambition may flummox Taurus, and fixed Taurus' bullheadness may frustrate Capricorn.

Your Boss: Your long-term goal may be to step into your Taurus boss's shoes if you are a Capricorn, but you probably respect her authority, as well as her management style, partly because Saturn, your planetary ruler, has bequeathed you his traditional values, and partly because the bull's earthy element is also yours. You may consequently respond well to Taurus' methodical, realistic way of thinking and insistence on paying attention to detail and staying within budget. It is the influence of Venus, her ruling planet, that gives her a head for figures, as well as the peaceable temperament that makes her easy to work for. Having been born under a more enterprising and energetic, cardinal sign, you may, however, sigh at her fixed-quadruplicity viewpoint and unwillingness to take the occasional risk.

You may find your Capricorn boss a little intimidating if you are a Taurus. Although her feminine polarity helps to ensure that she listens to your opinions, she may be a hard taskmaster, even if she leads by example. The problem may be that Capricorn's standards are difficult to live up to, with Saturn manifesting himself in her refusal to tolerate idleness or carelessness, and her cardinal quadruplicity also making her someone who is forceful and driven. As an earthy Taurus, you may be hard-working, reliable, and productive—all of which Capricorn demands in an employee—but because you are a child of Venus, you would no doubt prefer a more relaxed and kindly working atmosphere.

If you are a Taurus, although you are a hard worker, you also have a laid-back nature and will not necessarily push as hard as your Capricorn coworker to get to the top. You may think that she should take things easy once in a while!

Taurus and Capricorn in the Workplace: Both Taurus and Capricorn are dependable, diligent, and disciplined, which makes it unlikely that they will clash over their working methods. There may be a lack of understanding at a more personal level, however. If you are a Capricorn, you may not comprehend why Taurus can be so laid-back on the one hand, and so stubborn on the other; the explanation lies in being ruled by Venus and having a fixed quadruplicity. And if you are a Taurus, you may be baffled by Capricorn's determination to climb the career ladder as quickly as possible; this is due to the influence of Saturn and a cardinal quadruplicity.

Capricorn Birth Influences

Ruling planet: Saturn
Element: Earth
Polarity: Feminine
Quadruplicity: Cardinal

AQUARIUS
TAURUS

Although the very different talents and approaches of Taurus and Aquarius could cause friction in the workplace, this rarely happens, partly because Venus-governed Taurus loathes unpleasantness, and partly because the Aquarian element is congenial air. Both being fixed signs, they are equally determined when working toward a common goal, with Aquarius supplying innovative ideas and Taurus beavering away behind the scenes to transform them into practical reality.

Your Boss: The boredom factor is probably the downside of having Taurus as a boss if you are an Aquarius. Despite sharing a fixed quadruplicity, the additional input of his steady, realistic element of earth makes him more reluctant to embrace radical departures from convention than you, whose birth influences include the revolutionary Uranus and intellectual element of air. As a result, he may refuse to countenance investing in the cutting-edge software that you believe would improve your company's fortunes, not only because the Taurean maxim may be "If it ain't broke, don't fix it," but also because his planetary ruler is the money-conscious Venus. Nevertheless, you no doubt find this even-tempered character hard to resent.

You may find that there are advantages in working for Aquarius, if you are a Taurus, such as a genial boss who is both approachable and communicative, and who can match your staying power when a project really captures her attention. What may unsettle you, however, is her apparent tendency to switch off when you are trying to discuss the details inherent in a task that she has delegated to you, demonstrating the difference between your matter-of-fact element of earth and Aquarius' more restless, flighty element of air. Despite appearances, be reassured that Aquarius probably is paying attention, if only to thank her lucky stars that she can rely on you to spare her the burden of dealing with the minutiae that she finds so tedious and offputting.

Taurus and Aquarius in the Workplace: The Aquarian polarity is masculine, or active, that of Taurus being feminine, or reactive. Having Uranus as a planetary governor and air as an element makes Aquarius an ideas person, while Taurus is influenced by financially aware Venus and the sensible element of earth. Put Aquarius and Taurus together in a working context, and all of the bases are therefore covered. If you are an Aquarius, you may find Taurus frustratingly slow to come round to your forward-looking viewpoint, however, and if you are a Taurus, you may wish that Aquarius would stop raving on about what you consider to be totally unworkable concepts and would get down to some real work.

Aquarius Birth Influences

Ruling planet: Uranus; traditionally Saturn
Element: Air
Polarity: Masculine
Quadruplicity: Fixed

With Aquarius' innovative ideas being supported by Taurus' productiveness, this has the makings of a good partnership.

Taurus Birth Influences

Ruling planet: Venus
Element: Earth
Polarity: Feminine
Quadruplicity: Fixed

TAURUS

PISCES

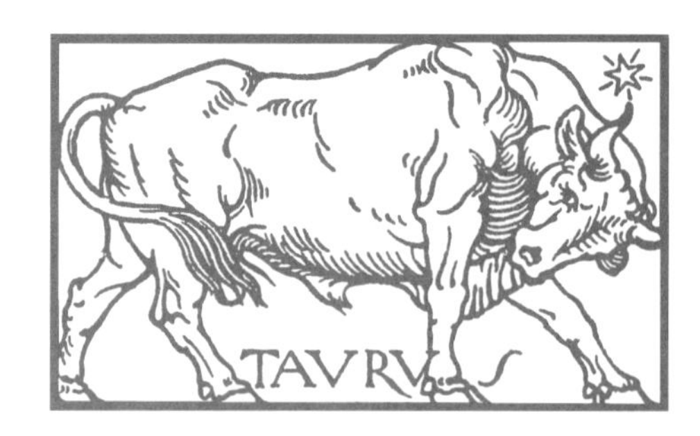

Taurus Birth Influences

Ruling planet: Venus
Element: Earth
Polarity: Feminine
Quadruplicity: Fixed

Although they may like each other as people, a working relationship between Taurus and Pisces can sometimes become rather fraught. Pisces may admire Taurus' practical skills, and the bull Pisces' creativity, but their differences may nevertheless give rise to friction, with Pisces considering Taurus unimaginative and unbending, and Taurus regarding Pisces as unrealistic and unreliable.

Your Boss: Taurus and Pisces' shared feminine polarity causes them to be receptive to those around them, but if you are a Pisces, your emotional element of water and your empathetic planetary ruler, Neptune, make you especially sensitive to others' moods, which is why you may be relieved to be working for an even-tempered Taurean boss who dislikes a tense atmosphere as much you do. Having been born under a mutable, or restless, sign yourself, you may, however, wish that Taurus wasn't so set in her ways, a characteristic that is derived from having a fixed, or unchanging, quadruplicity and a routine-loving element of earth.

You may find your boss kind, considerate, and flexible if he is a Pisces and you are a Taurus, but may still find him trying to work for at times. You may have two problems with Pisces in particular, the first being his lofty idealism—an attribute of Neptune that, being a down-to-earth type yourself, you may view as being hopelessly impractical—and the second being Pisces' dramatic mood swings, which may both puzzle and trouble you. These are the inevitable consequence of having water as an element and a mutable quadruplicity, so don't feel personally responsible when Pisces descends into gloom.

You may respect your Piscean boss's relaxed and adaptable nature if you are an easygoing Taurus, but may wish that he'd take his head out of the clouds and come down to Earth once in a while.

Taurus and Pisces in the Workplace: Taurus and Pisces are similar in many respects. Due to their common feminine polarity, both are quite introverted, while their ruling planets—respectively Venus and Neptune—give them a tendency to try get along with, rather than antagonize, those around them. This means that their interaction at work is unlikely to be peppered with heated arguments, even if tension between their different temperaments and approaches sometimes brings them both to simmering point. If you are a patient, steady, and methodical Taurus who likes to complete one job before starting on another, you may have trouble coming to terms with Pisces' love of variety, lack of staying power, and unpredictability, for example. And if you are a Pisces, you may be equally frustrated by stubborn Taurus' insistence on sticking firmly to facts and established procedures instead of going with the more imaginative, adaptable, Piscean flow.

Pisces Birth Influences

Ruling planet: Neptune; traditionally Jupiter
Element: Water
Polarity: Feminine
Quadruplicity: Mutable

GEMINI
GEMINI

Because theirs is a masculine, aggressive sign, and because their talents and instincts are so similar, it is possible that two Geminis may consider each other rivals in the workplace. That said, neither is particularly competitive or ambitious—except when it comes to dreaming up ingenious ideas—and each cannot help but have respect for the other's intellect. Being friendly, talkative, and playful types, both would far rather gossip and laugh together than stab one another in the back. The question is, will any work get done?

Your Boss: In many respects, you must be relieved that your boss is a Gemini if you are one, too. Your shared element of air gives you an equal dislike of rigid procedures and routines, which means that you must appreciate the relatively free hand that your boss gives you, and may applaud his impatience with office protocol and bureaucratic red tape. The combined influence of air, Mercury, and your mutable quadruplicity also means that you are both intellectually curious, think along the same rational and objective lines, and are inspired by innovative ideas. In practice, this probably means that your boss is willing to listen to your proposals with an open mind and that you have many stimulating and productive debates about how best to proceed. The trouble is, your working relationship may generally be all talk and no action, and on the days when your mutability makes either of you moody, there may be no meeting of minds at all.

Gemini and Gemini in the Workplace: If you and your coworker are both Geminis, you probably like each other a lot, even if you know that you often have a bad influence on one another. Your shared quadruplicity causes you both to thrive on variety, and if this is lacking, you quickly become bored and restless, which is when your airy, jokey, chatty side may kick in and you may relieve the tedium by encouraging each other to play pranks, tease those around you, or speculate about their personal lives. It's all great fun, but hardly conducive to making progress with the job in hand. When your joint attention is really captured by a project's potential, however, you may work together seamlessly, both of you expressing your viewpoints intelligently and articulately, displaying adaptability, and rarely taking offense if one of you disagrees with the other. But then one of you may lose interest and break the productive spell.

Gemini Birth Influences

Ruling planet: Mercury
Element: Air
Polarity: Masculine
Quadruplicity: Mutable

Two Gemini coworkers will keep each other entertained throughout a tedious day. These pranksters may find themselves in trouble, however, if they forget that there's a job to be done.

Gemini Birth Influences

Ruling planet: Mercury
Element: Air
Polarity: Masculine
Quadruplicity: Mutable

GEMINI
CANCER

Gemini Birth Influences

Ruling planet: Mercury
Element: Air
Polarity: Masculine
Quadruplicity: Mutable

A Cancer boss may be so concerned for his employee's welfare that Gemini finds his interest intrusive.

Cancer Birth Influences

Ruling planet: The Moon
Element: Water
Polarity: Feminine
Quadruplicity: Cardinal

The primary difference between Gemini and Cancer's attitude toward work is usually that Gemini regards it as a source of intellectual stimulation, while Cancer considers it a means of building up financial security, which is why Cancer is often more long-suffering than Gemini. With Gemini providing ideas, enthusiasm, and verbal skills, and Cancer creativity, thoughtfulness, and caution, they generally complement one another well, even if Gemini's capriciousness sometimes annoys Cancer, and Gemini is occasionally disconcerted by the combination of Cancer's sensitivity and forcefulness.

Your Boss: Although your cheerful, neutral Gemini boss must be hard to dislike, you may nonetheless find her exasperating if you are a Cancer. Your feminine polarity, lunar ruler, and watery element make you profoundly responsive to others, and because quick-thinking Gemini has a mercurial and mutable mind, trying to follow the rapid twists and turns of her way of thinking, however articulately she explains her logic, may make you feel dizzy. But then you may be relieved that Gemini is also impartial and adaptable, and is consequently willing to weigh up your views objectively and perhaps take them on board.

When you have problems at work, you must appreciate your boss's ability to listen and empathize if he is a Cancer and you are a Gemini, which is when you reap the benefits of his compassionate planetary ruler and element. Yet the same birth influences may sometimes drive you to distraction. Cancerian bosses often treat their charges as second families, encouraging them to share their feelings and details of their personal lives, while you are more comfortable in the realm of reason and prefer to discuss an intriguing new concept than people's loved ones, even yours.

Gemini and Cancer in the Workplace: Having been born under a masculine, or pioneering, sign, the typical Gemini is focused on the future, also welcoming change and being fascinated by the potential inherent in innovative ideas, whereas Moon-ruled Cancer is suspicious of the unfamiliar. If you are a Gemini, you may therefore be frustrated by Cancer's resistance to taking a leap into the unknown, but may also be shocked by the vehemence of cardinal Cancer's response when you push it too far. If you are that Cancer, you may in turn find Gemini's tendency to champion the latest big idea tiresome, and can probably add his or her mutable fickleness and fidgetiness to your list of gripes. Such niggles aside, Cancer may find Gemini a refreshing personality, while Gemini may often be grateful for Cancer's circumspection and understanding when things go wrong.

LEO — GEMINI

Although they may respect and like one another, a working relationship between Gemini and Leo can become tense under pressure. This is mainly due to conflict between their mutable and fixed quadruplicities, when Gemini's lack of staying power may infuriate Leo, Leo's inflexibility in turn exasperating Gemini. That apart, these masculine, enterprising zodiacal signs typically make a fine team.

Your Boss: You may find your Gemini boss both stimulating and frustrating to work for if you are a Leo—stimulating because she has a talent for firing up your imagination with an inventive idea, and frustrating because, having done so, she may then suddenly lose interest in it before you've had the chance to develop it. If so, this illustrates the interaction of Gemini's planetary ruler (the quick-thinking Mercury), the inspirational element of air, and a changeable nature, as well as the effect that this interplay has on fixed-sign Leo. Gemini is nevertheless probably hard to dislike, partly because she is adaptable, partly because she is persuasive, and also because she, like you, believes that work should be fun.

If you are a Gemini, your birth influences combine to give you an abhorrence of being forced to knuckle under by a stern authority figure, which is why you may have difficulty being a model employee if your boss is a commanding, Sun-ruled Leo who demands loyalty and hard work. Having been born under a fixed sign, he is no doubt decisive, disciplined, well-organized, and constant, and expects you to be the same, which is a tough demand to make of an airy, free-spirited Gemini. Despite this, the occasional fiery flare-up aside, you may find that you are grateful for his generally sunny outlook, and may also find yourself stimulated by his spontaneity, enthusiasm, and ambitious visions.

Gemini and Leo in the Workplace: When Gemini and Leo have equal status in the workplace, they typically get along well, not least because witty Gemini makes Leo laugh, while Leo's vitality and playfulness energize Gemini. If you are a Leo, you may also admire Gemini's gift for analysis and communication, and while some may brand his or her ideas outlandish, your experimental solar ruler and fiery element may make you see them as potentially trendsetting. Mutable Gemini's moodiness may try your patience at times, however, but then your coworker can probably counter this gripe by saying that you can be overbearing and unyielding. Yet what you may particularly appreciate about your Leo colleague, if you are a Gemini, is his or her confidence, willingness to run with an original idea, and tenacity in seeing it through to the end.

Leo Birth Influences

Ruling planet: The Sun
Element: Fire
Polarity: Masculine
Quadruplicity: Fixed

A free-spirited Gemini may find a Leo boss too demanding and authoritarian, even while admiring her enthusiastic, inspiring approach to work.

Gemini Birth Influences

Ruling planet: Mercury
Element: Air
Polarity: Masculine
Quadruplicity: Mutable

GEMINI
VIRGO

Gemini Birth Influences

Ruling planet: Mercury
Element: Air
Polarity: Masculine
Quadruplicity: Mutable

Both being mutable signs that have Mercury as a planetary ruler, Gemini and Virgo are generally on the same forward-looking, quick-thinking wavelength, and are analytical, adaptable, and articulate to boot. Yet airy, masculine-polarity Gemini is more of a pioneering presence in the workplace than earthy, feminine-polarity Virgo, who is more comfortable providing practical backup. As a result, they usually make an effective combination, even if their different approaches occasionally cause friction between them.

Your Boss: There may be many qualities that you admire in your boss if she is a Gemini and you are a Virgo, such as the confidence that is the bequest of a masculine polarity, or the ingenious ideas that are the gift of the element of air. And because you share the same ruling planet and flexible nature, you no doubt have little trouble staying abreast of Gemini's rapidly changing thought processes or juggling your workload to accommodate her latest request. You may, however, find her airy lack of attention to detail trying, but, having been born under an earthy, feminine sign, probably enjoy beavering away diligently behind the scenes to ensure that if her castles in the sky are to be translated into reality, they will be built on firm foundations.

You probably respect your Virgo superior if you are a Gemini, although it is unlikely that you regard him as an inspiring influence. What you may appreciate in Virgo—perhaps because you share these characteristics—are his sense of fair play, way of dealing with problems rationally and objectively, and ability to convey his instructions clearly and fluently. Your element of air makes you someone who likes to let your imagination fly free, while earthy Virgo operates strictly within the bounds of reality and feasibility, which is why you may nevertheless resent his tendency to bring you back down to earth when you propose a plan that you think is innovative and inventive, but he regards as being harebrained and impracticable.

If you are a Virgo, you are probably annoyed when your Gemini coworker stops what he's doing, sits back, and starts goofing around, but maybe he's just trying to inject a little fun into your day.

Gemini and Virgo in the Workplace: If you are a Virgo, you may find airy, restless Gemini a distracting person to work with, maybe because his or her low boredom threshold and urge to liven up a subdued working atmosphere often result in a volley of wisecracks being delivered in your direction. And if you are a Gemini, you may wish that serious, routine-loving Virgo would lighten up a little and stop trying to organize you. That said, you probably appreciate earthy Virgo's reliability, while Virgo may find your positive outlook refreshing.

Virgo Birth Influences

Ruling planet: Mercury
Element: Earth
Polarity: Feminine
Quadruplicity: Mutable

LIBRA
GEMINI

When airy Gemini and Libra share a workspace, there's sure to be plenty of animated discussion and lots of laughter, too, although how much actual work will be done is a different matter, partly because both are typically more interested in initiating ideas than pondering practicalities and also because both can lack staying power. They may not always be on the same wavelength, but their respective birth influences indicate that they generally get on well.

Your Boss: It may seem as though your Gemini boss's quick brain and motor mouth are never still, which you may find both stimulating and a little wearisome if you are a Libra—stimulating because you were born under an air sign and are thus inspired by his inventive ideas, and wearisome because Venus, your ruling planet, moves at a slower pace than Mercury, Gemini's planetary governor. Another minor gripe that you may have about mutable Gemini is his occasional moodiness, which you may find unsettling if, in common with most Librans, "balance" is your watchword, but you must be relieved that your boss is usually as easygoing as you are.

Overall, your Libra boss may be a joy to work for if you are a Gemini, in which case be grateful to your joint element of air and masculine, or pioneering, polarity, as well as indulgent Venus, all of which may make Libra sympathetic to, and often enthusiastic about, your ingenious contributions to brainstorming sessions. One of the few problems that you may have in working for Libra, however, is her insistence on meeting deadlines. This priority illustrates the difference between her cardinal sign, which bestows a sense of urgency upon Librans when it comes to meeting targets, and your more restless, less goal-focused, mutable sign.

Gemini and Libra in the Workplace: You probably rarely stop talking if you and your coworker are a Gemini and a Libra, but because your mutual airy element is as much associated with fun as it is with communication, gossip may feature the most in your verbal exchanges. If you are a Libra, you may admire the lightning speed at which Mercury-governed Gemini's mind operates, but may sometimes feel let down by your mutable colleague's unreliability. And if you are an objective Gemini, you may respect Libra's Venusian mediation skills when you are unable to talk your way out of a tight spot, but may bristle if you think that he or she is being two-faced when smoothing someone else's ruffled feathers.

Libra Birth Influences

Ruling planet: Venus
Element: Air
Polarity: Masculine
Quadruplicity: Cardinal

Your Mercury-governed, Gemini boss will certainly inspire you if you are a Libra. The meetings that she leads are likely to be lively and fun.

Gemini Birth Influences

Ruling planet: Mercury
Element: Air
Polarity: Masculine
Quadruplicity: Mutable

GEMINI
SCORPIO

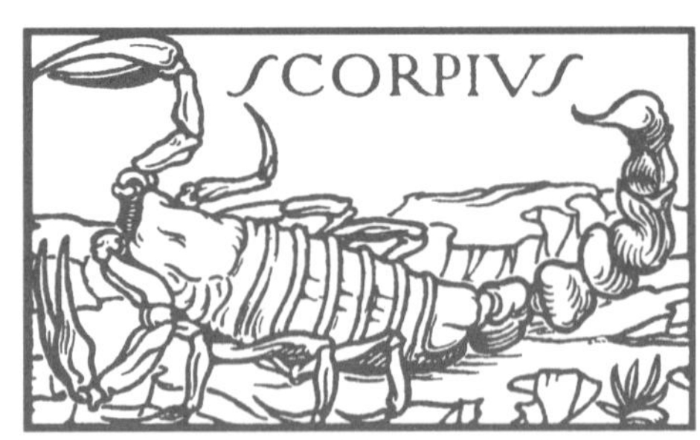

Gemini Birth Influences

Ruling planet: Mercury
Element: Air
Polarity: Masculine
Quadruplicity: Mutable

If you are a Scorpio, you may often feel like putting a sock in your Gemini coworker's mouth, especially when you're trying to finish a task. Gemini's gossip may often interest you, though.

Scorpio Birth Influences

Ruling planet: Pluto; traditionally Mars
Element: Water
Polarity: Feminine
Quadruplicity: Fixed

If they are both inspired and motivated by their work, Gemini and Scorpio can complement one another extremely well in the workplace. Information gathering and communication are Mercury-ruled, airy Gemini's fortes, while watery, Pluto-governed Scorpio's strengths include creativity and a gift for strategic thinking. Mutable Gemini is adaptable, but inconstant, and fixed-sign Scorpio is persistent, but inflexible—qualities that they may both admire and dislike in each other.

Your Boss: You may sometimes feel as though you are working for a butterfly if you are a zodiacal scorpion with a Gemini boss. Having been born under a fixed sign, you are blessed with formidable powers of concentration and like to see a project through to the end before starting on the next, unlike mutable Gemini, who thrives on variety, becomes restless if unenthused, and may then tend to tour the office talking to everyone. On the plus side, he is probably flexible, and because your feminine polarity and watery element make you receptive to others' vibes and give you a tendency to be wounded by indifference or criticism, you probably value Gemini's genial temperament, interest in your work, and habit of giving praise where praise is due.

Working for Scorpio may really keep you on your toes if you are a Gemini, not because your work is difficult, but more likely because his standards—which you may not share—are so high. His fixed nature makes him something of a planner and perfectionist, as well as a stickler for convention and a person with extraordinary staying power, whereas you find dealing with detail tedious. You also love experimenting with the new and often lack self-discipline when bored. Indeed, it may feel as though you are back at school under Scorpio's strict regime, but you may nevertheless be grateful that your boss is surprisingly understanding when you are struggling, for which you have his intuitive and compassionate element of water to thank.

Gemini and Scorpio in the Workplace: Most Geminis never stop talking, and your coworker's conversation may both entertain and exasperate you if you are a Scorpio. The benefits may include the welcome lightening of a fraught working atmosphere and the tidbits of gossip that you glean, for Pluto gives you an appetite for clandestine knowledge. The downside is being distracted from the job in hand. But then, if you are a Gemini, you may consider fixed-sign Scorpio to be overly earnest and someone who needs to be more open to diversity. Yet you may also appreciate Scorpio's dependability, and can be amazed by his or her original ideas and insights.

SAGITTARIUS
GEMINI

When Gemini and Sagittarius work together, there is often a meeting of minds. Their respective planetary rulers, Mercury and Jupiter, are both associated with the intellect, and their progressive masculine polarity gives them a fascination with cutting-edge concepts. Having been born under mutable signs, they are also adaptable and ready to countenance change. Their elements may sometimes cause friction between them, however, for airy Gemini is a rational thinker and may therefore throw cold water on some of fiery Sagittarius' impulsive proposals, while Sagittarius may be frustrated by Gemini's tendency to value logic over creativity.

Sagittarius Birth Influences

Ruling planet: Jupiter
Element: Fire
Polarity: Masculine
Quadruplicity: Mutable

Your Boss: Overall, you may find Gemini fun to work for if you are a Sagittarius. Not only does her airy element give her a light-hearted outlook that no doubt accords with your own optimistic nature (in your case, the gift of Jupiter), but, like you, she probably loathes routines, and her love of variety no doubt matches your own. You may also admire the speed with which her mercurial mind operates, and the articulacy with which she outlines her ideas, but may be disappointed that she doesn't always share your enthusiasm for your own suggestions. If so, it may be that this is due to a temperamental mismatch between Gemini's reliance on reason and Sagittarius' original, wide-ranging vision.

Although Gemini and Sagittarius share a mutable quadruplicity, which means that they can both be moody at times, Sagittarius' volatile spells are often sparked by the element of fire, causing hot-headed outbursts that you may find trying if you are a more dispassionate Gemini with an archer for a boss. But then these are probably mercifully brief interruptions in your normally good-humored working relationship, and may be outweighed by other Sagittarian traits, such as the fiery zeal and energy that you may find so motivating, as well as the inclusive way in which your boss treats you and your coworkers.

Although you generally make a happy and positive team if you are a Sagittarius and your coworker is a Gemini, your hot temper may sometimes get the better of you.

Gemini and Sagittarius in the Workplace: Mutable Gemini and Sagittarius colleagues usually have a natural rapport that is partly based on their gregarious personalities and partly on their need for intellectual stimulation. Gemini's predilection for passing on juicy nuggets of gossip spiced with witty observations may have you in stitches if you are a fiery Sagittarius, just as Sagittarius' novel and passionately expressed viewpoints may pique your interest if you are an airy Gemini. If one of you is not in the best of moods, however, Sagittarius may learn just how withering Gemini's tongue can be, while Gemini may be startled by Sagittarius' explosive temper.

Gemini Birth Influences

Ruling planet: Mercury
Element: Air
Polarity: Masculine
Quadruplicity: Mutable

GEMINI
CAPRICORN

Gemini Birth Influences

Ruling planet: Mercury
Element: Air
Polarity: Masculine
Quadruplicity: Mutable

A basic difference between Gemini and Capricorn is that Gemini works to live, and needs to have fun while earning a living, and Capricorn lives to work, and is prepared to endure almost anything in the quest to reach the top of the career ladder. They have different strengths: generating and communicating ideas number among mercurial, airy Gemini's skills, while saturnine, earthy Capricorn is formidably productive, meticulous, and well organized. They may not always see eye to eye, but recognize that each has talents that the other lacks.

Your Boss: Although you may find amiable, light-hearted Gemini hard to dislike, you probably disapprove of his working methods if you are a Capricorn. Having Saturn as a planetary ruler and earth as an element, you like to operate within structured routines and hierarchies, which means that airy, mutable Gemini's free-and-easy attitude to time-keeping and protocols may unsettle you. While Saturn moves slowly, Mercury, which governs Gemini, has the fastest rate of revolution around the Sun of all of the planets, as a result of which you probably prefer working at a far more unhurried pace than Gemini sets.

If you are a Gemini, you may not enjoy being Capricorn's subordinate, even though you may respect the air of authority that she projects, as well as the results that she achieves. Her go-getting, cardinal quadruplicity and straightforward, earthy element make her focused and impatient to accomplish her goals, whereas your mutable and airy birth influences give you a tendency to procrastinate, be it because you are beset by indecision or have been distracted by an intriguing diversion. And woe betide you if you miss a deadline, when saturnine Capricorn may call you into her office for a dispiriting lecture on collective responsibility and taking your job seriously.

If you're a Gemini with an unorthodox working style, your Capricorn boss may come down hard on you.

Gemini and Capricorn in the Workplace: If you are a Capricorn, you probably think that your Gemini colleague should talk less and work harder, and if you are a Gemini, you no doubt wish that Capricorn would lighten up and return your banter once in a while. Despite these mutual gripes, there must be certain qualities that you admire in one another, and may have cause to be thankful for, too. Gemini's objective, analytical, and quick-thinking mind may rapidly come up with ingenious solutions to problems that have long been preoccupying you if you are a Capricorn, while Capricorn's attention to detail and reliability may have saved your bacon more than once if you are a Gemini.

Capricorn Birth Influences

Ruling planet: Saturn
Element: Earth
Polarity: Feminine
Quadruplicity: Cardinal

AQUARIUS
GEMINI

Although Gemini's lack of staying power may annoy Aquarius, and Aquarius' dogmatism may frustrate Gemini, it is usually only the discrepancy between their mutable and fixed quadruplicities that causes this pair to exchange sharp words in the workplace. Not only are they both pioneering personalities, thanks to their shared masculine polarity, but their airy element makes them affable colleagues, logical thinkers, and gifted communicators. In addition, their planetary governors, Mercury and Uranus, give them an intellectual affinity, so that they usually respond well to each other's ideas.

Your Boss: If you are an Aquarius and your Gemini boss seems more like a friend than someone who has authority over you, this is probably due to the influence of your joint element of air. You airy types are typically good-natured, informal, and talkative, as well as people who are inspired by innovative concepts, which is why you may have such a natural rapport with Gemini, and may spend a lot of time brainstorming a variety of potential projects with your boss. You may, however, dislike his tendency to lose interest in a proposal which you believe could be groundbreaking and have worked hard on developing, for which you can blame his restless, mutable quadruplicity.

You may find Aquarius an inspiring boss if you are a Gemini, partly because she, like you, believes that work should be fun, and partly because she comes up with such cutting-edge ideas. As a quick-thinking, objective child of Mercury, you probably rapidly grasp the implications—both positive and negative—of her propositions, but because Aquarius is a fixed sign and yours is mutable, you may wish that she were more willing to accept the changes that you in turn propose. Indeed, although you are flexible, there may be times when her insistence on doing things her way irritates you immensely.

Gemini and Aquarius in the Workplace: The sound of silence is unlikely to be a regular feature of a working relationship between talkative Gemini and loquacious Aquarius, both of whom thrive on verbal interaction and are energized by exchanging opinions. Yet if you are a fixed-sign Aquarius, you probably wish that Gemini didn't have such a grasshopperlike mind and would stay on a topic long enough for you to be able to explain your radical theories in full. If you are a mutable Gemini, you in turn may be bored of hearing about how new technology will revolutionize office life in the future, and may be itching to switch the subject to something that interests you more.

Aquarius Birth Influences

Ruling planet: Uranus; traditionally Saturn
Element: Air
Polarity: Masculine
Quadruplicity: Fixed

While Aquarius and Gemini often shoot the breeze at work, Aquarius can sometimes be too stubborn for Gemini's liking.

Gemini Birth Influences

Ruling planet: Mercury
Element: Air
Polarity: Masculine
Quadruplicity: Mutable

GEMINI
PISCES

Gemini Birth Influences
Ruling planet: Mercury
Element: Air
Polarity: Masculine
Quadruplicity: Mutable

Not only do Gemini and Pisces share a mutable quadruplicity, but both can be said to be split personalities, exemplified by the two twins and two fishes—often moving in opposite directions—that symbolize their signs. This means that both airy, intellectual Gemini and watery, creative Pisces are versatile and respond well to diversity, but can also be moody and indecisive, which may sometimes cause friction between them. Yet genial Gemini and kindly Pisces usually get on well, and each generally has respect for the other's strengths.

Your Boss: Your livewire Gemini boss may occasionally throw you into a panic if you are a highly responsive Pisces. Her zodiacal sign is masculine, or proactive; mercurial, or quick-thinking; and airy, or communicative, whereas yours is feminine, or reactive; Neptunian, or dreamy; and watery, or pensive. You may consequently often feel overwhelmed by the volley of ideas that Gemini fires at you, and may become so flustered that you are unable to think straight, which may make mutable Gemini impatient. But then you, too, were born under a mutable sign, and are therefore able to go with the Geminian flow once you have spent some time alone to gather your thoughts.

Sharing as you do a mutable quadruplicity with your Piscean boss, you probably enjoy the informality and lack of structure that may typify his management style if you are a Gemini, for you also work best in a free-and-easy working environment. Your rational ruling planet and unemotional airy element make you more logical than Pisces, whose visionary planetary governor and intuitive element give him a tendency to think idealistically and laterally, so that you may frequently be astonished by the subtle brilliance of his unusual ideas. Yet because Pisces is more of a "feeling" person and less articulate than you, there may be times when you are frustrated by his vagueness.

You will probably enjoy the relaxed workplace culture of a Piscean boss if you are a Gemini.

Gemini and Pisces in the Workplace: If you are a Pisces, you are no doubt very sensitive to, and deeply affected by, others' moods, which is why you must be grateful to be working alongside cheerful, airy Gemini, who, although not immune to the odd bout of bad temper, rarely remains in negative mode for long. And what you may particularly appreciate in your Piscean colleague if you are a Gemini, is his or her readiness to drop everything for you if you need a helping hand, for which you have unselfish Neptune and the compassionate element of water to thank.

Pisces Birth Influences
Ruling planet: Neptune; traditionally Jupiter
Element: Water
Polarity: Feminine
Quadruplicity: Mutable

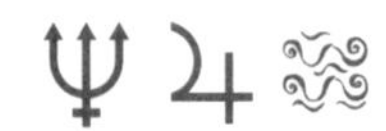

CANCER
CANCER

Having identical birth influences means that two Cancerian colleagues are generally on the same wavelength, instinctively understand and respect one another's thought processes and methods, and typically work to live rather than live to work. Although their feminine polarity in particular gives them a preference for quietly working away behind the scenes, their cardinal quadruplicity can make them remarkably focused, forceful, and fast when inspired by a goal or under pressure to meet a deadline.

Your Boss: Your lunar ruling planet and watery element may have given you a wonderful imagination if you are a Cancer, and you may be finding that your creative juices are flowing like never before if your boss is a fellow crab. The combined effect of the Moon and water can cause you to be oversensitive and vulnerable to criticism, which is why you must appreciate his or her preference for gently guiding you in the right direction rather than harshly reprimanding you when you have meandered off course. Because Cancer is a born nurturer, your boss probably treats you and your coworkers like family members by expressing concern for your welfare, encouraging you to fulfill your potential, and making time to listen empathetically to your problems, be they work- or home-related. You must be thriving in this caring and supportive atmosphere, but there may also be times when your days are a little fraught. Not only is your boss responsible for your team's success, but Cancer's cardinal quadruplicity imbues those born under this sign with a sense of urgency when working toward a target, so that your boss may sometimes push you harder than you would like. But because you are an empathetic person, and can similarly pull out all of the stops when necessary, you probably don't take your boss's occasional abruptness personally and carry out his or her instructions with determination and vigor.

Cancer and Cancer in the Workplace: You may consider your workmate a good friend if you are both Cancers. It is thanks to your planetary governor, element, and polarity that you are sensitive and compassionate characters who are usually ready to offer a sympathetic ear when one or other of you is upset or struggling. Due to your cardinal quadruplicity, you are also likely to give practical, as well as emotional, assistance. The one thing that may be lacking in your relationship, however, is the intellectual stimulation that comes from working alongside a completely different personality, but then you are no doubt surrounded by quite a few of those.

Cancer Birth Influences
Ruling planet: The Moon
Element: Water
Polarity: Feminine
Quadruplicity: Cardinal

Cancer colleagues will enjoy working together. They are also likely to be very supportive of one another.

Cancer Birth Influences
Ruling planet: The Moon
Element: Water
Polarity: Feminine
Quadruplicity: Cardinal

CANCER
LEO

Cancer Birth Influences
Ruling planet: The Moon
Element: Water
Polarity: Feminine
Quadruplicity: Cardinal

As long as Leo remembers that Cancer is a sensitive soul whose feelings must be respected, and Cancer gives the lion the respect that Leos consider their birthright, this pair will interact happily and productively in the workplace. Not only is Moon-governed Cancer kind-hearted and supportive, and Sun-ruled Leo a warm and jovial personality, but their respective elements and polarities make the crab an instinctive, creative "thinker," and the lion an energetic, inspirational "doer." Add Cancer's cardinal and Leo's fixed quadruplicities to the mix, and this is a team that has both ambition and staying power.

Your Boss: The Sun's influence means that most Leos regard themselves as natural leaders, their spontaneous, fiery element also causing them to resist being constrained by others' rules, which is why you may resent having to yield to your Cancer boss's authority if you are a zodiacal lion. That said, there may be a number of qualities that you admire in Cancer that often ignite your fiery enthusiasm, too, including the drive that comes from having a cardinal quadruplicity and his fertile imagination—the joint bequest of the Moon and the element of water. He is probably a good listener, and you may appreciate the empathy that he shows when you bring a problem to him, as well as the thought that he gives to finding a solution.

If you are a Cancer, you probably find that working for Leo can be exciting. Because your polarity is feminine, or receptive, and the Moon makes you impressionable, the combination of masculine-polarity Leo's dynamism, sizzling energy, and air of commanding authority must have a powerful impact on you. Indeed, you must feel motivated and vitalized by your positive, vigorous boss, and can probably forgive the occasional fiery rant—even though temperamental outbursts upset watery, emotional crabs—because you sense that stress, not meanness, has provoked the lion's roar.

If Leo offends her Cancer colleague with a tactless remark, he'll withdraw into his shell.

Cancers and Leos in the Workplace: Your Cancerian colleague may be a soothing presence at work if you are a Leo: quiet, thoughtful, sympathetic, and always ready to help out or to push you on to meet an impending deadline should your leonine laziness have caused you to fall behind. You may not like the crab's tendency to burst into tears or give you the silent treatment when you have somehow caused offense with an unthinking remark, however. Equally, if you are a Cancer, you may sometimes be pained by fiery Leo's hot-headedness or disregard for your feelings, but may otherwise enjoy working alongside such an energizing person.

Leo Birth Influences
Ruling planet: The Sun
Element: Fire
Polarity: Masculine
Quadruplicity: Fixed

VIRGO
CANCER

Both Cancer and Virgo are thoughtful, feminine-polarity signs, which means that these colleagues take pleasure in working behind the scenes and usually interact quietly and efficiently. Sensitive Cancer may need to be treated with kid gloves, however, and nit-picking Virgo may occasionally trigger a few Cancerian tears, but then Cancer's intuitive, touchy-feely way of operating may equally irritate cool, rational Virgo.

Your Boss: If you are a Virgo, you may find it hard to resent your caring Cancer boss, who probably seems intent on nurturing your professional progress, but you may nevertheless wish that he didn't keep asking if you are happy, which you may consider intrusive. The personal interest that Cancer takes in you is down to the influence of his ruling planet, the compassionate Moon, and his empathetic element of water, while his cardinal quadruplicity makes him ambitious on your behalf. Your own zodiacal sign is ruled by neutral Mercury, your element is resilient earth, and your quadruplicity is flexible, which, in combination, means that you probably don't mind doing whatever is asked of you, and can put up with a lot before your feelings become an issue at work.

Although you have to concede that your Virgo boss is focused and fair, she may upset you with her fault-finding if you are a Cancer who takes criticism very much to heart, in which case try to toughen up a little because Virgo almost certainly doesn't mean to wound you. Her ruling planet makes her objective, her earthy element, realistic, and her mutable quadruplicity, analytical, so when she points out where you may be going wrong, she is usually stating the facts as she sees them. She may well be right, so when she gives you unwelcome feedback, try to regard it as receiving an impartial helping hand.

Cancer and Virgo in the Workplace: You sometimes rub each other up the wrong way if you and your coworker are a Cancer and a Virgo, but otherwise probably have a satisfyingly productive working relationship. Cancer's strengths include creativity, intuition, and drive, while Virgo is logical, practical, and adaptable, so together you have most of the bases covered when it comes to generating ideas, making progress, and problem-solving. There may also be personal benefits in working together. Should watery Cancer become withdrawn when swamped by negative emotions, talkative, persuasive Virgo may be able to encourage the crab to re-engage with reality, while Cancer can instinctively sense when Virgo is feeling fraught and has an unrivaled ability to soothe.

Virgo Birth Influences

Ruling planet: Mercury
Element: Earth
Polarity: Feminine
Quadruplicity: Mutable

If you are a Cancer and your Virgo boss seems to criticize everything you do, try not to take it personally.

Cancer Birth Influences

Ruling planet: The Moon
Element: Water
Polarity: Feminine
Quadruplicity: Cardinal

CANCER
LIBRA

Cancer Birth Influences
Ruling planet: The Moon
Element: Water
Polarity: Feminine
Quadruplicity: Cardinal

Neither Cancer nor Libra enjoys a formal working environment, or one that is highly charged, although for very different reasons. Having been born under a feminine, watery, lunar sign, Cancer's creativity will usually only flow when coworkers seem like family members, and the crab definitely cannot cope with the stress of dealing with others' ego trips. Airy, Venus-ruled Libra, by contrast, thinks best when given freedom, and can be seriously distracted from a job in hand if ruffled feathers need soothing. These colleagues consequently generally interact harmoniously, even if they are not always on the same wavelength.

Cancer and Libra colleagues are more likely than most astrological pairings to find a way of working together harmoniously.

Your Boss: You may not consider your Cancer boss an inspiring leader if you are a Libra, but probably appreciate his understanding nature. The sign of the crab is feminine, or passive, whereas yours is masculine, or pioneering, and because Cancer's planetary ruler and element are both associated with the nebulous realms of emotions and instincts, and yours give you a more material, intellectual awareness, you will inevitably talk at cross purposes at times. That said, your natural charm and unwillingness to rock the boat may arouse watery Cancer's liking and sympathy, and he may therefore often choose to overlook your airy flightiness or Venusian self-indulgence.

Libra may be a delight to work for if you are a Cancer, even if you sadly suspect that she isn't that interested in you as a person. Having a masculine polarity gives her dynamic energy, the additional input of her airy element making her rational, yet funny, and that of Venus causing her to be relaxed. Because you respond so sensitively to people's personalities, you probably find her energizing, as well as someone who doesn't make you feel as though you are toiling in a pressure-cooker atmosphere, which may bring out the best in you when it comes to productivity. Yet most of your birth influences accentuate your emotions, so you may be disappointed that she is not inclined to dig beneath the surface to get to know the real you.

Cancer and Libra in the Workplace: Being essentially nonaggressive types, Cancer and Libra usually have a smooth working relationship, and if tension does arise, caring Cancer will soon withdraw his or her pincers and pacific Libra will revert to honeyed words in an attempt to restore calm. Your shared quadruplicity is cardinal, which means that you both rise to a challenge, with Cancer providing intuition and imagination, and Libra, logic and analysis, when working toward a common aim.

Libra Birth Influences
Ruling planet: Venus
Element: Air
Polarity: Masculine
Quadruplicity: Cardinal

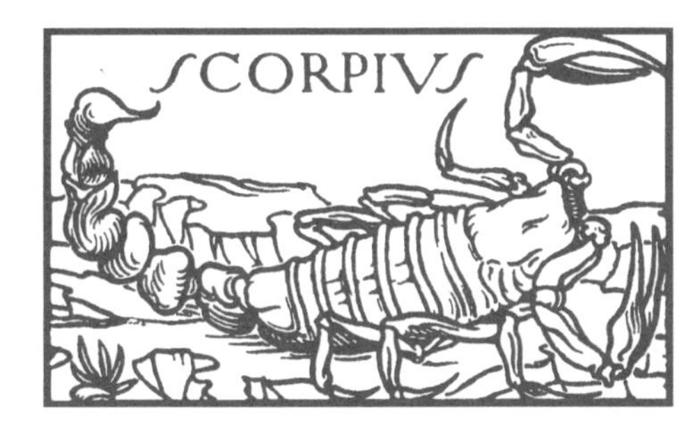

SCORPIO / CANCER

Cancer and Scorpio may have a feminine, or introverted, polarity and watery, or sensitive, element in common, but it is often the characteristics imparted by their different planetary rulers and quadruplicities that come to the fore in the workplace. The influence of the Moon and a cardinal quadruplicity makes Cancer both creative and driven, for instance, while that of Pluto and a fixed quadruplicity causes Scorpio to share information only on a need-to-know basis and to stick to a task in hand. They may therefore understand and complement each other, but may also occasionally upset one another.

Your Boss: However successfully you manage to mask your emotions under a veneer of professionalism if you are a Scorpio, you may have the uncomfortable feeling that your Cancer boss knows exactly how you are feeling. And no wonder, when you consider that Cancer not only shares your intuitive element of water and receptive feminine polarity, but is also governed by the hypersensitive Moon. Pluto, your own planetary ruler, may predispose you to secrecy, but don't worry too much that Cancer's disconcerting insight will work against you because she is an instinctively sympathetic person who has your welfare at heart, and not just when it comes to your career.

If you are a Cancer, you may sense that you and your Scorpio boss are on the same wavelength, but may feel that you don't connect with him as a person, in which case you're probably both correct and mistaken. Correct because you were both born under watery, feminine-polarity signs, which means that your Scorpio boss indeed shares your empathetic, thoughtful mindset. And mistaken because although he may like and understand you, being a protégé of Pluto, he is not one to pass comment on anything that is not directly concerned with your work.

Cancer and Scorpio in the Workplace: It is largely as a result of their joint birth influences that Cancer and Scorpio derive immense satisfaction from getting on quietly with their jobs and dislike being exposed to the often distressing distraction of bitchy gossip or hard-nosed office politics. Given the right conditions, both have the potential to be exceptionally imaginative, with Moon-ruled Cancer dreaming up visionary concepts and Pluto-governed Scorpio generating long-term strategies. If you are a Scorpio, you may frequently be thankful for the sense of urgency that cardinal Cancer injects into working toward a mutual goal, and if you are a Cancer, you may equally bless fixed-sign Scorpio's dogged perseverance.

Scorpio Birth Influences

Ruling planet: Pluto; traditionally Mars
Element: Water
Polarity: Feminine
Quadruplicity: Fixed

Although a typical Scorpio tends to be private, an empathetic Cancerian boss may have a positive influence on her days at work.

Cancer Birth Influences

Ruling planet: The Moon
Element: Water
Polarity: Feminine
Quadruplicity: Cardinal

CANCER
SAGITTARIUS

Cancer Birth Influences

Ruling planet: The Moon
Element: Water
Polarity: Feminine
Quadruplicity: Cardinal

Because they are opposites in many respects, Cancer and Sagittarius' strengths can complement one another well in the workplace. Masculine-polarity, Jupiter-governed, fiery Sagittarius may be more adventurous, far-seeing, and trendsetting than the feminine-polarity crab, but then watery, Moon-ruled Cancer possesses the creativity and intuition that are vital assets in the business world. And while mutable Sagittarius may be more flexible, yet also more restless, than the crab, having a cardinal quadruplicity means that Cancer is often far more focused and driven when under time pressure.

Although a typical Sagittarius may find his Canerian boss uninspiring, he will certainly appreciate the fact that he's willing to listen and help.

Your Boss: You probably like your Cancer boss if you are a Sagittarius, even if he doesn't often ignite your interest. Having a fiery element, there may be times when you need to feel that you have your boss's undivided attention, and must consequently be gratified by the way in which Cancer listens empathetically to your suggestions. But if you are a typical Sagittarius who is motivated by activity and risk-taking, you probably don't find the restrained and circumspect crab an inspiring leader. In fact, the only occasions on which Cancer may exert a vitalizing influence on you are when he is urging you on to meet an impending deadline.

Your Sagittarius boss must make quite an impact on you if you are a Cancer. Not only are you receptive to the personalities to whom you are exposed, but Sagittarians exude fire and energy, and because their ruling planet is the jovial Jupiter, also benevolence. Working for Sagittarius may therefore generally be an enlivening experience, and she may often provide the spark of inspiration that activates your fertile imagination. Being a sensitive soul, you may, however, wish that your fiery boss were more tactful and less outspoken.

Cancer and Sagittarius in the Workplace: If you are a Sagittarius, Jupiter, your ruling planet, makes you well disposed toward others unless they trigger your hot temper by acting arrogantly or aggressively, which is one of the reasons why you may get along with your serene Cancer colleague. You may also appreciate having an empathetic sounding board in the crab, but being more impatient, may not be able to return the favor when your colleague wants to talk. And if you are a responsive Cancer, you may frequently be unsettled by mutable Sagittarius' twitchiness when bored, and may sigh at his or her tendency to leave you to finish a joint assignment the instant a more diverting task presents itself. That said, Sagittarius' optimism and enthusiasm must frequently lift your mood.

Sagittarius Birth Influences

Ruling planet: Jupiter
Element: Fire
Polarity: Masculine
Quadruplicity: Mutable

CAPRICORN
CANCER

Although they have a driving, cardinal quadruplicity in common, the difference between Moon-governed Cancer and Saturn-ruled Capricorn is usually that the crab's ambition is to be emotionally fulfilled, while the goat's is to climb to stellar career heights. And because Cancer's element is sensitive water, and Capricorn's, resilient earth, it follows that the responsive crab reacts badly to fractious working relationships, while the stoical goat will put up with almost anything. Fortunately, these introspective, feminine-polarity individuals generally get on well, and have many complementary qualities, too.

Your Boss: Although you may query his methods, and the workings of his mind may be beyond your comprehension, you probably respect your Cancer boss if you are a Capricorn. Like you, he is no doubt a thoughtful, restrained person, who can nevertheless summon up the necessary sense of urgency when faced with a tight deadline, similarities that are due to your shared polarity and quadruplicity. But because the combination of Saturn and earth makes you someone who is realistic and practical, and Moon and water cause Cancer to be intuitive and creative, you are almost certainly poles apart when it comes to your ideas and approaches.

You may not find working for Capricorn an enlivening experience if you are a Cancer, but may be grateful that you know where you stand with your steady, straightforward boss. The receptiveness and sensitivity to the moods of those around you that are the joint bequest of the Moon and your watery element can cause tears to spring to your eyes if you find yourself at the receiving end of a temperamental outburst or barbed words, and sober, matter-of-fact Capricorn is unlikely to distress you in such ways. Indeed, because your watery element can fill you with insecurity, you may appreciate the stability that underpins your working life thanks to earthy, saturnine Capricorn's patience and love of routines, even if she isn't always as inspiring as you'd like.

Cancer and Capricorn in the Workplace: If you and your colleague are a Cancer and a Capricorn, you may be far more interested in getting on with your work than gossiping or seeking distraction, mainly because you are both self-contained, goal-oriented people. When it comes to collaborating, you must each have a significant contribution to make, Cancer's perhaps being imaginative ideas, and Capricorn's, practical proposals. But on a more personal level, Capricorn may occasionally inadvertently wound thin-skinned Cancer by dismissing a suggestion as being unfeasible, while Cancer's spirits may be dampened by Capricorn's pragmatic, long-suffering mindset.

Capricorn Birth Influences

Ruling planet: Saturn
Element: Earth
Polarity: Feminine
Quadruplicity: Cardinal

Because they are typically both ambitious and responsible, Cancer and Capricorn team mates will stay focused on their work when their boss is away from the office.

Cancer Birth Influences

Ruling planet: The Moon
Element: Water
Polarity: Feminine
Quadruplicity: Cardinal

CANCER
AQUARIUS

Cancer Birth Influences

Ruling planet: The Moon
Element: Water
Polarity: Feminine
Quadruplicity: Cardinal

In a working context, Cancer and Aquarius are more likely to respect each other's strengths than to disagree over their differences.

Aquarius Birth Influences

Ruling planet: Uranus; traditionally Saturn
Element: Air
Polarity: Masculine
Quadruplicity: Fixed

Although Cancer and Aquarius have a dramatically different impact on the workplace, and their interest and approaches are equally dissimilar, fireworks rarely flare between them. In many ways, they couldn't be more unalike, feminine-polarity, watery, Moon-governed Cancer being prudent, quiet, creative, and rather reactionary, and masculine-polarity, airy, Uranus-ruled Aquarius being pioneering, communicative, rational, and fascinated by the new. Yet because neither enjoys conflict, and both are united in the satisfaction that they often find in their work, they typically make a peaceable, productive pair.

Your Boss: The one thing that you may find frustrating about working for a Cancer boss, if you are an Aquarius, is the way that she sympathetically hears you out while you explain the benefits of installing cutting-edge technology at work, for instance, and then ignores your suggestions. As you've no doubt come to realize, the crab's lunar ruler, watery element, and feminine polarity may result in her being a good listener, but also more conservative, cautious, and generally more passive than you. That said, her cardinal quadruplicity may make her surprisingly go-getting on occasions, and it is at times like these when you may be motivated by the urgency of her lead.

If you are a sensitive Cancer, the last thing that you want in the workplace is to feel on edge, which is why you may be grateful for your airy, Aquarian boss's relaxed regime and cheerful, positive outlook. Because you are such a responsive person, you may also be invigorated by Aquarius' dynamic energy and the articulacy with which he puts forward his proposals. But because Aquarius is a logical and fixed, or dogmatic, sign, and yours causes you to be open to suggestion and to believe that others should be, too, you may sometimes be upset by the intransigence with which your boss sticks to his guns and won't be swayed by your alternative, intuitive viewpoint.

Cancer and Aquarius in the Workplace: You may not get on like a house on fire if you are Cancer and Aquarius coworkers, but then you probably don't antagonize one another either. Although you may wish that your self-contained Cancer colleague were more communicative if you are an Aquarius, you may appreciate the crab's palpable empathy when you feel sidelined by your boss, and may also have great respect for his or her insightful imagination. And if you are a Cancer, you may sometimes long to be given a break from airy Aquarius' constant chatter, but may admire his or her coolly logical mind.

PISCES

CANCER

That Cancer and Pisces are both highly creative types is due to their shared element of water and respective ruling planets, the instinctive Moon and dreamy Neptune, their joint feminine polarity making them thoughtful individuals, too. These are people who thrive in a friendly working environment, when it may seem as though they are in uncanny harmony with one another and communicate almost telepathically. In short, these colleagues generally click, even if cardinal Cancer's driving determination sometimes rattles Pisces, and mutable Pisces' lack of focus exasperates Cancer.

Pisces Birth Influences

Ruling planet: Neptune; traditionally Jupiter
Element: Water
Polarity: Feminine
Quadruplicity: Mutable

♆ ♃ ♒

Your Boss: You must be fond of, and feel comfortable with, your Cancer boss if you are a Pisces, perhaps because you are so similar in character that you are usually on the same wavelength. Not only that, but because his planetary governor is the motherly Moon, he no doubts treats those under his authority more like family members than underlings, and you may therefore find that the cozy, nurturing environment that he promotes prompts inspiring ideas to swim to the surface of your mind. And when an emotional setback has flooded you with confusion, he will probably listen to you with empathy. Yet because you are readily distracted and prefer to work at your own, unhurried pace, there may nevertheless be occasions when cardinal Cancer flusters you by pushing you to meet a looming deadline.

You probably enjoy being set targets if you are a cardinal Cancer, and this may be one area in which you find working for your mutable Pisces boss rather dissatisfying, for if she is typical of those born under this sign, she lacks organization and concentration and is not as goal-driven as you. Even so, there are probably other ways in which she motivates you, maybe by intuitively grasping the gist of an innovative concept that is slowly taking shape in your mind, but that you are having difficulty putting into words, and then by responding with praise and encouragement. If so, give thanks to your common watery element, which fills each of you with an unconscious understanding of, and sympathy with, the other's way of thinking.

Most people appreciate a boss who makes an effort to be understanding, and sensitive Cancer more than most, making Pisces a compatible boss for Cancer.

Cancer and Pisces in the Workplace: If you and your coworker are a like-minded Cancer and Pisces pair who share a workspace with colleagues born under other zodiacal signs, you probably naturally gravitate toward each other's soothing, undemanding company. But because you both have a feminine, or passive and inward-looking, polarity, you may not be that inspired or stimulated by one another either.

Cancer Birth Influences

Ruling planet: The Moon
Element: Water
Polarity: Feminine
Quadruplicity: Cardinal

LEO
LEO

Leo Birth Influences

Ruling planet: The Sun
Element: Fire
Polarity: Masculine
Quadruplicity: Fixed

As long as Leos feel enthused, admired, and valued, they will give their all in the workplace, but whether a working relationship between a pair of zodiacal lions is relaxed and mutually inspirational or hostile and competitive depends on whether they tend to circle one another suspiciously as rivals or are sufficiently united by a common cause to disregard their respective egos. And although the influence of the egotistical Sun primarily dictates the nature of their relationship, they generally have the same enthusiastic, determined, and pioneering outlook.

Your Boss: Because Leos are naturally commanding and expect the world to revolve around them—just as the planets rotate around their solar ruler—a Leo boss assumes an authoritative role as though born to it, while a leonine underling will generally strive to assert him- or herself. If you are a confident, masculine-polarity lion, you may therefore feel compelled to challenge your Leo boss if you disagree with him or her, feel that you are being ignored, or think that he or she has become lazy and complacent, which are certainly leonine traits. But if your boss is as excited by a project as you—particularly if it requires the creativity with which you are both blessed, thanks to the Sun and your fiery element—you may both forget your respective positions and galvanize one another with your dazzling proposals and sizzling energy. Never forget, however, that as your superior, your boss demands your respect, and that if you forget to defer to him or her and impulsively start taking the lead in a hot-headed moment, you will feel the full force of the proud, status-conscious lion's wrath.

A Leo boss demands hard work and respect, which a Leo underling may resent if he feels that his style is being cramped.

Leo and Leo in the Workplace: Given your Sun-bestowed desire to lead, uninhibited, masculine polarity, and aggressive element of fire, there may inevitably be a competitive undercurrent coursing through your relationship if you and your coworker are both Leos. Although there may consequently be occasions when one Leo's perceived arrogance inflames the other to the extent that he or she cannot suppress the lion's fiery temper, such leonine feelings of rage no doubt disappear as soon as they are vented. And when both of you are inspired by a mutual goal, you no doubt relish bouncing ideas off one another and pushing a concept to outrageous limits together. What's more, your joint fixed quadruplicity may make you equally tenacious, so that you may each earn the other's admiration by refusing to give up when you encounter an obstacle.

Leo Birth Influences

Ruling planet: The Sun
Element: Fire
Polarity: Masculine
Quadruplicity: Fixed

VIRGO
LEO

As long as Leo and Virgo don't take their differences personally, recognize that each has strengths that the other lacks, and welcome one another's input, these two are potential dream-team material. Sun-ruled, masculine-polarity, fiery Leo is raring to take the lead, and has the necessary energy, confidence, enthusiasm, and inspiration to do so, whereas Mercury-governed, feminine-polarity, earthy Virgo supplies indispensable support in the form of logic, analysis, caution, and practicality. Their respective fourth birth influences balance one another effectively, too, with Leo's fixed quadruplicity providing determination, and Virgo's mutable one, a flexible attitude.

Virgo Birth Influences

Ruling planet: Mercury
Element: Earth
Polarity: Feminine
Quadruplicity: Mutable

Your Boss: Your Leo boss may sometimes exasperate you if you are a Virgo, but you probably find her sunny nature cheering and may admire her vigor and self-assurance. It is mainly due to the commanding Sun, Leo's planetary governor, that directing others comes naturally to your charismatic boss, while your own passive, feminine polarity and adaptable, mutable quadruplicity may enable you both to accede to her authority and accommodate her demands. That said, you may wish that she thought things through to their logical conclusion before asking you to undertake a task that you suspect is overambitious, and, after thorough research, are sure is unworkable.

Your main problem with your Virgo boss, if you are a Leo, may have nothing to do with him as a person, but everything to do with your innate, Sun-bestowed sense of superiority and urge to take charge yourself. Your time will come, but in the meantime, you may struggle to comply with earthy Virgo's insistence on paying attention to detail, may not be motivated by his dry, unexciting management style, and may resent being pulled up short when you've been careless. You may, however, be grateful that he gives you responsibility for a variety of projects, which may at least make you feel as though you are your own boss—even if it is over a smaller kingdom that you'd prefer—and may also keep boredom at bay.

As long as Virgo and Leo respect their alternative styles, their partnership should be highly successful, for they both have different talents.

Leo and Virgo in the Workplace: There may be times when the arrogance that your authoritative leonine coworker exudes grates on you if you are a Virgo, but you may nevertheless choose to overlook the lion's bossiness, particularly if you respect Leo's staying power. But if you are a Leo, when Virgo does respond caustically to a brilliant idea that's just fired your imagination, you may be so offended by his or her lack of admiration that you may not be able to contain your temper. Thank goodness that neither of you nurse grudges!

Leo Birth Influences

Ruling planet: The Sun
Element: Fire
Polarity: Masculine
Quadruplicity: Fixed

LEO / LIBRA

Leo Birth Influences

Ruling planet: The Sun
Element: Fire
Polarity: Masculine
Quadruplicity: Fixed

Leo's inspirational leadership talents and Libra's analytical and diplomatic skills make this astrological combination a potentially outstanding partnership, provided that Libra deems the Sun-ruled lion worthy of following and Leo recognizes the value of Venusian Libra's balanced outlook and restraining hand.

Your Boss: If your boss is a Leo, Libra, he or she is a born leader who thrives on wielding responsibility over others. Decisive, courageous, and usually sunny-natured, your fiery boss has the potential to be motivational and generous, also being genuinely concerned about your welfare, as well as your performance. You'll respect his creative concepts, even when corners have been cut, and you'll never feel undervalued. Problems will arise, however, should your boss's elevated position go to his head, when he may overstep important boundaries or dismiss your advice.

The well-balanced Libra boss has a tendency to weigh up all options carefully before reaching a decision, a characteristic that you, if you are a Leo, may recognize as being sensible, but nevertheless find frustrating. Yet among your boss's many virtues is the Venusian ability to make you feel that your opinions have validity and are worthy of attention, and you'll purr delightedly when flattered. Be warned that your boss's love of orderliness will sometimes seem petty and stifling, however, and that his or her airy, dispassionate style may make you feel undervalued and unappreciated.

Leo and Libra should concentrate on bringing out each other's best qualities when they work closely together, and should try to make their differences work for them.

Leo and Libra in the Workplace: Both Leo and Libra are team players who are stimulated by personal interaction and relish a busy working environment. Each has distinct strengths: creative Leo has a talent for thinking outside the box and is an enlivening influence, for example, while Libra is a balanced thinker and a born diplomat who instinctively strives to smooth over differences of opinion. You'll work reasonably well together as long as you both respect each other's contribution to the common cause. If you're a Libra, try to turn a blind eye to Leo's bossy tendencies, and Leo, try not to be offended by Libra's airy objectivity or apparent lack of enthusiasm for your ideas. And if fiery does explode, Libra, call on the help of Venus to keep the peace, and don't inflame the situation by being coolly critical. Leo, draw on your fixed quadruplicity, and Libra, enlist your cardinal one, to concentrate on the task at hand and focus on finishing it rather than disagreeing.

Libra Birth Influences

Ruling planet: Venus
Element: Air
Polarity: Masculine
Quadruplicity: Cardinal

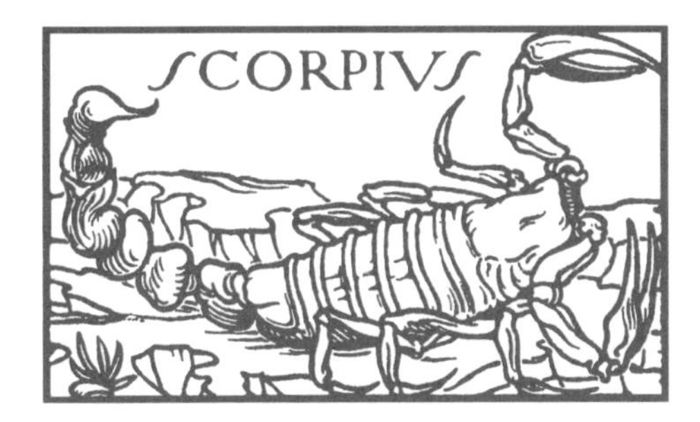

SCORPIO
LEO

Mutual respect is crucial if the proud lion and sensitive scorpion are to enjoy working together, but fortunately this is rarely lacking once each has benefited from the other's strengths. These include the tenacity that their shared fixed quadruplicity triggers in them both, fiery Leo's inspiration and enthusiasm, and watery Scorpio's creativity, shrewdness, and caution. Yet although they may interact effectively, these two may not always understand one another.

Your Boss: If you are a Scorpio, you may spend half your time trying to restrain your exuberant leonine boss and the other half diligently developing some of his dazzling concepts, and maybe adding some original touches of your own. You have a feminine polarity, and your boss, a masculine one, which means that you are receptive to his uninhibited influence, but are also more thoughtful, a trait that is deepened by Pluto, your intensity-bestowing ruling planet. Because your watery element blesses you with powerful instincts, you can probably sense when the impulsive or visionary aspect of Leo's fiery element has prevailed, and may therefore either be exasperated or motivated by Leo's experimental approach. Whichever is the case, you will probably always find it enlivening.

You would be an atypical Leo if the workings of your Scorpio boss's mind weren't a mystery to you. You are nothing if not open and outgoing, whereas the combination of secretive Pluto, a guarded element in water, and an introverted feminine polarity manifests itself in Scorpio as a tendency to communicate strictly on a need-to-know basis. You may find this frustrating if, like most Sun-ruled Leos, you consider yourself at least equal to your nominal superiors. You will probably be mollified, however, by Scorpio's disarming understanding of your need to exert control and her willingness to give you responsibility for those tasks for which a fixed sign's staying power is vital.

Leo and Scorpio in the Workplace: Given their different elements and polarities, the astrological indications suggest that Leo is a spontaneous doer, while Scorpio is a prudent thinker, and that while the influence of the Sun over Leo means that the authoritative lion may command the receptive scorpion's attention in the short term, the powerful will of Pluto-governed, Mars-influenced Scorpio will increasingly assert itself. If you are a Scorpio, you may consequently be enthused by Leo's more thought-provoking suggestions, and if you are a Leo, you may gradually come to realize that not only does your coworker have uncanny insight, but the scorpion is a force to be reckoned with.

Scorpio Birth Influences

Ruling planet: Pluto; traditionally Mars
Element: Water
Polarity: Feminine
Quadruplicity: Fixed

If you are a typically private Scorpio, make a conscious effort to keep your Leo colleague in the loop so that he or she doesn't feel that you're withholding important information.

Leo Birth Influences

Ruling planet: The Sun
Element: Fire
Polarity: Masculine
Quadruplicity: Fixed

LEO
SAGITTARIUS

Leo Birth Influences

Ruling planet: The Sun
Element: Fire
Polarity: Masculine
Quadruplicity: Fixed

Some workplaces demand vitality and courage as much logic and analysis. Where all of these qualities count, Leo and Sagittarius make a good, and mutually respectful, team.

Sagittarius Birth Influences

Ruling planet: Jupiter
Element: Fire
Polarity: Masculine
Quadruplicity: Mutable

A competitive undercurrent is usually a feature of a working relationship between Leo and Sagittarius—and no wonder, given that both of these colleagues have a masculine, or forceful, polarity and an equally aggressive element in fire. Sun-ruled, fixed-quadruplicity Leo may be the more assertive and unyielding of the two, but because they are generally on the same wavelength, and Jupiter-governed, mutable Sagittarius is positive, adaptable, and easygoing, fiery altercations may be few and far between. And while Sagittarius enthuses the lion by thinking big, Leo supplies the staying power that the archer often lacks.

Your Boss: Overall, you may enjoy working for Leo if you are a Sagittarius, even if there are occasions when your boss's behavior causes you to come perilously close to exploding with annoyance. Because you share a masculine polarity and fiery element, you may be inspired by Leo's boldly creative thought processes and trendsetting ideas, and may then be happy to follow the Sun-ruled lion's determined lead. What you may not appreciate, however, is Leo's unwillingness to take your alternative viewpoint on board, as well as her habit of either pulling rank or losing her temper if she feels that you are not according her due respect.

Being an underling is not a natural state of affairs for Sun-governed Leo, and if you were born under this sign, you may therefore resent having to follow orders when you are burning to issue them yourself. That said, you may not mind deferring to Sagittarius too much, particularly if Jupiter, his planetary ruler, endows him with an inclusive approach, and if his mutable quadruplicity gives him the flexibility that lets you do things your way (which may, in any case, also be his way, in view of your common birth influences). His changeability may sometimes rattle you, though, if, like most fixed-quadruplicity Leos, you prefer constancy.

Leo and Sagittarius in the Workplace: Leo and Sagittarius coworkers frequently have an instinctive affinity, mainly born of their joint polarity and element, but also because their respective strengths arouse one another's admiration. If you are a mutable Sagittarius, you may marvel at Leo's formidable concentration—a fixed-quadruplicity characteristic—and may be energized by the vitality that is the gift of the Sun. Likewise, if you are a Leo, you may be rather in awe of both the breadth of Sagittarius's Jupiterian vision and the mutable archer's analytical skills. Leo's obstinacy and Sagittarius's moodiness may not always be a happy combination, however.

CAPRICORN
LEO

At work, Sun-ruled Leo likes to be appreciated, while Saturn-governed Capricorn is usually a dependable worker, yet Capricorn requires just as much respect as Leo, and the lion is equally capable of seeing a job through to the bitter end as the goat. Their attitudes and approaches are otherwise very different, with fiery Leo contributing energy and inspiration, and earthy Capricorn, patience and practicality. They therefore have the potential to make a fine team, as long as each feels valued by the other and both are motivated by the same goal.

Your Boss: Although you may admire your Leo boss's confidence if you are a less assured, feminine-polarity Capricorn, you may sometimes think his self-certainty unjustified. Saturn, your planetary ruler, may tell you that nothing worthwhile is easily achieved, while your element of earth may make you realistic, so that you may be less than enthused by the prospect of proving solar, fiery Leo's impulsive notions unfeasible. Even so, you are probably energized by Leo's optimistic outlook, and may appreciate his habit of generously giving praise where praise is due.

You may be a little in awe of your boss if you are a Leo and she is a Capricorn, which is not a normal leonine reaction, but then few people are as upright, businesslike, and hardworking as the earthy, Saturn-ruled goat. As your superior, she may set extremely high standards, and not ones that you necessarily share, particularly if they focus on prudence and productivity, when you relish risk-taking and brainstorming. Still, you were born under a fixed sign, and it may be a matter of pride to you that she can't fault your perseverance when she sets you an assignment that fires you up.

Leo and Capricorn in the Workplace: If you are an earthy, feminine-polarity Capricorn working alongside a fiery, masculine-polarity Leo, you may spend much of your time trying to encourage your coworker to think through the implications of his or her latest bright idea, while simultaneously trying to make headway with your own workload. You probably can't help but warm to his or her vitality and fixed-quadruplicity tenacity, though. And if you are a Leo, you may sometimes sigh at Capricorn's limited imagination, but may secretly be grateful that your cardinal-quadruplicity colleague's sense of urgency gives you the impetus to make progress when you're working against the clock, particularly if the goat's dogged insistence inflames your competitive instincts.

Capricorn Birth Influences

Ruling planet: Saturn
Element: Earth
Polarity: Feminine
Quadruplicity: Cardinal

Capricorn and Leo people are often passionate about their jobs. When they focus on a common goal, theirs should be a powerful partnership.

Leo Birth Influences

Ruling planet: The Sun
Element: Fire
Polarity: Masculine
Quadruplicity: Fixed

LEO
AQUARIUS

Leo Birth Influences
Ruling planet: The Sun
Element: Fire
Polarity: Masculine
Quadruplicity: Fixed

Aquarius is a good communicator, and if you are a Leo with an Aquarius boss, you'll appreciate being addressed as an equal.

Aquarius Birth Influences
Ruling planet: Uranus; traditionally Saturn
Element: Air
Polarity: Masculine
Quadruplicity: Fixed

It would be unusual if a pair of Leo and Aquarius colleagues did not interact dynamically at work, if only because each is frequently inspired by the other's boldly experimental way of thinking. Yet because Sun-governed Leo is an authoritative type, and Uranus-ruled Aquarius is resolutely independent, tension may arise if Leo tries to limit Aquarius' intellectual freedom, or if Leo takes Aquarius' objectivity as a sign of disrespect. And having a fixed quadruplicity in common, both can be equally obstinate.

Your Boss: The union of the Sun, fire, and a masculine polarity within your Leo boss may manifest itself as total self-belief, infectious vitality, and unwavering confidence, a blend that you may find invigorating if you are an Aquarius, but occasionally also overpowering. You may not be intimidated by commanding Leo because your polarity is similarly masculine, so that you may share the lion's self-assurance. Because your airy element makes you impartial, and Uranus, nonconformist, you may perceive some of Leo's impulsive directives as being ill-considered, and may then boldly question them, possibly provoking a leonine roar of irritation. Your interest may nevertheless often be fired by Leo's creative concepts and approach, however.

If your boss is a typical Aquarius, and you are a proud zodiacal lion, you probably like the way that he talks to you as an equal and readily solicits your opinions. Not only is Aquarius' planetary ruler the egalitarian Uranus, which means that status is unimportant to him, but his airy element may cause him to be a gifted communicator, as well genuinely interested in others' views. There may consequently be times when you are thrilled that he picks up and runs with one of your ideas, but may otherwise be peeved when he coolly dissects your latest brainwave and cheerfully pronounces it unworkable, in which case blame the analytical influence of his element of air.

Leo and Aquarius in the Workplace: Leo and Aquarius coworkers generally enjoy an open and easy working relationship, which is partly down to their polarity, and partly due to Leo's sunniness and Aquarius' breeziness. Fiery Leo's spontaneous suggestions and Uranian Aquarius' maverick mind may be a mutually stimulating combination that conjures up ingenious solutions to workplace challenges, too. Whether you are a Leo or an Aquarius, your joint fixed quadruplicity gives you both tenacity, yet may also cause you to stick to your guns should you disagree, resulting in a deadlock that only your boss's intervention may resolve.

PISCES
LEO

Both Leo and Pisces work best in an unstructured environment, albeit for very different reasons. Sun-ruled, fiery Leo is assertive and demands freedom of action, while Neptune-governed, watery Pisces is hypersensitive and prone to becoming paralyzed with confusion when under pressure, for instance. As long as the conditions are right, they may enjoy an extraordinarily creative relationship, with Leo's eccentricity invigorating Pisces, and Pisces' intuition startling Leo. As a bonus, fixed-sign Leo is tenacious, while mutable Pisces is adaptable enough to follow the lion's lead, although stubbornness and changeability are more problematic aspects of their respective quadruplicities.

Pisces Birth Influences

Ruling planet: Neptune; traditionally Jupiter
Element: Water
Polarity: Feminine
Quadruplicity: Mutable

Your Boss: You have a feminine, or passive, polarity if you are a Pisces, and if your boss is a Leo, he has a masculine, or active, one, so you probably don't mind being subordinate to the authoritative lion. Indeed, if you have a tendency to be indecisive (and it is no coincidence that the fishes for which your zodiacal sign is named are traditionally depicted swimming in different directions), it may be a relief to be led by such a resolute, confident, and positive individual. That said, the few occasions when the fiery lion explodes with annoyance must upset you greatly, for your watery element makes you far more thin-skinned than resilient Leo.

If you are a commanding, Sun-ruled Leo, you may be burning to take over from your Pisces boss, maybe because you have an appetite for management, or else because her subtle, Neptunian style doesn't motivate you, or because her mutable quadruplicity makes her a ditherer. Still, you probably can't fault her kindness, and may be staggered by the depth of her insight into your feelings, especially if you've suffered a setback, when you may be especially grateful for the double dose of compassion that is the gift of Neptune and water.

If you are a Pisces, you will probably appreciate your fiery Leo coworker's creative input when your inspiration runs dry.

Leo and Pisces in the Workplace: Although it is unlikely that Leo and Pisces are always on the same wavelength at work, their originality usually establishes some common ground, with Leo's enterprising viewpoint sowing the seeds of inspiration in Pisces' fertile imagination, and Pisces' idealistic, abstract way of thinking similarly sparking ideas in Leo's pioneering mind. But the fixed-quadruplicity lion's dogmatism and insistence on doing things Leo's way may test your flexibility to its limits if you are a Pisces, while if you are a Leo, you may in turn be frustrated by mutable Pisces' lack of focus and concentration.

Leo Birth Influences

Ruling planet: The Sun
Element: Fire
Polarity: Masculine
Quadruplicity: Fixed

VIRGO
VIRGO

Virgo Birth Influences
Ruling planet: Mercury
Element: Earth
Polarity: Feminine
Quadruplicity: Mutable

They may not be that inspired by one another, but then the joint priority of a pair of Virgo colleagues is typically doing their job scrupulously and well, which is partly due to the restraint that their feminine polarity exerts over them, and partly down to the productiveness that is the gift of their earthy element. And because their mutable quadruplicity gives them flexibility, and Mercury makes them intelligent and quick-thinking, they usually interact smoothly, as well as sharing a talent for razor-sharp analysis. Yet despite having a similar mindset, their working methods may not always correspond, in which case each may feel the lash of the other's critical tongue.

Your Virgoan boss is not afraid of getting her hands dirty when it comes to menial tasks, which you may admire if you are also an earthy Virgo.

Your Boss: There may be many qualities that you appreciate in your Virgo boss if you were born under the same zodiacal sign, perhaps because they are part of your makeup, too. These may include a preference for juggling a number of projects simultaneously, due to your variety-loving, mutable quadruplicity, and an earthy, mercurial tendency to use logic and reason to untangle knotty problems. As a result, you may not only understand your boss's thought processes, but may sense that he or she approves of your own approach. One of the downsides of having the practical element of earth in common, however, may be that your hands-on boss delegates fewer tasks to you than you would like. If so, this is probably because he or she derives satisfaction from methodically imposing order on a welter of confused facts and figures, so don't take it as an indication that your boss doesn't trust you to do the same.

Virgo and Virgo in the Workplace: If you work alongside a fellow Virgo, you no doubt respect his or her capacity for hard work, incisive way of thinking, and communicativeness, but may wish that your coworker wasn't so meddlesome. Aren't you exactly the same, though? Earthy Virgoan individuals are renowned for their thoroughness and insistence on paying attention to detail, but not even Virgos are perfect, and it may consequently be that there are occasions when you cannot resist helpfully pointing out something that your colleague has missed or explaining why your own practices are more effective. Yet as you may be all too aware, feminine-polarity Virgos are not as confident as they seem, and criticism can send them into an agony of self-doubt, so do as you would be done by, and try to curb your urge to nitpick.

Virgo Birth Influences
Ruling planet: Mercury
Element: Earth
Polarity: Feminine
Quadruplicity: Mutable

LIBRA / VIRGO

Whatever their positions, Virgo and Libra have the potential to make a rather effective team, and a contented one to boot. While each is as bright as the other, thanks to the influence of Virgo's planetary governor, Mercury, and mutable quadruplicity, and Libra's element of air, feminine-polarity Virgo is apt to direct this intelligence inward, into research and analysis, while a masculine-polarity, cardinal-quadruplicity Libra tends to project it outward, so that it manifests itself as action. Already therefore complementary colleagues, mutable Virgo is furthermore adaptable, and Venus-ruled Libra, a peacekeeper, so that any disagreements are likely to be few and far between.

Libra Birth Influences

Ruling planet: Venus
Element: Air
Polarity: Masculine
Quadruplicity: Cardinal

Your Boss: If you are a Libra whose boss is a Virgo, you probably wish that she wouldn't take work so seriously, partly because, being a kind-hearted soul, you worry about the consequences for her health, but perhaps mainly because you sense that she feels that you should do the same, which may be expecting just a little too much from an airy, fun-loving child of Venus. Indeed, your straight-talking boss may even have told you as much, but although you want to please, you may find it difficult to sustain the steady, businesslike approach that comes so naturally to earthy Virgo. The exception may be when an assignment really interests you, when your driving, cardinal quadruplicity may take over, keeping you focused on your target.

You may find your Libran boss disarmingly charming if you are a Virgo, and may also respect his rational mindset, but may dislike being kept talking when your in-tray is calling for order to be imposed upon it. Although airy Libra may certainly enjoy a laugh or some inconsequential chatter (and there may be a lesson for you here in terms of achieving a healthy work–life balance), having a cardinal quadruplicity means that your boss is both brimming with ideas and needs goals to work toward. And because your polarity causes you to be thoughtful, and your earthy element, practical, he may value hearing your opinions before launching a new venture.

Are you annoyed when Libra is distracted by a phone call when you need to get through a pile of paperwork together, Virgo?

Virgo and Libra in the Workplace: You may be grateful that earthy Virgo is so hard-working and dependable if you are a sometimes lazy Libra, while you probably can't help but like your airy, Libran coworker if you are a Virgo. In addition, Virgo may enjoy beavering away on the tasks that Libra finds tedious, while cardinal Libra may be happy to take the initiative when mutable Virgo is beset by indecision.

Virgo Birth Influences

Ruling planet: Mercury
Element: Earth
Polarity: Feminine
Quadruplicity: Mutable

VIRGO
SCORPIO

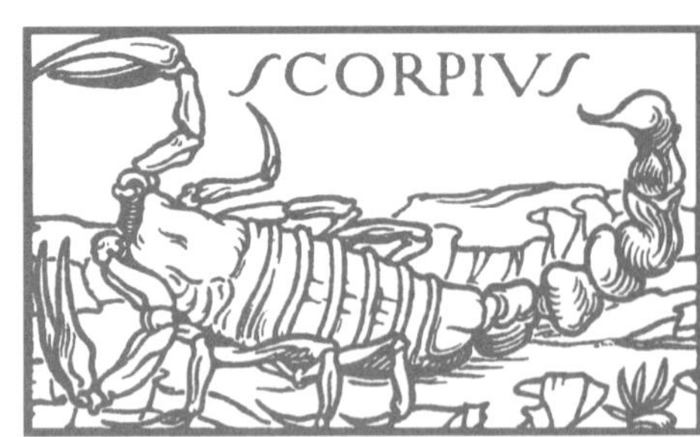

Virgo Birth Influences

Ruling planet: Mercury
Element: Earth
Polarity: Feminine
Quadruplicity: Mutable

Virgo and Scorpio both tend to take their work seriously and dislike going around in circles.

Scorpio Birth Influences

Ruling planet: Pluto; traditionally Mars
Element: Water
Polarity: Feminine
Quadruplicity: Fixed

Although Virgo's analytical, communicative approach can be an asset in the workplace, objective criticism will not always be well received by thin-skinned Scorpio. Similarly, while Scorpio's intuition and discretion can be a powerful combination, Virgo may not approve of people acting on hunches, or of them being withholding. Otherwise, they typically respect one another's diligence and staying power, and because mutable Virgo is flexible, watery Scorpio, empathetic, and they furthermore have a thoughtful feminine polarity in common, these two have the potential to be mutually supportive colleagues.

Your Boss: Mutable, Mercury-governed Virgos have an urge to gather and disseminate information, and if your boss is one of them, and you are a Pluto-ruled Scorpio who understands the value of hoarding nuggets of knowledge for future use, you no doubt like this trait. You may not appreciate your boss's openness so much when it's performance-assessment time, however, if, like many scorpions, your element of water can make you feel sensitive and insecure. Should dispassionate Virgo's fault-finding touch a raw nerve, try to accept that the underlying intention is almost certainly to help you to improve, not to shatter your ego.

Having a Scorpio as your superior may sometimes be frustrating if you are a mercurial Virgo who wants to be in full possession of the facts before embarking on an assignment. If it seems as though Plutonian Scorpio is deliberately keeping you in the dark, this may indeed be the case, but the reason for her reticence may not be that your boss distrusts you, just that she either operates on a strictly need-to-know basis or, being an intuitive person, doesn't think that the details need spelling out to someone as intelligent as you. This gripe apart, your straightforward, earthy side may respond positively to fixed-sign Scorpio's constancy, and you may be surprised and touched by her compassion when you encounter a setback.

Virgo and Scorpio in the Workplace: It is their shared feminine polarity that causes both Virgo and Scorpio to relish working diligently at the tasks that those born under masculine-polarity signs typically consider humdrum and unexciting. If you are a Scorpio, you may admire Virgo's incisive diagnostic skills and methodical mindset, as well as being thankful that your coworker is flexible. And it may be Scorpio's creative ideas and tenacity that particularly impress you if you are a Virgo, even if you wish that your colleague were less rigid, and also more talkative—but then maybe Scorpio is longing for more peace and quiet!

SAGITTARIUS
VIRGO

Most of Virgo and Sagittarius' respective birth influences are so diametrically opposed that they will either prove complementary or divisive in the workplace. Combine Mercury, earth, and a feminine polarity, and in Virgo you have a person who is neutral, practical, and risk-averse, for example, while Jupiter, fire, and a masculine polarity manifest themselves in Sagittarius as optimism, creativity, and a pioneering approach. They will therefore either respect or irritate one another, but thankfully their shared mutable quadruplicity typically gives them sufficient adaptability to interact well together.

Your Boss: You may sometimes leave Virgo's office simmering with frustration if you are a fiery Sagittarius. Perhaps you had a brilliant brainwave that earthy, Mercury-governed Virgo dismissed as being unrealistic or ill-thought-out, or maybe she confirmed your opinion of her as being innately negative or unable to see the wider picture, unlike a masculine-polarity child of Jupiter like you. That said, although Virgo may take her time to ponder a proposal, she will be objective, so there may equally be occasions when she approves of an idea of yours, and, being flexible, gives you the leeway to bring it to fruition yourself, albeit under her supervision.

If you are a responsive, feminine-polarity Virgo, you probably can't help but warm to your fiery, Jupiter-ruled, Sagittarian boss' enthusiasm and energy, and may also appreciate his inclusiveness in sharing his visions with you. The trouble may be that once you've set to work analyzing and researching how to proceed with his latest big idea, Mercury and your element of earth may soon make it clear that it is unfeasible, or at least ill-advised. But although breaking the bad news to Sagittarius may provoke a bark of annoyance, he may often relieve you by shrugging his shoulders and putting forward an alternative proposal, in which case you may be seeing your common mutable, or changeable, quadruplicity in action.

Virgo and Sagittarius in the Workplace: Sagittarius' interest is quickly fired, but can die down just as swiftly when attention to detail is required, and if you are a zodiacal archer, you may therefore be grateful when your earthy, methodical, Virgo colleague steps in to take care of that aspect of a joint assignment, even if you do not appreciate being criticized for your sloppiness. And if you are that Virgo coworker, you may enjoy imposing order on Sagittarius' work, but may wish that your workmate wouldn't take your helpfulness for granted. Still, you may find fiery, mutable Sagittarius an enlivening individual who inspires you, as well as someone with whom it is easy to communicate.

Sagittarius Birth Influences

Ruling planet: Jupiter
Element: Fire
Polarity: Masculine
Quadruplicity: Mutable

♃ 🔥

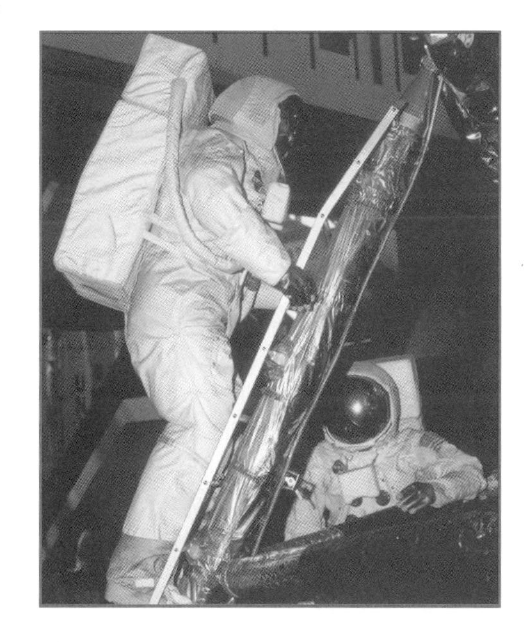

Virgo, you may respect your Sagittarian coworker's enterprising spirit, but then your own methodical and grounded approach is also essential for success.

Virgo Birth Influences

Ruling planet: Mercury
Element: Earth
Polarity: Feminine
Quadruplicity: Mutable

VIRGO
CAPRICORN

Virgo Birth Influences

Ruling planet: Mercury
Element: Earth
Polarity: Feminine
Quadruplicity: Mutable

It may sometimes seem as though you're back in school if you are a Virgo with a Capricorn boss, maybe because she insists on your figures adding up.

Capricorn Birth Influences

Ruling planet: Saturn
Element: Earth
Polarity: Feminine
Quadruplicity: Cardinal

Virgo and Capricorn colleagues usually respect one another's restrained style and practical, productive ways, which is hardly surprising, given that these are the gifts of their common feminine polarity and element of earth. Their remaining birth influences are different, however, and may therefore have either a positive or negative impact on each. Quick-thinking, Mercury-ruled Virgo may be irked by Saturn-governed Capricorn's slowness, for instance, yet may benefit from his or her determination, while cardinal Capricorn may appreciate mutable Virgo's adaptability, but not his or her appetite for change.

Your Boss: If you are a cardinal Capricorn with a Virgo boss, you may have your sights set on her job, but may not mind working for her. Indeed, sharing an earthy element may mean that you generally see eye to eye on basic matters, such as the importance of working within a limited budget, and your joint feminine polarity may also cause you both to give considerable thought to how to achieve this, so that in many respects you may feel that you are Virgo's equal. You may, however, frown on mutable Virgo's enthusiasm for the new, if, like many Capricorns, Saturn can make you quite conservative.

You probably know where you stand with your predictable Capricorn boss if you are a Virgo, and may be quite happy with this state of affairs, as long as he gives you the intellectual freedom that your mercurial side demands. And the reason why you may have no objection to sticking to Capricorn's routines is that your joint earthy element and feminine polarity may convince you that they offer a sensible framework within which to operate. Yet some of saturnine, cardinal Capricorn's characteristics may frustrate you almost to the point of tears, such as the agonizingly long time that he may take to reach a decision, and the one-track, goal-oriented mind that allows little room for diversity.

Virgo and Capricorn in the Workplace: Both Virgo and Capricorn enjoy being mentally occupied, but although they typically work alongside one another industriously and companionably, they don't always regard each other with unqualified approval. If you are a Capricorn, you may admire Virgo's flexibility, but may dislike being distracted by the urge to communicate that is also a mutable-quadruplicity trait. By contrast, you may occasionally be annoyed by Saturn-ruled Capricorn's reticence if you are a Virgo, particularly when you've persuasively presented a well-reasoned case for experimenting with a different method, for instance. That said, on other occasions you may be thankful for Capricorn's doggedness.

AQUARIUS

VIRGO

At best, Virgo and Aquarius colleagues' similarities give them an innate understanding, while their dissimilarities make them remarkably complementary. Perhaps the worst that could be said about their working relationship is that earthy Virgo's common sense can act as a dampener on Aquarius' airy spirits, and that fixed-sign Aquarius' obduracy may rankle with mutable, adaptable Virgo. Neither are emotional people, however, so they generally don't take their differences personally.

Your Boss: Your Virgo boss may seem more like your equal than your superior if you are an Aquarius, maybe partly because the influence of Uranus, your ruling planet, causes you to be indifferent to conventional hierarchies, and partly because you feel that you connect with him mentally. This is not surprising if you consider that the words "intelligent," "analytical," and "communicative" are all associated with your element of air and Virgo's planetary governor, Mercury, and mutable quadruplicity. But although your relationship with Virgo may be characterized by interesting exchanges of opinions, being an airy idealist, you may be frustrated by your practical, earthy boss's insistence on operating within feasible parameters, even if you know that this is an efficient approach.

You may find working for Aquarius simultaneously stimulating and exasperating if you are a Virgo. Stimulating, because Aquarius' eccentric, Uranian notions intrigue that mercurial, mutable mind of yours, and exasperating, because the earthy, realistic side of you may sometimes regard your airy, impractical boss as living in cloud-cuckoo-land. Indeed, there may have been occasions when Aquarius has, for example, instructed you to undertake an investigation into software that is still in its experimental stages, but that she believes could transform your working practices. You may not mind doing the research, yet may resent wasting time on an assignment that you suspect will come to nothing, but then maybe an Aquarian idea occasionally proves you wrong.

Virgo and Aquarius in the Workplace: If you are an Aquarius, your airy element and your Virgo coworker's mutable quadruplicity and governing planet may give you common ground in that they bestow an intellectual interest in your work upon you both. Yet while you have a pioneering, masculine polarity, Virgo's is feminine, or cautious, and his or her earthy element may also make your colleague more level-headed than you. You may consequently dislike Virgo's tendency to dismiss your brainwaves, just as you, if you are a matter-of-fact Virgo, may wish that fixed-sign Aquarius would stop stubbornly defending the indefensible and just get on with the job.

Aquarius Birth Influences

Ruling planet: Uranus; traditionally Saturn
Element: Air
Polarity: Masculine
Quadruplicity: Fixed

If you are a clever Aquarius, you probably find your intelligent Virgo boss easy to work with. You are both good communicators, and should therefore have little difficulty discussing your suggested plans of action, even if your approaches differ.

Virgo Birth Influences

Ruling planet: Mercury
Element: Earth
Polarity: Feminine
Quadruplicity: Mutable

VIRGO

PISCES

Virgo Birth Influences

Ruling planet: Mercury
Element: Earth
Polarity: Feminine
Quadruplicity: Mutable

They may have a pensive, feminine polarity and flexible, mutable quadruplicity in common, but a pair of Virgo and Pisces colleagues could otherwise hardly be more dissimilar. While Mercury and an earthy element typically result in Virgo being neutral, practical, and systematic, Neptune and water manifest themselves in Pisces as intuition, creativity, and disorganization. At best, this means that their strengths may both complement each other and compensate for one another's weaknesses. A worst-case scenario, however, may see them failing to interact happily or effectively.

Your Boss: If you are a Pisces, it may be that your watery element makes you feel rather at sea, in which case your Virgo boss's routines may give you a stable framework within which to operate, yet it may equally be that you find his businesslike ways so constricting that they dam up your imagination. Either way, you may admire his earthy capacity for hard work and mercurial intelligence, but may have a powerful hunch that he doesn't understand, or sympathize with, your intuitive methods. If you struggle to blink back the tears when he frowns on your haphazardness, for instance, try to toughen up a little because he almost certainly only wants to encourage you to be more productive.

Because you and your boss share a variety-loving, adaptable, mutable quadruplicity if you are a Virgo and she is a Pisces, you may welcome the diverse projects that she assigns to you, as well as her willingness to let you undertake them in your own, methodical way. You may nevertheless feel as though you are living on different planets, however, for while Mercury makes you especially articulate and communicative, Neptune may cloak Pisces in an aura of mystery that a watery element and feminine polarity reinforce with extra layers of reticence. Although you may regard her as an enigma, you may not be able to fault her caring and compassionate management style.

Virgo and Pisces in the Workplace: You may depend on your earthy Virgo coworker to keep you focused on a job in hand if you are a Neptunian Pisces who often lapses into daydreams when unenthused by tasks that don't inspire you, and may also respect that incisive Virgoan brain. And if you are a Virgo, you may be amazed and impressed by the original, insightful ideas that may often flow from Pisces' fertile mind, and may be touched by his or her sympathy when you're having a bad day. Even so, you're probably rarely on the same wavelength.

If you are a straightforward Virgo, you may find your Piscean boss's vague instructions baffling, and may be left wondering how to proceed.

Pisces Birth Influences

Ruling planet: Neptune; traditionally Jupiter
Element: Water
Polarity: Feminine
Quadruplicity: Mutable

LIBRA
LIBRA

When two airy Libras become colleagues, they'll probably have so much fun chatting about what they did the night before that any pretense of diligently applying themselves to the job in hand flies out of the window. Due to the influence of pleasure-loving Venus and a flighty, airy element, neither a self-denying work ethic nor staying power are Libran strong points, but then initiating pioneering ideas and looking after number one definitely are, thanks to this sign's masculine polarity and cardinal quadruplicity. In fact, despite their conciliatory approach, both of these people can be surprisingly steely where their own interests are concerned, sometimes resulting in the most understated of rivalries.

Your Boss: If you and your boss were both born under the zodiacal sign of the balance, it is likely that his informal management style encourages you to consider yourself his equal rather than an underling, which no doubt suits you very well. Being governed by Venus may mean that you both prefer a relaxed working atmosphere, your airy element furthermore blessing you each with intelligence and verbal fluency, so that your relationship is likely to be easygoing and focused on exchanging opinions, and perhaps also the latest gossip. That said, your boss's tolerance may occasionally lull you into forgetting his position, and if the cardinal quadruplicity that gives you both a desire to take the lead then surfaces strongly in you, you may feel an icy blast of Libran disapproval at your presumptuousness. Your shared cardinal quadruplicity may similarly manifest itself in your boss as driving ambition—at times personal, and at others on behalf of your team. But if his vision for your latest project doesn't arouse your interest, and you take your eye off the ball, you may find yourself receiving the subtlest of reprimands for your airy indifference or Venusian languor.

Libra and Libra in the Workplace: Having an extroverted, masculine polarity, a benevolence-bestowing planetary governor in Venus, and a gregarious element of air in common, you and your coworker may have an amicable relationship if you are both Libras. You may also share a positive outlook and an enjoyment of inconsequential chatter that may often lead you astray when you're supposed to be getting on with a tedious task, all of which may cause you to warm to your colleague. But your common cardinal quadruplicity and masculine polarity can make you both equally pushy and self-assertive, and when promotion is on the cards, for instance, neither of you may hesitate to try to outmaneuver the other, albeit in the most charming of ways.

Libra Birth Influences
Ruling planet: Venus
Element: Air
Polarity: Masculine
Quadruplicity: Cardinal

Libra coworkers often appreciate each other's easygoing style. Don't be fooled by his relaxed manner, though, for you may one day find that your colleague is up for promotion rather than you!

Libra Birth Influences
Ruling planet: Venus
Element: Air
Polarity: Masculine
Quadruplicity: Cardinal

LIBRA
SCORPIO

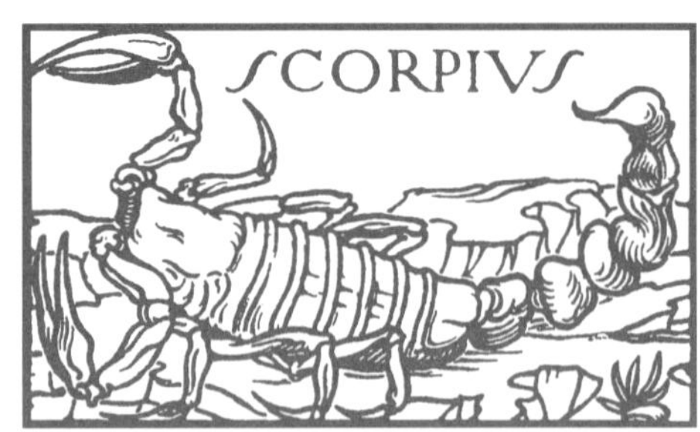

Libra Birth Influences

Ruling planet: Venus
Element: Air
Polarity: Masculine
Quadruplicity: Cardinal

When things are getting you down, Scorpio, your cheerful Libran colleague may raise your spirits.

Scorpio Birth Influences

Ruling planet: Pluto; traditionally Mars
Element: Water
Polarity: Feminine
Quadruplicity: Fixed

Libra and Scorpio can be remarkably complementary workmates, as long as they are enthused by the same mission or goal. Libra's strengths, for instance, include a Venusian talent for pouring oil over troubled emotional waters, an airy, rational viewpoint, a masculine polarity's optimism, and a cardinal quadruplicity's drive, while Scorpio contributes Plutonian concentration, watery creativity, feminine-polarity thoughtfulness, and a fixed quadruplicity's tenacity. But because Libra is progressive and open, and Scorpio, often conservative and closed, they may rarely establish a productive connection.

Your Boss: Although you may find it impossible to dislike your Libran boss if you are a Scorpio, you may not respect her that much, perhaps because you think that she lacks gravitas, or maybe because you disapprove of her management style. It is the combination of an airy element and Venus that makes Libra easygoing and peaceable, chatty and informal, which may soothe your watery, sensitive, Scorpionic soul, yet offend your rigid, fixed-quadruplicity side, which may also instinctively fend off her enthusiasm for the new. You probably cannot help but admire her airy articulacy and charm, though, as well as the cardinal-quadruplicity initiative that she displays in overcoming any obstacles in her path.

Your Scorpio boss may exasperate you if you are a Libra, even if you can see that he has many virtues, such as startling insight and astonishing perseverance, qualities bestowed on him by water and a fixed quadruplicity. The root of your problem may lie partly in the mismatch between the conciliatory, sociable influence of Venus and uncompromising, secretive Pluto, and partly in that between your active, masculine polarity and his passive, feminine one. Similarly, those born under airy, cardinal-quadruplicity signs like you are keen to communicate their opinions and to receive instant feedback, yet talking to reticent Scorpio give you the impression that you are transmitting your views into a black hole.

Libra and Scorpio in the Workplace: If you and your coworker are a Libra and a Scorpio, to say that you aren't on the same wavelength may be an understatement. If you are an airy, analytical Libra who likes to combine work with fun, intuitive, serious Scorpio may be an enigmatic and disheartening individual to work alongside. And if you are a private Scorpio, you may dislike the way that your curious, romantic Libran colleague tries to persuade you to spill the beans on your personal life. Yet you may nevertheless each be grateful for the other's support, be it in the form of Libra's kindliness or Scorpio's compassion.

SAGITTARIUS
LIBRA

Airy Libra and fiery Sagittarius typically inspire and enthuse one another with their inventive notions, but neither sign is renowned for its staying power, which is why there may be a lot of talk and preliminary action, but few concrete results, unless both are truly motivated by a task. These two have an affinity for one another, not least because they share a positive, masculine polarity, although Libra's conciliatory ruling planet and assertive, cardinal quadruplicity and Sagittarius' aggressive, fiery element and moody, mutable quadruplicity may sometimes be at odds.

Your Boss: Overall, you may like and respect your Libran boss if you are a Sagittarius. Although different birth influences—his element of air and your mutable quadruplicity—are responsible, you may both be articulate communicators who enjoy exchanging opinions and dislike formality, while your common masculine polarity may give you both an enterprising outlook, so that in many ways you may feel as though you are on the same, progressive wavelength. Yet because Venus-governed Libra hates causing offense and has a diplomat's way with words, you may sometimes feel that he is telling you what you want to hear rather than what he really thinks, which may irritate your honest and impatient, fiery side.

If you are a Libra, the combination of Venus and your unemotional element may cause you to shrink from both negativity and extreme displays of temperament, which may be why you generally enjoy working for your Sagittarian boss, except for those few occasions when you are at the receiving end of a frustrated, fiery outburst. Add optimistic Jupiter and the burning vitality of fire to your shared masculine, or confidence-bestowing, polarity, and the result is someone who both thinks big and is raring to go, which may frequently fire up your cardinal-quadruplicity ambition. You may be less keen on mutable Sagittarius' changeability, however, for it is not for nothing that Libra is called the sign of the balance.

Libra and Sagittarius in the Workplace: That you are both intelligent and talkative may be an asset and a hindrance in the workplace if you and your coworker are a Libra and a Sagittarius, in that you may spend so much time bouncing ideas off one another that nothing gets done. But should Libra's goal-oriented, cardinal quadruplicity come to the fore, fiercely individualistic Sagittarius may resist being pushed, and should fiery Sagittarius' dominating tendency manifest itself, Libra may respond with a cool display of airy independence.

Sagittarius Birth Influences

Ruling planet: Jupiter
Element: Fire
Polarity: Masculine
Quadruplicity: Mutable

If you are a Libra, you may wish that your fiery Sagittarian boss were more tactful when communicating with you.

Libra Birth Influences

Ruling planet: Venus
Element: Air
Polarity: Masculine
Quadruplicity: Cardinal

LIBRA
CAPRICORN

Libra Birth Influences
Ruling planet: Venus
Element: Air
Polarity: Masculine
Quadruplicity: Cardinal

You no doubt have to admit, Capricorn, that Libra's smiling face helps to brighten your day and calm you down when you're feeling stressed.

Capricorn Birth Influences
Ruling planet: Saturn
Element: Earth
Polarity: Feminine
Quadruplicity: Cardinal

Libra and Capricorn generally arouse one another's respect in the workplace, partly because they share a go-getting, cardinal quadruplicity, and partly because they recognize that each has strengths that compensate for the other's weaknesses. While airy, masculine-polarity Libra is analytical and enterprising, but often capricious and careless, earthy, feminine-polarity Capricorn is practical and steadfast, yet frequently unimaginative and overly cautious, and whereas Venus-governed Libra is easygoing, Saturn-ruled Capricorn is uncompromising. Although they may not always approve of one another's style and methods, their cardinal-quadruplicity focus on aiming toward a mutual goal may enable them to set aside their differences.

Your Boss: If you are a saturnine, feminine-polarity Capricorn, the esteem of your colleagues may be important to you, and worries may gnaw away at you if your boss seems critical or unappreciative of your performance, in which case you may find working for Libra satisfying. It is thanks to the element of air, Venus, and a masculine polarity that Libra is communicative, diplomatic, and positive, so that you may receive plenty of feedback, and almost certainly good. You may, however, suspect that he often rushes into a project without thinking through the implications, thereby having wasted everyone's time when it proves unfeasible.

Despite the admiration that you may feel for your tenacious, businesslike Capricorn boss if you are a Libra, her rigid regime may frequently remind you of school. Indeed, the combined influence of Saturn and earth may cause Capricorn to be a stern taskmaster who believes that routines aid productivity, which, as a relaxed child of Venus with a freedom-loving, airy element, may have a suffocating effect on you. Still, at least Capricorn is blessed with patience, and because you have a cardinal quadruplicity in common, may not be able to fault your motivation and drive when a crucial deadline needs to be met.

Libra and Capricorn in the Workplace: Your airy Libra colleague's tendency to question everything, as well as to chat away while working, may sometimes irritate you if you are a more phlegmatic, earthy Capricorn who has productivity targets to meet. Nevertheless, there may be times when you appreciate Libra's intelligent, incisive mind, cardinal-quadruplicity initiative, and Venusian tolerance. You may equally find Capricorn's matter-of-fact, prudent attitude rather boring if you are a Libra, yet may be grateful for his or her attention to detail, especially if a warning from your Capricorn colleague heads off a reprimand from your boss for being slapdash. You're probably having fun charming earnest Capricorn into lightening up, too!

AQUARIUS

LIBRA

It would be a rare Libra–Aquarius duo that didn't interact easily in the workplace. For while both share an informal approach and are united by their rational outlook, thanks to their common airy element, and are optimistic and energetic, due to their joint masculine polarity, it is well-nigh impossible to fall out with peaceable, Venus-ruled Libra, and because Uranus' rebellion-invoking influence over Aquarius is tempered by that of mature Saturn, the result is usually unconventional concepts rather than disruptive behavior. Nevertheless, cardinal-quadruplicity Libra's willingness to try anything if it promises success and fixed-quadruplicity Aquarius' dislike of change may sometimes be at odds.

Aquarius Birth Influences

Ruling planet: Uranus; traditionally Saturn
Element: Air
Polarity: Masculine
Quadruplicity: Fixed

Your Boss: You may forget about your Libra boss's superior status when you are discussing how best to initiate a new project if you are an Aquarius. Indeed, the double dose of your mutual, intellect-enhancing element of air and dynamic, masculine polarity, combined with Libra's urgency-bestowing, cardinal quadruplicity and the experimentation that is the hallmark of Uranus, your primary planetary ruler, may give your brainstorming sessions a sense of excitement that prompts you both to come up with pioneering ideas. Having a fixed, or straightforward, quadruplicity and honesty-preferring secondary planetary governor in Saturn, you may, however, dislike the tactfulness that is Venus' gift to Libra, which you may interpret as insincerity or even hypocrisy.

The eccentric workings of your Uranus-ruled, Aquarius boss's mind may be a source of endless fascination if you are an analytical, airy Libra. Indeed, she is probably so full of surprises, so confident that her ingenious theories will work, and so persuasive that you can't help but be inspired by her visions. But because your cardinal quadruplicity and rather lazy planetary ruler may cause you to suggest time-saving short-cuts, and her quadruplicity is fixed, giving her a preference for persevering with her tried-and-tested methods, her rejection of your streamlining proposals may sometimes rankle with you. In fact, it may seem as though there is one rule for your boss and another for you (not that you would ever make an issue of it if you are a typical, conciliatory, Venusian Libra).

Because you and your Aquarian boss share an airy, analytical mindset if you are a Libra, as well as an enterprising, masculine polarity, you probably both enjoy experimenting at work.

Libra and Aquarius in the Workplace: If you are one of a pair of Libra and Aquarius coworkers, you may get on well, perhaps partly because you think in the same logical manner, and partly because neither of you lets emotions intrude on your working relationship. Even so, Libra's desire for instant results and Aquarius' refusal to be pushed may occasionally give rise to muted mutual irritation.

Libra Birth Influences

Ruling planet: Venus
Element: Air
Polarity: Masculine
Quadruplicity: Cardinal

LIBRA
PISCES

Libra Birth Influences

Ruling planet: Venus
Element: Air
Polarity: Masculine
Quadruplicity: Cardinal

A fleeting look at Libra and Pisces' respective birth influences suggests that these colleagues will interact in a harmonious and complementary fashion in the workplace, for Venus is associated with conciliation, and Neptune with altruism; air equals logic, and water, creativity; a masculine polarity bestows enterprise, and a feminine one, pensiveness; and while a cardinal quadruplicity denotes initiative, a mutable one signifies flexibility. Looking closer, this relationship may not be perfect, however, particularly when one takes Libra's self-interest and Pisces' hypersensitivity into account.

Your Boss: You may rather rely on your Libra boss to keep you on track if you are a Pisces whose watery element and Neptunian ruler may often throw you into confusion, whose feminine polarity makes you more passive than proactive, and whose mutable quadruplicity infuses you with restlessness. Libra, by contrast, has an air-conferred factual and rational mindset, an energetic, masculine polarity, a go-getting, cardinal quadruplicity, and the winning charm of Venus, so that you may happily yield to her control. You may nevertheless feel a little hurt that she takes you for granted and doesn't seem to care about you as a person.

Although you may find it impossible to dislike your kindly, empathetic, Pisces boss, you may be exasperated by his chaotic management style if you are a Libra when, for example, his unstructured Neptunian ways and watery reliance on intuition appear muddled and irrational to your analytical, airy self. And whereas Venus gives you a balanced temperament, mutable Pisces' emotions may yo-yo, thereby interfering with your work and arousing your cardinal-quadruplicity impatience when delayed. Still, at least he may be willing to go along with you when you tactfully propose implementing some of your own ideas.

When you're caught up in chaos and mayhem, Pisces, you can count on cool-headed Libra to sort it out.

Libra and Pisces in the Workplace: The quality that you may most appreciate in your Libran coworker if you are a Pisces, is the generally tolerant, relaxed approach—the combined gift of Venus and air—that rarely makes you feel pressurized. You may also admire Libra's confidence and pioneering notions, but may be dispirited by his or her airy detachment if you long to establish a more profound connection with your workmate. And you may feel that you have to handle Pisces with kid gloves if you are a Libra, maybe having learned from experience that a playful comment may trigger a touchy response. That said, Pisces' unselfishness and thoughtfulness may earn your gratitude, and you may be awed by those Neptunian hunches that later prove spookily accurate.

Pisces Birth Influences

Ruling planet: Neptune; traditionally Jupiter
Element: Water
Polarity: Feminine
Quadruplicity: Mutable

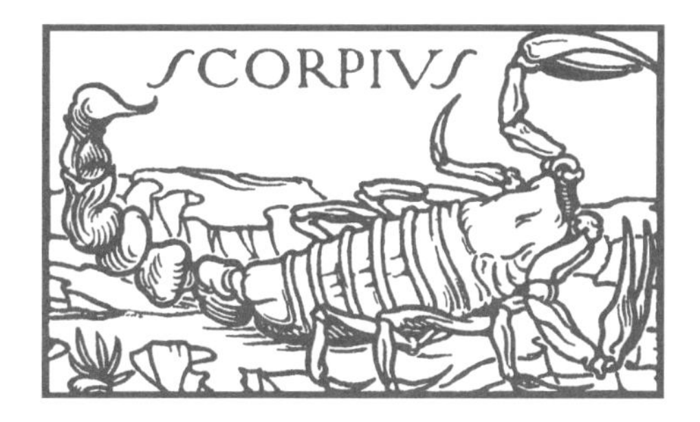

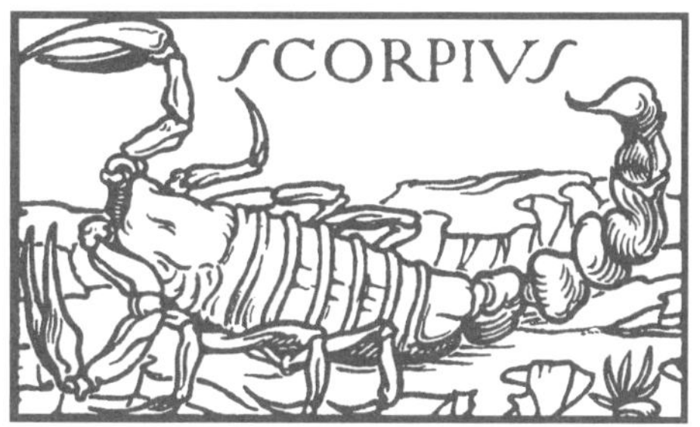

SCORPIO

SCORPIO

Sharing as they do the same birth influences, and consequently similar approaches and standards, it would be surprising if two Scorpio workmates didn't at least respect one another. It is unlikely that their relationship will take the form of an open and relaxed camaraderie, however, for their feminine polarity typically causes them to be reserved, a characteristic doubly reinforced by their element of water and secretive Pluto, their ruling planet, while their fixed quadruplicity gives them formidable focus and determination. Yet underneath their uncompromising façades lie soft and sensitive hearts, which means that they care about one another's welfare—even if they rarely show it—but are also wounded by perceived criticism.

Scorpio Birth Influences

Ruling planet: Pluto; traditionally Mars
Element: Water
Polarity: Feminine
Quadruplicity: Fixed

Your Boss: If you and your boss are both Scorpios, you may wonder why your coworkers complain that he or she is an enigma. Although it is true that feminine-polarity Scorpios are typically unforthcoming, the influence of Pluto may make you appreciate that knowledge represents power and is not to be shared indiscriminately, and your intuitive, watery element may furthermore provide you with an innate understanding of the creative way in which your boss's mind operates. And because you may well be as single-minded and tenacious as your Scorpio senior, due to your joint, fixed quadruplicity, you may sense that he or she regards you with kindly approval, even if you sometimes bristle when he overrides your decisions because they deviate from his or her tried-and-tested management blueprint. Don't let Scorpio's actions throw you into an agony of feminine-polarity, watery self-doubt, however, for they say more about your boss's resistance to change than they do about your judgment.

A typical Scorpio is naturally reticent, sometimes hiding his or her feelings or plans behind an enigmatic mask. Two Scorpios will understand and respect one another's need for privacy in the workplace, however.

Scorpio and Scorpio in the Workplace: You may not feel that you know everything about your Scorpio colleague if you are also a zodiacal scorpion, but then you may respect his or her privacy if you, too, would rather not share the intimate details of your personal life with your coworkers. Thanks to your shared, watery element, you may nevertheless each instinctively recognize when the other is feeling dispirited or upset, when you may unobtrusively offer your support, either by means of a few compassionate words or by quietly shouldering some of your fellow scorpion's workload. In normal circumstances, you may be grateful to be working alongside someone whose staying power matches yours, yet the downside of having a fixed quadruplicity in common may be the obstinacy with which you both stick to your guns when you disagree.

Scorpio Birth Influences

Ruling planet: Pluto; traditionally Mars
Element: Water
Polarity: Feminine
Quadruplicity: Fixed

SCORPIO
SAGITTARIUS

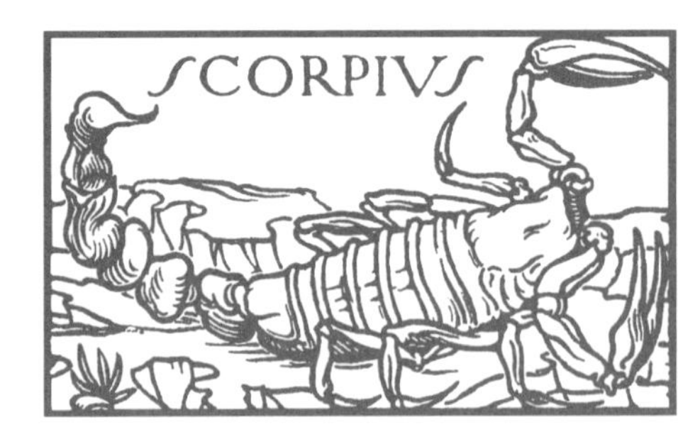

Scorpio Birth Influences

Ruling planet: Pluto; traditionally Mars
Element: Water
Polarity: Feminine
Quadruplicity: Fixed

Creative Sagittarius and tenacious Scorpio make an excellent team, provided that Sagittarius cooks up ideas and Scorpio takes care of details.

Sagittarius Birth Influences

Ruling planet: Jupiter
Element: Fire
Polarity: Masculine
Quadruplicity: Mutable

Scorpio's secretive Plutonian nature and watery sensitivity and Sagittarius' mutable-quadruplicity changeability and fiery bluntness are bound to act as irritants in a working relationship between the zodiacal scorpion and archer, which is not to say that they won't make an effective team. Indeed, Jupiter-ruled Sagittarius' big-picture visions, fiery energy, and masculine-polarity confidence may motivate Scorpio, who in turn typically contributes watery imagination, feminine-polarity backup, and fixed-quadruplicity determination to their joint ventures.

Your Boss: You may suspect that your Scorpio boss disapproves of you if you are a Sagittarius, and may not be that enthused by his leadership style either. It may be, for instance, that your mutable quadruplicity causes you to enjoy juggling a number of tasks at once and rapidly to become bored and antsy when required to concentrate your efforts on one project at a time, which may be precisely what inflexible, fixed-quadruplicity Scorpio expects of you. And because the triple injection of reticence bestowed on Scorpio by Pluto, water, and a feminine polarity may result in your boss being remarkably uncommunicative, he may rarely galvanize you into action, despite your pioneering, masculine polarity. Even so, on those rare occasions when you're feeling downcast, you may find watery Scorpio surprisingly empathetic.

If you are a Scorpio and your boss is a Sagittarius, you may have creativity in common, although you may take time to develop your notions, due to your intuitive, watery element and focused, fixed quadruplicity, and fiery, mutable Sagittarius' enterprising ideas may resemble lightning strikes: dazzling, ephemeral, and swiftly followed by others. Still, this may be one of the reasons why your boss often inspires you, others maybe including her optimistic, Jovian outlook, and infectious, fiery enthusiasm. That said, you because you have an emotionally vulnerable element in water and a pensive, feminine polarity, you may take her casual comments regarding your performance very much to heart if you perceive them to be critical.

Scorpio and Sagittarius in the Workplace: Feminine-polarity, fixed Scorpio's preference for working tenaciously behind the scenes collating and consolidating data, and masculine-polarity, mutable-quadruplicity Sagittarius' tendency to think up, seek out, or chase up new ideas can be remarkably complementary in the workplace. Sagittarius may respect Scorpio's staying power just as much as Scorpio admires Sagittarius' adaptability, too. They may find it difficult to communicate with one another, however, partly because Scorpio is reserved, partly because Sagittarius is impatient, and partly because they are usually on different wavelengths.

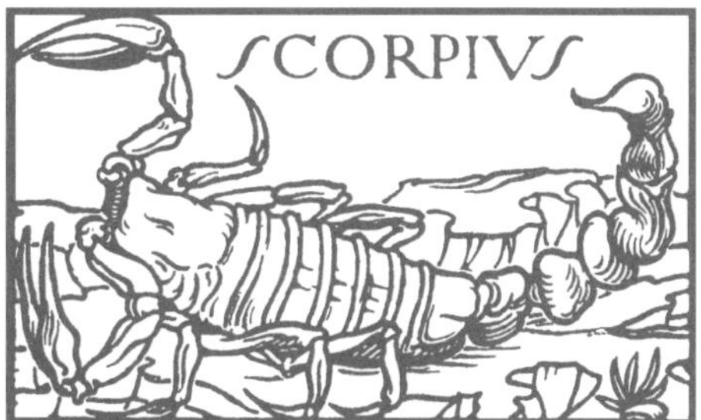

CAPRICORN
SCORPIO

Scorpio and Capricorn on the one hand display similar approaches in the workplace: their common, feminine polarity makes both thoughtful and conscientious, for example, while Scorpio's fixed quadruplicity and Capricorn's element of earth and saturnine planetary ruler cause them to be equally tenacious. On the other hand, Pluto-governed, watery Scorpio takes a strategic, as well as creative, long-term view, whereas earthy, cardinal-quadruplicity Capricorn has a more straightforward mindset and is often driven by urgency. As contrasting as they are, these qualities can be complementary, although Scorpio's watery sensitivity and Capricorn's single-minded ambition may not endear them to one another.

Your Boss: The workings of your enigmatic, Pluto-ruled, Scorpio boss's mind may be a mystery to you if you are a Capricorn, but you probably admire his determination and staying power, gifts of a fixed quadruplicity that may accord with your own Saturn- and earth-bestowed willpower and doggedness. And because you, too, have a reserved, feminine polarity, you may not mind Scorpio's uncommunicativeness, as long as he keeps you in the loop. Even so, his unwillingness to explain his decisions may rankle with you if you can't understand why they sometimes appear so illogical, in which case they either stem from his intuitive, watery element or may be steps in a Plutonian master plan to which you are not party.

It may seem as though your Capricorn boss has stepped straight out of the pages of a "model-boss" manual if you are a Scorpio. Indeed, thanks to the influence of Saturn and earth, Capricorn may set an impressive example, being patient, prudent, steady, and hardworking, characteristics that may be in harmony with your own Plutonian, feminine-polarity, fixed-quadruplicity practices. That said, because your element is water, earthy, cardinal-quadruplicity Capricorn may not be quite the perfect boss as far as you are concerned, maybe because you consider her unimaginative, or perhaps because she doesn't take your feelings or family commitments into consideration when pushing you to meet a deadline.

Scorpio and Capricorn in the Workplace: Although Scorpio and Capricorn may respect the serious and dedicated way in which each tackles tasks, it is unlikely that their relationship is anything other than strictly businesslike. If you are a level-headed Capricorn, you may feel that personal comments are best avoided on account of Scorpio's extreme touchiness (for which blame the scorpion's watery element), and if you are a fundamentally humane Scorpio, you may be alienated by cardinal Capricorn's narrow focus on prioritizing and accomplishing a workplace assignment.

Capricorn Birth Influences

Ruling planet: Saturn
Element: Earth
Polarity: Feminine
Quadruplicity: Cardinal

Scorpio and Capricorn are both determined individuals and no doubt make an efficient team. When they are at odds, however, neither is likely to change the other's mind easily.

Scorpio Birth Influences

Ruling planet: Pluto; traditionally Mars
Element: Water
Polarity: Feminine
Quadruplicity: Fixed

SCORPIO

AQUARIUS

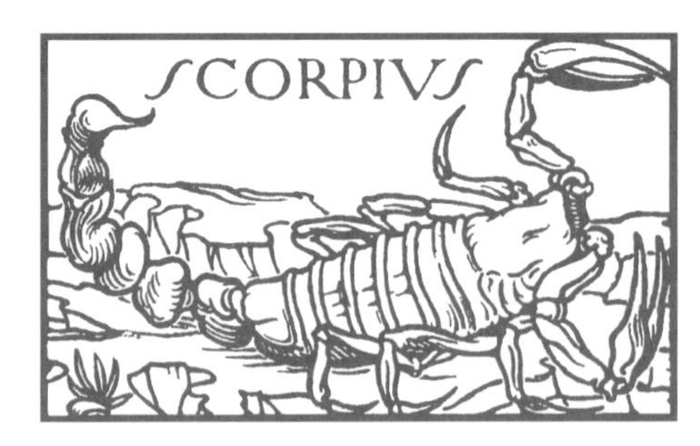

Scorpio Birth Influences

Ruling planet: Pluto; traditionally Mars
Element: Water
Polarity: Feminine
Quadruplicity: Fixed

♇ ♂ ♏

It is not only their common, fixed-quadruplicity tenacity that often makes Scorpio and Aquarius an excellent team, for their dissimilarities can be a boon, too. Watery, Pluto-governed Scorpio's creative, evolutionary way of thinking can provide an effective alternative to airy, Uranus-ruled Aquarius' logical, trailblazing mindset, for instance, while Aquarius' masculine-polarity enthusiasm can have a galvanizing effect on the more inhibited, feminine-polarity scorpion. Scorpio's profound reticence may sometimes irritate direct, communicative Aquarius, however, just as sensitive Scorpio may be bothered by Aquarius' cool indifference.

Aquarius, if you can bear to tear yourself away from your computer, take time to talk to Scorpio: she may impress you with her visionary ideas.

Your Boss: Your Scorpio boss may both interest and frustrate you if you are an Aquarius to whom Uranus and your element of air have bequeathed a double dose of curiosity. Secretive Pluto, an unforthcoming, feminine polarity, and the emotional vulnerability that is inherent in having a watery element may together cause Scorpio to be the most guarded of individuals, and if they seem incomprehensible to you, you may consequently long to understand the reasoning behind her decisions, and may be annoyed that she withholds information from you. You may have no trouble recognizing the strength of her will, however, if your shared fixed quadruplicity makes you equally determined.

You may be thankful that your airy, masculine-polarity, Aquarian boss is so friendly and upbeat if you are a Scorpio, especially if your dark planetary ruler and feminine, or negative, polarity make you feel somewhat isolated from your workmates or lacking in confidence, yet you may nevertheless be a little hurt that he seems more concerned with boosting your productivity than your self-belief. Personal issues aside, you may furthermore be impressed by Aquarius' radical, Uranian proposals should Pluto, your planetary governor, give you an appreciation of the need to shake things up at times, particularly when it comes to transforming outmoded working practices into more efficient ones.

Scorpio and Aquarius in the Workplace: Although you may respect Scorpio's staying power if you are his or her Aquarian colleague, you may wish that the scorpion were less taciturn and easier to get along with. That said, you may occasionally be startled by the depth of watery Scorpio's compassion when you're going through a bad spell, and may also be amazed by the original ideas that emanate from that fertile imagination. And if you are a Scorpio, there may be times when you think that Uranus-governed Aquarius has a closer relationship with his or her computer than with you, yet may nonetheless enjoy working alongside such a cheerful and affable person.

Aquarius Birth Influences

Ruling planet: Uranus; traditionally Saturn
Element: Air
Polarity: Masculine
Quadruplicity: Fixed

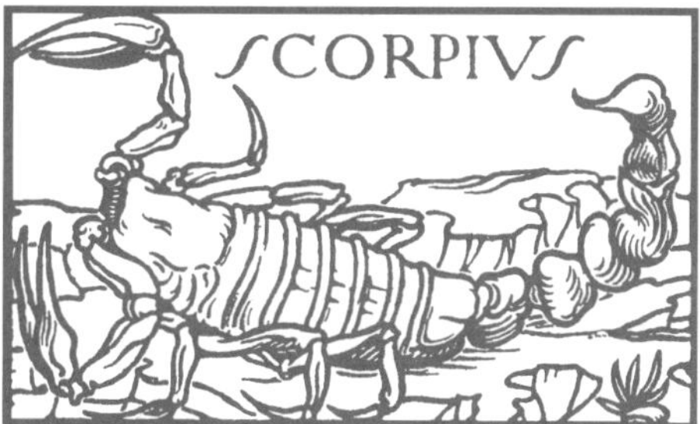

PISCES
SCORPIO

Their shared element of water may bless both Scorpio and Pisces with the gift of empathy, while their feminine polarity may make them quiet and thoughtful types. Although confrontational clashes may consequently be absent from their relationship, that doesn't mean that they won't vex one another once in a while, however. For Pisces, the primary irritants may be Pluto-ruled, fixed-quadruplicity Scorpio's secretive and unbending habits, for instance, while Scorpio may be frustrated by Pisces' Neptunian, mutable-quadruplicity vagueness and restlessness. Nevertheless, their equally creative mindsets, complemented by Scorpio's perseverance and Pisces' flexibility, may lead to a mutually productive—and even affectionate—partnership.

Pisces Birth Influences

Ruling planet: Neptune; traditionally Jupiter
Element: Water
Polarity: Feminine
Quadruplicity: Mutable

♆ ♃

Your Boss: His phenomenal powers of concentration and intense approach may arouse your awe if your boss is a fixed-quadruplicity, Plutonian Scorpio and you are a mutable-quadruplicity, Neptunian Pisces who is easily distracted and rather imprecise. He may be a man of few words, yet you may be able to sense his irritation when your attention's been diverted from a job in hand or you don't feel focused, but then his water-bestowed fellow feeling may be palpable when you're trying your best to do things his way. And you must feel as though you're on cloud nine when you receive a rare, heartfelt word of praise for having dreamed up an imaginative concept.

It may be hard for you to dislike your Pisces boss if you are a Scorpio, perhaps partly because you feel a bond with her as a result of your common polarity and element, and partly because Neptune infuses her with genuine altruism, in which case you may be touched that she genuinely seems to care about your welfare. Despite your watery intuition, you may sometimes find it difficult to comprehend exactly what she requires of you, however, for Neptune may confuse her thinking or her mutable quadruplicity may cause her constantly to change her mind. That said, when the light finally dawns, you may be inspired by her original visions.

Both having kind and insightful natures, Scorpio and Pisces colleagues enjoy working together.

Scorpio and Pisces in the Workplace: If you are a Pisces, you may be grateful to have such a compassionate and, above all, tenacious coworker in Scorpio, who may be someone who understands that you can't help lapsing into Neptunian daydreams and keeps you on track. Similarly, if you are a Scorpio, you may feel sympathy for kindly, well-meaning Pisces, and may appreciate your coworker's adaptability, if not his or her scattiness. Even so, each of you may have to do your best to suppress sighs of exasperation at times.

Scorpio Birth Influences

Ruling planet: Pluto; traditionally Mars
Element: Water
Polarity: Feminine
Quadruplicity: Fixed

SAGITTARIUS
SAGITTARIUS

Sagittarius Birth Influences
Ruling planet: Jupiter
Element: Fire
Polarity: Masculine
Quadruplicity: Mutable

Apart from a few fiery outbursts provoked, perhaps, when one self-assertive archer is briefly infuriated by the other's domineering tendencies, two Sagittarian colleagues typically both like and enthuse one another in the workplace. Thanks to Jupiter, their planetary governor, and their masculine polarity, these are broad-minded, positive thinkers whose fiery element gives them a knack for generating trendsetting concepts, yet may also cause their interest to wane almost as soon as it was kindled. Similarly, although their mutable quadruplicity makes them flexible and communicative, it fills them with restlessness, too, so that while their brain-waves may fire one another up, a change of tack may swiftly follow, with the result that this may not be the most efficient or productive of workplace pairings, with many loose ends being left.

When two Sagittarians work well together, the sky's the limit! A pioneering spirit helps them rise to any challenge, and they're adaptable enough to consider each other's ideas, too. Staying power is not a Sagittarian strength, though.

Your Boss: You may be pleased to have a Sagittarian boss if you are also a Sagittarius, not least if, sharing as she does your fiery element, masculine polarity, and mutable quadruplicity, she, like you, is impulsive, uninhibited, and easily bored. You may therefore never know what to expect when you arrive at work each day, and because your fiery element may infuse you with an insatiable appetite for stimulation, and the masculine-polarity side of you loves being challenged, this may suit you perfectly. As well as blessing her with wide-ranging vision, Jupiter may make her inclusive, too, which is why you may feel that she considers you more of an equal than an underling, which always gratifies somewhat egotistical, fiery people. In fact, the only occasions when you may be irritated with her are when your fiery creativity has been inspired by a certain assignment and she suddenly asks you to drop what you are doing to start on something new.

Sagittarius and Sagittarius in the Workplace: The problem with working alongside a fellow Sagittarius if you are also a zodiacal archer, is that you may spend so much time swapping enterprising ideas that you neglect those vital, yet tedious, chores for which you can't muster any enthusiasm, which may not be a drawback at all for you two, even if it is a headache for your manager. Thanks to the combination of jovial Jupiter, warm-hearted fire, an affirmative, masculine polarity, and an easygoing, mutable quadruplicity, you may rarely fall out with one another, but when you do, perceived bossiness and a refusal to be bossed around may be the triggers. Fortunately, neither of you tends to remain miffed for long, and your fuming frowns no doubt soon give way to laughter.

Sagittarius Birth Influences
Ruling planet: Jupiter
Element: Fire
Polarity: Masculine
Quadruplicity: Mutable

CAPRICORN

SAGITTARIUS

The fundamental difference between Sagittarius and Capricorn colleagues is that fiery, mutable-quadruplicity archers need to be stimulated by their work in order to sustain their enthusiasm and keep boredom at bay, while cardinal-quaduplicity, earthy Capricorns are set on climbing the career ladder and rather enjoy the mundane tasks that their Sagittarian coworkers consider so tedious. And if it seems as though they come from different planets, they do, with Jupiter infusing Sagittarius with an expansive outlook, and Saturn instilling a limiting approach in Capricorn, characteristics compounded by their opposite polarities. Different they may be, but the consequence is that Sagittarius' strengths may compensate for Capricorn's weaknesses and vice versa.

Your Boss: You may find your Sagittarian boss irritating if you are a Capricorn, maybe because, being a steady, earthy person, his mutable-quadruplicity unpredictability unsettles you, but perhaps primarily because you are driven, and he doesn't appear to take your career as seriously as you do. Indeed, fiery Sagittarian individuals tend to live for the moment and seek inspiration in spontaneity, and although Jupiter may cause them to encourage their staff to develop their knowledge and skills, you may feel that your work, and hence promotion prospects, are suffering through repeatedly being told to drop what you are doing in order to turn your attention to his latest bright idea. That said, you may admire his fiery creativity.

Capricorn may be a trial to work for if you are a Sagittarius, and not just because your fiery element gives you an innate resistance to being controlled, behavior that comes naturally to protégés of disciplinarian Saturn like your boss. The main problem may be that Capricorn's management style doesn't motivate you, for whereas you may see the wider picture, Capricorn homes in on the details—another mismatch between your planetary governors—and while your masculine polarity, fiery element, and mutable quadruplity may make you outgoing, adventurous, and easily distracted, Capricorn's corresponding birth influences may cause your boss to be introspective, cautious, and goal-oriented. The saving grace, however, may be Capricorn's cardinal-quadruplicity sense of urgency, which may activate your own masculine-polarity relish of a challenge.

Sagittarius and Capricorn in the Workplace: You are no doubt on totally different wavelengths if you and your workmate are a Sagittarius and a Capricorn, yet may nevertheless appreciate certain qualities in one another, such as mutable-quadruplicity Sagittarius' adaptability and amiability, and earthy Capricorn's productivity and patience.

Capricorn Birth Influences

Ruling planet: Saturn
Element: Earth
Polarity: Feminine
Quadruplicity: Cardinal

Your Capricorn boss may complain that you lack dedication if you are a Sagittarius. Is it because you like to throw caution to the wind, but the goat's prudent working style leaves you cold?

Sagittarius Birth Influences

Ruling planet: Jupiter
Element: Fire
Polarity: Masculine
Quadruplicity: Mutable

SAGITTARIUS
AQUARIUS

Sagittarius Birth Influences

Ruling planet: Jupiter
Element: Fire
Polarity: Masculine
Quadruplicity: Mutable

Airy Aquarius and fiery Sagittarius can make a dynamic team when the challenge is right. Unconventional and inspirational, they spur each other on to reach ever greater heights.

Aquarius Birth Influences

Ruling planet: Uranus; traditionally Saturn
Element: Air
Polarity: Masculine
Quadruplicity: Fixed

Although they have only a masculine, or positive, polarity in common, this is often enough to create an instinctive rapport between Sagittarius and Aquarius. The good news is that their remaining birth influences are generally sympathetic, so that while their personalities may be very different, they typically respond well to one another. The fiery archer's rather eccentric way of thinking may be stimulated by the water-carrier's unconventional, Uranian mindset, for instance, Sagittarius' mutable quadruplicity and Aquarius' element of air furthermore causing both to be smart and communicative. And the bad news is that mutable-quadruplicity Sagittarius' changeability may exasperate fixed-quadruplicity Aquarius, who may in turn be too inflexible for adaptable Sagittarius.

Your Boss: Overall, you may enjoy working for your jovial Sagittarian boss if you are an Aquarius, perhaps because, being blessed with a mutable-quadruplicity's flexible approach, he allows you the freedom to pursue your ideas that is so vital to an airy individual like you, or maybe because you find his enthusiasm infectious, especially when his imagination has been fired up by your inventive, Uranian proposals. Yet because you have a fixed quadruplicity, and Sagittarius' is mutable, and his fiery element may also make him impatient, you may be annoyed when he loses interest in a long-term project that you believe has potential.

If you are a Sagittarius and your boss is an Aquarius, your element of fire and Uranus, the water-carrier's planetary ruler, may result in you both being somewhat rebellious types who question convention, which is one of the reasons why you may warm to your "superior." Another is that your relationship may seem more like one of equals than of boss and underling, for your joint, masculine polarity's gift to you both is self-confidence, your fiery element and inclusive Jupiter may cause you to be disinclined to consider yourself inferior to anyone, and Uranian Aquarius is uninterested in status. All in all, you may feel as though you have a vibrant, intellectual connection with Aquarius, even if you are sometimes infuriated by his fixed-quadruplicity refusal to go along with some of your fiery, spur-of-the-moment suggestions.

Sagittarius and Aquarius in the Workplace: You and your coworker may have an amicable relationship if one of you is a Jovian Sagittarius and the other, an airy, even-tempered Aquarius. Your respective quadruplicities may trigger irritation at times, but then mutable-quadruplicity Sagittarius may come into his or her own when multitasking is required, and fixed-quadruplicity Aquarius may save the day whenever perseverance is needed.

PISCES
SAGITTARIUS

Although their shared, mutable quadruplicity may give Sagittarius and Pisces the necessary flexibility to accommodate one another's radically opposed mindsets and methods, it is unlikely that these two colleagues have an instinctive bond. For fiery, masculine-polarity Sagittarius' forcefulness can have an intimidating effect on watery, feminine-polarity Pisces, while Pisces' vagueness and uncertainty may infuriate confident Sagittarius. Yet their ruling planets and mutable quadruplicity indicate that both are visionary thinkers, and their respective elements suggest that they are original, too, so that this could be a highly effective working relationship if they can only make allowances for their differences.

Your Boss: If you are a Pisces, the best thing about having a Sagittarian boss may be that your common, mutable quadruplicity gives her an aversion to hide-bound practices that matches yours, particularly if the expansiveness of Jupiter, her ruling planet, accords with the abhorrence of boundaries that is the bequest of Neptune, your own planetary governor. Indeed, fiery Sagittarius may understand that creativity cannot flourish if it is hemmed in by rules and regulations, so you may find it easy to give expression to your ideas, especially when Sagittarius' Jovian optimism and fiery enthusiasm encourage you to shake off your inhibitions. That said, you may often keep your thoughts to yourself if you know from experience that your stream-of-consciousness approach may provoke a Sagittarian bark of impatience.

You may find him impossible to dislike if you are a Sagittarius and your boss is an unselfish, Neptunian Pisces, but he may nevertheless drive you to distraction. Whereas your masculine polarity may scream "action stations," his feminine polarity may signal "caution," and while your fiery element may instantly ignite a succession of brilliant ideas in your mind, his watery element may cause him to rely on nebulous instinct. Broad-minded Jupiter, an adaptable, mutable quadruplicity, and a positive, masculine polarity may enable you to go along with her lateral way of thinking, yet you may still burn to take charge yourself. But when you have been beset by personal problems, Pisces' profound compassion may touch you.

Sagittarius and Pisces in the Workplace: Thanks to their joint, mutable quadruplicity, neither Sagittarius nor Pisces are judgmental or inflexible types, which bodes well for their professional rapport, as does their appetite for diversity. Sagittarius' fiery aggression may nevertheless sometimes send you scurrying for cover if you are a tender Pisces, while watery Pisces' dreaminess may infuriate you if you are a Sagittarius who thrives on direct interaction.

Pisces Birth Influences

Ruling planet: Neptune; traditionally Jupiter
Element: Water
Polarity: Feminine
Quadruplicity: Mutable

♆ ♃ ≈

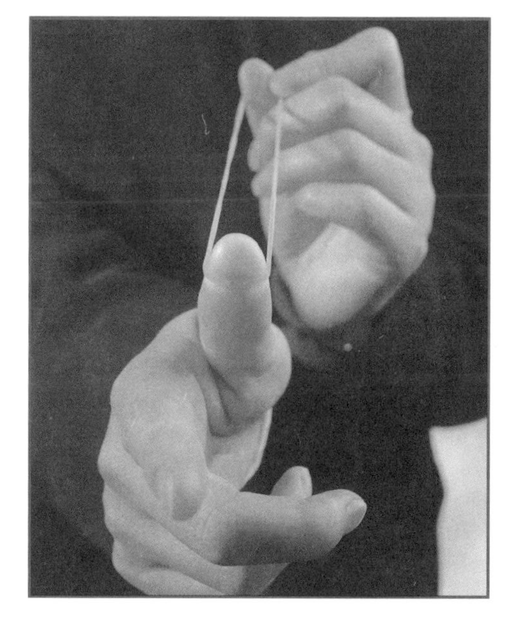

Both Sagittarius and Pisces are flexible and willing to bend the rules. The archer should try to respect Pisces' sensitive nature, however.

Sagittarius Birth Influences

Ruling planet: Jupiter
Element: Fire
Polarity: Masculine
Quadruplicity: Mutable

♃ 

CAPRICORN

CAPRICORN

Capricorn Birth Influences

Ruling planet: Saturn
Element: Earth
Polarity: Feminine
Quadruplicity: Cardinal

Capricorn coworkers are unlikely to be locked in a power struggle. Having a strong sense of responsibility, they are willing to work steadily and thoroughly together to do the job properly.

Capricorn Birth Influences

Ruling planet: Saturn
Element: Earth
Polarity: Feminine
Quadruplicity: Cardinal

Saturn-ruled Capricorn people's sense of self-worth is closely linked to their performance in the workplace, and although their cardinal quadruplicity may make them personally ambitious, two feminine-polarity Capricorn colleagues are rarely driven by the urge to compete directly with one another. That said, being earthy realists, one will no doubt seize an opportunity for promotion at the other's expense, yet this generally won't be taken personally, for neither is particularly sensitive, and both accept the dog-eat-dog dynamics of the business world. They are likely to respect one another, too, for both are equally steady, resilient, and industrious, thanks to their ruling planet and element, even if they aren't that enthused by each other.

Your Boss: You may be aiming to step into his shoes one day, but in the meantime, may find working for your Capricorn boss a satisfying experience if you were also born under the sign of the zodiacal goat. Unlike some of your coworkers, you may understand that the routines that your shared element of earth has prompted him to set in place provide a framework that aids efficiency, for you no doubt both believe that a lack of stability results in chaotic working practices and a consequent drop in productivity. And not only may his Saturn-bestowed diligence match yours, it is thanks to this same birth influence that your responsible boss may seem unwilling to exploit your conscientiousness to his own advantage. If you wish that he took more of an interest in helping you to develop your career plans, however, blame your joint, cardinal quadruplicity and feminine polarity, which may cause you both to be self-absorbed at times, as well as reticent.

Capricorn and Capricorn in the Workplace: You may be relieved to be working alongside a Capricorn if you are one, too, not least if you resent having your attention distracted from a task in hand by idle chatter or other people's overblown, emotional traumas. Like you, feminine-polarity Capricorn is probably quiet and thoughtful, and, thanks to Saturn and your earthy element, also serious, straightforward, and reliable. Despite the slow and cautious approach that may be common to you both, an advantage of sharing a cardinal quadruplicity is that it may infuse each of you with a sense of urgency when speed is vital, thereby enabling you meet a team deadline by working around the clock if necessary. Indeed, your only reservation about your fellow Capricorn's capabilities may be that your workmate isn't that imaginative, so that he or she may be of little help when a problem requiring a creative solution presents itself.

AQUARIUS

CAPRICORN

Capricorn and Aquarius could hardly be more dissimilar, which generally works to their advantage in the workplace, although it may inevitably give rise to differences of opinion, too. Whereas Capricorn is cautious, conventional, and practical, Aquarius is an enterprising, radical thinker, so that while Capricorn may temper some of Aquarius' more eccentric ideas with a hefty dose of common sense, Aquarius may inject energy and originality into a mutual project. Cardinal-quadruplicity Capricorn's urge to complete a task as quickly as possible may sometimes be thwarted by fixed-quadruplicity Aquarius' inflexibility, however, just as Aquarius' groundbreaking, Uranian impulses may be frustrated by saturnine Capricorn's repressive influence. Even so, these colleagues generally have a good-natured rapport.

Your Boss: You may feel a little ambivalent about your boss's predictability if he is a Saturn-governed, earthy Capricorn and you are an Aquarius, for you may be annoyed that he almost invariably rejects your trailblazing, Uranus-inspired proposals on the one hand, yet, on the other, may not mind fitting in with his routines, thanks to your stability-bestowing, fixed quadruplicity. Because he has a feminine, or passive, polarity and yours is masculine, or active, you may not be that motivated by him either—apart from when a deadline is imminent and his driving, cardinal quadruplicity takes over—even if you respect his earthy, businesslike manner.

You may be relieved that your airy, Aquarius boss is so approachable if you are a feminine-polarity Capricorn who can feel rather inhibited on occasions, and may furthermore approve of her fixed-quadruplicity tenacity if Saturn, your planetary governor, and your element of earth cause you to be similarly dogged and resilient. That said, because Saturn may give you conservative instincts, you may be deeply unsettled by her insistence that you get to grips with cutting-edge technology, for example, in which case blame pioneering Uranus.

Capricorn and Aquarius in the Workplace: If you are a pair of earthy Capricorn and airy Aquarius coworkers, each of you may be grateful that the other isn't easily upset, so that you don't have to choose your words carefully for fear of triggering a bout of weepiness or sulkiness. And you no doubt have plenty of disagreements, maybe because Capricorn is a realist who is wary of the new, while Aquarius is an idealist who is full of inventive suggestions, or perhaps because Capricorn can be forceful when necessary, and fixed-quadruplicity Aquarius, stubborn. Even so, the astrological indications suggest that earthy, placid Capricorn and airy, laid-back Aquarius workmates rarely make an issue of their differences.

Aquarius Birth Influences

Ruling planet: Uranus; traditionally Saturn
Element: Air
Polarity: Masculine
Quadruplicity: Fixed

Capricorn, you may feel frustrated when you're breaking your back trying to finish a task and your airy Aquarius boss is preoccupied with his grand plans. Aquarius probably knows that you'll keep your head down until the job is done.

Capricorn Birth Influences

Ruling planet: Saturn
Element: Earth
Polarity: Feminine
Quadruplicity: Cardinal

CAPRICORN

PISCES

Capricorn Birth Influences

Ruling planet: Saturn
Element: Earth
Polarity: Feminine
Quadruplicity: Cardinal

A Capricorn boss should try not to ignore Pisces' imaginative suggestions, or to hurt her feelings.

Pisces Birth Influences

Ruling planet: Neptune; traditionally Jupiter
Element: Water
Polarity: Feminine
Quadruplicity: Mutable

At best, Capricorn's strengths can compensate for Pisces' weaknesses in the workplace, and the other way around, of course, making this pair of colleagues a remarkable team, albeit a rather passive one, due to their joint, feminine polarity. Whereas mutable-quadruplicity, watery Pisces' thinking may be haphazard and muddled, cardinal-quadruplicity, earthy Capricorn's mindset may be goal-oriented and straightforward, but then Pisces may be blessed with the flexibility and creativity that is lacking in Capricorn, and may also have a Neptune-bestowed gift for seeing beyond the limits set by Saturn, Capricorn's planetary ruler. At worst, however, these may be colleagues who neither see eye to eye nor interact happily and successfully.

Your Boss: What you may like about your earthy, Capricorn boss if you are a Pisces, is firstly that she is even-tempered, and, secondly, that she is steady and predictable, for the combination of Neptune and water may make you ultrasensitive to others' moods, while your mutable quadruplicity may cause your own to swing wildly if exposed to dramatic changes. Yet because Saturn sets high standards in terms of productivity and precision, and having a cardinal quadruplicity may result in Capricorn being target-driven, her stern expectations may trigger a Neptunian longing in you to escape her repressive regime. You would, no doubt, prefer to let your watery imagination flow freely and work at your own easy pace.

Your Piscean boss may test even your long-suffering, earthy patience to its limits if you are a businesslike Capricorn. Saturn may prompt you to take your career very seriously, and your cardinal quadruplicity may give you the urge to make progress as quickly as possible, yet watery Pisces may be more interested in your feelings than in nurturing your ambitions, and may furthermore have an infuriating, mutable-quadruplicity tendency to prevaricate before eventually reaching what you consider to be an illogical decision. That said, at least he may be willing to go along with your practical proposals, and you probably have to admit that his way of thinking outside the box can have startlingly effective consequences.

Capricorn and Pisces in the Workplace: There are many reasons why you may be grateful to be working alongside one another if one of you is a Capricorn and the other, a Pisces. Your shared, feminine polarity makes you equally thoughtful for a start, and Pisces may furthermore be thankful for earthy Capricorn's stabilizing influence, while Capricorn may appreciate mutable Pisces' adaptability. Capricorn may have little sympathy with Pisces' intuitive thought processes, however, just as Pisces may find Capricorn's narrow vision limiting.

AQUARIUS

AQUARIUS

Whether these colleagues can stop talking long enough to get any work done is the big question when a pair of Aquarian individuals find themselves interacting in the workplace, for their element of air causes them to be both communicative and more keen on exchanging ideas than patiently plowing through a pile of paperwork, to which these dynamic, masculine-polarity people in any case have an aversion. Add Uranus, their planetary governor, to the mix, and here you have a pair of independent thinkers whose invigorating influence on each other can inspire them to come up with the most radical, if sometimes impractical, of propositions. Their fixed quadruplicity blesses them with staying power when necessary, too, although this may occasionally be a problem should it manifest itself as a mutual refusal to countenance one another's opinions or proposals.

Your Boss: If you are an Aquarius, having a fellow Aquarius as a boss may be enjoyable, and maybe even exciting. The combination of air and Uranus may infuse you both with a dislike of convention, while your masculine polarity may bless each of you with confident, outgoing natures, which suggests that you have a relationship of equals, despite your respective statuses. And if, as is likely, given your airy articulacy and intelligence, you frequently spend time brainstorming, you may be exhilarated when your boss urges you to express your thoughts freely and is then enthused by your innovative, Uranian theories, his unpredictable observations in turn maybe giving you fresh inspiration. You may, however, be irritated should, for instance, he disregard your modernizing suggestions because he prefers to stick to his tried-and-trusted ways, thereby illustrating how your common, fixed quadruplicity can give rise to obstinacy, and consequently friction.

Aquarius and Aquarius in the Workplace: Your shared, Uranian interest in new ideas or cutting-edge technology and your enthusiasm for discussing the latest developments with an airy, analytical someone whose eyes light up rather than glazing over may be a thrilling benefit of working alongside one another if you and your workmate were both born under the sign of the water-carrier. Your joint, airy element may furthermore give you both an easygoing attitude that you may each find refreshing, although you are also capable of minimizing the gossip in order to concentrate, fixed-quaduplicity style, on meeting a deadline when necessary. Yet you may occasionally have stubborn, fixed-quadruplicity-style standoffs, too, should one of you reject the other's viewpoint.

Aquarius Birth Influences

Ruling planet: Uranus; traditionally Saturn
Element: Air
Polarity: Masculine
Quadruplicity: Fixed

♅ ♄

Work can feel more like a social event when two Aquarians get carried away, but when a job calls for an unconventional approach, these two may form an ideal partnership.

Aquarius Birth Influences

Ruling planet: Uranus; traditionally Saturn
Element: Air
Polarity: Masculine
Quadruplicity: Fixed

AQUARIUS
PISCES

Aquarius Birth Influences

Ruling planet: Uranus; traditionally Saturn
Element: Air
Polarity: Masculine
Quadruplicity: Fixed

Eccentric Aquarius can be an inspiration to creative Pisces, provided that her lack of inhibition does not prove overwhelming.

Pisces Birth Influences

Ruling planet: Neptune; traditionally Jupiter
Element: Water
Polarity: Feminine
Quadruplicity: Mutable

Both Uranus and Neptune, Aquarius and Pisces' planetary governors, bless their protégés with the gift of transcendence, which means that these colleagues should be able to rise above their differences. And differences there certainly may be, for while airy, Uranian Aquarius is an analytical, radical thinker, watery, Neptunian Pisces may be intuitive to the point of vagueness, characteristics compounded by Aquarius' enterprising, masculine polarity and Pisces' cautious, feminine one, and whereas fixed-quadruplicity Aquarius can be stubborn, mutable-quadruplicity Pisces is flexible. Even so, because airy Aquarius is dispassionate and cool, and thin-skinned Pisces hates confrontations, their relationship is likely to be fairly peaceable.

Your Boss: One of the advantages of having an Aquarian boss, if you are a Pisces, may be that his airy, informal, management style and somewhat eccentric, Uranian ways may neither pressurize you nor suppress your creativity, for it may be that your watery imagination can only flow freely in a relaxed or unconventional working atmosphere. Her positive, masculine-polarity outlook and laid-back manner may also encourage you to overcome your feminine-polarity shyness and express yourself without fear of being ridiculed, and you may be thrilled should your Neptunian idealism whet her Uranus-bestowed appetite for experimentation. You may, however, be upset by her fixed-quadruplicity inflexibility should you want to change your working hours to suit your domestic duties, for instance.

Your Pisces boss's erratic, illogical decisions may intrigue the investigative, Uranian side of your nature if you are an Aquarius, even if they offend your airy reason and fixed-quadruplicity preference for constancy. He may also be a little too unforthcoming for a masculine-polarity, airy person like you, who may thrive on uninhibited verbal interaction, although once you've forged a connection and have understood his nebulous way of thinking, you may frequently be inspired by the potential inherent in Neptune-ruled Pisces' subtle, deeply original ideas.

Aquarius and Pisces in the Workplace: You may have learned that your airy, Aquarian coworker isn't that interested in you as a person if you are a Pisces, which you may find hurtful if you take a kindly, Neptunian interest in him or her. You may nevertheless be grateful to be working alongside someone who has such a calming effect on you, as well as a stabilizing one, thanks to his or her fixed quadruplicity. As for you, Aquarius, you may appreciate your unselfish coworker's readiness to drop everything to lend a helping hand if you've run into trouble, yet may be irritated by Pisces' tendency to sulk when you've inadvertently touched a raw nerve.

PISCES
PISCES

Pisces people are unlikely to impress their coworkers with their assertiveness, tenacity, or drive, yet their mutable quadruplicity does bless them with the invaluable gift of adaptability, their feminine polarity makes them thoughtful, and their element of water encourages a stream of imaginative concepts to flow from their fertile imaginations. And when it comes to dreaming up original ideas, two Piscean minds may seem as one, for Neptune, their ruling planet, gives them such a profound insight into one another's unconscious thought processes that it may often appear as though they are telepathic. Although these kindly, empathetic colleagues are therefore usually on the same wavelength, they may occasionally differ when their changeable, mutable quadruplicity sends them off in different directions.

Your Boss: You may consider your Pisces superior more of a friend than a boss if you share his zodiacal sign, maybe partly because you understand one another so well, and partly because, having a caring element in water, he is clearly anxious that you should be happy in your job. Indeed, you probably generally are, for not only may Neptune give you both a dislike of rules and regulations, but also a tendency to think the best of others, so that your unselfish boss may encourage you to believe that you have the ability to fulfill your dreams, be they work-related or personal. You may consequently be flourishing in this flexible, inspiring Piscean world, even if you are sometimes a little hurt when you're having a team meeting and your mutable-quadruplicity boss decides to go with a radically dissimilar proposal to the one that you've just made.

Pisces and Pisces in the Workplace: You may be deeply comfortable working alongside one another if you and your workmate are both Pisceans. You may each respect your watery, feminine-polarity need to withdraw into yourself in order to mull over a nebulous, Neptunian notion that may slowly be taking shape in your mind, for instance, and when you are ready to share it, may be equally enthused by its subtle potential. Your fellow Pisces may instinctively detect when you are feeling stressed or depressed, too, and may show his or her concern and support by offering to take over some of your workload. Because you are both easily swayed by the influence of others and furthermore enjoy variety, one of you may nevertheless unintentionally cause the other to feel excluded or isolated by appearing to side with someone with very different views.

Pisces Birth Influences

Ruling planet: Neptune; traditionally Jupiter
Element: Water
Polarity: Feminine
Quadruplicity: Mutable

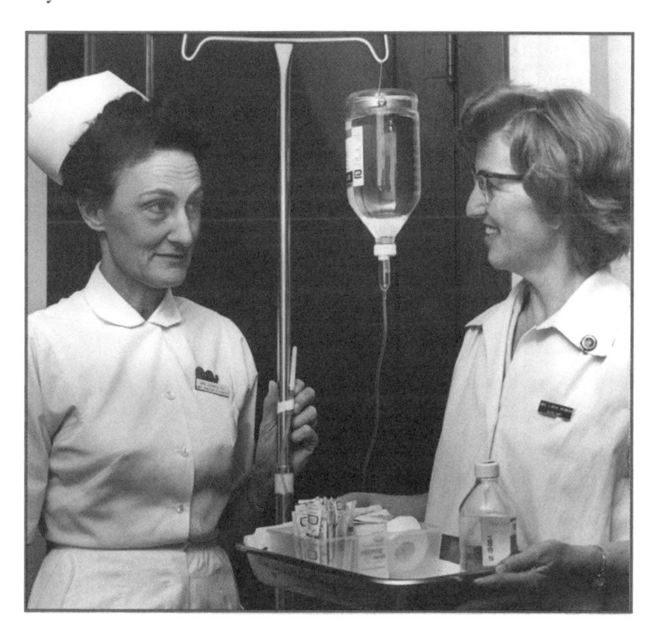

Your Piscean boss is probably quiet, kind, and knows how to encourage you to thrive and succeed if you are a fellow Pisces.

Pisces Birth Influences

Ruling planet: Neptune; traditionally Jupiter
Element: Water
Polarity: Feminine
Quadruplicity: Mutable

BIBLIOGRAPHY

Butler, Alan, *Build Better Zodiac Relationships*, Quantum, Slough, 2002.

Campion, Nicholas, and Eddy, Steve, *The New Astrology*, Bloomsbury Publishing Plc, London, 1999.

Cornelius, Geoffrey, and Devereux, Paul, *The Language of the Stars and Planets*, Duncan Baird Publishers, London, 2003.

Gibson, Clare, *The Ultimate Birthday Book*, Saraband Inc., 1998.

Huntley, Janis, *The Elements of Astrology*, Element Books Limited, Shaftesbury, 1993.

Huntley, Janis, *The Complete Illustrated Guide to Astrology*, Element Books Limited, Shaftesbury, 1999.

Miller, Sue, *Planets and Possibilities*, Time Warner Paperbacks, London, 2001.

INDEX

INDEX OF COMBINATIONS OF SIGNS

Family

Friends

Romance

Work